WILDERNESS MANAGEMENT
by

John C. Hendee
formerly Recreation Research Project Leader
Pacific Northwest Forest and Range Experiment Station
Seattle, Wash.
now U.S. Forest Service
Washington, D.C.

George H. Stankey
Research Social Scientist
Intermountain Forest and Range Experiment Station
Missoula, Mont.

Robert C. Lucas
Wilderness Management Research Project Leader
Intermountain Forest and Range Experiment Station
Missoula, Mont.

**University Press of the Pacific
Honolulu, Hawaii**

Wilderness Management

by
John C. Hendee
George H. Stankey
Robert C. Lucas

for U.S. Forest Service

ISBN: 1-4102-2231-4

Copyright © 2005 by University Press of the Pacific

Reprinted from the 1978 edition

University Press of the Pacific
Honolulu, Hawaii
http://www.universitypressofthepacific.com

Foreword

Wilderness preservation for the use and enjoyment of the American people is an important goal of public land policy. Under the Wilderness Act of 1964, Congress designates roadless tracts in the National Forests, National Parks, and Wildlife Refuges to be set aside for preservation in their natural state. The Eastern Wilderness Act of 1975 extended wilderness designation opportunities to National Forest lands in the East, and the Federal Land Policy and Management Act of 1976 extended the opportunity to the public domain administered by the Bureau of Land Management. In early 1977, there were 167 wilderness areas in 39 States, including more than 14 million acres. Another 24.4 million acres were proposed to Congress for classification, 23.7 million acres were in formal wilderness study areas, and numerous legislative proposals for additional wildernesses were being introduced in Congress—including vast additions in Alaska. The stage is set for the ultimate designation of a National Wilderness Preservation System exceeding 100 million acres.

Classification of areas as wilderness is only the first step, however. After classification, proper management is essential if the wilderness qualities of naturalness, solitude, and minimal man-caused impacts are to be preserved. This wilderness management challenge, which is the subject of this book, is becoming both more important and more difficult. The Wilderness System is growing as new areas are added by Congress, responding to the will of the people. Wilderness use is increasing rapidly as growing numbers of Americans hike or ride wilderness trails, paddle or float wild lakes and rivers, and seek inspiration from the beauty and opportunities for solitude found in wilderness. As the rest of our country becomes more developed and modified, the natural conditions preserved in wilderness will become more and more valuable to the American people, both for enjoyment and renewal, and also for scientific knowledge of ecological processes.

Wilderness Management may seem to be a contradiction in terms, but a variety of pressures make management necessary. To protect and perpetuate wilderness values, wilderness managers must make many difficult decisions to carefully balance impacts and benefits. Recreational use is one of the main wilderness values, but it must be kept in balance with protection of natural ecosystems and wilderness solitude. Some development for recreational use is needed in wilderness, such as simple trails and bridges at dangerous stream crossings, but, if not kept in balance, over-development can also destroy wilderness. Nonconforming uses are permitted in some wildernesses, including prospecting (until 1984), mining, grazing, and access to private inholdings, but these uses must be conducted in ways that do not destroy the area's wilderness qualities. These are but a few of the issues facing wilderness managers—issues that must be resolved with sensitivity and common sense, but within a management framework of doing only what is necessary to protect the wilderness, while using minimum impact methods and techniques.

The importance and complexity of wilderness management are described in this book, the first on the subject. It is a timely publication following almost 15 years during which the wilderness management agencies applied and tested management policies and approaches under the Act's direction. Reflecting this varied experience and emerging state of the art, the book describes the broad range of wilderness management issues and concerns, and alternative approaches to their resolution. Examples illustrate approaches used by all the wilderness management agencies. However, this is not a policy manual—specific policy endorsements are generally avoided in an attempt to set forth basic concepts and principles that apply to all wildernesses. These concepts and principles grow out of the wide ranging administrative experience, research, and literature reported in the book.

The principal authors of the book are three Forest Service research scientists, whose research during the past decade has included Department of the Interior lands, as well as National Forests. Four chapters are contributed by international experts in their respective, wilderness-related fields.

We are pleased to jointly endorse this book as a meaningful presentation of wilderness management issues, concerns, and concepts. It will be a positive stimulus to wilderness managers and users, resource policy makers, and concerned citizens, who must together face the wilderness management challenges in the years ahead.

CECIL ANDRUS
Secretary of the Interior

BOB BERGLAND
Secretary of Agriculture

June 1977

Preface

Wilderness is the topic of a substantial and growing amount of literature. A large number of books, articles, and brochures describe wilderness values (the rationale for preservation, public appeals, political movements), wilderness places (histories, geographies, noteworthy areas, biographies of people intimately linked with specific areas), and wilderness activities (how, where, and what-to-do guides). Faced with such a bewildering selection of wilderness readings, a reader could easily conclude that everything worth knowing about the wilderness has already been written. But when readers turn to wilderness management—how to preserve naturalness and opportunities for solitude in areas set aside for this purpose—they soon discover that readings are in short supply. This neglected and fragmented subject—wilderness management—seems to be widely scattered among short articles and research reports or relegated to graduate theses and government manuals.

For some time now, we have been concerned about the lack of any systematic, comprehensive synthesis of information about wilderness management, and our goal in preparing this book has been to provide such a volume. The importance of wilderness management cannot be overemphasized. In only the next few decades, most of the wilderness allocation decisions will have been made. Once the decision has been made to set aside a tract of land as wilderness, the long-term preservation of those values that originally led to wilderness legislation will depend on management.

This book is the first text and reference that specifically addresses the issues and problems of wilderness management. The material is organized into six sections, each intended to present a comprehensive summary and synthesis of pertinent information. The book's 16 chapters bring together both previously published as well as new information and viewpoints pertaining to wilderness management—writing which includes philosophy and concepts. research data, and management experience in Federal agencies. Specifically, our objectives include the following:

1. To sensitize readers to pressing wilderness management issues and the implications of alternative methods of dealing with them.

2. To distinguish issues of wilderness management from issues of wilderness allocation and management of related lands, and to describe their important interrelationships.

3. To introduce readers to pertinent literature and ongoing research on wilderness, focusing particularly on the management implications of such work.

4. To describe the evolution of the National Wilderness Preservation System from its philosophical and historical origins to its current size in number of areas and acres, with a speculative look at the future.

5. To propose principles and concepts from which management policy and actions to preserve wilderness might be derived, and to describe current management policies, procedures, and techniques that are available.

We recognize that among our readers there will be many diverse views about wilderness management, and we do not expect universal agreement with our treatment of a topic as emotion-laden as wilderness. Hopefully, we have avoided some of the polarity of opinion that commonly surrounds discussion of wilderness by attempting to maintain a broad, conceptual perspective on management problems. We have tried to identify alternative wilderness management perspectives and their implications. Where we do advocate a particular management direction, we try to state our position clearly and identify our line of reasoning. Both within individual agencies and among the public, there are varying orientations toward wilderness and its management, but we are gratified by what we think is some convergence of views in the past decade. We hope this book will stimulate the discussions and foster the consensus necessary to meet the challenge of wilderness management that faces government agencies and the interested public.

July 1977

John C. Hendee
George H. Stankey
Robert C. Lucas

Organization of the Book

The book contains 16 chapters that relate to one another in six main areas as follows:

Area one—the setting—contains an introductory chapter on the differences between allocation and management, the need for wilderness, and the philosophical and pragmatic bases for its management. The second chapter, contributed by Roderick Nash, professor of history and environmental studies, University of California, Santa Barbara, explores the history of the wilderness management idea and the beginning of its acceptance in the United States. Chapter 3, also by Roderick Nash, reviews international concepts of wilderness preservation, underscoring the unique cultural features of the concept as it has emerged in the United States.

Area two—legal basis for wilderness—contains three chapters explaining the enabling legislation and subsequent status of U.S. wilderness. Chapter 4 explains the wilderness acts; chapter 5, the wilderness classification process under the Acts; and chapter 6, the current and projected status of the National Wilderness Preservation System and related areas.

Area three—management concepts and direction—contains three chapters identifying some broad direction and concepts for managing wilderness. Chapter 7 proposes 11 general principles to guide wilderness management; chapter 8, by John Hendee and Russ Koch, graduate research assistant, University of Washington, College of Forest Resources, discusses the importance of planning to implement management and suggests a planning framework illustrated by excerpts from several actual plans; and chapter 9 reviews the basic concept of carrying capacity as applied to wilderness.

Area four—important elements for management—contains three chapters exploring aspects of wilderness that must be managed; that is, ecosystems, wildlife, fire. Chapter 10, by Jerry Franklin, principal plant ecologist, Pacific Northwest Forest and Range Experiment Station, Corvallis, Oreg., discusses wilderness ecosystems including a review of some basic concepts that control ecosystems everywhere, including wilderness. Chapter 11, by John Hendee and Clay Schoenfeld, joint professor of wildlife ecology and journalism, University of Wisconsin, Madison, reviews wilderness wildlife values and problems and proposes some management objectives and guidelines for wildlife in wilderness. Chapter 12, by Miron Heinselman, adjunct professor, Department of Ecology and Behavioral Biology, University of Minnesota, St. Paul, discusses the natural role of fire in wilderness and the need for management to maintain or restore this role.

Area five—wilderness use and its management—moves to the problems of visitor use and how to manage it. Chapter 13 reviews the ways in which wilderness is used and current and projected levels of use. Chapter 14 explores direct and indirect approaches to managing visitor behavior; chapter 15 discusses the variety of tools and techniques available to managers for site management to protect the wilderness environment.

Area six—problems and opportunities—offers a concluding chapter identifying some current issues and challenges Included is an appeal for an overall management system applied to wilderness and integrating efforts by universities and the public as well as the agencies. In addition, more research, increased professionalism, and improved funding are highlighted as necessary keys in realizing the potential of the National Wilderness Preservation System.

Throughout the book unfamiliar terms or words used in a particular way are explained where they occur in the text or as footnotes. Several recurring terms, however, will be defined here and then used without additional explanation.

Before 1964, the term *wilderness* was used to describe man's changing perception of unknown areas or lands modified primarily by natural forces, a subject explored by Roderick Nash in chapter 2. But, since 1964, while retaining this historic and familiar meaning, the word has acquired a new, more precise definition. The word refers to areas assigned by Congress to the National Wilderness Preservation System. For readability and clarity, we have elected to capitalize wilderness only when it is used as a proper noun, for example, the Bob Marshall Wilderness, the National Wilderness Preservation System, or the Wilderness Act. All other references to wilderness as a general term or in the legal sense, use a lower case *w*.

The term *Act*, used alone, might occasionally raise questions. As it is used in this book, if it applies to a period before January 1975, the term refers only to the Wilderness Act of 1964. After that date, unless the text clearly specifies otherwise, the term refers to the general intent or provisions of both the 1964 law and the so-called Eastern Wilderness Act of 1975, which extended provisions of the Wilderness Act to areas in the Eastern United States.

Authorship and Sponsorship

The authors have studied wilderness problems and worked closely with wilderness managers for many years. As this book was written, all three were Forest Service recreation research scientists. Many of their ideas were developed while the authors taught university courses in wilderness management—John Hendee at the University of Washington and George Stankey and Bob Lucas at the University of Montana.

The writing of this book has been sponsored by the U.S. Department of Agriculture, Forest Service, although the book is directed toward wilderness management in all the responsible agencies—the Forest Service and, in the Department of Interior, the National Park Service, the Fish and Wildlife Service and, as a result of 1976 legislation, the Bureau of Land Management. Our technical reviewers, case examples, and background material represent the expertise of all these agencies and, while we recognize specific policy differences among them, we have sought a level of technical presentation that transcends agency differences. This is not a book constrained by existing Forest Service policy—our goal is to provide leadership to management of a National Wilderness Preservation System now and in the future, but not bound to current organizational perspectives, policies, or practices.

Although each wilderness management agency has policy and Federal departmental guidelines directing its specific efforts, all operate under the Wilderness Act and seek high professional standards and aspirations for preservation of classified wilderness. Our many contacts with wilderness managers in all four agencies convince us that most are far more interested in getting the job done than defending or criticizing "company policy"—a healthy sign of professionalism and increasing maturity of wilderness management.

Preparation of this book spanned several years. The effort was originally conceived after a Forest Service-sponsored "Management Implications of Wilderness Research" symposium in Seattle during January 1973 that brought together managers, researchers, and environmentalists to discuss their mutual concerns for management of classified wilderness and the need for new and relevant information.

The volume is more than a book of readings, although we include four contributed chapters by colleagues on topics beyond our expertise—Roderick Nash on Historical Roots of Wilderness Management (chapter 2) and International Concepts of Wilderness Preservation (chapter 3); Jerry Franklin on Wilderness Ecosystems (chapter 10); and Miron "Bud" Heinselman on Fire in Wilderness Ecosystems (chapter 12). We are also grateful for the collaboration and coauthorship of Russ Koch on the Planning chapter (chapter 8) and Clay Schoenfeld on the Wildlife chapter (chapter 11). Except for these contributions, all parts of the book bear the imprint of all three coauthors. John Hendee provided overall coordination for writing, acquired technical reviews, and made administrative arrangements. He led the development of the photo plan, Preface, and chapters 1. Introduction, 7. Principles of Wilderness Management, 8. Planning, 11. Wildlife, and 16. Wilderness Management Issues and Opportunities. George Stankey had principal responsibility for chapters 4. The Wilderness Acts, 5. The Classification Process, 6. The Wilderness System, and 9. Carrying Capacity. He also oversaw the final preparation of the manuscript and photo plan. Bob Lucas headed work on chapters 13. Wilderness Use, 14. Visitor Management, and 15. Site Management.

To indicate leadership for preparation of individual chapters, the name of the author having that responsibility is noted at the end of each chapter.

Wherever the word *we* appears (outside of direct quotations), it refers to an opinion held by the three coauthors.

Even a casual reader of this book will notice that many of the specific examples—a disproportionate share, it might seem—are taken from the Forest Service experience in managing the wilderness. These selections do not reflect the preference or even the personal experiences of the authors. Rather, they express a reality that is documented throughout the book, particularly in chapters 5 and 6. So far, if only because of the acreage involved, Forest Service involvement with wilderness has been considerably more widespread than that of other agencies. Recent developments, for example, omnibus wilderness classification acts for National Parks and Wildlife Refuges and the Federal Land Policy and Management Act of 1976 giving the Bureau of Land Management wilderness management authority, indicate that this imbalance among the agencies in wilderness-related activities is narrowing.

Acknowledgements

We are particularly grateful to our many colleagues in universities, the Forest Service, Park Service, Fish and Wildlife Service, Bureau of Land Management, and the conservation community who provided encouragement and constructive review. A special note of thanks must go to Bob Buckman, Bob Harris, Bob Tarrant, Roger Bay, and Con Schallau of the Forest Service Research Branch for making this endeavor possible and to Pat Logie whose work helped shape the tone and format of the book. To the reviewers listed below we offer our sincere gratitude—their review and input was invaluable but they share no responsibility for our interpretations or statements. Those who reviewed all, or most of the book in outline or text, and provided valuable technical input are (in alphabetical order):

Del Armstrong, Assistant Regional Chief Scientist, National Park Service, Seattle, Wash.

Bill Barmore, Resource Management Staff, Grand Teton National Park

Dr. Richard Behan, Professor of Forestry, Northern Arizona University, Flagstaff

Dr. Perry Brown, Associate Professor, Forest Recreation, Colorado State University, Fort Collins

Edmund J. Bucknell, Resource Management Staff, Yellowstone National Park

Dr. Richard Bury, Professor of Parks and Recreation, Texas A&M University, College Station, Tex.

Dave Butts, Resource Management Staff, National Park Service, Washington, D.C.

Bob Cermak, Supervisor, North Carolina National Forests, Asheville

Dr. Ken Chilman, Associate Professor of Forest Recreation, Southern Illinois University, Carbondale

Richard Costley, Associate Professor, Landscape Architecture, University of Massachusetts (formerly Director of Recreation, Forest Service)

Jim Gillette, Wilderness Planner, Fish and Wildlife Service, Washington, D.C.

Mike Griswold, Asst. Director of Recreation, Forest Service, Washington, D.C.

Bill Holman, Division of Recreation, Forest Service, Washington, D.C.

Robert Jacobsen, Superintendent, Shenandoah National Park

Russ Koch, Doctoral student in Forestry, University of Washington

John Koen, Regional Director of Recreation, Forest Service, Albuquerque, N. Mex.

Diane LaCourse, Forestry Student, University of Washington

Allan Lamb, Regional Director of Recreation, Forest Service, San Francisco

Dr. Stephen McCool, Assistant Professor of Forestry, Utah State University

Mike Loeffler, Graduate student in Forestry, University of Washington

Dr. Larry Merriam, Professor of Forestry, University of Minnesota

Rosemary Perdue, Graduate student in Public Administration, University of Washington

Dave Redman, Graduate student in Geography, University of Washington

Dr. John Schomaker, Assistant Professor of Forest Recreation, University of Idaho

David Scott, Regional Director of Recreation, Forest Service, Atlanta

Dick Spray, Recreation Staff, Forest Service, Albuquerque

Stephen Wells, Biology Instructor (on leave), Principia College, Ill.

Peter Womble, Graduate student in Forest Sociology, University of Washington

Bob Wood, Resource Management Staff, Grand Teton National Park

Bill Worf, Regional Director of Recreation, Forest Service, Missoula, Mont.

For review or input to particular chapters:

Chapter 3, International Concepts of Wilderness Preservation

C. Frank Brockman, Emeritus Professor of Forestry, University of Washington

Chapters 4 and 5, The Wilderness Act and the Wilderness Classification Process

Clarance W. Brizee, Assistant Director of Forestry, Office of the General Counsel, Washington, D.C.
Bill Cunningham, The Wilderness Society, Washington, D.C.
Reynolds Florance, (retired) Director of Legislative Affairs, Forest Service, Washington, D.C.
Doug Scott, Pacific Northwest Representative, Sierra Club and Federation of Western Outdoor Clubs, Seattle

Chapter 8, Wilderness Management Planning

Bill Fessell, Recreation Staff, Mt. Baker/Snoqualmie National Forest, Seattle
Bill Gregg, Division of Legislation, National Park Service, Washington, D.C.
Jim Howe, Division of Legislation, National Park Service, Washington, D.C.
Tony Skufca, Regional Director of Recreation, Forest Service, Portland
Dick Walker, Wilderness Planner, Bitterroot National Forest, Forest Service, Hamilton Mont.
Don Warman, Planner, Division of Recreation, Forest Service, Portland
Dan Wood, Recreation Planner, BLM, Cañyon City, Colo.

Chapter 9, Wilderness Carrying Capacity

Dr. William R. Burch, Jr., Professor of Forestry, Yale University
Dr. Sidney Frissell, Associate Professor of Forestry, University of Montana
Dr. Bob Lee, Assistant Professor of Forestry, University of California, Berkeley
Dr. Jan Van Wagtendonk, Research Scientist, Yosemite National Park

Chapter 10, Wilderness Ecosystems

Dr. Steve Arno, Associate Plant Ecologist, Forest Service, Intermountain Forest and Range Experiment Station
    Missoula, Mont.
Dr. Sue Bratton, Research Biologist, Great Smoky Mountains National Park
Dr. Ted Dyrness, Research Project Leader, Institute of Northern Forestry, Forest Service, Fairbanks, Alaska
Dr. James Long, Research Associate, College of Forest Resources, University of Washington
Dr. Bob Pfister, Principal Plant Ecologist, Forest Service, Intermountain Forest and Range Experiment Station
    Missoula, Mont.
Dr. Dale Thornburgh, Professor of Forestry, Humboldt State University, Arcata, Calif.

Chapter 11, Wildlife

Dr. Durward Allen, Professor of Wildlife, Purdue University

James L. Baker, Wildlife Biologist, U.S. Fish and Wildlife Service, Washington, D.C.

Leon Cambre, Director of Legislative Affairs, Forest Service, Washington, D.C.

Roger Contor, Superintendent, Rocky Mountain National Park

David J. Dunaway, Wildlife Biologist, Forest Service, San Francisco

Boyd Evison, Superintendent, Great Smoky National Park

Peter Hayden, Aquatic Biologist, Grand Teton National Park

Dr. Larry Jahn, Executive Vice President, Wildlife Management Institute, Washington, D.C.

Harold C. Jordahl, Professor of Urban and Regional Planning, University of Wisconsin

William H. Kiel, Jr., Wildlife Biologist, King Ranch, Tex.

Dr. Robert McCabe, President, Wildlife Society; Professor and Chairman of Wildlife, University of Wisconsin

Clayton Partridge, Wilderness Ranger, Mt. Rainier National Park

Dr. James Peek, Professor of Wildlife, University of Idaho

Dale Potter, Recreation Research Staff, Forest Service, Pacific Northwest Experiment Station, Seattle, Wash.

Sheryl Stateler Smith, Forest Service, Land Use Planning Team, Sandpoint, Idaho

Richard Stroud, Executive Vice President, Sport Fishing Institute, Washington, D.C.

Dr. Fred Zwickel, Professor of Zoology, University of Alberta, Canada

Chapter 12, Fire in Wilderness Ecosystems

Dave Aldrich, Fire Planner, Forest Service, Northern Forest Fire Lab, Missoula

Dr. Bruce Kilgore, Associate Regional Director, National Park Service, San Francisco

Dr. Robert Mutch, Research Forester, Forest Service, Northern Forest Fire Lab, Missoula

Chapter 13, Wilderness Use and Users

Dr. David W. Lime, Forest Service, North Central Forest Experiment Station, St. Paul

Chapter 14, Visitor Management and Chapter 15, Site Management

Dr. Sidney Frissell, Associate Professor of Forestry, University of Montana

Dr. David W. Lime, Forest Service, North Central Forest Experiment Station, St. Paul

Bruce Moorehead, Biologist, Olympic National Park, Port Angeles, Wash.

Chapter 16, The Future: Wilderness Management Issues and Opportunities

Dick Benjamin, Forest Service Resources Planning Staff, Washington, D.C.

Dr. Jerry Franklin, Principal Plant Ecologist, Forest Service, Pacific Northwest Forest and Range Experiment Station, Corvallis, Oreg.

Dr. George Jacobson, University of Minnesota, 1976–77 AAAS Congressional Fellow with Senator Dale Bumpers, Arkansas

July 1977   *John C. Hendee*
                              George H. Stankey
                              Robert C. Lucas

Contents

Once an area becomes part of the National Wilderness Preservation System, the preservation of its future wilderness quality depends largely on its management. View southeast from Silver Pass in the John Muir Wilderness, Sierra National Forest, Calif.

1 The Need For Wilderness Management: Philosophical Direction

Introduction

The last two decades have been marked by significant progress in wilderness preservation in the United States. Because of the combined efforts of conservation organizations, concerned citizens, several Federal Agencies, and the U.S. Congress, progress toward the goal of preserving some lands as wilderness is being realized. From the perspective of many, this is a mark of social progress. Our society, through Congressional action in passing the Wilderness Act of 1964, insured that a portion of the country will remain unspoiled for future generations.

But, the final extent of U.S. achievements in wilderness preservation is yet unknown. Two challenges lie ahead. First, there remains the final selection and *classification* of lands which qualify for inclusion in the National Wilderness Preservation System. This process will continue for a number of years. The potential acreage involved will be examined in chapter 6. But building the size of the system is only part of the challenge. As George Marshall, brother of the famous Bob Marshall and former president of the Sierra Club,

notes, "At the same time that wilderness boundaries are being established and protected by Acts of Congress, attention must be given to the quality of wilderness within these boundaries, or we may be preserving empty shells" (Marshall 1969). This raises the second challenge, wilderness management—the formulation and implementation of management programs to achieve the objectives underlying decisions to allocate areas to wilderness purposes.

The subject of this book is wilderness management. Unless the wilderness management challenge is met, the National Wilderness Preservation System will fail to meet its objectives. The management challenge is increasingly important because of growing pressures of wilderness use and man's indirect impacts on all lands. The case for assigning a high priority to wilderness management has been stated in the following way:

> . . . in the controversy surrounding wilderness allocation, equally important questions about wilderness management are being slighted . . . simply allocating an area as wilderness does not assure its preservation.

1

Enlightened wilderness management also is needed.

Most of the areas to be set aside as wilderness will be staked out within the next few decades. From then on, the fate of those areas will rest *solely* upon their management. This is a sobering responsibility for resource professionals, and future generations will be our critics.

Resource professionals are challenged to develop effective approaches to wilderness management now—while there is still time to develop management policies and strategies by design—rather than wait until problems are racing out of control and our efforts can, at best, be reactions to pressing needs (Hendee 1974).

Wilderness and Other Land Uses

This book focuses on the management of *classified wilderness*—areas formally protected by the 1964 Wilderness Act, or its extension to eastern lands by the 1975 Eastern Wilderness Act and to the public domain by the Federal Land Policy and Management Act of 1976. Our ambition is to further the preservation of these legally designated areas through their proper management. However, we intend to avoid becoming embroiled in the controversy that surrounds issues of *how much* wilderness should be set aside, *where* it should be located, *how large* wildernesses should be, and so forth. We believe these wilderness allocation issues are primarily political and will be decided largely through the political process. Professional resource managers can best facilitate this process by helping define and assess the potential land use alternatives for areas proposed as wilderness.

We believe that providing a full spectrum of natural environments is a desirable and necessary goal to respond to the broad range of tastes and preferences in our society. An environmental modification spectrum ranges from the "paved to the primeval" (Nash 1973). Included are urban recreation areas, rural countryside, highly developed campgrounds, intensively managed multiple-use forests, National Parks, recreation and scenic areas, roadless wildland, and wilderness. Through the Wilderness Act, society has chosen to preserve, unimpaired for future generations, a selection of primeval environments as wilderness. The management challenge on which we focus in this book is insuring that these wilderness preservation goals are achieved once areas have been set aside as wilderness.

Wilderness is one kind of opportunity along a continuum of land uses. Some of these uses are compatible with wilderness; others are incompatible (Clawson 1975). Visualizing a continuum made up of both compatible and incompatible uses can help wilderness managers remain responsive to the interrelationships among activities and actions in adjacent areas.

We think this is a fundamental orientation for wilderness management. Resource management agencies in the United States that have wilderness management responsibilities—the National Park Service, Fish and Wildlife Service, Bureau of Land Management, and Forest Service—also manage other environments for other purposes and activities. Wilderness management is thus assigned to organizations having dynamic, ongoing relationships between wilderness and the administration of other land uses. At the very least, this requires that wilderness managers appreciate the intricate relationship of wilderness to other land uses.

Wilderness Management and Wilderness Allocation

There is a fundamental difference between wilderness allocation and wilderness management. *Wilderness allocation includes all processes and activities of government agencies and interested publics to identify areas potentially qualified for preservation as wilderness and to secure their classifications by Congress under the Wilderness Act. Wilderness management includes government and citizen activity to identify—within the constraints of the Wilderness Act—goals and objectives for classified wildernesses and the planning, implementation, and administration of policies and management actions to achieve them.* Wilderness management applies concepts, criteria, guidelines, standards, and procedures derived from the physical, biological, social, and management sciences to preserve naturalness and outstanding opportunities for solitude in wildernesses.

In brief, the wilderness allocation process typically operates as follows. (More detailed information appears in chapter 5.) In response to growing public interest in classifying a roadless portion of a National Forest, National Park, Wildlife Refuge, or BLM National Resource Land as wilderness, the managing agency will carry out a land-use study—including public input—to determine whether that land should be designated as an official wilderness study area. Selected study areas are then intensively studied by the agency to determine their suitability and the demand and need for their classification as wilderness. Based upon this study, a

Figure 1-1.—Wilderness allocation refers to agency and public actions taken to identify potential wilderness and to secure their protection through Congressional classification. Debate often becomes intense over what should or should not be classified, marked by protests such as this concerning wilderness protection for the French Pete drainage on the Willamette National Forest, Oreg.

wilderness proposal may then be submitted to Congress for its review and study, a step which often culminates in legislation classifying the area as wilderness.

The wilderness study and review process by Congress includes formal public hearings and extensive deliberation in Congressional committees as alternative bills are proposed, debated, revised, and finally enacted to legally set aside a specific area as wilderness. During this process, alternative wilderness proposals may be submitted to Congress by interested groups. As an example, a wilderness study on the Mt. Baker-Snoqualmie and Wenatchee National Forests in Washington State led to a Forest Service wilderness proposal to Congress for a 292,000-acre Alpine Lakes Wilderness—with the addition of 82,000 acres if money were allocated to purchase private land. However, the Alpine Lakes Preservation Society (ALPS) proposed a larger, 575,000-acre wilderness surrounded by a 437,000 National Recreation Area. Another organization,

representing industry and recreation vehicle interests, the Alpine Lakes Coalition Society (ALCS), proposed a 216,000-acre wilderness in two separate parcels. Congress studied all these proposals and through public hearings and Congressional debate finally passed legislation establishing a 303,508-acre Alpine Lakes Wilderness. An additional 86,000 acres of intermingled private and public land is defined as "intended wilderness" and Congress authorized (but did not appropriate) $57 million for acquisition of the 43,543 acres of private land needed to include the full "intended wilderness" in the Alpine Lakes Wilderness. The wilderness is surrounded by a protective management unit of 527,000 acres which will be managed by the Forest Service for multiple use purposes.

As the foregoing description illustrates, wilderness allocation issues are inherently political. Resource management proposals and advice are sought from federal management agencies by Congress during the allocation process, but this input may be given no more consideration than the formal proposals of vested interest groups. The determination of the public interest in wilderness allocation issues is arrived at through political processes—public debate, submission of alternative proposals, and ultimately a decision based on compromise.

Management, as we have argued, basically involves the application of guidelines and principles to achieve certain goals and objectives. It generally is not political. Nevertheless, there are important interdependencies between the political allocation process and management. Obviously, the management challenge facing the Agency is a direct function of the attributes of areas that are classified. You have to manage as wilderness what you inherit through the allocation process—and if the allocation process yields heavily impacted areas, with high levels of established use, the job of managing land for the maintenance of natural processes will certainly be tougher.

The Effects of Allocation Decisions on Management

Although we have described wilderness allocation as a separate and distinct process from wilderness management, in fact the two processes are interlinked. In general, management requires an overall strategy and series of actions to achieve the goals and objectives sought through the allocation process. Failure to achieve those objectives could reflect poor execution of the management job, but it could also mean that the

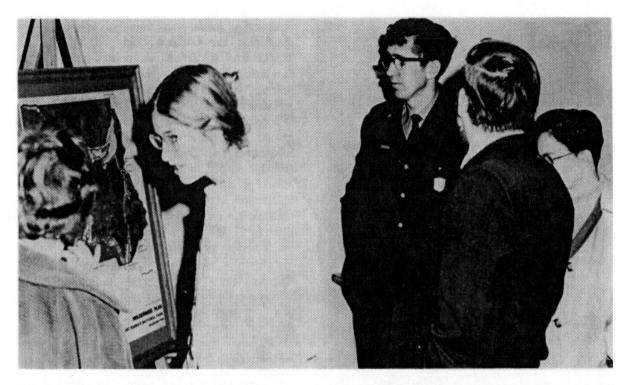

Figure 1-2.—Citizen participation in the wilderness allocation process is essential to gain resource and use data and ideas to determine public sentiment, and, ultimately, to make good defensible decisions. Public meetings, such as this one conducted by the National Park Service during its wilderness study of Mount Rainier National Park, have become a common part of the planning process.

objectives are unfeasible. Let's examine four major ways in which allocation affects the management job.

First, areas under study for possible wilderness classification must be managed during the review period in such a manner that the possibility of their being classified by Congress as a unit of the NWPS is not precluded. In other words, the decision to *study* an area for possible wilderness designation is also a decision to *manage*, at least temporarily, that area as a wilderness. The management of roadless lands to maintain their wilderness character is based on directives contained in the Wilderness Act stating that only Congress has the right to permit or deny any area's entrance into the NWPS. If interim management allows the wilderness character of a proposed area to deteriorate prior to Congressional review, then it has effectively narrowed a choice intended to be left open for legislative option.

Thus, Forest Service Roadless Areas, selected for intensive study as possible additions to the NWPS, are being managed (and used) essentially as wilderness, pending a classification decision. In the Act of 1975 that created wildernesses in the East, Congress specified that wilderness study areas established by the Act would " . . . be managed by the Secretary of Agriculture so as to

maintain their presently existing wilderness character and potential for inclusion in the National Wilderness Preservation System . . . " Despite the absence of an actual classification decision, then, the management options for these areas are limited to the choices available to managers of classified wilderness.

Second, wilderness allocation of areas requiring special management attention could serve to establish precedents affecting the management of other areas. For example, if an area classified as wilderness is not really pristine, some argue that the standards used in admitting that area set a precedent for all other areas (e.g., Costley 1972). Permitting an area which contains a road to be designated as wilderness could open the door to road construction in all other wildernesses, this argument goes.

However, we believe this concern about setting precedents can be adequately answered in two ways. First, established activities or facilities which may be included in an area with its classification as wilderness (airfields, for example) do not constitute a precedent for extending such activities or facilities to other classified areas. Second, the automatic application of lowered standards such as from established high levels of use to

4

other classified areas is inconsistent with the concept of nondegradation, a basic principle of air, water, and noise pollution management and a concept we also believe is applicable to wilderness (Mihaley 1972).

Under a nondegradation concept, management's obligation is to prevent *further* environmental degradation of individual areas and to seek rehabilitation of any areas at or below minimum standards. For example, the presence of high-use levels and significant resource impacts in the San Gorgonio Wilderness in California should not constitute a precedent that would permit similar conditions to evolve in a relatively pristine area such as the Selway-Bitterroot Wilderness in Idaho and Montana.

Third, the technical nature of the wilderness management job is often critically affected by characteristics of the area set aside. Areas classified as wilderness might present built-in problems for which technical solutions are limited, unavailable, or unfeasible. The location of boundaries in vulnerable or unwieldly locations has made the wilderness management job difficult in many places.

Figure 1-3.—Wilderness management includes the planning and implementation of policies and actions to achieve objectives of the Wilderness Act. To a substantial degree, it involves the management of human use and influence to preserve naturalness and outstanding opportunities for solitude in a wilderness. One important tool in the management of human use is wilderness rangers.

The Wilderness Act explicitly recognizes that the nature of allocation criteria will affect the management job; in Section 2(c)2, the Act prescribes the minimum size of a wilderness area: ". . . at least five thousand acres of land or . . . of sufficient size as to make practicable its preservation and use in an unimpaired condition." Below some minimum size, the Act is saying, management to preserve an area's wilderness qualities becomes extremely difficult. In addition, irregularities involving either substantial bulges or indentations; boundaries which do not follow easily recognized, natural features; and boundaries which adjoin areas of commodity production can all accentuate management problems. The Forest Service has attempted to keep wilderness boundaries along ridges or other easily recognized topographical features, arguing that such boundaries make management easier. Debate between the Forest Service and preservationists over the appropriate location of one section of boundary in the San Rafael Primitive Area reclassification tied up the wilderness proposal for over a year, even though the disputed area involved only 2,000 acres out of the nearly 150,000-acre total. In this case, managers favored a ridgetop boundary which facilitated fire protection of the wilderness but reduced its size; environmentalists favored a midslope boundary that enlarged the area.

Some areas cannot feasibly be managed as wilderness for other reasons. Marion Lake in the Mt. Jefferson Wilderness in Oregon illustrates the difficulties that can occur when an accessible and popular area is included in a wilderness. This lake, an easy mile hike from the road, had a long history of heavy use prior to its inclusion in the Wilderness System. Nonetheless, preservationists strongly supported its inclusion, even though a permanent Forest Service cabin already shared space at the lake with scores of private boats stored along the shoreline. The Forest Service contended it would be extremely difficult to scale back this established use to a level consistent with that required by the Wilderness Act. Congress disagreed and the area was included in the Mt. Jefferson Wilderness. Despite a substantial reduction in boating (accomplished in part by the sale of abandoned boats at auction and the burning of others) Marion Lake continues to attract heavy use. To deal with the undesirable impacts and resulting intensive management required at the lake, Oregon Senator Mark Hatfield sponsored legislation to remove Marion Lake from the Mt. Jefferson Wilderness. However, to date, his proposal has failed to attract the support necessary for enactment.

Finally, the allocation of an area to wilderness limits the range of management alternatives and techniques that might be considered. Areas managed as wilderness will provide only a limited portion of the total range of opportunities for outdoor recreation. Certain kinds of recreational activities (e.g., motorcycle riding) cannot be pursued in wilderness; certain management activities are likewise restricted by wilderness classification (e.g., use of mechanical equipment is generally disallowed).

The issue of what management actions, facilities, and equipment is allowed in wilderness bloomed as an important point of debate on the Endangered American Wilderness Act in 1977. Opponents of this bill, which sought to classify more than 20 new areas as wilderness, claimed that such designation would mean wildfires could not be suppressed, trails would be abandoned, and hunting and fishing drastically reduced. To clarify the issue of what you can and cannot do in wilderness, Congressman James Weaver of Oregon, a leading proponent of the bill, engaged the new Assistant Secretary of Agriculture, Rupert Cutler, in a colloquy of 12 questions and answers about Forest Service wilderness management policy. That colloquy, published in the Journal of Forestry, was an important clarification of the relationship of wilderness classification to management latitude. Actually, the colloquy exploded a number of misconceptions about the extreme purity of Forest Service wilderness management policy, which was much less restrictive than opponents of wilderness represented it (Weaver and Cutler 1977).

This restriction on permitted recreational and management activity means, then, that wilderness cannot supply the full range of primitive opportunities sought by visitors. As discussed earlier, wilderness is one point in the spectrum of alternative land uses. In order to provide diversity in both physical setting and recreational experience, the broadest range of overall settings should be offered. And, rather than attempting to provide many different kinds of opportunities under the heading of wilderness, it seems more appropriate to us to have a broadened range of land-use designations at the roadless end of the spectrum. How such areas are set aside—by administrative designation, as roadless area or backcountry, or by law as wilderness—is not our concern here. However, a wider range of settings, each with relatively clear standards for recreational and other uses and management seems needed, for at least two reasons. First, the public's tastes for widely diverse kinds of primitive recreation can best be met by a range of primitive settings. If wilderness is the only primitive setting offered in the land-use spectrum, it will be forced to accomodate all roadless recreation activities, including uses more appropriately carried out elsewhere. Second, the overriding goals of wilderness preservation are not advanced by classification of areas that cannot be successfully managed as wilderness.

The Need for Wilderness Management

Managing wilderness is a new idea. It has really become an issue only in the last 10 to 20 years. The early leaders of the wilderness movement, men like John Muir, Aldo Leopold, and Bob Marshall, whose roles will be discussed later in this chapter, were concerned with saving wilderness from development. They assumed that designating lands as wilderness and prohibiting road construction, logging, and similar uses would assure the preservation of wilderness—at least for the time being.

"Draw a line around it and leave it alone," pretty well describes the prevailing opinion not so long ago. Even today, it's shared by some. But a great many concerned people have concluded it just won't work with the kinds of pressures now descending on wilderness.

A Paradox

There is a paradox in managing a wilderness (Nash 1973). A wilderness is supposed to be an area where the influence of modern man is absent (or at least minimized as much as possible), but "management" implies man's controlling of nature. In most kinds of resource management man *does* alter and control nature. A dam changes a river into a lake. Forest management may change the number, size, distribution, and even species of trees growing in an area.

Many people react negatively to even a concept of wilderness management because they equate management with bulldozers and environmental manipulation (Burke 1969). However, wilderness management does not necessarily involve this kind of control of nature. *Wilderness management is essentially the management of human use and influence to preserve naturalness and solitude. It includes everything the persons responsible for a wilderness do in administering the area; for example, the formulation of goals and objectives for individual areas and all policies, standards, and field actions to achieve them.* Specifically, management includes the planning and implementation of such things as rules and regulations for controlling overuse; facilities such as trails and signs; decisions on access roads to the wilderness boundary; regulations for recreation stock and in some places commercial livestock grazing; wilderness patrol; public education including information provided in maps, brochures, and guidebooks. All these things are wilderness management. We will deal in much greater detail with components of wilderness management in subsequent chapters of the book.

Wilderness management does not need to be heavy handed. Wilderness managers are, in effect, guardians and not gardeners. Later we will discuss a key idea—that managers should not mold nature to suit people. Rather, they should manage human use and influence so that natural processes are not altered. *Managers should do only what is necessary to meet wilderness objectives, and use only the minimum tools, force, and regulation required to achieve those objectives.*

More Use — Less Area

Why is management necessary now if the founders of the wilderness preservation movement apparently weren't concerned about it? The reason is the overwhelming change in the number of users (Nash 1973, p. 263–273). At least 20 times as many people visit

wilderness now as in the 1930's, in the time of Marshall and Leopold. There is a real danger of people loving wilderness to death. Soils and vegetation take a pounding far beyond anything experienced a generation or more ago (Frome 1974, chapter 8). And some features of the wilderness experience—the quiet and solitude—have changed from something to be counted on to something difficult to find in many places and impossible to experience in others.

This enormous growth has many explanations: New developments in lightweight camping equipment and dried foods, changes in society such as higher education levels (the most distinguishing characteristic of wilderness visitors in every study), rising incomes, greater mobility, and growing interest in the environment, nature, and outdoor recreation. Heightened

Figure 1–4.—The need for wilderness management is growing, in part because of steadily increasing wilderness use and its impacts. Here users congregate at Red Pass in the Glacier Peak Wilderness, Mt. Baker-Snoqualmie National Forest, Wash.

interest and increased use of wilderness might even have been outgrowths of controversies and publicity over the classification of particular areas. And as Roderick Nash points out in chapter 2, the growth in wilderness use has been accompanied by a growing realization of the necessity for its management.

Paralleling increased use has been a decline in wilderness acreage. In fact, some of the growth in wilderness use must have been caused by displacement of users from areas that ceased to be wild, roadless, and undeveloped. The amount of potential additional wilderness is limited. Within any reasonable time span, new wilderness cannot be created. Classification as wilderness assures only that development will not occur; it does not create "new" wilderness or add capacity. The land was always there, and it was being used before it was classified. In order to gain the illusion of adding wilderness (i.e., the advantages that would accrue if new wilderness *could* be created), there is only one option: better management and protection of remaining wilderness (Zivnuska 1973; Simmons 1966). For wilderness (and other dwindling resources) our attention must broaden to include the intensive margin—better management of the existing supply—in addition to a continuing concern with the extensive margin—increasing the amount of wilderness (Lucas 1973).

Past Disruption of Nature

Quite apart from recreational requirements, there are other reasons wilderness management is needed. It is needed to restore the equilibrium which has been disrupted by man's interference with natural processes in wilderness. For example, the effectiveness of man's fire control has limited fire as a natural ecological force for about 50 years. This constitutes control of nature just as surely as does a dam across a brawling, wild river. Before man's control, fires typically occurred much more frequently than each 50 years in many areas. The effects of all the fires that have *not* occurred are cumulative in that unnatural conditions which could produce fires quite different from natural ones are building up. Fire management to restore natural conditions is needed in many areas and cannot be delayed indefinitely (see chapter 12).

To Give Classification Meaning

Finally, as mentioned earlier, some people who recognize the need for management, want to wait until all the wilderness classification decisions have been made. "We'll worry about management when wilderness designation is all done," is the gist of the position. We think this is an indefensible stand (Lucas 1973). First,

it will be a long time—at least 20 or 30 years—before all wilderness classification decisions are made. Use increased about 15-fold in the last 30 years, and a large increase will certainly occur in the next 30 years, especially if it is not restrained by management. Ecological change in such a long period would also be substantial.

Wilderness classification loses much of its meaning if subsequent management policies do not define, in effect, what classification will actually accomplish. Without management, wilderness classification verges on being an empty symbol—a mere name designation.

While the classification process goes on, nonconforming uses, inappropriate styles, and excessive levels of use can become well established and protected by their own vested interests. Irreversible damage can result from unmanaged use. Concentrations of numerous visitors can disastrously compact and erode wilderness soils. Threatened wildlife that depend on wilderness can be further jeopardized. Correction is always far more difficult and controversial than prevention. So, an important management task is preventing damage that would otherwise occur in the next 20 to 30 years. And these preventive measures must be taken while management is meeting pressing problems that require immediate correction in most wildernesses.

Alternatives to Management?

Is there any alternative to managing a wilderness? Two policies—both unacceptable—could avoid the necessity to manage. First, all use could be prohibited. Some problems, like fire control, would still require some thought, but essentially no use would make no management a possibility. But, as we will see later, the Wilderness Act and wilderness philosophy make clear that wilderness is for the *use* and *enjoyment* of people. Second, a completely laissez-faire attitude could eliminate the need for all management and planning. Just classify areas and forget about them. Any kind of use not clearly illegal under the Wilderness Act could be allowed in unlimited amount, and environmental damage or changes in the ecosystem would simply be accepted. Wilderness would vanish from most places (Frome 1974, chapter 7). This would also be a violation of the Wilderness Acts which require the protection and perpetuation—the preservation—of wilderness.

Not Whether, But How

The middle ground between these two extremes—no-use-allowed and classify-and-forget—requires management. We see no other justifiable course of action, and agree with Zivnuska (1973) that managed wilderness is the only possible kind. The real question is not *to manage* or *not to manage* but rather *how to manage*. That is the topic of this book. We may be able only to clarify the issue and identify some of its many parts. Wilderness management is frequently complex and necessarily subjective. But, since interest in wilderness management emerged, a considerable body of knowledge from experience and research has been developed. We think enough is known to greatly strengthen wilderness management. The knowledge is scattered; we have synthesized and summarized it for application to wilderness management.

What Is Wilderness?

What is wilderness? This is the crucial question for both allocation and management—the issue to which all allocation and management decisions must be related. At one extreme, wilderness can be defined in a narrow legal perspective as an area possessing qualities outlined in Section 2(c) of the Wilderness Act. At the other extreme, it is whatever people think it is; potentially, the entire universe, the *terra incognita* of people's minds. We can call these two extreme definitions legal wilderness and sociological wilderness.

There is little possibility of deriving a universally accepted definition of sociological wilderness because perceptions of wilderness vary widely. For some urbanites with scant knowledge of, or experience in, the natural environment, wilderness might be perceived in any undeveloped wildland, uncut forest, or woodlot.

On the other hand, legal wilderness as defined by the Wilderness Act of 1964 (Sec. 2c) is much more precise. "A wilderness, in contrast with those areas where man and his own works dominate the landscape, is hereby recognized as an area where the earth and its community of life are untrammeled by man, where man himself is a visitor who does not remain." This legal definition places wilderness on the "untrammeled" pole of the environmental modification continuum. Furthermore, the concept of legal wilderness in the Act is sanctioned by the tradition of this particular kind of land use in America and rests on ideas espoused decades ago.

For example, Aldo Leopold (1921) envisioned wilderness as "a continuous stretch of country preserved in its natural state, open to lawful hunting and fishing, big enough to absorb a 2 weeks' pack trip, and kept devoid of roads, artificial trails, cottages, or other works of man." Robert Marshall (1930) offered a similar definition:

. . . I . . . shall use the word *wilderness* to denote a region which contains no perma-

nent inhabitants, possesses no possibility of conveyance by any mechanical means and is sufficiently spacious that a person in crossing it must have the experience of sleeping out. The dominant attributes of such an area are: First, that it requires any one who exists in it to depend exclusively on his own effort for survival; and second, that it preserves as nearly as possible the primitive environment. This means that all roads, power transportation and settlements are barred. But trails and temporary shelters, which were common long before the advent of the white race, are entirely permissible.

This is a book about managing legal wilderness. Our definition of wilderness mirrors that outlined in the Wilderness Act (see the Preface). It is this definition that prescribes conditions for areas included in the National Wilderness Preservation System and the purposes that management programs for these areas are designed to achieve. It is these areas that are (as we discuss further in chapters 4, 5, and 6) legally classified for protection—set aside to be preserved as wilderness. The Act has lent both quantitative and qualitative substance to the traditionally elusive question, what is wilderness?

But while recognizing that wilderness has taken on added precision and clarity in its legal definition, we should not forget the evolution of the concept. Wilderness is still largely a phenomenon of 20th century North America. However, its recognition is spreading internationally, and in chapter 3 Roderick Nash describes in greater detail the status of such lands in Europe, Asia, and Africa and the cultural uniqueness of the United States wilderness concept. Even in the United States, the perception of wilderness has evolved from that of a repulsive landscape to a valued cultural resource.

It is not the intent or objective of this book to trace out in detail the origins of the word wilderness and its cultural evolution, or to annotate the extensive literature about the many values and philosophies of wilderness. Many other books and articles do this.[1] But it is important to give readers some appreciation for the origin and diversity of human values associated with the wilderness concept. This is necessary if they are to understand the Wilderness Act and be able to relate some of the diverse notions embodied in the 1964

[1] A comprehensive list of such books and articles is beyond the scope of this book. However, important examples would include Hans Huth, *Nature and the American*, Berkeley, Univ. of Calif. Press, 1957; Clarence Glacken, *Traces on the Rhodian Shore*, Univ. of Calif. Press, 1967; Roderick Nash, *Wilderness and the American Mind* (2nd ed.), Yale Univ. Press, 1973; and *Wilderness and Recreation—A Report on Resources, Values, and Problems*, Outdoor Recreation Resources Review Commission, Study Report 3, 1962, esp. chapter 1.

legislation to ways in which these values can be depreciated or enhanced through wilderness management. The next two portions of this chapter briefly review the origins of the wilderness concept and basic values that underlie its legal definition.

Historical Origins of the Wilderness Concept

There is a strong religious flavor in the early origins of the word wilderness. The word appeared in the 14th century English translation of the Bible from Latin and was used as a synonym for uninhabited and arid lands of the Near East (Nash 1973). Lands described as wilderness generally had three characteristics: (1) They were virtually uninhabited, (2) they were desolate and arid (less than 4 inches annual precipitation), and (3) they were vast (Outdoor Recreation Resources Review Commission 1962). In such lands, man could not long survive.

Because their inhospitality was due to the absence of precipitation, and because precipitation was beyond human understanding, such lands were perceived as evidence of God's displeasure. The wilderness was a cursed land, and when the Lord set out to punish, through act or parable, the wilderness was often the setting—witness the fate of Adam and Eve after being driven from the Garden of Eden. Conversely, the greatest blessing to be bestowed was to transform the wilderness—to make it "blossom like a rose."

The experience of the Israelites reinforced and added another dimension to the Judeo-Christian notion of wilderness. Wilderness was not only the setting for their 40-year wanderings inflicted as a punishment from the Lord for their misdeeds but it was also a place where they could prove themselves worthy of the Lord, and subsequently, the Promised Land. The wilderness, thus, was a place where one might purge and cleanse the soul, in order to be fit in the sight of God. Jesus' 40 days in the wilderness, fasting and resisting the temptations of Satan, was preparation for speaking to God (Nash 1973).

Wilderness, then, in early Judeo-Christian thought, was the place of evil—the antithesis of good. But even if wilderness had been seen as good—a place to enjoy oneself—early Christians would hardly have allowed themselves the luxury of a pleasure trip into the mountains. The mission of the early Christian was to forego worldly pleasures and seek salvation.

In its origins, Christianity was a highly man-centered religion (White 1967). God created Adam in his own image, and man stood distinctly apart from nature. But

Christian tenets gradually evolved until it became inappropriate or at least unnecessary to insist upon the dichotomy of man vs. nature. (The first proponents of this view were regarded as heretics. St. Francis of Assisi who insisted that animals, too, had souls, was excommunicated.) Rather than interpreting natural phenomena (storms, appearance of islands, earthquakes) as evidence of God's wrath, man came to see nature as a revelation of His handiwork. Eventually, with the rise of the physical and natural sciences, man associated inspiration (rather than terror) with wilderness, or he explained wilderness and other natural phenomena on the basis of natural rather than religious causes.

This new appreciation of nature was reflected in many ways. For instance, the symmetrical, formal gardens commonly found in the latter 1700's (e.g., the Garden of Versailles) gradually gave way to more informal and naturalistic settings. In art and literature the wild turbulent panoramas of the Alps became favorite scenes. A favorite literary hero became the man who knew how to live in harmony with nature (McCloskey 1966). This gradual evolution of thinking about man's relationship to the environment represented an important and necessary precondition to the recognition of wilderness as a source of human values and to the eventual development of programs for its preservation.

Wilderness and the Early American Scene

At the time the first European explorers reached what is now the conterminous 48 states, a continent of wilderness existed. In less than 500 years, this 1.9-billion-acre wilderness estate has been reduced by 98 percent. But concurrent with its diminishing size has been increasing appreciation for wilderness value. McCloskey (1966) and Roderick Nash in chapter 2 argue that scarcity of wilderness is a necessary precondition for recognition of its value. And, as Nash points out in chapter 3, both the American experience and that of other countries confirm that hypothesis.

Clearly, the wilderness was a barrier and a threat to 16th- and 17th-century settlers. It hindered movement, it harbored Indians, and it frequently possessed little that could help settlers prosper. But as the curtain of wilderness rolled back before the settlement of people, a movement began to retain some unmodified lands for perpetuity. Nash (1973) has argued that interest in maintaining some remaining wildlands was motivated in part by the desire to lend a certain distinctive quality to American culture. While literary and artistic accomplishments were almost nonexistent in the young Nation, we did possess one thing for which there was no European counterpart: wilderness. Thus, while there were still strong motivations to conquer the wilderness, there were also stirrings of countervailing opinions that valued its retention.

One early observer who foresaw the need for long term protection of the natural environment was George Catlin, a 19th-century lawyer, painter, and student of American Indians. Following a series of trips through the northern Great Plains, Catlin concluded that rapid slaughter of the buffalo, the deterioration of Indian cultures as they collided with the white man's, and the general disappearance of the primitive landscape were losses American culture could ill afford. Thus, in the early 1800's he called for establishment of "A *nation's park*, containing man and beast, in all the wild and freshness of the nature's beauty!" (cited in Nash 1973).

Catlin's remarks received little attention. But the seed was planted. In 1858, writing in *Atlantic Monthly*, Henry David Thoreau asked "why should not we . . . have our national preserves . . . in which the bear and panther, and some even of the hunter race, may still exist . . ." (cited in Nash 1973). Thoreau was a primary spokesman for a viewpoint that credited wilderness with the values most important in the molding of mankind— a perspective summarized in the oft-cited statement " . . . in wildness is the preservation of the world" (Thoreau 1851).

More than 100 years passed between the warnings of Catlin and Thoreau and passage of the Wilderness Act. During that time, numerous spokesmen argued for the preservation of some of the remaining wilderness landscape. Some important governmental acts indicated increasing recognition of the importance of reserving lands for public purposes. Yellowstone National Park was established in 1872, the first in a long series of significant reservations. Earlier, in 1864, the federal government had granted Yosemite Valley to the State of California "to hold . . . inalienable for all time" (Ise 1961). While it is almost certain that neither area was intended for wilderness purposes (see chapter 2 for more on this), they did provide a precedent for the federal government to set aside lands for nonexploitive purposes. Moreover, these reservations represented official recognition of values and philosophies expressed by people like Thoreau.

Historical Wilderness Themes and Values

The Wilderness Act of 1964 was the product of over 8 years of debate in Congress (see chapter 4). However, to fully understand the meaning of that legislation, one must reach back many generations. The Wilderness Act, and the movement leading to it, reflects a synthesis of diverse philosophical values that evolved over many years. As McCloskey (1966) notes:

> The evolution has blended many political, religious, and cultural meanings into deeply felt personal convictions . . . Those who administer that law must look to these convictions to understand why the law exists.

The diversity of motives and convictions among individuals and groups supporting the wilderness movement has been instrumental in its success. The contributions of many wilderness proponents, both early and contemporary, suggest several distinct themes or values around which the wilderness cause has been argued. While it is certainly true that wilderness is something a little bit different to everyone, an understanding of certain recurring themes is important for management which alone can assure their perpetuation. Following is a review of three consistent wilderness themes—experiential, mental and moral restoration, and scientific—and the key individuals associated with the various points of view.

Experiential

Certainly one of the central themes of the wilderness movement has focused on the experiences offered by unmodified natural settings—the wilderness experience. Historical writings highlight nature appreciation, education, freedom, solitude, simplicity, as well as spiritual, aesthetic, and mystical dimensions of the wilderness experience. An articulate and influential individual who identified experiential values of wilderness was John Muir, founder of the Sierra Club in 1892.

Muir was a Scottish immigrant, raised on a Wisconsin farm. Although a talented inventor, Muir was more intrigued by the ideas he found in science and literature. He was heavily influenced by the writings and philosophies of Thoreau and Ralph Waldo Emerson (Davis 1966–67). Nevertheless, he found them both wanting in some respects. Emerson had failed to express what Muir considered an appropriate amount of excitement after hiking in the mountains at Yosemite (Davis 1966–67) and he was amused that Thoreau, who had proclaimed "In wildness is the preservation of the world," could refer to orchards as forests (Nash 1973).

The essence of wilderness to Muir was the freedom, solitude, and beauty of the mountains, and these qualities, he felt, could satisfy all man's needs. The wilderness experience to Muir was spiritual—the forests were temples, the trees sang psalms. In the Sierra wilderness, "everything . . . seems equally divine—one smooth, pure wild glow of heaven's love." The wilderness also offered personal insight; during a raging windstorm in the California Sierras, Muir climbed a tree and lashed himself to it in order to experience nature more closely. The experience, he later recounted, led him to realize that "trees are travelers . . . they make many journeys . . . (so are) our own little journeys . . . only little more than tree wavings—many not so much" (Muir 1938).

The experiential theme was also reflected in many of the writings of Robert Marshall. Marshall was an extraordinary individual. In a brief (he died at 38) but frenetic life, he made major accomplishments for wilderness, including establishment of the U-Regulations in the Forest Service and the founding of the Wilderness Society in 1935. Wild scenery, Marshall felt, was similar to great works of art. In a major paper outlining the future of wilderness, he wrote "wilderness furnishes perhaps the best opportunity for . . . pure aesthetic rapture" (Marshall 1930).

Leopold, particularly in the early 1920's argued for wilderness designation because he felt it important to preserve a particular kind of recreational experience, the pack trip. Unless steps were taken to preserve large tracts of land, he stated, the day will come:

> When a packtrain must wind its way up a graveled highway and turn its bell-mare in the pasture of a summer hotel. When that day comes the packtrain will be dead, the diamond hitch will be merely rope, and Kit Carson and Jim Bridger will be names in a history lesson (Leopold 1925).

The experiential theme is present in the work of many contemporary authors. The Outdoor Recreation Resources Review Commission (1962) called upon Wallace Stegner, head of the Creative Writing Center at Stanford University, to comment on the significance of wilderness as "an intangible which has altered the American consciousness." Stegner's reply argued forcefully for the maintenance of wilderness for the sake of survival:

> Something will have gone out of us as a people if we ever let the remaining wilderness be destroyed; if we permit the last virgin forests to be turned into comic books and plastic cigarette cases; if we drive the few remaining members of the wild species into zoos or to extinction; if we pollute the last clear air and dirty the last clean streams and push our paved roads through the last of the silence, so that never again will Americans be free in their own country from the noise, the

exhausts, the stinks of human automotive waste.

Wilderness is needed, he concluded, because it is "a means of reassuring ourselves of our sanity as creatures, a part of the geography of hope" (ORRRC 1962).

The extensive writings of Sigurd Olson also reveal many of the important human values derived from wilderness. In a series of books published over the last two decades, Olson has articulated recorded wilderness experiences. He finds wilderness a source of inspiration, of insight, and of personal peace: "The singing wilderness has to do with the calling of the loons . . . it is concerned with the simple joys, the timelessness and perspective found in a way of life that is close to the past" (Olson 1957). While exploring the Knife River in the Quetico-Superior country, Olson found himself nearly overwhelmed by the environment around him: ". . . I was aware of a fusion with the country, an overwhelming sense of completion in which all my hopes and experiences seemed crystallized into one shining vision" (Olson 1963).

Mental and Moral Restoration

Closely related to experiential values is the notion that wilderness serves as a reservoir for renewal of mind and spirit. In some cases, it offers an important sanctuary into which one can withdraw, either temporarily or permanently, to find respite. Thoreau withdrew to the simple life of Walden; today, communes have sprung up in some wildernesses and many other wildland settings, their creation spurred by the desire of participants for a place to "do their own thing."

Muir advised townsmen to:

> Climb the mountains and get their good tidings. Nature's peace will flow into you as sunshine flows into trees. The wind will blow their own freshness into you and the storms their energy, while cares will drop off like autumn leaves (Teale 1954).

Aldo Leopold pressed for preservation of areas capable of providing a particular kind of recreational experience because he thought such experiences developed both individual and national character (Leopold 1921). Marshall also believed that wilderness experience produced great mental and moral values. Then, as now, one had to depend on his own resources to survive in the wilderness. Thus, wilderness demanded what society valued—self-sufficiency. Even then, civilization had taken a terrible toll on modern man as evidenced by increasing tension and unhappiness. People without the outlet of wilderness, Marshall reasoned, might turn to the "thrills" of crime and war

Wilderness, in Marshall's mind, offered a "moral equivalent to war" (Marshall 1930).

This moral-rejuvenation theme was also expressed by Arthur Carhart, the young Forest Service landscape architect, who in 1919 persuaded his superiors to abandon plans for development around Trappers Lake on the White River National Forest in Colorado. For instance, Carhart believed the primary value of forests was their potential for building individual and national character:

> Perhaps the rebuilding of the body and spirit is the greatest service derivable from our forests, for of what worth are material things if we lose the character and the quality of people that are the soul of America (Carhart 1955).

Strong moralistic values permeated Carhart's writing. To Carhart, recreation was not merely an incidental use of forests; it ranked among the highest of all possible uses because of the moral benefits associated with the particular kinds of opportunities if offered:

> Recreation in the open is of the finest grade. The moral benefits are all positive. The individual with any soul cannot live long in the presence of towering mountains or sweeping plains without getting a little of the high moral standard of Nature infused into his being . . . with eyes opened, the great story of the Earth's forming, the history of a tree, the life of a flower or the activities of some small animal will all unfold themselves to the recreationist . . . (Carhart 1920).

Carhart's immediate superior in Colorado was Carl J. Stahl. Stahl was a firm supporter of Carhart and helped back him on his Trappers Lake proposal. Like Carhart, he also saw forests as a source of moral values. Writing in the *Journal of Forestry* in 1921, he commented:

> An appreciation of nature, a stimulation of vigor of the mind and body, and the contentment of soul contributed by association with the forests, goes far toward making a useful and contented citizenry. If the American population can be made to feel contented and its effort directed to useful channels, enlistment in the Red organizations of this critical period of unrest can be averted. I can conceive of no more useful purpose the forests can be made to serve.

Thus, over 50 years ago, the moral character built by contact between man and nature was seen as an effective force to offset the perceived threat of socialist and communist philosophies and organizations to the American way of life.

An implicit notion of the rejuvenation theme is wilderness as a refuge. It is a place where one can go to "drop out" momentarily, to acquire a new perspective on life, and to simply slow down. In today's bustling world, it offers a place where important human values can be rediscovered and where a simpler, less complicated life exists, at least momentarily; it offers a chance to be rehumanized. Coupled with the opportunity to reestablish one's self-confidence through challenge is the possibility that a better man will emerge from the wilderness. This concept is institutionalized in current programs such as the National Outdoor Leadership School in which young people pit themselves against nature in order to gain the education and maturation that come from surpassing one's self-defined limits. Similar programs (e.g., Outward Bound) aim to instill self-confidence in individuals of all ages by posing challenges (e.g., rapelling a cliff or canoeing in rapids) that require participants to expand their previous limits. Many of these programs take place in designated wilderness because the kinds of physical challenge they frequently seek are particularly appropriate to an unmodified environment.[2] In a real sense, such programs fulfill a dream of Aldo Leopold. He believed that such areas should be places where primitive travel and subsistence skills could be perpetuated (Leopold 1949).

Wilderness can allegedly provide therapy to the emotionally run-down individual beset by the stresses of modern life (McKinley 1966) as well as the person beset by a severe mental disorder, such as schizophrenia (Bernstein 1972).

Scientific

A third wilderness theme relates to the scientific values wilderness holds for society. Because of its generally undisturbed setting, wilderness has been viewed as an important source of information about the world around us—how it evolved, how the impacts and changes introduced by civilization altered natural systems, and what the unmodified environment holds for us.

One commentator on the scientific value of wilderness was George Perkins Marsh. Marsh published a major volume describing the impact civilization had had on the earth. Entitled *Man and Nature; or Physical Geography*

---

[2] In some areas, serious management problems have developed around these programs. For instance, some wilderness managers have reported that after a survival school group passes through an area, few living creatures, such as frogs, can be found—they've all been eaten! Fortunately, cooperation between such groups and managing agencies has reduced such impacts.

as Modified by Human Action, March described numerous graphic examples of human misuse of natural resources. On parts of the world, he wrote:

> Man has brought the face of the earth to desolation almost as complete as that of the moon; and though, within that brief space of time which we call the "historical period," they are known to have been covered with luxurious woods, verdant pastures, and fertile meadows . . .

But,

> In countries untrodden by man, the atmospheric precipitation and evaporation, the thermometric mean, and the distribution of vegetable and animal life, are subject to change only from geological influences so slow in their operation that the geographic conditions may be regarded as immutable. These arrangements of nature are in most cases highly desirable to maintain, when such regions become the seat of organized commonwealths (Marsh 1907).

An ecological perspective, focusing on the intricate and complex interrelationships between all organisms, has been an important aspect of the scientific theme. Muir, for example, developed some important ideas on the subject. He received university training in the sciences, primarily geology, and was a careful observer of the natural scene. In wilderness, Muir argued, men could feel "part of wild nature, kin to everything" (Nash 1973). And it was Muir who expressed the fundamental principle of ecology: "Whenever you pluck up something, you find everything in the universe attached to it."

The scientific values of wilderness were particularly important to Aldo Leopold. In wilderness, Leopold saw the "perfect norm" for seeing how healthy land maintains itself. Paleontology offers abundant evidence that wilderness maintained itself for immensely long periods; that is, component species were rarely lost, neither did they get out of hand; weather and water built soil as fast or faster than it was carried away. Wilderness, then, assumes unexpected importance as a laboratory for the study of land health (Leopold 1941). In 1935, Leopold joined with Bob Marshall and others to found the Wilderness Society. It was through the Society that Leopold hoped to promote a new philosophical disposition—"an intelligent humility toward man's place in nature." Although Leopold had long valued wilderness for its important historical and recreational values (e.g., Leopold 1925), 1935 represented an important transition in his thinking to a predominantly

ecological and ethical justification for such areas (Flader 1974).

Because wilderness areas have remained undisturbed over long periods of time, they are reservoirs of genetic constructs following eons of evolution (Cowan 1968). In addition to its scientific significance, the genetic diversity inherent in a system of large, undisturbed tracts is important as a source of stability in animal and plant population (Ghiselin 1973–74). Such information once lost is impossible to replicate; yet it can offer the key to questions yet unasked. Similarly it is important to retain species whose chemical and biological make-up might be useful in the future—as the source of important drugs, for example.

The opportunity to analyze the complex processes in biological systems that have escaped man's impact is a necessary part of understanding man's relationship to the world around him. One observer (Loucks 1970) has commented that man's interference with the random rejuvenation of ecosystems (e.g., through fire control) is the greatest possible disturbance to them. Wilderness affords an important opportunity to witness ecosystems as they evolve outside man's influence. The understanding derived could help man avoid errors, at best careless and at worst catastrophic, as he shapes and modifies the earth to his purposes. As Leopold once noted, the first principle of intelligent tinkering is to save all the parts. The scientific understanding lent by the availability of a large and geographically representative collection of Wilderness tracts could be of immeasurable importance.

One major problem of the current system of wilderness reservations is that many important physical-biological systems are represented only poorly or not at all. A study by the National Park Service of the relative representation of various natural history concepts found many significant types had little or no representation. In many cases, the features, eradicated by man's activities, simply no longer exist (USDI NPS 1972). The Forest Service roadless area review and evaluation (RARE II), currently underway, includes an analysis of representation in the NWPS of the nation's ecosystems, landforms, and wilderness-associated wildlife. Roadless areas that would fill voids in the representation of these physical-biological phenomena will allegedly have priority as candidate areas for wilderness classification.

Wilderness is also valuable from a scientific perspective because a number of threatened species—for example, the grizzly bear and timber wolf—depend on large tracts of unmodified habitat. Wilderness is also necessary for the study of these species in order to assure their maintenance. These issues are discussed further in chapter 11, but it is important to note here that wilderness tracts have served as a laboratory for greatly increasing knowledge of the biota around us (Cain 1960). Studies of wildlife such as the wolves (Mech 1970; Allen 1974) and grizzly bears (Craighead et al. 1971; Cole 1974), carried out in wilderness settings have substantially enlarged our understanding of these animals. Similarly, the presence of extensive tracts of undeveloped land has made possible important baseline research on vegetative communities (Ohmann and Ream 1971), fire history (Heinselman 1973), and other natural biological systems that simply could not have occurred without such tracts.

Wilderness also provides an important scientific resource to scientists concerned with human behavior. Studies of how individuals relate to one another, how they cope in the face of stress and challenge, and how behavior is altered or modified in natural environments are important topics for wilderness research (Scott 1974). Ultimately, studies of wilderness users can reveal important insights on the experiential values of wilderness espoused by Muir, Marshall, Olson, and others. One of the very practical goals of wilderness user studies is insight into the importance of these human values and ways of increasing them through appropriate management.

Relating Wilderness Themes and Values to Management

This review of three major themes of wilderness values is necessarily broad. A more detailed inquiry would identify many more associated value concepts. For instance, McCloskey (1966) identified 11 valuations of wilderness that have emerged since arrival of settlers in North America. However, our purpose has been to simply outline something of the basic values of wilderness identified by both early and contemporary authors.

One point should be stressed. Most observers identified all three themes—experiential, mental and moral restoration, and scientific. For example, Muir's strong experiential philosophy was backed by an intense scientific curiosity. Similarly, Marshall recognized both mental values in wilderness and significant scientific contributions to be gained from such areas (Marshall held a Ph.D. degree in plant pathology). Leopold's ethical and scientific perspective was complemented by a well developed appreciation for the recreational values of wilderness. Supporting the credibility of these earlier observations are several studies of contemporary wilderness users, all of which have identified multiple

orientations and values in the relationship of use to wilderness.

The key to this discussion hinges on McCloskey's statement cited earlier: To understand the Wilderness Act, we must understand its historical and philosophical origin. The philosophies and perspective discussed above increase our understanding of what wilderness is, why we have it, and what it should provide society. These issues are important in applying the Wilderness Act—in the designation of wilderness and its subsequent management. Once wilderness allocation decisions have been made, the extent to which the values espoused by early philosophers like Muir, Marshall, and Leopold are realized will depend on wilderness management. It is essential that managers, educators, and citizens be guided in their efforts by a personal philosophy of wilderness that recognizes the basic values set forth by these early philosophers.

We turn now to a discussion of wilderness management philosophies and some of their consequences for realizing wilderness values.

Wilderness Philosophy and Wilderness Management

Each Federal agency assigned responsibilities under the Wilderness Act has developed policies and guidelines for its application. Such direction is important in order that wilderness management actions do not significantly deviate from place to place. However, it is simply not possible for agency policy to cover all the contingencies that might arise; moreover, it would be foolish to provide such detail. Managers need to retain some flexibility to respond to unique conditions occurring in individual areas. The gap that exists between specific policy and unanticipated contingencies—the need for broad guidelines on the one hand and flexibility on the other—is filled by the manager's philosophical perspective.

Because many different ideas exist about wilderness management, it is difficult to point to any one perspective and say "this is the right one." Each has its particular origin and set of consequences. In the following discussion, we will look at some wilderness management perspectives and try to identify their consequences, particularly their relation or their implications to the objectives of the Wilderness Act.

Wilderness Produces Human Values

Initially, we call attention to a fundamental principle discussed in more detail in chapter 7—wilderness is preserved and managed for the benefits and values it provides people. Many programs such as the Rare and Endangered Species Act, the Wild and Scenic Rivers Act, and the Wilderness Act have been enacted to protect and preserve the natural environment. These bills have been enacted not just for the sake of nature, but under the assumption that the retention of such natural features provides important human benefits and values. Even to say that some feature is unique and worthy of protection is a human judgment based on the belief that such things are valuable to man's pleasure, survival, and well-being (Murdy 1975).

Sometimes, but not always, the benefits of environmental preservation for direct consumption, vicarious enjoyment, or even as a future option for man's possible use can be assessed as economic values (Krutilla 1967). Thus, for example, retention of the Hell's Canyon portion of the Snake River in its natural state was found to be of greater economic value to society than was its development for hydroelectric power (Krutilla and Cicchetti 1972).

That wilderness is for use by people has clear statutory support. The Wilderness Act specifically notes that wildernesses shall be administered "for the use and enjoyment of the American people." But what kinds of use? The Act, of course, clearly rules out some types: Mechanized use, with some minor exceptions (aircraft use where previously established, motor boats in the Boundary Waters Canoe Area), is not permitted. But within the range of uses permitted by the Act, there is considerable diversity with regard to the styles of use and the accompanying facilities and developments. Simply arguing that wilderness is for use (e.g., DeFelice 1975) does little more than state the obvious. It does little to resolve the issues of what kinds of use and how much use. Obviously, one's philosophical perspective about wilderness and its values is important in considering the issue.

Anthropocentric and Biocentric Perspectives

Let's consider two alternative philosophical notions about wilderness and the basis for its values. On the one hand, there is the *anthropocentric* position that takes the "use and enjoyment" phrase of the Wilderness Act quite literally. Under this philosophy, programs to facilitate man's direct use of wilderness are paramount. Wilderness is viewed from primarily a sociological or man-oriented perspective; the naturalness of the wilderness is less important than its maximum direct use in ways pleasing to man. Programs to alter the physical environment to produce particularly desired settings are encouraged. Developments and facilities to increase

recreational use of wilderness are appropriate. In fact, increasing direct human use will increase human values and benefits. The character of wilderness will be amenable to man's desires and allowed constantly to evolve to contemporary standards of naturalness. There is no such thing as wilderness carrying capacity because man's ever changing preferences and adaptation to his environment and vice versa will continually change standards of crowding and naturalness. Wilderness is still one extreme on the environmental continuum, but a shifting extreme, ever relative to ubiquitous influence and not grounded in any absolute standards (Burch 1974). "Let's open up our wilderness areas" (Julber 1972) might serve as a slogan for believers in pure anthropocentrism.

Contrasted to the anthropocentric perspective is one that places an emphasis on the maintenance of the natural systems at the expense of recreational and other human uses if necessary (Hendee and Stankey 1973). The goal of this *biocentric* philosophy is to permit the natural ecological processes to operate as freely as possible because wilderness values for society ultimately depend on the retention of naturalness. To the extent that naturalness is distorted, the experiential, mental and moral restoration, and scientific values of wilderness are forfeited.

We recognize that labeling these alternative philosophical perspectives as "biocentric" versus "anthropocentric" might create a false distinction between "wilderness for man's sake" and "wilderness for wilderness' sake." As we discussed earlier, wilderness is for people. *The important distinction between these philosophies is the extent to which the human benefits of wilderness are seen as being dependent on the natural integrity of the wilderness setting.*

These alternative perspectives have been argued persuasively by their respective proponents. Before turning to a more detailed look at each, we should emphasize two points. First, these philosophies represent extreme polarized concepts about wilderness management, and it is unlikely either could be slavishly followed. But they do help highlight alternative orientations toward wilderness management. Second, it is difficult, if not impossible, to say that any philosophical position is wrong or right. It seems more important to ask that the long-range implications of each be examined and their consequences judged for appropriateness in light of the Wilderness Act objectives. With that concern in mind, let's look at each philosophical perspective more closely.

The Anthropocentric Philosophy

The principal emphasis of this orientation is to facilitate direct human use of wilderness. A manager who accepted this approach would emphasize recreation and other uses. Specific examples of actions might include development of high standard trail systems; artificial stocking of fish would be expanded to most wilderness lakes; the provision of campsite facilities such as tables, tent pads, and fireplaces; shelters, abundant toilets, and similar features seeking to increase recreational carrying capacity, aesthetic satisfaction, and user convenience. The most popular perception of wilderness—that held by the largest number of users—would be the important reference for managers.

This orientation—that sociological definitions of wilderness are more important than ecologically based definitions—would have important implications for both users and the environment. Initially the emphasis on the aesthetic and recreational qualities of wilderness settings could lead to a substantial alteration of the environment, particularly the vegetation. Given current knowledge and technology, it would be quite possible to engineer the wilderness scene to produce specific environmental conditions (Spurr 1966). For example, some have argued that a wilderness should represent a "picture" of some early point in our history—for example, the land as it was at the time the North American continent was first settled. To create such a situation, of course, would require sharp interference with natural processes in order to steer ecological successional processes in the desired direction. Fire, chemicals, or physical manipulations could do this. Some desirable results—from an anthropocentric point of view—might be achieved: for example, increased scenic views from well-cropped view points; additional forage for stock from intensively managed) perhaps irrigated and fertilized) range; increased high alpine meadow area maintained by physically uprooting invading conifers; more contact with wildlife stimulated by strategic salting, fertilizing favored vegetation, and prescribed burning to enhance habitat. Traditional forestry, silviculture, and habitat management would be in demand. Thus, theoretically at least, wilderness managers could be gardeners rather than guardians.

However, despite some desirable consequences from a recreational standpoint (in the view of adherents) an essential wilderness quality—naturalness—would be lost. Furthermore, such an approach (at least after a certain point) would be illegal in classified wilderness. The Act details quite clearly that wilderness should be a setting where the forces (processes) of nature operate free from man's influence. Man's influence on ecosystems is already pervasive worldwide, ranging from the introduction of pollutants into the atmosphere to direct recreational impacts. But as an ideal concept, minimal influence with natural evolution seems to be a clear intent of the Wilderness Act (Sec. 2a): "In order to insure that an expanding settlement and growing mechanization does not occupy and modify all areas within the United States . . . [and] . . . to secure for the American people of present and future generations the benefits of an enduring resource of wilderness." Meeting this goal under the "untrammeled" definition of wilderness in the Act would not seem possible to us under the degree of anthropocentrism described above.

An anthropocentric approach would also seem to be particularly detrimental to the scientific values of wilderness. The notion of wilderness as a genetic pool, an environmental baseline, and a refuge for the survival of species especially sensitive to man's influence would be lost in a wilderness manipulated and altered to fit evolving human tastes. Because the loss of naturalness would in many cases be irreversible, there would be incalculable costs in terms of foregone scientific opportunities.

Styles of recreation accommodated and facilitated by this management philosophy would be convenience-oriented. Because the production of recreational experiences is a primary goal, actions to increase access, to reduce difficulty and danger, and to facilitate use would be encouraged. Conversely, programs that hinder or restrict use would be rejected. The argument has been forcefully made by some authors (e.g., Behan 1972; Foote 1973; DeFelice 1975) that wilderness is for use and that programs that hinder use (e.g., wilderness permit systems, rationing, minimum standard trails, minimum party size) are bureaucratic hindrances that should be eliminated. Under an anthropocentric philosophy, then, if problems of environmental impact or excessive congestion did arise, the managerial response would involve such measures as engineering efforts to harden sites, revegetating, installing more facilities such as toilets, upgrading trails, and otherwise "gearing up" the wilderness to handle increased levels of use.

Management under this philosophy would be consistent with the views of some observers who argue that present day wilderness regulations discriminate against many people (e.g., the elderly, the ill) and, in effect, close off public (wilderness) lands to the majority of the public (Julber 1972; Netboy 1974). As an example of wilderness serving a large public, these authors point to the European Alps where large numbers of people are accommodated with relatively minor impact on the environment, through use of extensive road systems, cog railways, and mountain chalets. In this way, the authors argue, democratic values are retained, the environment is protected, and the greatest number of people are served.

The Biocentric Philosophy

The biocentric perspective places primary emphasis on preservation of the natural order. Its principal goal is to encourage management programs that most nearly approximate natural energy flows within wilderness ecosystems; that is, those that match the energy budgets of ecosystems as they existed in the absence of man's influence (Houston 1971). This requires controlling the introduction of unnatural levels of energy into the ecosystems through such sources as excess recreational use and eliminating restriction on normal energy flows through policies such as complete fire prevention and suppression. Thus, recreational use in wilderness would be consistent with this perspective only to the point that it does not unduly alter this energy balance. However, as with the anthropocentric philosophy, a biocentric approach also focuses on human benefits. The important distinction between them is the extent to which these benefits are viewed as being dependent on the naturalness of wilderness ecosystems.

This biocentric approach to wilderness management also has specific implications for both the environment and users. Over an extended period of time, we would expect to see evolving environmental conditions that reflect historical patterns of ecological succession. The natural processes (e.g., erosion, fire) that have shaped and altered the landscape would continue to operate much as they always have. One consequence of this is that a wilderness might often appear aesthetically unattractive. Insect infestation, erosion, fires, forest disease, and so forth would be allowed to run their course without man's interference; as a result, wilderness landscapes would sometimes reflect these natural perturbations. It would also mean that particularly desirable recreational features such as high mountain meadows, important stock forage areas, or areas of wildlife production would gradually shift with advancing ecological succession.

The management challenges offered would present little opportunity for traditional forestry skills. Silviculture, habitat management, and so forth would not be needed. Nature would roll the dice to determine ecological outcomes. Rather, much more emphasis would be placed on such things as monitoring the naturalness of conditions and the control of visitor behavior to preserve them.

The recreational use of a wilderness managed under a biocentric philosophical perspective would be secondary to maintenance of the natural order. Management actions to increase and facilitate use, such as improved trails and campsite facilities, would not be appropriate. In cases where use caused a significant impact on wilderness ecosystems, rather than instituting methods to absorb greater impact, management would curtail or disperse use. Moreover, appropriate management programs would promote opportunities with narrower appeal emphasizing the primitive environment, challenge, and solitude—activities contrasting with the more widely practiced recreational activities available on nonwilderness lands or emphasized under an anthropocentric philosophy. Under a biocentric philosophy, recreational opportunities require users to take wilderness on its own terms.

These alternative management perspectives represent extremes on a continuum of wilderness management orientations. As polar positions, we would not expect to see them translated directly into management programs. Our point in outlining them is to clearly distinguish two contrasting perspectives managers might consider in managing wilderness.

In Support of a Biocentric Approach

Which is the most appropriate philosophy? As we noted earlier, the question of which approach is right or wrong has no absolute answer. The answer must be related to the long-run implications for meeting the legal objectives set forth for the Wilderness System.

It seems to us that a philosophy which facilitates man's use of wilderness would gradually diminish the naturalness and solitude of wilderness, alter ecological regimes in subtle but drastic ways, and result in the loss of opportunity for human experiences dependent on wild and unaltered settings. The result would be a shrinking of the environmental continuum—the elimination of one extreme on the environmental modification spectrum—and a resulting loss of diversity of wildland settings.

To achieve the legal goals of the Wilderness System, it is our judgment that management should emphasize the natural integrity of wilderness ecosystems—we lean toward a biocentric philosophy. This position and its implications are most consistent with the legal mandate of the Wilderness Act, with the intent of the legislative debate that fashioned the Act, and with its historical-philosophical foundations that evolved over the past century. Consider the following arguments supporting a biocentric perspective.

First, in light of our knowledge of the diversity of

tastes held by recreationists, it would insure that those persons who prefer a wild and pristine setting would not be displaced in favor of users whose tastes can be met in many other locations. Some users really do depend on a pristine wilderness to achieve satisfactions important to them (Partridge 1975). The supply of pristine settings is diminishing, and a philosophy that maintains diversity of opportunity ought to be encouraged.

Second, recent research suggests that as people gain outdoor experience through such activities as car camping, they seek out progressively more demanding kinds of experiences (Krutilla 1967). There is, for instance, evidence that the demand for primitive styles of recreation is directly correlated with the amount of childhood camping experience (Burch and Wenger 1967). Thus, it is reasonable to expect that many persons now using car-campground facilities might in the future opt for wilderness. Increased demands on wilderness is virtually certain. Actions based on a biocentric philosophy will help insure the maintenance of opportunities to meet this increased level of demand.

Third, management responses to increasing use pressures can lead to unanticipated shifts in the kinds of recreational opportunity an area offers. Developments made to protect a site can attract a specialized clientele. This has been documented in campgrounds where developments to protect natural qualities of the site (e.g., tent pads, tables, fireplaces, toilets) attract a new clientele drawn not by nature but by the facilities, the sociability of other users, and other features of the location (Clark et al. 1971). Thus, the response of management can dramatically change the kind of opportunity offered and with it the people attracted. Applying a biocentric philosophy's criteria of naturalness and solitude would minimize the extent to which such artificially stimulated changes occurred. The extent to which new use opportunities would be allowed to evolve would be limited. But by no means would this be an unpopular approach. Studies document that a large proportion of users favor minimum campsite development in wilderness. A recent study of backcountry use in a National Park found Agency- and camper-constructed facilities related to user dissatisfaction (Lee 1975).

Fourth, a biocentric approach would preserve the greatest range of future options. Management decisions that increase use through facility development can accumulate into a series of irreversible decisions that narrow the range of available opportunities through elimination of the type of areas already in short supply. Additionally, this could mean the loss of important biological and scientific values.

Much debate has centered on certain sections of the Wilderness Act, particularly around the phrasing of Section 2(c), which defines wilderness as a place that ". . . has outstanding opportunities for solitude *or* a primitive and unconfined type of recreation." Clark (1976) has argued that the conjunction "or" means an area may provide either solitude or a primitive and unconfined kind of recreation. Either condition qualifies as an acceptable type of wilderness experience which managers might attempt to provide. And, he subsequently argues, to consider the "or" as an "and", making both solitude *and* a primitive and unconfined type of recreation necessary qualities of wilderness is a deliberate misrepresentation of the Act's intent and reduces the range of feasible management alternatives.

An alternative view of this phrasing is that the descriptive terms are essentially synonymous and were included to clarify the nature of the experiences wilderness was intended to offer (Worf et al. 1972). That is, the "or" is intended to add an elaboration on the nature of the experiences produced by wilderness. We endorse this interpretation. It is consistent, we believe, with both the legislative history of the Act as well as ensuing legislation. For example, the late Pennsylvania Congressman, John Saylor (1962), a leading supporter of the Wilderness Act described the wilderness experience in the following way:

> In addition, there is a composite value in wilderness recreation that cannot be reproduced anywhere short of an authentically rugged and big tract of undeveloped country. It derives from all the activities and experiences one enjoys or doesn't enjoy— camping, primitive travel, exhaustion, incomparable solitude, miserable weather—in a setting big enough for their simultaneous happenings with elbowroom.

The wilderness experience, in Saylor's view, was a composite one, comprised of various elements, including solitude. This view is also consistent with many of the other conceptions of wilderness voiced during debate on the Wilderness Act.

This interpretation is further supported by wording in the so-called Eastern Wilderness Act of 1975. In the statement of policy, the Act notes that wildernesses classified by the Act become a part of the National Wilderness Preservation System and that management shall "promote and perpetuate the wilderness character of the land and its specific values of solitude, physical and mental challenge, scientific study, inspiration and primitive recreation. . . ." Thus, management to provide a complex set of experiences seems called for, with solitude one of the important values management is to provide.

Obviously, the levels of solitude to be found within and between areas will vary, perhaps substantially (Stankey et al. 1976). The Wilderness Acts do not prescribe a single standard for solitude which all areas must meet. Moreover, the existing pattern of trails and campsites preclude such a standard anyway. Near trailheads, at popular locations, etc., use intensities will be higher and it seems neither necessary nor possible to manage for some uniform level of inter-party contact. The 1964 Act calls for provision of *"outstanding opportunities for solitude"* (emphasis added) and we interpret that to mean exactly what it says; there should be places and times within the NWPS and within individual wildernesses where visitors find little or no contact with others.

We fully recognize that the wilderness experience is a product of human perception and cannot be precisely described and packaged. But at the same time, managers need some guidelines as to the general nature and character of the experiences for which they are responsible for managing. To us, it seems the Wilderness Act, in Section 2(c)1, provides such guidelines. In answering the question "what distinguishes wilderness from other settings," we have sought an answer that would be true to Congressional intent and offer relevant criteria to guide managers. According to our definition, then:

> Wilderness is an area (1) featuring substantially natural ecological conditions and (2) offering the visitor outstanding opportunities for solitude in his pursuit of a primitive and unconfined type of recreation.

Two Qualifications

To repeat, the issue of what philosophy will underlie wilderness management is crucial to the future of the National Wilderness Preservation System. The Wilderness System we have in the year 2000 will be a direct product of the philosophy that guides the many related policy and management decisions. It is our judgment that a predominantly biocentric position is appropriate, necessary, and defensible. We think the recent wilderness management policy guidelines of the National Park Service and Forest Service reflect such a perspective.

However, our support for the biocentric approach is qualified in two important respects. First, because the biocentric philosophy, as we described it, represents an idealistic polar extreme, its implementation will have to be inhibited by practical constraints. For example, fire would ideally be allowed completely free rein under a strictly biocentric philosophy. But fires obviously cannot be allowed completely unchecked. In many areas, as a result of several decades of fire suppression, unnaturally large supplies of highly combustible fuels have accumulated. Fires in these areas might become extraordinarily intense, causing catastrophic damage to the wilderness resource and/or to resources outside the wilderness boundary. Because the National Wilderness Preservation System is composed of relatively small tracts of land scattered throughout areas managed for other purposes, nonwilderness considerations will always have a bearing on what happens inside the wilderness boundary—and vice versa. Thus, we endorse the biocentric philosophy, with the recognition that total achievement of its goals is unrealistic and impractical. Nevertheless, we feel that a management and policy orientation that judiciously strives toward the *intent* of biocentricity is proper and realistic.

The second qualification we must voice is that biocentricity, and even the entire wilderness preservation movement in a broader sense, is a viable philosophy only so far as it is accompanied by (1) an equitable provision of alternative outdoor recreation opportunities and (2) a comprehensive effort to humanize the places we work and live. With regard to the first point, we must be concerned about the elitist overtones of biocentricity; are we endorsing a philosophy that offers access only to a privileged few at the expense of the majority (Hardin 1969; Julber 1972; Behan 1976)? For example, some recreational organizations viewed the recent Alpine Lakes Wilderness classification as another loss of opportunity for their interests (Popovich 1976). Whatever the specific merits of their claim, their concern over the failure of land management agencies to provide a broad spectrum of opportunities is one we cannot ignore if we value the long term preservation of wilderness. Frankly, in a democratic society, we see little chance that a biocentric philosophy of wilderness management can survive unless an equitable range of alternative outdoor recreation opportunities is provided.

The second point is perhaps of even greater long term significance. As de Grazia (1970) has noted ". . . only if you give the city a pleasant and healthful outdoor environment, can you slacken the expensive, wasteful and self-destroying drive for the wilderness. Only the city can save the wilderness." Obviously, the citizens that press for .wilderness classification and the agencies that manage wilderness have only a limited capacity to change the poverty that plagues our inner cities, the social inequities that divide our people, the haphazard land use patterns and transportation systems that blight our landscapes, or the pollution that clouds our land, air, and water. But we all must make sure that even though wilderness is our primary focus, our perspective remains wide enough to grasp these broader issues. This broadened perspective is apparent in the increasing interest of wilderness organizations in such things as energy use and land use planning and in other programs of Federal agencies charged with wilderness management responsibilities that seek to provide outdoor opportunities for people of the inner city. Unless we as a society are able to achieve a "humanizing" environment (Dubos 1968), wilderness can be only a short run phenomenon.

A Common Sense Policy

We lean toward a biocentric, as opposed to an anthropocentric wilderness management philosophy, but we are not advocating an extreme orientation. We are calling for a biocentric emphasis, but with common sense application and responsiveness to local conditions. We emphasize the idea stated earlier that *wilderness management should not mold nature to suit people. Rather, it should manage human use and influences so that natural processes are not altered. Managers should do only what is necessary to meet wilderness objectives, and use only the minimum tools, force, and regulation required to achieve those objectives.*

Bearing in mind that direction will vary with the wilderness objectives at which it is directed, the above emphasis might be compared to direction put forth by Senator Frank Church, floor manager of the Wilderness Act when it passed the Senate, and former chairman of the Interior Subcommittee on Public Lands which oversees wilderness. In a recent "Wilderness Resource Distinguished Lecture," Senator Church argued the following:

> . . . it was *not* the intent of Congress that wilderness be administered in so pure a fashion as to needlessly restrict their customary public use and enjoyment. Quite to the contrary, Congress fully intended that wilderness should be managed to allow its use by a wide spectrum of Americans.

> There is a need for a rule of reason in interpreting the Act, of course, because wilderness values are to be protected. As I stated in 1972, while chairing an oversight

hearing of the Subcommittee on Public Lands:

> '. . . The Wilderness Act was not deliberately contrived to hamstring reasonable and necessary management activities. We intend to permit the managing agencies . . . latitude . . . where the purpose is to protect the wilderness, its resources and the public visitors within the area . . . (including, for example) minimum sanitation facilities . . . fire protection necessities . . . (and) the development of potable water supplies. . . . The issue is not whether necessary management facilities are prohibited; they are not. The test is whether they are necessary.'

> Thus, the wilderness management framework intended by Congress was for the agencies to do only what is necessary. The facilities just mentioned may be required—and restrictions on use may sometimes be needed to protect especially fragile locations. But in adopting regulations, common sense is required.

> In summary, if purity is to be an issue in the management of wilderness, let it focus on preserving the natural integrity of the wilderness environment—and not needless restriction of facilities necessary to protect the area while providing for human use and enjoyment. (Church 1977)

The statement by Senator Church, in essence, helps reduce the range for debate on biocentric versus anthropocentric emphasis in wilderness management. While clearly an appeal for less purity in wilderness management, and for wilderness use by a wide spectrum of Americans, the direction Senator Church advocates has elements of biocentric, as well as anthropocentric philosophy. We expect that in the years ahead debate over proper wilderness management philosophy will continue, but will be argued between these much narrower extremes. Our hope is that the wilderness management philosophy that ultimately prevails will emphasize the natural integrity of wilderness ecosystems, with common sense applications that are responsive to the needs of individual areas.

Conclusion

In conclusion, our objective for this chapter has been to set the stage for systematic and progressively more detailed discussion of material related to management of the National Wilderness Preservation System in the United States. So far we have focused on the broadest direction—the management philosophy.

More specifically, in this chapter we distinguished wilderness allocation from wilderness management issues and defined four relationships between them. The need for wilderness management was argued from several vantage points. To guide management, the meanings and definition of wilderness were explored in light of some basic, albeit overlapping, themes and values espoused by historical wilderness spokesmen.

Finally, two alternative wilderness management philosophies—anthropocentric and biocentric—were described and their applicability evaluated in light of objectives of the Wilderness Act. As the most fruitful direction for management of the National Wilderness Preservation System, we propose the judicious application of a biocentric philosophy—one that focuses on maintaining the historical flow of natural processes that formed wilderness.

Preparation of this chapter was shared jointly by John C. Hendee, George H. Stankey, and Robert C. Lucas.

Literature Cited

Allen, Durward.
1974. Of fire, moose, and wolves. Audubon 76(6):38–49.
Behan, R.W.
1972. Wilderness purism—here we go again. Am. For. 73(12):8–11.
Behan, R.W.
1976. Rationing wilderness use: an example from Grand Canyon. Western Wildlands 3(2):23–26.
Bernstein, Arthur.
1972. Wilderness as a therapeutic behavior setting. Therapeutic Recreation J. 6(4):160–61, 185.
Burch, William R., Jr.
1974. In democracy is the preservation of the wilderness. Appalachia 40(2):90–101.
Burch, William R., Jr., and Wiley D. Wenger, Jr.
1967. The social characteristics of participants in three styles of family camping. U.S. Dep. Agric. For. Serv. Res. Pap. PNW-48, 30 p. Pac. Northwest For. and Range Exp. Stn., Portland, Oreg.
Burke, Hubert.
1969. Wilderness engenders new management traditions. Living Wilderness 33(106):9–13.
Cain, Stanley A.
1960. Ecological islands as natural laboratories. In The meaning of wilderness to science, p. 18–31. David Brower, ed. The Sierra Club, San Francisco.
Carhart, Arthur H.
1920. Recreation in the forests. Am. For. 26:268–272.
Carhart, Arthur H.
1955. Timber in your life. 317 p. J.B. Lippincott Co., Philadelphia.
Church, Frank.
1977. Wilderness in a balanced land use framework. First Annual Wilderness Resource Distinguished Lecture, Univ. Idaho Wilderness Research Center, March 21, Reprinted as "Whither Wilderness," Am. For. 83(7):11–12, 38–41.
Clark, Roger N., John C. Hendee, and Frederick Campbell.
1971. Values, behavior, and conflict in modern camping culture. J. Leisure Res. 3:143–159.
Clark, Roger W.
1976. Management alternatives for the Great Gulf Wilderness Area. In Backcountry management in the White Mountains of New Hampshire, p. 2–27. William R. Burch, Jr., and Roger W. Clark, eds. [Working paper] 105 p. School of Forestry and Environmental Studies, Yale University, New Haven, Conn.
Clawson, Marion.
1975. Conflicts and strategies in forest land management. J. Soil and Water Conserv. 30(2):63–67.
Cole, Glen F.
1974. Management involving grizzly bears and humans in Yellowstone National Park. Bioscience 24(1):1–11.
Costley, Richard J.
1972. An enduring resource. Am. For. 78(6):8–11.
Cowan, Ian McTaggert.
1968. Wilderness—concept, function, and management. The Horace M. Albright Conservation Lectureship, Vol. XIII. 36 p. University of California School of Forestry and Conservation, Berkeley.
Craighead, John J., Joel R. Varney, and Frank D. Craighead, Jr.
1974. A population analysis of the Yellowstone grizzly bears. Bulletin 40, 20 p. Mont. For. and Conserv. Exp. Stn., School of Forestry, University of Montana, Missoula.
Davis, Millard C.
1966–67. The influence of Emerson, Thoreau, and Whitman on the early American naturalists—John Muir and John Barrows. Living Wilderness 39(95):19–23.
DeFelice, Vincent N.
1975. Wilderness is for using. Am. For. 81(6):24–26.
de Grazia, Sebastian.
1970. Some reflections on the history of outdoor recreation. In Elements of outdoor recreation planning. p. 89–97. B.L. Driver (ed.). University of Michigan Press, Ann Arbor.
Dubos, René J.
1968. So human an animal. 267 p. Scribner: New York.
Flader, Susan L.
1974. Thinking like a mountain: Aldo Leopold and the evolution of an ecological attitude toward deer, wolves, and forests. 284 p. University of Missouri Press, Columbia, Mo.
Frome, Michael.
1974. Battle for the wilderness. 246 p. Praeger Pub. Co., New York.
Foote, Jeffrey.
1973. Wilderness—a question of purity. Environ. Law 3(4):255–260.
Ghiselin, Jon.
1973–74. Wilderness and the survival of species. Living Wilderness 37(124):22–36.

Glacken, Clarence.
  1967. Traces on the Rhodian shore. 763 p. University of California Press, Berkeley.

Hardin, Garrett.
  1969. The economics of wilderness. Nat. Hist. 78(6):20–27.

Heinselman, Miron L.
  1973. Restoring fire to the Canoe Country. Naturalist 24(4): 21–31.

Hendee, John C., William R. Catton, Jr., Larry D. Marlow, and C. Frank Brockman.
  1968. Wilderness users in the Pacific Northwest—their characteristics, values, and management preferences. USDA For. Serv. Res. Pap. PNW–61, 92 p. Pac. Northwest For. and Range Exp. Stn., Portland, Oreg.

Hendee, John C., and George H. Stankey.
  1973. Biocentricity in Wilderness Management. BioScience 23(9):535-538.

Hendee, John C.
  1974. A scientist's view on some current wilderness management issues. Western Wildlands 1(2):27–32.

Houston, Douglas.
  1971. Ecosystems of National Parks. Science 172:648–651.

Huth, Hans.
  1957. Nature and the American. 250 p. University of California Press, Berkeley.

Ise, John.
  1961. Our National Park policy: a critical history. 701 p. The Johns Hopkins Press, Baltimore, Md.

Julber, Eric.
  1972. Let's open up our wilderness areas. Reader's Digest 100(60):125–128.

Krutilla, John V.
  1967. Conservation reconsidered. Am. Econ. Rev. 57(4):777–786.

Krutilla, John V., and Charles J. Cicchetti.
  1972. Evaluating benefits of environmental resources, with special application to the Hell's Canyon. Nat. Res. J. 12(1):1–29.

Lee, Robert G.
  1975. The management of human components in the Yosemite National Park ecosystem. [Final report to the Yosemite Institute and to the National Park Service.] 134 p. Dept. of For. and Conserv., University of California, Berkeley.

Leopold, Aldo.
  1921. The wilderness and its place in forest recreational policy. J. For. 19(7):718–721.

Leopold, Aldo.
  1925. Wildernesses as a form of land use. J. Land and Public Util. Econ. 1(4):398–404.

Leopold, Aldo.
  1941. Wilderness as a land laboratory. Living Wilderness. 6(6):3.

Leopold, Aldo.
  1949. A Sand County almanac and sketches here and there. 269 p. Oxford University Press, New York.

Loucks, O.L.
  1970. Evolution of diversity, efficiency, and community stability. Am. Zool. 10(1):17–25.

Lucas, Robert C.
  1973. Wilderness: a management framework. J. Soil and Water Conserv. 28(4):150-154.

Lucas, Robert C., and George H. Stankey.
  1974. Social carrying capacity for backcountry recreation. In Outdoor recreation research: applying the results. U.S. Dep.

Agric. For. Serv. Gen. Tech. Rep. NC-9, p. 14-23, North Central For. Exp. Stn., St. Paul, Minn.

Marsh, George Perkins.
  1864. Man and nature. 472 p. Charles Scribner, New York.

Marshall, George.
  1969. Introduction. In Wilderness and the quality of life, p. 13–15. Maxine E. McCloskey and James P. Gilligan, eds. Sierra Club, San Francisco.

Marshall, Robert.
  1930. The problem of the wilderness. Sci. Mon. 30:141-148.

McCloskey, Michael.
  1966. The Wilderness Act: its background and meaning. Oreg. Law Rev. 45(4):288-321.

McKinley, Donald.
  1966. Psychology of the wilderness. Mazama 48(13):33–35.

Mech, L. David.
  1970. The wolf. 384 p. The Natural History Press, New York.

Mihaley, Marc B.
  1972. The Clean Air Act and the concept of nondegradation: Sierra Club vs. Ruckelhaus. Ecol. Law Rev. 2(4):801–836.

Muir, John.
  1938. John of the mountains: the unpublished journals of John Muir. Linnie Marsh Wolfe, ed. 459 p. Houghton Mifflin, Boston.

Murdy, W.H.
  1975. Anthropocentrism: a modern version. Science 187(4182):1168–1172.

Nash, Roderick, ed.
  1968. The American environment: readings in the history of conservation. 236 p. Addison-Wesley Publishing Company, Reading, Mass.

Nash, Roderick.
  1973. Wilderness and the American mind. 300 p. Yale University Press, New Haven, Conn.

Netboy, Anthony.
  1974. Can we solve our high country needs like Europe? Yes. Am. For. 89(2):34, 36, 55.

Ohman, Lewis F., and Robert R. Ream.
  1971. Wilderness ecology: virgin plant communities of the Boundary Waters Canoe Area. U.S. Dep. Agric. For. Serv. Res. Pap. NC-63, 55 p. North Cen. For. Exp. Stn., St. Paul, Minn.

Olson, Sigurd F.
  1957. The singing wilderness. 245 p. Alfred A. Knopf, New York.

Olson, Sigurd F.
  1963. Runes of the North. 255 p. Alfred A. Knopf, New York.

Outdoor Recreation Resources Review Commission.
  1962. Wilderness and recreation: a report on resources, values, and problems. Study report 3. 352 p. U.S. Government Printing Office, Washington, D.C.

Partridge, Clayton.
  1975. Who needs wilderness? Signpost 10(2):10–12, 27.

Popovich, Luke.
  1976. Ah wilderness—an admiring look at Alpine Lakes. J. For. 74(11):763–766.

Saylor, John.
  1962. A report on wilderness. May–June 1962 Congressional Record.

Scott, Neil R.
  1974. Toward a psychology of wilderness experience. Nat. Res. J. 14(2):231-237.

Simmons, I.G.
    1966. Wilderness in the mid-twentieth century. U.S.A. Town Planning Rev. 36(4):249–456.

Spurr, Stephen H.
    1966. Wilderness management. The Horace M. Albright Conservation Lectureship, Vol. VI. 17 p. University California School of Forestry and Conservation, Berkeley.

Stahl, C.J.
    1921. Where forestry and recreation meet. J. For. 19(5):526–529.

Stankey, George H., Robert C. Lucas, and David W. Lime.
    1976. Crowding in parks and wilderness. Design and Environ. 7(3):38–41.

Teale, Edwin Way, ed.
    1954. The wilderness world of John Muir. 332 p. Houghton Mifflin, Boston.

Thoreau, Henry David.
    1851. The transcendental view. In The American environment: readings in the history of conservation, p. 9–13. Roderick Nash, ed. Addison-Wesley Publishing Company, Reading, Mass.

U.S. Department of the Interior, National Park Service.
    1972. Natural history: part two of the National Park System plan. 140 p. U.S. Government Printing Office, Washington, D.C.

Wagar, J. Alan.
    1974. Recreational carrying capacity reconsidered. J. For. 72(5):274–278.

Weaver, James W., and Rupert Cutler.
    1977. Wilderness policy: a colloquy between Congressman Weaver and Assistant Secretary Cutler. J. For. 75(7):392–394.

White, Lynn.
    1967. The historical roots of our ecological crisis. Science 155(3767):1203–1207.

Worf, William A., Glen Jorgenson, and Robert Lucas.
    1972. Wilderness policy review. 56 p. U.S. Dep. Agric., For. Serv., Washington, D.C.

Zivnuska, John A.
    1973. The managed wilderness. Am. For. 79(8):16–19.

Americans began to appreciate wilderness as it became scarce, especially after 1890 (the year the U.S. Census reported that urban population exceeded the rural population). Many Americans began to consider wilderness as a resource to be appreciated rather than an obstacle to be conquered. Early wilderness visitors, such as the above camper, did not have the advantages of lightweight equipment, portable gas stoves, or dehydrated food.

2   Historical Roots of Wilderness Management

Introduction

A designated, managed wilderness is, in a very important sense, a contradiction in terms. It could even be said that any area that is proclaimed wilderness and managed as such is not wilderness by these very acts! The problem is that the traditional meaning of *wilderness* is an environment that man does *not* influence, a place he does *not* control.

Before the era of herding and agriculture, say 15,000 years ago, no distinction was possible between wilderness and civilization. In a hunting and gathering condition man did not control his environment; he simply lived in it—like a bear or a buffalo. But with the beginning of herding and, subsequently, agriculture, *homo sapiens* began to experiment with the Pandora's box of environmental modification. Man domesticated (controlled) animals and, as an agriculturalist, managed (controlled) plants, soil, and water. In time, he built totally humanized environments called towns and cities. In the process he created wilderness by drawing a physical and—even more important—a mental distinction between the places he controlled and the places he did not control (Nash 1975).

Etymologically, the word *wilderness* is derived from the Old English "wild-deor-ness," the place of untamed beasts (Nash 1970b, 1973). "Civilization," conversely, was the place where man's controlling abilities had taken

This chapter was written by Roderick Nash, Professor of History and Environmental Studies, University of California, Santa Barbara.

effect. Understandably, since the advent of the civilization that created it, wilderness has stood for the dark, the chaotic, the unknown and fearful, the back of beyond. It was defined by the absence of the controlling structures of modern man's institutions and technologies. Outlaws and brigands of ancient times, like today's revolutionary guerillas, sought wild country for the same reason as do some of today's backpackers—escape from civilization's cloak of control.

The Intellectual Dilemma

The only wilderness true to the etymological roots of the word is that which man does not influence in any way whatsoever. The more man learns about wilderness, the more he visits it, maps it, writes about it—the less wild it becomes. From such a perspective, even knowledge about a region disqualifies it as wilderness in the true etymological sense.

The implications of this for wilderness management are not hard to understand. When a society, usually acting through a government agency, designates a wilderness, it cannot be wilderness in the most complete and traditional sense. Management of any kind is a further compromise of a region's wildness. Even maps, trails, and signs are a civilizing influence—steps toward ordering the environment in man's interest, toward lessening the amount of the unknown. The association of rangers, wardens, and search-and-rescue teams with a given area obviously detracts from its wildness. More subtle, but equally meaningful in this regard, are sophisticated management techniques. The notions of carrying capacity, use permits and quotas, regulations on behavior, prescribed fire, and fire control gradually erode the "wild" from "wilderness." It is virtually lost when recreational demand makes it necessary to secure permits a year in advance and, at the peril of arrest and fine, to maintain a rigid back-country travel itinerary so other parties, following a day behind, have places to camp. When these requirements exist (and the example is not as hypothetical as conditions in the Grand Canyon and the Middle Fork of the Salmon River testify), then wilderness is transformed into an open-air motel complete with registration and checkout times.

The intellectual dilemma posed by a managed wilderness is compounded by the fact that, in the last analysis, wilderness is a state of mind. Like beauty, it is defined by human perception. This can mean that, for some individuals, regulations for management will not be a distracting presence. But for others, just the *knowledge* that they visit an area by the grace of, and under conditions established by, civilization is devastating to a wilderness experience. It is ironic that the success of management in protecting the wilderness experience declines in proportion to its effectiveness. In the sense discussed here, the best managed wildernesses are the least wild.

Still, today, as explained in chapter 1, it is hard to deny the principle that wilderness management is essential if "wilderness" is to have any meaning at all. In the first place, it is undeniable that the "pure" definition of wilderness (no maps, no knowledge, a total blank space on the map) is, at least between the 60th parallels, a thing of the past. No one can ever again have the experience of a Lewis and Clark or a Jim Bridger or a John Wesley Powell. The best that can be hoped for in the American West, for instance, is a chance to be in beautiful and relatively natural country, away from roads, relatively alone, and dependent, in the short run, on one's own resources for comfort and survival.

Another factor compelling acceptance of managed wilderness is awareness by the user that, contradictory as it is, a man-controlled wilderness is better than no wilderness at all. The driving force behind this realization is the inescapable fact of the growth in popularity of wilderness recreation and the consequent certainty that without control what remains of its wildness would surely be loved to death (Nash 1973 pp. 266 ff.).

Destruction by Popularity—The Alternative

The harbingers of the destruction of wilderness by popularity are certain spectacular areas where the attention of the recreation-minded public focuses. Mt. Whitney, the highest peak in the United States outside Alaska, is a good example. It is located in an area of the Sierra Nevada that Sequoia National Park recommends for permanent wilderness status. But consider this: the peak was first climbed in 1873. In 1973, approximately 14,000 persons made the climb. A more dramatic illustration of the changes popularity has brought to Mt. Whitney comes from a man who on August 4, 1949, climbed the peak with his father. Proudly, they signed the summit register, the sixth and seventh individuals to have done so *that year*. On August 11, 1972, this same man climbed Mt. Whitney with his son. Upon signing

Table 2-1.—*Travel on the Colorado River through the Grand Canyon of Arizona*

Year	Number of People
1867	[1] 1?
1869–1940	44
1941	4
1942	8
1943	0
1944	0
1945	0
1946	0
1947	4
1948	6
1949	12
1950	7
1951	29
1952	19
1953	31
1954	21
1955	70
1956	55
1957	135
1958	80
1959	120
1960	205
1961	255
1962	372
1963–64	[2] 44
1965	547
1966	1,067
1967	2,099
1968	3,609
1969	6,019
1970	9,935
1971	10,385
1972	16,432
1973	15,219
1974	[3] 14,253

[1] Some contend that James White, a trapper fleeing Indians, floated through the Grand Canyon on a makeshift log raft 2 years before the famous expedition of John Wesley Powell.

[2] Travel on the Colorado River in these years was curtailed by the completion of Glen Canyon Dam upstream and the resultant disruption of flow.

[3] The downturn in visitation was the result of the institution by management of a quota system. The numbers applying for the available permits continued to rise sharply.

the register they noted with some shock that they were the 259th and 260th persons on record *that day!* Presumably there was less pride, and certainly less wildness, in the experience.

Additional testimony comes from the Grand Canyon of Arizona where the 300-mile float trip of the Colorado River is perhaps the most intensively supervised wilderness activity in the United States today. Close control by National Park officers is facilitated by severely limited access to the river and the expedition-level difficulty of the trip. As a result there exists an exceptionally complete set of visitation statistics (table 2-1).

Reviewing these figures and realizing that almost all the use of the resource occurs in the 3 summer months, it is clear that the quality of wilderness experienced by the early Grand Canyon river runners has declined precipitously. Some argue that, enjoyable as it is, the locale can no longer be considered wilderness. Disgustedly, they turn to the few remaining "wild" rivers, perhaps in Alaska and the Canadian northland. But many others comply, albeit reluctantly, with the strict management policies currently in effect for the Grand Canyon. The logic that persuades them might be illustrated by comparing the situation in the Grand Canyon and other popular wildernesses with that of obtaining playing time on tennis courts.

THE TENNIS COURT ANALOGY

Tennis players would obviously prefer to play when they wish, for as long as they wish. But the popularity of the game does not permit this luxury except on private courts which can be compared to the game reserves of medieval nobility. On public, tax-supported courts (comparable to publicly supported wilderness areas) demand frequently exceeds available space. Hence management devices are instituted such as sign-up sheets, time and frequency limitations, and rules regarding accepting waiting players in doubles games. Court monitors enforce the regulations.

Of course an alternative response to the tennis problem would be to have no management. Everyone who wished could squeeze onto a court. "Triples" would be common on the popular courts and, in peak-demand periods, a kind of volleyball-with-rackets with as many as 25 on a side could be played.

Acceptance, indeed preference, for management or self-restraint is understandable. Players recognize that tennis is a game that is played by two or four persons. So, out of respect for the integrity of the game, and with their own self-interest in mind, players support management. They sign up, wait their turn, and vacate the court at the appointed hour.

Wilderness recreation is also a "game" that cannot be played at any one time and place by more than a few persons. Moreover, it is a game that depends on the existence of a relatively unmodified natural and physical environment. These realizations prompt many to accept management. The resulting regulations may be distasteful, and clear violations of the traditional sense of wilderness, but they are the best hope of salvaging an approximation of the wilderness experience from the pressures of popularity.

The basis for any historical discussion of wilderness management is the recognition that management is a newcomer to the wilderness movement. There was preservation (allocation of land) long before there was positive management except for fire control and associated lookouts, trails, and guard cabins. For decades few even thought about managing wilderness. Perhaps this tendency sprang from the contradiction between the concepts of wilderness and management. Wilderness was not *supposed* to be managed. It was the region that began where management stopped. But certainly equal in importance was the fact that for years there were no significant management problems and none at all involving control of the number of recreational users that now dominate discussion. When, as late as 1949, only a dozen persons a season were climbing Mt. Whitney and about the same number running the Colorado River, their control could hardly be regarded as a pressing issue. So it was for a transitory, enchanted moment in American environmental history that recreational use of wilderness existed without the need for wilderness management.

Roots of Wilderness Appreciation

To review the first accounts of wilderness pleasure trips is to realize just how spectacularly empty the country was. Consider, as an example, the 625-mile hike that Joseph N. LeConte and three companions made in the southern section of the Sierra in 1890. The trip is interesting for its parallels with contemporary patterns of wilderness recreation. The four men, all in their early twenties, were students at the University of California in Berkeley. The trip was their summer vacation; they went into the mountains for fun. LeConte's excellent journal (LeConte 1972) permits comparisons between 1890 and our own time. One is struck, immediately, by the total lack of regulation. There were no permits in 1890, no regulations, no fish and game laws, not even clear maps. The students simply packed up (but they used burros rather than backpacks) and headed out. Much of the time

Figure 2-1.—Better access, light and efficient recreational equipment, population growth, and pressures of urban life are a few reasons for increased recreational use of wilderness. Visitors contemplate their trip to Green Lake in proposed wilderness of North Cascades National Park, Wash.

they had only a general idea of where they were. And a considerable part of their adventure stemmed from their recognition that no one was poised to bail them out of the trouble in which they regularly found themselves. In 1890, the wilderness was noteworthy for its emptiness. Except for a few miners on the lower Kings River and one of their geology professors conducting experiments above Yosemite Valley, they saw no people.

The Sierra was even emptier 20 years earlier when John Muir chalked up a first ascent almost everywhere he climbed. But even several decades after LeConte's trip, David Brower found virtually no one in the mountains. Even the Sierra Club's organized "outings," began under Muir's leadership in 1901, hardly compromised the Sierra's isolation. The use of pack animals restricted wilderness recreation to the easier routes and lower passes. "Off the beaten track" had a meaning that has been destroyed by the omnipresence of today's backpacking contingent.

The state of the art in wilderness recreational equipment also played a major role in restricting backcountry use until well into the 20th century. An oldtimer even today is astonished at what the outdoor equipment industry has wrought. In an earlier era, huge bedrolls, heavy tents, and the weight of canned foods sharply limited the places one could visit and the amount of time a party could spend in wilderness. So did the lack of portable, efficient gear for winter camping and rock climbing, the availability of which today has opened the

last hidden pockets. Then, too, in earlier years, the U.S. population was much smaller. And, compared to contemporary Americans, most of our ancestors had limited mobility (fewer cars, poor roads), along with less leisure and greater dedication to the "work" ethic.

But the principal reason why wild places were empty was that very few Americans cared to visit them. Even as late as World War II, wilderness appreciation was still in its infancy. The explanation lies in the heavy burden of suspicion and fear that wilderness carried as heritage from a pioneering past. It was not easy to appreciate something fought since the dawn of civilization. It was a matter of being too close to wilderness, of having too much of it. For appreciation to flourish, wilderness had to become a novelty, and this in turn depended on the rise of an urbanized, industrialized society. The United States was at the brink of the transition from a developing to a developed nation in the late 19th century. The frontier ended, according to the U.S. census, in 1890. Only then could large numbers of Americans begin to consider wilderness a resource to be enjoyed rather than an adversary to be conquered. (For extensive discussion of this attitudinal change see Nash 1973, pp. 141 ff.)

Evolution of Wilderness in the National Parks

Understandably, then, the first interest in wilderness for recreation took the form of what might be called the

30

"portal syndrome." People wanted wilderness but not too much. They preferred to be on its edge, to look at it but also to have the security and comforts of civilization. This was the context in which the first management decisions respecting wilderness were made. The reservation of the world's first National Park, Yellowstone, on March 1, 1872, for example, had little to do with providing a true wilderness experience for vacationing Americans. The intent of Congress, as stated in the text of the Act (U.S., *Statutes at Large*, 17, p. 32) was to create a "public park or pleasuring ground for the benefit and enjoyment of the people." Study of the intent of Yellowstone's proponents indicates that the "enjoyment" was expected to be derived from viewing scenic wonders such as geysers, hot springs, and waterfalls from the civilized vantage point afforded by luxurious lodges. Even Nathaniel P. Langford, a leading explorer and publicizer of the first National Park, enthusiastically predicted that it would not be long "before the march of civil improvements will reclaim this delightful solitude, and garnish it with all the attractions of cultivated taste and refinement" (Langford 1972). This was entirely consistent with the established pattern of nature tourism of the 19th century, which emphasized the edge of wildness, convenient transportation (usually railroads), and lavish hotel accommodations.

What did visitors to the early national parks expect? The brochures and promotional literature distributed by park promoters invariably featured the attributes of civilization: comfortable coaches, grand lodges, elegantly dressed tourists. Far from enticing the visitor with visions of wilderness camping, the advertisements tried to convince the tourist that there was no need to "rough it." Wildness was to be enjoyed—but at a distance. Too wild a park, it was rightly assumed in the late 19th and early 20th centuries, would be a deterrent to tourism. Interest in wilderness was growing, but it had not yet affected recreational tastes enough for wilderness management to exist, even as a concept.

As for the roads and hotels that "opened up" Yellowstone and the other early parks and determined their dominant use, park personnel or Congress did not *decide* to feature this mode of enjoyment. It wasn't even an issue. Everyone simply assumed that mass, mechanized recreation in a civilized context would be the park experience. The language used in the Yellowstone Act made such an interpretation easy. As long as the "timber, mineral deposits, natural curiosities, or wonders" were preserved "in their natural condition," there was no problem with developing the park for mass tourism. More exactly, Old Faithful and Yellowstone Falls were the objects of concern, not the wild backcountry of the park. As long as these "wonders" were kept in public ownership and free from vandalism, the 19th century purposes of the park were fulfilled.

Even the most ardent wilderness preservationists of the time, people like Sierra Club president John Muir, accepted this premise and its management implications. In 1913, Muir supported the admission of the first private automobiles into Yosemite Valley (Lillard 1968). His reasoning centered on the need to bring people into the parks in order to build citizen support for the park idea. Along with motorized people came their civilized lifestyles. Hotels, such as the posh Awahnee in the scenic heart of Yosemite Valley, and cars contributed to the people's outdoor pleasure as it was defined in the first decades of the 20th century. And because the National Parks were instructed by law to be "pleasuring grounds," who could object? Muir bitterly fought economic development of park wilderness. He opposed grazing, mining, logging, and, unsuccessfully, the 1913 decision in favor of hydropower development that inundated Hetch Hetchy Valley in northern Yosemite National Park. But Muir did not recognize development for recreation, for the public's pleasure, as a comparable threat to wilderness. He died (in 1914) before wilderness advocates began questioning creature comforts in parks and demanding corresponding changes in management.

The passage of the National Park Service Act on August 25, 1916, did not change earlier conceptions of the meaning, purpose, and appropriate uses of National Parks. Although the legislation stipulated that anything done in the parks must leave their scenery and wildlife "unimpaired," the whole reason for their existence was indisputably public enjoyment. And pleasure-seeking people could impair nature. The ambiguity inherent in the National Park Service Act has been the source of extensive commentary and still more extensive agony for subsequent park managers. But for Americans in 1916, there was considerably less inconsistency in the Act. As long as the spectacular natural wonders, those objects the parks were assumed to have been created to protect, were not impaired, high-intensity tourist development was not only allowable but desirable. Conversely, since wilderness protection and the provision of a wilderness experience were not recognized goals of park management, few questioned developments (such as roads and lodges) that eroded wildness. And why, after all, should they have? Hardly anyone went into the park backcountry at all at this time. Dramatic assertions (probably true) that over 90 percent of these early visitors saw only 3 percent of the park were not the result of any conscious management policy. They reflected quite accurately the tastes of recreation-minded

Americans in the early 20th century. Most people didn't *want* to experience park wilderness. The practical implications for management of these conceptions of park means and purposes can be found in a letter of May 13, 1918, from Secretary of the Interior Franklin K. Lane to Stephen T. Mather, the first Director of the National Park Service (USDI National Park Service 1970). In all probability the letter was drafted for Lane's signature by Mather himself.

It opens with the standard insistence that the parks be kept in "absolutely unimpaired form," but quickly makes compromises on behalf of public enjoyment. From the standpoint of wilderness preservation, the most damaging aspect of the Lane letter is the assumption that the public should be encouraged to enjoy the parks "in the manner that best satisfies the individual taste." There is, in other words, no attempt to define what kind of enjoyment is appropriate in a National Park, no effort to distinguish uses that are consistent with the mandate to leave park land unimpaired. In effect, Lane is saying that the citizen will bring his preferences to the parks and the parks will fulfill them. The 1918 letter makes clear that "automobiles and motorcycles will be permitted in all of the National Parks; in fact, the parks will be kept accessible by any means practicable." The implications of this statement are extraordinary and clearly work against wilderness. So does the Secretary's directive to encourage a full range of accommodations from "luxurious hotels" to "free campsites." Nothing was said about low density, offroad wilderness uses of the parks. The point, again, is that wilderness recreation was not recognized in the 1910's, and for some time thereafter, as being part of the statutory purpose of National Parks. And the American people of this period gave little evidence of being disappointed with such a definition and the resulting management policy.

Stephen T. Mather was the ideal director of the National Park System under the explicit and implicit mandates of the early 20th century. His talent was public relations, and he recognized that National Park survival and growth depended on skillful playing of the numbers (of visitors) game in the political arena. Immediately after passage of the 1916 legislation, Mather launched a vigorous program to boost National Parks. It included a series of publications, the work of Robert Sterling Yard, and the initiation or continuation of management policies designed to attract and please visitors. Mather and Yard knew that wilderness would not "sell" to their contemporaries. Instead they cultivated a resort or circus image of parks. Drive-through sequoias, cut initially in the 1880's, continued to be a tourist "must" at Yosemite. At Yellowstone, soap was regularly dumped into the

geysers to break their surface tension and cause eruptions at times convenient to tourists. In the case of Old Faithful, the symbol of America's National Parks in this period, colored spotlights from adjacent hotels illuminated night eruptions. During the hour between eruptions, tourists were entertained by radio music.

Yellowstone's famous roadside bears shared top billing with Old Faithful. By explicit direction of Director Mather and his assistant and subsequent director Horace M. Albright, the bears were regularly fed with hotel garbage before grandstands of camera-wielding tourists. In the 1920's, it must be remembered, bear feedings and caged wildlife around hotels did not violate National Park purpose—rather, they expressed it. Public "enjoyment" could easily be stretched to cover such activities.

At Yosemite National Park in the 1870's, the "firefall" replaced the "chicken fall" in which live chickens were tossed over the cliffs. It continued, under Mather and Albright, to dominate the park experience for most tourists. The firefall involved the construction of a huge wood fire on the lip of Glacier Point 3,000 feet above the floor of Yosemite Valley. As dusk fell, the crowds gathered. Music ("Indian Love Call" was a favorite) played, and at a voice signal, "Let the fire fall!," the burning logs and embers were pushed over the cliff. The potential of forest fire was fully recognized and carefully avoided, but for decades no one even questioned whether the firefall was an appropriate activity for management to sponsor in a National Park. No one asked if this was the *kind* of "enjoyment" parks were created to provide. It was not until the late 1960's that changing interpretations of the meaning and purpose of National Parks led to the abolition of the firefall and the replacement of the "resort" conception with more wilderness orientation in National Parks.

There had, however, been earlier indications of wilderness consciousness in National Park circles. In 1929 the phrase "original wilderness character" was used in certain versions of the bill establishing Grand Teton National Park. No hotels or new roads were to be permitted in the park. Although stricken from the final text of the bill (it became law on February 26, 1929), the omitted phrase clearly indicated a desire to emphasize wilderness in the Teton reservation. The first explicit recognition of wilderness in National Park history appeared 5 years later in the act establishing Everglades National Park. Section 4 of the May 30, 1934, measure specified that the Florida wetlands would be "permanently preserved as a wilderness." With an eye toward management, the bill went on to say that "no development of the project or plan for the entertainment of visitors shall be undertaken which will interfere with the preservation of the . . . essential primitive natural conditions now prevailing in this area" (Cammerer 1938).

Other evidence of some early awakening to the need to be concerned about management can be noted. In 1928 and 1929, George M. Wright of the National Park Service saw the need for an organizational unit to monitor impacts on wildlife found in National Park ecosystems. Wright organized a small group of individuals to begin a nationwide systematic survey of the status of wildlife in the Parks with development of a well-defined wildlife policy as its goal. The work of this group (Wright et al. 1932; Wright and Thompson 1934) provided an historic baseline of data concerning wildlife in the Parks, including such wilderness-dependent species as the wolf and grizzly bear. Wright's work led to the establishment of the Division of Wildlife Research in the National Park Service, with Wright as its first head.

The evolution of thinking—from allocation to management—was beginning to expand. One of the first written examples of this transformation as it concerned National Parks was a 1936 report of Lowell Sumner, a regional wildlife technician. In his policy recommendations for Sierra parks, Sumner wondered "how large a crowd can be turned loose in a wilderness without destroying its essential qualities." He realized that for wilderness to exist in the parks, the areas "cannot hope to accommodate unlimited numbers of people." Construction of tourist facilities would have to be restricted. And finally, Sumner's insights extended to the understanding that wilderness managers could also pose a threat to wilderness values. He urged that only "the very simplest maintenance activity" be undertaken in wilderness (Sumner 1936).

Sumner's thinking on these points matured so that 6 years later he could discuss the adverse effects of pack-stock grazing, fishing, and sheer numbers of visitors on the biological balances of wilderness areas. Then, in one of the first uses of the term, Sumner urged that use of wilderness be kept "within the carrying capacity or 'recreational saturation point'." His 1942 definition described this as "the maximum degree of the highest type of recreational use which a wilderness can receive, consistent with its long-term preservation." Wilderness managers should "determine in advance the probable maximum permissible use, short of impairment, of all wilderness areas." Here, in 1942, was the basic logic of modern wilderness recreation management (Sumner 1942).

Evolution of Wilderness in National Forests

While the National Parks of the early 20th century were playing to crowds that had little interest beyond visiting pleasuring grounds, the United States Forest Service took the first steps toward the explicit identification of wilderness as a specific recreational resource and the development of appropriate management techniques. While Gifford Pinchot headed the Division of Forestry (after 1905, the Forest Service), the emphasis was all resource commodity business. The forests were to be used, albeit carefully, as a constant source of valuable timber products. After Pinchot's departure from office in 1910 in the aftermath of the Ballinger-Pinchot controversy, the meaning of "products" underwent some expansion. Henry Graves, the new Chief of the Forest Service, began to conceive of the National Forests as valuable for recreation. Of course, in these early years, "recreation" meant almost every conceivable outdoor activity, but wilderness had a small and growing significance. For instance, in 1910 Graves asked Treadwell Cleveland, Jr., to write an essay on public recreation facilities for the American Academy of Political and Social Science. The resulting discussion of the use of logging roads, bridges, and trails by the hunter, angler, and picnicker was unprecedented in the history of American forestry. Cleveland made a significant prediction:

> So great is the value of national forest area for recreation, and so certain is this value to increase with the growth of the country and the shrinkage of the wilderness, that even if the forest resources of wood and water were not to be required by the civilization of the future, many of the forests ought certainly to be preserved . . . for recreation use alone (Cleveland 1910).

But, the Forest Service, like the National Park Service at this time, was constrained by the antiwilderness bias of public opinion. Few people wanted to rough it. Recreational development, therefore, consisted of the extension of forest roads and the leasing of sites for summer home and hotel construction. Chief Forester Graves was enthusiastic about progress in these areas in his 1912 report; and, 3 years later, he obtained permission from the Secretary of Agriculture to extend leases to 30 years. The result? More permanent structures were built. Wilderness suffered, but at the time nobody really cared.

In 1918 landscape architect Frank A. Waugh prepared a report for the Forest Service entitled *Recreation Uses* on the *National Forests*. It marked the emergence of full awareness that recreation was an established rationale for National Forests. William B. Greeley, who became Chief Forester in 1920, and his Associate Forester L. F. Kneipp gave increasing emphasis to this use and even secured budgetary appropriations for recreation beginning in 1922. Greeley, in particular, valued forest scenery and on several occasions in the early 1920's vetoed tourist development plans in its behalf. His most important decision of this kind affecting wilderness occurred in 1919 and involved the spectacular Trappers Lake, Colorado. This was National Forest land, and a young Forest Service landscape architect named Arthur H.

Carhart was assigned to survey the area for road access and several hundred vacation homes. The plan was entirely in keeping with Forest Service definitions of recreation, but Carhart was troubled. The beaver of Trappers Lake had been exploited in the 1850's, but otherwise it was untouched and reachable only by a tough 5-mile hike. Realizing the rarity of such wildernesses in the American West, Carhart had misgivings about developing Trappers Lake even for recreational purposes. So, after a summer allegedly spent surveying, Carhart had the courage to recommend doing nothing at all to Trappers Lake. Probably to his surprise, the Denver District Office of the Forest Service

Figure 2-2.—Arthur Carhart (*upper left*) and Aldo Leopold (*upper right*) were instrumental in setting aside 574,000 acres of the Gila National Forest in New Mexico (*opposite*) in 1924 as the first U.S. wilderness.

approved the idea. Trappers Lake was left alone (Baldwin 1972).

Arthur Carhart followed his prowilderness recommendation in Colorado with a similar one for the Superior National Forest in Minnesota. And late in 1919, he met with the young, iconoclastic forester Aldo Leopold. The disappearance of large roadless areas in Arizona and New Mexico was causing Leopold misgivings similar to Carhart's. Leopold's ideal, expressed in a 1921 publication, was for "a continuous stretch of country preserved in its natural state, open to lawful hunting and fishing, big enough to absorb a 2-week pack trip, and kept devoid of roads, artificial trails, cottages, or other works of man" (Leopold 1921). In 1924, Leopold had the satisfaction of seeing the Forest Service designate 574,000 acres of the Gila National Forest, New Mexico, as a reserve for wilderness recreation. The efforts of Carhart and Leopold produced the first allocation of public land specifically for wilderness values in American history, and indeed in the world.

The management consequences of establishing the Gila Wilderness Reserve were minimal. A laissez-faire approach prevailed. It was considered sufficient to administratively designate an area as wilderness, prohibit building roads and hotels, and then leave it alone. There was no attempt to determine what a wilderness experience should be and then manage positively to attain this goal. Wilderness was simply set aside.

William B. Greeley, then Chief Forester, exemplified this philosophy in action. He was enthusiastic about creating wilderness reserves on the National Forests largely, to be frank, because he feared that the aggressive leadership Stephen T. Mather was giving the National Parks threatened his own empire. If the Forest Service did not move to protect its spectacular scenery and develop its recreational resources, there was a good chance that some of its land might be turned over to the National Park Service. Such considerations unquestionably supported the intentions of some foresters to preserve wilderness simply because it was a good thing to do. In 1926, at any rate, Greeley formulated a policy for wilderness. Commercial use (grazing, even logging) of the areas could continue, but campsites, meadows for pack-stock forage, and special scenic "spots," as they were called (Gilligan 1953), would be protected. Greeley also instructed his assistant, L. F. Kneipp, to make an inventory of National Forest wilderness. The result showed 74 areas, each at least 360 square miles, in the 48 states. The Chief Forester's ideas of management stopped at this point. In a 1926 communication to his several Districts, he explicitly disavowed any intention to

regulate the numbers or the behavior of recreational users of wilderness: "I have no sympathy," he declared, "for the viewpoint that people should be kept out of wilderness areas in any large numbers because the presence of human beings destroys the wilderness aspect." "Public use and enjoyment," he continued, "were the only justification for having wilderness reserves at all." As for the numbers of visitors, "the only limitation should be the natural one set up by the modes of travel possible" (Gilligan 1953). Clearly, Greeley did not foresee the time when such limitations would not be sufficient to keep wilderness from being destroyed, ironically, by those who loved it. In the third decade of the 20th century there was little reason to worry about loving wilderness to death. The woods were still relatively empty.

At the 1926 session of the National Conference on Outdoor Recreation, Aldo Leopold made a strong plea for more systematic planning to protect wilderness (NCOR 1926). In Kneipp, he found a supporter close to the center of power in Washington. At last, on July 12, 1929, Kneipp issued Forest Service Regulation L–20, with the object of ordering and consolidating what had until then been piecemeal preservation. The directive, which was not law but only an expression of agency policy, standardized the term "primitive area" for a decade (see chapters 4 and 5). Interestingly, in view of the importance of American attitudes, the term "wilderness" was discarded because Kneipp and his colleagues thought the public would be repelled by its connotations (Pomeroy 1957). Kneipp also admitted that the term wilderness did not apply to regions that had been, and still were being, commercially exploited.

The L–20 Regulation plus the amendments and mimeographed instructions that followed it required the field staff to submit definite management plans for each primitive area (further discussion of the L-20 Regulation is found in chapter 4). Extremely vague, these first management instructions amounted to little more than a list of prohibited and permitted activities. Among the latter were virtually the full range of commercial endeavors customarily pursued in National Forests. A notable exception, however, was that section of the L–20 Regulation which established research reserves (after 1930, called experimental forests). These areas, usually small, embraced virgin forests of scientific importance. Commercial use of the research reserves was prohibited; even recreational use was discouraged. Here was at least implicit recognition that recreation could have an impact on the biological integrity of an area.

On the issue of recreational developments in the primitive areas, the L–20 Regulation raised important management questions. Some Forest Service officials responded to the instructions with an aggressive program of trail and shelter construction in order to compete with the civilized style of developments common in the National Parks and attractive to the majority of vacationers. Kneipp, for one, had a different conception of the meaning of wilderness management. On May 20, 1930, he wrote with some impatience to the field staff: "There should be no need for developing these areas to take care of the large numbers of people who are not capable of exploring wild country without considerable aid." Kneipp went on to direct his Forest Supervisors to stop plans for trail signs, latrines, corrals, and shelters in the wilderness. He recommended that the concept of "primitive simplicity" be used as a criterion for development decisions. "These primitive areas are for the class who seek almost absolute detachment from the evidences of civilization," he concluded (Gilligan 1953).

Such sentiments must have cheered Robert Marshall. The New York-born son of a millionaire lawyer, Marshall, devoted his entire life to wilderness. Professionally, he trained as a plant pathologist. For recreation, he penetrated the nation's wildest remaining corners including the Brooks Range in northern Alaska. A prodigious hiker (he regularly covered 50 miles a day), Bob Marshall resented any kind of convenience in wilderness, and his management ideas reflected this

viewpoint. From his position after 1933 as director of the Forestry Division of the U.S. Office of Indian Affairs, Marshall crusaded for the curtailment of road building in wild places. He was particularly offended by so-called fire roads. Easy to build, especially when the Great Depression brought thousands of job-hungry men under federal care, dirt roads threatened to divide and conquer the last really large wildernesses in the West. Marshall's greatest achievement, really a memorial because he died 2 months later at 38, was the promulgation of the U Regulations by the Forest Service on September 19, 1939. Superceding the L Regulations with respect to more than 14,000,000 acres of wilderness on the National Forests, the U rulings tightened protection (see chapter 4 for additional details on the U Regulations). In designated wilderness and wild areas (the term "primitive" was no longer to be used in classifying areas), there would be "no roads or other provision for motorized transportation," no lumbering, and no hotels, lodges, or permanent camps (Baldwin 1972). Very little was said about management either in the U Regulations or the subsequent instructions for their implementation. To preserve wilderness it seemed enough to exercise a caretaker function with an emphasis on guarding against outside influences. Wilderness inventory and allocation was the specialty of the 1930's. Marshall's walls were covered with maps and lists—a circle drawn around an area was supposed to be sufficient to preserve it.

Figure 2–3.—Many people contributed to the wilderness movement in the United States. Bob Marshall (*left*), the Chief of Division of Recreation and Lands in the U.S. Forest Service, led the establishment of the U-Regulations in 1939 creating wilderness, wild, and roadless areas, the immediate forerunner of today's National Wilderness Preservation System. Lowell Sumner (*right*) of the National Park Service helped inventory wilderness conditions in the Sierra Nevada of California in the 1930's and, at this early date, recognized that these fragile lands had a "saturation point" beyond which use could lead to irreversible damage.

Wilderness Management Ideas Among Conservationists

The same emphasis on circle-drawing and laissez-faire was also characteristic of citizen conservation groups in the 1930's. The Wilderness Society had its origins in 1934 and 1935 among a group of people, Marshall and Leopold included, whose declared objective was "holding wild areas *soundproof* as well as *sightproof* from our increasingly mechanized life" (Nash 1973). The whole thrust of this effort was to keep adverse influences *out* of wilderness rather than to understand and control what was happening *within* its borders.

The first recognition of an internal dimension to wilderness preservation began in this period. Robert Marshall's contribution to *A National Plan for American Forestry* (1933) (the so-called Copeland Report) contained sections on the overuse of backcountry campsites and the need to educate the recreational user in outdoor etiquette. Further recognition that management to preserve wilderness was as much a concern of management as was allocation came in the summer of 1937 when Marshall, the new Chief of the Division of Recreation and Lands in the Forest Service, toured the Sierra with members of the Sierra Club. On the trip the party visited high country severely damaged by the grazing of pack stock and the behavior of campers. Discussions begun on the trip led to Marshall's requesting Professor Joel H. Hildebrand, president of the Sierra Club, to organize a committee to advise the Forest Service with regard to wilderness management. Marshall provided the committee with key questions which revealed the direction of his thinking about wilderness. One question, for example, concerned the feasibility of distributing use—of zoning wilderness, in effect, to achieve certain ends. Specifically, Marshall was anxious that "certain areas may still be preserved in what might be termed a super wilderness condition, or, in other words, kept entirely free even from trails, in order that a traveler can have the feeling of being where no one has been before" (Hildebrand 1938).

The Hildebrand committee replied with a list of trails currently in the Sierra and a recommendation that construction of new trails be sharply limited and, if necessary, kept at a low (that is, primitive) standard. Responding to other questions from Marshall, the Sierra Club advised restricting trail signs and limiting the use and grazing of pack stock. Considering camping habits prevalent in the area, the committee recommended against cutting pine boughs for beds. To manage the wilderness and enforce their suggested regulations, they

suggested appointing high country rangers or guards. Finally, in a significant forecast, both Marshall and the Sierra Club expressed concern about making wilderness available to all the public by encouraging use by younger and poorer people. One idea discussed was making burros and camping equipment available on a rental basis.

The Marshall-Sierra Club interchange in 1937 opened a new era in wilderness management. Others developed ideas of positive, *internal* management of wilderness beginning in the 1940's. They recognized that recreation was only one value associated with wilderness and that, in the name of maintaining wild conditions, even recreation should be regulated and restricted. One of the earliest expressions was an article entitled "Certified Outdoorsmen" in *American Forests* for November 1940. The author, J.V.K. Wagar, began by observing that "nature once certified outdoorsmen." The weak, foolish, and careless just did not return from the wilderness they entered. "But now," he continued, "there is such ease of transportation and so much improvement in equipment that anyone can become a wilderness traveler." Wagar's point was that, as a consequence, many people are in the wilderness who do not know how to care either for themselves or for the country. His suggested remedy was a program conducted by rangers from the National Park Service and the Forest Service to certify outdoorsmen. Those attaining the rank of "Expert Outdoorsman" would be "safe to leave in the woods." Included in their knowledge would be the ability to respect and live gently on the land. In 1940, Wagar did not go so far as to suggest that *only* certified outdoorsmen would be admitted to designated wilderness areas, but the implication was clearly present. If the Park and Forest Services certified recreational users of the lands they administered, the next logical step was to require certification before admission to those lands in the interests of protecting the wilderness resource (Wagar 1940).

Wilderness enthusiasts had long recognized that too many people, even too many outdoorsmen, could spoil a particular place. As early as 1926, the *New York Herald Tribune* featured a before-and-after cartoon of a mountain lake. In the first frame, a lone horseman approached the lake, which was surrounded with pines and full of leaping trout; in the second, a solid rank of fishermen surrounded the lake and their camps obliterated the scenery. In this case the extension of a road to the lake was represented as the cause of the change. But by the 1930's, it was possible for some Americans to understand that, even without roads, wilderness values could be threatened by overuse. If that solitary horseman of 1926 were joined by 50 other riders and 100 backpackers, the problem would be much the same.

As a prime consumer of wilderness recreation, the Sierra Club continued to take keen interest in developing techniques of wilderness management. In 1947 the Club's *Bulletin* featured another article on recreational impact on wilderness. It was coauthored by Lowell Sumner of the National Park Service and Richard M. Leonard, the chairman of the Sierra Club's Outing Committee which, by this time, was coordinating a number of large, high-country trips each year. The particular focus of Sumner and Leonard was the mountain meadow of the Sierra, and their article included a photographic sequence depicting stages in the transformation of a lush grassland into a dustbowl. The cause was excessive recreational use. Discussing the problem under the heading "saturation of the wilderness," the authors declared "we need more than just a concept . . . We need a comprehensive technique of use that will prevent oversaturation of wilderness and still enable people, in reasonable numbers, to enjoy wilderness" (Leonard and Sumner 1947). Among the management tools suggested were rotation of camping and grazing sites, limitations on the length of permissible stay by one party in one area, and the use of transported oats rather than natural grasses for pack stock food. According to Sumner and Leonard, there already existed 24-hour limits for camping in some meadows. These must have been among the earliest such rules in wilderness management history.

In 1949, the Sierra Club sponsored a High Sierra Wilderness Conference. It has grown into the Biennial Wilderness Conference that flourishes today. At the initial one, about 100 Federal and State administrators, outing club representatives, and professional outfitters and guides from the Packers Association met to discuss a common concern: wilderness preservation. There was a consensus at the conference that the allocation and permanent protection of wilderness from outside influences such as roads and commerical development was only part of the problem. The other part was the impact of recreational users on wild country. The conferees, in other words, had the courage to recognize that they were part of the problem. By the time of the Fourth Wilderness Conference in 1955, a full range of wilderness management concerns was being discussed. So was the idea, still a decade away, for a National Wilderness Preservation System; but most commentators recognized that without proper management, the allocation of wilderness could well be meaningless. Also

implicit was the idea that it is not the wilderness as much as the wilderness *user* who needs management.

In the 1950's and 1960's, the related concerns of allocation and management continued to dominate the American discussion of wilderness. Inventory and designation of wild places progressed as well as the protection of established reserves. Notable here was the Echo Park Dam controversy involving Dinosaur National Monument and, many felt, the integrity of all National Parks (Nash 1973). Part of the price of the 1956 decision not to build a dam in Dinosaur was approval of one in Glen Canyon on the Colorado River. Its completion in 1963 intensified the efforts of both dam builders and wilderness protectors when the Grand Canyon itself became the subject of controversy 3 years later (Nash 1970a). The success of prowilderness forces in defending the Grand Canyon from dams, coming on top of the passage of the Wilderness Act and its establishment of the National Wilderness Preservation System (September 3, 1964) was encouraging. But this was limited to the external dimension of wilderness preservation—allocation. The internal one—how an allocated wilderness was used—continued to generate problems. The fact was that the National Park Service had not substantially departed from the management assumptions of the Mather-Albright era. Despite the establishment, at Sierra Club urging, of Kings Canyon in 1940 as a roadless National Park devoted to wilderness recreation (a 1939 version of the establishing act even used the name "Kings Canyon Wilderness National Park"), park management still emphasized visitor numbers, spectacles, and conveniences. This became clear in 1956 when the National Park Service launched Mission 66. This program was a response to rapidly increasing park visitation, but some feared it was the wrong response because the major thrust of Mission 66 was further development. More than a billion dollars were poured into the program, mostly for the construction of roads, visitors' centers, and motel-type accommodations. There was no thought of limiting visitation; the entire emphasis of Mission 66 was on improving the parks' capability for handling more tourists, and little was said about wilderness values and wilderness management. A management philosophy more appropriate to an amusement park or resort prevailed. The National Park Service was not alone in this posture. Operation Outdoors, the Forest Service's counterpart to Mission 66, similarly emphasized facilities and conveniences.

The facility and convenience orientation of Mission 66 and Operation Outdoors was also reflected in wilderness, although there was no clear policy directive to do so. In the early and mid-1960's, the laissez-faire philosophy of wilderness management, in which little at all was done, came to be replaced by management programs in which improvements that facilitated use were developed. For example, split log tables, iron fireplace grills, latrines, and drift fences were commonly provided. Trail standards were improved to promote access. In some California wildernesses, rakes were provided at campsites in order that visitors could clean up wood chips and debris (Snyder 1966).

But as agency policy about wilderness management has evolved, the recreation orientation of the early 1960's has gradually been replaced by a philosophy that calls upon the user to accept wilderness without benefit of numerous conveniences. Perhaps the best way to illustrate this is contained in a letter to the authors of this book from a Forest Service employee:

> An interesting result of the Wilderness Act and subsequent Forest Service direction is dramatized . . . in the John Muir Wilderness. I went through there in 1967 . . . and there were improvements and people evident everywhere. Tables, iron grates, stoves, hitch racks, toilets, bulletin boards, and even corrals were closely spaced along the heaviest used trails. In 1973, I went through there again . . . (The Wilderness Ranger) was just removing some of the last improvements (cast iron cooking plates) in the basin by shanks mare . . . People were not as evident because they had dispersed themselves . . . You could find them . . . but they were just not as visible due to the lack of centralized, formal camp improvements.[1]

Legislation for Management: The Wilderness Act

The Wilderness Act of 1964, covered in detail in chapter 4, was the first document in world history to accord statutory protection *specifically* to wilderness. The essential difference between the Wilderness Act, on one hand, and the Yellowstone Act of 1872 and the National Park Service Act of 1916 on the other, is contained in just a few words. Whereas the earlier legislation used the words *pleasuring* (1872) and *enjoyment* (1916), the 1964 law specified that the purpose of the protected land was *enjoyment as wilderness* (Public Law 88–577) [Italics added for emphasis]. The Wilderness Act did much to change the idea of wilderness from a residual resource (leftover land not useful for anything else) to a primary one central to national recreational policy.

Unquestionably the Wilderness Act has imperfections. The commitment to preserve wilderness is hedged in a variety of ways distasteful to the proponents of the law but essential to its passage in a society and a Congress still ambivalent about wild country. But the overriding significance of the Act is its specification of (1) the particular kind of opportunity for outdoor enjoyment that was to be protected, and (2) the preservation of natural conditions. This specification gives Federal personnel the mandate to manage positively on behalf of wilderness values and wilderness experiences. It clearly rules out many of the actions taken, in good faith, under the earlier park legislation. In this sense the Wilderness Act must be understood as an expression of American dissatisfaction with how the National Parks were being managed. The 1964 legislation reflects the evolution of the needs and tastes of increasing numbers of Americans toward the primitive. Wilderness is now valued in a way it could not have been in 1872 or 1916 when American civilization was qualitatively less complex and intense and when the nation was too near its pioneer roots. Similarly, the need for management including such things as recreational carrying capacity, use permits and quotas, and efforts to restore natural levels of fire have received acceptance as a result of changing times.

---

[1]Koen, John. 1975. Personal correspondence to John Hendee, George Stankey, and Robert Lucas. U.S. Dep. Agric. For. Serv., Intermt. For. and Range Exp. Stn., Missoula, Montana. [On file at For. Sci. Lab., Missoula, Mont.]

Literature Cited

Baldwin, Donald N.
   1972. The quiet revolution: the grass roots of today's wilderness preservation movement. 295 p. Pruett, Boulder, Colo.

Cammerer, Arno B.
   1938. Maintenance of the primeval in national parks. Appalachia 22(12):207–213.

Cleveland, Treadwell, Jr.
   1910. National forests as recreation grounds. Am. Acad. Polit. Soc. Sci. 35(3):241–247.

Gilligan, James P.
   1953. The development of policy and administration of Forest Service primitive and wilderness areas in the Western United States. Ph.D. diss. University of Michigan, Ann Arbor. 476 p.

Hildebrand, Joel H.
 1938. Maintenance of recreation values in the High Sierra: a report to the United States Forest Service. Sierra Club Bull. 23(5):85–96.

Langford, Nathaniel P.
 1972. Discovery of Yellowstone National Park. Aubrey L. Haines, ed. 125 p. University of Nebraska Press, Lincoln, Neb.

LeConte, Joseph N.
 1972. A summer of travel in the High Sierra. Shirley Sargent, ed. 144 p. Lewis Osborne, Ashland, Oreg.

Leopold, Aldo.
 1921. Wilderness and its place in forest recreational policy. J. For. 19(7):718–721.

Lillard, Richard G.
 1968. The siege and conquest of a national park. Am. West 5(1):28–31, 67, 69–71.

Leonard, Richard and E. Lowell Sumner.
 1947. Protecting mountain meadows. Sierra Club Bull. 32(5):53–62.

Nash, Roderick.
 1970a. Grand Canyon of the Living Colorado. 143 p. Sierra Club-Ballantine, New York.

Nash, Roderick.
 1970b. 'Wild-deor-ness', the place of wild beasts. In Wilderness: the edge of knowledge, p. 34–37. Maxine E. McCloskey, ed. Sierra Club, San Francisco.

Nash, Roderick.
 1973. Wilderness and the American mind. Rev. ed. 300 p. Yale University Press, New Haven, Conn.

Nash, Roderick.
 1975. The 'creation' of wilderness by herding and agriculture. In Program/journal of the 14th biennial wilderness conference, New York City, June 5–8, 1975. p. 51–55. Sierra Club/Audubon, New York.

National Conference on Outdoor Recreation.
 1926. Proceedings. 175 p. Washington, D.C.

National Plan for American Forestry.
 1933. Senate Doc. 12, 73rd Congress 1st Sess., March 13. 2 vols.

Pomeroy, Earl.
 1957. In search of the golden West: the tourist in western America. 233 p. Knopf, New York.

Snyder, A. P.
 1966. Wilderness management. J. For. 64(7):441–446.

Sumner, E. Lowell.
 1936. Special report on a wildlife study of the High Sierra in Sequoia and Yosemite National Parks and adjacent territory. Inservice report, National Park Service Archives, Washington, D.C.

Sumner, E. Lowell.
 1942. The biology of wilderness protection. Sierra Club Bull. 27(8):14–22.

U.S. Department of the Interior, National Park Service.
 1970. Administrative policies for natural areas of the National Park System. Washington, D.C.

Wagar, J. V. K.
 1940. Certified outdoorsmen. Am. For. 46(11):490–492, 524–525.

Wright, George M., Joseph S. Dixon, and Ben H. Thompson.
 1932. Fauna of the National Parks of the United States Fauna Series No. 1. 157 p. U.S. Government Printing Office, Washington, D.C.

Wright, George M., and Ben H. Thompson.
 1934. Fauna of the National Parks of the United States. Fauna Series No. 2. 142 p. U.S. Government Printing Office, Washington, D.C.

In some countries, the North American concept of wilderness does not exist. Following centuries of civilization, all but the most inaccessible locations have been modified by man. This area, in the Upper Yaque del Norte watershed in the Dominican Republic, shows the impact of generations of use and exploitation, but reforestation efforts are occurring.

3 International Concepts of Wilderness Preservation

The American Invention of Wilderness Preservation

Coca-Cola, basketball, and National Parks: American contributions to world civilization. With the 1872 designation of the Yellowstone region, the United States invented the National Park as a form of land use. Subsequently, the concept, first institutionalized in northwest Wyoming, spread to more than 1,000 reserves in over 100 nations (Nash 1970; IUCN 1971; Sutton and Sutton 1972; Brockman and Merriam 1973; Ise 1961). In 1924 and again in 1964, the United States pioneered another new idea in public land management: wilderness preservation. Of course National Parks in the United States and elsewhere often include wilderness, but its explicit designation (1924, in the Gila National Forest) and formal statutory preservation (1964, through the Wilderness Act) were American innovations. The United States also took the international lead in developing, implementing, and refining the principles and policies governing the management of wilderness.

The Scarcity of Wilderness

Compared to the spread of National Parks, explicit preservation and management of wilderness has had

This chapter was written by Roderick Nash, professor of history and environmental studies, University of California at Santa Barbara.

only limited international acceptance. One reason is that in many countries there is no wilderness (even liberally defined) left to protect. Indeed in languages like Danish, even the word for "wilderness" has disappeared. Switzerland is an example of a nation for which wilderness is not a part of preservation. From border to border this small nation has been modified by man's activity into a thoroughly humanized landscape. In this regard it is instructive to recount the experience of ecologist Raymond Dasmann. When he went to Geneva to assume a position with the International Union for the Conservation of Nature and Natural Resources, he brought with him his American-born love of wild places. In one of his first leisure moments in Switzerland, Dasmann opened maps of the nation and located the largest blank space, high up an alpine valley, where, he assumed, he could find wilderness. A few weeks later Dasmann gathered backpacking equipment and set off for the mountains with great expectations. After driving to the vicinity, he parked beside a country road and began to walk. His apprehension rose because the road never ended. Neither did the succession of cultivated fields, pastures, and dwellings. At last Dasmann reached the heart of his Swiss wilderness, the place he had planned to camp. He found himself in a barnyard. Cows stared curiously and children waved at the strange man with a pack on his back. Sadder but wiser, and with a deeper appreciation of the wilderness recreational opportunities in his own country, Dasmann drove back to Geneva and permanently retired his backpack to the closet.

Switzerland does have a national park. It is a scenically magnificent expanse of mountains and high valleys on the border of Switzerland and Austria at the headwaters of the Inn River. But, characteristic of European parks, the environment is not conducive to obtaining a wilderness experience. In the first place, the region had been intensely used for economic purposes from the Middle Ages until the early part of the 20th century. The land that became the park in 1914 supported mines, foundries, and chalk ovens. Today no such use is permitted; with the exception of regionally extinct wildlife, the natural qualities of the environment are returning. Under proper management, wilderness conditions could be recreated in this area, but it would require several centuries. And there is another problem. Had Raymond Dasmann sought out the Swiss National Park for recreational purposes he would, once again, have been disappointed. The park was established as a biological sanctuary, and its charter insists that it be "protected from all human influence and interference." It exists in the name of science, not recreation. Camping and mountain climbing are both prohibited. Visitors are permitted access only during daylight hours. They are further restricted to authorized paths. One can step off them, to sit down or eat lunch, for instance, only in areas a few yards square marked by yellow boundary posts. Even if wilderness qualities do return to this part of Switzerland, obtaining a wilderness experience in the American sense will be extremely difficult (Schloeth 1974; Reifsnyder 1974).

It is hard for persons, who know only American wilderness criteria, to understand the omnipresence of civilization in those parts of the world intensively used by agricultural and technological man for thousands of years. China and India offer examples as does the Matterhorn region on the Italian-Swiss border. Justly famous for its scenery, the Matterhorn area is almost totally devoid of wildness. The spectacular high valley leading to the picturesque resort town of Zermatt in Switzerland is laced with a web of civilization. Roads and railroads work their way along the river which is controlled by a chain of hydropower installations. Trams and lifts crisscross the narrow gorge. Tunnels pierce cliff faces. Clusters of buildings occupy every level nook, and farms extend upward to nearly impossible slopes. The presence of cattle has lowered the timberline several hundred feet in this region and generally throughout the Alps. Chalets of the wealthy and climbers' huts perch on highest outcrops. And, crossing the ridge-top divide, one finds the same paraphernalia of civilization extending up the other side. The civilizations of Switzerland and Italy

Figure 3-1.—In Switzerland, man's activities over many centuries have modified the landscape so there is no wilderness, as we know it, left to protect.

meet at the Theodulepass, connected by ski lifts, just a few thousand feet below the Matterhorn. There is no possibility of a frontier in the American sense of that term—a dividing line between civilization and wilderness. Man has been here a long time. Only the sheer rock faces of the peaks themselves are without human impact. Spectacular, yes; awesome, yes; dangerous, yes; wild, no. And the wildness is not absent just to American eyes. Even Europeans, with understandably lower standards for defining what is wild, do not think of the Matterhorn as wilderness. For technical rock climbing it is legendary, the birthplace of mountaineering. Wilderness is something else.

Faced for centuries with the absence of wilderness, Europeans have adjusted. It is common to observe that they are doing fine without wilderness. Outside the metropolitan areas, the European environment is generally scenic and charming. The mountain resorts are spectacular. And, some contend, Europeans do not miss what they have never experienced: wilderness and backpacking (as opposed to hut-to-hut hiking). But if the call of the wild really is gene deep, the product of a racial experience a thousand times longer than man's recent experiment with civilization, then Europeans (like New Yorkers) would be expected to feel its tug from time to time. The most intense interest in wilderness is commonly encountered under the most civilized conditions. At any rate, it is surely folly to deny cultural relativity by transposing European standards into the United States. The fact that Switzerland is getting along without wilderness is no argument for developing Washington's North Cascades as an alpine resort.

The experience of Great Britain furnishes additional evidence of why the American lead in wilderness preservation cannot be followed even if the culture would welcome islands of wildness in their midst. England, in a word, is a garden or at least a giant pasture. It is a totally utilized landscape, and it has been so for thousands of years (Trent 1956; Lowenthal and Prince 1964; Bonham-Carter 1959; Hoskins 1955). As a consequence, the movement for environmental conservation in Great Britain has never involved wilderness preservation. Its earliest manifestations in the 19th and 20th centuries concerned historic preservation and what the English call "access to the countryside." The latter amounts to nothing more than the right of people to walk across pastures and cropland which have been in the hands of large landlords since the enclosures of the 18th and 19th centuries. Camping, the self-sufficient backpacking type, was never an issue either because of taste (the English seem to prefer inns, pubs, and hostels) or because of geography (on this relatively small island no part of the countryside is more than few miles' walk from civilization).

After World War II, National Parks attracted the interest of the English. In 1949, the National Parks and Access to the Countryside Act created the statutory framework for establishing what now amounts to 10 National Parks. From the American point of view, the English parks are unusual because they include *a quarter of a million residents*. These are not rangers and employees of concessionaires, but ordinary citizens who either lived in the parks before their establishment or moved in afterwards (Darby 1961; Abrahams 1959). What in fact is being preserved in the National Parks of England and Wales is a rural lifestyle complete with traditional agricultural practices. There is, of course, nothing wrong with this, especially not to the English who value the human associations a landscape may contain (Lowenthal and Prince 1965). But the English situation demonstrates that by the time an old and intensely developed nation like Great Britain decides to establish parks and reserves there is no alternative but to include substantial amounts of civilization. Modern England did not have an option of preserving wilderness.

Cultural Relativity and the Wilderness Concept

Another factor that has limited the spread of wilderness preservation and management from its birthplace in the United States is the inability of some cultures which actually possess wilderness to recognize the fact. Such attitudes are often found in countries classified as underdeveloped and nontechnological. From the perspective of highly developed nations, the citizens of such countries live in wilderness. But the nontechnological societies find this point incomprehensible. Indeed they have no conception at all of wilderness or its preservation.

Turning first to an historical example of this attitude, Chief Luther Standing Bear of the Oglala Sioux commented in the 19th century on the difference between his culture's viewpoint and that of the transplanted European settlers of the New World who were replacing it: "We did not think of the great open plains, the beautiful rolling hills, and the winding streams with their tangled growth as 'wild.' Only to the white man was nature a 'wilderness' and only to him was the land 'infested' with 'wild' animals and 'savage' people. To us it was tame." (McLuhan 1971). As Standing Bear implies, only cultures which are based on controlling and modifying the environment are capable of distinguishing between wilderness and civilization. The hunter-gatherer, on the other hand, did not live by transforming wilderness into civilization and consequently saw no dichotomy between the two. For Standing Bear, every place was simply home.

The point here is that only residents of highly developed societies can conceive of wilderness. Ironically, a culture must lose its wilderness before wilderness preservation begins. The trick is to develop the pressure for preservation that only civilization can produce before all the wildness is gone. The United States was fortunate in this respect because the course of westward settlement created an intensive, urbanized civilization in the East while there was still unappropriated wilderness in the West. Thus a park like Yellowstone could be created simply by drawing lines on a map. When it came to creating wilderness reserves in the East after 1964, Americans experienced the kinds of difficulties familiar in the Old World nations (Nash 1970).

Chief Standing Bear represented a true hunting-gathering people that has few contemporary parallels. But underdeveloped countries still exhibit many of the same attitudes toward wilderness and its preservation. Most of them have difficulty conceiving of "wilderness" in the way that term is used in the developed world. Evidence stems from the fact that less developed societies commonly do not have the word "wilderness" or an equivalent in their languages. In Malaysia, among many African peoples, and even in outback Australia, there is no synonym for "wilderness." Stares of incomprehension or laughter invariably meet the question: "What is your word for 'wilderness'?" After considerable explanation by the questioner or an interpreter one might be offered a word equivalent to "forest" or "nature" but totally lacking the connotations of "wilderness." A Masai in East Africa, for example, offered "serenget" as in Serengeti Plains. It signifies an extended place. The concept that this place might be *wild* simply could not be communicated in Masai.

These differences in attitude between developed and less developed (in the sense of less technological and less urban) people explain why wilderness preservation and management has no meaning in many parts of the world. And, frustratingly, this is particularly the case in the very regions with the most wilderness. Many Africans, for instance, have lived with wild animals and in a wilderness environment for as long as they can remember. For them it is hard to understand the rationale for a wilderness reserve. It would be as if a proposal were made to a group of New Yorkers to create and manage an urban reserve between 32nd and 42nd streets in Manhattan. To the African, the restrictions on grazing, farming, and living that invariably follow proclamation of a wilderness area are perplexing. The New Yorker, to continue the analogy, would be similarly confused if, after the creation of the urban reserve, he were prohibited from driving and shopping there.

Conditions in Kenya's Northern Frontier District are representative of this dilemma. By almost every American standard, save one, this is splendid desert wilderness. The few outpost towns are lost in an immensity of space. In that country there are no roads, vehicles, stores, and electricity. Elephant, lion, rhinoceros, and the big Cape buffalo abound. Hippopotami and crocodiles swarm in the few water courses. Few white people have ever seen the region. But there are people in the Northern Frontier District. The Samburu, a northern Masai tribe of cattle and goat herders, have used the region quite intensively for generations. And, further back in the hills, the more primitive Dorobo subsist chiefly on wild honey and the game their snares bring down. So is the Northern Frontier District wilderness? Could a wilderness reserve be established there by the Kenyan Government? If so, what would become of the Samburu and the Dorobo? The difficulty of finding clear answers is one reason wilderness

preservation has not fared well beyond the borders of the United States.

Comparing Switzerland and England to Kenya illuminates the dynamics of global wilderness preservation. The plain fact is that the development that imperils wilderness is *precisely* the factor that creates a perceived need for wilderness. There are no shortcuts here. The road to wilderness appreciation and protection leads, inevitably, to and through a technologically sophisticated, urbanized society.

On an international level wilderness is an actively traded commodity. The following metaphor might be helpful in making the point.

THE EXPORTING AND IMPORTING OF WILDERNESS

Between the countries that have wilderness and those that lack it and want it there exists what might be termed an export-import relationship. Before development or in its developing phase a nation is a wilderness exporter. It "sells" wildness to the developed nations. Nature does not, of course, physically leave the country except in the case of animal trophies. The more common form of export today is through the minds, spirits, and cameras of tourists. But there are also "armchair" tourists who derive pleasure simply from the *knowledge* that primeval places exist. The concern of these vicarious consumers of wilderness for what they may never see has been an important source of support for world preservation.

Conversely the developed nation finds its wildness depleted and therefore imports it from less developed nations. The payment is in the currency that tourists spend to experience the primitive. The philanthropy that funds world nature protection organizations is an example of wilderness importing. So is the purchase of books, films, and television specials on foreign wilderness.

National parks, wilderness systems, and the personnel sent to manage them or train native managers might be thought of as the institutional "containers" that developed nations send to underdeveloped ones for the purpose of "packaging" the exportable resource of wildness.

It is quite true that underdeveloped nations may eventually evolve to an economic and intellectual position in which nature protection becomes important in its own right. But in the meantime the preservation of wild places and wildlife in the developing nations depends on the existence of the world wilderness "market." As a poster in Swahili frankly states: "OUR NATIONAL PARKS BRING GOOD MONEY INTO TANZANIA— PRESERVE THEM." Wilderness preservation, at least at the international level, is the game of the relatively well-to-do, the urban, and the sophisticated. They are the clientele of wilderness wherever it exists. They subsidize the decision of less developed nations to protect wildness. Without such subsidy the chances of wilderness surviving would be poor in the face of the economic aspirations of the developing world.

Recognition of the existence of this export-import relationship appears frequently in the discussion of international concepts of wilderness preservation. This relationship is the basis of the idea, expressed most frequently in the United States by Russell E. Train, of a World Heritage Trust (Train 1974). The principle here is that the developed nations should take steps to insure the preservation and proper management of extraordinary natural areas in the rest of the world. Of course this means financial underwriting as well as technical assistance and even political jurisdiction. It is the last point that has kept the World Heritage Trust from getting off the ground. Even if it comes with money attached, few nations welcome the idea of an internationally controlled enclave in their midst. But the developed world cannot be expected to invest in projects vulnerable to the winds of political chaos or economic development. Still, the point that the whole world has an interest in, say, East Africa's wildlife, that the wildlife does not belong exclusively to East Africa, is gaining acceptance. International stewardship of wildness is not inconceivable for the future.

While Princeton-educated, safari-addicted Russell Train is clearly at the importing end of the spectrum, it is possible to find wilderness exporters with the same ideas. Perez Olindo, the American-trained director of Kenya's National Parks, believes that the developed world should exercise its desire for wilderness preservation *in* the underdeveloped world. Specifically, Olindo proposed that Americans, frustrated at their inability to establish a tallgrass prairie National Park in the Middle West, create their park on the plains of Kenya (Olindo 1975).

England's conception of its parks and reserves is international. The English are eager importers of wildness and glad to support its preservation around the world with time and money. Indeed many of the international nature protection movements began in England. Reginald Hookway, Director of the Countryside Commission for England and Wales, explains that admittedly his own country has no more wilderness, but, the English who want the experience simply travel to Norway or Africa or New Zealand. This, he continues, doesn't amount to much more than a New Yorker journeying to California's High Sierra or Arizona's Grand Canyon (Hookway 1975).

Wilderness Around the World: Case Studies

The following review of some selected nations' experience with wilderness allocation and management is done with the broad brush of cultural generalization and does not emphasize legislative history. For more specific data see the previous bibliographic references, particularly Sutton and Sutton 1972; Brockman and Merriam 1973; and Ise 1961.

Japan

Japan's National Parks and wildernesses are unquestionably the most heavily used of any in the world. The nation has over 100 million people in an area smaller than California. The Japanese, moreover, are a highly urbanized people with the affluence and leisure necessary to exercise their need for nature. Cities like Tokyo, with all its urban problems, tend to drive people to wilderness. Within sight of the city, on one of its relatively few clear days (about 1 in 7), is Fujiyama. The Japanese prefer to give the 12,467-foot-high volcanic cone the more venerable name, Fujisan. It is part of Fuji-Hakone-Isu National Park, and, incredibly, over 70 million people visit the area each year. One million of them climb the final 5,000 feet (after the end of the road) to the summit of the big mountain. Due to heavy snow the climbing season is short, and in the peak summer months *25,000 people per day* make the ascent. There are five trails to the crater rim, and according to Tetsumaro Senge, Chairman of the National Parks Association of Japan, "every climbing route is filled with long queues of people so that no one can find space and time to stop and rest" (Senge 1973). This is literally the case. The lines of climbers wind up the switchbacks like huge, multicolored snakes. At night, with flares, they resemble glowworms. The individual is literally carried up and down the nation's highest peak in the flood of bodies.

Parts of the country with more difficult access have, proportionately, the same recreational pressures. What Tetsumaro Senge calls "roadless wilderness areas" (Senge 1974) are also thronged. In the Oze area of Nikko National Park, an alpine peat marsh was saved from a highway in the late 1960's only to be overwhelmed by 500,000 hikers (70 percent of them female) every year. The circuit through the marsh takes 2 days, and huts are used for the night, at least by the early arrivals. Similarly, it is "line up and wait" at most of the cliffs suitable for technical rock climbing such as those in the Chubu-Sangaku National Park. Helicopters regularly haul out the resulting trash from the tent areas in this alpine region. Only the northernmost Japanese island, Hokkaido, retains a vestige of what Americans would call primeval conditions, bears included. Daisetsuzan National Park embraces part of the area, and its relative remoteness from the main centers of Japanese population on the main island of Honshu has acted as a filter. But the leisure, wealth, and recreational tastes of an urban population is catching up even to Daisetsuzan which now hosts more than 3 million visitors annually. Their demands for fast motorized access led to the recent withdrawal of a proposal for a wilderness area in the park.

In the face of this kind of pressure on their limited wilderness, Japanese managers have turned to zoning. Under the 1972 Natural Environmental Protection Law, which updates the 1931 park organic legislation and its 1957 refinement and clarification, there is a mandate for inventory and subsequently designation of Primeval Nature Preservation Areas. These areas are completely closed to use, recreational or otherwise. The rest of the park is also categorized according to degree of wildness, and there is talk about a permit system based on a tripartite (physical, ecological, and psychological) concept of carrying capacity which was inspired by discussion of this issue in the United States (Oi 1970). The park zoning system established under the 1957 legislation will facilitate whatever is done in this direction. There are Special Protection Areas, Special Areas, and Ordinary Areas. The first category, the most protective, comprises only 11.4 percent of the total park area in Japan, but in some of the alpine parks the figure jumps to 38 percent. Grazing and lumbering are not allowed in the Special Protection Areas, and, in principle, hydroelectric development is forbidden. Yet hydropower installations have been constructed, and there is even talk of nuclear plants in the protected areas. When it comes to recreational facilities such as tramways, ski lifts, roads, hostels, and even lavish resort hotels, many Japanese see no conflict with preservation.

One reason why there is not much concern for wilderness in Japan is the lack of a clear distinction in the old culture between scenery and wilderness. The former might not be destroyed by a chair lift or lodge—indeed such developments often facilitate public enjoyment of *scenery*. But they destroy wilderness. Still it is worth noting that when proposals were made to construct a mechanized lift to the summit of sacred Fuji, a coalition of priests, citizen conservationists, and professional park administrators defeated this idea. And there is now a movement aimed at removing the ski lift from Mt. Eniwa on the island of Hokkaido that served the 1972 Winter Olympics (Simmons 1973). But such departures from the norm are rare.

A more subtle problem facing wilderness in Japan is, ironically, the superior ability of the Japanese to derive pleasure and meaning from nature. They don't *need* wilderness in the American sense; nature in miniature

will suffice. A long cultural tradition, steeped in the philosophies of Tao, Shinto, and Zen lies behind this ability. It is manifested in the Japanese love of garden art, of bonsai, of flower arrangement, and of the tea ceremony. All these interests reflect the idea that beauty, spiritual insight, and peace (satisfactions gleaned from the "wilderness experience" in our culture) come from *within* the beholder and not from the external environment. The process is intuitive and unexpected. It involves thinking metaphorically. It depends on placing oneself in the proper frame of mind, not on entering a particular environment. It follows, then, that huge, wild reserves are irrelevant to the Japanese quest. The Japanese can see in a single leaf what, for an American, would require a sequoia if not a park full of them. This is why the formal garden is so important in the Japanese tradition of nature appreciation. Here, in miniature, in metaphor, the whole is represented. The American, Walt Whitman, whose *Leaves of Grass* was published in 1855, and Whitman's transcendental teachers, Ralph Waldo Emerson and Henry David Thoreau, came closest to the Japanese position. Thoreau, after all, found all he needed in a small pond on the outskirts of a New England town. But for most Americans, the wild wide-open spaces have been essential. Not having the luxury of wilderness in this sense, the Japanese have long approached the problem of communion with nature with a different set of cultural assumptions (Watanabe 1974; Anesaki 1933).

From the management perspective, several conclusions can be drawn from the Japanese relationship to nature. One is that the external distractions that would ruin an environment for certain Americans are less of a problem for the Japanese. In a real sense, the crowds and the park developments are not "seen" in Japan. The people tend to look "through" these distractions to the meanings of nature. They concentrate on the internal environment of their own minds. So it is that a Japanese can have a deeply moving experience even in the heavily populated setting of Fuji, or he can simply contemplate the mountain from a distance and be satisfied. The values he seeks from nature do not depend on the degree of wildness that for an American may be a necessity. In Japan, in other words, personal sensitivity has increased to compensate for the lack of wildness. In regard to wildness, the mind makes up for what is missing in the environment.

The same phenomena of cultural relativity in the perception of wilderness can be observed in the United States by contrasting contemporary western and eastern attitudes toward statutory wilderness. People adapt to what is available. Easterners, in general, are far more willing to accommodate civilized intrusions in their conception of wilderness than are Westerners. Logging roads and second-growth forests, for instance, often disqualify an area as wilderness in the West. But in the East, where there is little alternative, preservationists readily accept such compromises of pure wilderness conditions. From the standpoint of preservation, the implication of such relativity is that a culturally induced reduction in expectations and needs might rationalize substantial environmental modifications. With the Japanese example in mind, it is possible to envision a day when Americans camping by the score in Kampgrounds of America (KOA) lots might honestly believe they were having a wilderness experience. With environmental limits in clear sight, we all must learn to get more out of less. But if the integrity of the land itself (not just visitor perception) is a consideration in wilderness preservation, then cultural relativity must not be an excuse to justify the determination of the resource.

New Zealand

Topography has been a strong ally of wilderness preservation on the island first known as "the long white cloud." Some of that whiteness was snow on high peaks; some was cloud gathered by New Zealand's mountainous backbone. On the South Island, the high country (Mt. Cook is 12,349 feet) drops directly into the sea without a coastal plain that would invite settlement. Milford Sound, a fiord which receives over 300 inches of rainfall in the average year, winds between mile-high peaks. Nowhere else in the world does the land meet the sea so abruptly.

This ruggedness and a low population-to-land ratio throughout the islands sufficiently retarded settlement and roads so that in 1952, when the National Parks Act consolidated park laws, there was an abundance of wilderness left to protect. The Act, which is burdened with the same ambiguities respecting preservation and public enjoyment that characterized the 1916 Organic Act of the National Park Service in the United States, refers specifically to wilderness. Section 34 empowers the various park boards (there is one for each National Park) to designate wilderness areas with the concurrence of the National Parks Authority. This process does not insure permanent preservation. In the first place, the attachment of wilderness status to an area within a park is an administrative decision only. There is no statutory authority for wilderness in New Zealand. Second, the park boards are composed of representatives of various local interests. many of which are not inclined toward preservation. The private landowners and grazers commonly included on the boards are generally in strong opposition as are members with ski and hydropower interests. Tourism is also represented on the boards, but it often works at cross purposes to the wilderness interest. At Mt. Cook National Park small planes, ski-equipped to land on snowfields, have long been part of the tourist scene. Their standard package is a half-hour flight that includes a landing on the snow in what would otherwise be superb wilderness well inside the park boundaries. Climbing huts, which in Mt. Cook are lavish and radio equipped as bases for search and rescue operations, also disqualify an area as wilderness under the terms of the 1952 legislation. This leaves only a few, less desirable, and often less scenic areas for wilderness designation within the parks.

The ski planes represent the tip of a much larger iceberg of New Zealand tourist development. Although not on a level with the African nations and Malaysia where foreigners constitute at least 90 percent of the visitors to Nature Reserves, New Zealand seeks the foreign tourist dollar. The Tourist Hotel Corporation is a government agency with full rights to develop facilities in any of the National Parks. At Mt. Cook National Park, it is the force behind the expansion of the park village and its reorientation toward luxury tourism. The bearing of this on wilderness is that self-sufficient backcountry users are pointedly discouraged in the park. Signs at the luxurious Hermitage Hotel warn them to keep their dirty boots off the carpets, but the biggest liability of the sleeping-bag set from the standpoint of the Tourist Hotel Corporation is that they do not spend very much money. It is far better, from this point of view, to cater to the charge-card-carrying, generally older person who supports the tourist industry. These assumptions, which are widespread in New Zealand, naturally work against wilderness allocation and management.

The pattern is plain at the huge (3 million acres) Fiordland National Park in the southwest corner of the South Island. Most of those who forsake the hotels at Milford Sound and Te Anau to see something of the park's vast backcountry do so on organized Tourist Hotel Corporation walks along the world-famous Milford Track. The essential idea here is excellent—the Track offers an alternative to the paved road for reaching Milford Sound. But from the standpoint of experiencing wilderness, there is much to be desired. All the walkers do is walk. Guides lead them along heavily signed trails. At the end of the day, huts complete with dining rooms, laundries, hot showers, and bunk space for as many as 40 persons await their arrival. At one hut, set in an otherwise wild valley, an airstrip has been carved, and a small plane arrives an hour before supper to give the walkers short rides at $10 per person. Of course, the Milford Track can be looked on as a threshold outdoor experience. And the intense organization, combined with the existence of the huts, virtually eliminates the problems caused by thoughtless or inexperienced campers. But wilderness is not a primary concern of management. In fact only one small coastal island in Fiordland has been officially designated as a wilderness area.

The place of wilderness in the New Zealand cultural context is well illustrated by the Lake Manapouri controversy. It began in the late 1950's when plans to construct an aluminum smelter on the South Island near Fiordland turned attention to the hydropower potential of Manapouri and its companion lake, Te Anau. By 1963, shocked conservation groups realized that the New Zealand Government had in effect contracted with the foreign smelter investors to raise the level of the lakes. The storm of protest (on the grounds of scenic beauty and ecological integrity, not of wilderness recreation) led finally to Manapouri's becoming a central issue in the 1972 elections. The victorious Labor party ran on a platform of not raising the lakes. Celebrations were widespread, but overlooked was the fact that a hydropower development which did not entail lake raising was being completed right in the heart of one of the wildest regions of Fiordland National Park. It resulted in the digging of a 6-mile tunnel 700 feet beneath a mountain wall for the purpose of draining Lake Manapouri into the ocean at Deep Cove. The influx of water from the lake turned the fiord fresh for 15 miles. But far from regarding it as a source of regret, New Zealand proclaimed the Deep Cove-Manapouri development an engineering wonder of the world and added it to the list of tourist attractions.

Recently, statements of New Zealand park leaders suggest that the management of outdoor recreational resources for nonwilderness purposes will at least be scrutinized. Speaking in 1970 at a parks planning symposium, the chairman of the Tangariro National Park board expressed dismay at the developments that were rapidly transforming the park into a downhill ski resort. The experience of the United States, he pointed out, showed that parks could be loved to death by an enjoyment-minded public. The answer to this problem, he related, could be found by applying a principle suggested by a biocentric philosophy—nature preservation ahead of pleasure. He concluded his remarks with a suggestion for all park entrance signs in New Zealand: "THIS IS A NATIONAL PARK. IF YOU CAN DO IT ANYWHERE ELSE, DON'T DO IT HERE" (McGlone 1970). The advice favors wilderness, but New

Zealanders might find it easier to apply in Nepal, where they are acting as advisers in the creation of Mt. Everest National Park, than on their home islands.

Sweden

The only part of Europe that approaches American standards of wilderness is the northern extremity of Norway, Sweden, and Finland. This area is relatively inaccessible. Just reaching it involves at least a day of foot travel. And the harsh 7-month winters contribute to the wildness of the land of the Lapps.

Sweden, in particular, has been active in wilderness preservation. As early as 1909 it became the first European nation to follow the American example of 1872, setting aside six National Parks. Today there are 16, and the northern ones like Sarek and Padjelanta equal Yellowstone in size. Hydroelectric installations have compromised parts of the parks, but no more than Hetch Hetchy Reservoir compromises the total wildness of Yosemite.

Recreational use of Sweden's wilderness parks (and they are called such by the Swedes) is extremely light— about 5,000 persons annually as of 1972. In Padjelanta National Park, the huts and cottages familiar in Europes's Alps to the south are present. But visiting the rugged mountains and glaciers of Sarek National Park necessitates American-style backpack camping.

Other than fish-and-game laws, Sweden has placed few controls on wilderness visitors. One deterrent to regulation is the common-law principle of *allemansrätten* or "every man's right." A product of the people's reaction against feudal landuse practices of the Middle Ages, it provides that everyone in Sweden may wander freely in open country, even on privately owned lands. Public rights extend to camping and gathering (berries, mushrooms). In view of this fiercely defended cultural tradition, some of the restrictions on visitation and behavior applied to wilderness in the United States seem unlikely to gain many converts in Sweden.

Perhaps the most difficult problem facing Sweden in its efforts to protect and manage wilderness is the presence of native peoples whose use of the recently reserved parkland is of long standing. The nomadic Lapps have pastured their reindeer herds, hunted, fished, and lived in Sarek and especially Padjelanta for generations. The Swedish Government recognizes their right to continue this use but is understandably dismayed at the Lapps' recent preference for snowmobiles over ski and dog sled travel. While a Lapp on skis might be an attractive feature of the park—a kind of "man of the wilderness" in the eyes of many visitors—a Lapp in a snowmobile is likely to offend the visitor who must walk into the area. It is a problem comparable to grazing in some American wildernesses. A mounted cowboy is not nearly as disturbing as an agribusinessman riding herd in a helicopter.

Clearly Sweden faces the necessity of weighing wilderness values against the interest of native peoples. The presence of the Lapps does not automatically disqualify the northern parks as wilderness, but their technological ambitions well might. Still if wilderness preservation involves forcing the continuation of primitive conditions on aspiring natives, the social and political pressures against wilderness are likely to reach intolerable levels (Esping 1972).

Union of Soviet Socialist Republics

The hunting reserves of feudal lords marked the beginning of Russia's experience with wilderness preservation and management. After the 1917 revolution, all land was nationalized and remains so. This total public control creates, in theory, a promising political framework for all kinds of conservation including that of wilderness.

After 1917, the U.S.S.R. began the creation of a nationwide system of *zapovedniki*—literally forbidden areas. One of the early calls for such reserved areas was made by V.P. Semenov-Tyan-Shanskiy in 1917, under the title "On the types of locales in which it is necessary to establish zapovedniki analogous to American National Parks" (Pryde 1972). The system expanded until, in 1951, there were 128 zapovedniki totaling more than 31 million acres. Their purpose was and is largely scientific. Zapovedniki are, in the words of a 1960 law, primarily "outdoor laboratories for the study of naturally occurring processes." It is true that some of the reserves are used for recreation, but most of them exist for the resident scientists and their research.

The zapovedniki, which presently amount to about 0.3 percent of the total area of the U.S.S.R., contain an extensive amount of wilderness. The wild area is not given legal recognition; in fact there is no word for "wilderness" in Russian. But increasing numbers of Russians are turning to the zapovedniki for wilderness forms of recreation. In some cases, they are not rejected. The Kavkaz zapovednik in the Caucasus near the Black Sea is open to camping, climbing, and hiking. This is wilderness by any standard with virgin forests, wolves, and snow leopards. Management of the area is not well defined and as a result, the resource is sometimes damaged by careless visitors. But because there is no single managing agency for zapovedniki and the staffs that exist are composed of natural rather than social scientists and planners, reform is not likely. The only

response of the government to recreational pressure on zapovedniki has been to launch plans for National (or "Natural") Parks. The movement, which did not begin until the late 1960's, has yet to do more than make an inventory of areas, primary among them the Lake Baykal region in eastern Siberia which now enjoys National Park status. If parks are established, indications are that they will have a wilderness core and a surrounding zone developed for mechanized tourist and administrative use.

The Soviet political context makes the creation of zapovedniki relatively easy compared, say, to the establishment of a wilderness under the 1964 Wilderness Act in the United States. But the same degree of central political control also facilitates their abolition. Centralized power is a two-edged sword. For example, in 1951, about seven-eighths of the reserved area was suddenly eliminated from the system. Some of the casualties were as large as Yellowstone National Park. Explanations generally point to economic needs associated with the fifth Five Year Plan. Since 1951, the system has been partially reestablished, and the growing demands of urbanized Russians for wilderness recreation suggest that pressure for expansion will increase. For the same reasons, it appears that restriction of reserved wilderness to scientific purposes will be increasingly difficult.

Australia

In contrast to New Zealand, geography has not supported wilderness preservation and management in Australia. The continent is old and worn. Its highest points are gently rounded plateaus under 8,000 feet. Compared to the difficulty of building in true alpine regions, roads are easily constructed everywhere on the continent. Another problem is that several needs and activities necessarily compete for the continent's limited rooftop. The classic case is the Kosciusko National Park in New South Wales where the same mountains are used for downhill skiing, a huge hydropower water-supply development, and wilderness preservation. On the vast desert reaches of the Australian Outback, wilderness qualities certainly exist, but only because motorists and pilots are few and far between. There is, in other words, a large area of wilderness but few designated wilderness areas. The Elliott Price Wilderness National Park is an example of the latter. Australia's island state, Tasmania, *had* the nation's largest extent of forested wilderness until the heart was cut from it by the Gordon River hydropower project. Finally, in sharp contrast to the situation in Japan, the sheer enormity and unrelieved emptiness of the Australian continent (roughly equivalent to the contiguous United States) and the small population (about 11 million, mostly concentrated on the southeast coast) have not created much pressure for the protection and management of wilderness. Like Canada (see below), Australia suffers in these respects from the assumption that its problems stem from too much, not too little, wilderness.

The Australian political system is also a factor in wilderness preservation and management. The central government in Canberra has jurisdiction in federal territories only. Each state government is supreme in its area and creates and manages "national" parks according to its own needs. Kosciusko National Park, for instance, is a creation of the government of New South Wales, not the government of Australia. Lamington National Park (and the Great Barrier Reef) "belong" to the Government and people of Queensland. Management policies differ in each state. Consequently, a national effort to preserve wilderness is extremely unusual. Most such pressures exist at the state level.

Still, there has been a handful of Australians, mostly inspired by Americans such as Theodore Roosevelt, Robert Marshall, and Aldo Leopold and by American legislation like the National Park Act and the Wilderness Act, for whom effective wilderness management was and is a pressing concern. The father figure was Myles Dunphy. His efforts, beginning in 1914 with his organization of the "bushwalkers" of Sydney, led to proposals during the 1930's for establishing wilderness areas in several of the National and State Parks of New South Wales. Dunphy was not dedicated to solitude or even low-density recreation. Provided one entered the area with a pack, prepared to be self-sufficient, he was welcomed into the camaraderie of "the people of the little tents" (Johnson 1974). In the case of the Mt. Kosciusko region, Dunphy and his colleagues in the National Parks and Primitive Areas Council directed most of their energies against grazers and the developers of both hydropower and tourist facilities such as downhill skiing. He proposed to separate such activities from wilderness by means of park zoning. Dunphy counted on the support of the scientific community for this idea, but here he was surprised. The scientists indeed wanted wilderness but only for the purpose of scientific research. In the course of time, the scientists and "bushwalkers," joined later by soil and water conservationists, learned the advantages of presenting a united front against development. On June 5, 1944, they enjoyed their first success when over a million acres in Australia's highest range was designated the Kosciusko State Park. This act of the New South Wales Government contained a provision authorizing up to one-tenth of the park as a Primitive Area. The criterion for such places was that the

primary aim of their management was preservation of natural conditions. This became exceedingly difficult after 1949 when the giant Snowy Mountains Hydro-Electric Authority moved into the park with an ambitious project aimed at transferring water from the eastern side of Australia's continental divide to the arid west. Grazing also continued to be widespread in Kosciusko (Hancock 1972).

By 1960, prowilderness forces resolved to use the authority of the 1944 statute to save what wilderness qualities remained in Kosciusko. Their plan entailed reserving the park's highest land (generally above 6,000 feet) as wilderness. In 1963, over heated protests of the hydropower interests, park authorities approved the plan (it was not statutory). By 1967, when Kosciusko was renamed a "National Park," it contained four wilderness areas. From the American viewpoint these were hardly wild, but they represented the best Australia could do in an accessible area subject to competition from a number of conflicting uses.

Where the competition has been less severe, Australians have done better by their wilderness. Lamington National Park in the subtropical rainforest of Queensland is roadless except for two widely separated lodges. The state intends that any further development occur on the edges of the park's wild core. Tasmania's Cradle Mountain-Lake St. Clair National Park offers a chance for a 5-day hike through indisputable wilderness. The only distracting feature is a system of huts, but these can be avoided by the self-contained backpacker. In the outback, there is an abundant wilderness, but the vastness and hostility of the country, not management, is primarily responsible for its preservation. The Simpson Desert National Park sprawls over the Queensland-South Australia border for some 30,000 square miles. In fact, Australia has the opportunity to create the largest wilderness reserve in the world from an Outback where distances between settlements can be more than a thousand miles. But much of this land has been declared a reserve for the aborigines; and in a time of social sensitivity over treatment of these people, the government is reluctant to make changes. It would be nice to think that the aborigines hunt and gather from this land; in fact they scarcely depend on it for their subsistence.

The example of the 1964 Wilderness Act of the United States and a growing sense of the disappearance of the primitive have in the last decade prompted a vigorous defense of wilderness on the part of a small group of Australians. Their finest efforts came in the early 1970's in an abortive effort to save Lake Pedder, in the heart of southwest Tasmania's virtually unexplored wilderness, from inundation as part of the Gordon River hydropower project. Still the Lake Pedder controversy, like America's Hetch Hetchy battle a half-century earlier, did much to rally wilderness defenders throughout the nation. One of the consequences was the appearance of *The Wilderness World of Olegas Truchanas* in 1975 (Argus 1975). The book celebrated a man, a photographer-explorer, with striking similarities to John Muir, and a country—Tasmania's recently ravaged Southwest. Its publication marked the emergence of an unabashed Australian love of the wildness of their continent. Another milestone was the 1974 appearance of *The Alps at the Crossroads* (Johnson 1974). Its purpose was the preservation in an Alpine National Park coterminous with Kosciusko National Park in New South Wales, of the remnants of Victoria's mountain wilderness. The book is really a history of the whole wilderness movement in Australia and concludes with recommendations for management of the proposed park. These recommendations recognize at the outset that "many types of recreation *do not* coexist successfully" (Johnson 1974). It followed that wilderness areas would be established within the park. Active management of these areas would facilitate the phasing out of the omnipresent Australian fire road. Future fire control would use helicopters or men on foot. Private vehicles would, of course, be barred and existing huts phased out. As for grazing, a traditional activity in the high country, the recommendations hedged but expressed the hope that long-term policy could be directed to removing cattle from designated wilderness.

The most interesting recommendations for management of wilderness in the proposed Alpine National Park concerned rules regarding backpackers. Quotas and permits were not favored. Management should allow people to go where they wished in the park backcountry because this freedom was the essence of wilderness adventure. In time, it was recognized, crowding might necessitate tighter restrictions, but for Australia this seemed a long way off. A related point concerned danger. This, too, was seen as an essential part of the wilderness experience. Management should content itself with providing information on weather conditions and checking equipment and experience. But no adult should be prevented from entering the backcountry for reasons of potential danger. Then followed a significant statement:

> If this most important principle of adventuring is to be upheld we must be prepared for death in the mountains. Inexperienced rock climbers will fall, canoeists will drown, ski-tourers will freeze and bushwalkers will die of exposure. It is payment in kind for the

pleasure that is sought. The subsequent risk to individuals engaged in search and rescue operations, and the expense of these, are unfortunate but necessary costs imposed on society by the need of individuals to breathe. (Johnson 1974).

Although only recommendations at this time, such ideas pioneer a frontier of wilderness management that even the United States has not fully explored. It boils down to whether a person has the right to put his life on the line. Most American thinking on this safety aspect of wilderness use emphasizes protection of the visitor. This concern often translates to a preference by management for the commercially guided party as opposed to the do-it-yourselfers. But a growing, countervailing position argues that overemphasis on professional guides threatens to create a "safari syndrome." Self-led, private parties, it contends, represent the most appropriate use of wilderness for recreation. It is not merely an academic matter. With the advent of visitor quotas in some wildernesses and several wild rivers in the 1970's, the division of the total user "pie" between the commercial and noncommercial sectors has become one of the most controversial management issues.

Canada

The Canadian experience furnishes added evidence for the paradox that the possession of wilderness is a *disadvantage* in the preservation of wilderness. In Canada's case it is the northcountry—unbelievably huge and empty, a continuing frontier that elicits frontier attitudes toward land. The result of having this vast reservoir of wildness to the north is that the urgency for wilderness protection is lessened. And there seems no need to devise and apply sophisticated techniques of wilderness management. "Why worry?" is the dominant Canadian response to these questions. "Our problem," they say, "is too much wilderness, not too little." Understandably, then, the wilderness preservation movement in Canada lags some two generations behind that in the United States, where the frontier vanished 80 years ago.

In the beginning the Canadian park movement was highly utilitarian just as it is today in places like East Africa. The 1885 reservation of the hot springs at Banff, Alberta, and the 1887 enlargement of this area under the Rocky Mountain Park Act were directed at creating a resort, not a wilderness (Nelson and Scace 1968). The Dominion Forest Reserves and Parks Act of 1911 was no better in this respect. The statute did not distinguish between wilderness preserves and commercially oriented forest reserves—it was an example of the same confusion that characterized American thinking in the

1890's. Canadian wilderness management in the subsequent decades consisted of advancing recreational development as fast as possible. Although he had a strong personal commitment to wilderness, James B. Harkin, the first Commissioner of the Dominion (later "National") Parks set the tone in 1922, proudly declaring that "the mountain parks are worth $300,000,000 a year to the people of Canada in revenue from the visiting tourists." This fact was vitally important to the survival of the park system, Harkin continued, because "we have to show that the movement will pay for the efforts many times over" (Harkin 1922). Just as it does today in Kenya and Tanzania, this meant providing opportunities for tourists to spend money. Inpark townsites (like Banff), hotels, swimming pools, tennis courts, golf courses, ski slopes, and campgrounds with laundromats became standard features in the Canadian parks. Wilderness was forgotten in the drive to make the parks economically respectable, socially acceptable, and politically viable. If anyone was concerned about wilderness, the stock suggestion was "go north." This was, of course, an excellent idea but not practical for the Canadian of average means and vacation opportunities. The far north, in other words, was wilderness but not *meaningful* wilderness in terms of the typical citizen's recreational pattern.

Beginning in 1930, when the National Parks Act mandated the preservation of parks in an unimpaired condition, people with a concern for wilderness started to struggle against the dominant currents of Canadian thought and policy. It was an uphill fight. Even in existing wilderness preserves (notably those of Yoho and Wood Buffalo National Parks) mining and lumbering continued into the 1950's. On the provincial level, as important in Canada as it is in Australia, Ontario passed a Wilderness Act in 1959. Although weak (it did not formally close the land to economic or recreational development), the Ontario law was a first step comparable to the United States Forest Service designations of the 1920's. Canadians concerned with wilderness organized the National and Provincial Parks Association in 1963. They took heart from a 1964 clarification of park purposes in the House of Commons: "National Parks cannot meet every recreational need; the most appropriate uses are those involving enjoyment of nature and activities and experience related to the natural scene" (Bryan 1973). One of the first crusades of the Association was to have the highly developed townsites in Banff and Jasper National Parks removed from park status and reclassified as some kind of mass-recreation area. The point was to rededicate National Parks to preservation, but the reclassification attempt has not yet

been successful. Indeed the Canadian parks continue to be perceived by society as quite civilized resorts for what the Canadians call "holidays."

One indication of the resulting confusion was a 1968 advertisement for Banff National Park distributed widely by the Canadian Pacific Railroad. The full-page spread featured a magnificent color photograph of Lake Louise and its mountain backdrop. No trace of civilization appeared and the caption read, "Ah, Wilderness." But just so prospective visitors did not get the idea that the parks dealt primarily in wilderness recreation, the ad continued:

> at Banff Springs Hotel, we have to put fences to keep the elk off our championship golf course . . . . At Chateau Lake Louise, you can swim in a pool filled with water melted from a 50,000-year-old glacier, and warmed to a languorous 72°. At Banff—and at Lake Louise . . . two of the continent's finest resort hotels await you . . . There's tennis and shuffleboard. There are movies and cocktail lounges and concerts. There's Continental dining and ballroom dancing. Ah, wilderness.

Such attitudes make the construction of ski and even hydropower projects in the Canadian parks all the easier because wilderness does not appear to the public to be an issue in park management. There was hardly a ripple of public protest, for instance, when in the 1950's dams seriously damaged wilderness areas in Tweedsmuir and Strathcona Parks, both in British Columbia. At the same time, by way of contrast, pro-wilderness groups in the United States raised a massive outcry against and blocked the proposed Echo Park Dam in Dinosaur National Monument.

Still the gap in attitudes and policy that separates the United States and Canadian relationship to wilderness is not permanent. In time Canadians will close it, particularly as the growing urban character of their civilization increases the need for the wild. Already there are signs in the nation of a maturing wilderness consciousness and resulting management refinements. One case is the appearance in 1970 of *Wilderness Canada* (Spears 1970; see also Littlejohn and Pimlott 1971). A lavishly illustrated, coffee-table book in the tradition of the Sierra Club's Exhibit Format Series, the volume is a paean to the wildness of Canada and a recognition of its impact on Canadian culture and character. Its discussion of the wilderness-inspired painting of Tom Thompson could today be supplemented with an analysis of the popular music of Gordon Lightfoot. In *Marked by the Wild* (1973), Canadians have an anthology of literature shaped by their wilderness (Littlejohn and Pearce 1973).

In the province of Alberta, a small wilderness preservation program has been initiated. Spurred on by the Alberta Wilderness Association, Willmore Wilderness Park at the north end of Jasper National Park was established in 1959 as a Wilderness Provincial Park of about 2,100 square miles contained within it. Since then, two reductions in size have reduced the area to only 1,700 square miles.

Although still a substantial area, Willmore is subject to a multiple use management philosophy that largely abrogates the wilderness designation. For example, the act establishing the area specifically notes that "nothing in this Act affects the administration and control of mines and minerals within the area of the Park" (Pimlott 1968).

Alberta also has a Wilderness Areas Act that has led to the establishment of three areas: the Seffleur, White Goat, and Ghost. However, the Alberta Wilderness Areas Act is clearly intended as a mechanism for the protection of ecological systems rather than for the retention of areas for recreational use. Under the Act, fishing, hunting, horseback travel, and even berrypicking are prohibited. These areas are more similar to the Research Natural Areas in the United States where preservation for scientific and educational purposes take precedence over recreation. Such stringent regulations have led Alberta wilderness proponents to call for creation of a "recreational" wilderness system to complement the "ecological" system currently established. Proposals for nine wildernesses along the eastern slope of the Rockies have been made. There is also support for a 350,000-acre Elbow-Sheep Wilderness near Calgary to meet the growing demands for primitive recreation stemming from that urban area.

A concurrent development related to the rise of wilderness appreciation in Canada is a start toward turning back the frontier traditions of exploiting unoccupied land. The recent establishment of vast wilderness reserves on Baffin Island and along the South Nahanni River were relatively painless, comparable to creating a National Park in the unoccupied Yellowstone region in 1872. More of a test for the Canadian commitment to preservation was the 1973 rededication of Quetico Provincial Park in western Ontario for wilderness recreation along with the elimination of logging and mining operations in the park. And the Quetico, benefitting from being one of the most studied wildernesses (often by Americans), has instituted sophisticated quota and permit systems designed to keep recreational use within the carrying capacity of this canoe

country. On the federal level, Canadian park authorities are using their power to impose visitor quotas where they are thought to be needed. But the motive for such management tends to be short-term, emergency situations occasioned, for example, by fire or wild animal (bear) danger. Occasionally, however, excessive recreational use has been the cause of restrictions. While temporary (a parks-are-for-people philosophy that resents any limitations remains strong in Canada), the use of management authority in this way points toward the emerging American pattern. So does the 1974 decision of Alberta voters to reject a $5 million ski development package for Lake Louise.

The science of wilderness management in Canada has closely followed the lead of the United States. Revisions in 1964 of National Park policies began a movement away from fixation on the recreational aspects of wilderness as well as from concentration on anthropocentric criteria for wilderness management. Indeed Canada's five-stage zoning system currently used in National Park master plans reaches a level of biocentricity comparable to that of the National Wilderness Preservation System in the United States. Indeed some parts of established wilderness in Canada are justified without regard to any human visitation (Bryan 1973).

East Africa

In East Africa there is a wildness without wilderness. Visitors to the National Parks and Game Reserves of Kenya, Tanzania, and—before political difficulties effectively closed it—Uganda are unquestionably brought face to face with the primeval. But it is not the objective of management to offer these people a wilderness experience. The guiding concept instead is to keep visitors at the edge of the wild or in enclaves of civilization (moving, as with vehicles; or stationary, in the case of lodges) within the wilderness.

This policy has several advantages from the East African standpoint. One is that it protects visitors from animal attacks. This danger is quite real, particularly for persons unaccustomed to coexisting with large, wild animals. For their own safety visitors must be strictly controlled. To permit self-sufficient backcountry camping would be to invite disaster.

A second reason for separating visitors from wilderness is the welfare of the *animals*. Foot travelers frighten animals; for some reason people in cars do not. It is ironical that the mode of transportation least appropriate for wilderness is, in East Africa, precisely the one best calculated to respect wilderness conditions. Vans and land rovers, moreover, can approach to within a few

Figure 3-2.—The presence of abundant undeveloped area, in places like Canada, can create the impression that civilization and development will never claim all the land, and reduce the priority assigned to wilderness preservation. An almost unlimited amount of wild country seems to remain beyond Peyto Lake along the Banff-Jasper highway, Alberta.

yards of animals without occasioning discomfort to either the viewer or the viewee. A walker would be lucky to see a lion or a rhino. A biocentric philosophy of wilderness management is thus served in East Africa by the use of mechanized transportation. Lodges play the same role. By concentrating visitors in areas to which animals become accustomed, there is much less disturbance than free camping would invite.

Third, the denial of a wilderness experience to visitors to the African reserves has an economic advantage. Backpackers are notoriously "low rollers" when it comes to consuming goods and services. Their whole objective, after all, is to take care of themselves and usually with equipment purchased in other localities. Such people avoid the guides, tours, and lodges that generate income for the region in whch a park exists. Consequently, in East Africa where wild places and wild animals are justified almost entirely for economic reasons (as

"exportable" commodities), those seeking a wilderness experience paradoxically jeopardize the future of wilderness.

So it is that East Africa has developed a unique way of bringing people and wildness together. Luxury lodges are the campsites and minibuses or land rovers the beasts of burden. Many visitors to the African reserves quite literally never set foot on the land. Vehicles deposit them on the doorsteps of hotels which they are repeatedly warned not to leave at peril of being hurt by a wild animal. But such restrictions pose no obstacle to seeing wild animals. On the balconies or through the lodge windows visitors confront animals at a range of just a few yards. The salt licks, water holes, and baiting arrangements incorporated into the siting and construction of the lodges insure an abundance of animal viewing opportunities. At the Ark in Kenya's Aberdare National Park a buzzer system in every bedroom summons sleepers in the event something "special" (a leopard, usually) approaches the lodge's floodlit salt lick. The famous Treetops Lodge uses human door knockers for the same purpose. It is a situation, according to one tourist, "where caged people watch free animals." And it works reasonably well from the standpoint of both parties but at the cost of a true wilderness experience.

Game "runs" are the highlight of the daytime for these tourists. Using a vehicle which, in theory, stays on established roads, groups of four or six individuals cruise the wilderness in search of animals. Getting out of the vehicle is strictly prohibited. The drivers try never to be more than a kidney capacity from a lodge bathroom.

Particularly for those accustomed to wilderness recreation in other parts of the world, it is easy to put down the East African parks and reserves as giant Disneylands. In fact, they do resemble the drive-through animal parks and new cageless zoos of the United States and Europe. But consider the realities of wilderness preservation in the African context. To survive in a society that has little interest in them, parks and wild animals have to pay. This means they must attract foreign visitors in quantity. Under American-type conditions of wilderness use this amount of contact would quickly disturb the major African resource: wildlife. Consider, too, that the great proportion of visitors to Africa have absolutely no complaints. Middle-aged, wealthy, and unaccustomed to wilderness living, they have no interest at all in walking through hot bush frequented by dangerous animals. Their objective is to see wild animals, not to experience wilderness. The Ark, Treetops, and the game runs answer their needs quite well. As Norman Myers put it, "the modern traveler likes raw Africa without becoming raw himself" (Myers 1972). To their credit, if their survival is a criterion, the East African parks have deliberately courted and won this clientele. Other user groups have unquestionably been displaced in the process, but their usefulness to the cause of African wilderness preservation at this time is very low.

Still, a few alternatives are beginning to appear in East African park management, and predictably, in undesignated areas without tight visitor controls. The Chief Warden at Tanzania's Serengeti National Park is worried about the kind of experience visitors receive regardless of its advantage from the standpoint of control, safety, and revenue raising. His plan for putting people in closer contact with the land calls at the outset for carefully supervised short walks. Wardens carrying rifles would lead the groups and a vehicle would follow as a kind of portable sanctuary. Huts could be erected for lunch and, as the program expands, for overnight use.

Zambian park officials have had success with 3-to-7-day foot trips. But they are all conducted by concessionaires. The possibility of a visitor just taking off with a pack and a map is not one of the options open in the African parks.

In the eastern portion of huge, dry Tsavo National Park (Kenya) a wilderness area has been designated. Mechanized transportation is essential, however, because one simply cannot carry enough water to cover the necessary distances between dependable water supplies. Almost all groups granted permits to enter the area have professional guides and pay dearly for the privilege of being the only party allowed in at one time. This kind of wilderness use does, of course, generate the revenue vital to preservation in Africa. But the Tsavo policy is unusual in its recognition of wilderness as part of the resource being managed (Sheldrick 1973).

It is important to realize that East Africa today can not afford the luxury of low-density, wilderness types of recreation. These do not yield enough revenue to float the concept of wilderness preservation on the sea of native indifference. This points up another problem facing recreational land managers in Africa today: Management based on carrying capacity and quotas is economically suicidal. A few African parks like Zaire's Virunga (formerly Albert) National Park do operate without regard to popularity. In Virunga's case, science provides the justification. But in most other parts of the emerging and ambitious nations of this continent, wilderness preservation understandably finds itself in very hot competition with economic development and the sheer pressure of an expanding population base. Simply stated, if the only reason a park exists is to generate revenue, then restrictions on revenue-producing tourism are difficult. The situation under-scores the need to put forward other arguments for wilderness.

The Value of America's Wilderness in Perspective

"Friends at home! I charge you to spare, preserve, and cherish some portion of your primitive forests; for when these are cut away I apprehend they will not easily be replaced" (Nash 1973). The year was 1851; the author Horace Greeley writing from England where wilderness was long since a memory. Greeley's call for action drew its force from the manifest scarcity of wilderness in the Old World. And since Greeley's time, the value of the American wilderness has increased due to the scarcity of wildness in other environments. As noted earlier, this by no means represents a complete summary of the status of wilderness on the international scene. Other nations have established programs to protect diminishing wilderness lands. In Switzerland, for example, the State owns about half of the land in the Alps, and 40 percent of this is retained as wilderness at least by the European definition (Graves 1973). To be sure, there are nations, such as Brazil, with more wilderness than the United States. But none equals America in having both wilderness and a statutory system for its protection and management. One explanation is the linear pattern of American development which permitted the emergence of wilderness appreciation (in the East) before the Western wilderness vanished completely. In any event, those portions of the world that care about such things look to the United States as an example and inspiration.

There will be special attention focused on America's last frontier: Alaska. Less than 1 percent of this State's 375 million acres is developed. Native peoples, some of them hunters and gatherers, roam the backcountry. Big-game populations comparable to those of East Africa complicate the task of recreational land-use planning. And many Alaskans subscribe to the old frontier biases against wilderness. In short, the United States will be faced in Alaska with the same kinds of wilderness problems that exist in many sections of the underdeveloped world.

On December 18, 1973, Secretary of the Interior Rogers C. B. Morton submitted to Congress a recommendation to place 83,470,000 acres of Alaska in four Federal land management systems: The National Park System, the National Wildlife Refuge System, the National Wild and Scenic Rivers System, and the National Forest System (Cahn 1974). Almost all this land is now de facto wilderness. Legislation currently pending, although intensely debated, gives promise. While the outcome is uncertain now, it appears that some lands in Alaska will eventually constitute statutory wilderness reserves that will rank among the world's largest and most spectacular. Given Alaska's circumstances, the pitfalls are many but so, for the same reasons, are the opportunities for continuing world leadership in wilderness preservation.

Wilderness allocation and management is truly a cultural contribution of the United States to the world. Although other nations have established programs to preserve and protect tracts of land, it is only in the United States that a program of broad scope has been implemented, largely because of the fortuitous combination of physical availability, environmental diversity, and cultural receptivity. Despite the continuing ambivalence of American society towards wilderness, the reserves should be regarded as one of the Nation's most significant contributions.

Literature Cited

Abrahams, Harold M., ed.
1959. Britain's national parks. 151 p. Country Life Limited, London.

Anesaki, Masaharu.
1971. Art, life and nature in Japan. 178 p. Greenwood Press, Westport, Conn.

Argus, Max.
1975. The Wilderness world of Olegas Truchanas. 143 p. Olegas Truchanas Publication Committee, Hobart, Tasmania.

Bonham-Carter, Victor.
1971. The survival of the English countryside. 240 p. Hoddert and Stoughton, London.

Brockman, C. Frank, and Lawrence C. Merriam, Jr.
1973. Recreational use of wild lands. 2d ed. 329 p. McGraw Hill, New York.

Bryan, Rorke.
1973. Much is taken; much remains. 305 p. Wadsworth Publishing Company, Inc., North Scituate, Mass.

Cahn, Robert.
1974. Alaska: a matter of 80,000,000 acres. Audubon 76(7):2–81.

Darby, H.C.
1961. National parks in England and Wales. In Comparisons in resource management. p. 8–34. Henry Jarrett, ed. Johns Hopkins Press (for Resources for the Future), Baltimore.

De Vos, A.
1968. Problems in national park management in East Africa. Unasylva 22(3):23–27.

Esping, Lars-Erik.
1972. Sweden's national parks. Natl. Parks and Conserv. 46(6):18–22.

Hancock, W.K.
1972. Discovering Monaro: a study of man's impact on his environment. 209 p. Cambridge of University Press, Cambridge, England.

Harkin, J.B.
1922. Conservation is the new patriotism. (Typescript, Sept. 1, 1922), Library of the Department of Indian Affairs and Northern Development, Ottawa.

Hoskins, W.G.
1955. The making of the English landscape. 240 p. Hoddert and Stoughton, London.

Ise, John.
1961. Our national park policy: a critical history. 701 p. Johns Hopkins Press (for Resources for the Future), Baltimore.

Ishigame, Kashiro.
1972. Pressure of exploitation: the case of Japan. In World national parks: process and opportunities. p. 289–295. Richard Van Osten, ed. Hayez, Brussels.

International Union for the Conservation of Nature and National Parks.

1971. United Nations list of national parks and equivalent resources. 2d ed. 601 p. Hayez, Brussels.

Johnson, Dick.

1974. The Alps at the crossroads: the quest for an Alpine National Park in Victoria. 207 p. Victorian National Parks Association, Melbourne.

Littlejohn, Bruce, and Jon Pearce, eds.

1973. Marked by the wild. 287 p. McLelland and Stewart Limited, Toronto.

Littlejohn, Bruce M., and Douglas H. Pimlott, eds.

1971. Why wilderness. 104 p. New Press, Toronto.

Lowenthal, David, and Hugh C. Prince.

1964. The English landscape. Geogr. Rev. 54(3):309-346.

Lowenthal, David, and Hugh C. Prince.

1965. English landscape tastes. Geogr. Rev. 55(2):186-222.

Matteissen, Peter, and Eliot Porter.

1974. The tree where man was born: the African experience. 247 p. E. P. Dutton, New York.

McGlone, U.P.

1972. Interpreting the National Parks Act. In New Zealand national parks planning symposium, Canterbury, New Zealand, August 20-23, 1970. p. 3-23. Department of Lands and Survey, Wellington, New Zealand.

McLuhan, T.C., ed.

1971. Touch the earth: a self-portrait of Indian existence. 185 p. Outerbridge and Dienstfrey (distributed by E.P. Dutton), New York.

Myers, Norman.

1972. The long African day. 404 p. Macmillan, New York.

Nash, Roderick.

1968. Wilderness and man in North America. In The Canadian national parks: today and tomorrow. Vol. I, p. 66-93. J.G. Nelson and R.C. Scace, eds. University of Calgary, Calgary, Alberta.

Nash, Roderick.

1970. The American invention of national parks. Am. Quart. 22(3):726-735.

Nash, Roderick.

1973. Wilderness and the American mind. Rev. ed. 300 p. Yale Univ. Press, New Haven, Conn.

Nelson, J.G., and R.C. Scace, eds.

1968. The Canadian national parks: today and tomorrow. 2 vols. 1027 p. University of Calgary, Calgary, Alberta. [A one-volume edition of selected papers, Canadian Parks in Perspective, 601 p. was published by Nelson in Montreal in 1969.]

Oi, Michio.

1970. Carrying capacity of national parks in Japan. Park Practice Trends 6(2):21-24.

Pimlott, Douglas H.

1968. Wilderness in Canada. Living Wilderness 32(103):5-21.

Pryde, Philip R.

1972. Conservation in the Soviet Union. 301 p. Cambridge University Press, Cambridge, England.

Reifsnyder, William.

1974. Foot-loose in the Swiss Alps. 443 p. Sierra Club, New York.

Schloeth, Robert F.

1974. Problems of wildlife and tourist management in the Swiss national park. Biol. Conserv. 6(10):313-314.

Senge, Tetsumaro.

1973. Nature, its conservation and utilization for outdoor recreation in Japan. 22 p. [Publication distributed at Expo '74, Spokane, Wash.]

Senge, Tetsumaro.

1974. Park facilities for the future. In Second world conference on national parks, Yellowstone and Grand Teton National Parks, Sept. 18-27, 1972. p. 126-137. Hugh Elliot, ed. International Union for Conservation of Nature and Natural Resources, Morges, Switzerland.

Sheldrick, Daphne.

1973. The Tsavo story. 288 p. Collins, London.

Simmons, Ian G.

1973. Parks and recreation in Japan. Recreation News Suppl. 10(12):26-30.

Spears, Borden, Ed.

1970. Wilderness Canada. 174 p. Clarke, Irwin and Co., Limited, Toronto.

Sutton, Ann, and Myron Sutton.

1972. Yellowstone: a century of the wilderness idea. 219 p. MacMillan Co., New York.

Train, Russell E.

1974. An idea whose time has come: the world heritage trust, a world need and a world opportunity. In Second world conference on national parks, Yellowstone and Grand Teton National Parks, Sept. 18-27, 1972. p. 377-381. Hugh Elliot, ed. International Union for Conservation of Nature and Natural Resources, Morges, Switzerland.

Trent, Christopher.

1956. The changing face of England. 224 p. Phoenix House, London.

Watanabe, Masao.

1974. The conception of nature in Japanese culture. Science 183(4122):279-282.

The Wilderness Acts of 1964 and 1975 provide the basic mechanisms by which Congress can legally set aside undeveloped Federal land as wilderness. Here President Johnson, surrounded by Cabinet officials, signs the Wilderness Act of 1964, Public Law 88–577.

Introduction

As Roderick Nash convincingly argues in chapter 2, wilderness management is a recent concept. Not until passage of the Wilderness Act in 1964 did a positive philosophy about wilderness management develop. Prior to that, a *laissez faire* attitude prevailed, justified in many cases by the widespread belief that there was no reason to be concerned about management.

But as Nash further points out, some important developments regarding management did come about during the two decades before World War II. Two of these were the establishment of the L–20 Regulation in 1929 and its replacement in 1939 by the U-Regulations. Both were forerunners of the 1964 Act which established a unique experiment in land use classification, and we should look at them in greater detail.

The L-20 Regulation

As Nash noted, the extent of the national wilderness resource was an early concern to both conservationists and resource managers. Just how much roadless land remained after nearly five centuries of development? The 1926 inventory of roadless lands ordered by Kneipp indicated that there were 74 tracts totalling 55 million acres, with the largest unit about 7 million acres.[1] From this inventory evolved the first systematic program to reserve tracts of land for wilderness purposes—administrative regulation L–20 in 1929. The L–20 Regulation authorized the Chief of the Forest Service to establish "primitive areas," defined as areas managed to maintain primitive conditions of "environment, transportation, habitation, and subsistence, with a view to conserving the value of such areas for purposes of public education and recreation" (ORRRC 1962).

From a conservationist viewpoint, the L–20 regulation was not very protective of the wilderness resource. As noted in chapter 2, it was primarily a list of permitted and prohibited uses. Timber harvesting was permitted in

[1] It's interesting to note the 1972 Forest Service inventory of roadless areas found about 56 million acres, virtually the same as in 1926. But, minimum size in the recent inventory was only 5,000 acres, compared to 230,000 acres in 1926. The 1972 inventory did not include areas already classified, but it is clear that much of the remaining roadless land in the country is contained in relatively small units.

primitive areas "since the utilization of such resources, if properly regulated, will not be incompatible with the purposes for which the area is designated" (USDA Forest Service 1929). For example, logging occurred in about 80,000 acres of the South Fork Primitive Area, one of the three primitive areas that originally comprised what is now the Bob Marshall Wilderness.

Neither was the L–20 Regulation very strictly enforced. The broad latitude in L–20 management stemmed from a belief on the part of the Forest Service that primitive area status did not represent a long-term commitment of resources. Rather, it was to be used to prevent haphazard road building and commercial development in areas of scenic and recreational attraction until such time as detailed management plans might be prepared (ORRRC 1962). Thus, primitive area designation was not viewed as a general measure for wilderness protection; rather, it was seen as an interim protective measure for certain key lands.

Additionally, some have contended that the L–20 Regulation was used as a strategy by the Forest Service to combat the loss of National Forest lands to the National Park Service (Gilligan 1953). Several new National Parks have been created during the 1930's, largely from National Forest lands. The primitive area classification was seen as one way of countering such losses, by giving the Forest Service a land use designation with which to compete with National Park classification.[2] On the other hand, former Forest Service Chief Richard McArdle discounts this argument, pointing out that the creation of National Forest wilderness has never prevented transfers of National Forest land to the National Park Service. For example, the Olympic Wilderness, administered by the Forest Service, was nevertheless transferred to Olympic National Park after its establishment in 1938 (McArdle 1975).

The U-Regulations

Dissatisfaction with the looseness of the L–20 Regulation led to its replacement with Regulations U–1, U–2, and U–3(a) in 1939 (Gilligan 1953) as a means of preserving unroaded lands on the National Forests. These new regulations were formulated largely under the influence of Robert Marshall, then Chief of the Division of Recreation and Lands in the U.S. Forest Service. Marshall was a dynamic proponent of

wilderness, and much of his career centered on efforts to strengthen wilderness preservation programs both inside and outside the federal government. Earlier, as Director of the Forestry Division of the United States Office of Indian Affairs, Marshall was responsible for the designation of 16 wilderness areas on Indian reservations (Nash 1973). He was instrumental, along with Aldo Leopold, in the establishment of the Wilderness Society in 1935. Joining the Forest Service in 1937, Marshall pushed forcefully for expansion of wilderness reserves on the National Forests. The U–Regulations represented a culmination of his efforts.[3]

The U–Regulations broadened the purpose of wilderness as earlier defined by the L–20 Regulations. The Forest Service Manual noted:

> Wilderness areas provide the last frontier where the world of mechanization and of easy transportation has not yet penetrated. They have an important place historically, educationally, and for recreation. The National Forests provide by far the greatest opportunity for wilderness areas. Suitable provisions for them is an important part of National Forest land use planning (USDA FS 1955).

Under the U–Regulations, three land use designations were recognized. Regulation U-1 established **wilderness areas**—tracts of land of not less than 100,000 acres. Acting upon the recommendation of the Chief of the Forest Service, the Secretary of Agriculture could designate such an area as wilderness. Only the Secretary could authorize any modification or elimination of a wilderness area.

Regulation U–2 defined **wild areas**—tracts of land between 5,000 and 100,000 acres which could be established, modified, or eliminated by the Chief of the Forest Service. Thus, in addition to their size, U–1 and U–2 areas were different in terms of who could establish, modify, or eliminate them; however, they were managed identically.

Finally, Regulation U–3(a) established **roadless areas.** These areas were to be managed principally for recreation use "substantially in their natural condition."

---

[2] The National Park Service was concerned with the increasing recreation awareness among some Forest Service officials. Consequently, Stephen Mather, Director of the National Park Service, frequently challenged the authority of the Forest Service to develop recreation programs, arguing that recreation was the sole responsibility of his agency. See pages 62-71 in Baldwin's *The Quiet Revolution.*

[3] Although Marshall's role as an innovator and enthusiastic supporter of wilderness cannot be minimized, the role of his assistant in the Division of Recreation and Lands, John H. Sieker, has not been fully recognized or appreciated. Sieker, a forester educated at Yale and Princeton, enjoyed a close professional relationship with Marshall, endorsing his ideas about wilderness preservation. He also was well respected in the Forest Service. Marshall, while dynamic and energetic, was frankly viewed by many as an eccentric. Moreover, he was not really a "member of the family," having only recently joined the Forest Service. As an insider, Sieker became an important cog in efforts to implement and gain acceptance for the U-Regulations. Sieker's role was briefly noted in a recent interview with Richard McArdle, former Chief of the Forest Service (1975) and in personal correspondence to the authors from Richard Costley, former director of the Division of Recreation and Lands, Forest Service.

Roadless areas over 100,000 acres could be established or modified only by the Secretary of Agriculture; areas less than 100,000 acres could be established or modified by the Chief of the Forest Service. The only areas ever classified under this Regulation were three separate tracts in the Superior National Forest in Minnesota which were consolidated in 1958 to form what is now the Boundary Waters Canoe Area (BWCA).

Under the terms of the U–Regulations, the 76 areas classified as primitive areas under L–20 were to be reviewed and reclassified in accordance with the new regulation. Before the outbreak of World War II, three had been reclassfied as wilderness, six as wild, and three were consolidated into the Bob Marshall Wilderness in Montana. No action on reclassfication occurred during the War. After the end of the War, reviews were begun again, but the slow rate of progress, coupled with dissatisfaction on the part of conservationists with the way in which wilderness was protected, led to pressure for a new method of wilderness designation.

Statutory Protection for Wilderness

Both the L–20 Regulation and the U–Regulation were administrative designations; they were implemented at the discretion of the Secretary of Agriculture or the Chief of the Forest Service. Responsible officials were free to protect wilderness (within the limits of these regulations) or to ignore it, if they chose.

Realizing that undeveloped lands would not necessarily receive the safeguards available through administrative regulations, some wilderness supporters sought additional protection for wilderness. However, discretionary leeway in applying the L-20 and U-Regulations was only one of several reasons for seeking more reliable protection for wilderness. Undeveloped areas in both parks and forests, as long as they were insufficiently protected, were attractive and vulnerable to a variety of uses. For example, wilderness backers worried that commodity producers would succeed in removing large blocks of acreage from primitive areas during their reclassifications under the U–Regulations (McCloskey 1966). Under a multiple-use system of resource management, was it even possible to preserve a system of large wilderness areas within the National Forests, they wondered (Gilligan 1953)? Could overuse of wilderness-type areas in National Parks be stemmed and reversed? The answer to all these concerns seemed to lay in legal, rather than administrative, protection.

Legal protection for wilderness was not a new idea. In the 1930's, Marshall supported the idea of establishing

wilderness areas by Congressional action (Nash 1973). At about the same time (and nearly 30 years before passage of the Wilderness Act), H. H. Chapman, Professor of Forestry at Yale University also argued that the precarious status of primitive areas, protected only by administrative regulation, pointed up the need for Congressional protection (Chapman 1938). Interestingly, Chapman also argued that management responsibilities over these lands should remain in the hands of the administrative agency—an arrangement which prevails today in the Wilderness Act.

The need for a legislatively protected system received additional support from a report issued by the Legislative Reference Service of the Library of Congress in 1949 (Keyser 1949). The report was requested by a Congressman from Ohio on behalf of Howard Zahniser of the Wilderness Society, and was facilitated by the fact that the Director of the Reference Service (the research arm of Congress) was Ernest Griffith, another leader of the Wilderness Society (Scott 1976). The report, which highlighted the widely disjointed programs of wilderness preservation, included opinions from a survey of numerous Federal, State, and nonpublic organizations. It reported substantial concern for the future of wilderness and widespread support for wilderness protection as secure as that of the National Parks.

Figure 4-1.—One of the strongest advocates of a national wilderness system was Howard Zahniser, Executive Director of the Wilderness Society. Zahniser's main theme was the need for a comprehensive program of wilderness protection.

In 1962, the Wildland Research Center, in its report to the Outdoor Recreation Resources Review Commission, recommended the enactment of legislation creating a wilderness system protected by law. Otherwise, the Center predicted, the wilderness resource would gradually be lost. Their pessimistic conclusion was based on the following observations:

1. Land-administering agencies could put wilderness to other uses.
2. Agencies lacked full jurisdiction over some land uses (e.g., mining) within wilderness.
3. There was a lack of coordinated control over wilderness uses.
4. There was a lack of distinctive management policy (ORRRC 1962).

One of the strongest advocates of a national wilderness system was Howard Zahniser, Executive Director of the Wilderness Society.[4] Zahniser's major theme was the need for a "persisting program" of wilderness preservation—a cohesive program that would eliminate the need for continual, fragmented holding actions against various threats. As early as 1949, he had outlined a wilderness system similar in structure to that eventually proposed in the first wilderness bill in 1956 (Hession 1967). At the Sierra Club's 1951 Biennial Wilderness Conference, he remarked:

> Let's try to be done with a wilderness preservation program made up of a sequence of overlapping emergencies, threats, and defense campaigns. Let's make a concerted effort for a positive program that will establish an enduring system of areas where we can be at peace and not forever feel that the wilderness is a battleground (Zahniser 1951).

Zahniser's goal was a Congressionally established national wilderness system that would encompass areas of adequate size and numbers to meet future needs and provide legal protection to insure the perpetuation of their primeval character (Zahniser 1964). To meet this objective he and leaders from the Sierra Club, National Parks Association, National Wildlife Federation, and the Wildlife Management Institute prepared a draft bill in 1955 at the urging of Senator Hubert Humphrey (D-Minnesota). In 1956, Senator Humphrey and eight other Senators introduced the first Wilderness Bill. Representative John Saylor (R-Pennsylvania) introduced similar

legislation into the House. The long struggle for establishment of a national wilderness preservation system was underway.

A Brief Legislative History of the Wilderness Act

It took 9 years for the final Wilderness Act to emerge from Congress. During that time, 65 different wilderness bills were introduced. Eighteen hearings were held across the Nation and many thousands of pages of testimony were printed (McCloskey 1966).

The Wilderness Bill was substantially changed as it moved from the initial version drafted by Zahniser to the Act signed into law by President Johnson (Public Law 88–577) on September 3, 1964. In the next few pages we will look at some of the issues that delayed passage as well as the major changes between the first draft and the final Act.

The initial Wilderness Bill would have set up a wilderness system that included lands from the National Forest System, National Park System, National Wildlife Refuges and Game Range System, and Bureau of Indian Affairs. Altogether, about 65 million acres would have been subject to study; as many as 35 to 45 million acres might actually have been classified (Hession 1967).

All 37 Forest Service areas classified as wilderness, wild, or roadless under the U–Regulations were to be automatically included in the system under the 1956 bill. In addition, the 44 remaining primitive areas were to be temporarily included *within* the system, and the Secretary of Agriculture was given 9 years to review the status of each and recommend an appropriate classification. Congress would then decide whether to expand permanent protection to each primitive area or exclude it from the system.

The Secretary of the Interior was directed to review all areas under his direction, also within 9 years, and to recommend areas that should be included within the system. Unlike the Forest Service lands, no Department of the Interior holdings were automatically included in the system. Qualified areas under Bureau of Indian Affairs jurisdiction could be included, but only with the consent of the tribal councils. No time limit was placed on classifying Indian lands.

The original Wilderness Bill would have provided comprehensive protection from development. For example, it would have prohibited lumbering, prospecting, dams, commercial enterprises, roads, motor vehicles, the landing of aircraft, the extension of motorboating to

[4] Zahniser died May 5, 1964, only 4 months before the Wilderness Act was signed. A definitive biography of his monumental contribution to wilderness has yet to be written. However, the 1964 Winter-Spring issue of *The Living Wilderness*, p. 3-7, includes a review of many of his accomplishments. Also see Doug Scott, "Howard Zahniser: architect of wilderness," *Sierra Club Bulletin* 61(9):16-17.

new areas, new mining, and new grazing. However, existing uses would have been respected.

The first bill would also have established a National Wilderness Preservation Council composed of the heads of the Forest Service, National Park Service, Fish and Wildlife Service, Bureau of Indian Affairs, Smithsonian Institute, and six citizen preservationists. Its functions would have been to receive and review all wilderness reports and recommendations from the Secretaries of Agriculture and Interior, transmit these reports to Congress, and advise Congress and the President during ensuing deliberations on the agency recommendations.

The Wilderness Council was viewed as one means of checking the broad executive discretion possessed by administrative agencies. The Council, if it thought a secretarial report was unsatisfactory, would have been in a good position to influence Congressional attitudes.

The function of Congress in this earliest version of the Wilderness Bill was to serve as a safeguard against any unwise and arbitrary action on the part of any Secretary undertaking a measure disregarding conservation. This safeguard took the form of a legislative veto that could be enacted by either house of Congress. When any Secretarial recommendation came before it, Congress had 120 days within which to register its objection. Otherwise, the Secretary's recommendation to support or oppose wilderness classification would become effective pursuant to the law. In other words, statutory protection of wilderness would come about in the absence of any *affirmative action* on the part of Congress.

It is important to note, in this first bill, the significant exchange of authority. Congressional authority to formulate and enact legislation was delegated to the Secretaries of Agriculture and Interior; that is, their recommendations became law if not vetoed. At the same time, the Chief Executive's role to oppose legislation through the veto was transferred to Congress. Disagreement with this procedure (executive department determination of wilderness classification) called forth the more basic question "Who should take the affirmative action in wilderness allocations?"

This question—one of the crucial issues during the evolution of the Wilderness Bill—assumed particular importance during consideration of the Bill's provisions for granting temporary wilderness status to Interior Department holdings and Forest Service primitive areas pending review and during the procedure for recommending their classifications as outlined in the Act. It should be noted that no one objected to the reviews. Argument centered on two questions: (1) Should these lands be included in the wilderness system initially (instead of remaining unclassified during their reviews),

and (2) should affirmative Congressional action—that is, a bill sponsored, debated, and passed like any other bill—be required before any inclusion in the wilderness system?

Representative Wayne Aspinall (D-Colorado), Chairman of the House Committee on Interior and Insular Affairs, argued strongly that each new area should be the subject of a separate Congressional evaluation and an individual bill. Aspinall and other conservative legislators saw, in this particular use of affirmative Congressional action, one way of halting the erosion of Congressional authority to the executive (Mercure and Ross 1970). Wilderness proponents, on the other hand, were concerned that requiring Congressional approval of each individual area would prove to be a cumbersome barrier to a rapid and equitable settlement of the wilderness allocation problem.

To force his position, Aspinall refused to allow hearings on the wilderness bill until legislation calling for a general review of all federal land management policies was agreed upon. As Chairman of the Interior and Insular Affairs Committee, Aspinall was able to make good on his threat. As a consequence, preservation groups agreed to support his proposed legislation to create a Public Land Law Review Commission on the condition that Aspinall report out a wilderness bill that could be debated and amended on the floor of the House.

As the Wilderness Bill neared the end of its long journey through Congress, final refinements were worked out in Congressional conference committee. The San Gorgonio Wild Area in southern California, originally eliminated from the wilderness system in order to permit construction of a ski area, was restored to the system. Forest Service authority to declassify existing primitive areas by administrative directive was eliminated. The Senate acceded to the House provision requiring affirmative Congressional action, while the House agreed to reduce the time period in which new mineral exploration would be allowed in wilderness from 25 years to 19 years. The House passed the final version by a vote of 373 to 1 while the Senate approved it by a margin of 73 to 12. The Act was signed September 3, 1964, by President Lyndon Johnson, who said passage of the bill was " . . . in the highest tradition of our heritage as conservators as well as users of America's bountiful natural endowments."

Contrasting the Wilderness Act with the original bill submitted in 1956 reveals a number of changes—compromises that had to be made in order to secure Congressional support. Major changes included the following:

1. Bureau of Indian Affairs Lands were excluded from the bill. In 1937, nearly 5 million acres of Indian land had been administratively reserved for wilderness purposes, largely through the efforts of Bob Marshall. During 1957-58, the Department of Interior eliminated this designation. The Bureau of the Budget (now the Office of Management and Budget) opposed including the Indian lands in the Wilderness Bill. Moreover, the Federal government did not possess title to these lands; the Indian tribes did. As a result, Zahniser dropped the areas from his Wilderness Bill.

2. The National Wilderness Advisory Council was eliminated. The Forest Service opposed the Council from the beginning, arguing that it created an unnecessary step in the review process (McArdle 1975). Agency opposition, based partly on the 6-to-5 layman-to-agency-head representation on the council, remained even after the suggested number of laymen was reduced to three in 1958.[5] Zahniser, who had initially insisted on the council, agreed to its removal and counted on the President to check Secretarial recommendations (Hession 1967).

3. The Forest Service primitive areas were not included within the initial Wilderness System created in 1964, and their classification required affirmative action by Congress. (Under the original bill, they would have been temporarily included within the system and a Secretarial recommendation regarding their classification would have gone into effect in 4 months in the absence of Congressional action to stop it.) This provision appears to have been a direct result of discussions between President Kennedy and Congressman Aspinall in 1963. By agreeing to the affirmative action proposal, the President hoped to gain needed Congressional support to move more of his legislative programs through the Congress prior to the 1964 election (Hession 1967).

4. The prohibitions on nonwilderness uses were less restrictive. As initially conceived, for instance, all new mining in wilderness would have been prohibited upon passage of the bill. As passed, the Act permitted prospecting to continue until December 31, 1983, and mining on claims

established prior to this date would be allowed to continue indefinitely. This was a major compromise, one apparently crucial to the bill's passage.

The Wilderness Act clearly was a product of compromise (Mercure and Ross 1970). However, without such compromises, it is unlikely the bill would have ever passed. The bill enjoyed the support of several Senators and Congressmen, without whose help it would probably have failed. Senators Clinton Andersen (D-New Mexico), Frank Church (D-Idaho), and Hubert Humphrey and Congressmen Saylor and Lee Metcalf (D-Montana) were key supporters (McArdle 1975). The role of Zahniser as a committed citizen advocate was also crucial. Together, their efforts were rewarded with the passage of a piece of legislation unique in American conservation history—Public Law 88–577, the Wilderness Act.

The Wilderness Act

The Wilderness Act is included, in full, in appendix A at the end of this chapter (see page 82). It has been our observation that many of the arguments and much of the confusion surrounding wilderness management stem from the lack of a careful reading and clear understanding of this important document. As the major piece of legislation guiding both wilderness classification and management, it contains many of the essential "do's and don'ts."

However, the Wilderness Act was not intended to be an all-inclusive guide. As is the case with other landmark legislation, parts of the Wilderness Act are subject to widely differing interpretations, depending on one's particular wilderness philosophy.[6] As mentioned in chapter 1, much of the current debate over interpretation of the Wilderness Act centers on *classification* rather than management implications.

In the following pages we will review the seven sections of the Wilderness Act in order to highlight important provisions. Where there are ambiguities and contrasing interpretations, we'll note them. *Remember:* The Wilderness Act provides only broad guidelines and directions; detailed guidelines are contained in special regulations issued by the Secretaries of Agriculture and the Interior.

As it is important that you understand the Wilderness Act, its areas of ambiguity, and its effects on the resource,

[5] Opposition to the Advisory Council was also founded on the belief that it might very well end up making most of the final classification decisions, given its influential advisory role to Congress and the President. See Richard J. Costley. 1976. *Looking backward into the future.* Unpublished paper. Department of Resource Planning. University of Massachusetts, Amherst.

[6] Many articles have been written about alternative interpretations of the Wilderness Act, particularly differing administrative and public views. For contrasting perspectives, see Jeffrey P. Foote "Wilderness - A Question of Purity," *Environmental Law* 3(4):255-260; and Richard J. Costley "An Enduring Resource," *American Forests* 75(6):8-11.

the public, and the administering agencies, most of the remainder of the chapter is devoted to explaining the intent and meaning of the law. We suggest you make frequent reference to the text of the law as you read, with special attention to the specific wording used in the Act itself. The Wilderness Act is organized into seven sections.

Section 1 — Title

Section 1 states that this Act shall be known as the "Wilderness Act."

Section 2 — Wilderness System Established

Section 2 provides a broad statement of policy, defines what is meant by the term "wilderness" and sets forth some of the conditions and implications of wilderness designation. Section 2(a) clearly states that the establishment and protection of wilderness is a policy of the U.S. Congress, reflecting a belief that because of population pressures, all areas of the nation will be occupied or modified—except those set aside in their natural condition.

Management is specifically referred to in this section, where the Act states that wilderness areas:

> . . . shall be administered for the use and enjoyment of the American people in such manner as will leave them unimpaired for future use and enjoyment as wilderness and so as to provide for the protection of these areas, the preservation of their wilderness character, and for the gathering and dissemination of information regarding their use and enjoyment as wilderness.

Note how the term "as wilderness" appears several times. While it is clear that Congress fully intended wilderness to be for people's use and enjoyment, it is also apparent that such "use and enjoyment" was to be contingent upon the maintenance of these areas "as wilderness," a condition which the Act later defines.

Section 2(a) also specifies that only Federal lands will be included in the National Wilderness Preservation System and that no Federal lands except those protected by the Act or by a subsequent Act shall be designated "wilderness." This provision was included to prevent the executive branch of government from designating wilderness, reserving that responsibility to Congress. However, section 2(a) merely prohibits *official designation* as wilderness by agencies other than Congress. It does *not* prohibit administrative agencies from *managing* lands for wilderness purposes. The Forest Service, for example, had such authority based on the Multiple Use—Sustained Yield Act of 1960. The Wil-

derness Act specifically indicates that none of its provisions shall interfere with the purposes of the MU-SY Act.

The Wilderness Act's provisions originally affected three Federal agencies: (1) the Forest Service (in the Department of Agriculture), (2) the National Park Service, and (3) the Fish and Wildlife Service (both in the Department of the Interior). Prior to 1964, the wilderness idea had been formally incorporated into Forest Service planning through the L–20 Regulation and U–Regulations. The National Park Service (NPS) had utilized a zoning system to protect wilderness values in undeveloped areas more than a half mile from roads (ORRRC 1962). Before the Wilderness Act, the Fish and Wildlife Service (FWS) had not managed any areas specifically for wilderness purposes because manipulation of habitat to enhance wildlife values often results in substantial modification of areas, thereby conflicting with wilderness values. Nevertheless, the FWS is charged with wilderness responsibilities under the 1964 Act, and the first Department of the Interior area to be admitted to the National Wilderness Preservation System was the Great Swamp Wildlife Refuge in New Jersey.

In late 1976, Congress passed the Federal Land Policy and Management Act, giving the Bureau of Land Management (BLM) in the Department of the Interior an organic act. The Act instructs the Secretary of the Interior to review those roadless lands of 5,000 acres or more and the roadless islands of the public lands administered by BLM and to make recommendations regarding the suitability or nonsuitability of these areas for wilderness designation. The inventory of potential wilderness lands is to utilize the wilderness characteristics specified in the Wilderness Act.

Although the BLM has only now come under terms of the Wilderness Act, they have managed a system of areas for wilderness preservation purposes which they refer to as "primitive areas" (not to be confused with National Forest areas of the same name designated under the L–20 Regulation) and natural areas. We will look at these areas in more detail in chapter 6. However, under terms of the Federal Land Policy and Management Act, any area formally designated as a primitive or natural area prior to November 1, 1975, is to be reviewed by the Secretary of the Interior for its suitability or nonsuitability for wilderness classification and a recommendation made to the President by July 1, 1980.

In addition to specifying which Federal lands shall constitute official wilderness, section 2(a) assigns management responsibilities. It specifies that each Federal agency charged with jurisdiction of wilderness will continue to manage those areas originally under their jurisdiction, after they have been made part of the National Wilderness Preservation System. This clause was included so that no new agency (e.g., a National Wilderness Service) would be created.[7]

The final subsection of section 2 defines wilderness, and it is this section that has probably led to more confusion and debate than any other. It first defines wilderness in an ideal, almost poetic, sense:

A wilderness, in contrast with those areas where man and his own works dominate the landscape, is hereby recognized as an area where the earth and its community of life are untrammeled by man, where man himself is a visitor who does not remain.

The word *untrammeled* was specifically chosen by Zahniser, even though he was warned that it might confuse the definition. Not to be confused with *untrampled*, *untrammeled* means "not subject to human controls and manipulations that hamper the free play of natural forces."

Section 2(c) then goes on to define wilderness in a legal sense—an area of undeveloped federal land retaining its primeval character and influence, without permanent improvements or habitation, and which (1) generally appears to have been affected primarily by the forces of nature, with man's imprint substantially unnoticeable; (2) has outstanding opportunities for solitude or a primitive and unconfined type of recreation; (3) has at least 5,000 acres of land *or* is of sufficient size to make practicable its preservation; and (4) may also contain ecological, geological, or other features of scientific, educational, scenic, or historical value.

The definition of wilderness in Section 2(c) gives important clues to the Congressional view of wilderness. Recognizing that the ideal concept did not exist, they added a working definition based on reality. Wilderness was clearly intended to be an area where man's impact was minimal and which was predominantly natural and unmodified. But, at the same time, the Act accommodates reality by stating these areas "*generally* appear" to be "*primarily* affected" by nature with man's imprint "*substantially* unnoticeable."

Nevertheless, there are some unresolved ambiguities with which we must contend. For example, if a tract of

modified land were considered for wilderness along with a contiguous area of essentially unmodified land, would the criterion "substantially unnoticeable" be based upon the aggregate area or upon the modified portion? The question hinges on the spatial scale to which the criterion is applied. The Forest Service, in particular, has argued that additions of modified areas, even to large contiguous tracts of unmodified wilderness, compromise the quality of the entire system (Costley 1972). Opponents argue that the entire unit of land must be considered and that small areas of modified land are "substantially unnoticeable" when viewed within the broader area.

This question has been an issue in a number of areas. As discussed in chapter 1, Forest Service officials and environmentalists differed over inclusion of the Marion Lakes area to the Mt. Jefferson Wilderness in Oregon. Many private boats and other developments at the lake caused the Forest Service to contend that their presence should preclude wilderness designation for the area. Congress classified the area as wilderness, but in a conference report, instructed the Secretary of Agriculture to remove the boats and facilities and to restore the wilderness character to the area.

It is important to remember that the intent of Congress was to establish a system of areas—an ideal—that embodied the values espoused by such early wilderness proponents as Muir, Leopold, and Marshall. Accordingly, the definition of wilderness in 2(c) should not be viewed as an open door subject to endless subsequent qualification. Yet, unreasonable rigid admission standards clearly were not Congress intent, either. As Congressman Saylor noted in 1963, the Act first describes Wilderness as an *ideal concept*, but then goes on to discuss wilderness *as it is to be considered* for the purposes of the Act.

Establishing admission criteria has been surrounded by a considerable amount of debate, particularly over what is known as the *purity argument*. The purity argument is hinged on the notion that only those areas that have never sustained any human impact and which show no evidence of human presence are eligible for designation as wilderness. Many preservation groups have argued that the Forest Service has used unrealistically rigid (and allegedly illegal) standards for recommending areas for wilderness classification. The agency's response has been that to justify the substantial opportunity costs (benefits foregone) of wilderness classification it is important that any area selected be of the highest quality. Admitting areas of lesser quality means the public is paying too much (Costley 1972).

This purity doctrine has been rebutted by many authors (e.g., Behan 1971; Foote 1973; Trueblood 1975;

---

[7] Some persons still argue that a National Wilderness Service is needed because wilderness lacks the kind of representation it needs. (For example, see Michael Frome, *Battle for the Wilderness*, New York: Praeger Pub., p. 199-202.) However, it is our opinion that such an agency would be a mistake. First, such an agency might find it difficult to manage wilderness in light of the many interrelationships that exist between wilderness and other resources (see our discussion in Chapter 7). Second, creation of a wilderness agency could lead to agitation for creation of other functional agencies (e.g., timber, grazing, mining), thus deepening the Federal bureaucracy as well as accentuating problems of coordination and planning for interrelated resources.

Church 1977). Moreover, key legislators who participated in the drafting and passage of the Wilderness Act have argued that an excessively pure stance with regard to classification was not their intent. For instance, Senator Frank Church (D-Idaho) has charged that neither the letter nor the intent of the Wilderness Act calls for exclusion of areas once impacted by human use and that agency claims to the contrary are simply evidence of resistance to Congressional will (Church 1977). Congressional actions support his conclusion.

In the Mission Mountains Wilderness in Montana and the Agua Tibia Wilderness in California, impacts judged by the Forest Service to preclude wilderness designation were ruled acceptable by Congress. In the Mission Mountains, about 2,000 acres of the old primitive area were salvage logged in the 1950's after an insect outbreak in order to recover insect-damaged timber. The Forest Service proposed excluding this area, managing it to restore wilderness values, and then proposing its inclusion in the wilderness system. Congress, however, included the impacted area. In the Agua Tibia Wilderness proposal, the Forest Service excluded an area containing a road used for fire protection purposes from an area recommended for wilderness. The road was closed to public use. However, Congress approved a bill including the road, ruling that such a development was permissable under the administrative-exceptions clause of the Wilderness Act (Section 4(c)).

Not all impacts are acceptable to Congress, of course. A 6,000-acre area containing a 22-mile-long access road to a mining claim in the Emigrant Basin Primitive Area in California was excluded by Congress from the wilderness bill it approved for this area. Congress instructed the Forest Service to reexamine the area at a later date in conjunction with the review of some roadless lands contiguous to the nearby Hoover Wilderness.

It is important to note that the challenges and problems of wilderness management are closely tied to decisions regarding such questions as what constitutes a "substantially unnoticeable" impact; that is, the greater the latitude in admission standards, the more urgent will be the need for rigorous management guidelines to enhance restoration and protection of the wilderness resource.

The definition of wilderness in Section 2(c) cites the importance of "outstanding opportunities for solitude or a primitive and unconfined type of recreation." This phrase is variously interpreted to mean that opportunities for either solitude *or* a primitive kind of recreation are required (i.e., either one would qualify an area) or that

the phrases are similar and that both are included to help clarify Congressional intent. As we discussed in chapter 1, it is our belief that the latter interpretation is appropriate.

The 5,000-acre minimum is often cited as absolute, but a careful reading of the Act clearly shows that it is a suggested guideline. The intent is that the area classified should be large enough to permit preservation objectives. Many authors (e.g., Wilm 1974) argue that wilderness is a function of attitudes, mood, and perception more than of physical criteria. Therefore, they contend, Congress should establish a system of *miniwildernesses*—areas of only a few acres.

Finally, the definition says wilderness *may* include ecological, geological, scenic, and other features. The important thing to note is that these values are not required for an area to be a wilderness; neither are they by themselves sufficient criteria.

Our interpretation of this multifaceted definition of wilderness is that the criteria of naturalness and solitude are the distinguishing qualities of classified wilderness. They also serve as principal criteria to guide the management of wilderness and are used throughout this book in that context.

Section 3 — *National Wilderness Preservation System — Extent of System*

Section 3, a five-part section of the Wilderness Act, describes the National Wilderness Preservation System and the procedures for admitting areas to the system.

Section 3(a) defines the areas that formed the core of the National Wilderness Preservation System. These included all Forest Service areas previously classified as wilderness, wild, or canoe. Fifty-four areas were so classified, covering 9.1 million acres. It also instructed the Secretary of Agriculture to file accurate boundary descriptions of all these areas and to make maps and records of these areas available to the public. No Department of the Interior lands were included in the initial wilderness system.

Section 3(b) instructs the Secretary of Agriculture, within 10 years of the passage of the Act, to review all Forest Service primitive areas for their suitability or nonsuitability as wilderness and to make a report on his findings to the President. In turn, the President is to send Congress his own recommendations to support, oppose, or modify the proposal. It also established a time table for the review of the 34 primitive areas (a total of 5.4 million acres at the time the Act passed), with one-third to be completed within the first 3 years after the Act's passage, two-thirds after 7 years, and the remaining areas within 10 years. Until Congress acts, primitive areas were to be administered as they were at the time of the Act's passage.

This subsection also describes the President's latitude for modifying proposals. At the time of his recommendation to Congress, he may make an addition to any existing primitive area of not more than 5,000 acres, as long as no single unit of added land exceeds 1,280 acres. Additions beyond the 5,000-acre limit require Congressional approval (McCloskey 1966).

Section 3(c) is similar to 3(b) in that it instructs the Secretary of the Interior to review all roadless areas of at least 5,000 acres in the National Park System and similar size holdings and *every* roadless island within the National Wildlife Refuges and Game Ranges and to submit a report regarding the suitability or nonsuitability of these areas for wilderness classification. The islands were specifically cited because, in spite of the small size of many of them, their isolation made preservation a practicable alternative. A 10-year review period was established as well as the same timetable described in Section 3(b); that is, one-third in 3 years, two-thirds after 7 years, and the remainder at the end of 10 years.

Section 3(d) provides guidelines for notifying public and local officials of recommendations the Secretaries of Agriculture and the Interior intend to submit to the President and provides for public hearings on these recommendations.

Finally, Section 3(e) describes the procedures for modifying or adjusting any wilderness boundary.

Section 4 — Use of Wilderness Areas

Section 4(a) indicates that the purposes of the Wilderness Act are "within and supplemental" to the purposes for which National Forests and units of the National Park and Wildlife Refuge Systems are established. It specifically states that the Wilderness Act in no way interferes with a number of specific acts such as the Multiple Use—Sustained Yield Act and the National Park Organic Act. By providing for wilderness preservation under the multiple-use umbrella, section 4(a) removes a major reason for conflict between these two potentially incompatible laws.

The responsibility of each managing agency to maintain the wilderness character of lands under its jurisdiction is reaffirmed in section 4(b). In addition, it states that, except as otherwise provided in the Act, wilderness shall be devoted to public purposes such as recreation, education, and conservation.

Section 4(c) is subtitled "Prohibition of Certain Uses" and describes facilities and activities that are not allowed in wildernesses designated by the Act. However, this section must be carefully read, for it opens with the statement "Except as specifically provided for in this Act, and subject to existing private rights . . .," before going on to catalog prohibited uses. As we shall discuss in more detail below, these exceptions are quite substantial.

Subject to the subsection's opening qualification, commercial enterprises and permanent roads are prohibited. Other prohibited uses (motorized vehicles and equipment, temporary roads, aircraft landings) are prohibited "except as necessary to meet minimum requirements for the administration of the area for the purpose of this Act" (including measures required in emergencies involving the health and safety of persons within the area).

Subsection 4(c) outlines illegal activities and administrative latitude. It permits administrators to carry out actions seemingly inappropriate in wilderness if it becomes apparent these actions are necessary to manage the area *as wilderness*. McCloskey (1966) has pointed out that the phrase "minimum requirements" seems to mean "essential or necessary." Defined in this way, the clause "except as necessary to meet minimum requirements for the administration of the area for the purpose of this Act" becomes somewhat redundant.

Nevertheless, the basic interpretation of this section is that administrators must provide evidence that an action *is* necessary in order to manage the area as wilderness. Simple convenience or cost advantage are not sufficient reasons to justify, for example, the use of mechanized equipment. If, however, the use of mechanized equipment clearly reduced the amount of impact the wilderness would sustain (e.g., during a major job of trail construction), then administrators would have the flexibility to use such equipment.

McCloskey also goes on to point out a second ambiguity. Does the phrase "for the purpose of this Act" refer just to the Act's objective ("to secure for the American people of present and future generations the benefits of an enduring resource of wilderness"), an objective limited to preservation *or* does it include a broader purpose—preservation *and* compatible human enjoyment? Differing interpretations of the phrase could lead to different administrative actions. The wording of the Act suggests that both use and preservation were intended, but it also suggests that any construction to facilitate use (e.g., bridges, shelters) must satisfy a *necessity* criterion; that is, are they necessary to meet minimum requirements for the administration of the area *as wilderness*? In general, facilities for the convenience and/or comfort of users do not meet this criterion and have not been provided.

As we mentioned above, however, there are important exceptions to the prohibited uses described in

Section 4(c). These exceptions, which are subject to existing private rights, are outlined in section 4(d) and constitute what we call allowable, but nonconforming uses; i.e., they are legal, but they are clearly incompatible with the goal of the Act. These nonconforming uses reflect some of the compromises in the original Wilderness Bill. Both subsections apply only to those areas of National Forest land designated as wilderness by the 1964 Act. They do not apply to areas designated by subsequent legislation, although in the interest of consistency, the provisions of section 4(c) and 4(d) are generally applied to these areas.

The following uses are expressly permitted in section 4(d):

1. Established uses of aircraft and motorboats;
2. Actions taken to control fire, insects, and disease outbreaks;
3. Any activity, including prospecting, for the purposes of gathering information about mineral or other resources, if carried out in a manner compatible with preservation of the wilderness environment;
4. Continued application of the U.S. mining and mineral leasing laws for National Forest wilderness until December 31, 1983;
5. Water resource development (authorized by the President if he determines that such use will better serve the country's interest than would its denial);
6. Livestock grazing, where established prior to the Act;
7. Management of the Boundary Waters Canoe Area under regulations laid down by the Secretary of Agriculture, which are generally less restrictive than the Wilderness Act (an issue clouded in legal debate, as we shall discuss shortly);
8. Commercial enterprises necessary for activities that are appropriate in wilderness (e.g., outfitting and guiding).

In summary, the Act recognized that certain existing uses—specifically air and motor—should be permitted to continue in places where they were established. However, the Act also noted that the Secretary of Agriculture may impose such restrictions as he deems necessary to protect the wilderness resource. So, while these uses are protected by the Wilderness Act, they can nonetheless be controlled by the administering agencies. Similarly, although the Secretary of Agriculture can undertake measures to control fire, insects, or disease, it is clear this authority is *discretionary*, i.e., it is not mandatory that fires be controlled, for example.

The discussion of mining in wilderness occupies a substantial proportion of Section 4(d). Basically the Act

Figure 4-2.—The Wilderness Act prohibits facilities and motorized equipment except as necessary to administer the area for purposes of the Act. Here a patrol boat and dock at Flat Mountain Arm provide for administration of proposed wilderness adjacent to Yellowstone Lake in Yellowstone National Park, Wyo.

specifies that prospecting and mining may continue in National Forest wilderness until December 31, 1983.[8] After that date, mining may continue only on valid claims existing prior to that date. In other words, one could not file a claim for mining after December 31, 1983, but could continue mining a claim that existed prior to that date. A patent conveying both surface and mineral rights may be taken on a valid claim located prior to the Wilderness Act; for a valid claim located after the date of the Wilderness Act, the patent conveys title to mineral rights only. The Secretary of Agriculture is instructed to issue *reasonable regulations* governing access to claims and related facilities such as transmission lines, roads, and buildings. Generally, these regulations impose more stringent standards for mineral operations in wilderness than on other National Forest lands. Under current regulations (Title 36, Code of Federal Regulations, Part 252—Minerals), mining operators in National Forests are required to prepare an operating plan which describes who is doing the work, where and

---

[8] This clause of the Wilderness Act refers to National Forest wilderness because most Department of the Interior lands are withdrawn from mineral entry. Until recently, however, six National Parks were open to mineral entry, including Death Valley National Monument, Crater Lake National Park, Glacier Bay National Monument, Coronado National Memorial, Mt. McKinley National Park, and Organ Pipe Cactus National Monument. In 1976, Congress passed legislation withdrawing these parks from further mineral entry and placed existing claims under stringent regulations issued by the Secretary of the Interior. Details about this legislation are in chapter 13.

when it will be done, the nature of the disturbance the work will create, and measures to be taken to protect other resources. Restoration is also called for at such time as the operation ceases. Surface resources, such as timber, may be used if needed for the mining operation and if founded on sound principles of forest management.

After January 1, 1984, but subject to valid existing rights, minerals in wilderness are withdrawn from entry.

This portion of the Act also instructs the Secretary of the Interior to develop, in consultation with the Secretary of Agriculture, a plan for recurrent surveys of the mineral values in any wilderness and to submit these findings to the public, Congress, and the President.

Mining in wilderness is a paradox, and its presence can make sense only when viewed as a necessary political compromise. Nevertheless, many view its presence as an internal contradiction within the Wilderness Act. In early 1973, U.S. District Judge Neville in Minnesota ruled that a proposed copper and nickel prospecting operation in the BWCA should not be permitted:

> It is clear that wilderness and mining are incompatible . . .

Figure 4–3.—The Wilderness Act provided for several allowable but nonconforming uses. For example, mining of claims established prior to December 31, 1983, will be allowed to continue; *upper left*, a mining operation in a portion of the proposed wilderness in Death Valley National Monument, Calif. Snow surveys to determine potential water yields are also permitted; *upper right*, rangers making measurements in the Selway-Bitterroot Wilderness, Mont. Grazing is also permitted within wilderness; *lower left*, in the Bridger Wilderness, Wyo.

If the premise is accepted that mining activities and wilderness are opposing values and are anathema each to the other, then it would seem that in enacting the Wilderness Act Congress engaged in an exercise of futility if the court is to adopt the view that mineral rights prevail over wilderness objectives . . . Mineral development . . . by its very definition cannot take place in a wilderness area . . .

There is an inherent inconsistency in the Congressional Act and it falls in the lap of the court to determine which purpose (mining or wilderness) Congress deemed most important and therefore intended. In this court's opinion, the wilderness objectives override the contrary mineral right provision of the statute (Sumner 1973).

An Appeals Court later ruled that because mining company officials had not made a final application to the Forest Service for entry into the BWCA to explore for minerals, the decisionmaking process had not been completed by the administrative agency authorized to make the decision. Because no administrative action had been taken, there was no basis for judicial review. The case was returned to the lower court without prejudice (meaning it could be heard by the Appeals Court at a later time). If the mining company applies for and receives a permit to mine, the case will almost certainly go back into court.

It is important to note that the action of the Appeals Court in returning the case to the lower court was related to a technical shortcoming rather than disagreement with the lower court's substantive analysis of the case. The Appeals Court ruling neither affirmed nor denied that analysis. The issue of mining in wilderness, then, remains unresolved. This particular case does not necessarily have widespread applicability. It is directed only at the BWCA, an area whose management is covered by several special provisions in the Wilderness Act (Haight 1974). Moreover, many public mining laws do not apply in the state of Minnesota. However, the key in Judge Neville's rationale was his resolution of two contradictory mandates (mining versus wilderness). The judge ruled that in cases where such apparent contradictions exist, if "Congressional intent is plainly discernible in the legislative history, it will override the 'inconsistent' terms of the statutes" (Haight 1974).

Thus, the future of mining in wilderness is clouded by legal questions. Federal legislation is pending which would terminate all future mining in such areas

Confounding the situation further is the current energy crisis. The push to develop American fuel sources might exert new pressures on wilderness minerals (Haight 1974).

Section 4(d) grants authority to the President to authorize programs for the development of water resources within National Forest wilderness, if he determines that permission for such developments would better serve the interests of the United States than their denial. Actions involved here could include reservoir construction, power projects, and transmission lines. The Act does not specifically refer to weather modification, a practice of questionable legality.[9]

Grazing is allowed in National Forest wilderness where it was established prior to the signing of the Wilderness Act. As with several other excepted uses, the Secretary of Agriculture is permitted to impose "such reasonable regulations as are deemed necessary." While the Secretary of Agriculture cannot prohibit grazing merely by reason of wilderness, he can restrict or eliminate such use based on principles of range management (McCloskey 1966).

Another controversial portion of section 4(d) involves the management of the Boundary Waters Canoe Area (BWCA) which was so designated in 1958. What is now the BWCA was originally three roadless areas designated under the U-3(a) Regulation: the Superior, Little Indian Sioux, and Caribou Roadless Areas. Section 4(d) specifies the BWCA will continue to be managed in accordance with regulations established by the Secretary of Agriculture. In general, the primitive character of the area is to be maintained, but certain other uses, including timber harvesting, are permitted.

The BWCA has traditionally been managed as two zones: the Interior or "no-cut" zone, and the Portal. The Interior zone was created in 1941 and all commercial timber harvesting is prohibited within it. However, vegetation manipulation involving administratively required cutting or burning is permitted. In the Portal zone, commercial logging is allowed along with related developments such as road building.

The BWCA area also receives protection from the Shipstead-Newton-Nolan Act of 1930 which requires

---

[9] In 1972 the Bonneville Power Administration announced their intent to seed clouds in western Montana. This would possibly have affected precipitation in the Bob Marshall Wilderness. The plans were opposed by the Forest Service as well as by the State of Montana, and the Montana Wilderness Association sought an injunction against the plan. However, heavy precipitation that winter prompted BPA to drop their plans and the case became moot. The Bureau of Reclamation has issued a position paper arguing that weather modification will not result in any significant alteration of natural processes and should be permitted in wilderness. See Position Paper on Weather Modification over Wilderness Areas and Other Conservation Areas, Bureau of Reclamation, U.S. Department of the Interior, 1974. 29 p.

that natural water levels be maintained in the area (thus prohibiting dam construction) and that logging be prohibited within 400 feet of all shorelines in order to protect scenic quality. Actually, as specific management policies evolved, logging has been generally restricted where it would be visible from waterways, farther than 400 feet from shorelines if necessary.

In 1964, shortly before passage of the Wilderness Act, a select committee, headed by Dr. George Selke, was appointed by the Secretary of Agriculture to study the BWCA and recommend appropriate management actions. Their report supported continuation of the two-zone management concept, but recommended changes in their relative size. The Interior zone was to be enlarged by 250,000 acres over a 10-year period, with the land being withdrawn from the Portal zone. Thus, by 1976, the Interior zone, originally the smaller of the two, would be enlarged to about 618,000 acres and the Portal zone would shrink to about 412,000 acres.

Over ½ million acres in the BWCA is still virgin forest (Heinselman 1973). It is the largest contiguous tract of virgin forest left in the 48 States and it is this uniqueness that has led to much of the concern about the appropriateness of logging anywhere in the BWCA. In 1973, the Minnesota Public Interest Research Group (MPIRG) brought suit against the Forest Service and several logging companies, seeking an injunction against further logging. However, it is important to note that the suit was based, at least originally, on the contention that the Forest Service had failed to file an Environmental Impact Statement (EIS) before extending contractual deadlines for the logging of certain areas. Therefore, this suit was not directly based on the Wilderness Act (Haight 1974).

The judge handling the case based his ruling on reasoning similar to Judge Neville's in the mining case:

> . . . logging and the various reforestation methods which follow it destroy the primitive character of the area involved . . . the area loses forever its 'primeval character and influence' and 'natural conditions' (Haight 1974).

In response to the argument that the Wilderness Act permitted logging, the Court noted "Where there is a conflict between maintaining the primitive character of the BWCA and allowing logging or some other uses, the former must be supreme" (Haight 1974). The Court ruled that logging under consideration by the Forest Service constituted a significant impact and, consequently, required the filing of an EIS. In later judicial action in 1975, an injunction was issued against logging in that portion of the BWCA still considered virgin forest (about ½ million acres). The injunction was based on the alleged conflict of logging with the Wilderness Act as well as on the inadequacy of the EIS prepared by the Forest Service. Ten existing timber sales and all future sales were halted by the injunction. However, the 8th Circuit Court of Appeals lifted the injunction in August 1976, ruling that the Wilderness Act did not prohibit logging in the Portal zone and that the EIS did meet the procedural requirements of the National Environmental Policy Act. The Appeals Court did rule that an environmental analysis of each of the 10 sales must be completed and terms for how the sales were to be conducted written into the contract. Future timber sales are still enjoined, pending completion of a new timber management plan and EIS.

The Act also legalizes another otherwise prohibited use, specifically for the BWCA, stating that nothing in its text "shall preclude the continuance within the area of any already established use of motor boats." The BWCA's management plan recognizes three zones: (1) a large-motor zone, where motors up to and including 25 horsepower can be used;[10] (2) a small-motor zone, where motors up to 10 horsepower are permitted; and (3) a no-motor zone. However, there are no limits on motor size for any lake that touches the periphery of the area. About 60 percent of the water acreage in the BWCA is open to motor use.

Snowmobiles are prohibited in the BWCA, even along approved motorboat routes. Although their use had been approved at one time, a decision in 1976 by the Chief of the Forest Service was made to discontinue their use in order to protect the primitive character of the area.

The BWCA is the only area currently in the National Wilderness Preservation System that has an air-space reservation. An Executive order, signed by President Harry Truman in 1949, prohibited flights within the BWCA at levels below 4,000 feet above sea level except for emergencies and for official business of the Federal, State, or county governments (Andrews 1953).

Recognizing that certain commercial services might be necessary to realize fully the recreational values of wilderness, section 4(d) permits activities such as guiding and outfitting, despite the general prohibition of commercial enterprises cited in section 4(c).

After noting that the Act does not touch upon the question of federal exemption from State water laws, section 4 concludes with a standard disclaimer that the Federal government recognizes State jurisdiction over wildlife on Federal lands.

---

[10] Two lakes in this zone—Lac La Croix and Saganaga—are excluded from this limitation so as to allow bona fide Canadian property owners safe access to their property

Section 5 — State and Private Lands Within Wilderness Areas

Section 5 describes the rules and procedures for access to private or State-owned inholdings within National Forest wilderness. It provides "such rights as may be necessary to assure adequate access" to such lands. It also indicates that such lands may be exchanged for federally owned property in the same State and of approximately equal value. However, unless the State or private owner relinquishes the mineral interests in the surrounded land, the U.S. Government will not transfer the mineral rights of any exchanged land.

The Secretary of Agriculture is permitted, subject to the appropriation of funds by Congress, to acquire private inholdings within wilderness if (1) the owner agrees to such acquisition and (2) if the acquisition is approved by Congress. Condemnation is not permitted by the Wilderness Act, an authority which was important to the development of legislation establishing eastern wilderness.

Section 6 — Gifts, Bequests, and Contributions

Both the Secretary of Agriculture and Secretary of the Interior are authorized to accept gifts in furtherance of the purposes of the Act. Such gifts might be land, money, or both. If the gift involves land adjacent to rather than within an existing wilderness, Congress must be notified 60 days before acceptance. Upon acceptance, the land becomes part of the wilderness. If they are consistent with the purposes of the Act, a donor may attach stipulations to his gift.

Section 7 — Annual Reports

The last section of the Wilderness Act instructs the two Secretaries to report jointly to the President at the opening of each session of Congress on the status of the National Wilderness Preservation System. These reports are a valuable source of information on the number of areas and acres in the National Wilderness Preservation System, changes in the system, regulations in effect, and the status of areas under consideration. They are available to the public from the Government Printing Office and from Congressmen.

The Eastern Wilderness Act

In general, the Wilderness Act has served well. However, in one area—the Eastern United States (generally defined as east of the 100th meridian)—the Wilderness Act has not established the amount and kind of wilderness many people expected. There have been a variety of problems. Many of the lands in this region have been substantially impacted by man's past activities. However, the greater regenerative capacity of ecosystems in the humid East has often minimized many of these impacts.

Congressional debate over eastern wilderness has focused on National Forest land because National Parks and Wildlife Refuges were more secure from competing uses. There are, of course, external threats to these latter areas. The first area of the Department of the Interior to be classified into the National Wilderness Preservation System (the Great Swamp Wildlife Refuge in New Jersey) was threatened by construction of a jet port. Wilderness classification substantially contributed to stopping construction (Schindler 1970). Other development plans would have led to draining water from Everglades National Park in order to facilitate construction of a jet port. However, neither parks nor refuges are subject to the level of resource development facing National Forest lands managed under a multiple use philosophy.

Arguing that, because of size and previous impacts, roadless lands in the East do not meet wilderness admission criteria, the Forest Service has generally pressed for some alternative kind of classification. Debate over this purity argument has been intense, centering upon the classification of areas significantly disturbed by man (see chapter 1 and Foote 1973). In fact, the Forest Service has argued that only a few areas in all the Eastern United States qualified for wilderness under the 1964 Act. As of 1973, only four areas under Forest Service jurisdiction had been classified in the East (the BWCA in Minnesota, the Great Gulf in New Hampshire, and Linville Gorge and Shining Rock in North Carolina).

Because of Forest Service resistance to the classification of eastern areas as wilderness under the 1964 Act, legislators and conservationists initiated their own actions. In early 1972, President Nixon directed the Secretaries of Agriculture and Interior to hasten efforts to identify areas having wilderness potential in the Eastern United States. Later that same year, Senators George Aiken (R-Vermont) and Herman Talmadge (D-Georgia) introduced Senate Bill 3973, recommending establishment of an Eastern National Forest Wild Areas System. The bill would have established a new system of eastern roadless areas, *separate* from the existing National Wilderness Preservation System. In addition, it would have referred all wilderness bills to the Senate Agriculture Committee, noted for its favorable attitude toward industry, rather than the Interior and Insular Affairs Committee (Smith 1976). Another bill (Senate Bill 316), introduced by Senators Henry Jackson (D-

Washington) and James Buckley (R-New York), would have extended the protection of the Wilderness Act to areas in the East.

In 1973, Senate Bill 3433 was introduced into Congress. It incorporated provisions from the two eastern wilderness bills introduced in 1972, but in general followed the philosophy of SB 316. A series of 19 "instant wildernesses" were to be established and 40 "study" areas were to be designated for review by the Secretary of Agriculture within 5 years, according to procedures outlined in the Wilderness Act. SB 3433 contained two particularly important clauses: (1) the Secretary of Agriculture was given the power of condemnation when private landowners failed to use their land in a manner compatible with wilderness (this was an important authority, absent from the 1964 Wilderness Act, included because of the large amount of private inholdings in eastern National Forests), and (2) all lands classified as wilderness or as wilderness study areas were withdrawn from mineral entry.

Similar legislation appeared in the House, differing only in the number of instant wildernesses and wilderness study areas established.

The issue of wilderness preservation in the Eastern United States was debated by legislators, administrators, and citizens throughout 1973 and 1974.[11] A final bill was agreed upon and signed by President Ford on January 3, 1975. Public Law 93–622 was enacted:

> To further the purposes of the Wilderness Act by designating certain acquired lands for inclusion in the National Wilderness Preservation System, to provide for study of certain additional lands for such inclusion, and for other purposes.

It is extremely significant that this act provides for the incorporation of eastern roadless areas into the National Wilderness Preservation System. This provides a major challenge for management because there are important problems associated with managing small tracts of land for wilderness purposes near major population centers.

A copy of the Eastern Wilderness Act is found in appendix B (see page 87). The Act has nine sections, although the first section, containing the statement of purpose is not numbered. Although commonly referred to as the Eastern Wilderness Act, the legislation in fact does not have a title.

---

[11] Contrasting opinions on the need for eastern wilderness legislation can be found in these two articles: "Wilderness East?—NO," Fred C. Simmons, *American Forests* 78(7):344-45; and "Wilderness East? Yes, Incontestably," Frank E. Egler, *Ecology* 54(4):721-722.

Figure 4–4.—The Eastern Wilderness Act of 1975 extended wilderness classification opportunities to areas east of the 100th meridian. Many of these areas are small, such as the 20,000 acre Presidential Range-Dry River Wilderness in New Hampshire. Although they have sustained minor impacts from logging, farming, or other activities, they have largely regained their wilderness character.

Section 2 — Statement of Findings and Policy

Section 2 states that although some wilderness has been established on the National Forests, Wildlife Refuges, and National Parks in the East, the increasing population and development of the region warrants additional reservations. Consequently, Congress "finds and declares that it is in the national interest" that additional areas of wilderness be preserved in the eastern United States.

Section 3 — Designation of Wilderness Areas

Section 3 catalogs those areas that, with passage of the Act, became *instant wildernesses*, part of the National Wilderness Preservation System.

Sixteen different areas in 13 States are included, totaling nearly 207,000 acres. Each area is identified in this section, the National Forests on which they lie are specified, their approximate size is noted, and a name is assigned.

Section 4 — Designation of Wilderness Study Areas

Section 4 instructs the Secretary of Agriculture to review the suitability or nonsuitability for inclusion in the National Wilderness Preservation System of a series of tracts called *wilderness study areas*. Seventeen areas, in nine States, are described, totaling 125,000 acres. A 5-year review period is specified.

This section indicates that areas other than those listed may also be designated for study by Congress, upon the recommendation of the Secretary of Agriculture. Such areas must be east of the 100th meridian and, upon their designation, they must be reviewed within a 10-year period. The section concludes with a statement that nothing in the Act limits the authority of the Secretary of Agriculture to manage, in accordance with the Multiple Use—Sustained Yield Act of 1960, those lands not designated for review by the Act. In other words, the Forest Service is not limited in its management of wilderness to areas that might be suitable for study but which were not specified in this Act.

Section 4 concludes with a statement that the President may alter the boundaries of, or recommend an addition to, any study area submitted by Congress.

Section 5 — Filing of Maps and Descriptions

As soon as possible after passage of the Act, maps and legal descriptions for each area must be prepared and made available for public inspection.

Section 6 — Management of Areas

Any area classified under this act is to be managed in accordance with the provisions of the 1964 Wilderness Act. The Eastern Wilderness Act does not establish a different system; it basically describes new *admission* criteria for areas east of the 100th meridian.

The bulk of discussion in section 6 describes the condemnation authority granted to the Secretary of Agriculture and the procedures for its implementation. Where private landowners use their land in a manner that is incompatible with wilderness purposes and show an unwillingness to discontinue such uses, the Secretary may institute condemnation proceedings.

Procedures for notifying the Forest Supervisor of impending transfers or for changes in land use are specified. Landowners are permitted to retain for themselves or their successors, rights of use and occupancy for noncommercial, residential, or agricultural purposes for 25 years or until the death of the owner or his spouse (whichever is latest). If property use violates these specified rights, the Secretary may terminate those rights.

Section 7 — Transfer of Federal Property

This section permits the transfer of jurisdiction of other Federal property within a wilderness to the Secretary of Agriculture.

Section 8 — Applicability

This Act refers to National Forest lands, east of the 100th meridian, unless otherwise provided by another act.

Section 9 — Authorization of Appropriations

A total of $5 million was authorized for acquisition of private lands within the "instant" wildernesses. This was a one-time authorization, although presumably additional funds could be obtained from Congress at a later date. In addition, $1.7 million was authorized for conducting the reviews of the designated study areas called for in section 4.

Original legislation proposing eastern wilderness called for the withdrawal of all lands classified as wilderness from mineral entry. As passed, the Act makes no mention of mining whatsoever. The bulk of the wilderness in the East are acquired lands and are not under jurisdiction of the General Mining Laws. Neither, as a consequence, are they subject to the restrictions and guidelines contained in the 1964 Act. Mineral rights on these eastern lands were generally retained in private ownership and owners may demand access and use of surface resources needed to develop the minerals. Although the Eastern Wilderness Act contains provisions that permit condemnation of land where activities incompatible with wilderness are practiced, the

Figure 4-5.—Not only are many of the wildernesses in the east small, but they often are adjacent to private lands used for agriculture or low density residential purposes. They thus do not provide the illusion of an unbroken expanse of wilderness commonly found in many western areas. Portions of the proposed Shenandoah National Park Wilderness adjoin private, agricultural settlements.

cost of acquiring condemned lands can be extraordinarily high, which often makes such a remedy impracticable.

Some Exceptions and Ambiguities in Wilderness Legislation

One additional feature of both the Wilderness Act and the Eastern Wilderness Act deserves comment. The directives and guidelines for management of areas in both Acts pertain only to those areas classified by that specific piece of legislation. In other words, the Wilderness Act imposed use restrictions only on the 54 National Forest areas designated wilderness upon its passage. It also provides that, pending designation as wilderness, primitive areas were to be managed under regulations in affect at the time the Wilderness Act was passed. Similarly, the Eastern Wilderness Act, in its discussion of management, refers only to the 16 National Forest areas designated as "instant wildernesses." Left in some confusion then is the status of the Department of the Interior holdings, the wilderness study areas specified in the Eastern Wilderness Act, and all other lands that

might be added in the future to the National Wilderness Preservation System.

Why Congress did not clearly specify the management direction for these other areas is not entirely clear. It does allow Congress latitude for adding special management provisions to the legislation classifying each individual area, perhaps in response to an area's unique features.

But wide use of special management provisions could also undermine one of the major reasons a wilderness bill was initially proposed—*consistency* (Zahniser 1951; Aspinall 1964). As a consequence, and in subsequent legislation, Congress has affirmed that wilderness areas not covered by the Act shall nonetheless be managed in accordance with the 1964 Act's provisions. In other words, although the Wilderness Act did not specifically prescribe the management for areas subsequently classified, Congress has extended its guidelines to these areas. Congress is expected to follow a similar procedure when considering areas under the Eastern Wilderness Act.

The Wilderness Act and the Eastern Wilderness Act have, as we have discussed, many ambiguities, weaknesses, and omissions. Contradictions (permitting mining in wilderness; failing to describe procedures for the review of National Forest roadless lands) and the general vagueness of many procedures have placed a substantial burden on administrative agencies, citizen advocates, and, especially, on the courts. At least one author has suggested that the contradictions and ambiguities may simply reflect political expediency. Congress simply avoided offending many competing interests, leaving the job of resolving these problems to others (Haight 1974).

The status of the BWCA has been unclear and the recent legal arguments over such things as logging, mining, and snowmobile and motorboat use reflect the uncertainty over the area's management. At present a legislative remedy is under consideration in the form of two contrasting bills in the U.S. Congress. Under legislation proposed by Rep. James Oberstar (D-Minn.), a National Recreation Area would be established around what is now the BWCA, with about 60 percent of the present wilderness protected by the Wilderness Act. The remaining area would be open to logging, mechanized recreation, and other developments. Alternative legislation, proposed by Rep. Donald Fraser (D-Minn.), would give full wilderness protection to the entire BWCA, negating section 4(d)5 of the Wilderness Act, the clause containing the current exceptions regarding the BWCA (Heinselman 1977). The Fraser bill would specifically prohibit logging, the administrative cutting of timber, the use of snowmobiles and motorboats, and mining. The prohibition of mining, in fact, would not only make the BWCA a full and equal member of the NWPS, but actually slightly more equal than other units where mining is still permitted.

Although the Eastern Wilderness Act was a major achievement for preservationists, it has not been without problems. Confusion over the status and use of private inholdings has led local residents to protest wilderness designation of one of the original units, the Bristol Cliffs Wilderness in Vermont. Less than a year after passage of the Act, legislation was introduced into Congress to modify the area's boundaries, excluding all private land. In April 1976, the President signed an Act excluding 2,900 acres of privately owned land and 720 acres of National Forest land from the wilderness.

Notwithstanding all the unresolved issues, the Wilderness Act and the Eastern Wilderness Act form the principal statutory foundation for wilderness preservation and management in the United States today. They define the broad goals, objectives, policies, and procedures through which an enduring resource of wilderness is to be provided. Nevertheless, alternative interpretations of the legislation exist, each with its alternative implications for management. We think it important to make explicit our interpretation of the legislation as well as the rationale for our interpretation.

Some Features in the Evolution of Wilderness Protection

As we review the progress in statutory wilderness protection, we can see at least three major changes.

First, the *permanency* attached to such efforts has been substantially enhanced. The L–20 Regulation afforded little if any permanency. In fact, as we noted earlier, it was clear that the primitive area designation was viewed as an interim measure to halt haphazard development. Longevity of protection was improved by the U-Regulations, but, as the history of the Wilderness Act demonstrates, administrative discretion to choose the level of protection was a major shortcoming. Similarly, although National Park or Wildlife Refuge designation assured protection from many kinds of development, it did not necessarily guarantee permanent protection of wilderness values. The Wilderness Act brought assurance that such values would be permanently protected.

Second, *permitted uses* of wilderness have been increasingly restricted. The L–20 Regulation contained little in the way of prohibited uses. Logging and other forms of resource development were permitted. The U–Regulations were developed to a great extent in order to exclude some permitted uses—which they did. However, because the U–Regulations were instituted at the admistrative rather than the legislative level, there remained the possibility that certain uses, inconsistent with wilderness, might be permitted.

While National Park or Wildlife Refuge designation prohibited certain uses, the prohibitions (and permitted uses) were not established with clear wilderness preservation objectives in mind. The Wilderness Act defined a more restrictive framework within which National Park and Wildlife Refuge development plans were to take place.

Finally, the evolution from the L–20 Regulation and U-Regulations to the Wilderness Act reflects a change in *purpose*. The L–20 Regulation was intended to establish a series of areas for the purposes of public education, inspiration, and recreation (ORRRC 1962). However, it appears they were primarily an interim designation to control haphazard development and road construction. The U-Regulations emphasized the importance of retaining the primitive quality of these lands, particularly with regard to the style of travel permitted. However, the major innovation was in regard to permitted uses and procedures for establishment and modification of wilderness areas. It is clear from a review of some of Marshall's earlier writings (e.g., Marshall 1933) that protection of the natural environment was an important purpose of the U-Regulation.

Similarly, the management guidelines for National Parks and Wildlife Refuges prior to passage of the Wilderness Act did not explicitly define the purposes of wilderness preservation. While a generally low level of development prevailed in many of these areas, the purposes which these areas were to serve lacked specificity and direction.

In the Wilderness Act, we find a new emphasis on the purpose for wilderness reservations. While public use and enjoyment are clearly provided for, they are to take place within the constraint of the preservation of these areas as wilderness. Wilderness, as defined by the Act, is a landscape where the earth and its community of life are untrammeled by man. Thus, the Wilderness Act established a national policy and purpose of maintaining a system of areas where natural processes could operate as freely as possible. Recreation use was an appropriate use of these areas, *only so long as it was consistent with this purpose.*

This evolution of purpose in wilderness preservation is, in our opinion, a key development. Wilderness preservation has evolved from a holding strategy for minimizing unplanned development until more carefully thought-out plans could be formulated to a carefully defined and legally sanctioned national system for protecting the ecological integrity of selected areas. Our endorsement of a biocentric philosophy of wilderness management rests on the belief that framers of the Wilderness Act clearly intended to create a system of areas where nature's way was allowed, as far as possible, to continue unhampered by man. We share the lawmakers' recurring insistence that human use of these lands must not interfere with the preservation of the area as wilderness. It is from these assumptions regarding purpose that our interpretation of the Wilderness Act flows and that our management recommendations are founded.

Among the co-authors, the author primarily responsible for preparation of this chapter was George H. Stankey.

Literature Cited

Andrews, Russell P.
1953. Wilderness sanctuary. (Inter-University Case Program No. 13) 10 p. Bobbs-Merrill Co., Inc., New York.

Aspinall, Wayne N.
1964. Underlying assumptions of wilderness legislation as I see them. Living Wilderness 86:6–9

Baldwin, Donald N.
1972. The quiet revolution: the grass roots of today's wilderness preservation movement. 295 p. Pruett Pub. Co., Boulder, Colo.

Behan, R.W.
1971. Wilderness purism—here we go again. Am. For. 78(12):8–11.

Catlin, George.
1960. An artist proposes a national park. In The American environment: readings in the history of conservation, p. 5–9. Roderick Nash, ed. 236 p. Addison-Wesley Pub. Co., Reading, Mass

Chapman, H.H.
1938. National Parks, National Forests, and wilderness areas. J. For. 36(5):469–474.

Church, Frank.
1977. The coming of a new deal? J. For. 75(7):388–389.

Costley, Richard J.
1972. An enduring resource. Am. For. 78(6):8–11.

Egler, Frank E.
1973. Wilderness east? Yes, incontestably. Ecology 54(4):721–722.

Flader, Susan L.
1974. Thinking like a mountain: Aldo Leopold and the evolution of an ecological attitude toward deer, wolves, and forests. 284 p. University of Missouri Press, Columbia.

Foote, Jeffrey P.
1973. Wilderness—a question of purity. Env. Law 3(4):255–260.

Frome, Michael.
1974. Battle for the wilderness. 246 p. Praeger Pub. Co., New York.

Gilligan, James P.
1953. The development of policy and administration of Forest Service primitive and wilderness areas in the western United States. Ph.D. dissertation. University of Michigan, Ann Arbor. 576 p.

Haight, Kevin.
1974. The Wilderness Act: ten years after. Environ. Affairs 3(2):275–326.

Heinselman, Miron L.
1973. Restoring fire to the canoe country. Naturalist 24(4):21–31.

Heinselman, Miron L.
1977. Crisis in the canoe country. Living Wilderness 40(136):12–24.

Hession, Jack M.
1967. The legislative history of the Wilderness Act. M.S. thesis. San Diego State College, San Diego. 228 p.

Keyser, C. Frank.
1949. The preservation of wilderness areas—an analysis of opinion on the problem. 114 p. Legislative Reference Service, Library of Congress, Washington, D.C.

Marshall, George.
1951. Robert Marshall as a writer. Living Wilderness 16(38):14–20.

Marshall, Robert.
1933. The forest for recreation. Senate Doc. 12. P. 463–487. U.S. Government Printing Office, Washington, D.C.

McArdle, Richard E.
1975. Wilderness politics: legislation and Forest Service policy. For. Hist. 19(4):166–179.

McCloskey, Michael.
1966. The Wilderness Act of 1964: its background and meaning. Oreg. Law Rev. 45(4):288–321.

Mercure, Delbert V., Jr., and William M. Ross.
1970. The Wilderness Act: a product of Congressional compromise. In Congress and the environment, p. 47–64. Richard A Cooley and Geoffrey Wandesforde-Smith, eds. 277 p. University of Washington Press, Seattle.

Nash, Roderick.
1966. The strenuous life of Bob Marshall. For. Hist. 10(3):18–25.

Nash, Roderick.
1973. Wilderness and the American mind. 300 p. Yale University Press, New Haven Conn.

Outdoor Recreation Resources Review Commision.
1962. Wilderness and recreation: a report on resources, values and problems. 352 p. U.S. Government Printing Office, Washington, D.C.

Schindler, George.
1970. New Jersey: conservation in a crowded state. Sierra Club Bull. 55(8):18–21.

Scott, Douglas.
1976. Howard Zahniser: architect of wilderness. Sierra Club Bull. 61(9):16–17.

Simmons, Fred C.
1972. Wilderness east?—NO. Am. For. 78(7):3,44–45.

Smith, Allen E.
  1976. Eastern wilderness: a small price for a large heritage. Sierra Club Bull. 61(9):18–22.

Sumner, David.
  1973. Wilderness and the mining law. Living Wilderness 37(121):8–18.

Trueblood, Ted.
  1975. The Forest Service versus the Wilderness Act. Field and Stream, Sept., 1975.

U.S. Department of Agriculture, Forest Service.
  1929. Supplement to Forest Service Administrative Manual. 1 p. U.S. Dep. Agric., For. Serv., Washington, D.C.

U.S. Department of Agriculture, Forest Service.
  1955. Wilderness areas. In Forest Service manual, section G; national forest protection and management, p. 23. U.S. Dep. Agric., For. Serv., Washington, D.C.

U.S. Department of Agriculture, Forest Service.
  1975. Mining in national forests: regulations to protect surface resources. Curr. Inf. Rep. No. 14. 20 p.

Wilm, Harold G.
  1974. Wilderness redefined. Am. For. 80(5):16–17.

Zahniser, Howard.
  1951. How much wilderness can we afford to lose. In Wildlands in our civilization, p. 46–51. David R. Brower, ed. 175 p. Sierra Club, San Francisco. [Speech was given in 1951; book was published in 1964.]

Appendix A — The Wilderness Act

Public Law 88-577
88th Congress, S. 4
September 3, 1964

AN ACT

To establish a National Wilderness Preservation System for the permanent good of the whole people, and for other purposes.

Be it enacted by the Senate and House of Representatives of the United States of America in Congress assembled,

Wilderness Act.

SHORT TITLE

SECTION 1. This Act may be cited as the "Wilderness Act".

WILDERNESS SYSTEM ESTABLISHED STATEMENT OF POLICY

Sec. 2. (a) In order to assure that an increasing population, accompanied by expanding settlement and growing mechanization, does not occupy and modify all areas within the United States and its possessions, leaving no lands designated for preservation and protection in their natural condition, it is hereby declared to be the policy of the Congress to secure for the American people of present and future generations the benefits of an enduring resource of wilderness. For this purpose there is hereby established a National Wilderness Preservation System to be composed of federally owned areas designated by Congress as "wilderness areas", and these shall be administered for the use and enjoyment of the American people in such manner as will leave them unimpaired for future use and enjoyment as wilderness, and so as to provide for the protection of these areas, the preservation of their wilderness character, and for the gathering and dissemination of information regarding their use and enjoyment as wilderness; and no Federal lands shall be designated as "wilderness areas" except as provided for in this Act or by a subsequent Act.

(b) The inclusion of an area in the National Wilderness Preservation System notwithstanding, the area shall continue to be managed by the Department and agency having jurisdiction thereover immediately before its inclusion in the National Wilderness Preservation System unless otherwise provided by Act of Congress. No appropriation shall be available for the payment of expenses or salaries for the administration of the National Wilderness Preservation System as a separate unit nor shall any appropriations be available for additional personnel stated as being required solely for the purpose of managing or administering areas solely because they are included within the National Wilderness Preservation System.

78 STAT. 890.
78 STAT. 891.

DEFINITION OF WILDERNESS

(c) A wilderness, in contrast with those areas where man and his own works dominate the landscape, is hereby recognized as an area where the earth and its community of life are untrammeled by man, where man himself is a visitor who does not remain. An area of wilderness is further defined to mean in this Act an area of undeveloped Federal land retaining its primeval character and influence, without permanent improvements or human habitation, which is protected and managed so as to preserve its natural conditions and which (1) generally appears to have been affected primarily by the forces of nature, with the imprint of man's work substantially unnoticeable; (2) has outstanding opportunities for solitude or a primitive and unconfined type of recreation; (3) has at least five thousand acres of land or is of sufficient size as to make practicable its preservation and use in an unimpaired condition; and (4) may also contain ecological, geological, or other features of scientific, educational, scenic, or historical value.

NATIONAL WILDERNESS PRESERVATION SYSTEM—EXTENT OF SYSTEM

Sec. 3. (a) All areas within the national forests classified at least 30 days before the effective date of this Act by the Secretary of Agriculture or the Chief of the Forest Service as "wilderness", "wild", or "canoe" are hereby designated as wilderness areas. The Secretary of Agriculture shall—

(1) Within one year after the effective date of this Act, file a map and legal description of each wilderness area with the Interior and Insular Affairs Committees of the United States Senate and the House of Representatives, and such descriptions shall have the same force and effect as if included in this Act: *Provided, however*, That correction of clerical and typographical errors in such legal descriptions and maps may be made.

(2) Maintain, available to the public, records pertaining to said wilderness areas, including maps and legal descriptions, copies of regulations governing them, copies of public notices of, and reports submitted to Congress regarding pending additions, eliminations, or modifications. Maps, legal descriptions, and regulations pertaining to wilderness areas within their respective jurisdictions also shall be available to the public in the offices of regional foresters, national forest supervisors, and forest rangers.

(b) The Secretary of Agriculture shall, within ten years after the enactment of this Act, review, as to its suitability or nonsuitability for preservation as wilderness, each area in the national forests classified on the effective date of this Act by the Secretary of Agriculture or the Chief of the Forest Service as "primitive" and report his findings to the President. The President shall advise the United States Senate and House of Representatives of his recommendations with respect to the designation as "wilderness" or other reclassification of each area on which review has been completed, together with maps and a definition of boundaries. Such advice shall be given with respect to not less than one-third of all the areas now classified as "primitive" within three years after the enactment of this Act, not less than two-thirds within seven years after the enactment of this Act, and the remaining areas within ten years after the enactment of this Act. Each recommendation of the President for designation as "wilderness" shall become effective only if so provided by an Act of Congress. Areas classified as "primitive" on the effective date of this Act shall continue to be administered under the rules and regulations affecting such areas on the effective date of this Act until Congress has determined otherwise. Any such area may be increased in size by the President at the time he submits his recommendations to the Congress by not more than five thousand acres with no more than one thousand two hundred and eighty acres of such increase in any one compact unit; if it is proposed to increase the size of any such area by more than five thousand acres or by more than one thousand two hundred and eighty acres in any one compact unit the increase in size shall not become effective until acted upon by Congress. Nothing herein contained shall limit the President in proposing, as part of his recommendations to Congress, the alteration of existing boundaries of primitive areas or recommending the addition of any contiguous area of national forest lands predominantly of wilderness value. Notwithstanding any other provisions of this Act, the Secretary of Agriculture may complete his review and delete such area as may be necessary, but not to exceed seven thousand acres, from the southern tip of the Gore Range-Eagles Nest Primitive Area, Colorado, if the Secretary determines that such action is in the public interest.

(c) Within ten years after the effective date of this Act the Secretary of the Interior shall review every roadless area of five thousand contiguous acres or more in the national parks, monuments and other units of the national park system and every such area of, and every roadless island within, the national wildlife refuges and game ranges, under his jurisdiction on the effective date of this Act and shall report to the President his recommendation as to the suitability or nonsuitability of each such area or island for preservation as wilderness. The President shall advise the President of the Senate and the Speaker of the House of Representatives of his recommendation with respect to the designation as wilderness of each such area or island on which review has been completed, together with a map thereof and a definition of its boundaries. Such advice shall be given with respect to not less than one-third of the areas and islands to be reviewed under this subsection within three years after enactment of this Act, not less than two-thirds within seven years of enactment of this Act, and the remainder within ten years of enactment of this Act. A recommendation of the President for designation as wilderness shall become effective only if so provided by an Act of Congress. Nothing contained herein shall, by implication or otherwise, be construed to lessen the present statutory authority of the Secretary of the Interior with respect to the maintenance of roadless areas within units of the national park system.

(d)(1) The Secretary of Agriculture and the Secretary of the Interior shall, prior to submitting any recommendations to the President with respect to the suitability of any area for preservation as wilderness—

(A) give such public notice of the proposed action as they deem appropriate, including publication in the Federal Register and in a newspaper having general circulation in the area or areas in the vicinity of the affected land;

(B) hold a public hearing or hearings at a location or locations convenient to the area affected. The hearings shall be announced through such means as the respective Secretaries involved deem appropriate, including notices in the Federal Register and in newspapers of general circulation in the area: *Provided*, That if the lands involved are located in more than one State, at least one hearing shall be held in each State in which a portion of the land lies;

(C) at least thirty days before the date of a hearing advise the Governor of each State and the governing board of each county, or in Alaska the borough, in which the lands are located, and Federal departments and agencies concerned, and invite such officials and Federal agencies to submit their views on the proposed action at the hearing or by no later than thirty days following the date of the hearing.

(2) Any views submitted to the appropriate Secretary under the provisions of (1) of this subsection with respect to any area shall be included with any recommendations to the President and to Congress with respect to such area.

Proposed modification.

(e) Any modification or adjustment of boundaries of any wilderness area shall be recommended by the appropriate Secretary after public notice of such proposal and public hearing or hearings as provided in subsection (d) of this section. The proposed modification or adjustment shall then be recommended with map and description thereof to the President. The President shall advise the United States Senate and the House of Representatives of his recommendations with respect to such modification or adjustment and such recommendations shall become effective only in the same manner as provided for in subsections (b) and (c) of this section.

USE OF WILDERNESS AREAS

Sec. 4. (a) The purposes of this Act are hereby declared to be within and supplemental to the purposes for which national forests and units of the national park and national wildlife refuge systems are established and administered and—

(1) Nothing in this Act shall be deemed to be in interference with the purpose for which national forests are established as set forth in the Act of June 4, 1897 (30 Stat. 11), and the Multiple-Use Sustained-Yield Act of June 12, 1960 (74 Stat. 215).

(2) Nothing in this Act shall modify the restrictions and provisions of the Shipstead-Nolan Act (Public Law 539, Seventy-first Congress, July 10, 1930; 46 Stat. 1020), the Thye-Blatnik Act (Public Law 733, Eightieth Congress, June 22, 1948; 62 Stat. 568), and the Humphrey-Thye-Blatnik-Andersen Act (Public Law 607, Eighty-fourth Congress, June 22, 1956; 70 Stat. 326), as applying to the Superior National Forest or the regulations of the Secretary of Agriculture.

(3) Nothing in this Act shall modify the statutory authority under which units of the national park system are created. Further, the designation of any area of any park, monument, or other unit of the national park system as a wilderness area pursuant to this Act shall in no manner lower the standards evolved for the use and preservation of such park, monument, or other unit of the national park system in accordance with the Act of August 25, 1916, the statutory authority under which the area was created, or any other Act of Congress which might pertain to or affect such area, including, but not limited to, the Act of June 8, 1906 (34 Stat. 225; 16 U.S.C. 432 et seq.); section 3(2) of the Federal Power Act (16 U.S.C. 796(2)); and the Act of August 21, 1935 (49 Stat. 666; 16 U.S.C. 461 et seq.).

(b) Except as otherwise provided in this Act, each agency administering any area designated as wilderness shall be responsible for preserving the wilderness character of the area and shall so administer such area for such other purposes for which it may have been established as also to preserve its wilderness character. Except as otherwise provided in this Act, wilderness areas shall be devoted to the public purposes of recreational, scenic, scientific, educational, conservation, and historical use.

PROHIBITION OF CERTAIN USES

(c) Except as specifically provided for in this Act, and subject to existing private rights, there shall be no commercial enterprise and no permanent road within any wilderness area designated by this Act and, except as necessary to meet minimum requirements for the administration of the area for the purpose of this Act (including measures required in emergencies involving the health and safety of persons within the area), there shall be no temporary road, no use of motor vehicles, motorized equipment or motorboats, no landing of aircraft, no other form of mechanical transport, and no structure or installation within any such area.

SPECIAL PROVISIONS

(d) The following special provisions are hereby made:

(1) Within wilderness areas designated by this Act the use of aircraft or motorboats, where these uses have already become established, may be permitted to continue subject to such restrictions as the Secretary of Agriculture deems desirable. In addition, such measures may be taken as may be necessary in the control of fire, insects and diseases, subject to such conditions as the Secretary deems desirable.

79 STAT. 892.
78 STAT. 893.

16 USC 475.
16 USC 528-531.

16 USC 577-577b.

16 USC 577c-577h.
16 USC 577d-l,
577g-l, 577h.

39 Stat. 535.
16 USC 1 *et seq.*

41 Stat. 1063.
49 Stat. 838.

78 STAT. 893.
78 STAT. 894.

(2) Nothing in this Act shall prevent within national forest wilderness areas any activity, including prospecting, for the purpose of gathering information about mineral or other resources, if such activity is carried on in a manner compatible with the preservation of the wilderness environment. Furthermore, in accordance with such program as the Secretary of the Interior shall develop and conduct in consultation with the Secretary of Agriculture, such areas shall be surveyed on a planned, recurring basis consistent with the concept of wilderness preservation by the Geological Survey and the Bureau of Mines to determine the mineral values, if any, that may be present; and the results of such surveys shall be made available to the public and submitted to the President and Congress.

(3) Notwithstanding any other provisions of this Act, until midnight December 31, 1983, the United States mining laws and all laws pertaining to mineral leasing shall, to the same extent as applicable prior to the effective date of this Act, extend to those national forest lands designated by this Act as "wilderness areas"; subject, however, to such reasonable regulations governing ingress and egress as may be prescribed by the Secretary of Agriculture consistent with the use of the land for mineral location and development and exploration, drilling, and production, and use of land for transmission lines, waterlines, telephone lines, or facilities necessary in exploring, drilling, producing, mining, and processing operations, including where essential the use of mechanized ground or air equipment and restoration as near as practicable of the surface of the land disturbed in performing prospecting, location, and, in oil and gas leasing, discovery work, exploration, drilling, and production, as soon as they have served their purpose. Mining locations lying within the boundaries of said wilderness areas shall be held and used solely for mining or processing operations and uses reasonably incident thereto; and hereafter, subject to valid existing rights, all patents issued under the mining laws of the United States affecting national forest lands designated by this Act as wilderness areas shall convey title to the mineral deposits within the claim, together with the right to cut and use so much of the mature timber therefrom as may be needed in the extraction, removal, and beneficiation of the mineral deposits, if needed timber is not otherwise reasonably available, and if the timber is cut under sound principles of forest management as defined by the national forest rules and regulations, but each such patent shall reserve to the United States all title in or to the surface of the lands and products thereof, and no use of the surface of the claim or the resources therefrom not reasonably required for carrying on mining or prospecting shall be allowed except as otherwise expressly provided in this Act: *Provided*, That, unless hereafter specifically authorized, no patent within wilderness areas designated by this Act shall issue after December 31, 1983, except for the valid claims existing on or before December 31, 1983. Mining claims located after the effective date of this Act within the boundaries of wilderness areas designated by this Act shall create no rights in excess of those rights which may be patented under the provisions of this subsection. Mineral leases, permits, and licenses covering lands within national forest wilderness areas designated by this Act shall contain such reasonable stipulations as may be prescribed by the Secretary of Agriculture for the protection of the wilderness character of the land consistent with the use of the land for the purposes for which they are leased, permitted, or licensed. Subject to valid rights then existing, effective January 1, 1984, the minerals in lands designated by this Act as wilderness areas are withdrawn from all forms of appropriation under the mining laws and from disposition under all laws pertaining to mineral leasing and all amendments thereto.

(4) Within wilderness areas in the national forests designated by the Act, (1) the President may, within a specific area and in accordance with such regulations as he may deem desirable, authorize prospecting for water resources, the establishment and maintenance of reservoirs, water-conservation works, power projects, transmission lines, and other facilities needed in the public interest, including the road construction and maintenance essential to development and use thereof, upon his determination that such use or uses in the specific area will better serve the interests of the United States and the people thereof than will its denial; and (2) the grazing of livestock, where established prior to the effective date of this Act, shall be permitted to continue subject to such reasonable regulations as are deemed necessary by the Secretary of Agriculture.

(5) Other provisions of this Act to the contrary notwithstanding, the management of the Boundary Waters Canoe Area, formerly designated as the Superior, Little Indian Sioux, and Caribou Roadless Areas, in the Superior National Forest, Minnesota, shall be in accordance with regulations established by the Secretary of Agriculture in accordance with the general purpose of maintaining, without unnecessary restrictions on other uses, including that of timber, the primitive character of the area, particularly in the vicinity of lakes, streams, and portages: *Provided*, That nothing in this Act shall preclude the continuance within the area of any already established use of motorboats.

(6) Commercial services may be performed within the wilderness areas designated by this Act to the extent necessary for activities which are proper for realizing the recreational or other wilderness purposes of the areas.

Mineral leases, claims, etc.

78 STAT. 894.
78 STAT. 895.

Water resources.

78 STAT. 895.
78 STAT. 896.

(7) Nothing in this Act shall constitute an express or implied claim or denial on the part of the Federal Government as to exemption from State water laws.

(8) Nothing in this Act shall be construed as affecting the jurisdiction or responsibilities of the several States with respect to wildlife and fish in the national forests.

STATE AND PRIVATE LANDS WITHIN WILDERNESS AREAS

SEC. 5. (a) In any case where State-owned or privately owned land is completely surrounded by national forest lands within areas designated by this Act as wilderness, such State or private owner shall be given such rights as may be necessary to assure adequate access to such State-owned or privately owned land by such State or private owner and their successors in interest, or the State-owned land or privately owned land shall be exchanged for federally owned land in the same State of approximately equal value under authorities available to the Secretary of Agriculture: *Provided, however,* That the United States shall not transfer to a State or private owner any mineral interests unless the State or private owner relinquishes or causes to be relinquished to the United States the mineral interest in the surrounded land.

Transfers, restriction.

78 STAT. 896.

(b) In any case where valid mining claims or other valid occupancies are wholly within a designated national forest wilderness area, the Secretary of Agriculture shall, by reasonable regulations consistent with the preservation of the area as wilderness, permit ingress and egress to such surrounded areas by means which have been or are being customarily enjoyed with respect to other such areas similarly situated.

Acquisition.

(c) Subject to the appropriation of funds by Congress, the Secretary of Agriculture is authorized to acquire privately owned land within the perimeter of any area designated by this Act as wilderness if (1) the owner concurs in such acquisition or (2) the acquisition is specifically authorized by Congress.

GIFTS, BEQUESTS, AND CONTRIBUTIONS

SEC. 6. (a) The Secretary of Agriculture may accept gifts or bequests of land within wilderness areas designated by this Act for preservation as wilderness. The Secretary of Agriculture may also accept gifts or bequests of land adjacent to wilderness areas designated by this Act for preservation as wilderness if he has given sixty days advance notice thereof to the President of the Senate and the Speaker of the House of Representatives. Land accepted by the Secretary of Agriculture under this section shall become part of the wilderness area involved. Regulations with regard to any such land may be in accordance with such agreements, consistent with the policy of this Act, as are made at the time of such gift, or such conditions, consistent with such policy, as may be included in, and accepted with, such bequest.

(b) The Secretary of Agriculture or the Secretary of the Interior is authorized to accept private contributions and gifts to be used to further the purposes of this Act.

ANNUAL REPORTS

SEC. 7. At the opening of each session of Congress, the Secretaries of Agriculture and Interior shall jointly report to the President for transmission to Congress on the status of the wilderness system, including a list and descriptions of the areas in the system, regulations in effect, and other pertinent information, together with any recommendations they may care to make.

Approved September 3, 1964.

LEGISLATIVE HISTORY:

HOUSE REPORTS: No. 1538 accompanying H. R. 9070 (Comm. on Interior & Insular Affairs) and No. 1829 (Comm. of Conference).
SENATE REPORT No. 109 (Comm. on Interior & Insular Affairs).
CONGRESSIONAL RECORD:
    Vol. 109 (1963):   Apr. 4, 8, considered in Senate.
                             Apr. 9,   considered and passed Senate.
    Vol. 110 (1964):   July 28,   considered in House.
                             July 30,   considered and passed House, amended, in lieu of H. R. 9070.
                             Aug. 20,   House and Senate agreed to conference report.

Appendix B — The Eastern Wilderness Act

Public Law 93-622
93rd Congress, S. 3433
January 3, 1975

AN ACT

To further the purposes of the Wilderness Act by designating certain acquired lands for inclusion in the National Wilderness Preservation System, to provide for study of certain additional lands for such inclusion, and for other purposes.

Be it enacted by the Senate and House of Representatives of the United States of America in Congress assembled,

National Wilderness Preservation System. Designation of certain acquired lands.

STATEMENT OF FINDINGS AND POLICY

SEC. 2. (a) The Congress finds that—

(1) in the more populous eastern half of the United States there is an urgent need to identify, study, designate, and preserve areas for addition to the National Wilderness Preservation System;

(2) in recognition of this urgent need, certain areas in the national forest system in the eastern half of the United States were designated by the Congress as wilderness in the Wilderness Act (78 Stat. 890); certain areas in the national wildlife refuge system in the eastern half of the United States have been designated by the Congress as wilderness or recommended by the President for such designation, and certain areas in the national park system in the eastern half of the United States have been recommended by the President for designation as wilderness; and

16 USC 1131 note.

(3) additional areas of wilderness in the more populous eastern half of the United States are increasingly threatened by the pressures of a growing and more mobile population, large-scale industrial and economic growth, and development and uses inconsistent with the protection, maintenance, and enhancement of the areas' wilderness character.

(b) Therefore, the Congress finds and declares that it is in the national interest that these and similar areas in the eastern half of the United States be promptly designated as wilderness within the National Wilderness Preservation System, in order to preserve such areas as an enduring resource of wilderness which shall be managed to promote and perpetuate the wilderness character of the land and its specific values of solitude, physical and mental challenge, scientific study, inspiration, and primitive recreation for the benefit of all of the American people of present and future generations.

88 STAT. 2096
88 STAT. 2097

DESIGNATION OF WILDERNESS AREAS

SEC. 3. (a) In furtherance of the purposes of the Wilderness Act, the following lands (hereinafter in this Act referred to as "wilderness areas"), as generally depicted on maps appropriately referenced, dated April 1974, are hereby designated as wilderness and, therefore, as components of the National Wilderness Preservation System—

16 USC 1132 note.

(1) certain lands in the Bankhead National Forest, Alabama, which comprise about twelve thousand acres, are generally depicted on a map entitled "Sipsey Wilderness Area—Proposed", and shall be known as the Sipsey Wilderness;

(2) certain lands in the Ouachita National Forest, Arkansas, which comprise about fourteen thousand four hundred and thirty-three acres, are generally depicted on a map entitled "Caney Creek Wilderness Area—Proposed", and shall be known as the Caney Creek Wilderness;

(3) certain lands in the Ozark National Forest, Arkansas, which comprise about ten thousand five hundred and ninety acres, are generally depicted on a map entitled "Upper Buffalo Wilderness Area—Proposed", and shall be known as the Upper Buffalo Wilderness;

(4) certain lands in the Appalachicola National Forest, Florida, which comprise about twenty-two thousand acres, are generally depicted on a map entitled "Bradwell Bay Wilderness Area—Proposed", and shall be known as the Bradwell Bay Wilderness;

(5) certain lands in the Daniel Boone National Forest, Kentucky, which comprise about five thousand five hundred acres, are generally depicted on a map entitled "Beaver Creek Wilderness Area—Proposed", and shall be known as the Beaver Creek Wilderness;

(6) certain lands in the White Mountain National Forest, New Hampshire, which comprise about twenty thousand three hundred and eighty acres, are generally depicted on a map entitled "Presidential Range-Dry River Wilderness Area—Proposed", and shall be known as the Presidential Range-Dry River Wilderness;

(7) certain lands in the Nantahala and Cherokee National Forests, North Carolina and Tennessee, which comprise about fifteen thousand acres, are generally depicted on a map entitled "Joyce Kilmer-Slickrock Wilderness Area—Proposed", and shall be known as the Joyce Kilmer-Slickrock Wilderness;

(8) certain lands in the Sumter, Nantahala, and Chattahoochee National Forests in South Carolina, North Carolina, and Georgia, which comprise about three thousand six hundred acres, are generally depicted on a map entitled "Ellicott Rock Wilderness Area—Proposed", and shall be known as Ellicott Rock Wilderness;

(9) certain lands in the Cherokee National Forest, Tennessee, which comprise about two thousand five hundred and seventy acres, are generally depicted on a map entitled "Gee Creek Wilderness Area—Proposed", and shall be known as the Gee Creek Wilderness;

(10) certain lands in the Green Mountain National Forest, Vermont, which comprise about six thousand five hundred acres, are generally depicted on a map entitled "Bristol Cliffs Wilderness Area—Proposed", and shall be known as the Bristol Cliffs Wilderness;

(11) certain lands in the Green Mountain National Forest, Vermont, which comprise about fourteen thousand three hundred acres, are generally depicted on a map entitled "Lye Brook Wilderness Area—Proposed", and shall be known as the Lye Brook Wilderness;

(12) certain lands in the Jefferson National Forest, Virginia, which comprise about eight thousand eight hundred acres, are generally depicted on a map entitled "James River Face Wilderness Area—Proposed", and shall be known as the James River Face Wilderness;

(13) certain lands in the Monongahela National Forest, West Virginia, which comprise about ten thousand two hundred and fifteen acres, are generally depicted on a map entitled "Dolly Sods Wilderness Area—Proposed", and shall be known as the Dolly Sods Wilderness;

(14) certain lands in the Monongahela National Forest, West Virginia, which comprise about twenty thousand acres, are generally depicted on a map entitled "Otter Creek Wilderness Study Area", and shall be known as the Otter Creek Wilderness; and

(15) certain lands in the Chequamegon National Forest, Wisconsin, which comprise about six thousand six hundred acres, are generally depicted on a map entitled "Rainbow Lake Wilderness Area—Proposed", and shall be known as the Rainbow Lake Wilderness.

(b) In furtherance of the purposes of the Wilderness Act, the following lands (hereinafter referred to as "wilderness areas"), as generally depicted on maps appropriately referenced, dated April 1973, are hereby designated as wilderness and, therefore, as components of the National Wilderness Preservation System: certain lands in the Chattahoochee and Cherokee National Forests, Georgia and Tennessee, which comprise about thirty-four thousand five hundred acres, are generally depicted on a map dated April 1973, entitled "Cohutta Wilderness Area—Proposed", and shall be known as the Cohutta Wilderness.

DESIGNATION OF WILDERNESS STUDY AREAS

SEC. 4. (a) In furtherance of the purposes of the Wilderness Act and in accordance with the provisions of subsection 3(d) of that Act, the Secretary of Agriculture (hereinafter referred to as the "Secretary") shall review, as to its suitability or nonsuitability for preservation as wilderness, each area designated by or pursuant to subsection (b) of this section and report his findings to the President. The President shall advise the United States Senate and House of Representatives of his recommendations with respect to the designation as wilderness of each such area on which the review has been completed.

(b) Areas to be reviewed pursuant to this section (hereinafter referred to as "wilderness study areas"), as generally depicted on maps appropriately referenced, dated April 1974, include—

(1) certain lands in the Ouachita National Forest, Arkansas, which comprise approximately five thousand seven hundred acres and are generally depicted on a map entitled "Belle Starr Cave Wilderness Study Area";

(2) certain lands in the Ouachita National Forest, Arkansas, which comprise approximately five thousand five hundred acres and are generally depicted on a map entitled "Dry Creek Wilderness Study Area";

(3) certain lands in the Ozark National Forest, Arkansas, which comprise approximately two thousand one hundred acres and are generally depicted on a map entitled "Richland Creek Wilderness Study Area";

(4) certain lands in the Appalachicola National Forest, Florida, which comprise approximately one thousand one hundred acres and are generally depicted as the "Sopchoppy River Wilderness Study Area" on a map entitled "Bradwell Bay Wilderness Area—Proposed";

16 USC 1131 note.
16 USC 1132 and note.

Report to the President.

(5) certain lands in the Hiawatha National Forest, Michigan, which comprise approximately five thousand four hundred acres and are generally depicted on a map entitled "Rock River Canyon Wilderness Study Area";

(6) certain lands in the Ottawa National Forest, Michigan, which comprise approximately thirteen thousand two hundred acres and are generally depicted on a map entitled "Sturgeon River Wilderness Study Area";

(7) certain lands in the Pisgah National Forest, North Carolina, which comprise approximately one thousand one hundred acres and are generally depicted on a map entitled "Craggy Mountain Wilderness Study Area";

(8) certain lands in the Francis Marion National Forest, South Carolina, which comprise approximately one thousand five hundred acres and are generally depicted on a map entitled "Wambaw Swamp Wilderness Study Area";

(9) certain lands in the Jefferson National Forest, Virginia, which comprise approximately four thousand acres and are generally depicted on a map entitled "Mill Creek Wilderness Study Area";

(10) certain lands in the Jefferson National Forest, Virginia, which comprise approximately eight thousand four hundred acres and are generally depicted on a map entitled "Mountain Lake Wilderness Study Area";

(11) certain lands in the Jefferson National Forest, Virginia, which comprise approximately five thousand acres and are generally depicted on a map entitled "Peters Mountain Wilderness Study Area";

(12) certain lands in the George Washington National Forest, Virginia, which comprise approximately six thousand seven hundred acres and are generally depicted on a map entitled "Ramsey's Draft Wilderness Study Area";

(13) certain lands in the Chequamegon National Forest, Wisconsin, which comprise approximately six thousand three hundred acres and are generally depicted on a map entitled "Flynn Lake Wilderness Study Area";

(14) certain lands in the Chequamegon National Forest, Wisconsin, which comprise approximately four thousand two hundred acres and are generally depicted on a map entitled "Round Lake Wilderness Study Area";

(15) certain lands in the Monongahela National Forest, West Virginia, which comprise approximately thirty-six thousand three hundred acres and are generally depicted on a map entitled "Cranberry Wilderness Study Area";

(16) certain lands in the Cherokee National Forest, Tennessee, which comprise approximately four thousand five hundred acres and are generally depicted on a map entitled "Big Frog Wilderness Study Area"; and

(17) certain lands in the Cherokee National Forest, Tennessee, which comprise approximately fourteen thousand acres and are generally depicted as the "Citico Creek Area" on a map entitled "Joyce Kilmer-Slickrock Wilderness Area—Proposed";

(c) Reviews shall be completed and the President shall make his recommendations to Congress within five years after enactment of this Act.

(d) Congress may, upon the recommendation of the Secretary of Agriculture or otherwise, designate as study areas, national forest system lands east of the 100th meridian other than those areas specified in subsection (b) of this section, for review as to suitability or nonsuitability for preservation as wilderness. Any such area subsequently designated as a wilderness study area after the enactment of this Act shall have its suitability or nonsuitability for preservation as wilderness submitted to Congress within ten years from the date of designation as a wilderness study area. Nothing in this Act shall be construed as limiting the authority of the Secretary of Agriculture to carry out management programs, development, and activities in accordance with the Multiple-Use, Sustained-Yield Act of 1960 (74 Stat. 215, 16 U.S.C. 528-531) within areas not designated for review in accordance with the provisions of this Act.

(e) Nothing herein contained shall limit the President in proposing, as part of his recommendations to Congress, the alteration of existing boundaries of any wilderness study area or recommending the addition to any such area of any contiguous area predominantly of wilderness value. Any recommendation of the President to the effect that such area or portion thereof should be designated as "wilderness" shall become effective only if so provided by an Act of Congress.

88 STAT. 2099
88 STAT. 2100

FILING OF MAPS AND DESCRIPTIONS

SEC. 5. As soon as practicable after enactment of this Act, a map of each wilderness study area and a map and a legal description of each wilderness area shall be filed with the Committees on Interior and Insular

Affairs and on Agriculture of the United States Senate and House of Representatives, and each such map and description shall have the same force and effect as if included in this Act: *Provided, however*, That correction of clerical and typographical errors in each such legal description and map may be made. Each such map and legal description shall be on file and available for public inspection in the Office of the Chief of the Forest Service, Department of Agriculture.

MANAGEMENT OF AREAS

SEC. 6. (a) except as otherwise provided by this Act, the wilderness areas designated by or pursuant to this Act shall be managed by the Secretary of Agriculture in accordance with the provisions of the Wilderness Act. The wilderness study areas designated by or pursuant to this Act shall be managed by the Secretary of Agriculture so as to maintain their presently existing wilderness character and potential for inclusion in the National Wilderness Preservation System until Congress has determined otherwise, except that such management requirement shall in no case extend beyond the expiration of the third succeeding Congress from the date of submission to the Congress of the President's recommendations concerning the particular study area.

(b) Within the sixteen wilderness areas designated by section 3 of this Act:

(1) the Secretary of Agriculture may acquire by purchase with donated or appropriated funds, by gift, exchange, condemnation, or otherwise, such lands, waters, or interests therein as he determines necessary or desirable for the purposes of this Act. All lands acquired under the provisions of this subsection shall become national forest lands and a part of the Wilderness System;

(2) in exercising the exchange authority granted by paragraph (1), the Secretary of Agriculture may accept title to non-Federal property for federally owned property of substantially equal value, or, if not of substantially equal value, the value shall be equalized by the payment of money to the grantor or to the Secretary as the circumstances require;

(3) the authority of the Secretary of Agriculture to condemn any private land or interest therein within any wilderness area designated by or pursuant to this Act shall not be invoked so long as the owner or owners of such land or interest holds and uses it in the same manner and for those purposes for which such land or interest was held on the date of the designation of the wilderness area: *Proposed, however*, That the Secretary of Agriculture may acquire such land or interest without consent of the owner or owners whenever he finds such use to be incompatible with the management of such area as wilderness and the owner or owners manifest unwillingness, and subsequently fail, to promptly discontinue such incompatible use;

(4) at least sixty days prior to any transfer by exchange, sale, or otherwise (except by bequest) of such lands, or interests therein described in paragraph (3) of this subsection, the owner or owners of such lands or interests therein shall provide notice of such transfer to the supervisor of the national forest concerned, in accordance with such rules and regulations as the Secretary of Agriculture may promulgate;

(5) at least sixty days prior to any change in the use of such lands or interests therein described in paragraph (3) of this subsection which will result in any significant new construction or disturbance of land surface or flora or will require the use of motor vehicles and other forms of mechanized transport or motorized equipment (except as otherwise authorized by law for ingress or egress or for existing agricultural activities begun before the date of the designation other than timber cutting), the owner or owners of such lands or interests therein shall provide notice of such change in use to the supervisor of the national forest within which such lands are located, in accordance with such rules and regulations as the Secretary of Agriculture may promulgate;

(6) for the purposes of paragraphs (7) and (8) of this subsection, the term "property" shall mean a detached, noncommercial residential dwelling, the construction of which was begun before the date of the designation of the wilderness area (hereinafter referred to as "dwelling"), or an existing agricultural activity begun before the date of the designation of the wilderness area, other than timber cutting (hereinafter referred to as "agricultural activity"), together with so much of the land on which the dwelling or agricultural activity is situated, such land being in the same ownership as the dwelling or agricultural activity, as the Secretary of Agriculture shall determine to be necessary for the enjoyment of the dwelling for the sole purpose of noncommercial residential use or for the agricultural activity, together with any structures accessory to the dwelling or agricultural activity which are situated on the land so designated;

(7) any owner or owners of property on the date of its acquisition by the Secretary of Agriculture may, as a condition of such acquisition, retain for themselves and their successors or assigns a right of use and occupancy of the property for such noncommercial residential purpose or agricultural activity for twenty-five years, or, in lieu thereof, for a term ending at the death of the owner or his spouse,

Acquisition.

88 STAT. 2100
88 STAT. 2101

Notice.

"Property"

whichever is later. The owner shall elect the term to be reserved. The Secretary of Agriculture shall pay to the owner the fair market value of the property on the date of such acquisition less the fair market value on such date of the right retained by the owner: *Provided,* That whenever an owner of property elects to retain a right of use and occupancy as provided for in this section, such owner shall be deemed to have waived any benefits or rights accruing under sections 203, 204, 205, and 206 of the Uniform Relocation Assistance and Real Property Acquisition Policies Act of 1970 (84 Stat. 1894), and for the purposes of those sections such owner shall not be considered a displaced person as defined in section 101(6) of that Act; and

42 USC 4623-4626.
88 STAT. 2101
88 STAT. 2102
42 USC 4601.

(8) a right of use and occupancy retained or enjoyed pursuant to paragraph (7) of this subsection may be terminated with respect to the entire property by the Secretary of Agriculture upon his determination that the property or any portion thereof has ceased to be used for such noncommercial residential purpose or agricultural activity and upon tender to the holder of a right an amount equal to the fair market value as of the date of tender of that portion of the right which remains unexpired on the date of termination.

88 STAT. 2102

TRANSFER OF FEDERAL PROPERTY

SEC. 7. The head of any Federal department or agency having jurisdiction over any lands or interests in lands within the boundaries of wilderness areas and wilderness study areas designated by or pursuant to this Act is authorized to transfer to the Secretary jurisdiction over such lands for administration in accordance with the provisions of this Act.

APPLICABILITY

SEC. 8. Unless otherwise provided by any other Act the provisions of this Act shall only apply to National Forest areas east of the 100th meridian.

AUTHORIZATION OF APPROPRIATIONS

SEC. 9. There are hereby authorized to be appropriated an amount not to exceed $5,000,000 for the acquisition by purchase, condemnation, or otherwise of lands, waters, or interests therein located in areas designated as wilderness pursuant to section 3 of this Act and an amount not to exceed $1,700,000 for the purpose of conducting a review of wilderness study areas designated by section 4 of this Act.

Approved January 3, 1975.

16 USC 1132 note.

LEGISLATIVE HISTORY:

HOUSE REPORT No. 93-1599 accompanying H.R. 13455 (Comm. on Interior and Insular Affairs).
SENATE REPORT No. 93-803 (Comm. on Agriculture and Forestry).
CONGRESSIONAL RECORD, Vol. 120 (1974):

May 31,	considered and passed Senate.
Dec. 18,	considered and passed House, amended, in lieu of H.R. 13455.
Dec. 19,	Senate concurred in House amendment.

The Wilderness Act instructed the Secretary of Agriculture to review, within 10 years, all administratively designated primitive areas to determine their suitability for classification as wilderness. Headwaters of East Fork of Boulder River, Beartooth Primitive Area, Mont.

5 The Wilderness Classification Process

Introduction

Although this is primarily a text about wilderness management, it is difficult, if not impossible, to ignore the allocation or classification process. Because there are important interdependencies between allocation (an inherently political process to decide what areas to preserve) and management (the application of concepts and techniques from various sciences to preserve wilderness values), this chapter will focus on the allocation process. In it, we will review how wilderness is classified as outlined by the Wilderness Act, how the classification process has been affected by various administrative and judicial decisions, and how these rulings bear upon wilderness management.

The Classification Process

Chapter 4 points out that classification procedures are outlined in Section 3 of the Wilderness Act. The Act provided for two types of wilderness lands: 1) Areas that were defined by the Act itself as wilderness and 2) areas which required agency application and argument, Presidential recommendation, and Congressional approval (so-called mandated lands, because Congress mandated their review). First, the Act established an "instant" wilderness system by proclaiming that all those lands administered by the Forest Service as wilderness, wild, or canoe areas prior to 1964 would be known

henceforth as wilderness areas. No Department of the Interior lands were included in the initial system.

Secondly, the Wilderness Act instructed the Secretaries of Agriculture and the Interior to review certain lands within their respective jurisdictions and to make recommendations to the President regarding the suitability of these lands for classification as wilderness. The Forest Service, through the Secretary of Agriculture, was instructed to review those lands previously designated as *primitive areas* (a total of 34 areas and 5.4 million acres) within 10 years of the passage of the Act. According to the Act's timetable, one-third of the primitive areas were to be reviewed in the first 3 years, two-thirds by the end of 7 years, and the remainder by the end of 10 years.

Similar instructions were addressed to the Secretary of the Interior. All roadless areas in the various units of the National Park System and the National Wildlife Refuges and Game Ranges in excess of 5,000 acres, as well as all roadless islands, were to be reviewed by the respective agencies, and recommendations regarding their suitability for Wilderness were to be forwarded to the President. The 10-year review period and timetable applied to both Forest Service lands and Department of the Interior holdings.

Despite its apparent clarity, Section 3 has been the source of numerous conflicts. Because it provided only broad direction and left specific details of execution to Agency action, the Act's implementation has been surrounded by controversy. A discussion of some of these allocation issues follows.

Review of National Forest Primitive Areas

The Forest Service's workload implementing the Wilderness Act of 1964 was substantial. First, the agency was faced with the enormous job of developing new policies and regulations for wilderness in light of the Act. By the end of 1964, a special four-man team of Forest Service officials had drafted these guidelines, but before they could be accepted, they had to be subjected to extensive in-service and citizen review. [1]

The Forest Service was faced with the responsibility of reviewing and recommending to the President the wilderness suitability of the existing 34 primitive areas totaling 5.4 million acres and ranging in size from the 7,400-acre Mount Baldy Primitive Area in Arizona to the 1.2-million-acre Idaho Primitive Area. One of the initial tasks before the Agency was to establish a schedule for review of these primitive areas. In accord with the timetable imposed by the Wilderness Act, 11 areas were to be reviewed in the first 3 years. Because it was necessary to develop the new wilderness guidelines at the same time that recommendations were drawn up for the first group of primitive areas, it was decided that the areas that appeared least controversial were to be reviewed first. Starting with the easiest areas would also give the agency an opportunity to refine its review procedures.

The extent to which the initial group of primitive areas proved easy to review is open to question. All of the primitive area reviews have involved conflicting proposals and substantial debate. Typically, a long time—2 years or more—has elapsed between agency recommendations and Congressional action in classifying the area. The first public hearings on the Spanish Peaks Primitive Area in Montana, for example, were held in September 1966. In July 1977, the area remained in primitive status, its wilderness classification stymied by debate over the potential addition of a contiguous roadless tract.

Nevertheless, the review of Forest Service primitive areas moved ahead on schedule and was completed within the 10-year period specified by the Wilderness Act. As the Forest Service reviewed each area, they considered one of three basic management options: Wilderness classification within the existing primitive area boundaries, wilderness classification with larger or smaller boundaries, or alternative management because the area was deemed not suitable for wilderness.

By the end of 1974 (the end of the 10-year review period prescribed by the Wilderness Act), 16 primitive areas totaling 1.8 million acres had been classified by Congress as wilderness. The Forest Service recommended wilderness classification for all the remaining 18 areas in proposals totaling 3.6 million acres. Proposals submitted by conservationist groups for these same areas totaled nearly 6 million acres.

The preliminary proposal prepared by the Forest Service followed a format prescribed by administrative policies. Typically, a proposal contained the following information:

1. General description of the area;
2. Topographic and scenic features;
3. An inventory and appraisal of resources including wilderness, recreation, wildlife, water, forage, timber, and minerals;[2]
4. Anticipated public reaction;
5. Management considerations; and
6. Reasons why the area should or should not be recommended for wilderness designation.

The preliminary proposal was submitted by the Regional Office to the Forest Service Washington Office where it was reviewed for conformity with agency and Departmental policies. Suggested revisions were returned to the Region for incorporation in a revised proposal which served as the document for public review. Input from public meetings was analyzed, the proposal was again altered to reflect public suggestions, and a final proposal was prepared for resubmission to Washington.

Prior to 1970, this would have constituted a complete description of the Agency's responsibility in preparing its final proposal. But after 1970, a second set of documents had to be drafted to support the wilderness classification proposal. Along with the preliminary proposal, for example, the agency has been required to prepare a Draft Environmental Impact Statement (DEIS) for submission to the Council on Environmental Quality, an executive office created by the National Environmental

---

[1] See *A Discussion Draft of Suggested Objectives, Policies, Procedures, and Regulations,* U.S. Department of Agriculture Forest Service, Washington, D.C., December 1, 1964, by Ed Slusher, Arnold Snyder, George Williams, and William Worf.

[2] The joint Senate-House conference committee on the Wilderness Act noted that provisions of the Act pertaining to mining and mineral leasing laws were, strictly speaking, limited to those areas designated by the Act as wilderness. However, they also noted these provisions should logically be extended to the primitive areas that in the future would be designated as wilderness. Moreover, the conference committee indicated it "expects" the mining industry and agencies of the Department of the Interior to explore existing primitive areas for their mineral potential so that Congress will have the benefit of professional technical advice regarding mineral availability when the primitive areas come up for reclassification. This "expectation" has led to the publication of a series of reports on the mineral resources of the various primitive areas. This information is a standard part of the data base used by Forest Service officials in the formulation of a preliminary wilderness proposal.

Policy Act (NEPA). This Act requires all Federal agencies to give full consideration to environmental effects in planning their programs (Anderson 1973). The DEIS must contain the following information:

1. Description of the proposed action;
2. Probable impact of the proposed action on the environment;
3. Probable adverse and unavoidable environmental effects;
4. Alternatives to the proposed action;
5. Relationship between local short term environmental uses and the maintenance and enhancement of long term productivity; and
6. Any irreversible and irretrievable commitments of resources following from the proposed action.

The draft EIS must also be reviewed. When the final agency proposal for wilderness classification is submitted to the Washington Office, the final EIS is submitted to the Council on Environmental Quality. At this stage, it must contain responses to significant comments and questions raised during its review.

After the final proposal is submitted to Washington, any further changes are negotiated between the regional and national offices. When agreement is reached, the Chief signs the proposal and submits it to the Office of the Secretary of Agriculture where it is subjected to further review. The Secretary can concur with the proposal or he can suggest changes. (So far, he has changed only one proposal; he revised the wilderness proposal submitted by the Forest Service for the Idaho and Salmon River Breaks Primitive Areas downward from 1.5 to 1.1 million acres. (U.S. Department of Agriculture 1974a.)) At this point, the proposal is transmitted to the Office of Management and Budget (OMB) which holds a 60-day Quality of Life Review. During this review, in addition to OMB's own examination, officials of various Federal agencies are asked to appraise the impact of the proposal on their programs. After receiving their comments, OMB may revise the proposal. It is then returned to the Secretary of Agriculture for his signature, for the preparation of draft legislation under his direction, and for submission to the President for his signature. (Although the President has authority to make revisions in the draft, this has not yet occurred.) Finally, as draft legislation, the proposal is sent to Congress.

Usually, it is introduced by Senators or Representatives who endorse the Presidential recommendation. Other Congressmen, typically from the State or States where the area lies, frequently offer alternative

proposals. Commonly, three basic legislative drafts are offered for a proposed wilderness area: A maximum-area proposal endorsed by conservationists, a moderate proposal backed by the Forest Service, and a minimum-acreage proposal supported by industry. All proposals are submitted to the Interior and Insular Affairs Committee in the House or Senate.

This process describes the submission of a proposal for reclassification of a primitive area. For areas other than primitive areas virtually the same process is followed—with two important exceptions. First, if the Secretary of Agriculture opposes the proposal submitted by the Forest Service, it is dropped at that point and no further official action can occur. (Of course, legislation supporting this, or any, area can be directly introduced by citizens groups into Congress, bypassing the Executive review process entirely.) Second, once a proposal for a non-primitive area passes through the OMB review

Figure 5-1.—Classification of an area as wilderness is a lengthy process requiring resource study; public involvement; suitable proposals; review by congressional committees, including public hearings; congressional debate over alternative wilderness legislation; and, finally, passage of legislation classifying an area with specific boundaries as wilderness.

95

process, it is transmitted directly to Congress, bypassing the President. (OMB is located administratively in the Office of the President.)

Congressional committees generally hold their own field hearings on wilderness proposals. These hearings provide opportunities to gauge public response to agency recommendations and to hear alternative suggestions before committee drafts of legislation are completed and submitted to the full Senate or House. Upon passage in one House, the legislation is sent to the other, where additional debate often occurs. Frequently, joint House-Senate conference committees are convened to iron out differences. In conference committees, disputes over boundary determinations are sometimes resolved through negotiations between local interested parties and agency officials. A Senator or Representative sponsoring the bill can seek such a meeting in order to incorporate desired compromises into his legislation. Any changes supported by a majority of the conference committee are again presented to the respective Houses of the Congress. Upon passage, the bill is sent to the President for his signature.

This is an exceptionally brief outline of what is in fact a long and complicated process. Below is a diagram of the typical steps in the process. To illustrate what might appear to be a ponderous, bureaucratic maze, let's look at how one area, the San Raphael Primitive Area in California, became a Wilderness.

Generalized Flow Chart of the Wilderness Classification Process

Field Review of Area by Agency, Including Citizen Input
↓
Preliminary Wilderness Proposal and Draft EIS Prepared by Agency
↓
Public Review
↓
Final Wilderness Proposal and Final EIS Prepared by Agency
↓
Submission of Final Wilderness Proposal to Secretary of Agriculture (Forest Service) or Secretary of the Interior (National Park Service, Fish and Wildlife Service, and the Bureau of Land Management)
↓
Review of Wilderness Proposal by Departmental Staff for Conformity with Policy. Revision by Agency if Necessary
↓
Submission by Department to Office of Management and Budget for "Quality of Life" Review
↓
Wilderness Proposal Revised and/or Approved by OMB and Returned to Secretary for Signature
↓
Draft Legislation Prepared for Wilderness Proposal
↓
Submission to President
↓
Submission to Congress
↓
Legislation Sponsored by Senators or Congressmen
↓
Congressional Committee Review, Study, Including Public Input, Possible Revision
↓
Congressional Debate and Vote on Legislation
↓
President Signs Into Law

The San Raphael Primitive Area Review—A Case Study

The San Raphael Primitive Area was one of 34 areas the Forest Service was faced with reclassifying after passage of the Wilderness Act. It contained nearly 75,000 acres and had been designated as a primitive area in 1932.

The Forest Service began field studies in the area immediately after passage of the Wilderness Act. The U.S. Geological Survey and U.S. Bureau of Mines prepared an assessment of the area's mineral potential, concluding " . . . no mineral deposits approaching commercial grade were recognized within the Primitive Area." Figure 5-2 shows the primitive area and the contiguous roadless areas that were studied. Under the Forest Service proposal, areas A and B (36,244 acres) were to be added to the primitive area and area 1 (831 acres) was to be withdrawn, because of a fuel break and a lookout tower.[3] Total acreage in the Forest Service proposal was 110,403 acres.

Approximately a year after beginning their review, the Forest Service held a public meeting to solicit public comment on its recommended proposal. At the hearing, conservation groups urged the addition of unit C, an area of over 29,000 acres. As originally drawn, the Forest Service boundary lay midslope between the Sisquoc River on the southwest and the ridge of the Sierra Madre Mountains on the northeast. Testimony from conservationists indicated that area C was important for the protection of the rare California condor (an endangered species). This area also included small grassy openings known as Potreros along the Sierra Madre ridge as well as Indian pictographs.

The same conservation groups also supported addition of unit D (2,500 acres) and opposed the deletion of unit 1. Testimony revealed the latter unit contained favorite camping spots and was also important as a resting spot for condors. Thus, initial testimony by conservation groups supported classification of approximately 158,000 acres—all of units A, B, C, D, and 1, shown in fig. 5-2.

Based on a review of both public testimony and management considerations, the Forest Service submitted a revised recommendation to President Johnson calling for classification of 142,722 acres as wilderness, an increase of 32,000 acres over their initial proposal. The President transmitted the recommendation, unmodified, to Congress on February 1, 1967, and strongly urged the Congress to give it "early and favorable approval."

The proposal, in its legislative form, was sponsored in the Senate by Thomas Kuchel of California and in the House by Charles Teague of California and John Saylor of Pennsylvania. In April 1967, the Public Lands Subcommittee of the Senate Committee on Interior and Insular Affairs held public hearings on the Senate version. Testimony by conservationists indicated their willingness to accept a reduction of some 13,000 acres from their original proposal (158,000 to 145,000 acres). They concurred with Forest Service exclusion of areas E and G (a total of 10,700 acres, see fig. 5-2) as well as with the reduction of 2,500 acres from unit F, an area that had been bulldozed to convert brush cover to perennial grasses for wildlife habitat, livestock forage, and fire control (Cutler 1968). Thus, during Senate committee hearings, the conservationists' altered request differed from the Forest Service proposal by only 2,200 acres, a tract located in unit F.

However, the 2,200-acre unit became a major stumbling block to final resolution of the proposal. Conservationists argued that inclusion of the area was needed to bring wilderness protection to several kinds of unusual mountaintop-meadow life zones and to four village sites of the extinct Chumash Indian Tribe. The area was also the site of some condor activity. The Forest Service argued that, because fire in the chaparral-type vegetation of the area was a major concern,[4] the area should be excluded to permit construction of a fire-break. In fact, in June of the preceding year, a fire that ignited from a small airplane crash burned more than 90,000 acres, 70,000 of which were in the proposed wilderness.

The Subcommittee on Public Lands reported out the 142,722-acre administration proposal without amendment and, in May 1967, the full Senate passed the bill unanimously but noted that unit F could be included within the wilderness at a later date if desirable.

Unlike the Senate Committee, the House Committee reported out a bill that *did* include the debated 2,200-acre parcel of unit F. In October 1967, the House approved this bill, and a joint House-Senate committee was named to resolve the differences between the bills passed by the two legislative bodies. In December 1967 the committee published House Report No. 1029 with a majority recommendation "That the House recede from its amendment," that is, that the House delete the 2,200-acre addition from its proposed bill and adopt the Senate (Forest Service) version. In House debate, an effort was

---

[3] The unit designations (A, B, 1, etc.) are taken from the Forest Service planning map (fig. 5-2).

[4] Fire in wilderness is a policy issue that has undergone considerable change in the past decade. At the time of the San Raphael proposal, most wilderness managers considered fire as something to be controlled in wilderness to prevent the loss of scenic or recreational resources. As Heinselman discusses in detail in Chapter 12, however, fire is being increasingly recognized as a natural and significant part of the wilderness landscape in the plans of the wilderness management agencies. Nevertheless, fire is a major concern in many California areas because of its intensity and its potential impact on adjacent nonwilderness lands.

AREAS CONSIDERED IN REACHING BOUNDARY CONCLUSIONS

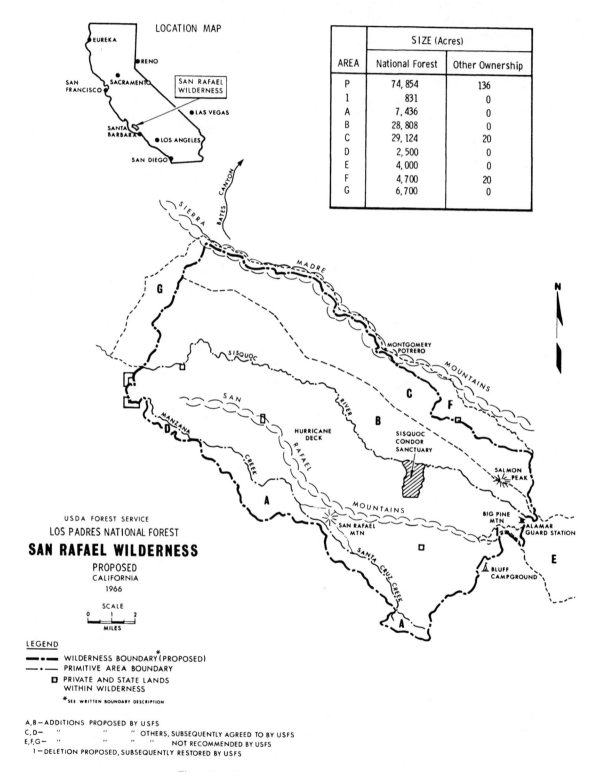

AREA	SIZE (Acres)	
	National Forest	Other Ownership
P	74,854	136
1	831	0
A	7,436	0
B	28,808	0
C	29,124	20
D	2,500	0
E	4,000	0
F	4,700	20
G	6,700	0

USDA FOREST SERVICE
LOS PADRES NATIONAL FOREST

SAN RAFAEL WILDERNESS

PROPOSED
CALIFORNIA
1966

SCALE
0   1   2
MILES

LEGEND
━━━ ▪ ━ ▪ WILDERNESS BOUNDARY (PROPOSED)*
━━ ▪ ━━ PRIMITIVE AREA BOUNDARY
▫ PRIVATE AND STATE LANDS
WITHIN WILDERNESS
*SEE WRITTEN BOUNDARY DESCRIPTION

A,B — ADDITIONS PROPOSED BY USFS
C,D —   "   "   " OTHERS, SUBSEQUENTLY AGREED TO BY USFS
E,F,G —   "   "   "   " NOT RECOMMENDED BY USFS
1 — DELETION PROPOSED, SUBSEQUENTLY RESTORED BY USFS

Figure 5-2.—Proposed San Rafael Wilderness boundaries.

98

made to return the question to conference committee. Those favoring recommittal argued that Congress, not the Forest Service, should be determining what areas were classified as wilderness. They supported their argument with reports of recent developments in the area. Plans for intensive recreational development and road construction had been dropped, they contended. Moreover, because fire danger was diminished it was no longer necessary to retain unit F as a nonwilderness fire control base.

Opponents to recommittal included Congressmen from the Forest Service district in which the San Raphael was located. They contended that fire was still a serious problem requiring firebreaks and roads. Opponents also denied that the Forest Service was usurping a Congressional responsibility (determining what areas should be wilderness). They pointed out that Congress was in fact debating the issue. In no way, they argued, had the executive branch taken away the responsibilities of the legislative branch, which retained final authority to classify or not classify the area as wilderness. On a roll call vote, the motion to recommit the conference report was defeated.

In a special White House ceremony in March 1968, President Johnson signed the San Raphael Wilderness bill into law.[5] It was the first addition to the National Wilderness Preservation System created in 1964. It had passed through the various steps and procedures prescribed by the Wilderness Act and required by Congress: (1) A preliminary agency recommendation, resting on substantial review (including field surveys and a mineral assessment), was revised following citizen review; (2) the revised recommendation was submitted through the Secretary of Agriculture to the President; (3) the President submitted the proposal to Congress, recommending passage; (4) Congressional committees considered several draft bills and held public hearings; (5) when the House and Senate approved different versions of the bill, a joint conference committee studied the differences and recommended the Senate version; (6) following defeat of a House motion to recommit the conference report, the committee-recommended bill passed both Houses; and (7) the President signed the legislation. Over 3 years passed between initial field investigation and final passage.

─────────────

[5] For a more detailed summary of the San Raphael Primitive Area Review, see the wilderness recommendation described in House Document No. 50, 90th Congress, 1st Session, "Communications from the President of the United States on the San Raphael Wilderness Area." 1967.

Classification of Nonreserved National Forest Lands

The procedures for reclassifying Forest Service primitive areas in accord with the Wilderness Act are relatively clear, as are those for Department of the Interior lands. However, one major block of lands potentially available for wilderness classification was not specifically mentioned at all in the Wilderness Act. These were the so-called *de facto* wilderness lands in the National Forest system, areas that are in fact wilderness in the general sense of the term; that is, roadless and undeveloped, but which lack explicit classification as wilderness. Since 1964 the future of these lands and their relationship to the Wilderness Act have been subjects of considerable controversy.

However, during debate on the Wilderness Act, *de facto* wilderness lands in the National Forests received very little attention. The Act's primary intent was not to bring about a major reform of natural resource management but to redefine the way in which wildernesses were allocated and protected. Supporters of the Act wanted Congressional, rather than administrative, protection for wilderness. Consequently, they were primarily concerned with the existing wilderness and primitive area system.

Although the Act itself did not specifically direct the Forest Service to review lands other than those designated as primitive areas, the authors of the Act obviously foresaw the possibility of the Act extending beyond these areas. For example, Section 3(b) states that "nothing contained herein shall limit the President in proposing, as part of his recommendations to Congress, the alteration of existing boundaries of primitive areas or recommending the addition of any contiguous area of National Forest lands predominantly of wilderness value." Consequently, it was the judgment of the agency that the Act did not *prevent* a review of existing roadless lands. Accordingly, the team of field personnel convened in 1964 to draft guidelines for the agency's wilderness management (see footnote 1) called for forest supervisors to "review each National Forest and identify, but not formally designate in any way, all potential new wilderness . . . by December 1966."

The Regional Foresters and the Chief of the Forest Service accepted the team's recommendation but allowed more time—until June 1970—for completion of the inventory. In 1969, when the review of existing primitive areas proved to be more time-consuming than expected, the deadline for identifying potential new wilderness was again extended, until June 1972.

The agency's decision to review *de facto* wilderness lands, in addition to lands specifically designated in the Wilderness Act, represented both the judgment of agency personnel that the Act did not *prevent* such a review and their recognition that conservationists would soon be demanding classification of additional wilderness lands not specified in the Act. This Forest Service-conservationist interpretation of the Wilderness Act's elasticity is shared by others including Howard Zahniser, one of the principal architects of the Wilderness Act. Although Zahniser wanted to give stability and permanence to the wilderness allocation process, neither he nor his colleagues regarded the Act's passage as ending the growth of the National Wilderness Preservation System.

Opponents of wilderness classification of nonclassified lands (e.g., Keane 1971) have argued a strict constructionist interpretation of the Wilderness Act. In their view, Congress did not intend that the Wilderness Act apply to any other lands than those specifically designated at the time the Act was passed. Therefore, wilderness classification should be limited to the wilderness, wild, canoe, and primitive areas on the National Forests and roadless units of the National Park, National Wildlife, and Game Range system. Citing testimony given during debate over the Act, they argued that Congress intended that the Wilderness Act apply only to those lands already classified. Senator Hart of Michigan, for example, noted ". . . this bill does not extend the wilderness classification to one additional acre of land that is not wilderness at the present time and is not already protected from commercial use" (cited in Keane 1971). Zahniser himself noted, "There is indeed not a single area included in the proposed protection of this measure that is now available for logging" (Zahniser 1958). Thus, to extend the Act to nonclassified areas, Keane argues, is to contradict not only Congressional intent but also the expressed intention of the Act's principal author.

However, it is our judgment that the opponents' arguments misread the intent of Congress. As we have already noted, the intent of the legislation was, in effect, to redefine the rules of the game, giving Congress, rather than administrative agencies, the right to classify wilderness. The Wilderness Act as passed applied only to designated areas, but nothing in the Act or in the extensive debate preceding its passage disclaimed the right of Congress to classify additional areas *in the future*. The applicability of the Act to nonclassified lands was demonstrated in the case of Parker vs. United States. Here, the U.S. District Court in Colorado ordered an indefinite halt to a proposed timber sale in the

nonclassified East Meadow Creek drainage, contiguous to the Gore Range-Eagles Nest Primitive Area. The judge ruled there was sufficient evidence of the area's wilderness character to require that the decision to classify or not classify the area as wilderness must remain open through the Presidential level (Foote 1973). Furthermore, the recent addition of nonmandated lands, such as the Scapegoat Wilderness in Montana clearly establish the applicability of the Act to these lands.

However, the East Meadow Creek suit did not actually extend the promise of wilderness classification to lands not covered by the Act. The land in question was nonclassified all right, but it was also contiguous to an existing primitive area. The Wilderness Act clearly included such lands within its provisions; that is, "nothing . . . shall limit the President . . . recommending the addition of any contiguous area of the National Forest lands predominantly of wilderness value (Section 3(b) of the Wilderness Act). The status of lands predominantly of wilderness value but noncontiguous to an existing primitive area was not resolved in the East Meadow Creek decision. It remained for the wilderness values of these lands to be protected in another way which will be discussed later.

Forest Service Criteria for the Evaluation of Potential Wilderness Additions

Three criteria were formulated to guide Forest Service managers faced with the task of identifying potential additions to the wilderness system. It is important to note that the Forest Service manual carefully pointed out that there was no formula for reaching these important decisions, but that the objective in each case was to determine the predominant public value within the meaning of the Multiple Use-Sustained Yield Act of 1960:

> with consideration being given to the relative values of the various resources, and not necessarily the combination of uses that will give the greatest dollar return or the greatest unit output.

The broad authority and responsibility of the Multiple Use Act, then, was used to buttress the Forest Service manual direction for wilderness studies. Three criteria were specified by the manual: (1) Suitability, (2) availability, and (3) need.

Suitability

The first criterion, suitability, indicated the area must meet the minimum conditions set forth in the definition of wilderness in the Act. It repeated the definition included in section 2(c) of the Wilderness Act. The Forest Service Manual also specified characteristics (not specifically mentioned by the Wilderness Act) that enhanced the opportunity for wilderness-dependent experiences:

1. *Land use factors.*—The area should be free of present or foreseeable nonconforming uses or activities that might damage the resource.

2. *Environment.*—The area should possess a wide range of subjective values, such as the potential for helping man discover freedom and spiritual renewal.

3. *Challenge.*—The area should possess outstanding opportunities for users to experience challenge, excitement, and self-reliance.

4. *Primitive recreation.*—The area should offer a variety of opportunities for primitive and unconfined types of recreation such as camping, ski touring, and hiking.

5. *Wildlife.*—The area should include abundant and varied wildlife.

6. *Scientific study.*—The area should possess opportunities for formal and informal education and scientific study.

Availability

The second criterion, availability, specified that wilderness designation must represent the highest and best use of the land over a long period of time. The tangible and intangible values of the wilderness resource had to offset the potential value of all resources that would be rendered inaccessible or unavailable if formal wilderness designation occurred. The availability measure, then, constituted an estimation of the opportunity costs incurred through wilderness classification; i.e., the total economic and noneconomic values that would be foregone by wilderness designation. These would include the value of the timber and minerals in an area, the economic value of nonwilderness recreation that is not developed, and the costs of administration of the area as wilderness.

Need

The third criterion, need, indicated that the requirement for wilderness must be measured and compared to that for other resources. It required clear evidence of current and future public need for additional, formally designated wilderness.[6]

---

[6]Need is a complex term and is often used in a simplistic fashion in recreation planning. *Need* can range from those qualities prerequisite to maintaining life (food, shelter) to those that enrich the quality of life (open space, cultural facilities). As used in the Forest Service Manual, need is closely related to demand. An interesting discussion on need is David Mercer's "The Concept of Recreational 'Need'," *Journal of Leisure Research* 5(1):37-50, Winter 1973.

Four assumptions underlay the need criterion:

1. Use of designated wilderness will increase with both an increasing population and a growing awareness and appreciation of wilderness values.

2. Undeveloped, nonclassified lands will diminish in availability, as pressures for other resource uses increase.

3. Some recreation use in wilderness is not dependent upon wilderness for its enjoyment.

4. Within limits, management can increase the capacity of wilderness without unacceptable depreciation of the resource.

Need was to be determined through a consideration of the location, size, type, and capacity of other wildernesses in the general vicinity, by local and national patterns and trends in wilderness use, and by the extent to which nonwilderness lands were available to provide dispersed recreation opportunities not necessarily linked to wilderness.

The Inventory of National Forest Roadless Areas

Many undeveloped and nonroaded lands in the National Forests held considerable wilderness potential. Agency personnel had recognized the potential value of an inventory and assessment of these areas. The question was: How to go about conducting such an inventory and assessment? One alternative was to rely upon the normal land-use planning process the agency utilized. As each roadless tract came up before the planning team, it would be studied for its various management potentials, including wilderness. However, some officials were concerned that this approach would stretch out the final disposition of the roadless areas over a long period of time. Lengthy delays could mean that roadless lands could be developed in unplanned and, possibly, undesirable ways. Moreover, the procedure of planning each roadless tract individually, carried out over a long time, could promote a polarization between preservationists, who would seek wilderness designation for each tract, and the agency, which would consider a range of management alternatives for these lands.

The Forest Service was experienced in confrontations with citizen groups. In the late 1950's, a group of citizens in Montana had begun agitating for protection of a ¼-million-acre tract known as the Lincoln Backcountry, contiguous to the southern boundary of the Bob Marshall Wilderness. Nevertheless, in the early 1960's the Forest Service proposed a development plan for the area that offered protection from roads and logging to only 26,000 acres—about one-tenth of the area. The plan was challenged by local citizens who requested a 10-year moratorium on the Forest Service plan. However, the moratorium was denied and, as a consequence, a citizen's conservation group began pressing for wilderness designation.

Conservationist-sponsored legislation requesting wilderness classification was introduced into both houses of Congress in 1964. The draft submitted to the Senate called for 75,000 acres; the House bill for 240,500 acres. Forest Service officials argued that wilderness classification was not appropriate for two reasons: The review process prescribed by Congress had not been followed and the necessary mineral studies had not been made. On the latter point, the agency was supported by Representative Wayne Aspinall of Colorado, Chairman of the House Interior and Insular Affairs Committee, who refused to permit consideration of the bill until mineral surveys in the area were completed. Moreover, he argued that the U.S. Geological Survey and Bureau of Mines had a prior responsibility to survey the primitive areas, a process that would occupy 10 years.

Citizen pressure on Congress finally loosened special funds for a mineral study of the area in 1970, a study which failed to reveal any appreciable mineral deposits. Finally, in August 1972, President Nixon signed a bill establishing the 240,000-acre Scapegoat Wilderness (named after Scapegoat Mountain in the middle of the area) the first de facto area to be classified after passage of the 1964 Act.

The debate, a long and costly one, appeared to set the stage for a series of potentially exhausting confrontations between citizen groups and the Forest Service. Millions of acres of Federal land (more than 200 times the acreage involved in the Montana quarrel) mirrored the wilderness potential of the Lincoln Backcountry. Thus, it seemed imperative to conduct a survey of National Forest roadless tracts as soon as possible while, at the same time, trying to resolve some major allocation issues. Such a survey, it was hoped, would serve as a first approximation of which roadless lands deserved careful, detailed study as to their potential for wilderness designation and which lands appeared to be more suited for alternative management. Beyond this, if a concensus regarding this division of land could be reached in relatively short time, the impending confrontations, presaged by the Lincoln Backcountry conflict, might be avoided.

Following the directions in the Forest Service manual, the inventory of roadless areas was begun in 1967. To be included in the inventory an area had to have (1) an absence of roads or other development and (2) a size of at least 5,000 acres if it did not adjoin existing wilderness or primitive areas. Smaller, undeveloped contiguous areas were also to be inventoried. (The inventory did not include the remaining primitive areas which were being separately evaluated for wilderness classification (USDA FS 1973)).

A total of 1,449 areas, containing about 56 million acres, was included in the Forest Service survey of roadless areas. The results of this inventory are shown in table 5–1.

After the inventory was completed, Regional Foresters were instructed to recommend by June 30, 1972, areas under their jurisdiction that should be considered for wilderness classification. Their judgments were to be based on the criteria of suitability, availability, and need, as well as extensive public review. The Chief planned to use their recommendations, in combination with other data, to compile a list of new study areas.

Along with the inventory of roadless areas, the Chief also requested that extensive data be compiled on each

Table 5–1.—*Summary of the Forest Service Roadless Area Inventory*[1]

Region	Number of areas	Gross acres	Commercial forest land acres	Annual allowable timber harvest
		- - - - Thousands - - - -		MM BF
Northern	283	7,612	4,768	457
Rocky Mountain	248	5,757	2,474	134
Southwestern	89	1,430	189	8
Intermountain	433	11,942	3,805	182
California	131	3,098	716	209
Pacific Northwest	255	5,592	3,169	699
Southern	2	37	23	<1
Eastern	0	0	0	0
Alaska	7	20,698	3,712	586
Puerto Rico	1	8	<1	0
Total	1,449	56,174	18,856	2,275

[1] From: Roadless and Undeveloped Areas—Final Environmental Statement. U.S. Department of Agriculture, Forest Service, 1973. p. 16.

area's characteristics and resources. To evaluate this enormous quantity of data along with the recommendations submitted by the Regional Foresters, the Chief assembled an interdisciplinary team. The procedure developed and used by the team, called the Roadless Area Review and Evaluation (RARE), became the principal analytical tool used to select the new study areas.

The RARE Process

Following are the principal objectives of the RARE selection process:

1. To obtain as much wilderness value as possible relative to the cost and value of the foregone opportunities to produce other goods and services for society.

2. To disperse the future wilderness system as widely as possible over the United States.

3. To represent as many ecosystems as possible so that the scientific and educational purposes of wilderness preservation are best served.

4. To obtain the most wilderness value with the least relative impact on the Nation's timber product output.

5. To locate some new wilderness areas closer to densely populated areas so that more people can directly enjoy their benefits.

There is a certain amount of conflict and overlap among these objectives, perhaps reflecting the public's diverse and mutually exclusive wants. Objectives 1 and 4 touch on the efficiency of allocation. But number 4 embodies a built-in contradiction. It simultaneously seeks two goals (maximizing wilderness values and minimizing impact on timber output) which are, if not mutually exclusive, at least inversely interdependent. Objectives 2 and 5 are statements of social goals, but 2 is largely unattainable. Wilderness is where we find it; there is no way we can distribute it spatially any more than we can equitably rearrange the Nation's iron ore reserves. Objective 3 recognizes the important scientific values of wilderness (Milton 1973).

To evaluate underdeveloped areas using the RARE technique, a number of quantitative and judgmental measures were obtained for each area. They included the following:

1. The total gross acres of roadless area. Size of area was judged to be an approximate indicator of carrying capacity.[7]

2. A quality index. Field personnel rated each area on three factors, using a 0 to 20 scale. The factors included:

---

[7] Although there is probably some gross relationship between size and capacity, many other factors enter into determining the carrying capacity of a wilderness. Topography, vegetative cover, and length-of-use season are examples of variables that affect the capacity calculations for an area (Stankey et al. 1976).

(1) Scenic quality (S), (2) isolation and likely dispersion of visitors within an area (I), and (3) variety of wilderness experiences and activities available (V). Each of these factors was weighted and used to calculate the quality index (QI) by the following formula:

$$QI = 4(S) + 3(I) + 3(V)$$

The maximum possible score on the QI equaled 200.

3. An effectiveness index. To derive this measurement, total gross acres were multiplied by the quality index.

4. Total opportunity costs. This index was composed of the sum of the following:

1. Budget costs for studies, establishment, operation, and maintenance.
2. Cost, if any, of acquiring private land.
3. Cost of replacing special-use improvements.
4. Mineral values.
5. Potential water development values.
6. Timber values.

Each roadless area was reviewed by the Chief and his staff in light of the data obtained from the preceding measurements. Roadless areas recommended for wilderness classification by Regional Foresters were given special attention. Following this analysis, all roadless areas were given one of two designations: Most desirable (high priority areas) and less desirable (low priority areas). Most desirable areas had at least one of the following characteristics:

1. Prior selection for New Study Area status. Four New Study Areas in Alaska had already been selected by the Chief. Four noncontiguous areas (and several adjacent ones) in Washington had been designated for wilderness review by the North Cascade Study Team (USDI–USDA 1965). Congress had already designated certain other areas for complete wilderness review. In addition, 47 roadless areas contiguous to the 11 primitive areas under review had been, or were being, studied in connection with the primitive area review.

2. Recommendation by Regional Foresters and having:

   a. General public support, or
   b. Quality indices greater than 155 (the top 25 percent of the QI's among all recommended areas), or
   c. A location contiguous to an established wilderness or a reviewed primitive area.

3. Ecosystems or subtypes that are relatively uncommon in the National Forest System (redwood, shinnery, Texas savanna, wet grasslands, annual

103

grasslands, Hawaiian grassland, tundra, muskeg, heath, Aleutian meadows, and desert).

4. Location in the East (Forest Service Regions 8 and 9) and Puerto Rico, both areas of low supply and high demand.

5. Unique features that make them highly desirable for study, e.g., habitat for rare or endangered species that depend on wilderness or other special factors.

To these areas located by the RARE method, the Chief added certain areas based on public response to the RARE-selected lands and on recommendations from Regional Foresters who had conducted the inventories. The result? The high priority areas gained 31 new members. And the Chief's initial proposal (his draft EIS of January 1973) called for the designation of 235 new areas covering 11 million acres (about one-fifth of the acreage inventoried) as new study areas—areas to receive early consideration for inclusion in the National Wilderness Preservation System (USDA FS 1973). Until the studies were completed, no management programs could be undertaken which would alter their undeveloped state.

Over 7,000 letters and documents were received in response to the draft EIS. Public involvement played a major role in shaping the changes incorporated in the final EIS.[8] Public input contained both facts and opinions—e.g., suggestions for areas to be added, deleted, expanded in size—relating to the Chief's proposed list. As public and official responses were analyzed, errors in the original data base were corrected and areas receiving particular interest were given special attention.

Following this analysis, 61 new study areas were included and 22 were deleted for a net gain of 39 new areas and a revised total (in the final EIS released in October 1973) of 274 areas and 12.3 million acres, an acreage gain of about 10 percent over the previously selected acreage in the draft EIS. Of this total, 46 areas and 4.4 million acres had already been officially committed for wilderness study prior to the announcement of the Chief's list.

The four principal variables—the ones on which marginal cases were decided and which the Chief and staff repeatedly used in making final decisions—were: (1) Public input, including sentiment of involved citizens and organizations, and the views of legislators and government agencies, (2) potential wilderness quality of the roadless areas as measured by the quality index, (3) cost effectiveness, reflecting the value of other resource uses foregone compared to relative wilderness values,

[8]John C. Hendee. 1974. Public involvement in the U.S.F.S. roadless area review: lessons from a case study. Prepared for Seminar on Public Participation, University of Edinburgh, Scotland.

and (4) an overall judgment factor resting heavily, but not entirely, on the recommendations of local, regional, and national decisionmakers (USDA FS 1973).

Many criticisms have been leveled at the roadless area inventory and particularly at the RARE process (e.g., Wilderness Society 1973; Milton 1975). Only 8 months elapsed between the Chief's initial list of new study areas and the final list. Opportunities for careful field review by both agency personnel and concerned citizens were seriously limited. Many preservationists viewed the compressed timetable as a deliberate attempt to thwart detailed investigations of proposed areas as well as other roadless tracts, thereby limiting the number of areas designated for wilderness study. The Forest Service argued that time was of the essence, that prolonged deliberation would unnecessarily delay orderly development of the National Forests, and that uncertainties over resource development could seriously harm local economies.

Quite apart from the speed of the review, the designation of roadless lands revealed a number of serious deficiencies in the RARE methodology itself. Several criticisms centered on the calculation of the quality index (QI) which was derived from the sum of three weighted scores that were each ranked on a 1 to 20 scale: (1) Scenic quality, (2) isolation and dispersion of use, and (3) variety of experiences available. Each of these components measured the primitive recreation potential rather than the ecological condition of an area, which is a more relevant measure, it seems to us, of wilderness quality.

Not only were the indices of quality one-dimensional, they were also subjective and very difficult to measure. Because no uniform guidelines or training existed for persons measuring the QI, reliability (consistency among different persons scoring the same area) was never clearly established. Judgments about the relative quality of individual areas were largely dependent on the values and perceptions of those performing the calculations.

The effectiveness index (EI) was calculated by multiplying the QI by area size. As a result, the value for the EI was almost wholly a function of size. Moreover, size was also indirectly used in the QI (as a measure of isolation and dispersal potential) and was thus represented twice in the EI.

Size plagued the calculations in other ways. Although size tended to be overemphasized in the calculations of the EI, it was often offset by the way in which roadless tracts were defined. Because the tracts were frequently defined along existing administrative boundaries, the aggregate size of large contiguous blocks of roadless lands that overlapped a number of administrative units (e.g., ranger districts) was diminished in importance because the area was treated as several separate smaller tracts.

The economic evaluation was made by opportunity cost analysis; (the value of opportunities foregone by choosing one mutually exclusive alternative over another). However, many values associated with preservation are nonquantifiable, and limit the applicability of an analytical technique that rests on objective measures of values assumed to be lost or gained.

Moreover, even the objective economic measures used in the analysis have been questioned. For example, the average high bid stumpage price used to calculate the value of timber on roadless lands probably led to overestimates in two ways. First, much of the old-growth timber on these lands is of marginal value, being of either low density, high harvest cost or low commercial value. Second, the average high-bid figure was based on the average of the 3 years, 1969 through 1971, during which timber prices jumped atypically upward, a surge from which they have now declined (Milton 1975).

The omissions and shortcomings of the RARE process are important to note and understand. But it is also important to keep in mind that the RARE process represents the first systematic effort to evaluate National Forest roadless lands for future use and to measure and relate benefits and costs to management alternatives. As far as possible, objectivity and quantification governed the procedure. At a minimum, the inventory and its evaluation clearly defined the realistic limits of the remaining roadless lands, highlighting the need for an increased emphasis on the development of management guidelines and programs for these lands, in addition to the continuing allocation efforts.

What of the remaining areas? The 274 areas selected for study constitute only 19 percent of the total number of areas inventoried and 23 percent of the acreage. In a 1972 lawsuit brought against the Forest Service, the Sierra Club charged that (1) the agency did not follow the appropriate procedures defined by NEPA and that (2) the procedures used in the inventory and selection of new wilderness study areas were inadequate. Later that same year, the Chief of the Forest Service directed Regional Foresters to file an EIS before conducting activities that might alter the wilderness character of *any* roadless area. He added that wilderness *must* be considered one of the viable management alternatives for *any* inventoried roadless area. In light of this action, the court dismissed the first charge in the Sierra Club's suit, ruling that the filing of Environmental Impact Statements would satisfy the requirements of NEPA. The second complaint was also dismissed because the

procedures cited as inadequate were, in fact, not yet completed.

Dismissal of the complaints did not resolve the issue. The complaints were dismissed without prejudice; i.e., the case can come before the court again. This might occur if, for example, local managers fail to follow the Chief's instructions to meaningfully consider wilderness as a management alternative in a roadless area.

Both the Forest Service and the Sierra Club hailed the outcome as a victory. The Forest Service pointed to the Chief's action in requiring an EIS as evidence of proper intent. Preservationists countered that they forced the Chief to undertake an action he would not have initiated without the specter of their lawsuit on his horizon. Regardless of these ongoing arguments, what is important, it seems to us, is that a systematic procedure has been prescribed to guide future management directives of the National Forest roadless areas.

RARE II — Another Look

Concern remains, however, about the amount of time involved before the management direction of the remaining roadless and undeveloped National Forest lands is resolved. Environmentalists, resource development interests, and the Forest Service share this concern. Thus, in mid-1977, Assistant Secretary of Agriculture Cutler announced a program to review again all the roadless, undeveloped lands in the National Forest System along with the data collected earlier on these areas. The purpose of this review—generally referred to as RARE II—is to categorize these undeveloped lands into three types, then to ask Congress for implementing legislation. One category would be those areas which should be immediately designated as wilderness. A second category would be those areas that require additional study before Congress can make a decision about whether wilderness designation is appropriate or not. The final category would be those lands which should be devoted to non-wilderness uses. Such a program would be designed to, at one time, relieve the concerns of environmentalists about the future management direction for much of the country's roadless resource and the uncertainties of the forest-related industries about future timber supplies (Cutler 1977). The review is to take about one year and will include a substantial program of public involvement.

Classification of Department of the Interior Roadless Lands

As noted earlier, the Wilderness Act provided clear descriptions of lands subject to wilderness classification.

Within the National Park System, Wildlife Refuges, and Game Ranges, these areas were all roadless lands in excess of 5,000 acres and all roadless islands. For those areas considered suitable for wilderness designation following agency study, wilderness proposals were to be developed for submission to Congress through the Department of the Interior, the Office of Management and Budget, and the President (see p. 96).

Operating with these guidelines, the Department of the Interior didn't have to decide what lands to consider or how to propose them for wilderness classification. But it *did* have to struggle with the problem of establishing criteria: Among its available candidates, which ones should be recommended as wilderness? On what basis? It was 8 years after the Act passed before official selection guidelines were established in Interior. In the meantime, a beginning had to be made.

Soon after passage of the Act, Interior estimated that 22.5 million acres of National Park System land and 24.1 million acres of Fish and Wildlife Service holdings were subject to becoming study areas—which increased as new units were added to the National Park and Wildlife Refuge Systems. The National Park Service eventually identified for review 63 units covering over 28 million acres while Fish and Wildlife Service identified 113 units and 29 million acres (U.S. Congress 1973).

The reviews themselves were very slow in reaching Congress. Only one area, the Great Swamp National Wildlife Refuge in New Jersey, was submitted and classified during the first 5 years of the Act. The first

Figure 5–3.—Within 10 years, the Secretary of Interior was instructed to review all roadless areas 5,000 acres or larger in the National Park System, to determine their suitability for wilderness. Hidden Valley looking northeast from ridge above Avalanche Lake, Glacier National Park, Mont., is within a roadless area reviewed by the Park Service and recommended to Congress for wilderness classification.

National Park Service areas, Craters of the Moon National Monument in Idaho (43,000 acres) and Petrified Forest National Park in Arizona (50,000 acres), were not added to the NWPS until 8 years after passage of the Act. However, by 1974, the end of the 10-year period, the Park Service had completed review and submitted wilderness proposals on 56 areas. Wilderness studies of NPS units added after the Act's passage were deferred for later study (13 areas as of 1975).

The absence of an explicit allocation procedure explains much of the delay and difficulty encountered by the National Park Service and Fish and Wildlife Service. Traditionally, the Park Service had zoned roadless and undeveloped tracts in the individual Park's Master Plans. For example, much of Yellowstone's 2.2 million acres is *de facto* wilderness which had been zoned roadless by the Park Service in Yellowstone's Master Plan. The problem the Department faced in meeting the obligations of the Wilderness Act was much the same as that faced by the Forest Service in the Roadless Area Review— determining specific boundaries for wilderness study.

In June 1972, Assistant Secretary of the Interior for Fish and Wildlife and Parks, Nathaniel Reed, issued a memo to the Directors of the National Park Service and the Fish and Wildlife Service defining criteria to be followed in determining an area's suitability for wilderness designation. In particular, the memo specified conditions that were sufficient or insufficient to exclude an area from wilderness designation. Among those conditions were the following:

1. Areas should not be excluded from wilderness designation solely because established or proposed management practices require the use of tools, equipment, or structures, if these practices are necessary for the health and safety of wilderness travelers, or the protection of the wilderness area.

2. Areas that otherwise qualify for wilderness will not be excluded because they contain unimproved roads created by vehicles repeatedly traveling over the same course, structures, installations, or utility lines, which can be and would be removed upon designation as wilderness.

3. Areas which presently qualify for wilderness designation but which will be needed at some future date for specific purposes consistent with the purpose for which the National Park or National Wildlife Refuge was originally created, and fully described in an approved conceptual plan, should not be proposed for wilderness designation.

These and other guidelines emerged as the basic allocation principles governing Department of the Interior recommendations. However, Interior officials and conservationists continue to disagree over official guidelines. For instance, the Wilderness Society (1974–75) argues that Interior's classification guidelines confuse the stringent management criteria in Section 4 of the Wilderness Act with the flexible entry criteria in Section 2. As a result, they argue, Interior officials interpret wilderness classification as a decision to cease virtually all management activity unless specific authorization is given in the wilderness legislation for an area. Based upon this interpretation, wilderness designation would be rejected in many areas because it would end management activities needed to accomplish objectives of the legislation originally establishing the Park or Refuge. The Wilderness Society suggests that a management activity need meet only a minimum necessity test (administrators need demonstrate only that a management activity is the minimum necessary for proper administration of the area both for the purposes for which the Park or Refuge was originally established and as wilderness). If the activity meets this test, it does not constitute a sufficient reason to disqualify an area for classification as wilderness.

The Department of the Interior also recognizes what are called potential wilderness additions. This was originally conceived of as a designation for areas where clearly nonconforming uses were present (e.g., structures), but which would clearly qualify for wilderness designation once the nonconforming use was removed. In omnibus legislation passed in late 1976, eight National Park units, containing 53,506 acres were identified as potential wilderness additions. Most of these areas were so labeled because of grazing and it is not altogether clear why they could not have been included in the wilderness because grazing is allowed in wilderness when it is a preexisting right. However, under this designation, the Secretary of the Interior will have authority to establish them as formal wilderness at such times as the nonconforming use ceases.

The relationship between the original legislation establishing a Park or Refuge and subsequent wilderness designation within these areas has also created problems, particularly on National Wildlife Refuges and Game Ranges. Many of the proposals submitted by the Fish and Wildlife Service following review of their roadless areas recommend against wilderness designation. For example, only about 29,000 acres of the 40,000-acre Red Rock Lakes National Wildlife Refuge in Montana was recommended for wilderness (USDI FWS n.d.). The remaining 11,000 acres were judged not suitable because of existing and planned developments to manage waterfowl, especially the trumpeter swan. Field studies of the 45,000-acre Laguna Atascosa National Wildlife

Refuge in Texas revealed that, although a portion of the area did qualify as wilderness, such designation would conflict with the primary objective of the Refuge, which is to provide habitat for waterfowl. Wilderness designation was not recommended (USDI FWS 1970). Congress concurred in substance with both recommendations, designating 32,350 acres of the Red Rocks Refuge as wilderness and concurring with the Fish and Wildlife Service recommendation against designation at Laguna Atascosa.

These examples of agency reluctance to recommend wilderness illustrate a recurring conflict between the goals of different legislative enactments. In chapter 11, we discuss the difficulty of reconciling wilderness management needs with the need for facilities and improvements required to fulfill wildlife management objectives of the original legislation establishing the Refuge or Game Range.

Conflicts between legislative objectives exist despite the declaration in Section 4(a) of the Wilderness Act that wilderness designation is "within and supplemental to" the purposes for which National Forests, National Parks, Wildlife Refuges, and Game Ranges were established. Where a legitimate conflict exists between the goals of wilderness and those of the basic enabling legislation, the organic legislation is apparently predominant. For example, where wilderness classification might restrict necessary wildlife management practices on a Game Range, wilderness designation is either limited, rejected, or made with special recognition of the intrusion.

Olympic National Park Wilderness Review—A Case Study

A summary of the wilderness study in Olympic National Park will help illustrate the review procedure prescribed by the Wilderness Act for roadless areas 5,000 acres or larger in the National Parks, Wildlife Refuges, and Game Ranges.

It has been the policy of the National Park Service to prepare a General Management Plan (formerly called Master Plan) for each area of the National Park System to provide the framework for its overall management, public use, and physical development. To help determine future use, a land classification plan based upon area resources is included in the master plan.

In classifying land, the National Park Service uses the six land classes developed by the Outdoor Recreation Resources Review Commission. These six classes, modified for applicability to the National Park System, include: Class I—High-density recreation areas, Class II—General recreation areas, Class III—Natural envir-

onment areas, Class IV—Outstanding natural areas, Class V—Primitive areas, and Class VI—Historic and cultural areas. Roadless areas within a Park (typically Class V Primitive Areas, but sometimes Class III, IV, and VI lands) have usually been managed and preserved in a roadless, natural condition prior to review and proposal for classification as wilderness. Because of the close relationship between National Park General Management Plans and wilderness areas within a Park, the review of Park lands to develop a recommendation for wilderness designation has usually been carried out in conjunction with a major public review and updating of the Park General Management Plan. Such was the case in Olympic National Park. Along with the review and updating of the Park General Management Plan, roadless portions of the 870,200-acre Park were formally reviewed in a wilderness study. The chain of events leading to a wilderness recommendation for Olympic National Park proceeded as follows.

During 1972 and early 1973, with the help of a National Park Service master planning team comprised of members from the local Park staff, the Regional Office, and the Planning Division in the National Park Service Denver Service Center, the draft of a new Master Plan and preliminary wilderness proposal were prepared for Olympic National Park. The initial proposal called for 93 percent of the Park to be classified as wilderness. The park contained four roadless units 5,000 acres or larger, and most of the acreage in three of them was proposed for wilderness classification. One unit included the majority of the Park (816,650 acres); the other two units were elongated strips of land along the Pacific Ocean comprised of 13,160 and 5,080 acres respectively. A fourth unit, the 26,800-acre Mt. Angeles Roadless Area, was not proposed for wilderness classification in order to retain long-range options for alternate access development. Also excluded from the preliminary proposal were two 20-acre enclaves in the roadless interior intended for permanent hostels furnishing both food and lodging to future visitors.

In August 1973 this preliminary proposal (along with the new Master Plan and accompanying draft Environmental Impact Statements) was released to other agencies and the public. Public meetings on the General Management Plan and wilderness proposal held in October and November were attended by 500 people. Altogether, nearly 6,000 agencies, persons, and organizations responded to the National Park Service's preliminary wilderness proposal. From November 1973 through early spring 1974, the National Park Service analyzed and evaluated their responses and prepared both a final wilderness recommendation and an altered General Management Plan.

The final wilderness recommendation eliminated the small areas intended for hostels and recommended the addition not only of these two enclaves but also of most of the Mt. Angeles unit for wilderness classification. With other minor additions and exclusions as a result of boundary adjustments, the final wilderness recommendation included 862,139 acres, about 96 percent of the Park.

The final wilderness recommendation for Olympic National Park was submitted by the Regional Office to the Washington Office in June 1974 and was rapidly transmitted from the National Park Service to the Department of the Interior and the Office of Management and Budget. Later that same month, a recommendation for wilderness classification of the four units in Olympic National Park, along with 15 other Parks and Wildlife Refuges, was included in a White House message to Congress. Early in 1975, Senate Bill 1091 called for designation of an Olympic National Park Wilderness identical to that proposed in the National Park Service recommendation. About the same time, a bill calling for designation of a slightly larger wilderness (HB 5823) was introduced in the House. These bills, and perhaps others, will be the subject of hearings before both House and Senate Interior and Insular Affairs Committees. When reported from committee, the bills will be debated and perhaps amended on the floor of Congress or recommitted prior to passage of legislation classifying any of the roadless areas within Olympic National Park as wilderness.[9]

Alaska—A Special Case?

It is ironic that Alaska, composed of 90 percent *de facto* wilderness and the epitome of the last frontier, contains only about 75,000 acres of classified wilderness. This vast area (375 million acres) is worth special attention if only because it appears to be a cornucopia of natural resources including wilderness. It's also a study in special problems related to the disposition of public lands to Alaskan natives, the State, and Federal land management agencies. And, of course, construction of the Alaskan oil pipeline complicates the problems of land and resource allocation and management.

In 1958, the Alaska Statehood Act permitted the State to select 103 million acres (more than a quarter of the State's total of 375 million acres) from the public domain.

The Alaska Native Claims Settlement Act, signed in 1971, authorized the passage of another 40 million acres (more than a tenth of the State's total) to the ownership of native villages or newly formed native corporations. Each Alaskan village is permitted to withdraw 23,040 acres (36 square miles). In addition, each of the 12 native corporations is allowed to withdraw an amount of land prescribed by formula in the law. The Native Claims Act defines the procedure for protecting these areas. The bulk of the remaining lands, some 230 million acres (about two-thirds of the total State) will remain under Federal jurisdiction. The Secretary of the Interior is authorized to set aside up to 80 million acres for additions to the National Park, Wildlife Refuge, Forest, and Wild and Scenic River systems. He is also authorized to set aside other unreserved and unappropriated public lands for study and classification to protect the public interest in such lands.

In 1973, the Secretary of the Interior announced his recommendations and submitted proposed legislation to Congress. Included were 18.8 million acres in new National Forests, 32.3 million acres in new National Parks, and 31.6 million acres in new National Wildlife Refuges. In addition, 20 new units in the National Wild and Scenic River System were recommended (USDA FS 1974b).[10]

Several other proposals for the disposition of Alaskan public lands have been made. Bills currently before Congress would designate varying amounts of land for National Park, National Forest, and Fish and Wildlife management. For example, the National Interest Lands Reservations Act, introduced by Congressman Udall (Arizona) and Senator Jackson (Washington) would place 47.8 million acres in the National Park System, 43.2 million acres in the National Wildlife Refuge System, and 1.6 million acres in the National Forest System. In addition, 1.6 million acres would be proposed for the Wild and Scenic River System and 11.9 million acres would be jointly managed as ecological reserves by the National Park Service and Fish and Wildlife Service.

Pending Congressional action on these proposals, it is difficult to predict how much land might eventually receive wilderness designation. The Secretary's recommendations do not discuss wilderness classification; it is the responsibility of the respective agencies to conduct wilderness studies on their new holdings.

However, almost 30 million acres of National Park and National Wildlife and Game Range lands in Alaska were mandated for wilderness review under the

---

[9] For a more detailed summary of the Olympic National Park Wilderness proposal, see Final Environmental Impact Statement for Proposed Olympic Wilderness. Olympic National Park, Washington. 164 p. On file, Pacific Northwest Regional Office of the Park Service, Seattle, Wash. 1974.

[10] Although these acreages exceed the 80 million acre figure the Secretary was authorized to set aside, Congress is the final arbiter of what will be established. The Secretary's estimate should be viewed as one set of possible alternatives.

Wilderness Act. The reviews have been delayed for a variety of reasons. Native villages located within existing Wildlife Refuges or Game Ranges are entitled to select up to about 70,000 acres from these areas for native ownership. The Interior Department has held that wilderness reviews should be delayed until such claims are made and settled. The disposition of wilderness areas near potential oil reserves is certain to be surrounded by controversy. Finally, State claims overlap some areas withdrawn by the Secretary of the Interior. The State, claiming priority under the Statehood Act, is suing the Federal Government (Deane 1972).

Debate over wilderness classification in Alaska also centers on the kinds of use many *de facto* areas now receive. Many remote areas are accessible only by airplane. Because of the hostile environment (e.g., inclement weather, bears), permanent cabins have been built on the shores of many backcountry lakes. There are more than 145 in the two Alaskan National Forests alone (Pardo 1970). Under Forest Service interpretation, use of these cabins would be restricted or, if continued, would disqualify such areas from wilderness classification.

Wilderness advocates argue that Alaska is different. The unique qualities of the State, they argue—its size, weather, and wildlife—should exempt the area from standards that might be reasonable in the lower 48.

For our purposes, the Alaskan situation should be viewed in light of the principles discussed in Chapter 7 where we argue that wilderness is part of a broad spectrum of environmental opportunities. We propose, for example, that wilderness management should be governed by a nondegradation principle; that is, establishing facilities or standards to meet local conditions does not constitute a precedent for other areas. If this principle is accepted, certain features (for example, air access and wilderness cabins) will remain peculiar to Alaska and not be endorsed for other wildernesses.

Maintaining local differences within the Alaskan wilderness might also provide one way of practicing the notion of decentralized management. Agency officials in Alaska who believe in this concept will retain the options and flexibility to cope with local conditions. Such decentralization is important in order to assure the local management commitment necessary for the success of wilderness preservation efforts.

Legal Issues in Wilderness Classification

Although the Wilderness Act directly involved only two branches of government, the executive and the legislative, the government's third branch, the judicial, has played a significant role in furthering wilderness preservation. The courts have become involved for a variety of reasons including the reluctance of some public officials to implement the Wilderness Act as well as legitimate differences of opinion over the law's provisions and uncertainty about Congressional intentions.

Legal decisions regarding wilderness have focused primarily on the classification process rather than management issues. However, because allocation is tied to management in a variety of ways, it seems important to discuss briefly some of the more significant judicial decisions.

One of the most significant court cases involved the classification of *de facto* wilderness land. It grew out of a proposed timber sale in the East Meadow Creek Valley in the White River National Forest in Colorado, an unroaded area contiguous to the Gore Range-Eagles Nest Primitive Area. Except for one short section of road, the valley was undeveloped.

Early in 1969, a group of people in Vail, Colo., along with several other individuals and organizations, initiated a lawsuit against the Forest Service and the expected purchaser of the timber, Kaibab Industries. Later that year, a hearing was held on defendants' motion to dismiss the trial. The motion was denied and the judge agreed to hear evidence (Kain 1970).

Before plaintiffs were allowed to bring suit, they had to demonstrate "standing," i.e., that they were "aggrieved" or adversely affected by the agency decision and therefore entitled to challenge the decision. In general, the Supreme Court holds that standing may be based not only on direct economic interests, but on recreational or conservation interests as well (Moorman 1974). While the question of the East Meadow plaintiffs' standing was before the judge, a similar case concerning the Sylvania tract in Michigan affirmed plaintiffs' standing there. This precedent was followed in the East Meadow Creek ruling.

A second hurdle faced by the plaintiffs concerned the doctrine of sovereign immunity. Basically, this doctrine holds that the U.S. Government can be sued only with its consent. It derives from early English law where the King could literally do no wrong (Moorman 1974). However, Congressional statutes make the actions of public officials subject to judicial review. For example, the Administrative Procedures Act permits the overturn of decisions found to be arbitrary, capricious, or abusive of discretion granted by Congress. Although the doctrine of sovereign immunity often shields governmental actions

Figure 5–4.—Nearly 1,500 tracts, 5,000 acres or larger, were inventoried during 1972-74 in a national roadless area review and evaluation (RARE) by the Forest Service; and 274 of the areas were reserved for formal study as to their suitability for wilderness classification. One new study area is the Hoodoo unit in western Montana, a 158,000 acre unit extensively burned in the early 1900's. Now another roadless area review and evaluation (RARE II) is underway.

from citizen review in the courts, judicial decisions are stripping away the armor of sovereign immunity. In the East Meadow Creek case, the defendant (the Forest Service) was denied such protection because the absolute discretion once held by the Secretary of Agriculture over the wilderness classification process (prior to 1964) had been removed by the Wilderness Act. The decision to log East Meadow Creek was seen by the court as evidence of the abuse of the discretion granted to the Secretary by Congress, thus eliminating the protection of sovereign immunity.

The plaintiffs argued their case on two merits. First, they contended that logging in the area would violate the Multiple Use-Sustained Yield Act of 1960 (Harris 1969). Second, and the major concern here, the plaintiffs argued that the Forest Service had failed to give the area adequate consideration as wilderness as required by the Wilderness Act. Section 3(b) of the Act notes:

Nothing contained herein shall limit the President in proposing, as part of his

recommendations to Congress . . . the addition of any contiguous area (to an existing primitive area) of National Forest lands predominantly of wilderness value.

Additionally, Forest Service regulations also required that a wilderness value study be made of *de facto* wilderness lands contiguous to primitive area. Thus, by logging the area (the proposed sale covered 357 acres and 4.3 million board feet), the Forest Service would eliminate the opportunity for the President and the Congress to consider the area as a potential addition to the NWPS and would also violate their own administrative regulations.

In early 1970, the judge handed down his decision. He found for the plaintiffs on all points. The Wilderness Act, he concluded, explicitly required that, for areas of predominantly wilderness value contiguous to a primitive area, "the decision to classify or not classify them as wilderness *must remain open through the Presidential level*" (Kain (1970). Furthermore:

111

Whereas here the contiguous area (East Meadow Creek) is shown by the evidence to have wilderness character, it thwarts the purpose and spirit of the Act to allow the Forest Service to take abortive action which effectively prevents a Presidential or Congressional decision (Kain 1970).

The decision was sustained on appeal. The East Meadow Creek decision (also called the Parker decision, after one of the plaintiffs) clarified a number of legal issues and established important precedents for similar legal tests.

The decision on the East Meadow Creek case was resolved in favor of the plaintiffs because the land was contiguous to an existing primitive area and the responsibility of the Congress and the President in the classification of such lands was clear. Noncontiguous lands, however, are another matter. It has been the judgment of the Forest Service that nothing in the Act prohibits the administrative review of land for possible wilderness classification by Congress. However, as wilderness proposals on noncontiguous undeveloped lands emerge and conflicts between wilderness proponents and opposing interests grow, the legal basis for such classification will receive increased attention.

Summary

This chapter has reviewed the mechanisms used to classify wilderness, a system founded in the Wilderness Act but broadened and clarified by administrative and judicial decisions.

Currently, over 14 million acres have been classified as wilderness. Substantial acreages for addition to the NWPS have been proposed but are still pending Congressional decision. It appears certain that the wilderness classification process will continue for a number of years. In chapter 6, we take a close look at the current and proposed extent of wilderness. Additionally, we consider alternative land use designations for some of the proposed wilderness lands.

Among the co-authors, the author primarily responsible for preparation of this chapter was George H. Stankey.

Literature Cited

Anderson, Frederick R.
   1973. NEPA in the courts—a legal analysis of the National Environmental Policy Act. 324 p. The Johns Hopkins Press (for Resources for the Future), Inc., Baltimore, Md.

Cutler, M. Rupert.
   1968. San Raphael Wilderness signed by President. Living Wilderness 32(101):37–44.

Deane, James G.
   1972. Alaska in transition. Living Wilderness 33(116):25–36.

Foote, Jeffrey P.
   1973. Wilderness—a question of purity. Environ. Law 3(4):255–260.

Harris, Don.
   1969. Conservation and the courts. Sierra Club Bull. 54(9):8–9.

Kain, Peter I.
   1970. The great chicken-little case. Am. For. 76(6):38–40.

Keane, John T.
   1971. The Wilderness Act as Congress intended. Am. For. 77(2):40–43, 61–63.

Lee, Robert.
   1975. The management of human components in the Yosemite National Park ecosystem. [Final report to the Yosemite Institute and the National Park Service.] 134 p. Department of Forestry and Conservation, University of California, Berkeley.

Mercer, David.
   1973. The concept of recreational "need". J. Leisure Res. 5(1):37–50.

Milton, William John, Jr.
   1973. A critique of the methodology of the Forest Service roadless area inventory study. M.F. thesis, University of Montana, Missoula. 49 p.

Milton, William J., Jr.
   1975. National Forest roadless and undeveloped areas: develop or preserve? Land Econ. 51(2):139–143.

Moorman, James W.
   1974. Bureaucracy and the law. Sierra Club Bull. 59(9):7–10, 39.

Pardo, Richard.
   1970. The confrontation. Am. For. 76(9):32–35, 52–56.

Stankey, George H., Robert C. Lucas, and David W. Lime.
   1976. Crowding in parks and wilderness. Design and Environ. 7(3):38–41.

Slusher, Ed, Arnold Snyder, George Williams, and William Worf.
   1964. A discussion draft of suggested objectives, policies, procedures, and regulations. U.S. Department of Agriculture, Washington, D.C.

U.S. Congress.
   1973. 9th Annual Wilderness Report. House Document 93–194. U.S. Government Printing Office, Washington, D.C.

U.S. Department of Agriculture, Forest Service.
   1974a. A proposal—Salmon River Wilderness and Idaho Wilderness. U.S. Dep. Agric., For. Serv., Washington, D.C.

U.S. Department of Agriculture, Forest Service.
   1974b. New National Forests for Alaska. Curr. Inf. Rep. No. 12. 12 p. U.S. Dep. Agric., For. Serv., Washington, D.C.

U.S. Department of Agriculture, Forest Service.
   1973. Final environmental statement: roadless and undeveloped areas. 690 p. U.S. Dep. Agric., For. Serv., Washington, D.C.

U.S. Department of the Interior, and U.S. Department of Agriculture.
   1965. The North Cascades: a report to the Secretary of the Interior

and the Secretary of Agriculture. 190 p. North Cascades Study Team, U.S. Government Printing Office, Washington, D.C.

U.S. Department of the Interior, Fish and Wildlife Service.
1970. Laguna Atascosa Wilderness study area. 12 p. U.S. Dep. Inter., Fish and Wildl. Serv.

U.S. Department of the Interior, Fish and Wildlife Service.
[n.d.] Red Rock Lakes Wilderness proposal. 16 p. U.S. Dep. Inter., Fish and Wildl. Serv.

Wilderness Society.
1973. National wilderness on the line. Living Wilderness 58(3):9, 24.
Wilderness Society.
1974–75. The Wilderness system: a report covering every existing or proposed wilderness. Living Wilderness 38(128):38–47.
Zahniser, Howard.
1958. The case for wilderness preservation legislation. In Soc. Am. For. Proc., p. 105–110. Washington, D.C.

Upon passage of the Wilderness Act, 54 Forest Service areas became "instant wildernesses" in the National Wilderness Preservation System. Thirty-four Forest Service primitive areas were designated for study within 10 years. The North, Middle, and South Sisters comprise the Three Sisters Wilderness in Oregon, one of the original Forest Service "instant" wildernesses.

6 The National Wilderness Preservation System And Related Areas

Introduction

This chapter examines the extent of the National Wilderness Preservation System (NWPS)—how much there is, where it is, and who manages it. We also discuss the early origins and possibilities for growth of the NWPS as well as complementary Federal and State systems.

Wilderness and the Environmental Modification Spectrum

As discussed in chapter 1, it is helpful to think of recreational settings as arrayed along a continuum or spectrum, ranging from the highly developed to the primitive, or as Nash (1973) has labeled it, "from the paved to the primeval." Passage of the Wilderness Act led to creation of an official system of national areas at the primitive end of the spectrum. But protected primeval areas are not limited to those making up the NWPS. Through a series of laws and administrative regulations, other areas also have been preserved and managed because they possess certain unique natural values. For example, rivers designated as "Wild" under the Wild and Scenic Rivers System (P.L. 90-542) are assured protection against dams and other developments along their shorelines. Because these other areas also lie

at the primitive or undeveloped end of the spectrum, it is important to understand their relationship to wilderness, how they complement it, and how they differ.

The National Wilderness Preservation System

In Chapter 4, we discussed the directives of the Wilderness Act with regard to the NWPS. Upon passage of the Act, a core of 54 areas, encompassing 9.1 million acres, all administered by the Forest Service in the U.S. Department of Agriculture, was immediately brought into the system. No Department of the Interior lands were included at the outset.

The Act directed the Secretary of Agriculture to initiate reviews of the 34 primitive areas of the Forest Service (5.4 million acres) in order that recommendations regarding their future management direction be completed within 10 years of the Act's passage. Similarly, the Secretary of the Interior was instructed to review lands of the National Park System and Fish and Wildlife Service, also within 10 years, and make recommendations to Congress regarding their suitability as wilderness. As we discussed in Chapter 5, the Act allows additional undeveloped and unroaded lands to be added to the NWPS. In 1975, the Eastern Wilderness Act provided entry into the NWPS for areas east of the

Table 6-1.—*Location, size, and administration of units of the National Wilderness Preservation System, December 31, 1976*

State	Name	Acres	Administration	State	Name	Acres	Administration
Alabama	Sipsey	12,646	FS	Colorado	Mount Zirkel	72,472	FS
Alaska	Bering Sea	41,113	FWS		West Elk	61,412	FS
	Bogoslof	390	FWS		Rawah	26,674	FS
	Tuxedni	6,402	FWS		La Garita	48,486	FS
	St. Lazaria	62	FWS		Maroon Bells-		
	Hazy Islands	42	FSW		Snowmass	71,060	FS
	Forrester Island	2,630	FWS		Weminuche	400,907	FS
	Chamisso	455	FWS		Flat Tops	235,230	FS
	Simeonof	25,141	FWS		Eagles Nest	133,910	FS
Arizona	Galiuro	55,717	FS		Black Canyon		
	Chiricahua	18,000	FS		of the Gunnison	11,180	NPS
	Sierra Ancha	20,850	FS		Great Sand Dunes	33,450	NPS
	Mazatzal	205,137	FS		Mesa Verde	8,100	NPS
	Superstition	124,117	FS	Florida	Island Bay	20	FWS
	Petrified Forest	50,260	NPS		Passage Key	20	FWS
	Mount Baldy	6,975	FS		Pelican Island	3	FWS
	Pine Mountain	20,061	FS		Cedar Keys	375	FWS
	Sycamore Canyon	47,757	FS		Bradwell Bay	23,432	FS
	Chiricahua (National				Florida Keys	4,740	FWS
	Monument)	9,440	NPS		St. Marks	17,746	FWS
	Saguaro	71,400	NPS		Chassahowitzka	23,360	FWS
Arkansas	Caney Creek	14,344	FS		N. N. "Ding" Darling	2,825	FWS
	Upper Buffalo	9,912	FS		Lake Woodruff	1,146	FWS
	Big Lake	2,600	FWS	Georgia	Okefenokee	343,850	FWS
California	Marble Mountain	213,743	FS		Blackbeard Island	3,000	FWS
	Yolla Bolly-Middle Eel	109,091	FS		Wolf Island	5,126	FWS
	South Warner	68,507	FS	Georgia, South			
	Thousand Lakes	15,695	FS	Carolina and			
	Cucamonga	9,022	FS	North			
	San Gorgonio	34,644	FS	Carolina	Ellicott Rock	3,332	FS
	Hoover	47,915	FS	Georgia and			
	San Jacinto	20,565	FS	Tennessee	Cohutta	33,776	FS
	Caribou	19,080	FS	Hawaii	Haleakala	19,270	NPS
	Minarets	109,483	FS	Idaho	Craters of the Moon	43,243	NPS
	John Muir	484,673	FS		Sawtooth	216,383	FS
	Dome Land	62,206	FS		Hells Canyon	193,840	FS
	Mokelumne	50,400	FS	Idaho and			
	San Rafael	142,722	FS	Montana	Selway-Bitterroot	1,240,618	FS
	San Gabriel	36,137	FS	Illinois	Crab Orchard	4,050	FWS
	·Ventana	95,152	FS	Kentucky	Beaver Creek	4,756	FS
	Desolation	63,469	FS	Louisiana	Breton	5,000	FWS
	Lava Beds	28,460	NPS		Lacassine	3,300	FWS
	Lassen Volcanic	78,982	NPS	Maine	Moosehorn	7,501	FWS
	Farallon	141	FWS				
	Agua Tibia	15,934	FS				
	Emigrant	104,311	FS				
	Joshua Tree	429,690	NPS				
	Pinnacles	12,952	NPS				
	Point Reyes	25,370	NPS				
	Kaiser	22,500	FS				

Table 6–1. (Continued)

State	Name	Acres	Administration
Massachusetts	Monomoy	2,340	FWS
Michigan	Seney	25,150	FWS
	Huron Islands	147	FWS
	Michigan Islands	12	FWS
	Isle Royale	131,880	NPS
Minnesota	Boundary Waters Canoe Area	747,840	FS
	Agassiz	4,000	FWS
	Tamarac	2,138	FWS
Missouri	Mingo	8,000	FWS
	Hercules-Glades	12,315	FS
Montana	Bob Marshall	950,000	FS
	Cabinet Mountains	94,272	FS
	Anaconda-Pintlar	157,803	FS
	Gates of the Mountains	28,562	FS
	Scapegoat	239,295	FS
	Mission Mountains	73,877	FS
	Red Rock Lakes	32,350	FWS
	Medicine Lake	11,366	FWS
	UL Bend	20,890	FWS
Nebraska	Fort Niobrara	4,635	FWS
Nevada	Jarbidge	64,667	FS
New Hampshire	Great Gulf	5,552	FS
	Presidential Range-Dry River	20,000	FS
New Jersey	Great Swamp	3,750	FWS
	Brigantine	6,603	FWS
New Mexico	Gila	429,546	FS
	San Pedro Parks	41,132	FS
	White Mountain	31,221	FS
	Pecos	166,790	FS
	Wheeler Peak	6,027	FS
	Salt Creek	8,500	FWS
	Bosque del Apache	30,850	FWS
	Bandelier	23,267	NPS
North Carolina	Linville Gorge	7,575	FS
	Shining Rock	13,350	FS
	Swanquarter	9,000	FWS

State	Name	Acres	Administration
North Carolina and Tennessee	Joyce Kilmer-Slickrock	14,033	FS
North Dakota	Chase Lake	4,155	FWS
	Lostwood	5,577	FWS
Ohio	West Sister Island	85	FWS
Oklahoma	Wichita Mountains	8,900	FWS
Oregon	Mountain Lakes	23,071	FS
	Eagle Cap	293,476	FS
	Mount Hood	14,160	FS
	Three Sisters	199,902	FS
	Strawberry Mountain	33,003	FS
	Gearhart Mountain	18,709	FS
	Kalmiopsis	76,900	FS
	Diamond Peak	36,637	FS
	Mount Washington	46,116	FS
	Mount Jefferson	100,208	FS
	Three Arch Rocks	17	FWS
	Oregon Islands	21	FWS
South Carolina	Cape Romain	28,000	FWS
South Dakota	Badlands	64,250	NPS
Tennessee	Gee Creek	2,493	FS
Vermont	Bristol Cliffs	4,495	FS
	Lye Brook	12,430	FS
Virginia	James River Face	8,703	FS
	Senandoah	79,019	NPS
Washington	Goat Rocks	82,680	FS
	Mount Adams	32,356	FS
	Glacier Peak	464,258	FS
	Pasayten	505,524	FS
	Washington Islands	179	FWS
	Alpine Lakes	303,508	FS
	San Juan	355	FWS
West Virginia	Dolly Sods	10,215	FS
	Otter Creek	20,000	FS
Wisconsin	Wisconsin Islands	29	FWS
	Rainbow Lake	6,388	FS
Wyoming	Bridger	392,160	FS
	North Absaroka	351,104	FS
	Washakie	686,584	FS
	Teton	557,311	FS
	Fitzpatrick	191,103	FS
Total		14,443,705	

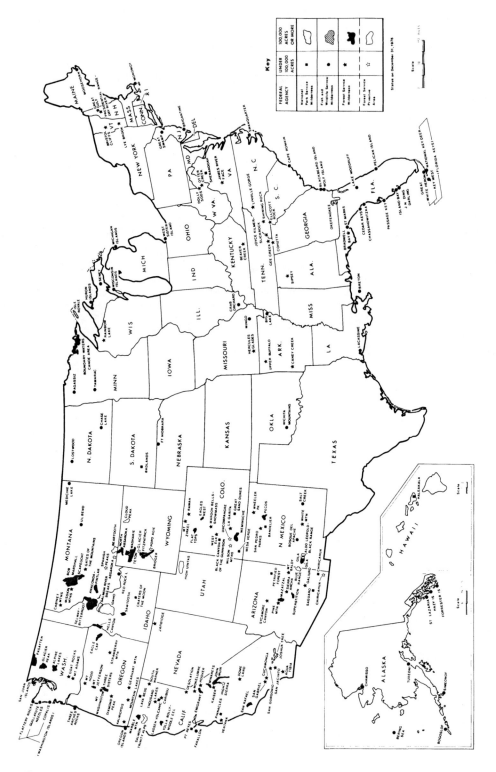

Figure 6-1.—The National Wilderness Preservation System, July 1, 1977.

100th meridian that did not qualify under prevailing interpretation of the Wilderness Act's entry criteria. Finally, in 1976 Congress passed the Federal Land Policy and Management Act giving BLM the responsibility and authority to study and recommend areas for wilderness designation. From all these sources, then, the NWPS is being built.

Where do we stand today? Table 6–1 presents the NWPS at the end of 1976; figure 6–1 shows the national distribution of the system. It contains 161 areas, covering over 14 million acres. The size of the average wilderness is about 90,000 acres. Only 36 areas exceed that figure (but they account for 11.6 million acres or 81 percent of the total acreage), as the large size of a few (e.g., the Selway-Bitterroot Wilderness is 1.2 million acres) inflates the average. Eliminating these few large areas lowers the average size to a more representative 22,400 acres.

The actual growth of the NWPS has been quite slow. In retrospect, it is probably not surprising that little occurred in the period immediately after passage of the Act. During this time, the three Federal agencies were busy establishing procedures for review of potential wilderness lands. While the Forest Service was directed to review their existing primitive areas, the National Park Service and Fish and Wildlife Service were faced with developing criteria and procedures for the review of *all* undeveloped lands over 5,000 acres.

The first additions to the NWPS were made in 1968, 4 years after passage of the Act, when four Forest Service primitive areas, totaling 784,000 acres, were added. In 1969, two more primitive areas, containing about 159,000 acres were added. In 1970, upon urging from the Nixon Administration to hasten the review process, the first omnibus bill was passed. It simultaneously classified 19 wildlife refuge units, 2 National Park Service units, and 1 Forest Service primitive area, a total of nearly 180,000 acres. No units were added in 1971. In 1972, nine additional units totaling 897,000 acres entered the NWPS. Again, in 1973, no additions were made (Haight 1974).

In 1974 (the end of the 10-year review period), 34 areas, totaling nearly 1.3 million acres, were classified. In 1975, one Forest Service primitive area, covering 235,000 acres, was classified and the 194,000-acre Hells Canyon Wilderness was added as part of the legislation creating the Hells Canyon National Recreation Area. Finally, in 1976, 1.9 million acres in 35 units were designated wilderness.

Of the 161 areas classified as wilderness by the end of 1976, 92 were administered by the Forest Service, 52 by the Fish and Wildlife Service, and 17 by the National

Park Service. On an acreage basis, the Forest Service manages 12.6 million acres (87 percent) of the NWPS, the Fish and Wildlife Service, 718,000 acres (5 percent), and the National Park Service 1.1 million acres (8 percent). It is important to remember, of course, that the system is not complete. Many of the areas reviewed by the National Park Service and Fish and Wildlife Service are currently before the Congress and as action is taken, agency representation will even out somewhat.

Wilderness in the National Forest System

As discussed in Chapter 4, the first official Forest Service-wide system of wilderness reservations was created by the L-20 Regulation in 1929, that established primitive areas. Earlier, some areas had been set aside and called "wilderness areas" by the District Foresters (the forerunner of todays Regional Forester); with the L-20 Regulation, however, these were renamed primitive areas (e.g., the Gila Wilderness, informally designated in 1924, became the Gila Primitive Area in 1933).

The L-20 Regulation was in force for 10 years. During this period, the number of acres reserved for wilderness purposes grew rapidly. As figure 6–3 shows, the primitive area system grew from 360,444 acres in 1930 (three areas) to 14.2 million acres in 75 areas in 1939. In 1939, the L-20 Regulation was replaced by the more exacting U-Regulations (see the discussion in Chapter 4), and a gradual process of review and reclassification under the new guidelines was begun. It is interesting to note that between 1939 and 1964 (when the Wilderness

Figure 6–2.—The Fish and Wildlife Service has 36 classified wilderness areas that average about 15,000 acres each. Nearly 30 million acres are to be reviewed by the agency. Pictured is False Pass in Isanotski Strait of the Unimak Island Proposed Wilderness, Aleutian Islands National Wildlife Refuge, Alaska.

Table 6–2.—*Reclassification of Forest Service primitive areas to wilderness, wild, or roadless status, 1939 to 1964*

	Primitive Areas		Wilderness Areas		Wild Areas		Roadless	
	Number	Acres[1]	Number	Acres[1]	Number	Acres[1]	Number	Acres[1]
1939	75	14.2	—	—	—	—	—	—
1944	60	11.3	4	1.4	9	.3	2	.8
1949	58	11.2	4	1.4	12	.5	3	.8
1954	53	9.5	8	2.9	15	.5	3	.8
1959	42	8.2	12	3.9	26	.9	[2]1	.8
1964	34	5.4	54	9.1	[3]		[3]	

[1] Acres in millions.
[2] In 1958, the three Superior Roadless Areas were collectively renamed the Boundary Waters Canoe Area.

[3] Under terms of the Wilderness Act, all areas designated under the U–Regulations were automatically made units of the NWPS and called wilderness.

Act passed), the system of reserved land grew by only 382,000 acres and 13 areas, or less than 3 percent. In fact, it was frustration with this slow rate of growth that many preservationists credit with bringing about a Congressionally designated wilderness system.

Table 6–2 outlines the progress of primitive area reclassification between 1939 and 1964, at 5-year intervals. Under the U–Regulations, three types of areas could be designated: Wilderness areas, defined as areas in excess of 100,000 acres; wild areas, defined as areas between 5,000 and 10,000 acres; and roadless areas, defined as areas managed principally for recreation use and primarily in their natural condition.

In the 25 years between establishment of the U–Regulations and the passage of the Wilderness Act (1939 to 1964), slightly more than half of the primitive areas were reviewed. Typically, areas that met the criteria of the more stringent U–Regulations were reclassified with only a change in name from primitive area to wilderness area. However, some areas were not reclassified because of developments that had taken place under the permissive guidelines afforded by the L–Regulations. For example, the Forest Service established the 1.8-million-acre Selway-Bitterroot Primitive Area in 1936. In 1963, 1.2 million of its acres were redesignated as a wilderness under the U–1 Regulation. Approximately 216,000 acres of the old Selway-Bitterroot Primitive Area were redesignated as the Salmon River Breaks Primitive Area and the remaining 411,000 acres were declassified either because they were not suitable for wilderness or because other resource values exceeded the wilderness values. In addition, the Forest Service noted that the deleted areas had been originally designated under the "less exacting standards for Primitive Areas" (Cunningham and Scott 1969). In other cases, several small primitive areas were consolidated into one large wilderness unit. For example, the present Bob Marshall Wilderness in Montana was established in 1940 from three primitive areas: The South Fork, the Pentagon, and the Sun River.

World War II slowed progress on the reviews considerably. Twelve areas had been studied between 1939 and 1941 (Outdoor Recreation Resources Review Commission 1962b); only five were completed between 1941 and 1949. Progress through the early 1950's was also slow and, as discussed in Chapter 4, concern over this delay in completing classifications served to help establish the National Wilderness Preservation System. When the Wilderness Act finally passed, 34 primitive areas totaling about 5.4 million acres still had not been reviewed.

Since passage of the Wilderness Act, 39 new Forest Service areas have been classified as wilderness. Nineteen of these resulted from review of primitive areas as required by the Act; 16 were designated under the 1975 Eastern Wilderness Act. One other, the Scapegoat Wilderness in Montana, was added in response to prolonged citizen pressure (see Chapter 5).

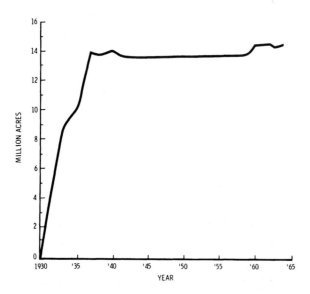

Figure 6–3.—Growth of Forest Service Wilderness, 1930 to 1964.

State	Name	Acres[1]
Arizona and New Mexico	Blue Range	177,239
California	High Sierra	10,247
	Salmon-Trinity Alps	223,980
Colorado	Uncompahgre	53,252
	Wilson Mountains	30,104
Idaho	Idaho	1,224,793
	Salmon River Breaks	216,870
Montana	Absaroka	64,000
	Beartooth	230,000
	Spanish Peaks	63,300
New Mexico	Gila	130,637
	Aldo Leopold-Black Range	188,095
Utah	High Uintas	237,177
Wyoming	Cloud Peak	136,905
	Popo Agie	71,320
Total Acreage		2,057,919

[1] Includes only that in existing primitive areas; does not include any land added or deleted in administrative or citizen wilderness classification proposals.

The remaining three areas were designated by Congress after mandated reviews by the Forest Service.

Presently, the largest designated wilderness in the country is the Selway-Bitterroot, containing 1.2 million acres along the Idaho-Montana border. All but three of the large wildernesses in the NWPS (over 100,000 acres) are under Forest Service administration. However, proposals for some of the National Park Service and Fish and Wildlife Service units will be quite large. For example, two units in Glacier National Park proposed for wilderness encompass 500,000 and 400,000 acres, respectively; a unit in Yellowstone National Park covers nearly 500,000 acres and one suggested for Olympic National Park is over 800,000 acres.

Until passage of the Eastern Wilderness Act in 1975, Forest Service wilderness was almost entirely in the West. Only four areas lay east of the 100th meridian: The Boundary Waters Canoe Area in Minnesota (747,840 acres), the Great Gulf in New Hampshire (5,400 acres), and Linville Gorge (7,655 acres) and Shining Rock (13,400 acres) in North Carolina. Most of the areas added by the Eastern Wilderness Act are small. Total acreage is 207,000 acres, with the average unit about 13,000 acres.

The situation surrounding the remaining primitive areas is a bit complex. Fifteen areas remain for Congressional review (see Table 6-3). In addition, two other primitive areas previously examined (the Glacier

Primitive Area in Wyoming and the Emigrant Basin Primitive Area in Colorado) were recommended and eventually designated as wilderness. The Glacier Primitive Area was redesignated originally as the 197,600-acre Fitzpatrick Wilderness, but in other wilderness legislation passed the same day, approximately 6,000 acres were withdrawn from the wilderness and retained as the Glacier Primitive Area, pending further study by the Secretary of Agriculture. Designation of the Emigrant Wilderness in 1974 similarly left out a portion of the Emigrant Basin Primitive Area for later study.

Wilderness in the National Park System

As of December 31, 1976, 17 areas under National Park Service jurisdiction had been classified as wilderness (see table 6-1). They total 1,120,213 acres. In accordance with the Wilderness Act, the National Park Service has conducted wilderness suitability reviews on nearly 28 million acres. Thirty-three areas, including some of the major wilderness parks (see table 6-4) currently await Congressional attention. The preliminary wilderness proposal for Glacier National Park (USDI 1974) recommends over 900,000 acres in three units, while the preliminary wilderness proposal for Yellowstone (USDI 1971) recommends nearly 2 million acres in 10 units.[1] The National Park Service did not recommend any wilderness classification in three areas—Wupatki National Monument in Arizona, Mammoth Caves National Park in Kentucky, and White Sands National Monument in New Mexico—and conservationists are pressing for wilderness protection for portions of these areas. Additionally, a new wilderness review has been requested for Grand Canyon National Park. The wilderness study in McKinley National Park has been postponed pending completion of the area's general management plan. Finally, eight new National Park wilderness study areas have been designated for review (these areas were included in the National Park System after passage of the Wilderness Act) (see table 6-5). Several of the Park Service units pending wilderness designation are in the East, including Everglades (Florida) and Great Smoky Mountain (Tennessee and North Carolina).

Wilderness in the National Wildlife Refuge System

Currently, the Fish and Wildlife Service administers 52 areas within the NWPS totaling 718,087 acres (see table 6-1). The average size is about 14,000 acres. A

[1] The three units in Glacier National Park contained 503,000-399,000; and 24,000 acres respectively. In Yellowstone, the 10 units ranged from 7,500 acres to 418,000 acres.

Table 6–4.—*National Park System wilderness proposals awaiting Congressional action*

National Park System Unit	State	Proposed Wilderness Acres[1]
Arches National Park	Utah	62,060
Assateague National Seashore[2]	Maryland	6,500
Big Bend National Park	Texas	559,600
Bryce Canyon National Park	Utah	21,520
Canyonlands National Park	Utah	274,810
Capitol Reef National Park	Utah	183,040
Carlsbad Caverns National Park	New Mexico	30,530
Cedar Breaks National Monument	Utah	4,830
Colorado National Monument	Colorado	10,300
Crater Lake National Park	Oregon	122,400
Cumberland Gap National Historic Park	Kentucky, Tennessee, Virginia	13,610
Death Valley National Monument	California	1,914,900
Dinosaur National Monument	Colorado, Utah	175,615
Everglades National Park	Florida	1,378,400
Glacier National Park	Montana	930,910
Glacier Bay National Monument[3]	Alaska	2,210,600
Grand Teton National Park	Wyoming	136,657
Great Smoky Mountains	Tennessee, North Carolina	390,900
Guadalupe Mountains National Park	Texas	46,850
Gulf Islands National Seashore	Florida, Mississippi	4,070
Hawaii Volcanoes National Park	Hawaii	130,950
Katmai National Monument	Alaska	2,603,566
Kings Canyon-Sequoia National Parks	California	790,770
Lake Mead National Recreational Area[4]	Arizona, Nevada	469,300
Mount Rainier National Park	Washington	210,865
North Cascades National Park	Washington	528,158
Olympic National Park	Washington	863,097
Organ Pipe Cactus National Monument	Arizona	309,700
Rocky Mountain National Park	Colorado	240,314
Theodore Roosevelt National Memorial Park	North Dakota	29,095
Yellowstone National Park	Wyoming, Idaho, Montana	2,022,221
Yosemite National Park	California	646,821
Zion National Park	Utah	129,660
Total		[5] 17,452,619

[1] In many areas, the proposed wilderness acreage shown is contained in more than one unit in the park. Roadless units may be separated by roads, developments, or lands where future nonwilderness actions are scheduled.

[2] Of the 6,500-acre total, 5,200 acres are managed by National Park Service and 1,300 acres by Fish and Wildlife Service.

[3] Recommendation has been deferred pending mineral survey.

[4] Recommendation has been deferred pending reclamation study.

[5] Total figure based upon acreage called for in either the preliminary proposal or in the final recommendation, whichever is the most up-to-date figure.

number of areas are quite small. As discussed in chapter 4, the Wilderness Act directed the Secretary of the Interior to review areas in excess of 5,000 acres as well as *all roadless islands*. The latter part of the phrase was specifically directed at the Fish and Wildlife Service which administers many island areas in its refuge system. In fact, among the currently designated areas, 10 are units smaller than 100 acres, and the Fish and Wildlife Service enjoys the distinction of managing the smallest unit in the NWPS—the 3-acre Pelican Island Wilderness in Florida.

The Fish and Wildlife Service has reviewed nearly 30 million acres in 113 units. Recommendations for wilderness include over 7 million acres. Currently, 47 units are before Congress awaiting action (see table 6–6). Of these units, the Fish and Wildlife Service has found 15 areas unsuitable for classification. Whether this

recommendation will prevail will depend on Congress, of course. Additionally, reviews of 17 million acres within five National Wildlife Refuges in Alaska have been

Table 6–5.—*National Park Service units awaiting wilderness review as of December 31, 1976*

National Park System Unit	State	Gross Acreage of Unit
Glen Canyon	Arizona, Utah	1,236,880
Buffalo River	Arkansas	94,196
Big Cypress	Florida	570,000
Canaveral	Florida	67,500
Cumberland Island	Georgia	36,876
Voyageurs	Minnesota	219,128
Cape Lookout	North Carolina	24,732
Big Thicket	Texas	84,550
Total		2,333,862

Table 6-6.—*Fish and Wildlife Service wilderness proposals awaiting Congressional action, December 31, 1976*

Refuge	State	Proposed Wilderness Acreage
		acres
Aleutian Islands	Alaska	1,395,357
Anaho Island	Nevada	747
Bear River	Utah	N.S.[1]
Blackwater	Maryland	N.S.
Bombay Hook	Delaware	2,000
Bowdoin	Montana	N.S.
Cabeza Prieta	Arizona	833,500
Cedar Island	North Carolina	180
Charles M. Russell	Montana	155,288
Charles Sheldon Antelope Range	Nevada	321,400
Crescent Lake	Nebraska	24,502
Chincoteague	Virginia	1,740
Deer Flat	Oregon, Idaho	N.S.
Desert	Nevada	1,443,300
Hart Mountain	Oregon	15,500
Havasu	Arizona, California	2,510
Hawaiian Islands	Hawaii	1,742
Horicon	Wisconsin	N.S.
Imperial	Arizona, California	12,010
Izembek[2]	Alaska	301,451
Kenai	Alaska	829,000
Klamath Forest	Oregon	N.S.
Kofa	Arizona	570,600
Laguna Atascosa	Texas	N.S.
Little Pend Oreille	Washington	N.S.
Malheur	Oregon	30,000
Martin	Maryland	N.S.
Mattamuskeet	North Carolina	590
Mille Lacs	Minnesota	0.6
Missisquoi	Vermont	2,165
National Bison Range	Montana	N.S.
National Elk	Wyoming	N.S.
Noxbuee	Mississippi	1,200
Oregon Islands	Oregon	492
Parker River	Massachusetts	3,110
Pea Island	North Carolina	180
Rice Lake	Minnesota	1,406
Salt Plains	Oklahoma	N.S.
Santee	South Carolina	163
Savannah	Georgia, South Carolina	N.S.
Semidi	Alaska	256,000
Sheldon National Antelope Range	Nevada	20,000
Turnbull	Washington	N.S.
Unimak	Alaska	973,000
Upper Mississippi	Illinois, Iowa, Minnesota, Wisconsin	N.S.
Valentine	Nebraska	16,317
White River	Arkansas	975
Total		7,216,425

[1] N.S.: Recommendation by Fish and Wildlife Service indicates area is not suitable for wilderness designation. Of course, Congress may disagree.

[2] Although a wilderness recommendation has been submitted to Congress, final resolution is pending settlement of the Alaskan Native Claims Settlement Act.

postponed pending settlement of the Alaskan Native Claims Settlement Act (see chapter 5). The five refuges include Arctic, Clarence Rhode, Hazen Bay, Kodiak, and Nunivak.

Future of the National Wilderness Preservation System

One major concern about the future of the NWPS centers on the slow rate at which Congressional review of areas proposed for wilderness has taken place (McCloskey 1972). The Forest Service submitted all its required primitive area proposals to Congress within the specified 10-year review period, as did the National Park Service and the Fish and Wildlife Service. However, many areas are still before Congress awaiting its recommendations.

To speed Congressional review, it seems probable that omnibus legislation, whereby a number of units are classified at one time, will be increasingly used (Haight 1974). Instead of a single bill per area, recent submissions

Figure 6-4.—Although only a few National Park Service areas have been added to the NWPS, many outstanding areas have been studied and proposed to Congress for wilderness classification—such as this area in Mt. Rainier National Park, Wash.

Table 6–7.—*The Wilderness System as of January 1977, wilderness proposals, wilderness study areas designated by Congress and the agencies, and remaining roadless lands that are potential wilderness*

Agency	Total agency jurisdiction	Classified wilderness		Proposals to Congress	Congress-mandated study areas	Administratively established study areas	Remaining roadless areas (potential wilderness)	Total
	Million acres	*Number of areas*	*Million acres*	*Million acres*	*Million acres*	*Million acres*	*Million acres*	
FS	187.6	92	12.6	3.2	1.6	10.9	42.2	70.5
NPS	31.1	17	1.1	14.0	10.6	.3	—	26.0
F&WS	32.1	52	.7	7.2	—	—	13.8	21.7
BLM[1]	450.0	—	—	—	.3	—	89.5	89.8
Total		161	14.4	24.4	12.5	11.2	[2]145.5	208.0

[1] The BLM figures reflect the following: 120-140 million acres, including some of the roadless lands, may be withdrawn or assigned to other agencies under the Alaska Native Claims Adjustment Act. The study areas are BLM primitive and natural areas which total 307,000 acres. Remaining roadless lands are minimum estimates, cited from House Report 94–1163.

[2] Excluding any proposed allocations under the Alaska Native Claims Adjustment Act, these remaining roadless lands include the following agency estimates of acreage in Alaska: USFS, 18.1 million acres; NPS, none; F&WS, 13.6 million acres; BLM, a minimum of 64 million acres. Thus, a total of 95.7 million acres of these roadless lands are in Alaska and 49.8 million acres in the other States.

to Congress by the President have included between 10 and 20 areas each.

A number of observers have made projections of the eventual size of the NWPS. These projections are difficult to compare because some have included Alaska; others have not. Some include the Bureau of Land Management even though that agency was, at the time of the projection, not covered by the Wilderness Act. McCloskey (1966) estimated the NWPS might reach about 48 million acres, but his estimate did not include the BLM. In a later projection, Stankey (1971) forecast that the NWPS could total slightly over 70 million acres, including contributions from BLM and Alaska. However, his effort preceded completion of the 1973 Forest Service roadless area inventory and his estimates of *de facto* acreage were low. A compilation by the Sierra Club (Gillette 1972) of the gross acreage, either in the NWPS or under review by the wilderness management agencies or Congress, totaled slightly over 67 million acres. This did not include about 1.6 million acres of *"de facto"* land proposed for wilderness status by preservationists. In a recent paper, Fredsall (1974) predicted the wilderness system might eventually encompass nearly 240 million acres. The size of his estimate—more than twice as large as the others—reflects his belief that about 120 million acres of BLM land in Alaska will be designated wilderness.

We can gain some idea of what size the NWPS might eventually reach by looking at the amount of land currently classified and under review. Table 6–7 presents the situation in January 1977.

The total amount of land—more than 200 million acres—shown in Table 6–7 represents our best estimate of the remaining roadless estate of the Nation. We can only speculate about how much of this land will actually become wilderness. But the figures in Table 6–7 serve the useful purpose of telling us the status of roadless areas with regard to the NWPS and something about the extent of the roadless lands. The amount of land finally receiving wilderness designation is an open question particularly with regard to the 134 million acres we categorize as other roadless Federal land available for wilderness classification.

The major significance of the acreage estimate, it seems to us, is in pointing out that additions to the NWPS cannot be continued infinitely into the future. While the exact amount of land in the NWPS and the time when such additions are completed is unknown, it will increasingly be *management* of existing areas, not *classification* of new ones, that will determine the manner in which the goals of the Wilderness Act will be achieved.

Factors Affecting the Final Size of the NWPS

As we note above, it is Congress that will ultimately decide the size of the NWPS. However, it seems that the outcome of five issues will have a particularly important bearing on that decision. Some of these factors, previously discussed, will be reviewed again.

Forest Service Roadless Areas

The Forest Service inventory of roadless tracts in 1973 identified about 56 million acres of potential wilderness land in the National Forests. Of this total, 12.3 million acres in 274 areas have been designated as New Study Areas; their suitability for wilderness will be officially studied under provisions of the Act. It is reasonable to assume that a major share of these lands will be recommended for wilderness classification by the agency. The remaining 44 million roadless acres will be studied in the recently proposed RARE II review. Thus, it is likely that additional roadless lands will be recommended for classification as wilderness.

Legislation was introduced into the 94th Congress in 1976 that would have given wilderness status to nine National Forest areas totaling nearly 1.1 million acres and would have mandated wilderness study of six additional areas covering nearly one-half million acres. Entitled the "Endangered American Wilderness Act of 1976," the bill primarily affected areas not chosen by the Forest Service for wilderness study; i.e., land not given New Study Area status.

Alaska

The great uncertainty about future jurisdictions of Alaskan lands is the second factor obscuring estimates about the eventual size of the NWPS. The State of Alaska, the Alaskan natives, and the Federal Government are all involved in the resolution of who gets what (see Chapter 5). Much land is involved; the State covers about 375 million acres and most of it is still *de facto* wilderness. The uncertainty is further confounded by debate over admission criteria for areas in Alaska—is Alaska different enough to warrant some special exceptions, such as allowing bushplane access and rustic cabins as concessions to its vast size, harsh climate and wildlife hazards? Until such time as questions of jurisdiction and qualifying criteria are resolved, the extent of classified wilderness in the state, and subsequently the size of the NWPS, will be difficult to predict.

Bureau of Land Management

Although not originally covered by terms of the Wilderness Act, the BLM is now required by the Federal Land Policy and Management Act of 1976 to conduct an inventory and review of all its roadless lands over 5,000 acres and its roadless islands and to submit recommendations regarding the wilderness suitability or nonsuitability to the President by 1991. Currently, the BLM has about 234,000 acres designated as primitive areas in six western States (Haverfield 1976). Under terms of the Federal Land Policy and Management Act, these areas must be reviewed for their wilderness suitability by 1980.

As we note in Table 6–7, estimates as to how much BLM land will be subject to wilderness study vary considerably from about 50 million acres to as much as 90 million acres. Many of the BLM holdings have been impacted by previous human activity and livestock grazing. In addition, much of the public domain is laced with primitive, low-standard roads. The impact of these

developments on the definition of what lands should be reviewed has yet to be determined.

Wilderness in the Eastern United States

With passage in 1975 of Public Law 93–622, commonly referred to as the Eastern Wilderness Act, 16 areas, containing 207,000 acres, of National Forest land east of the 100th meridian received wilderness designation. An additional 17 areas totaling 125,000 acres were identified for review by the Secretary of Agriculture.

The more lenient admission criteria included in this legislation could result in some additonal small areas being added to the NWPS in the East. However, most, if not all, the larger remaining eastern roadless tracts were included, either as instant wildernesses, or as study areas in the 1975 legislation. Few large roadless tracts remain in the East. For example, the 1962 ORRRC study of potential recreation sites in New England found that 98 percent of randomly selected sites located by air photo analysis were within ½ mile of a road (ORRRC 1962a). It would seem, then, that total wilderness acreage stemming from classification under the Eastern Wilderness Act would be relatively small, although particularly important, given the relative scarcity of wilderness opportunities in that part of the country.

Expansion of Primitive but Nonwilderness Opportunities

One of the most important determinants of the eventual size of the NWPS is the extent to which primitive, but nonwilderness, recreational opportunities are provided. Studies of wilderness visitors (Hendee et al. 1968; Stankey 1973), suggest that many users' experiences are not dependent upon wilderness; however, because local opportunities for such an experience are nonexistent or visitors are unaware of their existence, it is only in classified wilderness that they can find the kind of roadless recreation experience they desire. If wilderness is the only land that supplies roadless recreation opportunities, we anticipate very strong pressure to designate the maximum amount of wilderness. However, this would mean that wilderness often would be required to be something other than the Wilderness Act intended.

Without trying to answer the question "How much wilderness do we need?", we believe it would be very unfortunate if provisions are not made for roadless—but nonwilderness—use. First, failure to respond to the legitimate demands for roadless recreation might force many people to use land intended and managed for another purpose: To maintain natural ecological processes. This, in turn, could lead to management actions (for example, the hardening of sites, the construction of facilities) that threaten the long-term objectives of the Act or that promote excessively tight controls (for example, rationing) on users in order to protect the wilderness resource. Second, the unavailability of roadless recreation opportunities could lead to a growth in illegal activities (for example, trailbike riding) in wilderness as visitors attempt to find places to pursue their favorite dispersed recreation activities.

It is our judgment that, in addition to wilderness, roadless recreation areas are also needed. A variety of names have been suggested for such areas, including backcountry areas, pioneer areas, and frontier areas. These relatively unmodified settings would enhance a variety of opportunities such as camping, fishing, and hiking. These areas would be distinguished from wilderness by the greater degree of development and management permitted to increase recreational capacity, the kinds of recreational activities, and the low priority assigned to maintaining natural ecological processes. Such areas could reduce the level of impact on classified wilderness while meeting the needs of many users.

For example, we find many users of wilderness today who are drawn mainly for the fishing. As we will discuss later, fishing can be an important part of the wilderness experience. Fishing is not an activity, however, that wilderness managers should typically promote. In areas managed primarily for primitive (but not wilderness) recreation, it would be perfectly appropriate for managers to emphasize this kind of activity, perhaps by stocking lakes or developing impoundments to create new fishing opportunities. Many educational, mountaineering, and survival schools could be better accommodated in nonwilderness areas. Although most discussion about such a primitive recreation system is based upon the prohibition of roads, some areas could be developed that would provide trailbike and snowmobile trails for off-road vehicle users. Perhaps, in some areas, limited amounts of resource development (e.g., logging) could be done, but we believe that normally the economic value of such activity would be so small as to make it impractical. Some limited cutting might be done to improve scenic views, maintain meadows, or similarly enhance the visitor's recreational experience.

There are a variety of ways in which such roadless recreation areas could be provided. One alternative is the creation of a formal system, protected by law, analogous to the NWPS. Many preservationists believe this would be necessary because classification without the weight of law is an insufficient guarantee of longterm protection. Another alternative would be development of an administrative system of roadless recreation areas. Finally, such opportunities could be offered through an improved land-use planning program in which a full range of recreation settings is provided by the Federal, State, and private sectors. This would probably necessitate coordination with other suppliers of recreation, as no one supplier has either the capability or authority to do everything. In response to those who believe that protection under the second and third alternatives is inadequate, we believe adequate protection is available through NEPA (Wambach 1976).

The idea of a system of roadless recreation areas, however established, has failed to attract much support, possibly because various interest groups see little reason to support it. Commodity interests see it as only another lockup of resources on the public lands while wilderness proponents doubt its permanence under any kind of protection short of law.

Related Areas

In addition to formally classified wilderness, a variety of other areas complement or supplement wilderness purposes. Although some areas serve purposes closely related to wilderness, others are quite different. Nevertheless, all are located at the primitive end of the environmental modification spectrum and their relationship to designated wilderness is worth our attention.

Bureau of Land Management Primitive Areas

We have previously mentioned the change in the status of the BLM with regard to the Wilderness Act. However, the BLM has had an administrative designation to manage lands for wilderness preservation purposes since 1964. This authority was originally derived from the Multiple Use and Classification Act of 1964 (passed only about 2 weeks after the Wilderness Act), but more recently based upon regulations issued by the Secretary of the Interior.

Under these regulations, the BLM designated 11 primitive areas covering 234,003 acres (see Table 6–8). Of course, these areas should not be confused with National Forest areas similarly labeled under the 1929 L–20 regulation. The BLM's use of "primitive areas" is in part a response to the clause contained in the Wilderness Act restricting the use of the name "wilderness" to only those areas covered by the 1964 Act. BLM primitive areas are, nevertheless, intended to be equivalent to units of the NWPS, with the BLM Manual indicating that primitive areas will be managed to maintain the same quality as lands in the NWPS (Foster 1976). Criteria

Table 6–8.—*Bureau of Land Management primitive areas, January 1, 1977*

State	Name	Acres
Arizona	Aravaipa Canyon	5,080
Arizona	Paiute	35,092
California	Chamise Mountain	3,941
Colorado	Powderhorn	40,400
Montana	Beartrap Canyon	2,761
Montana	Centennial Mountains	24,165
Montana	Humbug Spires	7,041
Utah	Dark Canyon	57,248
Utah	Grand Gulch	24,080
Utah and Arizona	Paria Canyon	27,515
Wyoming	Scab Creek	6,680
Total		234,003

used to define primitive areas are the same as those used by the Wilderness Act. They differ from formal wilderness primarily in that they are the product of an administrative rather than statutory process. In one paradoxical way, they are somewhat better protected than legally designated wilderness because primitive areas are withdrawn from all mineral entry while wilderness is open until December 31, 1983.

The National Trails System

In 1968, Congress established a National Trails System (P.L. 90–543):

> In order to provide for the ever-increasing outdoor recreation needs of an expanding population and in order to promote public access to travel within, and enjoyment and appreciation of the open-air, outdoor areas of the nation.

The system includes three different types of trails: (1) National recreation trails, (2) national scenic trails, and (3) connecting or side trails. Some of these trails would overlap with wilderness or areas proposed for wilderness designation.

National Recreation Trails

National recreation trails are intended to provide a variety of outdoor recreation uses near urban areas. The Secretary of the Interior or the Secretary of Agriculture may establish a national recreation trail with the consent of any other jurisdiction (e.g., State, other Federal Agency) whose lands would also be involved. Trails on State lands may also be designated as national recreation trails by the Secretary of the Interior, with consent of the State.

Criteria for designating national recreation trails have been adopted by the Secretaries of the Interior and Agriculture. Such trails may be relatively short (perhaps

Figure 6–5.—Many different kinds of areas offer recreational opportunities that complement those found in officially designated wilderness. Here a couple enjoys an afternoon hike along a section of the Appalachian National Scenic Trail.

½ mile) but must be continuous. Some trails might be exclusively for the handicapped. National recreation trails are to be available to large numbers of people; consequently, locations such as stream valleys, utility rights-of-way, abandoned railroad rights-of-way, and levees or dikes are likely candidates. They may be designed solely for one use (e.g. hiking or outdoor recreational vehicle (ORV) use), but opportunities for multiple use are to be explored. Before designation of a trail, the administering agency must provide the appropriate Secretary (Interior or Agriculture) assurance that the trail will be available to the public for at least 10 consecutive years. Currently, 69 national recreation trails have been established, including the Sugar Loaf Mountain Nature Trail in Arkansas, the King Ranch Trail in California, and the Laurel-Snow Trail in Tennessee.

National Scenic Trails

National scenic trails differ from recreation trails in several respects. First, they can be designated only by an Act of Congress. Public Law 90–543 established two such trails: The 2,000-mile Appalachian Trail and the 2,350-

mile Pacific Crest Trail. In addition, 14 other trails totaling over 15,000 miles were identified for review as potential scenic trails.[2]

National scenic trails must possess superior scenic, historic, natural, or cultural qualities in combination with maximum outdoor recreation potential. They should avoid contact with developments such as transmission lines, highways, and industrial facilities; have adequate public access; and follow principal historic routes. Generally, they will be several hundred miles in length. Use of motorized vehicles on these trails is prohibited.

Connecting and Side Trails

The principal purpose of connecting and side trails is to provide additional points of public access to national recreation or national scenic trails or to join them. Such trails can be designated and administered either by the Secretary of the Interior or the Secretary of Agriculture and may be located on lands under other jurisdictions if approval from those jurisdictions is secured.

There is substantial need for a progressive program of trail construction and the development of opportunities for pleasure walking and hiking. Walking for pleasure is a major outdoor activity for many Americans. The Bureau of Outdoor Recreation (USDI BOR 1972) estimates that about 30 percent of the U.S. population 12 years and older walk for pleasure. However, trail opportunities are declining. In the United States today there are only about 100,000 miles of trails—less than 1 yard per citizen—and the trend appears to be downward. For example, trail mileage on National Forests, where much of the current opportunity exists, has declined over one-third since 1945 as roads and other developments have replaced trails (Lucas and Rinehart 1976).

The importance of walking and hiking, coupled with the static or declining opportunities for these activities has important implications because in many areas, the major trail opportunities are in wilderness. An increased level of impact on wilderness trails and camps can often occur, not *because* of the wilderness setting but simply because that's where the trails are.

In some wildernesses, units of the National Trail System overlap areas of the NWPS. For instance, the Pacific Crest Trail runs through several wildernesses in the Cascade and Sierra Nevada Mountains. Managers of these areas are faced with conflicting objectives when wilderness and national scenic trails overlap. Wilderness is managed for naturalness and solitude; national scenic

trails can attract many users (e.g., Scouts on endurance hikes) whose primary interest is not in wilderness values. Generally, the more restrictive management standards for wilderness will prevail, but the conflicting objectives and the heavier use attracted to national trails does create management problems. For example, where the Pacific Crest trail passes high mountain lakes, these attractive spots can become overused by hikers. Wilderness managers have encouraged rerouting of the Crest Trail away from fragile wilderness settings where possible, but it has been impossible to eliminate all the potential conflicts.

What seems needed is a broader range of types of trail settings. In particular, there is a need for lowland trails that offer roadless recreation opportunities. Such opportunities could often be provided on lands where commodity production or developed recreation take place, but which nevertheless provide opportunities for hikes to points of special interest. Nonwilderness trails would fill a major void and provide a great deal of enjoyment for users (Askham et al. 1974). Moreover, they could divert some use from wilderness. Such a program would provide an important complement to wilderness. This need, like the need for roadless, nonwilderness areas, illustrates the importance of understanding wilderness in relation to the total outdoor recreation spectrum.

The Wild and Scenic Rivers System

The Wild and Scenic Rivers Act of 1968 (P.L. 90–542) protected certain rivers throughout the country in order to assure their free and unimpaired flow and preserve their outstanding scenic, recreational, geological, fish and wildlife, historic, and cultural values. Originally promoted as a means of countering Federal dam construction programs, the Act evolved into an effort to limit development in general along rivers and their banks in the name of recreation (Tarlock and Tippy 1970).

The Act designated portions of eight rivers and adjacent lands as immediate members of the system.[3] Another 27 rivers were specified for study within 10 years for possible inclusion in the system; 18 to be studied by the Department of the Interior and 9 by the Department of Agriculture.[4]

---

[2] Trails to be reviewed include the Continental Divide Trail, the Potomac Heritage Trail, Old Cattle Trails of the Southwest, Lewis and Clark Trail, Natchez Trace, North Country Trail, Kittanning Trail, Oregon Trail, Sante Fe Trail, Long Trail, Mormon Trail, Gold Rush Trail, Mormon Battalion Trail, and the El Camino Real.

[3] The eight rivers include the Middle Fork of the Clearwater, Idaho; Eleven Point, Mo.; Middle Fork of the Feather, Calif.; Rio-Grande, N.M.; Rogue, Oreg.; Upper Saint Croix, Minn: and Wis.; Middle Fork of the Salmon, Idaho, and the Wolf, Wis.

[4] Rivers that were to be studied by the Interior are: Allegheny, Pa.; Bruneau, Idaho; Buffalo, Tenn.; Clarion, Pa.; Delaware, Pa. and N.Y.; Gasconade, Mo.; Little Beaver, Ohio; Little Miami, Ohio; Maumee, Ohio and Ind.; Missouri, Mont.; Obed, Tenn.; Penobscot, Maine; Pine Creek, Pa.; Rio Grande, Tex.; Lower St. Croix, Minn. and Wis.; Suwannee, Ga. and Fla.; Upper Iowa, Iowa; and the Youghiogheny, Md. and Pa. Rivers that were to be studied by Agriculture are: Chattooga, Ga., N.C., and S.C.; Flathead, Mont.; Illinois Oreg.; Moyie, Idaho; Pere Marquette, Mich.; Priest, Idaho; St. Joe, Idaho; Salmon, Idaho; and Skagit, Wash.

Designation of rivers under the Wild and Scenic Rivers Act can occur in two ways. First, specific legislation by Congress can be enacted to protect a river. Second, a river can be added to the System by the Secretary of the Interior, provided certain nomination procedures are followed by the state in which the river is located and provided there is no administrative cost to be borne by the Federal Government (Peters 1975).

Since passage of the Wild and Scenic Rivers Act, seven of the original study rivers have been officially designated by Congress (the Lower St. Croix, Little Miami, Chattooga, Little Beaver, Flathead, Missouri, and Obed). In addition, the Allagash Wilderness Waterway in Maine was designated by the Secretary of the Interior. Three other rivers (the New, Rapid, and Snake) have been added by Congress. Two other rivers (Suwannee and Upper Iowa) have had review studies completed and their final disposition is pending. Three rivers (Alleghany, Clarion, and Maumee) were studied and found not suitable for inclusion in the national system. In early 1975, 29 new rivers were designated for study. Currently, the National Wild and Scenic Rivers System contains 19 designated rivers.

The Act recognizes three classes of rivers:

1. Wild rivers.—Those rivers or sections of rivers that are free of impoundments, and generally inaccessible except by trail, with watersheds or shorelines essentially primitive, and waters unpolluted. These represent vestiges of primitive America.

2. Scenic rivers.—Those rivers or sections of rivers that are free of impoundments, with shorelines or watersheds still largely primitive and shorelines largely undeveloped, but accessible in places by roads.

3. Recreational river areas.—Those rivers or sections of rivers that are readily accessible by road or railroad, that may have some development along their shorelines, and that may have undergone some impoundment or diversion in the past.

Currently, 24 states have passed legislation establishing wild and scenic river systems under State jurisdiction. Twenty have implemented programs, resulting in over 115 rivers being designated at the state level. Louisiana has 35 rivers so protected (Lime 1975).

Designation of a river under the Wild and Scenic Rivers Act combined with wilderness designation over the river and adjacent lands could have very important complementary benefits. Wilderness designation generally affects broad reaches of land and would protect the broader watershed of which the river is a part. Wild and Scenic River designation, on the other hand, provides some important protection not afforded by the

Figure 6–6.—Originally designed to prevent dam development along some of our remaining wild rivers, the Wild and Scenic Rivers Act became an important law providing for a variety of river-related recreational activities. Rafters on Idaho's Selway River ride through heavy white water.

Wilderness Act. First, it provides complete protection against dam construction and other water development projects. Such facilities can be developed in classified wilderness if judged by the President to be in the public interest (see Chapter 4). Second, the Wild and Scenic Rivers bill prohibits construction of power transmission lines; such facilities can be developed in wilderness. Third, although the Wilderness Act does not allow for the condemnation of private inholdings, the Wild and Scenic Rivers Bill permits administering agencies to condemn private land, if less than 50 percent of the entire river area is owned by Federal, State, or local government. However, land within a city, village, or borough cannot be condemned if valid zoning ordinances protecting the river areas are in effect. Finally, while lands in the NWPS are open to mineral entry until 1984, there is a complete withdrawal from mineral entry of lands within ¼ mile of the bank of any river designated for management under the wild category of the Wild and Scenic Rivers system (Tarlock and Tippy 1970).

State Wildernesses

So far, we have dealt with legislation designed to preserve and protect only Federal lands. However, we know of several States that have enacted legislation to establish State wilderness systems. In addition, since 1885, the State of New York has given statutory protection to a portion of its Forest Reserve to assure that these lands remain forever wild. The State of Maine also maintains a wilderness park, protected by law. A number of States have sponsored programs reflecting public interest in wildland preservation; e.g., the New Jersey Open Space Recreation Plan, the program of dedicated nature preserves in Indiana and Illinois. State wildernesses and related programs can be a valuable complement to the National Wilderness Preservation System and could help relieve pressures on currently overused areas. Such programs could play an especially important role in the Eastern United States, where Federal lands are limited. It has been estimated that more than 16 million acres of land under State ownership remain in a substantially natural condition in the East today (Cutler 1972). Below, we look at three examples of state wilderness systems—those of California, Michigan, and Maryland—and the New York and Maine programs.

California

In 1974, the California legislature passed Senate Bill 1498, creating a California Wilderness Preservation System. Three basic criteria govern admission to the system: (1) The land must be State-owned; (2) the area must remain in, or have been returned to, or have substantially reestablished its principal, natural character and influence; and (3) the area must be of sufficient size to make its preservation practical. About 5 million acres appear subject to review.

Two areas totaling nearly 97,000 acres have been established in Anza Borrego Desert and Mt. San Jacinto State Park. Another 1,500 acres, currently State inholdings within the boundaries of existing Federal wilderness, was added to the State system on January 1, 1977, unless exchanged for Federal lands.

Restrictions on use are similar to those in the Federal Act. Also, the California bill leaves jurisdiction of areas in the State system to the agency controlling them at the time they are designated wilderness. Each agency must prepare regulations for managing the areas consistent with the Act's objectives. The Secretary of the Resources Agency is instructed to review all State-owned roadless areas within 3 years of the Act's passage and report his findings regarding suitability or nonsuitability of these lands as State wilderness to the State legislature. The

State legislature has authority to classify areas under the Act.

Michigan

The Michigan "Wilderness and Natural Areas Act" of 1972 is also quite similar to the 1964 Federal Wilderness Act. It established three land use designations: (1) wilderness areas, (2) wild areas, and (3) natural areas. The first two designations are similar to the earlier designations of Forest Service lands under the U-Regulations of 1939. Wilderness areas are defined as tracts of undeveloped State land, administered by the State Department of Natural Resources. Further, such areas must:

1. Have at least 3,000 acres, or be an island of any size;
2. Generally appear to have been affected primarily by forces of nature, with the imprint of man's work substantially unnoticeable;
3. Have outstanding opportunities for solitude or a primitive and unconfined type of recreation; and
4. Contain ecological, geological or other features of scientific, scenic, or historical value.

Criteria 2, 3, and 4 are drawn verbatim from the Federal Wilderness Act.

Wild areas are distinguished from wilderness areas primarily by size, being less than 3,000 acres. In addition, they have "outstanding opportunities for personal exploration, challenge, or contact with natural features of the landscape and its biological community." Further, they must meet one of the criteria—2, 3, or 4—for wilderness areas. As far as possible, such areas are to be established near urban centers with populations over 100,000.

Finally, natural areas are State lands that have retained or reestablished their natural character or possess unusual flora, fauna, or biotic, geologic, scenic, or other features of educational or scientific value. Such areas must have been identified and verified through study by qualified observers. They may be part of an existing State wilderness or wild area.

Natural areas are designated by the Natural Resources Commission (a citizen board) upon approval of appropriate committees in the State legislature. The commission is advised by the Wilderness and Natural Areas Advisory Board, a citizen group appointed by the Governor, representing the geographic regions and interests within the State.

At present, 12 areas totaling about 44,000 acres have been designated under the Michigan Act. However, nearly 40,000 acres of this total are contained in the State's one wilderness area—the Porcupine Mountains Wilderness. The remaining 11 areas (3,000 acres) are all managed under the natural area designation.

Maryland

The objectives of the Maryland Wildlands Preservation System Act of 1971 closely parallel the Federal Wilderness Act. The bill required the Secretary of the Department of Natural Resources to review all roadless state lands 500 contiguous acres or more in size and to report their suitability as a State wildland to the Governor. The review of roadless tracts was completed in 1974. According to criteria developed by the Department of Natural Resources, 162 areas were evaluated for suitability as wildland areas. These guidelines included the presence of roads or structures, intensive resource management programs, and private inholdings. The presence of any of these factors eliminated the area as a candidate for wildland classification. This analysis identified 38 potential areas totaling 44,776 acres. Detailed field studies of each area will determine if wildland classification would be appropriate.

To date, only one area has been formally established—the Big Savage Mountain Wildland, a 2,000-acre area in the Savage River State Forest. No management plan has been developed, and the lack of specific managment guidelines makes it hard to judge the relationship of the Maryland system to its federal counterpart.

New York

The New York Forest Preserve is one of the oldest areas protected by legislation in the country. It was established to correct logging abuses in the Adirondack Mountains and protect the area's watershed (Thompson 1963; Nash 1973). In 1885 the State legislature created the Forest Preserve, declaring:

> The lands of the state, now owned or hereafter acquired, constituting the forest preserve as now fixed by law, shall be forever kept as wild forest lands.

The preserve was ostensibly for resource protection, but many people felt the area should be designated a park. Thus, in 1892 the legislature established a 3-million-acre Park "open for the free use of all the people for their health and pleasure" (Nash 1973). In 1894 protection of the area was embodied in the State constitution. In pressing for an amendment to the constitution, proponents cited the need not only for protection of the valuable watershed but also for the preservation of lands where people could find peace and quiet.

Further additions to the Adirondack Park brought its total acreage to about 6 million acres. The area is a unique park from an American perspective because about 60 percent of it is privately owned and with a resident population of nearly 125,000 people. To manage and coordinate uses within the area, an Adirondack Park Agency has been created which has responsibilities for both private and public holdings.

The State currently owns 2.3 million acres of the Park. Of this total, 1 million acres have been designated as a "wilderness" where mechanized equipment is prohibited. Additionally, a few thousand acres have been set aside as "primitive" where wilderness standards will be followed but where more time is needed to recreate wilderness conditions. Fifty-four lakes and ponds have been designated as a "canoe area," with motorboats prohibited. A small amount of land is devoted to intensive campground development and ski areas. Finally, 1 million acres were designated as "wild forest" for uses such as group camping, snowmobiling, and trail rides (Davis 1976).

The 3.7 million acres of private land were also zoned. Existing communities were classified as hamlets, with future development at the discretion of the local government. Existing industrial use areas were also identified. Locations where future residential growth was likely were classified as moderate intensity use areas where housing development could not exceed one unit per 1.25 acres. Low intensity use areas were also designated, permitting residential construction within a one unit per 3.25 acres constraint. These four designations, equalling about 13 percent of the total private land, represent the total that was judged capable of fairly intensive development (Davis 1976).

The remaining 87 percent of private land, considered unable to withstand intensive development because of natural resource considerations or because the land was needed as open space, was divided into two categories. First, rural use areas were defined as permitting no more than one building every 8.5 acres. Resource management lands, to be generally devoted to forest management and agriculture, were limited to one building every 43 acres (Davis 1976).

Today, the Adirondack Park represents one of the largest undeveloped tracts in the East. Although heavily interspersed with private lands, over 2 million acres of predominantly wild land remain. Combined with the 250,000-acre Catskill Forest Preserve 50 miles south, it constitutes a substantial block of undeveloped country in the most populous region of the country (Sutton and Sutton 1974).

Maine

In 1931, former Governor of Maine Percival P. Baxter donated nearly 6,000 acres of land to the State for use as a park. The land, he specified, "shall forever be kept and remain in the natural state." Over a period of 30 years, additional donations by the Governor brought the total size of the area, known as Baxter State Park, to 200,000 acres.

The area is surrounded by a perimeter road system, with short branching roads leading to nearby destinations in the interior. Most of the area is accessible only by trail, however, and under the existing management plan, no further expansion or improvement of the road system, except for reasons of safety, will be permitted. Camping is carefully regulated. During the winter, camping and mountain hiking and climbing are allowed only with a special use permit issued by Park officials.

The Park is clearly intended to provide a rather special set of recreational experiences linked to enjoyment of the natural, undeveloped environment. Uses not dependent upon such a setting are to be accommodated elsewhere. Although named a State park and supported by state funds, it is not a unit of the existing State Park System and is to be managed according to the directives outlined by Governor Baxter over 40 years ago. Along with the Adirondack Preserve to the south, it represents one of the relatively few remaining areas in the Northeast where natural conditions still prevail.

These five States illustrate the efforts being made at the State level to preserve the wilderness character of certain remaining undeveloped lands. Other States will probably follow their lead. Such State-level actions reaffirm the validity of the wilderness idea and help support an optimistic view of its future.

Research Natural Areas

In 1966, the Department of the Interior, as part of the United States' participation in the International Biological Program (IBP), established the Federal Committee on Research Natural Areas. The committee was composed of representatives of the major Federal land management agencies along with liaison representatives from the Department of Defense, Atomic Energy Commission, and Tennessee Valley Authority. Its purpose was to inventory and prepare a directory of natural areas on Federal lands.

Research natural areas are related to wilderness because one of their key objectives is the maintenance of natural processes and because they serve an important

research and education role. Their specific objectives include the following:

1. To assist in the preservation of examples of all significant natural ecosystems for comparison with those influenced by man.

2. To provide educational and research areas for scientists to study the ecology, successional trends, and other aspects of the natural environment.

3. To serve as gene pools and preserves for rare and endangered species of plants and animals (Federal Committee on Research Natural Areas 1968).

In general, six basic characteristics of natural areas can be identified (Moir 1972):

1. They are examples of the natural environment;
2. Their natural features have been disturbed as little as possible by man;
3. They are defined by ecological criteria;
4. They are assured the greatest possible degree of preservation and permanency;
5. Their withdrawal is for scientific and educational purposes; and
6. They harbor genetic stock of possible value to society.

Research natural areas range from 1 acre to over 100,000 acres. As of late 1976, 383 areas containing nearly 4.5 million acres throughout the United States were included in the system. They generally are surrounded or buffered by Federal land. Research on these areas must be essentially nondestructive and reasonably consistent with the purpose and character of the surrounding land. Studies involving manipulation of the environment are generally not permitted.

Recreational use of research natural areas is, by definition, limited and subordinate to the scientific and educational objectives for these areas. They nevertheless do serve as important recreational settings for activities that emphasize learning and environmental awareness (Hendee 1970). More importantly, they supplement the scientific and educational objectives of the NWPS.

Biosphere Reserves

The most recently instituted program of nature preservation is the Biosphere Reserve Project. The Project was established in 1973 under the auspices of the United Nations Educational, Scientific, and Cultural Organization (UNESCO). The purpose of the program is to establish an international network of protected areas, representing the major natural regions of the world. These areas would be set aside for the conservation of genetic diversity, ecological research, monitoring, and education. Biosphere reserves include two categories: natural ecosystems where human influence is slight and man-modified ecosystems. The Biosphere Reserve Project is different from other conservation and preservation programs in that it provides for the testing and demonstration of various resource management practices (Franklin 1977).

In the United States, the Project is jointly coordinated by the National Park Service and the Forest Service. In 1976, the first areas officially recognized as Biosphere Reserves were designated. Three National Parks were designated: Great Smoky Mountains National Park in Tennessee and North Carolina, Everglades National Park in Florida, and Virgin Islands National Park; and three National Forest areas: Coweeta Experimental Forest in North Carolina, Hubbard Brook Experimental Forest in New Hampshire, and Luquillo Experimental Forest in Puerto Rico. Another 22 areas have been approved for Biosphere Reserve designation but have not yet been officially recognized by UNESCO. Selection of these areas is based on the significance and representativeness of their features and on their history of biotic presentation, ecological research, or both (Franklin 1977). Like Research Natural Areas, Biosphere Reserves will play an important complementary role to wilderness in terms of providing educational and scientific values.

Specially Designated National Forest Lands

A variety of administrative designations are available to set aside National Forest lands for special purposes. These areas are broadly labeled Special Interest areas. Originally, they were designated by authority of the U-3 Regulation of 1939 (see Chapter 4) which established roadless areas, managed primarily for their recreational values. Such authority is now contained in regulations issued by the Secretary of Agriculture.

Six different kinds of areas can be established by such administrative designations: Scenic areas, geological areas, archeological areas, historical areas, botanical areas, and other special interest areas. Each designation gives added protection for an area possessing certain special qualities. Designation can be made by National Forest supervisors. Areas established under these regulations can be managed at least as restrictively as wilderness. For example, management guidelines for the Jewel Basin Hiking Area in western Montana prohibit the use of stock; all access must be on foot.

A major concern about such administrative designations centers on the degree of protection they provide. Because they are established administratively at local or regional levels, they can also be eliminated at those levels. This was also the situation with wilderness under the U–Regulations. It was one of the compelling reasons conservationists sought Congressional protection for wilderness, and it is one of the major objections to administrative designation of a roadless recreation area or a backcountry system to supplement wilderness. We look at this issue in greater detail in Chapter 16.

Wilderness on Private Lands

Although wilderness is typically associated with public lands, some efforts to maintain large tracts of undeveloped land in private ownership can be cited.

In Upper Michigan, the 21,000-acre Sylvania tract has remained largely undeveloped since the turn of the century. Originally purchased by U.S. Steel Corporation as an exclusive fishing and hunting club, the area later passed into the hands of the Fisher family of auto-body fame. Although some development occurred, the area remained essentially unmodified into the 1960's when the Forest Service purchased it. Now in public ownership and managed principally for its primitive recreation values, the substantially natural conditions were protected for over half a century by private individuals.

In Tennessee and North Carolina, the Bowater Southern Paper Corporation has initiated a "Pocket Wilderness" program on their lands. About 1,800 acres have been set aside, in areas ranging from 100 to 700 acres to be maintained—except for simple trails—in their natural state. Areas, chosen on the basis of natural and scenic values, have been selected by a process that involves input from both citizens and company officials (Streetman 1976). Several other private forest product companies have expressed interest in the program and taken the first steps to implement similar programs.

The achievements of the Nature Conservancy should also be noted. Organized as a nonprofit corporation, it has located and provided funds to purchase natural preserves of land across the country. Because of its nonprofit status, the Nature Conservancy is able to raise substantial sums, often in a short period. This is particularly important when quick acquisition of property is needed to prevent development. Typically, lands acquired by the Nature Conservancy are later sold to public agencies, with the conditions to insure preservation specified by contract. If the conditions are violated, the land reverts back to the Nature Conservancy. The organization has acquired some 10,500 acres on a cooperative basis with the Forest Service; several State parks have also worked with it. Areas such as Walcott Preserve (Connecticut), Battle Creek Cypress Swamp (Maryland), and St. Vincent Island (Florida) owe their preservation to Nature Conservancy efforts.

Conclusions

Although the NWPS has grown relatively slowly since passage of the Wilderness Act, it has considerable potential for growth. Trade-offs must be made by resource managers and citizens to answer the question "how much is enough." Although forecasting is hazardous, it seems reasonable to expect the NWPS to increase from its present 14 million acres to something between 50 and 70 million acres. For instance, the recently submitted Forest Service program required by the Forest and Rangeland Renewable Resources Planning Act of 1974 (RPA), calls for a total allocation of National Forest land to wilderness designation of between 25 and 30 million acres by the year 2020 (USDA 1976). Additions, of course, will also be made by the National Park Service, Fish and Wildlife Service, and the Bureau of Land Management.

Whether this is "enough" wilderness is open to debate; "enough" for what purposes is the key question. Some key ecosystems are currently poorly represented— or, in some cases, not represented at all—in wilderness. Some observers have argued that cave environments should be represented within the NWPS and have proposed inclusion of Flint Ridge Cave System in Mammoth Cave National Park in Kentucky (Watson and Smith 1971). Proposals for underwater wilderness have also been made. The "need" for wilderness is a complex and confusing issue. It is clear to us, however, that wilderness alone cannot supply all the environmental values and recreational opportunities the public seeks at the primitive end of the outdoor opportunity spectrum. Other roadless, nonwilderness settings must also be provided, either by administrative regulations or statute, to more adequately meet public desires. Full development of the National Trails System, the Wild and Scenic Rivers System, Research Natural Areas, and provision for roadless areas managed intensively for recreation will have an important bearing on what happens in wilderness in the future (Towell 1976). The quality of tomorrow's wilderness will depend as much on our success in fully developing the outdoor recreation opportunity spectrum as on our achievements in developing and implementing innovative wilderness allocation and management programs.

The author primarily responsible for preparation of this chapter was George H. Stankey.

Literature Cited

Askham, Leonard R., Kathleen P. Warfield, and Gladys I. Biglor, eds.
1974. Proceedings of Washington's first symposium on recreation trails. 117 p. Cooperative Extension Service, Washington State University, Pullman.

Cunningham, William P., and Douglas W. Scott.
1969. The Magruder Corridor controversy. Living Wilderness 33(107):36–39.

Cutler, M. Rupert.
1972. Preserving wilderness through state legislation. *In* Action for wilderness. p. 104–112. Elizabeth R. Gillette, ed. Sierra Club, San Francisco.

Davis, George D.
1976. Meeting recreational, park and wilderness needs. Am., For. 82(3):12–13, 63.

Federal Committee on Research Natural Areas.
1968. A directory of research natural areas. Addendum to the 1968 directory dated November 1972. 129 p. U.S. Government Printing Office, Washington, D.C.

Franklin, Jerry F.
1977. The biosphere reserve program in the United States. Science 195:262–267.

Fredsall, R.M.
1974. Land withdrawal situation report. Unpublished report to Western Wood Products Association, Portland, Oreg. 6 p.

Gillette, Elizabeth R., ed.
1972. Action for Wilderness. 222 p. Sierra Club, San Francisco.

Haight, Kevin.
1974. The Wilderness Act: ten years after. Environ. Affairs 3(2):275–326.

Hendee, John C., William R. Catton, Jr., Larry D. Marlow, and C. Frank Brockman.
1968. Wilderness users in the Pacific Northwest—their characteristics, values, and management preferences. USDA For. Serv., Res. Pap. PNW–61, 92 p. Pac. Northwest For. and Range Exp. Stn., Portland, Oreg.

Hendee, John C.
1970. Recreational values, use and management of natural areas. *In* Natural areas-needs and opportunities, p. 35–38. William J. Dittrich and James M. Trappe, eds. Northwest Sci. Assoc.

Hendee, John C.
1974. A scientist's views on some current wilderness management needs. Western Wildlands 1(2):27–32.

Lime, David W.
1975. Back-country river recreation: problems and research opportunities. Naturalist 26(1):2–6.

Lucas, Robert C. and Robert P. Rinehart.
1976. The neglected hiker. Backpacker 4(1):35–39.

McCloskey, Michael.
1966. The Wilderness Act: its background and meaning. Oreg. Law Rev. 45(4):288–321.

McCloskey, Michael.
1972. Is the Wilderness Act working? *In* Action for wilderness, p. 22–28. Elizabeth R. Gillette, ed. Sierra Club, San Francisco.

Moir, William H.
    1972. Natural areas. Science 177(4047):396–400.
Nash, Roderick.
    1973. Wilderness and the American mind. 300 p. Yale University Press, New Haven, Conn.
Outdoor Recreation Resources Review Commission.
    1962a. Potential new sites for outdoor recreation in the Northeast. ORRRC Study Rep. 8, 132 p. U.S. Government Printing Office, Washington, D.C.
Outdoor Recreation Resources Review Commission.
    1962b. Wilderness and recreation—a report on resources, values, and problems. Outdoor Rec. Res. Comm. Study Report 3, 352 p. U.S. Government Printing Office, Washington, D.C.
Peters, Clay E.
    1975. A national system of wild and scenic rivers. Naturalist 26(1):28–31.
Stankey, George H.
    1971. Myths in wilderness decisionmaking. J. Soil and Water Conserv. 26(5):183–188.
Stankey, George H.
    1973. Visitor perception of wilderness recreation carrying capacity. USDA For. Serv., Res. Pap. INT-142, 61 p. Intermt. For. and Range Exp. Stn., Ogden, Utah.
Streetman, Clarence.
    1976. Industry's approach to wilderness values management, 10 p. Paper presented at Winter Meeting, Alleghany Section, Society American Foresters, Dover, Del. (In press.)
Sutton, Ann, and Myron Sutton.
    1974. Wilderness areas of North America. 406 p. Funk and Wagnalls, New York.
Tarlock, A. Dan, and Roger Tippy.
    1970. The Wild and Scenic Rivers Act of 1968. Cornell Law Rev. 55(5):707–739.

Thompson, Roger C.
    1963. Politics in the wilderness: New York's Adirondack Forest Preserve. For. Hist. 6(4):14-23.
Towell, William E.
    1976. Eastern Wilderness: Big "W" or little "w"? Am. For. 82(4):6-7, 48.
U.S. Congress.
    1970. Sixth annual report, National Wilderness Preservation System. 91st Congress, 2nd Session, Document No. 91-372, 22 p.
U.S. Department of Agriculture Forest Service.
    1975. The nation's renewable resources—an assessment, 1975. 345 p. U.S. Government Printing Office, Washington, D.C.
U.S. Department of Agriculture, Forest Service.
    1976. A recommended renewable resource program. 658 p. U.S. Government Printing Office, Washington, D.C.
U.S. Department of the Interior, National Park Service.
    1971. Yellowstone National Park Wilderness proposal. 24 p. U.S. Dep. Inter., Nat. Park Ser.
U.S. Department of the Interior, Bureau of Outdoor Recreation.
    1972. The 1970 survey of outdoor recreation activities: preliminary report. USDI Bur. Outdoor Recreation. 105 p. U.S. Government Printing Office, Washington, D.C.
U.S. Department of the Interior, National Park Service.
    1974. Glacier National Park Wilderness proposal. 34 p. U.S. Dep. Inter., Nat. Park Serv., Washington, D.C.
Watson, Richard A., and Philip M. Smith.
    1971. Underground wilderness: a point of view. Int. J. Environ. Studies 2(3):217–220.

Eleven wilderness management principles serve as conceptual tools from which more specific direction and policy can be derived. A first principle is to recognize that wilderness is one extreme of the land use spectrum where naturalness and outstanding opportunities for solitude are legally mandated. Wolf Peak in the Beartooth Primitive Area, Mont., looking south.

7 Some Principles Of Wilderness Management

Introduction

The practice of wilderness management is necessarily an imprecise science. Seldom will there be clear and unequivocal answers for managers faced with problems. Rather, they will be interpreting information and choosing among alternative solutions to problems.

Because judgments have to be made, it is important to define a clear rationale and basis for such decisions. This chapter sets forth a set of principles—fundamental assumptions—that offer a logical and consistent framework within which the difficult decisions that daily confront managers can be made. It is from such principles or fundamental assumptions that more specific management direction and policy are derived.

The following principles, arranged along a general-to-specific continuum, offer basic perspectives on the nature of the wilderness resource, its use, and its place in the spectrum of land uses. By no means should this list be considered final. However, the following include many basic concepts needed to guide wilderness management decisionmaking.

Principle 1: Wilderness Is One Extreme on the Environmental Spectrum

One of the most important fundamental concepts available to wilderness managers is that of the environmental modification spectrum—sometimes called the outdoor recreation opportunity spectrum. The concept describes a continuum of environmental settings ranging from the "paved to the primeval" (Nash 1973); that is, from heavily modified, urbanized environments to those that are—relatively speaking—remote and pristine. By virtue of the range in modification from a developed to a primitive condition, the spectrum offers a wide variety of experiences to users. The notion is that the experience available to users—even those who vicariously appreciate the setting as long distance spectators—will vary based on such things as the area's degree of naturalness, the intensity of human visitation, and the level of facility development (Lloyd and Fisher 1972; Lucas and Stankey 1974).

Through the Wilderness Act of 1964 and the so-called Eastern Wilderness Act of 1975, our society has elected to preserve selected areas nearest the primeval end of the spectrum in a National Wilderness Preservation System (NWPS). The concept that wilderness is a point to be preserved on the environmental modification spectrum is implied in the stated purpose of the Wilderness Act (P.L. 88-577, Sec. 2a).

> ". . . to assure that an increasing population, accompanied by expanding settlement and growing mechanization, does not occupy and modify all areas within the United States . . . leaving no lands designated for preservation and protection in their natural condition . . ."

This first principle, recognizing that wilderness is one extreme on the environmental modification spectrum, has important ramifications for wilderness management. It defines wilderness in relation to more modified lands and, by implication, recognizes a range of successively more modified environments that are *not* wilderness. For example, as discussed in chapters 1 and 6, there are roadless but nonwilderness lands; roaded wild land set aside for park, wildlife, recreation and scenic uses; multiple use lands providing for dispersed road recreation and development-oriented activities at campgrounds, ski areas, interpretive centers, and other facilities related to commodity production.

Most of those examples are not confused with wilderness, although debate preceding classification of any given wilderness may feature heated arguments over merits of allocating the area to these alternative uses. Even after an area is classified as wilderness many forces can still erode the primeval qualities of naturalness, solitude, and the relative absence of environmental modification that distinguish it as wilderness. Among the inappropriate alterations and uses currently suggested for many wildernesses are snowmobiling; trail biking; downhill skiing; chalets; overnight shelters; comfort stations; and retreats for teaching religion, mountaineering, survival, and environmental education. All these pressures threaten to erode the threshold on the environmental modification spectrum that separates wilderness from other land uses. A fundamental objective of wilderness management is to maintain the thresholds between wilderness and other land uses.

In essence, wilderness management consists of regulating human use and influence so as to preserve an area's relatively unmodified condition—its wilderness character defined by the Wilderness Act (Sec. 2c) as

> ". . . a place where the earth and its community of life are untrammeled by man . . . Land retaining its primeval character and influence without permanent improvements or human habitation . . . (that) generally

appears to have been affected primarily by the forces of nature with the imprint of man's work substantially unnoticeable; has outstanding opportunities for solitude or a primitive and unconfined type of recreation."

To achieve this goal, we need to resist pressures seeking to increase the environmental modification of wilderness.

To preserve wilderness naturalness and solitude requires that demands inconsistent with the area's wilderness character be met elsewhere. Wilderness use is thus interrelated with all other land uses. Many activities and demands are easily diverted to wilderness because there are insufficient opportunities for them on other lands. The best example of this infringement of marginally related activities on the wilderness is the demand for roadless, dispersed recreation which has escalated during the past three decades. Many roadless activities do not *depend on wilderness conditions* but do require or benefit from a roadless setting: Snowmobiling; trailbiking; family day-hiking; visitation to points of interest such as scenic views, waterfalls, hot springs, or easy-to-reach lakes; fly-in fishing and hunting; organized group hiking and camping; cross country skiing; and environmental education. Wilderness simply cannot meet all of these demands without either directly violating provisions of the Act or compromising the qualities of naturalness and solitude that distinguish wilderness from other lands.

In conclusion, although wilderness is a discrete part of the environmental spectrum, it is nevertheless linked to other lands. To the extent that these related lands are lacking, the displaced uses may be diverted to classified wilderness where they may result in excessive or inappropriate demands. An expanded range of opportunities for roadless recreation would thus help insure the preservation goals established for the NWPS and help meet the public's diverse tastes and needs. The ultimate quality of the NWPS will depend in part on provision of alternative (nonwilderness) opportunities for activities that do not require the degree of naturalness and solitude provided in classified wilderness.

Principle 2: The Management of Wilderness Must Be Viewed in Relationship to the Management of Adjacent Lands

This second principle—that management of wilderness is related to the management of adjacent lands—is also related to the environmental spectrum. Here, however, the concern is broadened from outdoor recreation opportunities to a variety of other resource uses and management practices. Simply put, wilderness does not exist in a vacuum—what goes on outside of, but adjacent to, a wilderness can have substantial impacts inside the boundary. Conversely, the designation of a tract of land as a wilderness can substantially affect the management of adjacent areas.

Many examples illustrate the interrelationship between wilderness and adjacent land use. Probably the most obvious are the impacts on wilderness resulting from timber harvesting and its accompanying road development. The building of logging roads to the edge of a wilderness boundary can dramatically affect the amount and character of its recreation use by making access easier. Resulting impacts on physical-biological conditions can detract from the goal of maintaining natural conditions. Reducing the number of roads, lowering road standards, and closing roads after timber harvesting are ways in which these impacts might be offset.

Similarly, the development of high-density recreational facilities (e.g., youth camps, picnic areas) immediately adjacent to wilderness or undeveloped backcountry can bring serious management problems as users of these facilities penetrate the immediately adjacent roadless lands for hiking, fishing, or other activities. For example, one of the most heavily used entrances into the San Gorgonio Wilderness in southern California is the South Fork Meadows trail. Formerly, access to the wilderness boundary was over a route called "Poopout Hill," an appropriate name for a climb that required considerable effort. Today, the hill is topped by a paved road and lined by numerous summer camps. Because of this improved access and the added visitation from the youth camps, use impacts in the area reached such a level that entry at that trailhead had to be rationed beginning in 1973 (Hay 1974). The example illustrates how excessive visitation and inappropriate recreation activity can be diverted to wilderness when access is made easier and alternative opportunities are lacking.

However, impacts can also move from wilderness to nearby nonwilderness areas. For example, programs to reestablish natural fire regimes in wilderness could cause smoke pollution and possible fire losses in adjacent areas managed for commodity production. Wildlife that thrive on summer range in high wilderness meadows compete with domestic stock for scarce forage in the lower valleys during winter.

Relating the management of wilderness to that of adjacent lands is a complex and controversial issue. One commonly suggested possibility is creating a buffer zone—a band of land around the periphery of wilderness that would absorb impacts and help avert conflicts. Some

managers and commodity-resource users oppose this as a solution, however, arguing that any needed buffer should be included within the wilderness boundary. Regardless of where the buffer is located, wilderness can be protected from impacts originating on surrounding lands only through comprehensive land-use planning that anticipates potential conflicts and addresses the complementary and competitive relationships between wilderness and adjacent lands (Stankey 1974).

In planning the various forest resource uses, activities that demonstrate little compatibility with one another should be carefully defined and steps taken to keep these incompatibilities at a minimum (Clawson 1975). Integrating the various recreational resources can probably best be achieved through a concentric-circle concept, with high-density, facility-oriented sites located around the periphery of a planning region and environment-oriented and primitive-style opportunities, such as wilderness, located in the core. This gradation of uses would protect the environmental quality of the interior roadless land or wilderness and would facilitate access to the development-oriented opportunities (Gould 1961; Carhart 1961; Hart 1966). To do otherwise invites problems when the more intensive uses impinge on the less developed areas.

Explicitly defined use zones also help protect against the phenomena of invasion, succession, and displacement of primitive-site recreation users by new and more numerous developed-site recreationists. The displaced recreationists successively move on · to other more primitive sites and can start a new wave of invasion, succession, and displacement by the users they displace to even more remote settings.[1] The ultimate impact of this invasion, succession, and displacement can lead to excessive wilderness visitation and impacts if uses of surrounding areas are not carefully planned and coordinated. Managers may facilitate undesirable impacts from this "ecology of recreation use" if they respond to every increase in use with development to accommodate it; for example, if they encourage campgrounds, large parking lots, or resort developments at the edge of wilderness. Furthermore, the most remote sections of a wilderness—highly prized by the most discriminating users—can have their naturalness and solitude impaired if wilderness managers are not aware of use interrelationships. Actions such as building trails in areas that are currently visited only by cross-country travelers seeking the greatest possible isolation may

---

[1]The phenomena of invasion, succession, and displacement in a recreation context is described in Burch and Wenger 1967; Hendee and Campbell 1969; Clark, Hendee, and Campbell 1971; Stankey 1974.

ultimately eliminate the most remote part of the recreation spectrum.

Principle 3: Wilderness Is a Distinct, Composite Resource with Inseparable Parts

To describe something as a resource is to recognize that it has utility for society, that it serves a function (Zimmerman 1933). Many of our resources are so defined by their economic value, but the definition of a resource is not limited by such a measure. On the contrary, the judgment by society that something has a worth or value, even though it lies outside our capacity to assign an economic measure to it, is the necessary prerequisite to the labeling of such an object as a resource.

Wilderness is an excellent example of something that has acquired such a value in our culture. To the early settlers, the abundant wilderness was something to be eliminated; it served only to hide Indians and wild animals and to hinder progress. In the last two or three generations, however, its growing scarcity has highlighted its unique qualities and prompted efforts to insure its preservation. It was not the physical presence of flora and fauna that made these lands wilderness; it was the recognition of their unique worth when preserved in their natural condition that supported their definition as a resource. Zimmerman's (1933) famous definition of a resource notes, "Resources are not, they become"; the physical qualities of the land that we once strove to overcome have now achieved a measure of utility and value that constitute definition as the "wilderness resource".

Wilderness has clearly achieved the status of a resource in our society by virtue of its cultural values and the legal sanctions attached to those values by the Wilderness Act. The Act refers to ". . . an enduring resource of wilderness" (Sec. 2a). From a management standpoint one important attribute of the wilderness resource is the natural realtionship among all its ecosystem parts; i.e., vegetation, water, forage, recreation, wildlife, geology. *It is a composite resource with inseparable parts, and the central focus of its management must be on the interrelationships of the whole, not on those component parts.*

This has important planning implications. For a wilderness one should not develop isolated management plans for vegetation, wildlife, and recreation; rather, one single wilderness plan must deal simultaneously with the interrelationships between these and all other component parts of the resource. Likewise, criteria controlling the use of wilderness should be based on the maintenance of these natural relationships. For instance, wilderness fishing might be limited by its potential

effects on shoreline vegetation and soil and the solitude afforded visitors as well as the impact on the fish populations. Other wilderness recreation use might be controlled, not only by physical capacity, but by expected tolerance of vegetation, wildlife distribution and behavior, and water quality.

If wilderness is viewed as a resource, what can be said about its renewability? To a considerable degree, renewability is a relative question. For example, timber is normally considered a renewable resource because the rotation length between harvests is relatively short while minerals are considered non-renewable because, for all practical purposes, once they are used, they are gone. But, this is accurate only in light of a reasonable time horizon. Given a geological time frame, even minerals are renewable; coal, for instance, is constantly being renewed as vegetative matter decomposes.

Where does wilderness fit into this renewability perspective? Clearly, commercial exploitation of its component parts would destroy what we define as the wilderness resource. But just as clearly, the passage of time, coupled with a restriction on further disturbance, would eventually lead to a reestablishment of primitive, naturally appearing conditions—although perhaps without some component of the original ecosystem such as a particular plant or animal species. In this sense, then, wilderness is renewable only to a degree. And, depending on the type of environment, renewal could require many human generations or centuries.

Renewability of the wilderness resource was a major theme in debate over the Wilderness Act. Many proponents pointed to the importance of the Act as a mechanism whereby the wilderness characteristics of disturbed sites might be allowed to recover. As Senator Frank Church (1972) noted: "This is one of the great promises of the Wilderness Act, that we can dedicate formerly abused areas where the primeval scene can be restored by natural forces." Thus, it is not easy to describe wilderness's precise status on the renewable-to-nonrenewable continuum. But even when management seeks to restore wilderness conditions, the focus must be on protecting the naturalness of relationships between its ecosystem parts.

Principle 4: The Purpose of Wilderness Management Is To Produce Human Values and Benefits

Wilderness is for people. This is a principle that bears restating. The preservation goals established for such areas are designed to provide values and benefits to society; as the Act notes: "It is . . . the policy of the Congress to secure for the American people of present and future generations the benefits of an enduring resource of wilderness."

The human values and benefits of wilderness are set forth as a management principle because it is so easy to forget that wilderness is not set aside for the sake of its flora and fauna, but for people. Wilderness management must aim at producing the important and—in the judgment of some—necessary, benefits they yield to people.

How human values and benefits are derived from wilderness is an important question. Direct benefits may result to wilderness visitors from the pleasure or therapy coincident to their wilderness recreation. Others might vicariously appreciate or indirectly benefit from wilderness, simply by knowing it is there or reading about it. Other indirect benefits can accrue to society from increased scientific knowledge derived from research in wilderness. These values and benefits are not easily measured, nor is there evidence that they are optimally or exclusively produced in wilderness. Nevertheless, concepts of human values and benefits to be derived from wilderness preservation and use are implicit in the wilderness ideology and philosophy which led to passage of the Wilderness Acts and the allocation of federal resources to serve such purposes. The continued protection of these human values and benefits must be a fundamental goal of wilderness management.

Two extreme orientations illustrate widely differing management positions, both aimed at enhancing the human values of wilderness. (See our discussion in chapter 1.) One perspective, the biocentric, emphasizes the degree of naturalness of wilderness—ecological integrity—as the basis for its human values and benefits. This perspective rests on the idea that because wilderness is prized as the antithesis of urbanization and civilization, compromising its naturalness will ultimately decrease its values to man. An alternative perspective, called anthropocentric (man-centered), implies that human values and benefits of wilderness rest on the direct aesthetic pleasure man receives from it. Under this view, this aesthetic potential should be facilitated by managing natural processes to enhance their aesthetic features (e.g., meadows and scenery) and by encouraging visitation so that the largest number of direct users will obtain them.

These philosophical orientations are related to *how* human values and benefits of wilderness can be enhanced by management. But they are stated in extremes and too much should not be made of the distinction. New national agency policy guides issued by both the National Park Service and Forest Service indicate both agencies are fairly pure in their orientation toward wilderness (USDI 1975; USDA 1976). In their management directions these new guidelines reflect a commitment to maintain high standards of naturalness and opportunities for solitude. The guides suggest that a deliberate effort must be made to ensure that wilderness stands out in marked contrast to environments already modified by human activity. It is from the primeval attributes of wilderness that its human values and benefits are derived; attempts to facilitate their enjoyment by making them easier, more convenient, or simultaneously accessible to too many people at one time can ultimately diminish them. While we think this calls for a biocentric leaning in wilderness management policy, this issue is political and controversial. (See chapter 1.) It is extremely important that the management philosophy be applied with common sense to avoid extreme purity, which can trigger a purity backlash.[2]

Principle 5: Wilderness Preservation Requires Management of Human Use and its Impact

The very idea of wilderness management is, in many ways, a paradox. On the one hand, wilderness conveys impressions of freedom, of land beyond the control of man. Management, on the other hand, suggests control and manipulation. However, this is only an apparent contradiction. In today's world, preservation of wilderness areas can be achieved *only* by deliberate management to minimize man's influence.

The need for management of wilderness users hardly needs to be argued (see chapter 1). National statistics point to a steady, upward growth in use. Specific examples of site impacts and deteriorated wilderness conditions can be found in virtually any area. Man's influence extends even to the most remote wilderness environments. Man's indirect influence is evident in unnatural vegetation patterns from fire prevention and suppression and a resulting unnatural distribution of wildlife. The fragile, sometimes irreplaceable qualities of these areas, are easily lost unless thoughtful, deliberate management protects against the direct impacts of use and the indirect but pervasive influence of civilization. Increasing the size of the NWPS offers only temporary or short-term protection. Ultimately the preservation of wilderness, and the values and benefits it offers people, will depend on the management of wilderness areas after they have been set aside.

The principal goal of wilderness preservation is the maintenance of long-term ecological processes. *Thus, wilderness management is basically concerned with*

---

[2]Discussions by Church (1977) and Weaver and Cutler (1977) illustrate some of the consequences of too pure an approach to wilderness management.

management of human use and influence to preserve natural processes. Recreational impacts are currently among the most critical, unnatural influences in wilderness. Therefore, managers are challenged to influence, modify, and if necessary, directly control use to minimize its impact (Lucas 1973).

Some resource-management professionals view the designation of land for wilderness purposes as an abdication of management responsibility. Nothing could be more wrong. Currently, wilderness management emphasizes people management. But ecological problems are also growing and wilderness managers will be increasingly challenged to monitor the naturalness of wilderness. Fire, for example, needs to be restored to a closer approximation of its historial role.

Principle 6: Wilderness Management Should Be Guided by Objectives Set Forth in Area Management Plans

Wilderness management actions must be guided by formal plans that include statements of goals and objectives and explain where, when, how, and why actions will take place to achieve them. Without such clear prescriptions, management can become uncoordinated and even include counterproductive measures that could thwart the preservation goals of the Wilderness Act. Wilderness management plans allow both local managers and the public to address the varying qualities and situations of individual areas so management strategies—consistent with legislative goals and national policy—can be determined.

As will be explained in chapter 8, wilderness management plans establish a hierarchy of guidelines for individual areas. Beginning with the broad, general goals contained in the Wilderness Act, these guidelines proceed to more explicit Departmental regulations and then to national agency policy. The hierarchy of direction in an area plan culminates with specific objectives for a given area and the policies and management actions needed to achieve them. This planning process permits local agency officials and citizens to review the varying situations of individual areas and develop management strategies consistent with broad legislative goals, Departmental regulations and agency policy, yet still remain responsive to specific local conditions.

Wilderness management plans must be clear statements of objectives that describe desired wilderness conditions. Every proposed management action must be evaluated for its potential contribution to a specific objective. Clear objectives, and the commitment to be guided by them, are important for several reasons.

Management actions can have enduring—even irreversible—results. The philosophies, perceptions, and definitions of wilderness can vary widely among managers. Plans with clear, formally stated objectives are needed to guide judgments about what management actions are necessary; to provide continuity when managers are replaced; and to prevent potential damage from independently conceived plans, no matter how well intentioned. Excessive or poorly conceived management actions can be as damaging to wilderness values as the absence of necessary management. For example, the accumulation of a series of relatively minor decisions formulated outside an overall planning framework might result in too many trails built to unnecessarily high standards, an excessive number of signs, or unnecessary restrictions on user activities. In the aggregate, these independent actions can depreciate wilderness values.

Objectives are also useful criteria for evaluating the success of wilderness management. If an objective is not reached, an evaluator needs to know why. Lack of feasibility? The need for different policies or implementing actions? The need for a different kind of, or a more conscientious, administration?

Because the goals of the Wilderness Act are so broad, it is very difficult to write clear objectives for all the various aspects of wilderness management. But because of their usefulness, it is crucial to develop, through an orderly planning process, the clearest and most specific objectives possible and to use them as constant guides to management. Only actions necessary to achieve objective should be implemented.

Principle 7: Wilderness Preservation Requires a Carrying Capacity Constraint

The capacity or ability of wilderness to absorb the impacts of use and retain its wilderness qualities is limited. As use increases or as damaging patterns of use develop at specific places or during particular times, those qualities that define the wilderness resource will disappear, sometimes gradually, sometimes with startling swiftness. The concept of carrying capacity— the use an area can tolerate without unacceptable impact occurring—offers a framework for limiting use in order to preserve wilderness qualities.

Change from natural ecological processes occurs inevitably in wilderness. The purpose of management is not to hold ecosystems in any kind of static condition, but to allow *natural* change to occur, with an absolute minimum of human-induced change. Both ecological conditions and available wilderness experiences are subject to such change. As described in greater detail in chapter 9, the standards of ecological integrity and solitude that are established for an area help define the carrying capacity of an individual wilderness.

Figure 7-1.—Wilderness requires a carrying capacity constraint for its preservation. Too many visitors can depreciate the quality of the wilderness environment and the solitude available to others. Trailriders east of Cloudy Pass near Lyman Lake, Glacier Peak Wilderness, Wash.

The concept of carrying capacity has two important parameters when applied to wilderness. (1) Physical and biological dimensions describe the amount and kind of use an ecosystem can sustain without undue evidence of unnatural impact. Campsite deterioration and expanding impact resulting from soil compaction, the denuding and proliferation of paths near locations of concentrated human use, exposed and protruding tree roots, the appearance of multiple trails across meadows, and unnatural behavior and distribution of wildlife are some signs that can reflect unnatural change from the physical impact of use. (2) Social or psychological dimensions refer to the levels and concentrations of human use an area can accommodate before the kind of solitude which helps define wilderness experiences is diminished. It is important to note here that "outstanding opportunities for solitude" are required by the Wilderness Act. Several studies document that solitude—privacy from persons in other parties, particularly from large parties of users encountered near one's campsite—is an important attribute of the wilderness experience desired by many users. Concentrations of wilderness visitors and resulting congestion at popular wilderness attractions such as hotsprings or lakes might indicate that the social carrying capacity is being approached or exceeded.

Carrying capacity will be discussed in more detail in Chapter 9, but here four major points should be stressed: (1) Carrying capacity is a relative term. It is not an absolute, inherent number that lies waiting for discovery by managers and researchers (Wagar 1968). Its range

depends on specific objectives that are established for an area. (2) Capacity must be established by managerial judgment—there is no magic yardstick to tell when it has been exceeded. (3) Capacity is tied to (a) the quality of the physical-biological environment and (b) the human experience offered by wilderness. (4) The development of capacity limits is a necessary part of the wilderness management planning process.

Unless use is limited to levels an area can tolerate without changing unnaturally, the long-term goals of wilderness preservation will slip through our fingers.

Principle 8: Wilderness Management Should Strive To Selectively Reduce the Physical and Social-Psychological Impacts of Use

The National Wilderness Preservation System under the Wilderness Act was not established primarily to provide for recreational needs. Rather, the Act's objective is to preserve an enduring wilderness resource characterized by naturalness and outstanding opportunities for solitude; and, only with these goals as an overriding constraint, to provide for primitive types of recreation and other permitted uses. Implicit in these legislatively established goals is the requirement that recreation use be curtailed if it interferes with preserving established standards of naturalness and opportunities for solitude. Controls on use are already being implemented in some of the more heavily used wildernesses and at certain popular locations in many others. Whenever such restrictions are contemplated, several difficult questions must be faced: Who should be restricted? Under what conditions and criteria? How should restrictions be implemented?

This principle calls for selective restriction—use restrictions should focus on specific *impacts* of use on the wilderness environment and the wilderness experience of other visitors. It calls for a site specific orientation rather than an across-the-board approach that would impose restrictions everywhere in a wilderness to solve problems that might be only local or temporary in nature.

Obviously, not all uses produce equal impacts. Accordingly, all types of wilderness use and activities can be ranked according to their relative physical and social-psychological impacts; when restrictions are necessary, those activities having the greatest impact can be the first ones controlled. For example, various types of wilderness use might be ranked, in the absence of an actual study, in the following order of decreasing environmental and social-psychological impact: Large parties of horse users, small parties of horse users, large parties of overnight campers, small parties of overnight campers, small

143

parties of overnight campers not building fires, small parties of day hikers. Additional criteria—such as visitor's skill levels—might be used to establish or modify priorities among users (Behan 1976).

In addition, the unacceptable impact from various users might require regulation only in a few locations in a wilderness. Furthermore, the vulnerability of the resource is greater at different times, such as in early spring with its lush and easily damaged vegetation or on peak weekends when use is heaviest. Thus, to minimize excessive environmental and social-psychological impacts, restrictions should be selective—aimed at times, places, and users having the greatest potential for damage—rather than enforcing wholesale restrictions.

This principle of selective restriction strives to promote equity by specifying those conditions under which uses will be regulated; i.e., what kinds of use, where, and when. Discrimination against certain types of use, such as horse parties or large, organized groups of hikers, is based on their respective impacts on the wilderness environment. Wilderness managers are relieved from deciding arbitrarily on a certain mix of horse users, organized groups, hikers, and so forth; or alternatively, from deciding that because they cannot make such choices, everyone—or no one—must be restricted.

Principle 9: Only Minimum Regulation Necessary To Achieve Wilderness Management Objectives Should Be Applied

The themes of freedom, spontaneity, and escape have emerged as important components of the wilderness experience. However, as discussed earlier, to preserve the unique qualities of wilderness, specific restrictions are sometimes required. It is important to remember that these regulations can significantly alter the experience of users.

Use regulation, of course, encompasses a broad range of actions. It is helpful to think of a continuum of use-management actions ranging from those that are subtle, light-handed, and indirect to those that are direct and authoritarian (such as telling users where they can travel and camp and how long they can stay). As we will explain in chapters 14 and 15, both indirect and direct types of use-management actions are legitimate techniques; the decision as to which approach is most appropriate depends on managers' judgments about the degree of regulation necessary to achieve wilderness management objectives.

The principle of minimum regulation calls for the use of only that level of control necessary to achieve a specific

Figure 7–2.—Public education is one of the most important tools for wilderness managers. Supplying visitors with information can help prevent many undesirable impacts, thus postponing the need for more stringent regulations. This is consistent with the principle of using only the minimum level of regimentation necessary to achieve wilderness management objectives. Here, a wilderness ranger contacts users to seek their help in preserving the area.

objective.[3] If, for example, managers wish to bring about a more even use distribution, they might first seek the cooperation of informed users. To achieve this, they might provide users with information about current use distributions, alternative trailheads or areas they might use, times when concentrations are lowest, and so forth. However, if current impacts are so severe that this light-handed, indirect approach seems inadequate or if it fails to bring about the desired redistribution of use, then a more restrictive, direct-action approach might be needed. A manager might need to limit camping at damaged sites, assign entry quotas for each trailhead, or even assign campsites. *The guiding principle is that only the minimum regimentation necessary to achieve established wilderness management objectives is justified.* Use controls applied more widely than necessary, for administrative convenience or for any other reason, are not justified if the National Wilderness Preservation System is to be used as fully as possible while it is being preserved.

Wilderness managers are challenged to develop, test, and implement as many indirect approaches as possible in order to delay and minimize the need for direct controls. Some of the less regimenting approaches include visitor education, appeals for self-compliance and low-impact camping practices, and location of trailheads

---

[3]Minimum regulation is directly related to the so-called "minimum tool" rule which specified that when managing wilderness biota to simulate or supplement natural processes, the minimum device necessary to accomplish the objective should be used. (See chapter 11 for its application to wildlife.)

and trails to minimize impact on fragile areas. In the beginning, direct controls could be limited to on-site management of overused locations to educate and disperse users. Only as a last resort, when a battery of specific and successively restrictive measures has failed, is direct control of visitation to the entire wilderness justified.

However, managers must balance the regimenting effects of limiting entry against the aggregate impact of numerous controls on particular activities within an area. The attempt to preserve all possible opportunity for visitation to a wilderness might produce a nightmare of activity and site-specific restrictions such as only hikers on this route, no camping at these locations, and no fires at others. For this reason, some managers favor limiting numbers of visitors in order to preserve the freedom of those who are admitted. Under this approach, once an individual gains entry to the wilderness, there is a minimum of control over where he goes, when, how he travels, and so forth. By controlling numbers, types, and distribution of users at the entry point, the need for control over behavior within the area is minimized. The inverse relationship between numbers of users and individual freedom is an important perspective. In every area there is some threshold beyond which the individual wilderness experience becomes so diluted by additional restrictions that it is in danger of being completely lost. It is at this point—which must be subjectively determined by managers—that rationing entry must begin.

Principle 10: The Management of Individual Areas Should Be Governed by a Concept of Nondegradation

We have described wilderness as part of an environmental modification spectrum ranging from the paved to the primeval, i.e., from heavily urbanized environments to those which are relatively remote and pristine. Through the Wilderness Act of 1964 our society has elected to preserve, unimpaired for future generations in a National Wilderness Preservation System, selected primeval areas. But even within the part of the environmental spectrum that includes wilderness there is a range of settings. It is obvious that not all areas classified as wilderness are identical in their primeval qualities. Areas vary in the degree to which their naturalness has remained unspoiled or their opportunity for solitude undiminished by current, established uses. The definition of wilderness changes, depending on the nature of surrounding areas. The relativity of wilderness was reflected in debates over the so-called Eastern Wilderness Act of 1975 and the subsequent classification of areas in the East that some feel did not meet the quality criteria of the Wilderness Act of 1964. The concept of nondegradation has emerged as a basic principle of air- and water-quality management and offers a framework to cope with variation in wilderness quality as well.

Basically, the nondegradation concept calls for the maintenance of present environmental conditions if they equal or exceed minimum standards, and the restoration of below-minimum levels. For example, where air quality is currently higher than that required by the Clean Air Act, that higher level shall be preserved and not allowed to deteriorate to minimum standards established under that Act. Thus, minimum standards of air quality do not constitute an acceptable level to which air quality everywhere will be allowed to deteriorate; rather, the objective is to maintain high standards, to prevent further degradation, and to restore below-minimum situations to acceptable levels (Meyers and Tarlock 1971; Mihaley 1972).

As applied to wilderness, this nondegradation principle seeks recognition of the variation in the level of naturalness and solitude available in individual wildernesses. The objective is to prevent further degradation of current naturalness and solitude in each wilderness and restore substandard settings to minimum levels rather than letting all areas in the National Wilderness Preservation System deteriorate to a minimum standard.

For example, the existence of wildernesses that possess only minimum levels of naturalness and solitude need not be regarded as setting a precedent to which areas of higher quality will be allowed to descend. The near-pristine areas in the Intermountain West should not be allowed to decline to the substantial level of impact found in some southern California wildernesses. Likewise, wilderness classification of heavily impacted areas in the Eastern United States does not mean that the level of naturalness and solitude found in those areas should constitute an acceptable level for areas in the West. To a certain reasonable degree, under the nondegradation principle, the conditions prevailing in each area when it is classified establish the bench mark of naturalness to be sought by management.

The nondegradation concept also does not rule out the opportunity to upgrade or restore quality. Where existing conditions are judged to be below minimum acceptable levels, an appropriate priority of management is to promote restoration of the wilderness to minimum quality levels. This does not automatically imply that wilderness restoration will involve the active manipulation of the resource such as scarifying campsites, planting natural materials, fertilizing, and watering. There are numerous opportunities to promote restoration through the control of use numbers, the timing of use, and other management measures designed to facilitate restoration by natural processes.

The issue of just how pure to manage each wilderness has plagued wilderness management on the National Forests for years. Hopefully, the recent adoption of the nondegradation principle will help resolve the issue.[4]

Principle 11: In Managing Use, Wilderness-Dependent Activities Should Be Favored

Wilderness serves as the setting for many activities ranging from scientific study to recreational pursuits such as fishing, backpacking, and picnicking. Some of these activities depend to a significant degree on wilderness conditions, a primeval setting, for their conduct. For example, some types of scientific study are dependent on the availability of a substantially unaltered ecosystem, perhaps covering a large area. Conversely, other activities such as certain kinds of hunting and fishing are not dependent upon a wilderness situation at all, although they can be enhanced by such a setting. Whenever one or more uses conflict, the principle of dependency, that calls for favoring activities that depend the most on wilderness conditions, is used to resolve use conflicts and prevent overuse. This principle is intended to assure optimum use of wilderness resources.

As noted above, different uses can be categorized by the degree to which they depend on wilderness conditions for their enjoyment. Some are specifically wilderness dependent; others are only coincidentally linked to wilderness and can be pursued elsewhere. These transferable activities, by definition, have a relatively large number of alternative settings where they can be enjoyed whereas wilderness-dependent activities have relatively few. Resolving conflicts among competing wilderness uses in favor of those that are highly dependent, then, will have a net positive effect on social welfare because it prevents the displacement of those users who depend on wilderness, while the displaced users will suffer less because their interests can be satisifed elsewhere. This requires, of course, an adequate supply of nonwilderness-type opportunities.[5]

Defining an activity as wilderness-dependent can be difficult. Often, an activity itself is not dependent, but the particular style or form in which it is pursued might be. For example, hunting is not necessarily wilderness-dependent. However, certain styles of hunting, such as pursuing game under the most natural conditions away from roads or stalking a Dall Sheep are highly dependent on wilderness settings. It is the assumed or actual need for primitive conditions, not the mere quest for game,

---

[4]Letter from M. Rupert Cutler, Assistant Secretary of Agriculture, to John McGuire, Chief, Forest Service, summarizing wilderness management policy on the National Forests. August 11, 1977. 5 p.

[5]The dependency argument has its root in the concept of minority rights championed by Bob Marshall (Marshall 1930; 1937). A more recent paper casts the argument as "A Sociological Criterion for Outdoor Recreation Resource Allocation" by Joseph Harry, John Hendee, and Robert Stein. Paper presented to Joint Session of annual meeting of the Rural Sociological Society and American Sociological Association, August 1972, New Orleans. 14 p. mimeo. See also Partridge (1975).

Figure 7-3.—An important principle of management is to feature wilderness-dependent recreational activities. Many activities can be wilderness-dependent if naturalness and solitude are essential parts of the experience. *Left:* Rider in the Sycamore Canyon Wilderness, Ariz., *right:* Fisherman at Lower Aero Lake in the Beartooth Primitive Area, Mont.

that defines certain kinds of hunting as wilderness-dependent (see chapter 11 for discussion).

Likewise, while fishing can be pursued in a wide variety of settings, certain styles of fishing might be dependent upon wilderness for their enjoyment. Fishermen who desire remote, difficult-to-reach lakes where one can fish under natural conditions without meeting many other people must rely on wilderness for such opportunities. Many users report that fishing is an important part of their wilderness experience, enhancing other important satisfactions such as nature appreciation and contemplation.

Thus, favoring wilderness-dependent activities might call for reducing or discouraging—rather than eliminating—certain *forms* of some activities. One is reminded again of the interdependency of wilderness with the rest of the outdoor opportunity spectrum. The key to favoring wilderness-dependent activities in classified wilderness is the availability of alternative non-wilderness lands to which inappropriate activity can be diverted.

Summary

These 11 principles provide the base from which much of our subsequent discussion about wilderness management is derived. As suggested at the outset, the principles are not necessarily comprehensive nor do they, by themselves, insure quality wilderness management. What they do provide is a broad conceptual foundation from which the wilderness management job can be approached and from which solutions to specific problems might be derived. At the very least, for those in search of consistent wilderness management policies and actions, they provide a basis for reviewing and evaluating solutions to problems.

Among the co-authors, the author primarily responsible for preparation of this chapter was John C. Hendee.

Literature Cited

Behan, R.W.
    1976. Rationing wilderness use: an example from the Grand Canyon. Western Wildlands 3(2):23–26.
Burch, William R., and Wiley D. Wenger.
    1967. The social characteristics of participants in three styles of family camping. USDA Forest Serv. Res. Paper. PNW–48, 30 p. Pac. Northwest For. and Range Ex. Stn., Portland, Oreg.
Carhart, Arthur.
    1961. Planning for America's wildlands. 97 p. The Telegraph Press, Harrisburg, Pa.
Church, Frank.
    1972. [Preservation of wilderness areas]. Wilderness Rep. 9(5).
Church, Frank.
    1977. Wilderness in a balanced land use framework. First annual Wilderness Resource Distinguished Lecture. Univ. Idaho Wilderness Research Center, March 21, 18 p. Reprinted as "Whither Wilderness," Am. For. 83(7):11–12, 38–41.
Clark, Roger N., John C. Hendee, and Frederick Campbell.
    1971. Values, behavior, and conflict in modern camping culture. J. Leisure Res. 3(3):143–149.
Clawson, Marion.
    1975. Conflicts and strategies in forest land management. J. Soil and Water Conserv. 39(2):63–67.
Gould, Ernest M., Jr.
    1961. Planning a recreational complex. Am. For. 67(8):30–34.
Hart, William J.
    1966. A systems approach to park planning. IUCN Publ., New Series: Supplementary Pap. No. 4. 118 p. Morges, Switzerland.
Hay, Edward.
    1974. Wilderness experiment: it's working. Am. For. 80(12):26–29.
Hendee, John C.
    1974. A scientist's views on some current wilderness management issues. Western Wildlands 1(2):27–32.

Hendee, John C., and Frederick Campbell.
    1969. Social aspects of outdoor recreation—the developed campground. Trends in Parks and Recreation 6(4):13–16.
Hendee, John C., and George Stankey.
    1973. Biocentricity in wilderness management. Bioscience 23(9):535–538.
Lloyd, R. Duane, and Virlis Fischer.
    1972. Dispersed versus concentrated recreation as forest policy. Paper presented to the Seventh World Forestry Congress. Buenos Aires, Argentina, Oct. 4–18, 1972, 16 p.
Lucas, Robert C.
    1973. Wilderness: a management framework. J. Soil and Water Conserv. 28(4):150–154.
Lucas, Robert C., and George H. Stankey.
    1974. Social carrying capacity for backcountry recreation. *In* Outdoor recreation research: applying the results. USDA Forest Service Gen. Tech. Rep. NC-9, p. 14-23. North Central For. Exp. Stn., St. Paul, Minn.
Marshall, Robert.
    1930. The problem of the wilderness. Sci. Mon. 30(2):141–148.
Marshall, Robert.
    1937. The universe of the wilderness is vanishing. Nature 29(4):235–240.
Meyers, Charles J., and A. Dan Tarlock.
    1971. Water Pollution. *In* Water resource management, p. 677–708. Charles J. Meyer and A. Dan Tarlock, eds. Foundation Press, Mineola, N.Y.
Mihaley, Marc B.
    1972. The Clean Air Act and the concept of nondegradation. Sierra Club vs. Rukelhaus. Ecol. Law Rev. 2(4):801–836.
Nash, Roderick.
    1973. Wilderness and the American mind. 2d ed., 300 p. Yale University Press, New Haven, Conn.
Partridge, Clayton.
    1975. Who needs wilderness? Signpost (1-2):10–12, 27.

Stankey, George H.
    1974. Criteria for the determination of recreational carrying capacity in the Colorado River Basin. *In* Environmental management in the Colorado River Basin, p. 82–101. A. Berry Crawford, and Dean F. Peterson, eds. Utah State University Press, Logan, Utah.
U.S. Department of Agriculture, Forest Service.
    1976. Chapter 2320: Wilderness management (national wilderness policy guidelines). *In* Forest Service manual. Washington, D.C.

U.S. Department of the Interior, National Park Service.
    1975. Chapter VI: Wilderness and preservation and management. *In* Management policies. Washington, D.C.

Weaver, James W., and Rupert Cutler.
    1977. Wilderness policy: a colloquy between Congressman Weaver and Assistant Secretary Cutler. J. For. 75(7):392–394.

Zimmerman, Erich.
    1933. World resources and industries. 832 p. Harper and Brothers, New York.

The management direction for individual wildernesses, under the constraints of the Wilderness Act, are set forth in wilderness area management plans. Wilderness management to preserve an area's distinctive qualities of naturalness and solitude can be no better than the underlying planning process. Pole Creek-Rio Grande National Forest.

8 Wilderness Management Planning

The management of wilderness needs to be guided by formal plans that prescribe the what, where, when, how, and why of proposed management actions. It is through management plans for individual wildernesses that the hierarchy of applicable direction, i.e., legislation, departmental regulation, and agency policy, is translated into action.[1]

The Need for Planning

Without management plans, derived from an orderly planning process, wilderness management can be no more than a series of uncoordinated reactions to immediate problems. That kind of management by reaction can be counter-productive to overall wilderness preservation goals because management direction can be easily shaped by a succession of minor decisions—a tyranny of small decisions—one leading to another, with

[1]The authors wish to thank Bill Fessel, Dick Walker, and Dan Wood for providing material from their planning efforts at Glacier Peak Wilderness, Anaconda-Printlar Wilderness, and Browns Canyon Primitive Area, respectively.

This chapter was written by John C. Hendee and Russ Koch, graduate research assistant at the University of Washington, College of Forest Resources.

cumulative results which are at best undesirable and which at their worst might sometimes be irreversible. Unplanned management can be recognized by a shifting focus on problem after problem as each becomes pressing; inconsistent, conflicting actions; and a loss of overall direction toward wilderness preservation goals.

In the planning process, differences in management philosophy and ideas can be consolidated prior to taking actions which have long-range effects upon the wilderness resource. Formal plans protect the consistency and continuity of management direction even if philosophies, perceptions, and definitions of wilderness differ widely between individual managers. Formal plans that establish clear objectives for an area, and the policies and actions by which objectives will be pursued, are essential to guide wilderness management toward consistent outcomes. Good plans can stabilize management, despite changes in personnel or the simultaneous influence of several managers on wildernesses governed by more than one administrative unit. The planning process also gives the interested public an opportunity to learn about, evaluate, and provide input to management. It makes planning explicit and visible. Thus, the effectiveness and consistency of wilderness management, as well as the involvement of the public and their acceptance of that management, are highly dependent on plans and the planning process.

The Federal wilderness managing agencies increasingly recognize the importance of planning as a process and as a set of methods that will help them meet their legislative mandates. The first wilderness management plans were developed by the Forest Service shortly after passage of the Wilderness Act to guide management of the "instant" wildernesses created by that legislation. Likewise, the National Park Service began to develop backcountry management plans for their roadless areas that would ultimately be reviewed for wilderness classification and which were attracting increasing use. Both agencies are planning the management of roadless lands that will ultimately be considered for wilderness classification to insure that they retain their wilderness character until Congress determines their future use. And, as will be explained, the Fish and Wildlife Service and the Bureau of Land Management also have a planning process to guide and direct management of their classified, proposed, and potential wilderness.

Planning Flexibility and Effectiveness

Despite these initial efforts, wilderness (and back-country) management planning processes are still in an emerging, formative stage. A variety of approaches and styles of plans have been developed, ranging from brief documents providing only the most general direction to detailed plans that lose the reader with specific details. This diversity is healthy to the extent that it provides the flexibility needed to address the complexity of management problems posed by different areas. On the other hand, too many planning approaches may indicate the need for more consistency based on the acceptance and application of established planning principles.

The consistency, quality, and utility of wilderness management plans can be improved with the development of planning frameworks specifically adapted to wilderness. In our opinion, there is room for flexibility in format and detail of different wilderness plans as long as they translate the legislative mandate of the Act into specific objectives for individual areas so that necessary management actions can be identified and implemented.

In the coming decades the wilderness management efforts of all the agencies will depend on the quality of plans that summarize management policies and actions for individual areas. Tightly reasoned plans are necessary to identify what needs to be done and how it might be achieved, and to provide a basis for discussion with interested citizens. Ultimately, the responsiveness of

agencies and Congress in appropriating manpower and money for wilderness management will depend on the internal logic of these plans in identifying acceptable objectives and the management efforts necessary to achieve them.

In this chapter we (1) review the wilderness management planning processes applied by the National Park Service, Forest Service, Fish and Wildlife Service, and Bureau of Land Management; (2) suggest a terminology expressing a hierarchy of directions around which plans can be developed; (3) suggest a goal-achievement framework and format for preparing wilderness management plans; (4) provide excerpts from actual plans to illustrate application of the suggested framework; and (5) discuss problems that arise in preparing wilderness management plans.

Wilderness Management Planning in the Federal Agencies

Following is a description of the current management planning process applied by the Federal agencies that administer backcountry, classified, proposed, and potential wilderness areas.

National Park Service

Management direction for wilderness in the National Park System comes from the Wilderness Act, the National Parks Act of 1916 (as amended), legislation establishing individual parks, and Congressional Acts designating wilderness within a particular park. Interpretation of this legislation is found in Department of the Interior Guidelines for Wilderness Proposals by USDI agencies, and Management Policies of the National Park Service. A statement by the National Park Service Director to Congress in 1975 summarizes Park Service National Wilderness Guidelines (Everhardt 1975).

Congressional intention reflected in the laws and the federal department and agency interpretation of those laws are implemented predominantly through two levels of planning applicable to all National Parks, National Recreation Areas, Historical Sites, and National Monuments administered by the National Park Service: (1) General management plans and (2) implementation plans.

1. *General management plans* (formerly known as master plans) are the basis for National Park Service planning. These documents, which address an entire

park, provide the framework for long-range visitor use, resource management, and development within the bounds of law and agency policy. For each park, the general management plan identifies overall purpose; land classifications; management objectives; significance, interrelationships, limitations, and capabilities of park resources and their relationship to the region; and visitor programs required to achieve the desired objectives of the park. The management objectives set forth in the plan address the two most important park management challenges: (1) Resource preservation and (2) management of visitor use.

An approved plan and, if significant impacts will result, a final environmental impact statement drafted in conformity with the National Environment Policy Act are required before any development program or certain other management decisions may be carried out.

2. *Implementation plans* are the National Park Service's second level of planning. These plans describe methods for achieving general management objectives. Implementation plans may deal with portions of a park, such as a wilderness, backcountry area, or development zone. Sometimes they are involved with a specific park-wide subject like fire management, interpretive programs, or concessions. Wilderness and backcountry management plans in National Parks fall under the Park Service category of implementation plans.

It is Park Service policy that each administrative unit of the National Park System containing backcountry, classified wilderness, or proposed wilderness prepare a management plan for each of these areas (USDI NPS 1975). The purpose of these plans is to give management direction that will assure that the specific purposes of backcountry and wilderness are achieved and that the desired public benefits are realized. Each plan should identify all problem situations such as overcrowding, stock damage to trails and tundra, human waste, visitor safety, or grizzly bears—along with actions proposed to eliminate, lessen, or otherwise deal with each problem.

Preparation and approval of wilderness or backcountry management plans proceed in the following sequence. Plans are prepared by managers and staff assistants at the respective park under the direction of the Park Superintendent. The first level of certification or approval is given by the Superintendent when he recommends approval of the plan and forwards it to his regional office. Following policy review by regional staff and the Washington office, final approval is granted by the regional director.

Forest Service

Management direction for wilderness in the National Forest System comes from the Multiple Use—Sustained Yield Act which established Congressional philosophy and policy for management of the National Forests, the Wilderness Act, and sometimes legislation establishing individual wildernesses in the National Forests. Further direction is contained in U.S. Department of Agriculture regulations, and in Forest Service policy guidelines for wilderness management, chapter 2320 of the Forest Service Manual and its supplements (USDA FS 1976).

The Forest Service has three levels of planning which relate to wilderness: (1) regional planning guides or area guides, (2) wilderness resource plans, and (3) ranger district wilderness action plans (USDA, Forest Service 1973; 1976).

1. *Regional Planning Guides.* Planning for all resource management programs on the National Forests is given general conceptual direction by regional area guides which also coordinate regional National Forest resources with Federal, State, and local agencies, population needs, and trends. The guides recognize National Forest wildernesses within the region as special zones which require separate planning. The regional planning guide may include a special zone chapter on wilderness that gives a brief statement of management objectives and coordination requirements for all wilderness in that region (USDA FS 1976).

2. *Wilderness Resource Management Plans.* In accord with the regional planning guide a wilderness resource management plan is prepared for each wilderness. This plan is the direction-setting document establishing management objectives, specific policies, and actions for that wilderness. The responsibility for developing the wilderness management plan is vested in the Supervisor of the National Forest containing the wilderness. It is usually written by his recreation staff with involvement and technical assistance by the district rangers and their staffs who will ultimately implement management on the ground. Because many wildernesses occupy more than one National Forest and several ranger districts, sometimes a special planning team is appointed to prepare the plan. When completed to the satisfaction of the responsible Forest Supervisor(s), the plan is submitted to the Regional Forester who has authority for final approval.

An addition to the above procedure involves grazing, an allowed use in National Forest wilderness, which takes place under 10-year permits issued to private individuals. A range allotment management plan is required as a supporting measure for all grazing permits, even for permits in wilderness. However, overall management direction for wilderness forage will be contained within the wilderness management plan.

3. *Wilderness Management Action Plans.* Ideally the wilderness management plan concerns itself primarily with translating national and regional direction into objectives and specific policy applicable to a given wilderness. Although it can set forth some of the specific on-the-ground actions (what will be done and where) to implement policies and achieve objectives, the detailed field activity (the when, how, and by whom) is spelled out in wilderness management action plans. The Forest Service manual provides this guideline: "Plans for the year-to-year or day-to-day operation of the wilderness as the guidance for wilderness management personnel and District Ranger will be prepared only as needed and in the manner and format best suited to meet such need. They will follow direction stated in the management plan" (USDA, Forest Service 1976, Chapter 2322.3). Several programs or sets of related actions affecting a particular aspect of a wilderness can be included under the heading of action plans, that is, a fire management plan, a trails or transportation plan, a signing plan, visitor control plan, structure maintenance or removal plan.

The need for action plans will depend on the complexity of the wilderness management challenge in a particular area. All or some of the action plans listed above might be prepared or updated annually by each ranger district having all or part of a wilderness to administer. The Anaconda-Pintlar plan provides for "resource compartment plans" to establish "site specific actions" called for in the overall wilderness management plan. (See footnote 3.)

By whatever name or focus, action plans spell out when and how directions set forth in the wilderness management plan will be implemented. When needed actions are identified and assigned priorities, the costs of their implementation should also be estimated. Such data facilitate budgeting. Depending on annual appropriations, this part of the plan helps determine how many actions are undertaken and which ones are carried out first.

Fish and Wildlife Service

Management direction for wilderness in the National Wildlife Refuge System comes from the Wilderness Act, from the Wildlife Refuge System Administration Act of 1966 and its supplemental amendments, and from legislation establishing individual units of the Refuge System except where the areas were purchased or withdrawn from public lands under Executive order. Further national direction comes from published regulations for Wilderness Preservation and Management (50 CFR, part 35), U.S. Department of the Interior guides, and agency national policy for wilderness management.

Congressional direction in the form of laws, and their interpretation in Federal departmental guides and national agency policy, is implemented through two levels of planning. Land use plans are prepared for each refuge unit and can include separate plans for management of hunting and fishing, grazing, public use, fire control, and other important activities. Wilderness management plans for each wilderness are prepared as an element of the land use plan.

Bureau of Land Management

As explained in chapter 6, the Federal Land Policy and Management Act of 1976 calls for the review of all Bureau of Land Management roadless areas and roadless islands within 15 years, to determine their suitability or nonsuitability for inclusion by Congress in the National Wilderness Preservation System. Prior to 1976, the BLM had established, by its administrative authority, a natural and primitive areas system. All such areas established prior to November 1, 1975, must be reviewed and recommendations regarding their future status as wilderness made to the President by July 1, 1980. Because these lands might eventually be classified as wilderness, their current planning and management is directed at preserving their wilderness qualities. The BLM manual, in a section on primitive area policy, sets more specific management direction.

"It is the Bureau policy that . . . BLM primitive areas will be managed to maintain the same quality as lands included in the National Wilderness Preservation System" (USDI BLM 1971, section 6221.06).

The BLM has two planning documents which guide management of primitive areas: The management framework plan and the activity plan.

1. *Management Framework Plan (MFP).* The MFP guides management for larger areas called planning units. A primitive area can be part of one planning unit. Each resource area (similar to a Forest Service ranger district) is divided into planning units. Criteria for determining planning unit boundaries include topography, types of resources, transportation routes, and so forth. These planning unit boundaries are not political

boundaries but logical or natural boundaries from the field manager's point of view.

If a large roadless area of 5,000 acres or more is identified within a planning unit, the MFP can recommend the area be designated as a primitive area. This recommendation would be based upon inventory information identifying the area as one with primitive values as defined in BLM Manual, chapter 6221. The MFP thus sets overall goals for primitive area management.

2. *Activity Plan.* Once the management goal for a roadless area is identified in the MFP, management prescriptions are defined in the activity plan. This document identifies specific management actions and programs to be carried out in the primitive area.

Management framework plans and activity plans pertinent to primitive areas are prepared in the appropriate BLM district office and reviewed in the State and Washington offices prior to approval by the State director.

As mentioned earlier, the Federal Land Policy and Management Act of 1976 provides for the classification of BLM areas into the NWPS. While the description of BLM planning processes focuses on their administratively designated primitive areas, similar processes will no doubt be applied to proposed and classified wilderness areas as they are identified by the agency and classified by Congress.

As the foregoing summary indicates, wilderness management planning is a formal activity within the respective agencies. Planning is important for management of proposed as well as classified wilderness—any area where the land management objectives are to preserve wilderness qualities and provide related benefits. We move now into a discussion of planning concepts and a suggested framework that will be useful in writing wilderness management plans.

Planning Terminology and the Hierarchy of Direction

Wilderness management plans reflect a hierarchy of direction. These plans are the product of increasingly specific descriptions of desired conditions. A particular plan should set forth basic direction and objectives for a particular wilderness. This direction comes not only from the Wilderness Act but from other legislation such as the managing agency's organic act or the law establishing an individual wilderness.

The planning framework offered in this chapter adapts basic planning principles to wilderness management; it emphasizes planning as a decisionmaking process that seeks the attainment of clearly stated management goals and objectives (Webber 1969; Wheaton 1970; Alston 1972). After defining goals and objectives, the plan should state the management mechanisms (policies and actions) to be used for their attainment. The goals and objectives stated in the plan serve two purposes: (1) They are *criteria* for determining what management policies and actions are necessary and (2) they are *standards* against which the effectiveness of wilderness management can later be judged.

Regardless of the particular organization or format that is used in a wilderness management plan, certain basic planning concepts are needed. When labeled, these concepts provide a terminology for discussing the hierarchy of direction ranging from general goals to specific actions. We recognize that some of the terms we use can have variations in meaning, but we urge acceptance of our definitions here so readers can follow the way the concepts are used in the planning framework that follows.

Goals are a portrait of ideal ends or effects. Goals, although not attainable, give direction and purpose. They provide direction and limits to the range of potential objectives. They are often lofty statements of intent. One example from the Wilderness Act is ". . . to secure for the American people the benefits of an enduring resource of wilderness." We have heard many discussions arguing whether a particular statement is a *goal* or an *objective.* Our view is that the distinction rests on specificity and attainability; objectives, which *are* attainable, are more specific than goals.

Broad goals for the National Wilderness Preservation System are found in the Wilderness Act although, as explained earlier, other legislation pertinent to different agencies and particular areas can also influence direction by helping shape goals.

Objectives are statements of specific conditions to be achieved—reference points that, if attained, will assure progress in the direction of established goals (Young 1974; USDA 1974). In the suggested planning framework that follows, objectives are used to describe wilderness conditions to be achieved and/or maintained through management.

Objectives are shaped by the goals they serve. As descriptions of the field conditions sought through management, objectives serve as criteria for identifying the management policies and actions necessary to achieve them. Clearly stated objectives are the key to effective management plans. We suggest that plans include objectives for all important aspects of the wilderness resource and its use. For example, objectives might be stated for topics such as trails and travel, fish and wildlife, fire, and recreation.

Current situation and assumptions are statements that define local conditions and expectations with regard to any particular aspect of the wilderness covered by the plan. Because areas in the National Wilderness Preservation System vary in their characteristics, level of use, and other local conditions, important information about current situations and assumptions about how things will change in the future should be identified. This information can be helpful, both in specifying feasible objectives and in identifying measures necessary to achieve them. For example, current heavy use by hikers in a portion of a wilderness, combined with expectations for future increases in use, might influence objectives as well as the policies and management actions deemed necessary to achieve them.

Management Mechanisms is a collective term that refers to *policies, programs, actions,* and *standards.* These are the manager's arsenal of tools to be applied as needed to achieve objectives.

Policies are explicit expressions of intent describing what will be done in order to attain objectives. Sometimes, a policy describes what will not be done or otherwise prescribes constraints on management activity.

Programs are sets of related actions that are combined to help achieve particular objectives within the constraints of established policy.

Actions are specific practices applied to achieve objectives, but within the constraints of established policy and programs.

Standards serve as performance criteria, indicating acceptable norms, specifications, or quality of actions.

Following is an example of how *goals* and *objectives, current situations,* and *assumptions* about the future, and *management mechanisms* are organized in a hierarchy of direction that should be contained in plans.

To assure progress toward the *goal* of ". . . minimizing the impact of man and his technology upon the wilderness resource," specific objectives must be established and met. An *objective* for recreational use, one particular aspect of wilderness that would usually be covered explicitly in a management plan, might be to "provide opportunity for primitive recreation featuring naturalness of the wilderness environment, solitude,

Figure 8–1.—The most important elements of good management plans are clearly stated objectives. Objectives serve as criteria both for determining necessary management actions and for later evaluating how well they were achieved. Here National Park Service and Forest Service wilderness managers discuss a planning problem involving coordination between the agencies.

physical and mental challenge, and inspiration, consistent with the long-range preservation of natural conditions and opportunity for solitude in the wilderness." This objective is a statement of a condition to be achieved through management. Although the achievement of such a condition might not be directly measurable and might not even be apparent to a layman, it *is* attainable. Theoretically, at least, a team of experts could study the situation and judge whether the objective had been reached.

One *current situation* statement describing conditions in the wilderness might point to a large amount of litter at several heavy-use locations, and an *assumption* might be that recreational use of the wilderness will increase. Litter, a form of human debris, is clearly contradictory to the naturalness of wilderness. An obvious *policy* would thus direct management to "take necessary action to see that litter is removed from the wilderness." *Programs* aimed at removing litter could be prescribed, such as the "pack it out" program that encourages wilderness users to "pick up and pack out" their litter and garbage. Under the pack-it-out program, a number of *actions* might be included, such as posting signs at wilderness trailheads; a pack-it-out message issued with wilderness permits; and wilderness ranger contacts to ask, remind, and explain the need for visitors to pack out their litter and other debris. *Standards* define acceptable results of these actions. Some pertinent standards here might include definitions of acceptable cleanliness in the wilderness and the prescribed format and information content for antilitter posters to be placed at trailheads.

The substance of the above example is not the important point here. What is important is the internal logic reflected in the planning framework through which a hierarchy of direction was implemented; that is, goals leading logically to objectives—interpreted according to the current situation and assumptions about the future—which were used as criteria for deriving necessary policy and programs of actions to meet established standards.

The elements of wilderness management planning thus consist of the following: Managers, with their concerned publics, must conceive and agree on feasible objectives that are consistent with NWPS goals, suitable to local conditions in particular areas, and acceptable under the agency management guidelines that interpret the Wilderness Act. The objectives established in the plan, considering current situations and assumptions about the future, must lead to logical policies, programs, actions, and standards. Prescribed actions or programs that do not appear necessary to achieve established objectives should be seriously questioned. They may call for excessive management that could detract from wilderness values.

A Framework for Writing Wilderness Management Plans

The outline below describes a framework for organizing and writing wilderness management plans using the foregoing concepts and terminology. This particular format—a goal-achievement framework—is closely related to management-by-objectives frameworks (Koch 1974). It seeks simplicity using straightforward statements of goals and objectives followed by prescription of the management mechanisms needed to achieve them.

A GOAL-ACHIEVEMENT FRAMEWORK FOR WILDERNESS MANAGEMENT PLANNING—A SKELETON OUTLINE

Goals	Broad statements of intent, direction, and purpose, found in: legislation—The Wilderness Act; Departmental regulations; Agency national policy and philosophy that interprets legislation and establishes management direction.
Objectives	Statements which describe specific conditions sought in a particular wilderness serve as criteria for deciding what management mechanisms are needed, and are used as standards in later evaluation of management.
Current Situation and Assumptions	Statements of local conditions and situations, and predictions about changes, help determine feasible objectives and the need for specific management mechanisms.
Management Mechanisms	Policies, programs, actions and standards, through which objectives for a given wilderness are achieved.

An expanded outline of the skeleton framework with additional detail necessary to relate it to the organization of an actual wilderness management plan is shown below. These outlines imply one specific organization for wilderness management plans using the framework. This is not necessary. The organization and format might be dictated by agency or personal preference. These outlines are merely *one* format for focusing a hierarchy of direction on a wilderness by defining national goals and direction; stating area objectives, current situations, and assumptions for important aspects of wilderness management in a particular area; and finally prescribing the management mechanisms to achieve objectives.

A GOAL-ACHIEVEMENT FRAMEWORK FOR WILDERNESS MANAGEMENT PLANNING— EXPANDED OUTLINE FOR ORGANIZING AND WRITING A PLAN

PLAN FRAME-WORK	SECTION OF PLAN	CONTENT
	Introduction	Brief description of the area and purpose and organization of the plan.
	Summary and overview of overall situation and management strategy	An overview or summary of current conditions affecting management such as use levels and patterns; special situations; personnel; general management strategy.

PLAN FRAMEWORK	SECTION OF PLAN	CONTENT
Goals	National direction	Concise summary of legislative requirements, Departmental guidelines, National Agency policy and philosophy.
	Overall[1] area goals	A statement of goals for the management of the particular wilderness.
Objectives[2]	Objectives for all important aspects of wilderness management.	Specific wilderness conditions sought for all important aspects of the wilderness such as vegetation, recreation, wildlife, fire, trails, and travel. (Topics may vary by agency or area.)
Current Situation and Assumptions[2]	A. Current situation	A. Summary of trends and conditions pertinent to each objective.
	B. Assumptions	B. Judgments about future trends, pressures, and problems pertinent to each objective.
Management Mechanisms[2]	C. Management policies	C. Guiding policies that—considering current situation and assumptions about the future—are necessary to guide actions toward established objectives.
	D. Management actions	D. Programs, actions, and standards that are judged necessary to achieve established objectives.

[1] See example from the Glacier Peak Wilderness Management Plan.

[2] A separate section in the plan covers each important aspect of the wilderness and includes related current situations, assumptions about the future, policies and actions. Examples from actual plans appear later in this chapter.

Applying the Framework — Examples from Plans Using the Framework

Following are examples from management plans built around the goal-achievement framework. The overall goals and the table of contents from the management plan for the Glacier Peak Wilderness in the Mt. Baker-Snoqualmie and Wenatchee National Forests are presented below.[2] Also shown are sections of

[2] U.S. Department of Agriculture, Forest Service. 1976. Wilderness management plan for the Glacier Peak Wilderness, Mt. Baker-Snoqualmie and Wenatchee National Forests. 54 p. mimeo. USDA For. Serv., Pac. Northwest Region, Portland, Oreg.

the Anaconda-Pintlar Wilderness plan giving objectives, current situation and assumptions, and prescribed management policy and actions for "Signing" and "Collection of Resource and Use Information," two aspects of wilderness covered in that plan.[3] A final example from a plan using the suggested framework is the "Visitor Use Structures and Facilities" section from the Browns Canyon Primitive Area plan in Colorado.[4] This last example, from a small, arid area managed by BLM, illustrates how the framework can be adapted to meet differing agency and area needs.

Readers are cautioned to view the examples as illustrative of format more than content. The substantive content of these plans comes from management direction determined by local managers for those particular areas. Alternative management direction can appear in a plan using the goal-achievement framework when different goals and objectives—and of course different policies and actions—are specified.

Overall Goal for the Glacier Peak Wilderness

The Glacier Peak Wilderness will be managed under the Wilderness Act to minimize the impact of man and his technology upon the Wilderness resource. Management will seek to minimize the impact of use rather than use per se. In this area, man will be a temporary visitor who leaves no permanent imprint of his use. The forces of nature will dominate the landscape and man's activity will be limited to that of an unobtrusive observer. Manipulation of the flora, fauna, or the surface of the land destroys the wilderness resource and will be allowed only to the extent necessary to meet the provisions of the Wilderness Act.

Wilderness exemplifies freedom, but is defined more by the absence of human impact than by an absence of human control. Management will seek to preserve spontaneity of use and as much freedom from regimentation as possible while preserving the naturalness of the wilderness resource and opportunity for solitude, primitive recreation, scenic, scientific, and historical values.

To the extent that the wilderness resource is not impaired, the Glacier Peak Wilderness will be managed to provide opportunities for primitive recreation featuring solitude, physical and mental challenge, freedom from the intrusion of unnatural sights, sounds, and odors; the chance to experience unmodified ecosystems, and to travel and live without mechanized aids in an environment where one's success and failures are directly dependent upon his abilities, knowledge, and initiative.

[3] U.S. Department of Agriculture, Forest Service. 1976. Wilderness management plan for the Anaconda-Pintlar Wilderness. Beaverhead, Bitterroot, and Deerlodge National Forests. 99 p. July 1977. (plus 42 p. public involvement summary). U.S. Dep. Agric., For. Serv., North Reg. Missoula.

[4] USDI Bureau of Land Management. 1976. Browns Canyon Primitive Area activity plan. 69 p. mimeo plus appendix. BLM Upper Arkansas Planning Unit, Royal Gorge Resource Area Cannon City, Colo.

GLACIER PEAK WILDERNESS
MANAGEMENT PLAN
Table of Contents

---

[1] In the Glacier Peak Plan, each topic is followed by the same four subtopics listed under Administration. In order to conserve space, they are omitted here.

ANACONDA-PINTLAR WILDERNESS MANAGEMENT PLAN
(Signing Objective)

IV. SIGNING

MANAGEMENT OBJECTIVE: To provide signs when necessary to protect the Wilderness resource such as to protect especially fragile endangered areas and for visitor orientation to help disperse use where desired.

A. *Current Situation*

The presence of many existing signs conflicts with goals of this plan to preserve the naturalness of the Wilderness resource and to allow the forces of nature to dominate the landscape. For example, some signs have been installed primarily for visitor orientation.

Present Forest Service Wilderness signing policy specifies the use of rustic lumber signs with characters that are lightly charred to enhance their readability. Only a few of the existing signs in the Wilderness meet this standard. Some signs are mounted on posts, the remainder of the signs within this Wilderness are mounted on trees.

Present information and administrative signing at Wilderness portals is inadequate.

B. *Assumptions*

A new Anaconda-Pintlar map and brochure will reduce the need for the existing number of signs in the area. Costs will be a critical factor in the preparation and distribution of this map/brochure.

There will be conflicting views, expressed by the public as to what will be signed, and where they will be placed

C. *Management Policy*

1. Signs will not be provided solely for user orientation, convenience, education, or interpretation. The need for signs will be minimized by developing accurate maps and brochures which will include up-to-date descriptions of management expectations for appropriate visitor behavior and activity.

2. Signing at Wilderness entries will be limited to trail direction signs, Wilderness boundary signs, and such official information display as fire prevention, regulations governing use of the Wilderness, and suggested Wilderness behavior.

3. Signing needed for management and regulation of use will be installed so as to minimize the physical and psychological impact of the signing system upon the Wilderness resource.

4. Existing signs will be evaluated on a case-by-case basis to determine if they meet the objective.

5. To facilitate permanent mounting, the standard Wilderness signs will be placed on trees wherever possible.

6. Wilderness boundary signs and an information signboard will be posted at all known entry points.

D. *Management Actions*

1. Develop a coordinated signing plan for the Anaconda-Pintlar Wilderness by _____

2. Existing signs will not be removed until a new Anaconda-Pintlar Wilderness brochure and topographic map is distributed to the public, no later than _____

3. Coordination with I&E Objectives will assure the development of suitable brochures and interpretative material to replace the need for descriptive and interpretative signs of a nondirectional nature.

4. Signs may be placed at:
   a. System trail junctions
   b. Wilderness restoration sites
   c. Area and/or trail closures

5. Signs will not be placed:
   a. In trailless areas
   b. On nonsystem trails
   c. To identify natural features or distances
   d. To provide for onsite interpretation.

6. The signing standards designated for the Anaconda-Pintlar Wilderness shall prevail if the Continental Divide Trail becomes a component of the National Scenic Trails System (P.L. 90-543). The marker and symbol for this trail will continue through the Wilderness, except that modification of the sign material may be required to subdue its contrast.

7. A Wilderness portal information signboard will be designed by the Bitterroot National Forest prior to Dec. 31, 1976. These information signboards will be installed at all major portals during the next field season.

ANACONDA-PINTLAR WILDERNESS MANAGEMENT PLAN
(Collection of Resource Data and Use Information)

XIV. *COLLECTION OF RESOURCE DATA AND USE INFORMATION*

MANAGEMENT OBJECTIVE: To collect in a nonobtrusive manner consistent with the preservation of the Wilderness resource, resource and recreational use information necessary to: (a) gain information needed to achieve and monitor the attainment of the objectives of this plan, and (b) acquire baseline knowledge needed to assess long-range natural changes in the Wilderness ecosystem, and man's direct and indirect influence on it.

A. *Current Situation*

A self-registration system is in effect and provides a fair estimate of visitation from 1969 to the present.

Vertical aerial photos are available in color, infrared, and black and white for the entire Wilderness, as are oblique black and white and color photographs. Earth satellite monitoring images are also available for the Wilderness. A few permanent photo points have been established for subsequent monitoring of heavy use locations.

B. *Assumptions*

Basic resource and use information will be needed to achieve the objectives of this plan and to monitor progress towards its objectives.

Funding will be a limiting factor. The need for resource and use information will have to be prioritized.

Use information will continue to come primarily from Wilderness registrations data, correlated with electronic trail counters.

C. *Management Policy*

1. Because recreational use is judged as posing the greatest immediate threat to the naturalness of Wilderness and opportunities for solitude, information about the amount and impacts of use have high priority.

D. *Management Actions*

    1. Identified resource data (inventory) and use (information) needs by priority are as follow:

        a. Collection of information on extent and location of use from summaries of Wilderness portal registration and Wilderness Ranger data.

        b. Completion of a Code-a-Site inventory of all established campsites in the Wilderness. At heavily used sites, permanent photo points will be established to evaluate impacts on the resource occurring over time, and to determine if the objectives for vegetation, soil, and recreation are being achieved. More detailed vegetation and soil data will be collected by managers using permanent transects in areas where unnatural vegetation change is suspected or indicated. A pilot vegetation transect and soil movement study was initiated during the summer of 1975 on the Sula Ranger District to establish a baseline for selected lake-associated campsites. More detailed research will be encouraged at these locations by university and Government researchers to assist assessment of vegetation change, related to amount and kind of use.

        c. Complete a fuels inventory which will provide a basis for development of a fire management plan.

        d. Initiate a cultural history inventory.

        e. Collection of information about wildlife species composition, population, distribution, and behavioral characteristics relative to Wilderness visitor density and distribution.

        f. Monitoring of water quality.

BROWN'S CANYON PROPOSED PRIMITIVE AREA MANAGEMENT PLAN[1]
(Visitor Use Structures and Facilities)

VISITOR USE STRUCTURES AND FACILITIES

OPERATIONAL OBJECTIVE: Visitor use structures and facilities will be constructed when needed for the protection of the area rather than for the comfort and convenience of users.

Present Situation:

    With the exception of a primitive road through the area, there are no visitor use structures or facilities in the Primitive Area.

    The boundary between the adjacent National Forest and Primitive Area is identified by a barbed wire fence in reasonably good repair.

Assumptions:

    1. As use increases, requests for facilities will increase by some visitors; e.g., more trails, sanitation facilities, etc.

    2. Any facilities constructed will attract additional use to their location.

Policy Summary

    No facilities will be made which are primarily for the comfort and convenience of visitors. Facilities needed for protection and management of the area will be primitive, rustic in design, and built without motorized equipment.

    Trailheads — Development of trailhead facilities should be approached with extreme caution due to the increased use and change in use patterns they create.

    Trails — Due to the irreversible nature of trails constructed in Brown's Canyon, construction will be approached with extreme caution. When constructed, trails will avoid fragile areas such as gulch meadows and areas of high erosion potential. Whenever possible, trails will be built out of sight of popular camping areas. Constructed trails will be maintained.

    Development of new trails is not an acceptable answer to dispersing heavy public use. At best, new trails afford temporary relief to overuse problems only to create new problems in more areas. Other methods of dispersal will be employed before new trail construction.

    Bridges — Bridges will only be constructed when absolutely necessary for visitor safety or for protection of stream banks. When constructed, bridges will be small, inconspicuous, and of rustic design.

    Signs — Signing in the Primitive Area will be minimized and used only when absolutely necessary to indicate trail direction, distances, and regulations. They will not be used for interpretive or educational purposes. When needed, signs will be as small as possible and of rustic design.

---

[1]Slightly revised (edited) to reduce space.

Actions:

1. Evaluate the feasibility, impact, and costs of locating a trail through the Primitive Area. This proposed trail would enter at Ruby Mountain and utilize the existing road which extends into the National Forest. Then, in the vicinity of Green Gulch on the National Forest the trail would leave the old road and extend southerly to terminate either at Hecla Junction or at the community of Brown's Canyon.

This trail study should be done in close cooperation with the U.S. Forest Service and Colorado Division of Wildlife. A decision should be made as to when and where to build the trail by fall of _____.

See proposed trail location in appendix of this plan.

Preparing Wilderness Management Plans: Problems and Suggestions

Some issues and problems in wilderness management planning warrant comment.

Writing the Plan

The actual writing of certain portions of a plan has some pitfalls. One trap is to invest too much effort into stating current situations and assumptions about the future. Some of each are needed, but, if too detailed, they can become the focus of the plan. In extremes, this can give the plan a problem-solution focus because problems are often described in current situation statements, and assumptions can forecast a worsening of the situation. This orientation can lead to prescriptions to fulfill assumptions, whether or not they are well-founded. In many cases, accurate data is lacking, so that assumptions about the future are no better than guesses.

Situation and assumption statements are easy to dwell on because they are easier to write than management objectives, but this will result in a plan lacking objectives as the real criteria for deriving management policies and actions and later judging their effectiveness. For example, a current situation statement describing heavy use, combined with assumptions predicting substantial increases in use, could lead directly to very restrictive policies and actions. While these might ultimately be necessary, a recreation-use objective that described *intended* conditions would provide a better basis for prescribing policies and actions (where, when, and how use must be restricted) aimed at achieving or maintaining the desired conditions. This approach is also easier to explain and justify to critics because debate and disagreement over wilderness management can be focused on the stated objectives and actions deemed necessary to achieve them rather than on the accuracy of situation and assumption statements or on individual policies or actions that, considered in isolation, might not appear necessary.

We believe that the key to good wilderness management plans is clearly stated objectives. But such objectives are particularly difficult to write for wilderness because of the subjective nature of the resource and the experiences it offers. It is nevertheless important to state objectives as clearly as possible so they can serve as guiding criteria for policies and actions. It is helpful to think of objectives as statements of wilderness conditions or experience opportunities that management seeks to preserve or provide.

How specifically the individual objectives can be stated will vary, depending on what aspect of wilderness they pertain to. Objectives for "structures allowed in the wilderness"—if that is an aspect singled out for an objective—might be more specifically stated than an objective for "fish and wildlife," "vegetation," or "water." In either case, it is important to understand the distinction between generality and vagueness of a stated objective. Objectives can be stated in broad, general terms, and still retain fairly definite implications about the kinds of policies and actions needed to achieve them. Vague objectives, on the other hand, regardless of their generality, lack clear implications for management direction, policy, programs or actions. While an acceptable objective might be general, it should *not* be vague: that is, its management implications should be clear.

It is also important to recognize that the specificity of goals and objectives is directly related to their location in the hierarchy of direction. The closer to the field-action level an objective is, the more specific it should be. Compared to the lofty goals of the Wilderness Act such as "to preserve, unimpaired, a wilderness resource," management objectives for one particular aspect of wilderness will seem quite specific; for example, "to provide for primitive recreation only to the extent that naturalness, outstanding opportunities for solitude, physical and mental challenge are preserved." And, further down the hierarchy, a field manager's objectives may be to implement very specific actions derived from goals, objectives, and policies formulated higher up in the planning process. For example, one field

162

manager indicated that the objectives he was interested in were the number of signs to be posted that summer, number of campsites to be relocated, and miles of trail to be cleared or maintained. To him, the objectives stated in the plan for the entire wilderness were so general they appeared to be goals rather than attainable objectives. Perspective varies down the hierarchy. At lower levels in the planning and management process, field objectives *are* statements of actions to be carried out—but actions that are derived from goals, objectives, and policies set forth at higher levels of the planning process. If there is internal logic in the plan, it should be possible to trace any field actions reflecting field manager objectives to higher levels of the planning process. This can be done by asking *why* the activity is being carried out. Thus, the field manager above should be able to trace logically the reasons for the proposed actions (such as posting a certain number of signs, relocating campsites, or clearing and maintaining trails) to particular policies and objectives in the wilderness management plan. Of course, this describes an exemplary situation that might not be as simple or straightforward in the real world, but it is a general guide.

The level of detail to be contained in wilderness management plans is an important consideration. A plan containing 200 pages of single-spaced typing will be so overwhelming that even managers might never read it. On the other hand, except for the most simple circumstances, a plan of only eight pages will not contain enough details even though it might give general direction. Some balance of generality and detail is needed, depending on the size, complexity, level of use, and problem situations in the particular wilderness. Our view is that the plan should contain sufficient detail to describe all objectives, policies, and the what and where of particular actions; but the when, how, and by whom level of detail is more appropriately included in action or work plans formulated at field levels. The Forest Service planning process provides for this division in action plans prepared at the ranger district level. Other agencies also have work planning procedures which permit details to be worked out at field levels.

As a general guideline, management plans are most useful if they are straightforward, well organized, and readable documents. They should clearly inform managers and users of the management direction for the wilderness, what this will entail in policies that will govern field actions, and what kind of major actions will be carried out at particular locations. The plan should not be so long and detailed that only its authors or the affected managers are willing to read it. If a plan becomes

ponderous, a separate summary should be provided for the public.

Zoning

The wilderness management strategy for many wilderness areas is beginning to include zoning—delineating particular areas where different management policies, actions, or restrictions on user behavior apply. Examples are no-camping zones, trail-less zones (where only cross-country travel and special minimum-impact camping practices are allowed), and special management zones having particular problems (high-use sites, impacted locations, or perhaps sensitive wildlife areas). Other designations include portal, primitive, and pristine zones to identify locations of increasing degrees of naturalness and solitude. Sacrifice areas, characterized by relatively dense concentrations of visitors and use-impacts, are also a kind of zoning. The resource compartments established in the Anaconda-Pintlar management plan might also serve a zoning function[3]

These and other zoning methods are appropriate to different situations. While it isn't possible to judge one better than another, we offer two criteria for judging

Figure 8-2.—Wilderness management plans may identify particular locations where special management is needed, such as travel corridors, heavy-use locations, unusual attractions, or vegetation zones where special restrictions apply. For example, a no-fire regulation in high alpine zones may help preserve esthetic features such as this ancient whiteback pine snag in the John Muir Wilderness, Calif. It might otherwise be used as firewood.

their utility and appropriateness. First, to be effective, any zone that requires different visitor behavior must be made known to the users by some reliable means such as through a use permit or map. Second, a distinction should be made between zoning for special management or user practices to maintain wilderness standards throughout the area, and zoning to designate sacrifice locations where *lower standards* and special management objectives will apply. Particularly when designating locations such as portal zones, managers should clarify whether they are establishing lower standards for the zone (a sacrifice concept), or merely recognizing a location's unusual sensitivity, and likely impacts which will require special management to maintain the standards applicable elsewhere in the wilderness.

It seems unwise to us to set substantially lower standards anywhere in a wilderness and expect to successfully confine the spread of impact to the rest of the wilderness. However, it may often be necessary to identify zones where special management will be needed.

The example below from the Glacier Peak plan illustrates the use of vegetation types and special management situations to designate areas where different policies might be necessary to maintain established standards.

GLACIER PEAK WILDERNESS MANAGEMENT
PLAN
Vegetation Types and Special Management Situations

This management plan does not recognize zoning based on user density or ease of access (FSM 2322.12) but does recognize *three distinct vegetation types and two special management situations* that are designated so the manager can tailor policies to the resource. The vegetation types and special management situations can be described in brochures and on maps so special regulations applicable to them can be readily communicated to visitors.

The three vegetation types are: *Alpine* areas of ice, rock, snow and meadow, *subalpine* areas characterized by clumps of high elevation fir and meadow, and *coniferous forest* composed primarily of mountain hemlock and pacific silver fir on the westside of the Cascade Crest and subalpine fir and pacific silver fir on the east side. The distinct characteristics of each vegetation type, and the potential need for restrictions applicable to only one or more of them, dictate that management be capable of focusing on them collectively or separately.

As an example, potential use controls necessary to preserve the wilderness resource in fragile *subalpine* areas may need to be more stringent than those necessary in the *coniferous forest*. In subalpine areas the short growing season heals campfire scars very slowly and natural accumulations of firewood are not readily replenished. Where the impact of use threatens the wilderness resource

in *subalpine* areas there may be a need to ban campfires, even though campfires might continue in the *coniferous forest* because of its longer growing season and plentiful supply of dead and down wood.

Within these three vegetation types, the plan recognizes two special situations requiring different management approaches: (1) *trail corridors* and associated *user activity areas* such as campsites, observation points, and shelters; and (2) *heavy use areas* currently being subjected to concentrated use pressures and impact.

Ten heavy use areas are now recognized in the Glacier Peak Wilderness: Kennedy Hot Springs, Image Lake, Lime Ridge, White Pass, Buck Creek Pass, Lyman Lake, Canyon Creek Shelter, Hart Lake, Holden Lake, and Ice Lakes. These heavy use areas require and are receiving special management to reduce impacts, such as restrictions on horse use, numbers of parties allowed to camp at one time, and restrictions on camping and fires.

Such special management approaches have been established because the influence of human activity is present in some portions (i.e., heavy use areas and trail corridors) of the wilderness to a greater degree than in others. Such measures would be inappropriate in other wilderness locations where they are not needed.

Public Involvement and Plan Review Processes

Involving the public in resource planning is increasingly important, and wilderness management planning is no exception. The public is a source of ideas, a sounding board for the acceptability of proposed management direction and policy, and potentially a partner in its formation. Ultimately they too have to live with the results of the planning efforts. However, many managers are reluctant to involve the public in wilderness planning because of their fear that the public, not understanding the legal constraints on wilderness management, will seek to lower wilderness standards. Regardless of these fears, it seems unrealistic these days to think about any kind of planning without public participation. We know of successful public involvement efforts in several wilderness management plans. Wilderness users are diverse, and while there might be pressure to relax standards from groups with special interests such as horsemen, outfitters, or local resort owners, it is likely to be countered by pressure from conservationists and others committed to higher standards of naturalness and solitude.

Study of public participation in resource decisions indicates that managers who hesitate to involve the public are often those who haven't tried it or who doomed their public involvement efforts to failure by their own anxiety or negative attitude towards it Hendee and others 1973; Hendee 1977). Most managers who have successfully used public involvement are impressed with its helpfulness in making better decisions and in deriving policies that have a higher chance of withstanding public criticism. Many user groups are affected by wilderness management: Hiking and climbing clubs, conservation groups, high-country hunters and fishermen, horsemen, photographers, youth organizations, and outfitters. They deserve to be involved in its planning. Without the understanding and support of the involved public, wilderness management will fall short of its goals.

Certain successful strategies for securing public involvement seem to have widespread applicability. Two of these, used in connection with the Glacier Peak and Anaconda-Pintlar Wilderness management plans, are described below. Either procedure could be amended to fit different circumstances.

• Public involvement in the Glacier Peak Wilderness management plan indicated, on balance, strong support for maintaining high standards of wilderness quality as well as some excellent suggestions about objectives, policies, and implementing actions. Perhaps most importantly, proposed objectives, policies, and actions were tested for public acceptability before publishing the final plan. One factor managers must be prepared for is the large amount of time required to get public input, incorporate it into new drafts, and then get agency staff and the public's response to the revisions. Note in the following example from the Glacier Peak plan that public review occupied a full year.

February-April 1975—Drafts 1 and 2 of management plan prepared by agency.

Mid-April 1975—Availability of draft 2 for public review announced in news release and notices to interested organizations. Copies of the plan furnished to individuals and important interest groups.

May 30-31, 1975—Public workshop, Friday evening and all day Saturday, to review draft 2 of the plan—17 persons in attendance Friday and 8 on Saturday. Entire plan reviewed, page by page; comments and reactions recorded.

June-July 1975—Draft 3 prepared incorporating public input.

August-November 1975—Agency review of draft 3; preparation of draft 4 incorporating additional input by managers.

December 1975—News release of availability of plan (draft 4) for public review. Circulation of plan (draft 4) to all concerned organizations and members of the public requesting a copy (70 copies distributed). Thirty pages of written comments, received in 11 formal letters, responding to, or suggesting additional changes in, the plan. Draft also sent to the regional office for pre-approval review.

May 1976—Plan revised in response to public input and regional office review comments, both of which called for more detail about management actions to implement the policies prescribed in the plan under each objective. Twenty-seven major concerns appearing in the public input—and managers' response to them—are summarized in the plan's appendix.

Public involvement in preparation of the Anaconda-Pintlar Wilderness management plan in Montana followed a slightly different track, beginning before writing was started. In October 1975, 400 people and organizations known to be interested in the wilderness were mailed public-response sheets identifying 13 topics for which management alternatives were being considered. Letters and 134 response sheets were received, containing 1783 individual comments addressing 72 specific areas of concern. A summary of the response to each topic was included in the first draft of the plan—May 1, 1976. A section of the draft plan on public involvement (p. 65-131) summarized input on each topic, keyed to the page in the plan where it was addressed. For example, one of the items to which the public was asked to respond was the following (item 12)[5]:

> Two management concepts that can be applied to impacted sites in wilderness are sacrifice areas versus user rotation. An example of the former would be to designate a lakeshore campsite for all use, realizing that the site will be greatly altered over time. The other option recognizes, by plant indicator species, when use on a site should be curtailed and another site chosen.

Response to item 12 was summarized as follows:
> Statement 12
> A very clear majority of the public response favored site rotation over sacrifice areas on highly impacted sites within the Wilderness. The methods favored for determining when a site needed rest rotation ranged from use of good judgment to the use of plant indicator species.

Public input during the fall of 1975, such as that described above, was invaluable to managers and helped them prepare a strong first draft plan for the Anaconda-

[5]Example from Public Response Form Summary, p. 67-68; in May 1976 draft of Anaconda-Pintlar Wilderness management plan. The final plan is cited in footnote 3.

Pintlar Wilderness. In May 1976 a draft of the plan, including the summary of public input, was sent to interested persons and organizations, asking them for additional input prior to September 1, 1976. Following additional public input, a final draft was prepared for submission to higher officials for approval. The final plan, with a separate public involvement summary, was published in July 1977.

Public involvement was an essential ingredient in the development of management plans for both the Glacier Peak and Anaconda-Pintlar Wildernesses. Each used a different approach. No doubt many other different approaches have been used successfully elsewhere. We conclude that public involvement in wilderness management is essential and valuable; a variety of approaches is possible; the time required makes it necessary to extend the planning period from 18 months to 2 years.

While most of the preceding discussion focuses on public involvement, it is important also to highlight the considerable technical and policy review of plans that take place at different levels of the agency hierarchy and by other public agencies. It is essential that any other governmental units such as fish and wildlife, forestry, environmental, or other resource protection and management agencies be given a chance to review and provide input to plans. From both the public and agencies, the challenge is to secure optimum review and input that afford managers the benefit of adequate information and opinion prior to implementing the plan but without unduly dragging out the planning process. The necessary review and time required will vary with the situation, but we suggest that planners address these questions when beginning a plan. How can public involvement and review of the plan be streamlined to get what is needed and desired within an optimum period of time? What are the most efficient times in the planning process to involve the public? How can the number of drafts of the plan that will need to be circulated be minimized? By addressing these questions, planners can help keep the planning process the means to a feasible, effective management plan and not let the planning process become an end in itself.

Criteria for Evaluating Wilderness Management Plans

Increasing professionalism of wilderness management and public involvement assure that wilderness management plans will come under increasing scrutiny by persons other than agency bureaucrats performing review and approval functions. What are appropriate criteria for reviewing plans—regardless of format or specific agency requirements? In our view, several minimum standards might be applied.

1. Management direction and its origin. Does the plan summarize or explain key provisions of the Wilderness Act, Departmental guidelines, and national agency policy that will direct management of the area? This will relate management of one wilderness to the entire NWPS, of which it is a part.

2. Are the local conditions that will affect, and be affected by, management of the wilderness described and explained?

3. Is the general management strategy explained, including how the wilderness is administered by various units of the agency, the numbers of managers and their responsibilities, and key user requirements such as a permit system?

4. Are there internal logic and a hierarchy of direction in the plan linking prescribed actions to policies and objectives? It is essential that there be some kind of framework through which management actions and policy are prescribed on the basis of their necessity to achieve objectives or some stated condition in the area. Clearly stated management objectives are the key to a plan's internal logic.

5. Does the plan address coordination needs among other resource management activities or nonconforming uses? A National Scenic Trail crossing the wilderness is one example; grazing in National Forest wilderness is another. Coordination with others affected, such as adjacent landowners, is essential. For example, National Park Service and Forest Service wildernesses are often adjacent. There is also an obvious need to coordinate plans with other organizations such as the State game departments that are responsible for managing fish and wildlife in National Forest wilderness.

6. Does the plan specify when and by whom the plan will be reviewed and when and by whom the necessary updating and revision will be carried out? How can changes in the plan be made? Who will initiate them? Who will approve them? Including this information will help keep a plan from stagnating at field offices.

Conclusions

Good planning is essential to good management. Planning is a formal process of thinking ahead about the purposes of management and alternative methods for attaining them. Management involves selecting appropriate policies and actions, fitting them to local situations, implementing and explaining them. In this chapter we have described some elements of good planning and a framework for executing plans. We have been concerned here with a process for applying the principles of wilderness management proposed in Chapter 7. In remaining chapters we move on to substantive wilderness topics, information that must be focused on wilderness management through planning. These topics include visitor carrying capacity; ecosystems; fire, wildlife, visitor, and site management.

Literature Cited

Alston, Richard M.
 1972. Forest: goals and decisionmaking in the Forest Service. USDA For. Serv. Res. Pap. INT-128, 84 p. Intermt. For. and Range Exp. Stn., Ogden, Utah.
Erber, Ernest, ed.
 1970. Urban planning in transition: an introductory essay. In Urban planning in transition, p. xi–xxviii. Grossman Publishers, New York.
Everhardt, Gary.
 1975. Congressional wilderness hearing [Statement of Director Everhardt to Congress]. Natl. Park Serv. Newsl. 10(20):7–10.
Hendee, John C.
 1977. Public involvement in the United States Forest Service roadless area review: lessons from a case study. p. 89–103 in Public Participation in Planning. Terrance Coppock and Derrick Sewell, eds., John Wiley. [Reprinted from paper presented at the Seminar on Public Participation sponsored by the University of Edinburgh, School of the Built Environment and the Centre for Human Ecology, Edinburgh, Scotland, July 1974.]
Hendee, John C., Robert C. Lucas, Robert H. Tracy, Jr., Tony Staed, Roger N. Clark, George H. Stankey, and Ronald A. Yarnell.
 1973. Public involvement and the Forest Service: experience, effectiveness, and suggested direction. 163 p. Government Printing Office, Washington, D.C. [NTIS Accession No. PB2 234 244/AS].
Koch, Russell W.
 1974. A goal achievement framework to guide wilderness management planning. M.F. professional paper, University of Washington, Seattle. 30 p.
U.S. Department of Agriculture, Forest Service.
 1973. Chapter 8200: land use planning. In Forest Service manual. Washington, D.C.
U.S. Department of Agriculture, Forest Service.
 1974. A planning, budgeting, and management information system for USDA. Washington, D.C.
U.S. Department of Agriculture, Forest Service.
 1976. Chapter 2320: wilderness. In Forest Service manual. Washington, D.C.
U.S. Department of Interior, Bureau of Land Management.
 1971. Section 6221: primitive areas. In BLM manual. Washington, D.C.
U.S. Department of the Interior, National Park Service.
 1975. Chapter IV: wilderness preservation and management. In National Park Service, management policies. Washington, D.C.
Webber, Melvin.
 1969. Planning in an environment of change: Part II: permissive planning. Town Planning Rev. 38(4):277–295.
Wheaton, L.C., and Margaret F. Wheaton.
 1970. Identifying the public interest: values and goals. In Urban planning in transition, p. 152–164. Ernest Erber, ed. Grossman Publishers, New York.
Young, Robert C.
 1974. Establishment of goals and definitions of objectives. In Elements of outdoor recreation, p. 261–272. B.L. Driver, ed. University Michigan Press, Ann Arbor.

The carrying capacity of wilderness is the amount, kind, and distribution of use that can occur without leading to unacceptable impacts on either the physical-biological resource or the available wilderness experience. By establishing use limits, the experiences uniquely offered by wilderness, such as shown here in the Three Sisters Wilderness, Oreg., can be protected.

Introduction

In 1975, 15,600 visitor-days of use were reported for the rugged 64,000 acre Absoraka Primitive Area in south-central Montana. In the same year, the Desolation Wilderness in California, just 531 acres smaller received 256,100 visitor-days of use, or nearly 17 *times* that of the Montana area![1]

Is the Desolation Wilderness being overused? Or, is the Absoraka Primitive Area being far underutilized? These questions address the perplexing problem of wilderness carrying capacity. In chapter 7, we advanced, as a fundamental principle of wilderness management, the notion that the preservation of those qualities defining an area as wilderness required a carrying capacity constraint. Our concern is with determining at what point use conditions become inconsistent with the social and environmental qualities generally associated with wilderness and required by the Wilderness Act. The carrying capacity question is one of the most basic problems confronting wilderness managers today. Theoretically and practically, each set of wilderness conditions and experiences that are sought as management objectives implicitly carry with them some limit in the kinds and amounts of recreation use that can be tolerated as well as the need for various policies and actions to see that these limits of tolerances are not

exceeded. In this chapter, we explore the origins of the carrying capacity concept, consider the concept's application to wilderness, and briefly review what is known about it. In addition, we present a general model of carrying capacity and describe its possible application to wilderness.

As we will discuss in more detail in chapter 13, wilderness use has grown steadily over the past three decades and, even though annual growth rates may be diminishing somewhat, future increases in absolute numbers are expected. As use grows, so will problems of resource damage and congestion. For instance, the presence of 1,000 people camped in the South Fork Basin of the San Gorgonio Wilderness in Southern California on a single day hardly offers the kind of solitude seemingly called for by the Wilderness Act (Hay 1974). Nor do trails eroded 6 feet deep by recreational use in the Selway-Bitterroot Wilderness in Montana seem consistent with the notion of an area managed to retain its primeval character (Helgath 1975). Severe resource damage and increasing numbers of people in some wildernesses has led one observer to write an article in the Los Angeles *Times* entitled "National Wilderness Areas—They Exist In Name Only" (Fradkin 1971).

Some have argued that undesirable impacts could be offset by rapid expansion of the National Wilderness Preservation System, thus making more acres available to the increased numbers of users. Growth of the

---

[1] The contributions of Dr. Sid Frissell, School of Forestry, University of Montana, are gratefully acknowledged.

Figure 9–1.—Where use limits have been established wilderness experiences can be protected. However, excessive use can lead to both resource damage and to a loss in the type of experience associated with wilderness. *Left:* Grassy Lake, John Muir Wilderness, Calif.; *right:* Image Lake, Glacier Peak Wilderness, Wash.

Wilderness System will, of course, occur and will help absorb some impacts due to increased use. But, adding more acres to the system to solve the problem of increased use has two important limitations. First, as discussed in chapter 6, it is only a short-run solution at best because the amount of acreage suited for wilderness classification is limited. As of December 31, 1976, 14.4 million acres of classified wilderness existed; possibly, the system will expand threefold or fourfold beyond this. But, at some point there will simply be no more land for consideration as wilderness. A second problem is that adding new acres to the Wilderness System does not necessarily increase capacity in a net sense because many of these acres already sustain substantial amounts of wilderness-type use.

Expanding the supply of wilderness as a solution to the accommodation of increasing use is an important part of the total package of tools available to citizens and resource managers to preserve the resource. But, in the face of limited supply and increasing demand, more attention needs to be devoted to making optimum use of a fixed supply. Intensified management will be required to make the limited wilderness resource yield more benefits, consistent with the constraints and objectives imposed by the Wilderness Act. As noted in chapter 7, the preservation of wilderness depends upon maintaining a balance between supply and demand; a balance achieved through a carrying capacity constraint. Thus,

the management concept of carrying capacity becomes increasingly important.

The Concept of Carrying Capacity

Carrying capacity, a fundamental concept in natural resource management, is the limitation on use of an area, set by various natural factors of environmental resistance (e.g., food, shelter, or water). Beyond this natural limit, no major increases in the dependent population can occur (Odum 1959). For example, a particular range might be capable of supporting 100 deer. In other words, when 100 deer live on the range, there is a balance between animal numbers and available food, shelter, and water. If that balance is upset, perhaps by a substantial growth in numbers of deer, the productive capabilities of the range suffer. Food resources become depleted, and perhaps even destroyed, as animals search for nutrition. In such a situation, herd numbers exceed the range's carrying capacity and its ability to maintain deer will decline, even though a temporary increase in population might have occurred. In extreme cases, the imbalance may lead to longterm environmental impacts that are virtually irreversible.

As defined above, carrying capacity is seemingly uncomplicated. In fact, it is not. For instance, the preceding example involved deer; if the species had been elk or sheep, the numbers of animals capable of being

170

supported on the same range would have been quite different. So, we can see that capacity limits vary according to the type of *consumer* we are talking about. Also, the limits were those naturally imposed. Had management intervened (e.g., by supplemental feeding or irrigation of natural forage), the range would have been capable of supporting a greater number of animals. Thus, carrying capacity is not an inherent, fixed value of the land. It can be diminished by unregulated overuse or enhanced by thoughtful management.

In recreation management terminology carrying capacity has become a common, if not altogether well understood, term (Chubb and Ashton 1969). Generally, it is used in two different ways. First, it is used to describe the ability of the physical-biological environment to withstand recreation use. Various studies have been made of the impact of use on vegetation and soils (Willard and Marr 1970), water (Barton 1969), and wildlife (Schultz 1975). Second, carrying capacity has been used to express the amount of use that is consistent with some measure of quality in the recreational experience (Wagar 1964). Studies of social carrying capacity have focused on such things as the impacts of increasing use on the recreational experience (Shelby and Neilson 1975) and the impacts of conflicts between user groups (Lucas 1964).

Efforts to measure the carrying capacity of recreation lands have been pursued with considerable enthusiasm, at least partially with the belief that once the magical figure was found, the task of recreation management would be made easier (Wagar 1968). But just as carrying capacity is not a simple notion for the range or wildlife manager, neither is it for the recreation manager. Several problems can be noted. For instance, recreation lands are used by many different people (consumers) seeking many different, and sometimes conflicting, experiences. Some want solitude, others look for companionship; what is appropriate for one represents congestion or loneliness to another. Thus, theoretically at least, there would be a different carrying capacity for every type of experience provided.

Impacts on physical-biological resources are not precise indicators of overuse, either. Any use of an area produces some change; in fact, studies measuring resource impacts from recreation use generally report that light use produces substantial unnatural change (Frissell and Duncan 1965; Wagar 1964; Merriam et al. 1973). Thus, if a manager elects to allow only use that will produce little or no change, it will be necessary to restrict use at very low levels (Wagar 1968). Finally, capacity, considered from either the biological or the social perspective, is a function of more than simple

numbers of users. In fact, use intensity by itself seems to be a fairly poor predictor of impact (Stankey 1973); variables such as seasonality of use (LaPage 1967) and habitat type (Helgath 1975) are more effective in predicting impacts on the resource, while type of use encountered (Lucas 1964, Lime 1975) and the location of encounters (Stankey 1973) are particularly important in assessing impacts on users.

In light of these problems, some have argued that carrying capacity either has little to offer managers or is so complex that it cannot be made operational (Wagar 1974; Bury 1976). In part, these arguments rest on the concern that efforts to determine the magic number implied by carrying capacity divert attention from a wide variety of alternative management strategies. This is a very real possibility and while we have chosen to stick with the term carrying capacity, it is important that we explicitly define how we view its role in wilderness management.

Definitions of the carrying capacity concept as applied to recreation and wilderness management abound. One recent annotated bibliography listed over 20 articles defining the term (Stankey and Lime 1973).

We believe a useful definition of carrying capacity in the context of wilderness is its capability to produce wilderness-dependent experiences. Our focus is on the human experience for it is, after all, the ultimate product of all resource management programs (Wagar 1974). While management input can be employed to enhance capacity, it nevertheless must be used sensitively and conservatively, given a legislative mandate which calls for substantial preservation of the historic ecological processes that shaped the physical-biological community. Those experiences related to enjoying, appreciating, and learning about these natural processes deserve emphasis in management as do those that relate to "solitude or a primitive and unconfined type of recreation" as outlined by the Wilderness Act. Thus, wilderness carrying capacity represents those use configurations[2] consistent with the long-term maintenance of opportunities for wilderness-dependent experiences.

The term carrying capacity has been criticized as an inappropriate, inadequate, and possibly even misleading concept in recreation and wilderness management. Rather than taking part in the debate surrounding the term, we think it more important to promote understanding of the underlying *intent* of the concept. If we are to preserve those social and ecological qualities that constitute wilderness, we need to balance use with its

---

[2] Use, which is more than a matter of simple numbers, varies also by type, time, space, and behavior. We use the term *use configuration* to refer to some specific combination of these variables (Frissell and Stankey 1972).

Figure 9–2.—Managing visitor behavior is essential for protecting the quality of wilderness and maintaining the carrying capacity within acceptable limits. Tying horses to these trees in the Eagle Gap Wilderness, Oreg., has resulted in severely impacted sites. Techniques for accommodating horse use are discussed in Chapter 15.

associated impact on these qualities. Carrying capacity is the general framework we use to do this.

From this definition, we offer four caveats, or qualifications, that govern the application of carrying capacity to wilderness planning.

The determination of carrying capacity is ultimately a judgmental decision.

Perhaps the most fundamental point to be made about carrying capacity is that it is a product of management judgment rather than a precisely defined measure—it is a decisionmaking concept rather than a scientific concept. Whether we are measuring physical-biological impact or social impact, the relationships between use and the resultant impact are typically described by continuous curves that lack abrupt and clearly defined changes (Frissell and Duncan 1965; Wagar 1964; Stankey 1973). Information about use impacts will not define capacity limits; it will describe the consequences associated with different use conditions. Such decisions must rest on the judgment of managers as to whether these consequences, either actual or anticipated, are acceptable.

Such a situation clearly limits the role of the researcher or scientist in the capacity calculation. The researcher, rather than prescribing how much is too much, is the source of information about the stream of consequences of alternative use configurations on the ecological,

physical, and social elements of a setting. From such information, standards can be formulated and criteria prescribed for identifying factors that might limit use (Pfister and Frenkel 1975). As far as possible, these standards should be measurable or quantifiable conditions in order that logical and defensible decisions about use limitations can be made.

Although the establishment of carrying capacity standards should have a base in scientific knowledge, the judgmental nature of the carrying capacity definition still leaves open the possiblity of decisions that are arbitrary or illogical. Our second qualification deals with this concern.

Carrying capacity decisions depend on clear management objectives

Management objectives—the definition of the environmental and social conditions that have been chosen to prevail at a specified location—provide the basis from which carrying capacity determinations are made. As Wagar noted (1974), decisions about objectives involve value choices based on normative judgments of what *ought* to be or *should* be as opposed to technical decisions about what *can be*. Being value judgments, they are less dependent on the technical expertise of resource management professionals than on their agreement with broad social goals defined as desirable by public consensus.

Only when these goals are reduced to specific area *management objectives*—formal statements of the environmental and social conditions that management either seeks to maintain or to restore—can logical carrying capacity decisions be made. Statements of management objectives should thus be precise and site specific so they can serve as criteria for making carrying capacity decisions. Chapter 8 described the importance of management objectives in planning any wilderness management action and the factors that influence how objectives are formulated. Here we see their function in resolving the carrying capacity question.

In making carrying capacity decisions, the range of available alternative opportunities must be taken into account

Decisions about carrying capacity, like similar judgmental decisions, should be considered in the context of a broad spectrum of outdoor recreation and leisure opportunities. Such decisions should be resolved in light of other opportunities existing within a regional area. Only when wilderness is viewed as one part of a broader outdoor opportunity system is there an equitable and defensible rationale for preserving the relatively low density use commonly associated with wilderness. In order to adequately meet the diverse tastes of people, a range of opportunities is needed, varying in terms of such things as interpersonal contact, access, and development (Lloyd and Fischer 1972). Carrying capacity thus represents a general management strategy for maintaining a particular set of conditions within a system of recreational opportunities (Lime and Stankey 1971)—a strategy that is a direct consequence of the decision(s) to preserve a range of different opportunities. But the maintenance of these conditions, particularly where direct limitations on use may have to be implemented, can be justified only if alternative settings meet people's needs. In our view, maintaining carrying capacities for wilderness without providing and managing for nonwilderness recreational opportunities will be, in the long run, politically unacceptable.

Carrying capacity is a probabilistic concept, not an absolute measure

Our fourth qualification is that carrying capacity can be stated only in terms of what is probable, not in terms of what can be assured. This generalization simply points out that in no way can all the contingencies affecting capacity decisions be predicted or accommodated. The vagaries of weather, changing user behavior, and so forth will always mean that unanticipated impacts will occur. Carrying capacity is not intended to anticipate all such events. Rather, it is intended to serve as a framework that accommodates the most probable pattern of events.

As an example, capacity calculations might be made assuming that normal weather patterns will prevail. However, a sudden spell of unseasonably rainy weather that turned trails into muddy mires would obviously upset these calculations and force managers to reassess the anticipated impacts of use on these trails. While the carrying capacity determination for an area serves as a basic outline of the use-impact relationship managers can reasonably expect to occur, it does not eliminate the need for continuous monitoring of conditions or the need for good professional judgment in the face of changing conditions. Establishing carrying capacity standards for an area will not give managers an impersonal formula to which they can turn in order to make difficult decisions (Wagar 1968).

In summary, carrying capacity is ultimately a judgmental determination rather than the product of some absolute and measurable characteristic of the environment. In specifying carrying capacity, we are prescribing the use configuration consistent with the social and ecological conditions we wish to prevail at a location. These conditions are formalized in area management objectives derived from managerial judgment and citizen input, tempered by various constraints, such as laws. Definitions of appropriate

capacity levels need to be derived in light of a spectrum of outdoor opportunities in order that diversity and equity be achieved. Finally, capacity is a probabilistic concept; it is neither possible nor necessary that all contingencies be accommodated.

As we discussed above, the role of science in the determination of carrying capacity levels is one of providing information about the probable outcomes, changes, or consequences anticipated from different use configurations. Giving administrators accurate, reliable information on which to base their decisions is a responsibility of the researcher; the decision as to how much change is too much is an administrative responsibility.

Ecological Research on Wilderness Carrying Capacity

Wilderness and other minimally impacted lands have been the setting for a variety of studies of human impact on ecosystems. (See Liddle 1975 for a good review.) Although more work is needed, some important guidelines have begun to emerge. The following is a review of studies to identify the degree to which recreational use alters natural conditions.

Impacts on Vegetation and Soil

Perhaps the most significant conclusion concerns the relationship between increasing use and associated impacts. Several studies (Wagar 1964; Frissell and Duncan 1965; Merriam and Smith 1974) have reported the presence of a curvilinear relationship between use and impact on vegetation and soils, with substantial amounts of impact occurring with only light use. For example, Frissell and Duncan found that over 80 percent of the ground cover was lost at campsites in the Quetico-Superior with only light recreation use. (They defined light use as from 0 to 30 days use per season.) Similarly, in a 5-year study of impact on newly opened sites in the Boundary Waters Canoe Area, Merriam and Smith (1974) reported that most site impact occurred within the first 2 years, then leveled off for the remainder of the study period.

In Olympic National Park, Bell and Bliss (1973) found that cover and productivity changes declined exponentially. On sampled strips of vegetation, total cover declined 59 percent and annual productivity, 46 percent with only five applications of treading per day. They noted that the quantity of living plants on a site could be greatly reduced before the effects were particularly noticeable to the casual observer. Based upon this data, they estimated that 80 percent of the plant cover on certain locations could be destroyed in only 2 weeks, with as few as 50 people per day passing over the area.

It is also clear that different kinds of use produce impacts at different rates and that use level, computed solely as some measure of intensity (such as visitor-days), is a poor predictor of impact (LaPage 1967). In an investigation of trail deterioration in the Selway-Bitterroot Wilderness, for example, Helgath (1975) reported that the amount of use on trails was less strongly and consistently related to deterioration than expected. She noted, as others have observed, that much of the impact seemed to occur with only limited use, and she attributed part of this phenomenon to the early loss of vegetation, promoting soil erosion and instability.

In a series of experiments, Dale and Weaver (1974; Weaver and Dale [in press]) have examined the impact of various kinds of recreational users on trails. They found that typically only a relatively narrow band of vegetation is impacted along trail sides. In contrasting the relative impacts of hikers, cyclists, and horses on vegetative cover, trail width, trail depth, and soil compaction, they report the following findings (Weaver and Dale [in press]):

Vegetative cover. (1) Vegetative cover was reduced by trampling; (2) vegetative loss was more rapid on sloping sites than on level sites (also see Helgath 1975); (3) vegetative loss was more rapid in dwarf shrubs than in grassy vegetation; (4) on level ground, impact increased from hiker to cyclist to horse; and (5) on slopes, hikers were less destructive than cyclists or horses.

Trail width: (1) Trail width increases with increased use to some equlibrium width; (2) equilibrium trail widths are wider on sloping sites than on level sites; and (3) on both level and sloping sites, trail width increases from hiker to cycle to horse.

Trail depth: (1) Trail depth increases with increasing use, with possibly no equilibrium depth; (2) depths are greater on slopes than on level sites; (3) depths tend to be greater in stone-free meadow soils than in stony forest soil; and (4) depth increases from hiker to cycle to horse.

Soil compaction: (1) Soil compaction increases with trampling; (2) compaction is greater on slopes than on level sites; and (3) compaction increases from hiker to cyclist to horses.

Weaver and Dale also reported that while cycle damage was greatest when machines moved uphill, hiker and horse damage was greatest traveling downhill, due to the plowing and braking action as the hiker or horse attempts to hold back.

The variable impact of different types of recreation users also was apparent in a study of campsite impact in

the Spanish Peaks Primitive Area in Montana by Frissell (n.d.). At campsites predominantly occupied by visitors using stock, an average 42 percent of the campsite surface was devoid of vegetation, organic litter, or humus; at sites used primarily by hikers, about 6 percent of the cover was gone. In addition, horse party camps averaged about 10 times the impacted area of hiker camps. Using a site condition typology developed in his report, Frissell reported that one-half of the sampled campsites were in a condition of deterioration calling for close management attention.

A major shortcoming of many impact studies is their failure to follow impact over an extended period (Speight 1973). One major exception is a 5-year study of visitor impact on newly developed campsites in the Boundary Waters Canoe Area (McCool et al. 1969; Merriam et al. 1973; Merriam and Smith 1974). Using a composite of site conditions to calculate an impact stage for campsites, they found that most new sites reached a maximum level of impact in about 2 years. Although there was no significant difference in tree growth between on- and off-site trees, this apparently was due to the fact that most root systems had penetrated through the thin soil mantle into underlying rocks and were thus protected from trampling. However, Magill (1970) also reported that growth rates of trees in California campgrounds used for over 30 years did not appear to be affected by recreation use. Soil compaction reached a maximum in

Figure 9-3.—Horses generally create more impact than do an equal number of hikers. Especially near fragile lakeshores, horses can inflict severe environmental damage. Horses are now prohibited at Reflection Pond in the Glacier Peak Wilderness, Wash., before irreversible damage occurs.

about 2 years and the author's estimates, as well as others (Thorud and Frissell 1969), suggest recovery might take as long as 6 years.

Merriam and Smith (1974) also reported that, among 21 new campsites studied, 10 expanded 50 percent in size and 4 expanded over 100 percent. Only one site showed no expansion during the 5-year study.

Impacts on Water Quality

Recreation impacts on water quality in backcountry and wilderness areas have not been studied in any detail. Merriam and Smith (1974) noted that coliform bacteria counts were higher near campsites than at control points and that phosphate and turbidity levels were also increased near camps. However, other parameters of water quality (e.g., temperature, dissolved oxygen) were not affected and they concluded that recreational impacts on water quality were generally small.

McFeters (1975) also found little impact on water quality in watersheds sampled in Grand Teton National Park. In fact, he reported that in studies of microflora in the water of two adjacent watersheds near Bozeman, Mont., one open to public use and the other closed to public entry for the past 50 years, the closed watershed produced consistently higher bacterial counts than the open watershed. He attributed the difference to the fact that wild animals contribute significantly to microflora content in water and that the presence of people in the open watershed had disturbed these animals, causing them to move from their natural habitat to new territories within the closed watershed.

Impacts on Wildlife

Although wildlife comprises an integral part of the wilderness (see our discussion in chapter 11), very little systematic research has been devoted to the impacts of wilderness use upon animal numbers, distribution, and behavior (Speight 1973; Stankey and Lime 1973). It is clear that wildlife populations, including the large ungulates and carnivores as well as smaller species of mammals and birds, are affected by backcountry recreation use, particularly when this use is concentrated in critical habitat areas. The potentially fatal consequences of recreational use in grizzly bear habitat areas is probably the best example of conflict between the backcountry user and wildlife. Research is underway to provide data to minimize visitor intrusion into grizzly habitat. (Craighead and Craighead 1971; also see the discussion in chapter 11.)

Recreation impacts upon wildlife are probably particularly significant where the species has a limited habitat in which it can survive and/or a habitat that is attractive to recreationists. However, our knowledge of these impacts is limited. Although typical wilderness uses, such as backpacking, probably have a fairly brief and relatively minor impact on wildlife, increases in this use will raise the level of harassment on wildlife populations. (Harassment is defined as any activity of man and his associated domestic animals which increases the physiological costs of survival or decreases the probability of successful reproduction.) (Neil et al. 1975).

In summary, our understanding of the ecological consequences of backcountry and wilderness use is limited. What information we do have is generally descriptive in nature. We generally lack the ability to predict, in quantitative terms, the consequences of alternative levels, types, and patterns of use on the physical-biological environment, a serious shortcoming in our efforts to develop the potential of the carrying capacity concept.

Physical-biological impact is a complex phenomena. It does not bear a direct linear relationship to use; in fact, use intensity is less helpful than other variables (e.g., method of travel, season of use) in explaining the degree of impact sustained. With the onset of recreation impact, substantial alterations in vegetation and soil occur, generally followed by a state of equilibrium. At this equilibrium point, there is typically a major shift in the composition of the vegetation, with delicate and fragile species disappearing, to be replaced by hardier, more resistant species (Verburg 1974). Thus, ecosystems can adapt to recreation pressures through a process of succession. However, while this kind of adaptation could aid managers of developed campgrounds (e.g., see Magill 1970 and Merriam and Smith 1974), such succession is a major problem in wilderness where a key management objective is the preservation of natural conditions. We will return to this issue shortly.

For the purposes of our discussion, the key point is that recreation impacts on ecosystems can lead to a departure from naturalness along a number of specific dimensions: The level of vegetation loss and its subsequent replacement by non-native species, soil erosion and compaction, water quality impacts, and impacts on wildlife behavior and population levels. Such departures, then, represent conditions where carrying capacity constraints may have to be imposed to prevent an unacceptable loss in wilderness quality.

Social Research on Wilderness Carrying Capacity

Concerns about use impacts are not limited to changes in the physical-biological environment; there is also concern about how use affects the quality of the visitor's experience. If we define wilderness carrying capacity as representing those conditions conducive to wilderness-dependent experiences, we can cite a number of studies that provide information on how varying use conditions impact visitor experiences.

Use Levels and Type of Group

Several studies have reported that visitors prefer relatively few encounters with other parties, a preference consistent with the importance of solitude as a management objective in wilderness. Lucas (1964) found that canoeists in the Boundary Waters Canoe Area preferred much lower use levels than did motorboaters. He also noted that canoeists perceived two critical levels of use intensity—first where anyone was met, and second at a point where between 6 and 10 groups were seen in a day. In terms of preferred types of encounter, canoeists indicated they could accommodate seeing anywhere from zero to five canoeists, but they preferred no contact at all with motorboaters.

Lucas' study points out an important finding reported in several other investigations; the impact of use intensity or use level is extremely difficult to dissociate from the *type* of use involved. The level of use people report as preferred or tolerable is not independent of the type of use involved. We will see this relationship in other studies reported below.

Lime (1975) also has studied use in the BWCA and his work corroborates that of Lucas and earlier studies. Although use in the BWCA is heavy, it is also highly variable in both space and time. Lime found that some visitors encountered 40 times as many users as did other visitors, even though only a short distance separated the two groups. Nearly three-fourths of the canoeists reported they saw too many others on at least 1 day of their trip; typically, about three encounters per day was considered the maximum level of contact before the sense of being in the wilderness was impaired. As Lucas discovered, however, most canoeists (90 percent) preferred to meet no motorboaters.

In a study of capacity perception by wilderness visitors in four areas, Stankey (1973) found a declining level of preference for increased levels of use contact. While about 75 percent of the visitors to three western areas (the Bob Marshall Wilderness, Mont.; the Bridger Wilderness, Wyo.; and the High Uintas Primitive Area, Utah) indicated that having no contact with backpackers was a pleasant experience, only 20 percent felt the same about four encounters. Although a lower level of preference was expressed for contacts with horse parties, the difference was not great.

Unlike backpackers, canoeists in the BWCA seem to prefer a low level of contact with other canoeists to none at all. About half of them indicated a preference for contact with no other canoeists, and about two-thirds preferred two encounters. However, for two contacts with motorboats, it declined quickly to 20 percent.

Following the methodology used by Stankey, Badger (1975) studied crowding problems in the Rawah Wilderness, Colo. Most visitors (67 percent) felt that the amount of use encountered was about right, while the remaining one-third thought it was too crowded. Badger also examined the levels of use people preferred to encounter as well as the amount they would tolerate. In general, about a 1:2 ratio existed between the two measures; that is, they preferred a level of contact only about half of that they would tolerate. Additionally, tolerance for increasing use levels was greater when the contact involved hikers rather than horse users.

The idea that the quality of the wilderness experience automatically declines with increasing use levels is not altogether accurate, however. Stankey (1973) reported that users generally prefer encounter levels of one or two other groups to a zero level of contact. Pfister and Frenkel (1974) report a similar finding among visitors on the Rogue River, Oreg., with half again as many persons preferring one contact to zero contact. At least a minimum opportunity for socialization and interaction with others seems important even for wilderness visitors.

However, higher than preferred contact levels do not necessarily detract from the wilderness experience. Shelby and Neilsen (1975) found that measures of overall trip quality were unrelated to actual river contact level among visitors on the Colorado River in the Grand Canyon. Also, they did not find any significant relationship between perceived crowding and reports of satisfaction.

Like physical-biological impact, the impact of use on the wilderness experience is a complex phenomenon. As the preceding discussion indicates, the amount of use one encounters can alter the experience, but the relationship is not necessarily linear. The kind of use contacted is clearly one variable that must be specified. Another important factor is where the encounters occur. Stankey (1973) found that reactions to encounters along the periphery of the wilderness differed in their impact on users from those occurring in the interior. The impact of those occurring along the outer edges of the wilderness was apparently tempered by the expectation of most visitors to meet other people in this area. Once in the interior, however, encounters had a subsequently greater impact. Impacts from encounters also varied according to whether they occurred along the trail or at the campsite, with the latter being more stressful.

Badger (1975) also examined the effect of encounter location and found similar results. Most visitors showed greater tolerance for encounters near the trailhead than near their destination and for encounters along the trail rather than at the campsite. He also found greater tolerance for groups camped further away than for those nearby.

The importance of relative solitude at the campsite has been hypothesized as a possible bottleneck on overnight capacity (Hendee 1967; Stankey 1973; Badger 1975). Dunwiddie and Heberlein (1975) found strong and consistent support for such an hypothesis. In observing actual campsite selection behavior in the Bridger Wilderness, Wyo., they found that experienced visitors distinguished themselves from novices by selecting campsites that were: (1) Further from other visitors; (2) further from the nearest campsite, whether it was occupied or not; and (3) in an area with few other sites. Knowledgeable visitors were more likely to spread themselves out from all other parties. The authors also concluded that beyond certain density levels, the more experienced visitors were crowded out.

Another important characteristic of use was group size. Although large parties typically comprise only a small percentage of total use (e.g., in the Boundary Waters Canoe Area, groups of more than 10 people are only 5 percent of the total use) (Lime 1972; chapter 13), they may have a disproportionate impact on both the wilderness resource and the wilderness experience of others they encounter. Most users studied have reported that they prefer small, rather than large, groups. Definitions of small and large vary from study to study, but generally parties of less than 10 to 12 persons are regarded as small. Stankey (1973) found that users generally preferred contacts with small, rather than large, groups, even when given a choice between meeting only 1 large party per day as opposed to 10 small parties per day. Pfister and Frenkel (1974) found similar results. Most users felt that seeing large parties reduced the feeling of being in a wild river area. Persons in large groups tended to be more tolerant of other large groups. Badger's work in the Rawah Wilderness (1975) also confirmed visitor preference for smaller groups.

Because most visitors travel in small groups, parties that violate the small-party norm probably seem more conspicuous and the individuals making up such groups might be perceived as different from most visitors. Such perceptions stem from concerns about resource impact, crowding, or simply the feeling that such groups are inappropriate in a wilderness setting (Stankey 1973).

Whatever the reason, the fact that members of small groups do not readily identify with members of large groups is an important finding, especially in view of the work of Lee (1975) who reported that the expressed satisfaction of trail users in the Yosemite National Park backcountry depended on the extent to which visitors perceived one another as being *similar*.

Visitor Behavior

In determining the impact of use on the wilderness experience, the behavior of persons might be more significant than are such things as total use, party size, and travel methods used by the groups encountered. Lee (1975) found that, both along the trail and at the campsite, important influences on visitor satisfaction were the demeanor, friendliness, and courtesy of people they met. Many of the potential conflicts between user groups probably can be mitigated if visitors abide by accepted norms of wilderness behavior. For example, selecting a campsite out of sight and hearing of another occupied camp respects the privacy and solitude many users seek and, thereby, lessens the prospect of conflicts between visitors. Research on campsite spacing to avoid unnecessary noise intrusions have been developed that allow managers to develop guidelines to reduce such conflicts (Daily and Redman 1975).

The physical evidence of inappropriate or illegal behavior—most likely littering—is also a serious impact on the wilderness experience. Stankey (1973) found that virtually all persons sampled in four wildernesses objected to the presence of litter. Additionally, most felt that a littered campsite represented a more disturbing condition than seeing too many people.

Badger (1975) reported that inappropriate behavior was overwhelmingly more disturbing than a less-than-desired distance between one's own campsite and that of another. People were also more disturbed by seeing litter or other environmental damage than they were by seeing other people or experiencing conflicts because of travel methods, group size, or the location of the encounter.

In the Yosemite National Park backcountry, Lee (1975) also reported that visitor satisfaction was related to the absence of litter on trails and at campsites. He noted that the presence of unnatural objects left by previous visitors (e.g., makeshift tables) was more disturbing to visitors than deterioration of the immediate physical environment.

In summary, then, a variety of use-related variables must be examined in order to accurately measure the consequences of use on the wilderness experience. While increasing use is clearly one of the important variables, other parameters of use must also be examined and may be more significant than total use. As was the case with ecological impact, use intensity is best described as a necessary, but not a *sufficient*, variable in the determination of the social impact of wilderness use. Violations of acceptable behavior and conflicts over appropriate styles and methods of use often will be the critical variables on which managers must focus their attention. As Lee (1975) notes, social relations between wilderness campers were more important to the satisfaction of those users than was the condition of the physical environment. Therefore, encouraging appropriate wilderness behavior might be the most important action managers can undertake.

The research on visitor perceptions of crowding and overuse must be carefully interpreted. Much of the research on the effects of increasing use on visitor satisfaction has involved hypothetical situations and questions of preferred, rather than actual, contact. Studies reporting responses to use levels actually encountered have generally reported little association between the level of contact and visitor satisfaction. This work has been done in a variety of wildland settings: Lee (1977) in the Yosemite National Park backcountry, Shelby and Neilson (1975) on the Grand Canyon of the Colorado River, Heberlein (1977) on the Brule River in Wisconsin, and Lucas (1978) in the Desolation Wilderness. Each of these investigators has found little statistical or substantive relationship between the amount of use visitors actually encountered and the level of satisfaction they reported with their experience. Does this mean that solitude is not important in wilderness?

In response to this rhetorical question, we would say, "no." First, the Wilderness Acts specifically call for wilderness management to offer opportunities for solitude. Perhaps more important, the lack of an observed relationship between use and satisfaction has several potential explanations, not necessarily exclusive of one another. The level of contact with other people is only one of the components of the wilderness experience and its relative importance surely varies among users. Also, even for those to whom solitude is important, other aspects of the wilderness experience may compensate (in a sense, increase in their relative importance) when use levels are high enough that solitude is difficult to find. Thus, although the level of use might be fairly high, there are other features of the trip that still made it worthwhile: new acquaintances were made, the scenery was superb, the hike was challenging, and so forth.

We also need to recognize that the investigations of visitor ideas about crowding may be simply missing those users to whom solitude is especially important. For these people, conditions may have already exceeded some critical threshold of sensitivity and they have already sought other places where use conditions are still consistent with their desires. These displaced persons represent a measure of the cost involved when a carrying capacity constraint is not imposed.

Finally, reports of satisfaction need to be understood in the context of what was expected. Where expectations are poorly defined (e.g., a first-time visitor has little basis for knowing what to expect), satisfaction with the experiences are difficult to assess. Crowding is generally recognized as a personal judgment or assessment about some physical condition measuring people per unit of space (Altman 1975). The context of the situation also is important. Judgments about whether the number of people present in a situation—the density—is a crowd or not depends on the nature of that situation. A cocktail party can have too few people; a wilderness campsite can have too many, even though the same number of people might be involved in both situations. And, what is judged to be appropriate is largely a function of the norms (rules, either written or unwritten) that govern the situation. Thus, where norms are poorly defined or poorly understood (e.g., as by a novice wilderness user) the evaluation of use conditions as being crowded, just right, or underused will be inconsistent and variable.

What the lack of association between use and satisfaction does suggest is that the notion of managing wilderness to "maximize satisfaction" is probably not a very effective or useful management idea. Why not? Satisfaction is a very general, inclusive concept; the difficulty of using it to guide carrying capacity decisions is that it will probably continue to rise over time because people will continue to report, typically, that they enjoy their outdoor experience. However, at the same time, we must recognize that the nature of the experience is changing constantly—there is a *shift in product* from a wilderness-dependent experience to one simply enhanced or incidental to a wilderness setting.

This change in the nature of the opportunity and the kind of experiences offered is central to the carrying capacity issue. Rather than managing to maximize satisfaction or uncritically accepting the argument that because there is little observed relationship between increasing use levels and satisfaction, solitude is not important, the task of wilderness managers ought to be to develop policies to insure preservation of opportunities producing wilderness-dependent experiences. Solitude is an important feature of the wilderness experience to many people and is backed by a legislative mandate. Increasing use restricts the degree to which visitors can find solitude and although there are various techniques or mechanisms that people can adopt to achieve solitude (e.g., going during the off-season, traveling cross country), the opportunity to find solitude will eventually diminish if use continues to grow. Rather than attempting to define capacity through some quantitative estimation of satisfaction, the challenge is to develop area management plans that insure maintenance of opportunities where the ranges of human contact normally prevailing is low.

Applying the Carrying Capacity Concept to Wilderness

There are various definitions of carrying capacity used by biologists, range managers, and others. In general the concept is used to describe the relationship between the productivity of a resource and the ability of that resource to maintain its productivity. For instance, the long term range productivity is diminished if intensified grazing exceeds the natural regenerative capacity of the range.

We can apply this same principle to wilderness management. In wilderness, the product of management programs is a set of human experiences that are linked to the naturalness of the environmental setting, and thus to a very low level of development, and to a generally low level of contact with others. These elements appear to be basic attributes of the wilderness experience, even though the term refers to what is, in fact, a complex and diverse set of experiences that different individuals might or might not share.

The qualities of naturalness and solitude are subject to change. As recreational use increases, opportunities for solitude decline while the probability of substantial modification of ecosystems increases. Excessive change might be reflected in the form of a social cost (e.g., congestion with resulting impacts on the wilderness experiences), an environmental cost (e.g., loss of water quality, vegetation impact, disturbance of wildlife population), or a combination of the two (e.g., a severely impacted campsite that represents a substantial modification of an ecosystem as well as an aesthetically unattractive scene). Any of these impacts represent a loss in wilderness carrying capacity because they adversely affect the long term capability of the resource to produce the kinds of wilderness-dependent experiences required by the Act.

Change can come from a variety of sources. The most significant source is recreation use. However, other sources of change must also be considered.

Change-A Key Element

Pervasive, global pollution (a source of change over which managers have little control) represents a particularly odious type of influence because of its subtle character and the difficulty of tracing its origins. Radiation, pesticides, and air pollution are examples. For instance, flouride pollution from the Anaconda Aluminum Company plant near Columbia Falls, Mont., has caused vegetation damage as far away as 10 miles in the Flathead National Forest and Glacier National Park (Carlson and Dewey 1971).

Wilderness boundaries serve as very poor shields against many impacts. Management programs and other practices on adjacent nonwilderness lands can have profound impacts on runoff, microclimate, or nutrient availability in nearby lands supposedly protected by the Wilderness Acts. Developments on nonwilderness lands can alter the distribution, behavior, and, often, even numbers of wilderness wildlife species. The development of roads close to the wilderness boundary can lead to significant changes in the patterns and style of use within the wilderness. As discussed in chapter 7, it is important to encourage a holistic view of wilderness, one that encompasses not only the wilderness proper, but surrounding lands as well.

Management decisions within wilderness itself can also introduce stress. For instance, with a few notable exceptions, current policies in the wilderness management agencies generally call for complete control of fire. The control of fire—one of the most significant natural forces in wilderness—has had decided impacts on the evolution and development of wilderness ecosystems (see chapter 12). Other management policies affecting activities, such as commercial and recreational stock use, have similar impacts on ecosystems.

In many areas, the presence of activities and facilities established prior to wilderness classification can represent a significant loss in capacity. For example, sheep and cattle grazing still occur in much of the Bridger Wilderness in Wyoming, and the dust, vegetation loss, and odor are major sources of complaints from many visitors (Stankey 1973). Most of these changes are protected as preexisting rights under the Wilderness Acts. Nevertheless, they should be viewed as permissive and necessary political compromises, not as measures of the intent of wilderness classification.

Thus, many forces lead to change in wilderness. The term preservation does not refer to the maintenance of a static picture of the American landscape at some point in time; rather, it refers to the preservation of conditions that allow natural ecological forces to operate as they

Figure 9–4.—Wilderness is continually changing in response to ecological forces. Carrying capacities indicate those use levels that will not severely disrupt natural processes. Here campers in a fragile meadow can accelerate environmental impacts and disturb normal ecological succession.

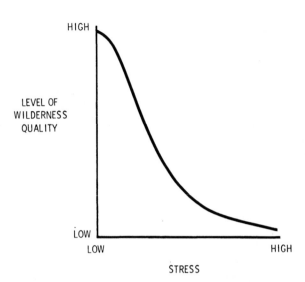

Figure 9–5.—Impact of increasing stress on wilderness quality.

have for eons—as far as possible, beyond man's control. Our concern with change of the sort described in this chapter centers on the extent to which the natural process of change is disturbed, restricted, or altered. In wilderness management, we are primarily concerned with controlling and minimizing man-induced change, rather than with change per se.

Change is a natural characteristic of wilderness and is a key element in understanding carrying capacity. It is the norm; conditions change constantly in response to natural forces. Also, as we noted in the earlier review of literature on ecological impact, only small amounts of stress (e.g., recreation use) can produce large amounts of change both socially and ecologically. Graphically, this relationship between stress (use) and change, either social or ecological, can be shown as in figure 9–5. As stress increases, the qualities of naturalness and solitude are diminished. Although the slope of the curve varies according to the specific conditions involved, the overall implication is that use, allowed to increase unchecked by a carrying capacity constraint, will eventually reduce, or even eliminate, wilderness quality.

Another implication of this general relationship between use and change is that the decision to allow any use in wilderness is also a decision to allow some amount of unnatural change. Moreover, if we seek to keep man-induced change at a bare minimum, it will be necessary to

restrict use at extraordinarily low levels; perhaps in some areas it would mean no use at all (Wagar 1968).

But Wilderness Acts tell us that use is consistent with the wilderness concept. Moreover, it is unlikely that extremely tight restrictions on use would be politically acceptable (e.g., see DeFelice 1975).

Thus, it seems that use will occur and that use-related change—either in environmental quality or in the kind of experience available—will be a fact of life with which managers must contend. The question the manager must confront is not "Do I allow change to occur?" but "How much change can occur without impairing the qualities that made this area a wilderness?" What constitutes excessive change? How can a manager make a decision that is not arbitrary and capricious? It is a difficult job; there are no readily available measures that warn managers that "use cannot exceed this point." But the situation is not hopeless. Carrying capacity can become an effective tool for wilderness managers, as the following discussion indicates.

The Role of Management Objectives

The key to dealing with carrying capacity lies in explicit and detailed management objectives. As discussed in chapter 8, a major shortcoming in most wilderness management plans is the lack of objectives that allow managers to explicitly state the conditions they seek and to measure performance with regard to achieving those objectives. Failure to develop such objectives is also the reason that specifying wilderness carrying capacities has remained an elusive task.

Management objectives define the physical, biological, and social conditions within wilderness that management programs seek to create, restore, or maintain. These objectives serve as criteria for management policies and actions to achieve these conditions. Thus, the objectives for recreation use, trails and travel, fish and wildlife, and so forth serve as the criteria for establishing carrying capacities and the policies and actions needed to hold use consistent with these capacities. Objectives are prescriptive; they tell what conditions *should* be like. This characteristic allows managers to review conditions at any given point in time in order to determine the discrepancy (if any) between the conditions desired and the conditions that exist. To the extent that a discrepancy does exist, management policies and actions can often be applied to lessen the difference. Similarly, objectives serve as criteria that allow managers to review the likely outcome of different use configurations and to judge whether the probable consequences are compatible with established objectives.

Obviously, management objectives must be both site-specific and detailed. Vague statements, such as "Management will seek to insure preservation of native fauna" are too imprecise to permit managers to assess their progress toward that goal. As discussed in chapter 8, the lack of precision, specificity, and detail in stated objectives is the source of many management problems, and it is certainly at the root of the difficulty encountered in attempting to formulate wilderness carrying capacities.

Management objectives provide managers with several critical pieces of information. The information provided describes the nature of the experience to be produced, serves as the operational objectives by which all management decisions must be formulated (see chapter 8), defines what tools and strategies are appropriate for use by managers, and serves as a check to test progress toward their achievement.

In the case of wilderness, we are attempting to manage areas that show minimum evidence of man, that provide visitors with an opportunity to see nature's forces with as little confinement and regulation as possible, and that minimize intergroup contact. These are admittedly general aims, but they do give us some pretty definite clues as to the types of experiences we ought to provide in wilderness. Certain actions are also ruled out that might be appropriate and customary in other resource management. For instance, reseeding impacted sites with hardy, tolerant grasses, exotic to the area, is inappropriate in an area managed for naturalness.

This chapter has considered the causes and impact of stress on wilderness and the resulting physical and social changes it produces. Management objectives have also

been discussed—the role they play and some guidelines for their formulation. To tie these elements together, we now consider a framework within which the basic question facing wilderness managers attempting to determine carrying capacity can be addressed. "Given the inevitability of change, what are the limits of acceptable change that may occur without the loss of those qualities that led us to define this land as wilderness?"

Defining the Limits of Acceptable Change

Change is a fact of life with which wilderness managers must contend. Natural ecosystems are constantly evolving and our wilderness management programs should permit this natural evolution. Man-caused change, on the other hand, brought about either by direct impacts of man (e.g., recreation) or through management policies (e.g., fire exclusion), is something management should minimize. Similarly, the social aspects of wilderness also change. Absolute solitude (the complete absence of other people) is seldom experienced—the social environment that characterizes wilderness is usually modified. Likewise, the natural environment will almost always show some signs of modification and the human satisfactions gained from the enjoyment of pristine nature may be correspondingly lessened. In either case, excessive change alters the capability of the wilderness resource to offer the kinds of experiences associated with wilderness; in other words, it reduces wilderness carrying capacity.

Change, occurring in both the ecological and social realm, is not only continuous, it is also complex and interdependent. The biological changes (e.g., soil compaction) which have obvious ecological implications, also affect visitor satisfaction. Likewise, social changes (e.g., increased congestion around lakes) have impacts that are both biological and social. Let's take a closer look at these ecological and social systems and attempt to bring some order to this complexity.

Establishing Ecological Limits of Change

Ecosystems evolve with regard to both character and rate. By *character*, we mean the composition of the biological system: The species, the relative frequency of the different species, and so forth. Man's influence can affect the character of ecosystems by introducing some exotic species, eliminating other native species. Additionally, the composition or character of any ecosystem changes over time and the *rate* of this change can be influenced (either retarded or accelerated) by man. Man's impact, then, can lead to variations in both ecosystem character and the rate of evolution beyond what we would expect to occur under long term averages.

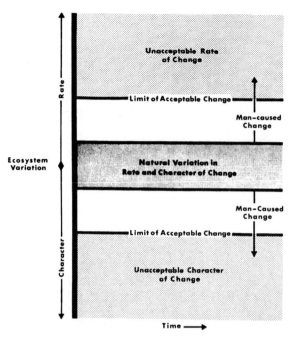

**Model of Acceptable Ecological
Variation in Wilderness**

Figure 9–6.—Model of acceptable ecological variation in wilderness.

Figure 9–6 presents this relationship. The central band labeled "Natural Variation in Rate and Character of Use" represents the natural range one would expect to occur without man's influence. But as we have discussed, man's pervasive influence has altered the natural order. Thus, some man-caused change in both character and rate is expected and accepted. However, at some point this change becomes excessive; that is, the conditions that prevail no longer represent wilderness. It is at this point that the ecological carrying capacity of the area is exceeded. The definition of the point at which an area is still representative of wilderness while accommodating its maximum use (i.e., its carrying capacity) is incorporated within the area's management objectives and the accompanying standards for measuring performance toward achievement of those objectives.

This, of course, is a very simplified model of what in reality is very complex. (See chapters 10, 11, and 12.) Ecosystems are composed of numerous diverse components that are interrelated in ways that are often poorly understood. Changes occur in each individual resource element. The introduction of any particular use configuration leads to change in soil bulk density, percentage of ground cover at campsites, wildlife

behavior patterns, and so forth. Thus, our model of ecological carrying capacity actually must be repeated for each of these elements as well as for any other variables that can be isolated for study. The most sensitive indicator becomes the limiting factor. For example, the wilderness manager might establish a series of standards for a given area in order to measure performance toward achievement of the area's management objectives. These would clearly and precisely specify the environmental conditions desired at the location in order to achieve area's management objectives. The maximum amount of ground cover that would be permitted to be lost at campsites, the level of coliform bacteria permissible in lakes, the extent of intrusion of exotic plant species, and so forth, might be indicated. Such standards might be derived from data generated in studies in the area, by interpreting from data generated elsewhere, or from judgment based on experience.

For each environmental parameter, a limit of acceptable change should be established (Frissell and Stanley 1972). Managers would then be alert for a change in conditions that exceeded the established limit. Conditions that exceed limits (or give managers strong reason to believe that excessive change is imminent) would call for a change or new emphasis in policies and actions to minimize the impact. The change might range from a light-handed restoration to restrictions on visitor numbers. (See chapter 14 and 15 for specific techniques of site and visitor management.)

How does one go about setting limits of acceptable change? There are no clearcut procedures. In some cases, however, managers might be able to make a relatively easy decision. Consider, for example, situation A in figure 9–7, a hypothetical diagram of the relationship between total use and environmental change along a trail.

Up to a certain point, the environmental change recorded is low and relatively stable. Then, there is an abrupt shift upwards. (Such information on the amount and rate of change could be obtained through such techniques as permanent photo points, systematic trail condition reports, or even judgments of field personnel. More detail on these techniques are in chapters 14 and 15.) Managers might establish standards that specify that conditions will not exceed those beyond the abrupt shift in the curve. In such a case, the basis for establishing the limit of acceptable change becomes a relatively easy task.

In many other cases, however, there will be no readily apparent point beyond which change should not be allowed. For example, change might be steady and constant as in situation B of figure 9–7. There is no obvious point at which an abrupt or noticeable shift occurs; managers are faced with establishing the limits of

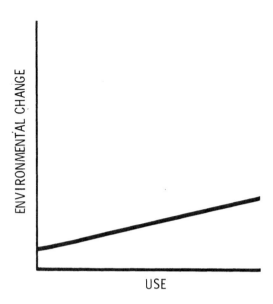

SITUATION A   Here an abrupt shift in the rate of change helps define the limits of acceptable change.

SITUATION B   Here a continuous low rate of change provides no clear evidence where the limits of acceptable change should be established.

Figure 9-7.—Hypothetical relationship between use and environmental change.

acceptable change in the absence of any distinct discontinuities. Management judgment becomes a crucial part of the carrying capacity process, a subject to be discussed in more detail shortly.

Establishing Social Limits of Change

The model we have described for ecological carrying capacity can be repeated for establishing social limits of change. It is somewhat more difficult to describe our starting point for social change than it is for ecological change, however. What is loosely referred to as the wilderness experience is, in fact, a composite of diverse human experiences related to wilderness. For some people, solitude is the key value. For others, it is the challenge offered by an area where man is on his own. For still others, it is the opportunity to anticipate or witness the untrammeled processes of nature. Thus, rather than viewing the wilderness experience in figure 9-8 as some fixed, unbending definition, it is better to think of it as a generalized and hypothetical concept.

For purposes of discussion, let's assume that the perfect wilderness experience offers the user complete solitude, an opportunity to appreciate and study completely undisturbed ecosystems, the ultimate in challenge, and the absence of facilities or aids. In reality,

of course, wilderness in North America does not offer such conditions. Wilderness has been tamed in varying degrees. Nevertheless, the Wilderness Acts are clear in terms of their general intent: Wilderness should offer low intensities of use, a relatively unmodified setting, challenge, and a chance for discovery. Constantly meeting others along the trail does not seem a part of the wilderness experience, nor do bare and dusty campsites and trampled vegetation. To accommodate these variables, the model in figure 9-8 recognizes two important factors for establishing social use limits: Human contact and visitor perception of resource quality.

There is probably relatively good agreement on the general nature of the essentials of the wilderness experience. The principal difficulty does not emerge until an attempt is made to develop more precise guidelines. At what point does contact with others change from being a pleasant and even welcome interlude to an unwelcome invasion of privacy? The question centers on a value judgment, but whose values: Users or managers? Whose judgment should predominate? These two groups often hold very different views (Hendee and Harris 1970; Hendee and Pyle 1971). Resolving in favor of the user doesn't always help because wilderness users

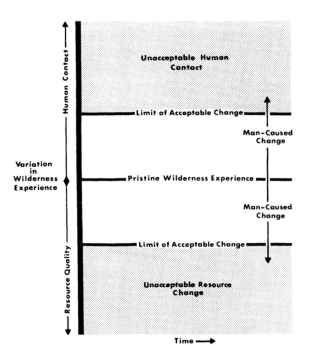

Model of Acceptable Variation in Wilderness Experience

Figure 9–8.—Model of acceptable variation in wilderness experience.

are spread across a wide spectrum, ranging from the inveterate enthusiast to the onetime, casual dropin. Assuming a single standard for judging acceptable change is wrong, striving for an average is also unrealistic.

Several efforts have been made to deal with problem. Lucas (1964) argued that BWCA managers give more attention to the attitudes of canoeists than to motorboaters because their behavior was more in keeping with area management objectives. They were canoeing, rather than using a motor, in an area established primarily to provide an opportunity for wilderness canoeing. The Outdoor Recreation Resource Review Committee's wilderness report (1962) used amount of past wilderness experience as a measure of commitment. Hendee et al. (1968) and Stankey (1973) used attitude scales to differentiate users on the basis of the purity of their attitudes toward wilderness, arguing that the standards ascribed to by those scoring high in purity should be given particular attention by decision-makers.

These examples illustrate a management guideline advocated in chapter 7—feature wilderness-dependent activities. The process of defining the primary clientele group is something managers cannot avoid. The principle of featuring wilderness-dependent activities offers a logical and systematic procedure for helping to define this group. By assigning first priority to the needs of users who, by their behavior and/or attitudes reveal a dependent relationship to wilderness (that is, those whose use and experiences can be satisfied only, or at least largely, by the primitive, unmodified, and low-use-density setting offered by wilderness) managers can most effectively use public input to guide carrying capacity decisions.

As with the ecological model of capacity, the social model involves a number of specific elements, any one of which might define an area's social carrying capacity. A manager will want information about total number of encounters, the number of encounters with other kinds of users, crowding at campsites, and so forth. Judgments about acceptable limits for each element comprise standards; when approached or reached they constitute a limit on further use. For example, managers might suggest that, on the average, wilderness parties should not meet more than three other parties per day. If information obtained by wilderness rangers or through use surveys indicates that most parties encounter five other groups per day, managers might decide to remedy this through a program of use redistribution by giving visitors information about use conditions so that people concerned with solitude can alter their routes. If this technique doesn't reduce encounters, direct rationing of use might have to be instituted. The point is, management actions are taken as part of a logical and visible process intended to help achieve an established objective.

The social aspects of wilderness must be meshed with the ecological. The two models described must be considered together so that neither the unique environmental qualities of wilderness nor the special human experiences available in wilderness are lost. Consider examples of the way such a composite model of wilderness carrying capacity might work.

An Example of Carrying Capacity Determination

Imagine that managers of the Red Mountain Wilderness have written a management plan with management objectives and have developed accompanying standards that specify limits of acceptable change for the major ecological and social parameters of the area. One management objective concerns campsites in the area: Wilderness campsites shall be managed to preserve the naturalness of vegetation, continuity of groundcover, and opportunity for solitude at individual sites. This objective is further clarified by policies that include specific standards:

Figure 9–9.—Low impact camping regulations can be used to increase the capacity of a wilderness for visitor use. These campers in proposed wilderness within Shenandoah National Park, Virginia, follow requirements to camp out of sight and sound of trails and other camper parties, and not build a campfire.

1. The maximum extent of groundcover loss to be tolerated at any campsite shall not exceed 50 percent of the amount within the general area of the fire circle and tent location.

2. Campsites will offer, wherever possible, an opportunity for visitors to camp out of sight and sound of other camps and will take advantage of vegetation and natural barriers. Use levels at campsites should be such that parties shall generally not need to camp within sight or hearing of one another.

Both of these standards have been developed from data generated in studies of the area by a local university. When groundcover losses exceed 50 percent, natural recovery by the following year is generally not possible. Campsite solitude has been cited by visitors as an expecially important part of the experience; consequently, an attempt has been made to physically locate sites away from one another. Where one site is located within sight or sound of another, the policy calls for limiting use levels so that normally both sites will not need to be occupied.

As use builds up through the summer, wilderness rangers report that a number of campsites are close to losing 50 percent of their groundcover and the rangers report that they anticipate substantially greater loss if use continues unabated. Given the management objective and policies noted above, then, these sites are approaching their ecological capacity.

Managers now have several alternative actions they might consider. They could close off those sites to any further use. They could reduce total use in the area to such a point that the sites could begin to recover. They might also consider restoration of the camps (e.g., scarifying the sites, planting native grasses).

In this case, managers choose to close those sites in danger of losing over 50 percent of their groundcover. This is accomplished through a program involving information distribution about the closure to users and enforcement of the closure through site restrictions, enforced by information and education contacts by wilderness rangers. No control over total use is imposed.

With the number of available campsites now reduced, demand for the remaining sites grows. Wilderness rangers begin reporting that on most evenings, several parties have set up camp around existing sites and it is not uncommon to have three or four other camps within

185

sight and hearing of one another. Here, the second policy is in danger of being exceeded. The limits of acceptable change established for campsite solitude has been exceeded and management action is called for. Now, a social factor controls capacity; the physical-biological resource is not threatened at present and might even be capable of supporting more use. But in this case, visitor solitude is the most sensitive indicator of capacity and is the cue managers use to take action by implementing a policy.

As was the case in deciding how to prevent excessive vegetation loss at campsites, several alternative actions are open to managers. They could attempt to redistribute use to new campsites. Obviously, they would need some measure of how many new or potential sites exist. This problem will be examined in greater detail in chapter 15. Or, regulations could be imposed that simply prohibit camping near others. To prevent congestion, managers could begin assigning users to campsites. They might, as has been done in the Shenandoah Wilderness, restrict all camping within sight or sound of trails or other camping parties. Finally, total use could be controlled. Deciding the most appropriate course of action is a manager's job. Each action has certain costs and benefits associated with it; there is no simple answer. The principles described in chapter 7 will prove useful in making this decision.

The preceding examples demonstrate how either ecological or social elements might lead to a judgment that a wilderness carrying capacity limits had been reached. In both examples, managers determined that conditions were inconsistent with established wilderness objectives. It is especially important to note that research data did not, by itself, reveal what decision should be made. Rather, in light of what was known, managers had to weigh the apparent consequences of alternative decisions and then choose the most appropriate course of action. This is why management objectives play such an important role in the carrying capacity equation. They provide the framework within which the consequences and implications of decisions can be reviewed and tested for appropriateness.

Summary

There are three key ideas to keep in mind in the application of the carrying capacity concept to wilderness management. First, establishing carrying capacities is not a process of developing magic numbers that tell how much use should be allowed. Rather, it is a matter of determining what kind of social and environmental conditions we want to provide (that is, establishing management objectives), reviewing the probable consequences of different use configurations on that desired outcome, and prescribing policies and actions that will attain those objectives. Management judgment is the key element in this process. Judgment is a product of experience, research data, basic inventory information, and good common sense. Computers and other sophisticated analytical tools are just that—tools. They help managers do a better job of accumulating, reviewing, and evaluating information, but they do not make decisions—people do.

Judgments can still be arbitrary and capricious, particularly if made in the absence of any substantive information. Thus, the second basic idea is that establishing carrying capacities is dependent upon the formulation of explicit management objectives that provide precise measures of desired conditions. These objectives and their associated policies define the limits of acceptable change for as many ecological and social elements of the wilderness as can be identified.

Finally, either ecological or social factors can lead to a determination that an area has reached its capacity. The point at which the most sensitive indicator, or weakest link, is reached becomes the point at which managers must take action. Their response can vary widely, from merely implementing policies to changing the management objective (thus changing the definitions of the limits of acceptable change). Management objectives, together with the principles described in chapter 7, help determine what policies and actions are most appropriate to achieve them.

Among the co-authors, the author primarily responsible for preparation of this chapter was George H. Stankey.

Literature Cited

Altman, Irwin.
  1975. The environment and social behavior. 256 p. Brooks/Cole Publishing Co., Monterey, Calif.
Badger, Thomas J.
  1975. Rawah Wilderness crowding tolerances and some management techniques: an aspect of social carrying capacity. M.S. thesis, Colorado State University, Ft. Collins. 83 p.

Barton, Michael A.
  1969. Water pollution in remote recreational areas. J. Soil and Water Conserv. 24(40):132-134.

Bell, Katherine L., and Lawrence C. Bliss.
  1973. Alpine disturbance studies: Olympic National Park, USA Biol. Conserv. 5(1):25-32.

Bury, Richard L.
1976. Recreation carrying capacity—hypothesis or reality? Parks and Recreation 11(1):22–25, 56–57.

Carlson, Clinton E., and Jerald E. Dewey.
1971. Environmental pollution by flourides in Flathead National Forest and Glacier National Park. 57 p. U.S. Dep. Agric., For. Serv., North. Reg., Missoula, Mont.

Chubb, Michael, and Peter Ashton.
1969. Park and recreation standards research: the creation of environmental quality controls for recreation. Report to the National Recreation and Park Association. Tech. Rep. No. 5, 76 p. Rec. Res. and Planning Unit, Dep. Park and Rec. Res. Michigan State University, East Lansing.

Craighead, John J., and Frank C. Craighead, Jr.
1971. Grizzly bear-man relationships in Yellowstone National Park. Bioscience 21(16):845–857.

Daily, Tom, and Dave Redman.
1975. Guidelines for roadless area campsite spacing to minimize impact of human-related noises. USDA For. Serv. Gen. Tech. Report PNW-35, 20 p. Pac. Northwest For. and Range Exp. Stn., Portland, Oreg.

Dale, D., and T. Weaver.
1974. Trampling effects on vegetation of the trail corridors of North Rocky Mountain forests. J. Appl. Ecol. 11(2):767–772.

DeFelice, Vincent N.
1975. Wilderness is for using. Am. For. 81(6):24–26.

Dunwiddie, Peter, and Thomas A. Heberlein.
1975. Crowding and campsite selection at a high mountain lake. [Paper presented to the annual meeting of the Rural Sociological Society, San Francisco, Aug. 21–24.] 27 p.

Fradkin, Philip.
1971. National Wilderness areas—they exist in name only. 5 p. Los Angeles Times Reprint, Aug. 15.

Frissell, Sidney S.
[n.d.] The impact of wilderness visitors on natural ecosystems. (Completed report to the USDA For. Serv., Intermt. For. and Range Exp. Stn., Missoula, Mont., 60 p.)

Frissell, Sidney S., and Donald P. Duncan.
1965. Campsite preference and deterioration. J. For. 63(4):256–260.

Frissell, Sidney S., and George H. Stankey.
1972. Wilderness environmental quality: search for social and ecological harmony. In Proc., Soc. Am. For. Annu. Meet., Hot Springs, Ark. p. 170–183.

Hay, Edward.
1974. Wilderness experiment: it's working. Am. For. 80(12):26–29.

Heberlein, Thomas A.
1977. Density, crowding, and satisfaction: sociological studies for determining carrying capacities. In Proceedings river recreation management and research symposium, p. 67–76. Gen. Tech. Rpt. NC-28, 455 p. U.S. Dep. Agric., For. Serv. North Central For. Exp. Stn., St. Paul, Minn.

Helgath, Sheila F.
1975. Trail deterioration in the Selway-Bitterroot Wilderness. USDA For. Serv. Res. Note INT-193, 15 p. Intermt. For. and Range Exp. Stn., Ogden, Utah.

Hendee, John C.
1967. Recreation clientele—the attributes of recreationists preferring different management agencies, car campgrounds or wilderness in the Pacific Northwest. Ph.D. diss., University of Washington, Seattle, Wash. 290 p.

Hendee, John C., William R. Catton, Jr., Larry D. Marlow, and C. Frank Brockman.
1968. Wilderness users in the Pacific Northwest—their characteristics, values, and management preferences. USDA For. Serv. Res. Pap. PNW-61, 92 p. Pac. Northwest For. and Range Exp. Stn., Portland, Oreg.

Hendee, John C., and Robert W. Harris.
1970. Foresters' perception of wilderness user attitudes and preferences. J. For. 68(12):759–762.

Hendee, John C., and Robert M. Pyle.
1971. Wilderness managers, wilderness users: a problem of perception. Naturalist 22(3):22–26.

LaPage, Wilber F.
1967. Some observations on campground trampling and ground cover response. USDA For. Serv. Res. Pap. NE-68, 11 p. Northeast For. Exp. Stn., Upper Darby, Pa.

Lee, Robert G.
1975. The management of human components in the Yosemite National Park ecosystem. 134 p. The Yosemite Institute, Yosemite, Calif.

Lee, Robert G.
1977. Alone with others: the paradox of privacy in wilderness. Leisure Sciences. 1(1):3-19.

Liddle, M.J.
1975. A selective review of the ecological effects of human trampling on natural ecosystems. Biol. Conserv. 7(1):17–36.

Lime, David W.
1972. Large groups in the Boundary Waters Canoe Area—their numbers, characteristics, and impact. USDA For. Serv. Res. Note NC-142, 4 p. North Central For. Exp. Stn., St. Paul, Minn.

Lime, David W.
1975. Sources of congestion and visitor satisfaction in the Boundary Waters Canoe Area. Proc. Third Boundary Waters Canoe Area Inst., Duluth, Minn., May 9, 1975, p. 68–82. Quetico-Superior Foundation, Duluth, Minn.

Lime, David W., and George H. Stankey.
1971. Carrying capacity: maintaining outdoor recreation quality. In Recreation: symposium proceedings. Syracuse, N.Y., Oct. 12–14, 1971, p. 174–184. U.S. Dep. Agric., For. Serv., Northwest For. Exp. Stn.

Lloyd, R. Duane, and Virlis Fischer.
1972. Dispersed versus concentrated forest recreation as forest policy. [Paper presented to the Seventh World Forestry Congress, Buenos Aires, Argentina, 16 p. (Oct. 4–18, 1972).]

Lucas, Robert C.
1964. The recreational capacity of the Quetico-Superior area. USDA For. Serv. Res. Pap. LS-15, 34 p. Lake States For. Exp. Stn., St. Paul, Minn.

Lucas, Robert C.
1978. The characteristics of visitors to wilderness and related areas USDA For. Serv. Res. Pap. LS-15, 34 p. Lake States For. Exp. Stn., St. Paul, Minn.

Magill, Arthur W.
1970. Five California campgrounds . . . conditions improve after 5 years' recreational use. USDA For. Serv. Res. Pap. PSW-62, 18 p. Pac. Southwest For. and Range Exp. Stn., Berkeley, Calif.

McCool, Stephen F., Lawrence C. Merriam, Jr., and Charles T. Cushwa.
1969. The condition of wilderness campsites in the Boundary Waters Canoe Area. Minn. For. Res. Notes No. 202, 4 p. University of Minnesota, Minneapolis.

187

McFeters, Gordon A.

1975. Microbial studies of a high alpine water supply used for recreation. Final report to the USDI, National Park Service on research contract CX 12004 BO25. 12 p. Dep. Microbiol., Montana State University, Bozeman.

Merriam, L.C., Jr., and C.K. Smith.

1974. Visitor impact on newly developed campsites in the Boundary Waters Canoe Area. J. For. 72(10):627–630.

Merriam, L.C., Jr., C.K. Smith, D.E. Miller, Ching tiao Huang, J.C. Tappeiner II, Kent Goeckermann, J.A. Bloemendal, and T.M. Costello.

1973. Newly developed campsites in the Boundary Waters Canoe Area: a study of 5 years' use. Agric. Exp. Stn. Bull. 511, 27 p. University of Minnesota, St. Paul.

Neil, P.H., R.W. Hoffman, and R.B. Gill.

1975. Effects of harassment on wild animals—an annotated bibliography of selected references. Special Report No. 37, 21 p. Colorado Division of Wildlife, Denver.

Odum, Eugene P.

1959. Fundamentals of biology. 546 p. W.B. Saunders Co., Philadelphia.

Outdoor Recreation Resources Review Commission.

1962. Wilderness and recreation: a report on resources, values, and problems. Outdoor Recreation Resour. Rev. Comm. Rep. 3, 352 p. U.S. Government Printing Office, Washington, D.C.

Pfister, Robert E., and Robert E. Frenkel.

1974. Field investigation of river use within the wild river area of the Rogue River, Oregon: Interim Report to Oregon State Marine Board, 112 p. Salem.

Pfister, Robert E., and Robert E. Frenkel.

1975. The concept of carrying capacity: its application for management of Oregon's Scenic Waterway System. 50 p. Water Resour. Res. Inst., Oregon State University, Corvallis.

Schultz, Richard D.

1975. Responses of national park elk to human activity. M.S. thesis, 57 p. Dep. Fish. and Wildl. Biol., Colorado State University, Ft. Collins.

Shelby, Bo, and Joyce McCarl Neilsen.

1975. Use levels and user satisfaction in the Grand Canyon. [Paper presented to the annual meeting of the Rural Sociological Society, San Francisco, Aug. 21–24.] 31 p.

Speight, M.C.D.

1973. Outdoor recreation and its ecological effects: a bibliography and review. Discussion papers in conservation No. 4, p. 35. University College, London.

Stankey, George H.

1973. Visitor perception of wilderness recreation carrying capacity. USDA For. Serv. Res. Pap. INT-142, 61 p. Intermt. For. and Range Exp. Stn., Ogden, Utah.

Stankey, George H., and David W. Lime.

1973. Recreational carrying capacity: an annotated bibliography. USDA For. Serv. Gen. Tech. Rep. INT-3, 45 p. Intermt. For. and Range Exp. Stn., Ogden, Utah.

Thorud, D.B., and S.S. Frissell.

1969. Soil rejuvenation following artificial compaction in a Minnesota oak stand. Minn. For. Res. Note No. 208, 4 p. University of Minnesota, Minneapolis.

Verburg, K.

1974. The carrying capacity of recreational lands: a review. Occas. Pap. No. 1, 70 p. Planning Division, Prairie Region, Parks Canada.

Wagar, J. Alan.

1964. The carrying capacity of wildlands for recreation. For. Sci. Monogr. No. 7, 23 p. Society of American Foresters, Washington, D.C.

Wagar, J. Alan.

1968. The place of carrying capacity in the management of recreation lands. Rocky Mt.-High Plains Parks and Recreation J. 3(1):37–45.

Wagar, J. Alan.

1974. Recreational carrying capacity reconsidered. J. For. 72(5):274–278.

Weaver, T., and D. Dale.

1977. Trampling effects of hikers, motorcycles, or horses in meadows and forests. J. Appl. Ecol. (In press.)

Willard, Beatrice E., and John W. Marr.

1970. Effects of human activities on alpine tundra ecosystems in Rocky Mountain National Park, Colorado. Biol. Conserv. 2(4):257–265.

Wilderness ecosystems are constantly changing as a result of normal successional processes and patterns of periodic disruptions. Wilderness management should insure that natural processes proceed in as uninterrupted a fashion as possible. Here, clusters of subalpine fir are naturally invading a meadow near Big Agnes Mountain in the Mount Zirkel Primitive Area, Colo.

10 Wilderness Ecosystems

Introduction

This chapter considers major features of wilderness ecosystems of concern to managers and contrasts them with ecosystems significantly altered by modern man. The emphasis is on the dynamic nature of ecosystems, their strong internal linkages and the ways various human activities have affected and continue to affect the "naturalness" of wilderness ecosystems. Only when ecosystem dynamics, including interrelationships with man, are fully understood can an assessment of the consequences of alternative management strategies be made.

Some readers may think that ecosystem concepts are only marginally related to wilderness management because so much of the previous material concerns people management. However, there is a large body of literature to remind us that ignorance of ecosystem concepts—internal linkages among environment, plant, and animal, and successional dynamics—lies at the root of many wilderness and park management problems. Concern about fire-control policies throughout much of the West (e.g., Kilgore 1973, Habeck 1970, and Habeck and Mutch 1973) and in the Lake States (Heinselman 1973, Wright 1974, and Frissell 1973) is based on

This chapter was written by Jerry F. Franklin, Principal Plant Ecologist, Pacific Northwest Forest and Range Experiment Station, Corvallis, Oreg.

ecosystem considerations. (See chapter 12.) Management of large ungulates (bighorn sheep, elk, or caribou) or predators, such as grizzly bears, inevitably must be based on ecosystem concepts. (See chapter 11.) Even the limits of human use under the naturalness constraint of the Wilderness Act—physical carrying capacity—rests on ecosystem concepts. (See chapter 8.) Finally, the entire notion of regulated human use and management of wilderness so as to not distort naturalness, the idea of man as an integral but not dominant part of wilderness, is an ecosystem concept.

Some readers without natural science backgrounds may find this chapter difficult reading for it contains a cram course in ecology. However, the basic ecological concepts discussed are essential for understanding the implications of the subsequent chapters on fire and wildlife.

Man's Historic Role in Wilderness

One point should, perhaps, be dealt with at the outset—is man an integral component of the wilderness? Are man and his influences natural or unnatural? The answer to this is clearly relative rather than absolute. Primitive man unquestionably played a role in shaping the wilderness landscapes of North America including those formally recognized today as components of the National Wilderness Preservation System. He burned and hunted, raised crops, and built settlements. With rare exceptions (man's role in extinction of Pleistocene mammals may be one of these), however, aboriginal man did not exist in sufficient numbers nor did he have the technology to control and direct the forces of nature. He was an influencing factor, but only one of many, and negative feedback mechanisms existed which kept his populations and impacts in check. For example, when resources were exhausted or depleted or when climatic changes occurred, primitive man generally died or moved on. He could not dominate his environment nor could he delay or alter these negative feedbacks.

This situation has changed with the rise of technological civilization. Current human technology has grown extremely powerful and, in the short term, is capable of buffering man from the effects of strong negative feedback. "Natural" human influences might be considered those which have been elements in the long term evolution of the presettlement ecosystems— present for hundreds, thousands, and even tens of thousands of years. The impacts of modern man are *not* this type. The wilderness ecosystems we are concerned with here—those in designated wilderness—did not evolve under the influence of these forces and are not adapted to them. Uncontrolled, modern man's influences alter the historical direction and rate of ecosystem evolution. The contrast between primitive and modern man in the ability to control and alter natural forces and ecosystems is so great it does not require elaboration. Modern technology has allowed us to impact every single point on the globe (consciously or unconsciously) and influence even the most basic and powerful natural forces such as climate. Finally, our technology allows us to avoid, delay, or control the negative feedback mechanisms which kept primitive man in check. Nature will probably exact her full price for each act of modern man but the feedback is typically neither as direct nor as rapid (at least in so far as we perceive it) as it was for primitive man. In most instances we have overcome the negative feedback of nature with modern technology, at least in the short run.

To conclude on this point it can perhaps be said that man is a natural part of wilderness but, because of their recent origin, strength, pervasiveness, and ability to buffer rapid feedback, the technological forces at his control are *not*. We cannot accept modern man—or more specifically the forces he controls—as a "natural" component of wilderness. In an historical context, they are not natural. Legally, tolerance to them is restricted by the Wilderness Act. Nevertheless, modern technology is impacting the wilderness and will increasingly do so. We will use technology to manage wilderness—to perpetuate or create desired conditions, sometimes to substitute

for a natural process such as wildfire or predation. Because of the pervasive and powerful nature of the forces we generate (and sometimes command) it is critical that we understand their effects as a guide to minimizing them and, in the case of management, use these forces to mimic natural forces or processes no longer present.

Ecosystems and Their Characteristics

An ecosystem includes all the organisms of an area, their environment, and a series of linkages or interactions between them. As Odum (1971) summarizes, "The ecosystem is the basic fundamental unit in ecology, since it includes both organisms . . . and abiotic environments, each influencing the properties of the other and both necessary for the maintenance of life . . . . "

The *abiotic environment* includes climatic conditions such as temperature and moisture regimes and inorganic substances supplied by mineral soil. The *organisms* include *autotrophs* and *heterotrophs*. *Autotrophic organisms* are the green plants which provide the ecosystem's entire energy base by fixing solar energy and using simple inorganic substances to build up complex organic substances. *Heterotrophic organisms* (animals, microbes, and fungi, for example) utilize these complex substances as a food base and rearrange or decompose them. Heterotrophs can be divided into (1) ingestors (macroconsumers, biophages) that feed on live materials—bear, deer, squirrels, butterflies, and slugs, for example, and (2) decomposers (microconsumers, saprophages) such as bacteria, fungi, and some insects that feed on dead material such as leaf litter, fallen logs, and feces.

A wilderness ecosystem has a series of attributes which are fundamentally the same as those in any other ecosystem. First, at a given point in time there is a particular *compositon* and *structure*. That is, there is an array of plant and animal species in various proportions. Each biological component contains given amounts of biomass or energy, nutrients, and other materials—the compartments or states recognized in computer models of ecosystems (fig. 10–2). The elements are spatially arranged to produce an ecosystem we recognize as forest or meadow or savanna.

Within this ecosystem various *processes*— photosynthesis, transpiration, consumption (by ingesters), decomposition—are going on. These processes are driven by *environmental* factors (the *driving forces* of ecosystem models) such as moisture supply, temperature, and sunlight. Not all processes are carried out exclusively by organisms, however; weathering of parent

Figure 10-1.—Many different kinds of ecosystems are represented currently in, or pending designation in, the National Wilderness Preservation System. These ecosystems range from the semiarid lands of the Gila Wilderness, N. Mex. (*lower left*), the deciduous forests of the Presidential Range-Dry River Wilderness, N.H., (*lower right*), to the moon-like landscape of Craters of the Moon Wilderness, Idaho (*upper left*).

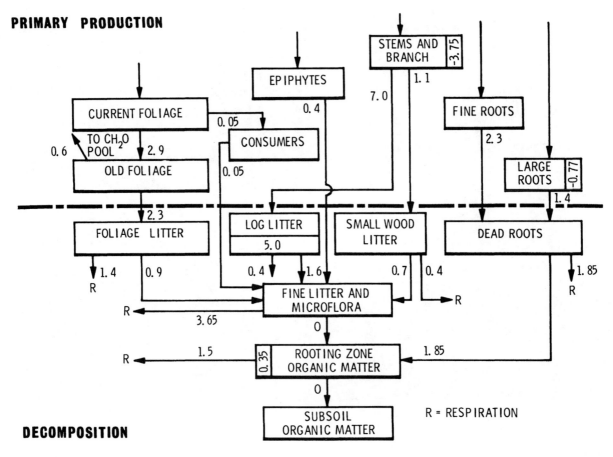

PRIMARY PRODUCTION

DECOMPOSITION

Figure 10–2.—Any ecosystem, such as a forest or meadow, contains a number of individual components possessing given amounts of biomass, energy, nutrients, or other material. Each of these components is linked to others in the same system.

materials, erosion, and evaporation are examples of essentially physical processes. Likewise, not all environmental or abiotic· factors are the classical climatic influences of light, temperature, and moisture. Fire and flood are examples of periodic driving forces.

The *linkages* or *flows* (fig. 10–2) between parts of an ecosystem are characteristics of special importance to resource managers. Energy, water, nutrients, and other substances do not remain indefinitely in any one place or state. They are transferred through the ecosystem along a series of flow pathways. Organic materials are generally degraded or broken down into simpler substances as they flow from primary producers to consumers and decomposers. Materials are ultimately recycled within the system or lost from it by leaching, volatilization, or other processes. Environmental factors are important in controlling the rates at which the flows take place; biologic composition and spatial arrangement largely determine the flow paths. These fundamentals are extremely important, for man exerts his most profound

influences on ecosystems when he alters the paths and rates of these flows. As an example, can you imagine what would happen to a forest ecosystem if, somehow, decomposition rates (breakdown of dead organic matter with the release of energy and nutrients) were significantly reduced?

There are short-term fluctuations—diurnal, seasonal, and annual—in rates of each process whether it is photosynthesis, herbivory (ingestion of plant materials by animals), or water runoff. Ecosystem science has progressed further in simulating these relatively short-term dynamics than it has in approximating longer term changes (see, for example, U.S. Natl. Comm., Inter. Biol. Program (1974). However, long term changes in ecosystem states, processes, flowpaths and rates are also occurring. These are changes associated with successional development of the ecosystems.[1]

---

[1] For a concise, theoretical analysis of successionally related changes in ecosystems, see Odum (1971).

To summarize and relate these ecosystem characteristics to the real world, let's look at them in the context of a lodgepole pine stand. This stand has a complement of plant and animal species of varying abundance which define its biological *composition* (e.g., lodgepole pine, dwarf huckleberry, fungus, squirrel, Stellers jay). These organisms and their parts have a spatial arrangement defining the stand *structure* (e.g., an overstory canopy, shrub layer, litter layer, rooting zone). By combining elements of composition and structure we can define the major boxes or *compartments* (e.g., leaves, stems, roots, primary or plant consumers, secondary consumers or predators) each containing a certain amount of biomass, nutrients, and water. Flows or transfers of energy or materials are taking place from one compartment to another—from the leaves and branches to animals by grazing, for example, or from live green plants to the decomposing organisms by litter fall. Processes and transfer rates are largely controlled or driven by *environmental or abiotic factors* such as temperature and moisture availability. All of the elements of the lodgepole pine stand are linked together by the paths of energy and material flow—tree, bird, deer, nematode, bacterium. Changes in composition, structure, climate, and so forth will alter the rates and/or paths of energy and material flow. Therefore, the basic functions carried out by the ecosystem are expressed in terms of production of organic matter (energy fixation) and use and conservation of water and nutrients.

One attribute of ecosystems we have not considered is the size or, more generally, how the boundaries of an ecosystem are defined. Basically, an ecosystem can be as large or as small as we want it to be, depending on our objectives. It can be an aquarium, forest stand, watershed, an entire park or wilderness, a biome, or the entire world. It is necessary only that the area have the characteristics defined by Odum—constituent organisms interacting with their environment, energy flow, material cycles. Scientists often find a watershed a useful unit for ecosystem study because it is relatively easy to define the physical boundaries and to measure many of the flows into and out of the ecosystem; it also incorporates both terrestrial and aquatic elements and allows study of their interaction. In summary, an ecosystem can be of widely varying size depending on the objectives of the work.

In wilderness management the size of the ecosystem unit of interest will also vary. In some cases it might be an individual stand or community such as a meadow. When locating camping areas or determining carrying capacity, it might be a small lake basin or watershed—or the "heavy use areas," "trail corridors," or "subalpine zone" as described for planning purposes in chapter 8. Manage-

ment of habitat for large ungulates, such as elk, might necessitate that the relevant ecosystem be defined as a large river basin. And, of course, the entire wilderness can be the ecosystem unit for many planning and management activities. Determining the size of the ecosystem unit or the number to be recognized in a wilderness will depend on management's objectives (see chapter 8) and the kinds of problems facing the manager.

Dynamics of Ecosystems

There are two basic concepts about ecosystems for a land manager to keep continually in mind. First is the interrelatedness of all the parts; that is, you can not do just one thing for any given action ramifies to a greater or lesser degree throughout the whole ecosystem. Such linkages are typically responses for extensive, unexpected, and sometimes undesirable effects of a given activity. One example is the accumulation of pesticides in food chains leading ultimately, not to the demise of the target pest, but rather to declines in organisms high in the trophic chain, such as brown pelicans, peregrine falcons, and bald eagles. Another is the subtle and complex interactions of red alder with a forest soil that lead to changes in total soil nitrogen, nitrates, soil acidity, Actinomycete populations, and, ultimately, the ability of a root rot such as *Phellinus* to survive (Trappe 1972).

The second outstanding attribute is the dynamic character of an ecosystem over long time periods—as opposed to short-term cyclical changes. These longer term trends are often referred to as successional[2] changes. Long-term plant succession is a familiar concept for land managers and particularly important for those who propose to manage or maintain natural landscapes. It suggests there is no one answer to the question, "what should a wilderness look like?" The ecosystem of any given wilderness—if allowed to remain natural—is continually changing.

The classical successional sequences are described as either primary or secondary (Daubenmire 1968) (fig. 10–3). Primary succession is normally considered a much slower process than secondary succession because it involves amelioration of extreme site conditions by gradual alterations brought about by the organisms. An

[2] Odum (1971) defines succession as an orderly process of community development involving changes in species structure and community processes with time. It is directional and predictable and results from modification of the physical environment by the community. Succession culminates in a stabilized ecosystem with maximum biomass and linkages between organisms per unit of energy flow. Daubenmire (1968) describes succession as any unidirectional change that can be detected in changes in proportions of species in a stand or the complete replacement of one community by another.

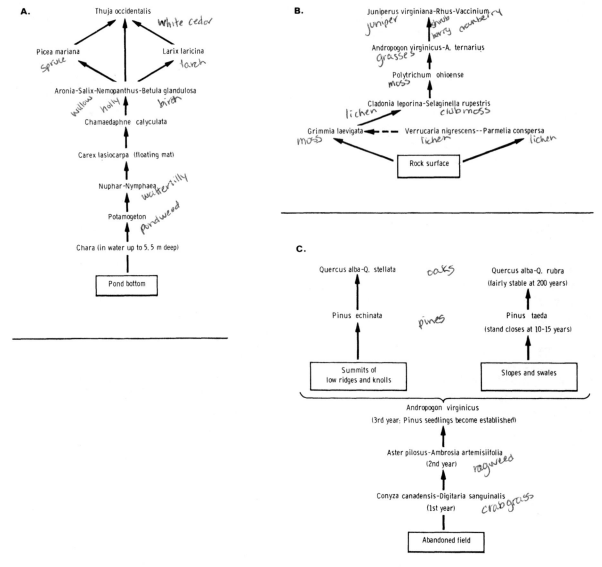

A.

Thuja occidentalis — *white cedar*

Picea mariana — *spruce*   Larix laricina — *larch*

Aronia-Salix-Nemopanthus-Betula glandulosa — *willow, holly, birch*

Chamaedaphne calyculata

Carex lasiocarpa (floating mat)

Nuphar-Nymphaea — *waterlilly*

Potamogeton — *pondweed*

Chara (in water up to 5. 5 m deep)

Pond bottom

B.

Juniperus virginiana-Rhus-Vaccinium — *juniper, shrub, berry, cranberry*

Andropogon virginicus-A. ternarius — *grasses*

Polytrichum ohioense — *moss*

Cladonia leporina-Selaginella rupestris — *lichen, clubmoss*

Grimmia laevigata — *moss*   Verrucaria nigrescens--Parmelia conspersa — *lichen, lichen*

Rock surface

C.

Quercus alba-Q. stellata — *oaks*   Quercus alba-Q. rubra (fairly stable at 200 years)

Pinus echinata — *pines*   Pinus taeda (stand closes at 10-15 years)

Summits of low ridges and knolls   Slopes and swales

Andropogon virginicus (3rd year: Pinus seedlings become established)

Aster pilosus-Ambrosia artemisiifolia (2nd year) — *ragweed*

Conyza canadensis-Digitaria sanguinalis (1st year) — *crabgrass*

Abandoned field

Figure 10–3.—Classical successional sequences are described as either primary or secondary. In *A*, the common sequences of dominants in pond succession found in an area in lower Michigan is shown; in *B*, the principal stages of succession in shallow depressions in granite rock found in eastern North Carolina is outlined; and in *C*, successional trends in the Piedmont plateau are shown. (Taken from Daubenmire 1968).

example of *primary succession* is a lake filling in and being replaced consecutively with marshes, shrub-fields, and finally forests. Another illustration is colonization and development of vegetation on bare rock surfaces, sand or talus. *Secondary succession* can be seen in the fairly rapid changes following cutting or burning of a forest or removal of grazing animals from a depleted range.

Secondary succession has been extensively described (Daubenmire 1968). For example, following fire or clearcutting, forest lands are dominated by opportunistic, shade-intolerant herbaceous species (fireweed) which

are replaced in turn by shrubs and ultimately, a stand of shade-intolerant, pioneer tree species. In time, tree species that are more shade tolerant seed in under the canopy and reproduction of intolerant trees fails in the shaded environment. Over several centuries the stand proceeds through a gradual compositional change to a stable climax forest composed of shade-tolerant species capable of perpetuating themselves indefinitely.

This is a useful concept based on the assumptions of: Orderly progression toward a stable climax following a disturbance; gradual elimination of less shade-tolerant competitors by more tolerant species; and, often, the necessity for a hardier pioneer species to prepare the way for less hardy species. This classical view of forest succession may, then, be viewed as being largely dependent upon intrinsic processes—amelioration or preparation of severe sites by pioneering species and their eventual elimination by the less hardy climax species through competition.

As a concept, forest succession is based largely on inferences drawn from size- or age-class distributions, however, and many situations do not fit classical concepts when examined closely. For example, the assumption that pioneer trees *must* precede climax tree species, making the environment more suitable for the latter, simply does not hold in many situations. Given an adequate seed source, both tree species can often invade a bared area simultaneously and the stand structure 100 years later reflects differing growth or competitive abilities, not necessarily later arrival of the smaller tolerant species or its dependence on site amelioration by the pioneer species. Age structure analyses are showing more and more that inferences drawn from size structure analyses can lead to erroneous conclusions about successional developments.

Likewise, we encounter some forests where there is no change in the composition of the tree species over time. Some ponderosa or lodgepole pine forests are of this type. In these situations, only one tree species is capable of surviving, and if it happens to be intolerant, then regeneration of the species must await openings in the canopy as the stand grows older. For example, even in the renowned Douglas-fir region of the Pacific Northwest there are dry habitats where Douglas-fir is both the main pioneer and climax tree.

The important things to remember are these: There are a variety of processes involved in forest succession including opportunity (seed source), site amelioration, and competition; and a climax species can be tolerant or intolerant depending on the site.

Bearing all of these qualifications in mind, it is still useful to think of successional change as a reasonably ordered sequence of plant species culminating in a stable or climax (self-perpetuating) type over much of our wildland. Such changes occur regardless of the causes. Thus, an ecosystem can be considered to have a *trajectory* or general direction of change over time. If the system is destroyed or set back in the sequence by a disturbance it will presumably begin evolving again toward the same end point or climax state provided the climate has not changed, the site has not been significantly degraded, and the same organisms are available to reinvade the site.

The fact is, of course, that because of periodic disturbances—fire, flood, storm, avalanche, pathogens,

or geomorphological processes (such as mass soil movements)—very few of our natural ecosystems ever reach a stable climax state. *Therefore, an important corollary to the dynamic successional nature of ecosystems is that periodic disturbances of some type almost inevitably intercede before an end point or climax state is reached.* In the Lake States, most of the ecosystems in the West, and interior Alaska, fire is the primary disruptor and it occurs at fairly frequent intervals thereby initiating new successional sequences— as will be explained more fully in chapter 12. In the redwood region, both flood and fire have been intrinsic environmental elements which periodically altered the ecosystem (which in no way suggests they are essential for perpetuating redwood itself). Hurricanes function as periodic disrupters (or rejuvenators) of forest ecosystems in much of the eastern temperate forest, as do typhoons in Japan and strong winter winds along the northern Pacific coast. Pathogens (for example, mountain pine beetle, lodgepole needleminer, dwarfmistletoe, and stem cankers) are the periodic disturbers of some wildland ecosystems such as some lodgepole pine forests that escape fire.

What is important is the realization that ecosystems are adapted to a particular set of disruptions. The patterns of disturbance are as much a part of the wild landscape as a successional sequence or trajectory.

To summarize, long term ecosystem dynamics are the consequence of normal successional processes (colonization, competition, site alterations by organisms, etc.) and patterns of periodic disruption (caused, for example, by fire, insect, disease, storm, and avalanche). Through knowledge of these successional forces and relevant ecosystem characteristics, the trajectory or general direction of natural change over time is apparent to the wilderness manager. The job of wilderness management is often to insure that the dynamics of the ecosystem and the resulting successional change—the natural trajectory of the ecosystem—proceed without disruption or distortion by man. If the trajectory is to be altered by human intervention it should be as a consequence of conscious choice and with full understanding of the consequences.

Human Influences on Ecosystem Dynamics in Wilderness

The mosaic of ecosystems in a wilderness reflects the basic environmental conditions (soil, macroclimate and microclimate), the array of organisms available for occupying the sites, and the pattern of disturbances— types, time, and areal extent. If *any* of these are altered by modern man, then the mosaic will be altered to an unnatural state to a greater or lesser degree.

What are some of the changes which modern man has brought about in wilderness areas? A visible and well-known example is fire control. Fires at some interval are a natural feature of almost all of our forest ecosystems. It has been argued that western coniferous forests have actually evolved in such a way as to increase flammability and insure periodic burning. Certainly many of the species of great interest to us depend upon fire for their perpetuation—giant sequoia (Kilgore 1973), Douglas-fir and ponderosa pine on some sites (Habeck and Mutch 1973, Cooper 1960) red and white pine in the Lake States (Frissell 1973), and the closed-cone (serotinous) pines of the West such as knobcone pine (Vogl 1973). (See chapter 12.)

Elimination of fire, when periodic low-intensity fires are naturally part of an ecosystem's environment, can have catastrophic consequences. First, a successful fire control program will change the composition of the forests, in many cases. Succession will proceed further before disruption than it would under natural conditions. Not only will the plant composition of the forest change but the suitable habitat for many animal species will also be altered with consequent changes in the animal composition of an area. Within a forest community, changes will also take place in stand structure and in paths and rates of material flow. Organic matter and nutrients accumulate in slowly decomposed woody plant material on the forest floor. Continuity develops between the crown and ground fuels as the density of saplings and poles increases. One result is likely to be not just a loss of earlier successional communities and less tolerant tree species, but ultimately a catastrophic fire to which the ecosystems in the area are *not* adapted.

The coniferous forests on the western slopes of the Cascade Range offer an interesting contrast with most other coniferous forest regions. Here, fire appears *not* to have been primarily a chronic or frequent disturber of the forests; *rather*, infrequent catastrophic fires, often affecting large areas, seem to have been the rule.

Grazing by domestic animals is another influence in wilderness ecosystems introduced by modern man. Concentrated grazing by sheep or cattle (or even large wild ungulates, such as elk or mountain goats, introduced to regions where they are not native) is not part of the natural regimen under which many of our wilderness meadows and savannas have evolved. Consequently, they are often poorly adapted to it. When large-scale grazing is introduced, changes in the composition of the meadows occur due to preferential feeding on, and/or sensitivity of, some plant species. The site may be physically altered due to compaction and accelerated erosion, and changes in water table level can also occur. Exotic plant species, introduced with livestock and horsefeed, may take advantage of the altered conditions to establish themselves. Animal pathogens may be introduced into native ungulate populations (just as the white man brought measles to the Indian) with catastrophic results—such as when scabies, a disease of native sheep, was introduced into bighorn sheep populations.

Some of the changes—addition of exotic species and site degradation—can be particularly significant because they can permanently alter the potential of the site, that is, its ability to return to its original natural state. An outstanding example of the effects of grazing on the ecosystem is found in the sagebrush-bunchgrass and Palouse prairie types of eastern Washington and Oregon (Daubenmire 1970). Heavy grazing by large herbivores reduces the vigor of and can eliminate the bunchgrass dominants such as bluebunch wheatgrass and Idaho fescue. Cheatgrass or Kentucky bluegrass invades and once these exotic species occupy habitat vacated by native plants there is no evidence that the native species can ever again successfully recolonize the sites. Grazing can thus bring about permanent changes in ecosystems even in the absence of site degradation.

Modern man has altered—and continues to alter—wilderness ecosystems by eliminating or reducing populations of specific species. The best known examples are the elimination of predatory animals—for example, wolverine, grizzly bear, cougar, raptor. Populations of such species have been eliminated from some wildernesses, reduced in others. In any case, the composition of these ecosystems is not what it was originally. It should be noted that in terms of *some* ecosystem functions—their ability to fix energy and conserve nutrients—the loss of such organisms may not be particularly significant. However, in terms of a human's perception of a tract as a pristine landscape, the loss is very significant. Further, loss of some predators, such as the wolf, can have significant ecological impacts when they, as natural controls on large herbivore populations, are lost[3] although the report "Wildlife Management in the National Parks" concludes that

---

[3] It should also be noted that because predators high on the trophic chain are, relatively, so strongly affected by human activities, they are very good indicators of the degree of naturalness of a particular area. This is not always the case; chronic perturbation of an area by pollutants such as SO compounds and ozone can appear first in the compositional changes in plants or animals or even rates of productivity or decomposition. Nevertheless, because of the direct impacts of human activities on large predators (such as, hunting, elimination of dangers) plus their position at the end of long food chains, they are often among the first organisms affected.

Figure 10–4.—Wilderness ecosystems can be ranked according to their ability to sustain use impacts. Many ecosystems are quite fragile and can be easily impacted. Examples include: (*upper left*) proposed wilderness in the San Juan Islands Refuge, Wash.; (*upper right*) high alpine country, Beartooth Primitive Area; and (*lower left*) the desert country of the Desert Game Range Wilderness, Nev. Other ecosystems are quite resilient, such as the eastern hardwoods found in such areas as (*lower right*) the Monongahela National Forest, W. Va.

" . . . predation alone can seldom be relied upon to control ungulate numbers . . . ." (Leopold et al. 1969).

Losses of species are not confined to higher animals, however. Plant species have also been eliminated or drastically reduced in some areas. These losses significantly alter the ecosystem's structure and its basic functions of energy fixation and nutrient conservation. Disregarding grazing and fire, losses in plant species are most frequently caused by human introduction of exotic pathogens. Outstanding examples which affect designated wildernesses include the nearly complete loss of American chestnut to chestnut blight and substantial losses of whitebark and other five-needled pines to white pine blister rust. Exotic pathogens of this type can have extremely profound effects on otherwise pristine landscapes for, once introduced, they are uncontrollable and, if the host species lack significant genetic or other mechanisms for resistance, effects (alterations) are essentially permanent.

Consider the effects of balsam woolly aphid on Pacific coast true firs, *Phytopthora* root rot on Port-Orford-

cedar, and white pine blister rust on western white pine. Balsam woolly aphid, an insect introduced from Europe, has reduced the vigor and attractiveness of subalpine fir and Pacific silver fir in many parts of their range and has effectively eliminated them in some areas. For example, subalpine fir is now essentially absent from many locations in the southern Oregon Cascade Range. *P. lateralis*, a root rot introduced on horticultural stock, is easily spread by spores transported along roads, trails, and streams. Port-Orford-cedar has no resistance to this pathogen and infected stands are suffering 100-percent mortality. Only the isolation of some stands and the fact that the spores may possibly be short lived (viable for only a few years) offer any hope of survival of the species in its natural habitat; certainly it will never again have the importance it once did in the virgin stands of the southern Oregon Coast Ranges. The effects of white pine blister rust, another introduced pathogen, are well known to the forest managers of the northern Rocky Mountains. The blister rust probably causes relatively little mortality in large mature trees but can be

199

devastating in young stands and will greatly reduce the importance of western white pine in future forests. Whitebark pine is extremely susceptible to this pathogen (the most susceptible of all five-needled pines) and both young and old trees may be eliminated in infected areas.

Besides introducing pathogens, man has purposely added specific organisms to pristine landscapes in order to make them more attractive recreationally. The introduction of sport fish to originally barren lakes and streams is an outstanding example here. There can be no question that when fish introductions of this type are successful the affected aquatic ecosystem is significantly changed. An entirely new compartment may be added (if a fish at the same trophic level was not previously present). Native fish may be displaced or eliminated entirely; hence, the native brook trout in Great Smoky Mountains is now found only in high, isolated streams. In any case, alterations in the composition of other organisms and paths and rates of energy and nutrient flows are to be expected. There are many other examples mostly involving exotic game or food species; managers' attitudes towards exotic pests as opposed to introduced fish and game species are, to put it mildly, philosophically inconsistent.

There are a number of other human impacts which have altered the dynamics and states of wilderness ecosystems. There are the direct effects of human use, although these tend to be concentrated in relatively small areas—compaction of soil, destruction or alteration of vegetation at camping sites. Although heavily impacted locations may be small relative to the total area, they may be among the most popular, aesthetic, and frequently visited. Clearly, input of human wastes can reach sufficient levels in local areas to cause significant pollution; health problems probably become a management consideration before the effects of eutrophication in such cases.

In wilderness in the East, past human activities have sometimes included logging, road building, and clearing of land for agriculture. Modern man is introducing a variety of substances (plastic and other refuse; petroleum products in the Boundary Waters Canoe Area where motors are allowed) by his activity in wilderness and, on a far larger scale, by activities outside of the wilderness. Pollutants present in the atmosphere may be deposited in rain or as dust or brought in by migrant organisms. Pesticides and SOx compounds are such materials. In a few cases, sources of atmospheric pollution are sufficiently close to wilderness to directly affect air quality and cause pathological effects on organisms (e.g., damage to trees in the Los Angeles basin and several southern California wildernesses). Miller (1973) described the accelerated mortality of ponderosa pine in the San Bernardino Mountains as an example of the type of damage that can occur.

Natural Versus Man-Influenced Ecosystems

A key feature of wilderness ecosystems and a focal point of the Wilderness Act is "naturalness"—freedom from significant influences of modern technological man. Can the ecologist define naturalness or is it a quality, like solitude, which is largely in the eye of the beholder?

At the outset we must recognize there are no completely unaltered ecosystems left on this planet. The effects of modern man and his products are pervasive. This is as true in the Antarctic, where DDT is found in the tissues of penguins, as it is in Central Park in New York City. None of the world remains unaltered and the examples given in the previous section should make it clear that even in areas we perceive as pristine, modern man has already had a significant impact.

Human activities can affect several key attributes of ecosystems. First, they can affect the *functional ability* of the ecosystem, the capacity to perform key actions—to fix and cycle energy, conserve and cycle nutrients, and provide suitable habitat for an array of inhabiting species. Second, they can affect the *structure*, or spatial arrangement of the parts, of the ecosystem—whether it is a savanna, meadow, even-aged or uneven-aged forest, or some other type. Third, they can affect the *composition* and population structure, that is, the number of species and their relative abundance as well as the densities and age- and size-class distributions of individual species. Finally, human actions can alter the basic *successional patterns*, or trajectories, characteristic of a given site.

The ecological significance of human activity is based on the magnitude and permanence of its effects. In assessing its importance, one needs to know if the change in one of the four attributes (function, structure, composition, dynamics) is very large or small and if it is transient or essentially permanent. As will be seen, it is the changes in structure and composition which are most easily perceived by the manager and visitor; although changes in function and dynamics may be more important in the long run, they are often very difficult to identify until they have progressed beyond correction.

The human activities which bring about changes in ecosystem attributes can be placed in a relatively few general categories:

(1) Introduction of an exotic organism such as chestnut blight, a sport fish, or cheatgrass;

(2) Elimination of a native organism such as grizzly bear, American chestnut, or wolf;

(3) Addition of materials, especially foreign substances such as a pesticide or SOx compound;

(4) Removal of materials, especially energy- or nutrient-rich substances, as in grazing and logging or by erosion;

(5) Physical alteration of site, for example, trail or road construction and compaction of soil from recreation use;

(6) Alteration of the natural patterns and level of disturbance, for example, control of natural fires or insect epidemics; and

(7) Alteration of the basic environmental regime of the site, for example, by weather modification projects, reduction of the ozone layer, or addition of noise, none of which has its origin within the wilderness itself.

Any of the activities included in these seven categories can have profound effects on ecosystem function, structure, composition, and dynamics. But the significance of the alteration, as measured by its magnitude and permanence, may be far different from the degree to which it is sensed as unnatural by the layman. The following are some examples.

Introduction of the chestnut blight resulted in permanent elimination of the American chestnut. The hardwood ecosystems of which it was a part underwent a permanent change in composition and population structure, not only as a result of the loss of a dominant tree but also because of adjustments in animal species dependent upon it for food. Alterations also occurred in rates of energy and nutrient cycling, forest structure and successional sequences as the ecosystems adjusted and other species filled the gaps. Despite these changes, visitors to forests from which chestnuts have been eliminated do not typically perceive these as unnatural or man-altered ecosystems. Likewise, presence of planted sport fish is rarely perceived as an unnatural influence although the effects on the structure and function of the largely unseen lake, pond, or stream ecosystem may be significant and permanent.

On the other hand, visitors are more likely to be aware of the elimination of grizzly bears and wolves from many wildernesses. Composition (the diversity of these ecosystems) has been changed permanently but the effect on their structure and function is probably relatively minor.[4] However, because visitors are much

more aware of large animals of this type, their absence is more likely to be perceived as an unnatural influence.

Logging has been a factor in some wildernesses in the East producing profound changes in the structure of forest ecosystems quite aside from the roads that were required for access. Composition and ecosystem functioning were also drastically altered. Many aspects of system function, such as conservation of nutrients, quickly recovered to near prelogging levels as succession proceeded, however. These ecosystems are returning to approximations of their former structure and composition at a slower rate but, barring site degradation, will generally recover. This is not to say that such logged areas will ever have exactly the same composition and species population structure; conditions (environmental and biological) are never exactly the same at the initiation of a successional sequence as they were before disturbance. It is probable that the duration of the logging impacts on structure and composition are substantially less in the moderate, summer-wet forest environments of the Appalachian Mountains with their rapid vegetative regrowth than would have been the case in much of the more arid western coniferous forest.

Logging disturbance, and especially clearcutting, is perceived by all visitors as highly unnatural and, of course, it is. Nonetheless, in many habitats, while effects are long term, they are not necessarily permanent in terms of composition, ecosystem functions, structure, or successional trajectory.

Interferences in patterns of natural disturbances, for example, fire control programs are much more subtle in their effects. Yet they are equally unnatural, leading (if successful) to permanent alteration in ecosystem function (for example, paths and rates of nutrient cycling), composition, and successional trajectory. Effects are gradual and, initially, not as drastic and noticeable as logging impacts. Yet they may be much more profound.

It would appear that the ecologist can provide some measurements of the naturalness of the landscape. These measurements are based on the degree to which modern man has altered the functional abilities (energy fixation and nutrient conservation) of the ecosystems, their composition and structure, the successional trajectories and the historic pattern of natural disturbances. The larger and more permanent the alteration, the greater its significance as an unnatural influence.

This also suggests that recreationists, managers, and ecologists will not necessarily see eye-to-eye on an area's degree of naturalness or, more likely, unnaturalness. Ecologically, a dramatic but transient disturbance such as a road might be judged less of an unnatural influence

---

[4] The relative importance of the ecological role of the wolf to overall ecosystem function was probably highly variable; in ecosystems with large populations of large ungulates such as moose or caribou its role has been considered critical. In many other areas it probably was not. Current ecological theory suggests that, in general, predator populations are not the major factor controlling prey population levels.

than permanent loss of a plant or animal species which might not be apparent to the untrained eye.

Thus, ecological and sociological perceptions of the naturalness of wilderness can differ widely. This perspective can lead to the conclusion that, in ecological terms, as far as naturalness is concerned, there is not as sharp a distinction as many have assumed, between the previously impacted wildérnesses in the East and the more primitive areas in the West. Exotic species have been introduced and native dominants have been lost in both areas. And it is an open question whether the wilderness areas in the West have been more permanently changed and are more unnatural after nearly 70 years of fire control programs and extensive grazing than the forest sites of the Appalachian Mountains which were logged 50 or more years ago.

Ecologically, the most significant human alterations of natural ecosystems are not necessarily the most obvious. What a visitor perceives as natural may have been profoundly and permanently altered. *The degree of naturalness in ecological terms is a function of knowledge about ecosystem factors and, if quantified, will often differ from the lay visitor's perception of naturalness.*

This conclusion should not obscure the fact that we have purposely selected as our wildernesses those tracts of land within each biotic region which both the ecologist and laymen view as among the most natural and unaltered by modern technology. For this reason, they are extremely valuable for determining environmental and ecological baselines in each biotic region in which they occur. Not only is there more naturalness to be lost in wilderness than elsewhere but also there are greater opportunities to maintain, and learn from, this environment—opportunities which might be just as important a loss if they disappear. It can be argued that because these are our most natural environments we need to minimize both broad, external impacts (such as pollutant inputs via the atmosphere or climatic changes due to weather modifications) and specific activity impacts within the area (such as predator reduction, fire control, and grazing of domestic livestock). Because wildernesses are the most unaltered landscapes in each biotic region, it seems important to at least maintain each area level of naturalness, and the naturalness of some could stand to be enhanced.

Ecological Knowledge in Interpreting and Managing Wilderness

Knowledge of ecosystems and ecosystem dynamics is important for wilderness managers; the key question is what information is needed and how does the manager go about getting and using it. There are some general principles by which a manager should be guided:

(1) *In developing a management plan for a wilderness, key ecological data are essential,* although the

Figure 10–5.—Sixty years of natural ecological change is illustrated in these two photos of Red Buttes near Maroon Lake on West Maroon Creek in a new wilderness study area near the Maroon Bells-Snowmass Wilderness, Colo. *Left,* taken in 1916; *right,* taken 1976.

detail needed may vary with management objectives and problems. These data include at least a general knowledge of the ecosystems and their properties: (a) What kinds of ecosystems are present? (classification); (b) where are they located? (distribution, mapping); (c) what are their biological and physical characteristics? (e.g., characterizations of biotic composition, climate, etc.); (d) what are their dynamic properties? (rates and directions of change or successional trends); and (e) what are the key factors affecting the dynamics?

(2) *Periodic monitoring of changes within, and at the ecotones between, key ecosystems is essential to assess their naturalness.* Inventories which provide essential descriptive data at one point in time must be supplemented by repeated measures over time to *monitor* change.

(3) *The levels of ecological inventory and the needed monitoring will vary with the ecosystem.* The most important considerations are the rate at which the ecosystem is likely to change and its importance in the total wilderness landscape. In addition, each ecosystem must be considered in terms of the specific objectives for management of that wilderness and the current conditions and assumptions about the future which combine to identify problems (see chapter 8). Features requiring intensive levels of inventory and monitoring include meadows, lakes and streams, and some animal components, for example. These are ecosystems or elements which can change relatively rapidly and are focal points of visitor interest and use. Forest ecosystems, on the other hand, often provide a landscape background and usually undergo relatively slow changes.

(4) *The best ecologist and ecological information in the world do not substitute for clear management objectives.* The wilderness manager must decide what the ecological objectives of the management will be—the degree of naturalness desired. Many alternatives are available such as maintenance of status quo, return to presettlement condition, and perpetuation of a particular species, ecosystem, or community mosaic. Ecological information can tell the manager what is present, how it is changing and, possibly, why. Such information can also indicate biologically feasible options or potentials, constraints and dangers, and alternative management strategies. But the manager must decide what is desired in types and distribution of ecosystems; ecological information will then indicate if that is attainable, and if so, the necessary management actions to achieve it.

Identifying Wilderness Ecosystems

There can be no argument that, at some level of detail, ecological inventory is essential to the wilderness manager. It is absolutely essential to management planning and operations to know what ecosystems are present, where they are, and the direction and rate at which they are changing. There will be a great deal of variation in the detail needed based on management objectives and problems and available manpower, money, and technology. There will also be significant philosophical differences among professionals about the appropriate techniques and emphases.

Certainly, we can agree at the outset that, in a given wilderness, we want to know the vegetation types or communities and their locations. As examples we have the timber and range type maps of the forester and range manager. General classifications and maps of this type are arrived at through relatively simple standard procedures such as mapping on aerial photographs with appropriate ground checking. It is important to realize that indexing the communities as to location, most often by mapping, is essential. The best statistically designed, point-sample inventory or survey of a wilderness can tell you a particular vegetation type is present and its extent with a quantitative error term, but nothing about where it is or how it is spatially oriented with regard to other communities. This has been a traditional problem with many timber inventories, leaving the manager with the knowledge he has x-acres of stands suitable for thinning but no idea of their locations.

In wilderness and other natural areas the ecologist will usually begin with ground sampling of the communities using some design which may be statistical or subjective. Aerial photos are often used to locate stands of different types. The stand data collected are subjected to statistical and/or subjective analyses, and a classification or ordination of the communities will be the final product. This initial stratification can be used as a basis for mapping of the community types on aerial photographs or topographic maps or for establishing relationships between environmental factors (slope, aspect, soil type, landform, elevation) and vegetation.

Knowledge of the existing vegetative communities or cover types is essential, but this is not enough information to monitor and assess the naturalness of change. The wilderness manager needs a stratification of his landscape into basic environmental or habitat units. Existing vegetation may or may not provide a good index to areas which vary in basic environmental and ecosystem characteristics. Perhaps an example will make the contrast between habitat type and cover type (or existing vegetation) clearer. There are many types of ponderosa pine forest in western North America. A survey of existing communities may establish that there is a ponderosa pine/shrub community. In fact, this community may occur in several habitats, distinctive in their environmental conditions. As a consequence, on one, the pine forest is climax while on another it is subject to replacement by more tolerant species due to better moisture conditions.

The point here is that the wilderness manager needs to know both the kinds and distribution of existing communities and the basic habitat types. Approaches to identifying and classifying the basic habitat types or environmental mosaic of a landscape are many and diverse, however, and here is where ecologists often part company—among themselves and with other specialists.

Remember, at this point, that the objective is to identify natural landscape units which are relatively homogeneous in biological and physical characteristics. This allows the manager to categorize his lands according to their use potential, management problems, and response to various natural or artificial perturbations or treatments. To do this, knowledge of *both* the existing communities and the basic environmental mosaic (habitat types) is needed.

In the Western United States major emphasis is on the use of stable or near-climax vegetation to identify habitat types.[5] Pfister (1975) has outlined the philosophy, potential use, and current progress of this approach which is based upon the concepts developed and demonstrated by R. Daubenmire in the northern Rocky Mountains (Daubenmire and Daubenmire 1968). The self-perpetuating tree species and selected understory species are used to stratify the landscape into basic habitat types. This can be termed the use of potential natural vegetation for identifying the environmental mosaic. Obviously, when a wilderness is occupied largely by successionally advanced communities, a map of existing vegetation provides a good index to the environmental mosaic. However, where communities are mainly early successional types, maps of existing community types may look very different from those of habitat type or potential natural vegetation.

The *habitat-type approach* works well for stratifying broad areas into relatively homogenous units. Inferences about environmental conditions and the potential and limitations of the types for various uses can be accurately and quickly drawn and easily extrapolated across the landscape. Nevertheless, there are limitations. The current or existing vegetative cover may not receive sufficient attention. In addition, it is necessary to integrate the habitat-type classification with soils and landform data for a complete ecosystem classification. Also, in the classification process some information is lost about an individual stand as it is lumped into a type with other similar but not identical stands. Mapping must follow the classification to make it useful in land planning, it cannot be carried out until the initial classification is completed.

An alternative approach has been developed by Kessell (1977 [in press]) in Glacier National Park in which *gradient models* of the vegetation and fire fuels are combined with a hectare-by-hectare resource inventory using aerial photographs and topographic maps in a computerized storage and retrieval system. By means of sampling, community characteristics (composition and structure of the vegetation, nature of the fire fuels, etc.) are related to six gradients: Elevation, topographic-moisture, time since last burn, primary succession, alpine wind exposure, and specific subdrainage. Once the gradient models are constructed, the inventory process proceeds. Topographic and fire history maps and aerial photographs are used to determine the location of each hectare of ground on the six gradients. This information is stored in a computer and, when combined with the gradient models, predicts what the characteristics of the community are within that hectare. Depending upon the data collected in the field survey, a wide range of information, from fire fuel loadings to number of trees per hectare by species, can be generated. This approach was developed specifically to produce real-time, fire-behavior models upon which managers could base fire-control decisions.

This approach is the first direct application of vegetation gradient models to management inventory and decisionmaking. The key element is the computerized data storage and retrieval system which makes it possible to handle the tens of thousands of information bits associated with a hectare-by-hectare inventory of a large wildland area. Obviously, the manager must have available (and know how to operate) a computer terminal if the system is to be fully utilized, although computer-generated maps can partially overcome this limitation. An inventory of this intensity and detail may not be needed to fulfill all management objectives. Finally, an important concern is the accuracy of the gradient models upon which the predictions of stand conditions are highly dependent. The successional gradient, which in the broadest application must relate current stand condition to time since last disturbance, is a particularly difficult problem. Factors of history (chance), availability of seed source, and intensity of disturbance can play major roles in providing for different successional patterns under similar environmental

---

[5] A habitat type is defined as the collective area which is presently or potentially occupied by the same plant association or climax community.

conditions. Nevertheless, as a flexible and comprehensive inventory system, Kessell's approach offers an alternative to the habitat-type approach.

In the Eastern United States the emphasis has been on using data on existing vegetation, combined with soils, landform, slope and aspect, to provide the basic landscape classification (e.g., Ohmann and Ream 1971a, 1971b, Ohmann et al. 1973). Reasons for using this approach in the East include the early successional nature of many of the communities (i.e., the difficulty of identifying climax types and relating seral types to them), the tendencies toward broader, more gradual ecotones between types (less discrete communities, more gradual gradients in moisture and temperature), and tradition (philosophy and sampling methods). It also appears the classification and mapping of soils in biologically meaningful ways is more possible in the East than in the rugged mountains of the West.

Experience suggests that an ecosystem classification should ultimately be based on vegetation, soils, and landform. The vegetation component should consider both the dominant and less conspicuous species because the dominants define the existing community while less conspicuous species are often more sensitive indicators of environmental conditions. The relative emphasis on each component—vegetation, soils, and landform—in developing the environmental, or habitat-type, classification will vary from area to area depending on the relative contribution each can make in a particular landscape.

In the West, the habitat-type approach, with some modification to recognize existing communities or cover types, appears well suited for stratification of wilderness tracts. The direct-gradient-analysis approach also appears to offer substantial promise, but it will require further testing in areas other than Glacier National Park. It is essential, however, that this approach be combined with adoption of a computerized data storage and retrieval system. Both habitat-type and direct-gradient approaches will benefit from stratification into relatively homogenous (climatically and geomorphically) large drainages with greater use of soils when subdividing major units. In the East, various approaches utilizing existing vegetation, soils, and landform are probably suitable; Ohmann and Ream's (1971a) community stratification is a good example.

Characterizing Wilderness Ecosystems

The inventory of the ecosystems in a wilderness is only the beginning. Each ecosystem type must, to some degree, be characterized biologically and physically. A good deal of information, but probably not enough, will have been gathered while obtaining the samples for the classification. The types of data valuable for management interpretations of the ecosystem units include the following:

1. *Floristic composition,* including measures of importance (e.g., frequency and cover of understory and density of trees by size classes) rather than simply presence and absence;

2. *Faunistic composition,* such as permanent and transient vertebrates and information on how each uses and depends upon the particular ecosystem. Numerous studies have shown the value of relating faunistic composition and utilization to major vegetation types (see Ohmann et al. 1973, Thomas et al. 1976); in this way the character and potential of animal habitation and utilization can be rapidly extrapolated over broad areas. In any case, because of large fluxes in populations, absolute data on densities are probably of a much lower order of priority than relative abundance and thorough species lists.

3. *Environmental features and controls* such as temperature, moisture, and snow regimes. These indexes of nutrient status range from very crude approximations (extrapolations from climatic situations or inferences from vegetative composition) to detailed analyses. Some characterization of the environmental regime of an ecosystem unit is essential to understanding its behavior and management potential. An example of one approach to environmental characterization is offered by Zobel et al. (1976). Physical and chemical characterizations of the soil may be included here if not separately handled as part of a soil survey (mapping unit characterization) effort.

4. *Rates of key processes* such as productivity and decomposition. The objective here is to obtain a measure of the "metabolic rate" of each ecosystem unit. Again, very crude indices may be applied because definitive data on processes such as productivity and decomposition are difficult and expensive to obtain. A site index measurement (tree height at an index age such as 100 years) is sometimes a useful index for a forest ecosystem. Clipping can be used in herbaceous communities to obtain some estimate of productivity. In any case, it is desirable to get some feeling for rates of energy fixation and nutrient cycling in major ecosystems because this information provides insights into the rapidity with which areas will recover from various disturbances. Site productivity or growth potential is a key element in recovery.

Successional Characterization of Ecosystems

Characterizing the rate and direction of change in the ecosystem units is particularly important. The objective is to be able to forecast expected changes in composition and structure of an ecosystem type over a unit of time and with alternative patterns of disturbance (e.g., none, frequent fire, heavy grazing).

A variety of techniques can be used. In forests, one of the simplest is size-class analysis of the tree species present. The general concepts are well known, for example, the tree species well represented in reproduction size classes are considered likely candidates for late successional or climax status (Daubenmire 1968). Dominants which are failing to reproduce are, on the other hand, typically considered to be pioneer or seral species. The contrasting interpretations are illustrated in table 1.

Age-class analyses can add considerably to size-class analyses in interpreting successional trends. Size and age are by no means perfectly correlated and the small incense-cedar saplings and dominant Douglas-firs in a hypothetical stand may be the same age. The increasing numbers of stand-age structure data are greatly improving our interpretations of stand development. A study of two Engelmann spruce-subalpine fir stands on southern Utah plateaus (Hanley, Schmidt, and Blake 1975) showed that both species are climax with Engelmann spruce essentially an all-aged species and subalpine fir uneven-aged species (wavelike pattern of reproduction) (fig. 10–6). Similarly Viers has demonstrated the all-aged characteristic of coast redwood on the

Table 10–1.—*Examples of size-class distributions (stand tables) and their interpretation*

A:—*Numbers of trees by size class and species in 15-by-25 m plot at Santiam Pass in central Oregon Cascade Range*[1]

| Species | < 5 | | Size class (diameter in cm) | | | | |
	< 1 m tall	> 1 m tall	5–10	10–30	30–50	50–70	70–90
Subalpine fir (dead)				4	2		
Lodgepole pine (dead)				2	1		
Pacific silver fir	3,720	15	4	9	1		
Mountain hemlock	8	2	3	19	6	1	
Western white pine				1			

[1]Two early successional species (subalpine fir and lodgepole pine) have been eliminated while the longer-lived western white pine is still present but failing to reproduce. Mountain hemlock currently dominates but is reproducing very poorly and will apparently be replaced by abundantly reproducing Pacific silver fir (from Franklin and Mitchell 1967).

B:—*Population of trees on 1 hectare near Lake Itasca, Minn.*[2]

| Species | Size class (diameter in cm) | | | | |
	0–10	10–20	20–30	30–40	> 40
Sugar maple	220	86	35	6	—
Basswood	175	81	7	11	3
Eastern hophornbeam	460	20	[3]3	—	—
American elm	47	16	55	—	—
Northern red oak	14	7	3	–3	—
White ash	100	10	3	—	—
Bur oak	17	7	—	—	—
Quaking aspen	[4]39	94	55	43	—
Paper birch	[4]53	50	7	3	—
Eastern white pine	260	—	—	3	3
Balsam poplar	—	—	7	—	—
Yellow birch	—	4	—	—	—
White spruce	3	—	—	—	—
Bigtooth aspen	2	—	—	—	—
Slippery elm	30	—	—	—	—

[2] The first seven species are interpreted as climax species or permanent occupants, the next five as seral species or disappearing relics of an earlier successional stage, and the last three as unsuccessful invaders (from Daubenmire 1968).

[3] Approximate maximum size of the species in this region.
[4] Root or stem-base suckers, no seedlings.

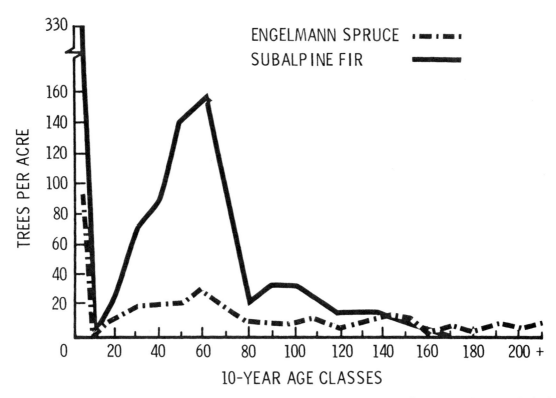

Figure 10-6.—Stand age-class distribution of Englemann Spruce and Subalpine fir in Deer Hollow study location, Utah. (From Hanley, Schmidt, and Blake 1975).

northern California coast (due to limited but regular establishment of reproduction while associated Douglas-fir typically reproduces in pulses following major stand disturbances).[6]

Historical analyses, such as reconstruction of the fire history of a wilderness from stand ages and records, can provide major insights into rates of successional change and the disturbance factors which formed and controlled the landscape mosaic (Heinselman 1973).[7] Fire-scar analysis can be a particularly useful part of such a study. Old journals, books, newspapers, photographs, and interviews with longtime residents of regions also can be useful.

Data on successional rates can be obtained by looking at a series of natural stands which are of different ages but occupy the same basic environment (as indicated by

slope, aspect, soil, landform, etc.). Rates of primary succession on new land surfaces can be obtained by looking at community development on a series of land surfaces that differ in age. This was carried out very effectively on glacial tills at Glacier Bay. Rates of soil development have also been studied using similar chronosequences of land surfaces, such as, age sequence of mudflows in northern California (Dickson and Crocker 1953a, 1953b, 1954).

Modern computer techniques are being developed which will allow simulation of successional changes over decades or even centuries and with different types and intensities of disturbance. The use of computer-based simulations will probably be limited to a very few wilderness tracts for the near future although the potential is substantial and the capabilities exist. The availability of money is the limiting factor. Forest-stand simulators predict changes in composition, biomass, and structure, due either to the dynamics of the ecosystem or to disturbances of various types (e.g., a fire of specific intensity; destruction of selected portions of the stand by an insect, disease, or wind). They are analogous to the various stand simulation and management alternative

---

[6] Viers, Stephen. 1976. Personal communication.

[7] Care must be taken in using these historical records as a basis for future fire management programs, however. Ahlgren (1976) has suggested, for example, that reintroduction of fire in Lake States' forests will rarely provide suitable conditions for reestablishment of successful red and eastern white pine stands which would be one objective of such a reintroduction. Buildup of aspen stands, presence of white pine blister rust, and lack of abundant pine seed trees are offered as reasons. Ahlgren concludes that these species, at least, cannot be restored by natural means (including fire restoration programs) to their previous positions.

models, such as RAM which currently is used on the National Forests.

Two general types of simulation models are available: The *regional landscape model* which simulates probable changes in the relative proportions of various community types over time and under alternative disturbance patterns, and the *stand simulation model* which simulates changes in environmental conditions, composition, structure, and biomass within an individual stand.

Regional models (which could apply to a wilderness) require (1) a classification scheme which separates ecosystems into important and definable categories; (2) tabular data for the area of interest which defines the initial conditions, for example, acreages by the defined ecosystem categories; and (3) data on the rate at which an ecosystem is changing from one category to another. Such models have been developed for the western Great Lakes and Georgia Piedmont regions (Burgess and O'Neil 1975). The compartment model and results of a 40-year simulation are illustrated in figure 10-7.

For simulating dynamics in wilderness ecosystems, the best stand simulator is probably one which is driven by environmental conditions on a site, such as the Hubbard Brook forest simulator (Botkin, Janak, and Wallace 1973). This model matches the environmental conditions on the site with the known environmental tolerances and optima of potentially inhabiting species to introduce (reproduce), grow, and remove (as mortality) trees in the stand. The basis for the growth prediction is an optimum growth curve for each species. Appropriate reductions from this curve are made when the light, soil, and temperature conditions experienced by each tree are less than optimum. Growth is also limited by maximal diameters and heights. Reproduction, in the Hubbard Brook model is a probabalistic (stochastic) process of introducing seedlings based on environmental (especially light) conditions within the stand. Death is conditioned by occurrence of both minimal growth and maximal species age. The long term successional patterns simulated by this model fit very well with those developed by experienced ecologists in the area in which it was applied (fig. 10-8). One particular advantage of the stand-level model is the opportunity to simulate ecosystem behavior if only a part of a stand (say a single species) is disturbed with the remainder left intact. The

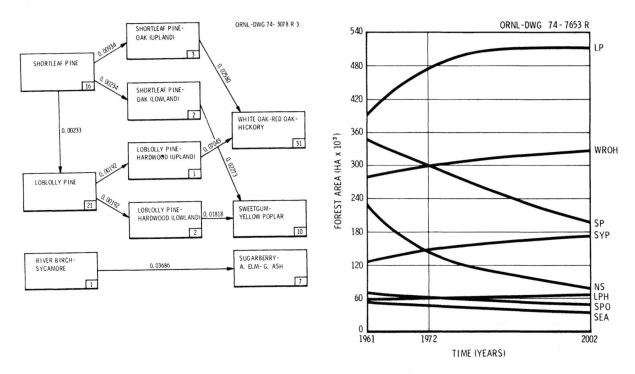

Figure 10-7.—Compartment model and simulation of change in forest type in Georgia. *Left*, annual natural succession is shown, with coefficients indicating the percentage land area in donor compartment transferred to recipient department. Number in lower right of each compartment is percent of undisturbed plots. *Right*, the change in forest type in North-Central Georgia is simulated for the period 1961–2002. Species abbreviations along right margin: LP, loblolly pine; WROH, white oak-red oak-hickory; SP, shortleaf pine; SYP, sweetgum-yellow poplar; NS, non-stocked; LPH, loblolly hardwoods; SPO, short-leaf pine-oak; SEA, sugarberry-American elm-greenash. (From Burgess and O'Neill 1975).

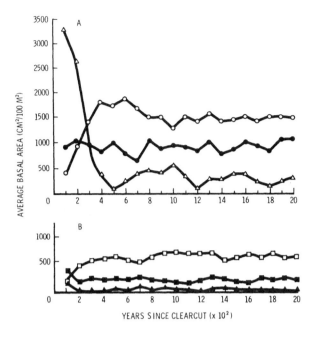

Figure 10–8.—Long-term prediction of average basal area for six species under constant climate and good, well-drained soils; (a) includes those species typical at lower elevations: ●, sugar maple; ○, beech; △, yellow birch. (b) includes those species more typical of higher elevations: ■, balsam fir; □, red spruce; ▲, white birch. Each line represents the average of 100 plots. (From Botkin, Janak, and Wallace 1973.)

effects of a loss of an individual species, such as in an insect or disease epidemic, can therefore be simulated.

These models are mentioned here because they illustrate a class of "tool" which will be available to develop wilderness management information integrating large amounts of ecological data to simulate successional trends in stands and landscapes under a variety of natural disturbances and management regimes. As tools, they are comparable to the wilderness-use simulation model described in chapter 14 for developing information on acceptable levels of visitor use under different criteria. The most challenging step in formulating either the stand or regional simulation models is development of the data on transfer rates—birth and death rates in the former and rates of change from one community to another in the latter. Data on the frequency and intensity of natural disturbances (e.g., fire or windthrow) are also challenging and difficult to develop but essential to realistic simulations of various management alternatives.

Levels of Detail for Inventorying and Monitoring

It was mentioned earlier that the level of resolution or detail appropriate in inventorying and monitoring

wilderness ecosystems will vary. The manager needs at least a crude understanding of the ecosystems over the general landscape and their characteristics. However, he needs much more detailed knowledge of initial conditions and frequent updating on changes in certain locations, particularly where human activities concentrate and/or when rapid biologic or physical changes occur, either from human or natural causes.

Subalpine meadows are the classic example of ecosystems for which detailed information might be needed, particularly in heavily used areas. Documented instances of compositional changes and rapid tree invasion of meadows are abundant. Some of these have been ascribed to natural causes such as tree invasion in the subalpine meadows of the Pacific Northwest (Franklin et al. 1971) resulting from climatic change. More often, man and domestic livestock are responsible. Lodgepole pine has invaded Sierran and Rocky Mountain meadows as a result of reduced wildfire, grazing by livestock, changes in the meadow moisture regime (due to erosion and/or trail trenching), and climatic change. Grazing, trampling, and compaction have altered meadow composition in many wildernesses.

Meadows, margins of lakes and ponds, and timberline forests are examples of fragile ecosystems particularly likely to be heavily impacted by visitors. They should receive special attention in inventory and, especially, monitoring programs. The initial state (e.g., composition) of these ecosystems needs to be known in greater detail. Greater numbers of permanent sample plots and photo points are appropriate and they should be remeasured more frequently than heavily forested and lightly used ecosystems.

An example of a pioneering effort in monitoring such sensitive areas (and of the value of such an effort) is Thornburgh's (1962) study of the Image Lake area in the Glacier Peak Wilderness. Significant deterioration of the vegetation was apparent at that time. Thornburgh provided lists of use-susceptible and use-resistant species and recommended exclusion of livestock from the area. Remeasurements of 25 permanent transects made in 1966 and 1971 have served as a basis for management programs to rehabilitate damaged sites and control types and intensity of use allowed in the lake basin. Shifts in impact areas from the vicinity of the lake shore to higher benches (use of the immediate lake shore area was restricted) were detected by continuous monitoring. Similar studies at other locations in the North Cascades National Park and research on techniques for rehabilitating damaged sites (such as seeding native plants or using plug transplants) have been a major spinoff from the Image Lake study.

Figure 10-9.—Alpine meadows and lake shorelines are particularly sensitive to impact because of easily damaged vegetation and short growing seasons which limit the restoration of damaged areas. Upper Florence Lake in the Alpine Lakes Wilderness, Wash., shows considerable evidence of human use. (Note trail on the left.)

Depending on the objectives, there are many possible techniques for monitoring ecosystems. For purposes of this discussion we are thinking mainly of monitoring biological changes, such as changes in vegetation composition and structure, on permanent plots or transects. Inferences drawn from the initial inventory on rates and directions of change are useful, but they are no substitute for observing actual changes on permanent, long term samples.

We won't attempt to outline the many possible strategies for setting up a series of permanent plots, points, and photo points for monitoring. Some principles apply, however: (1) Sample more intensively and remeasure plots more frequently in areas where changes are likely; (2) when sampling areas likely to be heavily impacted, have comparable control monitoring sites for the same ecosystems in areas which have little or no visitor use, that is, don't put all your monitoring

stations for an ecosystem type in areas which will be disturbed leaving you without a control; (3) ecotones between different types of vegetation—such as, forest and meadow—are sensitive locations for monitoring biological changes; and (4) permanently locate or reference monitoring sites on the ground; document their location and the techniques used in detail.

With the great emphasis on meadows and similar areas of special visitor attraction, the need for monitoring of changes in forest ecosystems is often overlooked. It is important that at least some monitoring be carried out in forested areas over long periods to identify actual, not inferred, trends in forest structure and composition. Representative sites for major forest ecosystem types are obvious choices for permanent plots. Careful documentation and referencing of plot location are critical because of the long time spans and difficulty of relocating plots in forested landscapes. Frequency of remeasurement will depend on objectives and likely rate of change. Seral forests of short-lived species (e.g., aspen and alder) and fire types where fire intervals are (or were) frequent obviously require more frequent attention than the conifer forests in wetter parts of the Pacific Northwest which are composed of long-lived species and have long return intervals for fire. When dealing with forest (or even shrub-dominated) ecosystems, it is extremely important to pay close attention to entries or "births" of new individuals.

A final word on the present state of monitoring, or baseline data collection, in wilderness is in order. At best, it is woefully inadequate; in most areas, it is essentially absent. What little monitoring is being done is generally not part of a systematic, comprehensive plan. Documentation is poor. Most work is focused on "sores" which are immediate management problem areas; such sites obviously have high priority but perpetuate a tendency to lose perspective on monitoring and baseline data needs over the wilderness as a whole. No other natural resource managers would ever tolerate such an inadequate inventory base in their programs. In timber management programs, for example, there are extensive systems of continuous inventory plots, comprehensive stand examinations, simulation models, and complex data storage and retrieval systems. Certainly, this type and intensity of inventory and monitoring is not advocated for wilderness. But it should make the wilderness manager aware of the total inadequacy of past efforts and the imperative for improving a data base in the future. Even provision for periodic high quality aerial photography of wilderness tracts, something sorely lacking for many areas, would be a major improvement.

Literature Cited

Ahlgren, Clifford E.
　1976. Regeneration of red and white pine following wildfire and logging in northeastern Minnesota. J. For. 74(3):135–140.
Botkin, Daniel B., James F. Janak, and James R. Wallis.
　1972. Some ecological consequences of a computer model of forest growth. J. Ecol. 60(3):849–872.
Burgess, Robert L., and Robert V. O'Neill, eds.
　1975. Eastern deciduous forest biome progress report September 1, 1973 to August 31, 1974. 252 p. Oak Ridge National Laboratory Environmental Sciences Division Publ. 751 (EDFB–IBP 75–11). Oak Ridge National Laboratory, Oak Ridge, Tenn.
Cooper, C.F.
　1960. Changes in vegetation, structure, and growth of southwestern pine forests since white settlement. Ecol. Monogr. 30(2):120–164.
Daubenmire, R.
　1968. Plant communities. 300 p. Harper and Row: Evanston and New York.
Daubenmire, R.
　1970. Steppe vegetation of Washington. Wash. Agric. Exp. Stn. Tech. Bull 62, 131 p., illus. Wash. Agric. Exp. Stn., College of Agriculture, Washington State University, Pullman.
Daubenmire, R., and Jean B. Daubenmire.
　1968. Forest vegetation of eastern Washington and northern Idaho. Wash. Agric. Exp. Stn. Tech. Bull. 60, 104 p. Wash. Agric. Exp. Stn., College of Agriculture, Washington State University, Pullman.
Dickson, B.A., and R.L. Crocker.
　1953a. A chronosequence of soils and vegetation near Mt. Shasta, California. I. Definition of the ecosystem investigated and features of the plant succession. J. Soil Sci. 4(1):123–141.
Dickson, B.A., and R.L. Crocker.
　1953b. A chronosequence of soils and vegetation near Mt. Shasta, California. II. The development of the forest floors and the carbon and nitrogen profiles of the soils. J. Soil Sci. 4(1):142–154.

Dickson, B.A., and R.L. Crocker.
　1954. A chronosequence of soils and vegetation near Mount Shasta, California. III. Some properties of the mineral soils. J. Soil Sci. 5(2)173–191.
Franklin, Jerry F., and C.T. Dyrness.
　1973. Natural vegetation of Oregon and Washington. USDA For. Serv. Gen. Tech. Rep. PNW–8, 417 p. Pac. Northwest For. and Range Exp. Stn., Portland, Oregon.
Franklin, Jerry F., and Russell G. Mitchell.
　1967. Successional status of subalpine fir in the Cascade Range. USDA For. Serv. Res. Pap. PNW–46, 16 p. Pac. Northwest For. and Range Exp. Stn., Portland, Oreg.
Franklin, Jerry F., William H. Moir, George W. Douglas, and Curt Wiberg.
　1971. Invasion of subalpine meadows by trees in the Cascade Range, Washington and Oregon. Arctic and Alpine Res. 3(3):215–224.
Frissell, Sidney S., Jr.
　1973. The importance of fire as a natural ecological factor in Itasca State Park, Minnesota. Quaternary Res. 3(3):397–407.
Habeck, James R.
　1970. Fire ecology investigations in Glacier National Park. 80 p. Department of Botany, University of Montana.
Habeck, James R., and Robert W. Mutch.
　1973. Fire-dependent forests in the northern Rocky Mountains. Quaternary Res. 3(3):408–424.
Hanley, Donald P., Wyman C. Schmidt, and George M. Blake.
　1975. Stand structure and successional status of two spruce-fir forests in southern Utah. USDA For. Serv. Res. Pap. INT–176, 16 p. Intermt. For. and Range Exp. Stn., Ogden, Utah.
Heinselman, Miron L.
　1973. Fire in the virgin forests of the Boundary Waters Canoe Area, Minnesota. Quaternary Res. 3(3):329–382.
Kessell, Stephen R.
　1977. Gradient modeling: a new approach to fire modeling and resource management. *In* Ecosystem modeling in theory and

practice: an introduction with case histories. Charles Hall and John Day, eds. Wiley, New York. (In press.)

Kessell, Stephen R.
1977. Wildland inventories and fire modeling by gradient analysis in Glacier National Park. Proc. Joint Tall Timbers Fire Ecol. Conf.—Intermt. Fire Symp., Oct. 1974, Missoula, Mont. No. 14. Tall Timbers Res. Stn., Tallahassee, Fla. (In press.)

Kilgore, Bruce M.
1973. The ecological role of fire in Sierran conifer forests. Quaternary Res. 3(3):496–513.

Leopold, A. Starker, Stanley A. Cain, and Clarence M. Cottam.
1969. Reports of the special advisory board on wildlife management for the Secretary of the Interior, 1963–1968. (No pagination). Wildlife Management Institute, Washington, D.C.

Miller, Paul L.
1973. Exidant-introduced community change in a mixed conifer forest. Am. Chem. Soc. Advances in Chem. No. 122, p. 101–117, illus. American Chemistry Society, Washington, D.C.

Odum, Eugene P.
1971. Fundamentals of ecology. 574 p. 3d Ed. W.B. Saunders Company, Philadelphia.

Ohmann, Lewis F., and R.R. Ream.
1971a. Wilderness ecology: a method of sampling and summarizing data for plant community classification. USDA For. Serv. Res. Pap. NC–49, 14 p. North Central For. Exp. Stn., St. Paul, Minn.

Ohmann, Lewis F., and R.R. Ream.
1971b. Wilderness ecology: virgin plant communities of the Boundary Waters Canoe Area. USDA For. Serv. Res. Pap. NC–63, 55 p. North Central For. Exp. Stn., St. Paul, Minn.

Ohmann, Lewis F., Charles T. Cushwa, Roger E. Lake, James R. Beer, and Robert B. Brander.
1973. Wilderness ecology: the upland plant communities, woody browse production, and small mammals of two adjacent 33-year-old wildfire areas of northeastern Minnesota. USDA For

Serv. Gen. Tech. Rep. NC–7, 30 p. North Central For. Exp. Stn., St. Paul, Minn.

Pfister, Robert D.
1975. Land capability assessment by habitat types. Proc. Soc. Am. For. Annu. Meet., Washington, D.C. p. 312–325.

Sollins, P., C.C. Grier, K. Crnock, Jr., F. Glenn, and R. Fogel.
1977. The internal nutrient cycle of an old-growth Douglas-fir stand in western Oregon. Ecol. Monogr. (In press.)

Thomas, Jack Ward, Rodney J. Miller, Hugh Black, Jon E. Rodick, and Chris Maser.
1976. Guidelines for maintaining and enhancing wildlife habitat in forest management in the Blue Mountains of Oregon and Washington. Proc. 41st North Am. Wildl. and Nat. Resour. Conf. Wildlife Management Institute, Washington, D.C. (In press.)

Thornburgh, Dale.
1962. Image Lake report. 51 p. (Unpublished Master's thesis. University of California, Berkeley.)

Trappe, James M.
1972. Regulation of soil organisms by red alder: a potential biological system for control of *Poria weirii*. In Managing young forests in the Douglas-fir region, Vol. 3, p. 35–51, Oregon State University, Corvallis.

U.S. National Committee for the International Biological Program.
1974. U.S. participation in the International Biological Program 166. p. National Academy of Sciences, Washington, D.C.

Vogl, Richard J.
1973. Ecology of knobcone pine in the Santa Anna Mountains of California. Ecol. Monogr. 43(2):125–143.

Wright, H.E., Jr.
1974. Landscape development, forest fires, and wilderness management. Science 186(4163):487–495.

Zobel, D.B., W.A. McKee, G.M. Hawk, and C.T. Dyrness.
1976. Relationships of environment to composition, structure, and diversity of forest communities of the central Western Cascades of Oregon. Ecol. Monogr. 46(2):135–156.

Wildlife are a part of all wilderness ecosystems and their distribution abundance and behavior reflect the naturalness of a wilderness.

11 Wildlife In Wilderness

"Great Wilderness has two characteristics: Remoteness and the presence of wild animals in something like pristine variety and numbers" . . .

Lois Crisler (1950) in *Arctic Wild*.

Introduction

Many wildlife species and wilderness go together. Ecologically, they are symbiotic; culturally, they are firmly linked in the minds of people. But wildlife in wilderness is a source of some of the more controversial and complex issues in wilderness management because of laws that pertain to wildlife in the National Forests, Parks, and Wildlife Refuges in which wilderness is located. Thus, any wilderness management text must

deal with wildlife as it promotes or restricts management options.[1]

Wildlife is but one aspect of the composite wilderness resource as is vegetation, water, or scenery. As pointed out in chapter 7, one basic principle is that wilderness management be comprehensive and not focused on any one aspect of the wilderness resource at the expense of other components. Thus, we do not speak of wildlife management in wilderness—but of wilderness management relating to wildlife. But, within this constraint of a comprehensive perspective, there are functional problems and issues such as those involving wildlife. A major goal of this chapter is to propose wilderness management objectives and guidelines to maintain or restore

This chapter was written by John C. Hendee and Clay Schoenfeld, Joint Professor of Wildlife Ecology and Journalism, the University of Wisconsin-Madison.

[1] For contributions to this chapter we are indebted to the many reviewers listed in the preface, and particularly to: Roger Contor, Superintendent of Rocky Mountain National Park; Laurence Jahn, Vice President of the Wildlife Management Institute; Robert McCabe, Chairman, Department of Wildlife Ecology, University of Wisconsin-Madison, and President, The Wildlife Society; Sheryl Stateler Smith, USDA Forest Service Land Use Planning Team, Sandpoint, Idaho. An expanded book version of this chapter is Schoenfeld, Clay, and John C. Hendee. 1978. Wildlife Management in Wilderness, Wildlife Management Institute by Boxwood Press. 170 p. illus.

and thus assure the natural place of wildlife in classified areas of the National Wilderness Preservation System.

We write from a perspective suggesting the reciprocal importance of wilderness and wildlife values and the need for appropriate management to protect and enhance those values. In the following, we (1) define the wilderness wildlife resource, (2) discuss important wilderness/wildlife relationships and values, (3) identify some of the wildlife-related problems in wilderness management, and (4) provide a manager's perspective on some wilderness-wildlife issues, contributed by Roger Contor of the National Park Service. Finally, (5) we propose some wilderness management objectives for wildlife, and (6) we conclude with recommended management guidelines we think are necessary to attain those objectives.

The Wilderness Wildlife Resource

From an ecological perspective a number of definitions of wilderness wildlife have been suggested. Dasmann (1966) defined wilderness species as those that are "obligate members of a climax community or wilderness area." Among his illustrations of wilderness species were the passenger pigeon, caribou, musk-ox, bighorn sheep, and grizzly bear. Hochbaum (1970) would include many species of migratory waterfowl, like swans and geese, which require wilderness wetlands for nesting purposes. Starker Leopold (1966) identified the following North American ungulates as associated primarily with climax forage types: caribou, bighorn sheep, mountain goat, musk-ox, bison, peccary, tapir, and brocket.

Aldo Leopold (1933) considered wilderness wildlife as species harmful to or harmed by economic land uses. He named seven species that met this criterion—wapiti, caribou, bison, grizzly, moose, mountain sheep, and mountain goat. Each of us might enlarge this list in his own way, adding perhaps brown and polar bear, whales, musk-ox, puma, wolf, wolverine, sea turtle, passenger pigeon, some species of seals, some warblers, condors, and eagles, for example. Durward Allen (1966) labeled the cougar, grizzly, and wolf as the true wilderness animals because they are capable, wide-ranging, and at odds with the livestock industry.

From an esthetic perspective, Michael Frome (1974) argues that any wilderness wildlife list should not be limited to large birds and mammals and that other wildlife forms such as insects and snails are also indispensable in the wilderness cycle of life. He points out that our proper concern is "all creatures great and small," not just the grizzly, wolf, sea turtle, whale, and eagle.

For purposes of this chapter we define wilderness wildlife as *those species naturally found in classified or proposed areas of the National Wilderness Preservation System*. While not wishing to slight the small creatures, our focus is on those larger mammals, birds, and fish that clearly reflect the characteristics of classified wilderness— naturalness, solitude, and relative absence of permanent human activity. While it may be true esthetically that salamanders and butterflies are as important in wilderness as mountain lions and eagles, as a practical matter the ungulates and carnivores at or near the top of their food chains serve as indicators of the health of lower trophic levels. The relative stability of a pine marten population in turn reflects the stability of the vegetative components of the particular wilderness ecosystem (Koehler et al. 1975). Hence, our greater emphasis on dominant species.

Categories of Wilderness Wildlife

Wilderness wildlife may be usefully categorized as (1) wilderness-dependent wildlife, (2) wilderness-associated wildlife, and (3) common wildlife found in wilderness. As a practical matter, we recognize the difficulty of pinpointing the status of any particular species within any single category—at least for the entire NWPS— because of overlap, regional and local variation, and exceptions that don't fit neatly into compartments. However, these three categories are useful for discussion, at least, because they suggest something about the relationship of the species to the unaltered habitat found in wilderness.

Wilderness-dependent wildlife includes species vulnerable to human influence, whose continued existence is dependent on and reflective of the relatively wild, undisturbed habitat characteristics of classified or proposed wilderness. Wolves, grizzly bear, pine marten, and wolverine are a few examples, although sometimes even these species are found in modified environments. Inspection of lists of threatened and endangered species suggests that more than a hundred species of mammals, birds, fish, reptiles, and amphibians may appear—at least seasonally—in classified or proposed areas of the NWPS. Considering any particular area, many locally or regionally rare species might be dependent on the continued naturalness of their habitat and thus be placed in the wilderness-dependent category. For example, in or near proposed wilderness areas in Idaho's Panhandle National Forests are such locally or regionally rare species as grizzly bear, mountain caribou, native cutthroat trout, Canada lynx, wolverine, mountain goat,

Richardson's blue grouse, fisher, marten, peregrine falcon, bald and golden eagles, osprey, mountain sheep, and northern white-tailed ptarmigan.[2]

Wilderness-associated wildlife includes species commonly associated (in fact and in human perception) with habitat characteristics of classified or proposed wilderness. This category includes wildlife common in the high elevation habitat of the Western United States, which is characteristic of much of the Wilderness System, and species associated with conditions characteristic of Wilderness in the East such as southern swamps and remaining roadless reserves or hardwood forests. A list of wilderness-associated species would be illustrative, not exhaustive, and would identify species linked with wilderness both by human perception and ecological reality.

For example, a list of wilderness-associated species would include hoary, Olympic, and yellow belly marmots; pika; heather moles, Clarks nutcracker, grey jay, golden eagles, and grey-crowned rosy finches; deer, bear, elk, moose, mountain sheep and goats; rainbow, cutthroat, and golden trout, greyling and whitefish. There may be regional variation in the public's perception of wilderness associated species based on relative wildness of the surrounding territory. For example, while black bear and bobcat are not strongly associated with wilderness in the West, they are more impressive indicators of wild conditions in the minds of easterners. Some other species commonly perceived as wilderness-associated might also appear in the wilderness-dependent category (such as mountain and woodland caribou, pine marten, fisher, wolves, southern bald eagle, grizzly and polar bears, Florida panther, eastern cougar, and others).

Common wildlife found in wilderness includes species that happen to be found there but which also live in many other more modified environments. Their relationship to wilderness is incidental. They are not associated in fact or in human perception with especially wild places like wilderness. Some examples are deer, coyote, bobcat, raccoon, rabbits, muskrat, mink; a host of rodents like squirrels, field mice and rats; and many species of birds including raptors, grouse, woodpeckers, sparrows, juncos, and thrushes.

Unlike the other two categories, the relationship between these common wildlife species is not specific. They are not dependent on wilderness nor do they enjoy any real or perceived association with wilderness. But when found in wilderness, they are not less important in

their natural role. In fact, these common species, since they are adaptable to more modified environments, may reveal through their natural place in the wilderness scheme, the extent to which they have adapted elsewhere.

The foregoing categories may be useful to guide inventories of wilderness wildlife and the characteristics of natural habitat on which they depend. This information is essential for management and is also useful in assessing some of the values hinging on an area's proposed classification.

First Management Steps

Managing all three categories of wilderness wildlife will of necessity be an extensive rather than an intensive operation. This is dictated not only by financial realities but by the terms of the Act calling for preservation of the areas' wilderness character—naturalness, solitude, and with man's imprint substantially unnoticeable—even when managing for such other allowed purposes as endangered species preservation.

Later in the chapter we propose broad wilderness management guidelines for wildlife. But here we can suggest some specific first steps that should be taken after any particular area is classified as wilderness. First in importance is an inventory of all the wilderness-dependent species found in the area and the characteristics of the natural habitat on which they depend. Wilderness management should assign a high priority to monitoring and preserving these *natural* conditions. In many cases a good start on this inventory task may have been accomplished during the wilderness study preceding the area's classification.

Likewise, an inventory should be taken of the wilderness-associated species and their habitat. Lowest priority should be accorded an inventory of common species found in the wilderness.

We are not blind to the financial limitations that may prevent the completion of these inventories by paid agency personnel. But we call for initiative and innovativeness by managers to solicit volunteers, cooperating educational institutions, and interested scientists and conservationists to join in the endeavor. Ultimately, the aggregation of inventories of wilderness-wildlife species, dependent or associated with the habitat of individual areas, will define more completely the role and relationship of wildlife to the National Wilderness Preservation System, and vice versa. Even more important, data for individual areas will be available for identifying wilderness wildlife management needs and priorities.

---

[2] U.S. Department of Agriculture, Forest Service. 1975. Idaho Panhandle National Forest land use plan, Part I. 108 p. [On file at Northern Regional Office, Missoula, Mont.]

Wilderness–Wildlife Relationships

As we have said, wilderness and wildlife go together. The crucial ways in which they do so provide a framework for wilderness wildlife management and suggest both management directions and constraints.

Wildlife as a Measure of Wilderness Quality

The distribution and numbers of its various wildlife species can be a measure of the naturalness of a wilderness. Wildlife reflects ecological conditions and their changes over time, so wildlife can serve as a monitor of wilderness quality—in fact and in human perception.

Culturally, for many people the concept of wilderness is frequently linked to some form of wildlife. For example, when the Muries wrote of their American elk studies in Wyoming, they called their book *Wapiti Wilderness*. Likewise, Andy Russel entitled his book on Canadian wilderness *Grizzly Country*. In William Faulkner's novel, *The Bear*, it is literally Old Ben, the bear, that represents the disappearing American wilderness, cornered in places like Mississippi's Big Bottom. The presence of particular kinds of wildlife always suggests the comparative absence of human influence and the existence of primitive harmonies. Simply knowing that such wildlife is present is important to the meaning of wilderness. "If key wildlife is removed, although everything else remains visibly the same, the intensity of the sense of wilderness is diminished" (Nash 1970).

The emerging land ethic of Aldo Leopold, early spokesman for "designated" wilderness, expanded from wildlife to wilderness, and then on to the total environment. He dates the moment of evolution quite precisely. As described in *A Sand County Almanac* (Leopold 1949), the incident occurred about 1920 during Leopold's Forest Service days in the Southwest. Shots rang out from the rimrock, and, Leopold writes:

> We reached the old wolf in time to watch a fierce green fire dying in her eyes. I realized then, and have known ever since, that there was something new to me in those eyes—something known only to her and to the mountain. I was young then, and full of trigger-itch; I thought that because fewer wolves meant more deer, that no wolves would mean hunter's paradise. But after seeing the green fire die, I sensed that neither the wolf nor the mountain agreed with such a view.

Leopold experienced the same feeling—that eliminating wildlife diminishes wilderness—after the demise of an old grizzly, the last of its kind roaming the Arizona high country. When a government hunter shot the bear for bounty, Leopold wrote a benediction:

> (Mount) Escudilla still hangs on the horizon, but when you see it you no longer think of bear. It's only a mountain now (Leopold 1949).

The extent to which wildlife is used as a wilderness criterion is striking. Asked to describe the Alaskan wilderness, John P. Milton (1972) used wildlife species as one of his parameters. It is caribou that carry "the soul of the Alaskan wilderness," says Milton. They require freedom and vast space in which to range. When they migrate "it is as if the land itself grows restless." The wolf and the wolverine also carry "the very essence" of wilderness in them, he goes on. They are the first species to vanish from wilderness under human pressure. Too, the Yukon Flats and Delta are the source for a vast circulation of migratory waterfowl throughout North and South America; destroy the living heart of these flyways "and the pulse of the wilderness will cease." In brief, Milton concludes, Alaska's wildlife is "the very web of wilderness that graces the space, the openness, the silence of the North."

The wolf, to Hochbaum (1970), perhaps more than any other species, is "a criterion of wild country." "The wild laughing tremolo of the reverberating choruses" of the common loon is, to Sigurd Olson (1963):

> the crowning symbol of lake country, the sound that more than any other typifies the rocks and waters and forest of wilderness.

Appropriately enough, the loon is distinctly intolerant of human activity. Lakes attracting boat traffic tend to lose nesting loons. Wildlife, to Buchheister (1963), is:

> the crowning symbol of wilderness: a beach without sanderlings is an empty beach; a mountain without eagles may lose none of its height above sea level, but it will be less inspiring to men who wonder about the ways of eagles.

These examples suggest the importance of wildlife as an indicator of wilderness quality in human perception. We previously pointed out the importance of wildlife, as a quality indicator from an ecological standpoint. The concept of certain wildlife serving as wilderness indicator species has been proposed as a means of assessing human impact on ecosystem reserves, a case in point being grizzly bear and mountain caribou in Glacier National Park in British Columbia (Hamer 1974). Particularly, carnivores at the top of their food chain may serve as indicators of the stability of lower trophic levels. But the environmental barometer value of wildlife is not limited to carnivores. Other species sensitive to human influence and requiring unaltered habitat also serve such a function. For example, the Big Thicket National Preserve in Texas owes much of its appeal not only to the fact that it contains a virgin cypress grove but also to the possibility that it is one of the last refuges of the ivory-billed woodpecker—not sighted for 10 years, yet still believed by some to exist in this 300,000-acre remnant ecosystem (Farney 1974).

Wildlife's Role in the Wilderness Web

Wildlife is one of the inseparable parts of the composite wilderness resource. In fact, it is biologically essential to much wilderness as we know it. Wildlife plays a vital role in the development and maintenance of the skin of soil and vegetation that covers wilderness topography:

> Wildlife directly affects the soil and vegetation mantle in key ways: Dispersal, planting, and germination of seeds; fertilization; conversion of dead plants into organic matter more usable by living plants; pollination; and modification of vegetation and soil (Talbot 1970).

Illustrative is the symbiotic relationship of the saguaro cactus and whitewinged dove. To spread pollen from one cactus to another, saguaros depend considerably on whitewings attracted by nectar. The whitewings come back to eat the resulting fruit, and then deposit the saguaro seeds beneath distant mesquite trees, which in turn provide the shade essential to young saguaros. The saguaro also has a partnership with the Gila woodpecker. The pulpy saguaro provides housing for woodpecker nests; the woodpecker in turn lives off the beetle larvae and other insects which carry diseases that could in time overcome the cactus.

The Everglades Wilderness owes many debts to the alligator; none is more important than the benefits that accrue from the alligator's relentless search for water in the dry season. Alligators seek low places where the water table lies just below the surface and work either to deepen the existing water hole or to excavate a new one, breaking the caked earth with their powerful tails and shoveling away the debris with their broad snouts. During the worst droughts, alligators have been known to dig their way down through 4 feet of compacted mud and peat before coaxing water from the porous substrate. Such gator holes, found throughout the parched Glades, attract many thirsty creatures ranging from otters to herons, and soon become biological microcosms of the

whole region. The alligators, conserving energy and living on their own fat, largely ignore the boarders; the refugees sustain life on the gator hole's remaining fish, insect life, and vegetation, and live side by side in a relative state of truce. When the rains finally return, it is from these gator-made oases that the various species go forth to repopulate the Everglades (Carr 1973).

One of the best examples of wildlife's role in a natural ecosystem has been recorded during several years of study by Durward Allen (1974), appropriately summarized recently in an article titled "Of Fire, Moose and Wolves." Here, the principal predator, the wolf, insures the survival of moose by controlling the size and vigor of the herd, thus keeping it within carrying capacity of its range.

The Wilderness Role in Wildlife Preservation

Wilderness may be crucial to the survival of some wildlife species, particularly those with highly specialized habitat needs. While many species with an affinity for wilderness conditions may in fact hammer out survival in less pristine habitats, they live most naturally in wilderness.

The Alaskan brown bear, for example, "requires all of the ingredients of the Alaskan wilderness to survive" (Troyer 1973). Another example, the northern spotted owl, is one of several species absolutely dependent on the mature Douglas-fir forest stands characteristic of some wilderness in the Pacific Northwest. Such species have evolved into specialists requiring the stability and mosaic which only old-growth forests can provide (Meslow and Wight 1975). The wild flamingo is another species that requires remote stretches of undisturbed country during the breeding season. To be sure, a civilized version lives in the Hialeah race track, but the true wild bird needs great open areas in the Caribbean in which to nest (Buchheister 1963). In the Great Smokies black bears may den 30, 40, or even 60 feet above the ground which requires overmature trees whose existence is guaranteed in very few places not given wilderness protection.[3] Pine marten survival during Western winters requires climax spruce-fir communities older than 100 years with a canopy cover greater than 30 percent. As a barometer of the health of a coniferous forest wilderness ecosystem, the marten may be unsurpassed (Koehler et al. 1975). On the other hand, of course, the presence of pine marten in a particular area does not necessarily signify wilderness. In Mount Rainier National Park, for example, the pine marten has been noted hanging

---

[3] Evison, Boyd. March 1976. Personal correspondence. [Mr. Evison is superintendent Great Smoky Mountains National Park.]

around ranger stations, raiding kitchens and garbage cans, and living in attics.[4] Likewise, grizzly bears can become habitues of campground dumps, although under natural conditions they serve as a barometer of wilderness conditions.

Wilderness can serve as essential seasonal habitat. For instance, the extensive Arctic wilderness provides summer breeding grounds for much of the continental population of whistling swans, white-fronted geese, snow geese, brandt, eiders, and scaup (Pimlott 1974). Wilderness in the West helps play seasonal host to herds of biggame animals seeking summer range in the high meadows. Such wilderness can function as a wildlife bank. For example, between 1892 and 1962 many of the elk ranges of the West were restocked with over 10,000 surplus elk live-trapped in Yellowstone, one of our greatest wilderness-type National Parks (Leopold, A.S. et al. 1969).

Even more significant, though less obvious, is the role of wilderness as a hidden trove of those recessive genes necessary for genetic adaptability in the face of environmental change. These recessive traits represent a stock of variability which can be brought into play, sometimes within a single generation. Who is to say what obscure wilderness species harbors the genes mankind will ultimately call on for his survival? A vaccine for leprosy distilled from the armadillo, quinine and cortisone derived from certain jungle plants, a type of rubber from the guayule plant, potential help for hemophilia gleaned from the blood of the manatee, the thrifty beefalo developed from bison—such contributions are already with us. Classified wilderness in particular protects habitats which have been modified but little from the conditions under which their biotic communities evolved. No ecologist can yet judge the total consequence of destroying the habitat of a single species, and hence of destroying that species. We simply do not know enough. The function of wilderness as a reservoir of genetic variability can be crucial. Wilderness wildlife is "an investment in a biological currency we cannot specify, a hedge against a biological need we cannot name" (Ghiselin 1973–1974).

For example, the extinction of the Tule Elk would result in the irreversible disappearance of a valuable gene pool. The Tule is a dwarf subspecies, reduced to some 400 animals in three areas of California, which has adapted itself to a semiarid environment with great variations in climate and topography. There may be a strong demand in the future for such an animal—as "a converter of for-

age in large areas of the world which have similar habitats" (Ciriacy-Wantrup and Phillips 1970).

Although legally classified wilderness is not always essential for the survival of the species, it may be extremely beneficial. In classified wilderness, species can at least work out their destinies under the most natural conditions available in the country.

The Wilderness Acts, by greatly limiting habitat management flexibility, may ultimately restrict conditions most beneficial to the largest number of game species. But, on the other hand, wilderness areas may offer a vegetative condition that eventually may be missing or limited on private and other public lands. In some regions, they may well offer islands of habitat that otherwise would not be available, particularly for wildlife species dependent on old-growth forests, since these are increasingly being preempted for intensive uses. In the East, particularly, designated wilderness may provide habitat to accommodate the needs of some species on at least a seasonal basis. Wild turkeys, for example, may benefit from the availability of mature woods, particularly if suitable stands are absent outside the wilderness. Deer also may benefit in winter, if adequate stands of mature trees otherwise are missing from their mobility range. Migratory or mobile species will be best equipped to take advantage of such habitat, should it satisfy their seasonal needs (Poole 1976).

In spite of the obvious benefits wilderness provides many species, it is hazardous to generalize about the wilderness role in wildlife preservation in general, since environmental conditions favorable to one species may be highly unfavorable to another. David Smith (1973) puts it in this way:

> Animal populations are ultimately controlled by the vegetation on which they most directly or indirectly feed. The larger herbivorous mammals and birds which include most game species thrive best feeding on low vegetation. Therefore, low, young forests actually have far more game than tall, old, and magnificient ones. This observation is sometimes extended to statements that old forests are biological deserts, but it might be more correct to call them game deserts. Old forests probably support as much or more animal life as young ones, but there may be a higher proportion of small birds, squirrels, insects, and other organisms that inhabit the high foliage canopy or the soil. The old forest usually has a more diverse fauna than the young, thus it is more intriguing for the birdwatcher but less so for the hunter.

[4] Partridge, Clayton, April 15, 1976. Personal correspondence. [Mr. Partridge has worked as a wilderness ranger in Mt. Ranier National Park.]

Wilderness Wildlife as an Environmental Baseline

The wilderness-wildlife web can provide a mean datum plane for collecting and assessing evidence suggestive of human influence on the planet. As indicators of comparable biological change caused by water and air pollution and measurement of environmental health, wilderness ecosystems have no substitute. Wilderness provides a standard against which the alteration of developed lands can be measured. Leopold (1949) frequently stated the case for wilderness as a model of ecological perfection: "A base-datum of normality, a picture of how healthy land maintains itself as an organism." Wild places, Leopold said, reveal "what the land was, what it is, and what it ought to be." Evolution operates there without hindrance from man, providing "standards against which to measure the effects of violence." Each biotic province, he declared, "needs its own wilderness for comparative studies of used and unused land."

Thus the wilderness-wildlife web has intrinsic value as a natural laboratory where relationships among species and habitat can be observed and studied. Several flourishing national magazines as well as TV series and specials attest to the importance of popularized wilderness-wildlife ecology as a means of widespread vicarious enjoyment and environmental education (Schoenfeld 1971; 1976). More fundamental are the scientific reports, based on the population dynamics of wilderness inhabitants, that would be impossible in the absence of designated areas serving as living wilderness-wildlife laboratories. For example, a careful survey throughout the Boundary Waters Canoe Area in Minnesota has shown that some 500,000 acres have never been significantly affected by modern civilization. Because of its large size and undisturbed character, this virgin forest is a unique laboratory for the study of large-scale ecological processes (Wright 1974). Another prime example of major ecological research that can be accomplished in a definitive way only in a large natural area is the study of the habitat and behavior of the moose and timber wolf, conducted over the past 18 years at Isle Royale by Durward Allen (Allen 1974). Mech and Pimlott on wolves, Geist on wild sheep, Hornocker and associates on mountain lions, McClelland on forest ecosystems, Koehler and associates on pine marten, Peek on moose, Herrero on bear-human interactions, the Craigheads and Cole on grizzlies, Keith on grouse, Raveling on geese—such studies are representative of basic research that requires long-time investigations in relatively undisturbed ecosystems. If we can discover how to measure the rate of activity or metabolism in free-living individuals of populations in intact wilderness ecosystems, we will have taken a giant step toward better understanding of the whole structure and function of nature (Odum 1969).

The history and stability level of a natural ecosystem can be studied only when none of the dominant components have been artificially removed or significantly disturbed in an unnatural way. Such systems have matured through ages beyond our reckoning. If we are to learn how natural communities really work and survive, we must continue ongoing research and establish many more long-range studies in undisturbed wilderness laboratories. One noted ecologist has defined and summarzied the potential contributions of wilderness and wildlife:

> . . . a biological standard of comparison for measuring those other biotic communities which are much more influenced by man, a reservoir and holding ground for genetic material, and a dynamic and complex natural laboratory for the development of modern ecological theory and knowledge (Spurr 1963).

Recreational, Economic, and Esthetic Values

As will be pointed out in chapter 13, recreational use of wilderness has increased rapidly in recent years, faster than other forms of outdoor recreation. The presence of wildlife is surely part of the wilderness lure. Many people come simply to view or photograph native species in natural settings. In season, others come to hunt or fish under primitive conditions. Millions of Americans enjoy wilderness wildlife vicariously by appreciating it through friends, stories, and photos, through television and movies; or simply by knowing that it is there. Even those who have never been within sight of real wilderness . . .

> have at least some vision of its enchantment,
> due in part to the rich profusion of books
> celebrating its beauty in picture and poetry
> . . . and to a strong instinct for maintaining
> some residual hold upon a more primitive life
> (Robinson 1975).

The number of articles on wilderness wildlife listed in the *Readers Guide to Periodical Literature* more than doubled from 27 in 1971 to 55 in 1975.

The value of incidental contact with wildlife to outdoor recreation experiences is indicated by a study in which 96 percent of all campers interviewed said that the opportunity to see wildlife in their natural setting added to their outdoor experience (Lime and Cushwa 1969). The fact that many people are not deliberately seeking contact with wildlife in wilderness makes little difference; the incidental contact—the chance observation under natural conditions—can enrich immeasurably the many satisfactions that accrue to wilderness users from their overall experience:

> Something about sighting wildlife and watching it changes the atmosphere. There is a suppressed air of excitement, a pleasant tension, and a keenness of looking forward to the morrow (Russell 1971).

For some, even *danger* can be an important positive aspect of the wilderness experience, either by direct confrontation with wildlife and the elements, or simply by knowing that the possibility exists.

Can we quantify this lure of wilderness wildlife? Should we try? The California condor is an endangered species. Only an estimated 60 birds are left. How much is the condor worth? That is a difficult question to answer because most condor conservation benefits are extra-market; that is, they aren't subject to direct dollar exchange, yet they are no less real.

As Bishop (1972) has pointed out, many people receive satisfaction each year from seeing the live condors, from viewing them in pictures and movies, and from reading about them in books, newspapers, and magazines. Many people who will never see a condor or otherwise benefit directly from its continued existence still support efforts to save it and pay something each year to express this preference through activities of the National Audubon Society. The Audubon Society has supported three research projects to study the bird and its problems. Condor affairs receive the full-time attention of one National Audubon Society employee as well as considerable amounts of time from other personnel. Concern about the birds has led to extensive research and management activities at the Federal and State levels of government.

It is impossible to say what the condor is worth today relative to other goods and services, and who can say what it will be worth in years to come. No doubt the world could survive without the bison, without the heath hen, without the condor, without the grizzly, and without you-name-it. There are direct costs in trying to preserve them—and immeasurable costs in losing them. Where do we stop?

Suppose, for instance, we want to try to save the last mountain caribou herd in the lower 48 States—about 20 animals in the Selkirk Mountains north of Priest Lake, Idaho. The forest habitat must be managed for lichen production, which means restrictions on timber harvest. Poaching and harrassment must be eliminated, particularly in winter ranges, which means closing roads and apprehending violators (Freddy 1973). At best, the future of this small, peripheral herd of mountain caribou is precarious. Is it worth the costs of trying to save it? After all, there are abundant mountain caribou in Alaska.

Political Values of Wilderness Wildlife

In our kind of society, wilderness preservation could not have come to pass in the absence of a viable political constituency. While this constituency has been composed of many groups, for 100 years sportsmen have played an important role, spurred by their recognition of wilderness as a fish and wildlife refuge (McHenry and Van Doren 1972).

It was the Northwoods Walton Club and the new outdoor magazine, *Forest and Stream*, that took the lead in the pioneer New York State campaign that culminated in setting aside the Adirondacks Forest Preserve in 1885. The major 132-million-acre expansion of U.S. National Forests came during the Presidency of a founder of the Boone and Crockett Club, that vigorous exponent of hunting, Theodore Roosevelt, who believed forest conservation and game conservation to be synonomous. It was the Boone and Crockett Club that urged the passage of the Yellowstone Park Act of 1894, designed to protect Yellowstone wildlife from poachers and establishing the precedent of the National Parks as game preserves (Reiger 1975).

Within the U.S. Forest Service the concept of inviolate wilderness tracts bloomed at a meeting in Denver in 1919 between Arthur H. Carhart, a Service landscape architect who supplemented his income writing articles and books about biggame hunting, and Aldo Leopold, a forester and ardent hunter. The remarkable array of U.S. National Wildlife Refuges has largely been identified by sportsmen groups and, where lands were purchased, paid for in part with revenues from special waterfowl hunting stamps. When a Wilderness bill was first introduced in Congress in 1956, among its charter supporters were the National Wildlife Federation and the Wildlife Management Institute (Mercure and Ross 1970).

The desire to save wildlife threatened with extinction or associated with the wilderness of particular areas has been a major impetus in the proposal for or classification of individual wildernesses. Today, if you want to block a dam, a highway, a mine, or a ski resort that threatens any part of wilderness, you will usually find hunters, fishermen, and other wildlife supporters at your side.

Take the recurring struggle on Idaho's Salmon River, for example. Leading the array of conservation groups opposed to damming and developing the river were the National Wildlife Federation, the National Rifle Association, the Wildlife Management Institute, Trout Unlimited, and every sportsmen's club in the State.

Figure 11–1.—Carried out in an appropriate style, fishing can be an important part of an overall wilderness experience. An angler tries his luck at Johnson Lake in the Anaconda-Pintlar Wilderness, Mont.

Why? Any dam on the Salmon River would wipe out one of the most important remaining spawning areas for steelhead and salmon in the entire Columbia River drainage. The proposed solution? A 2.3-million acre River of No Return Wilderness that protects deer, elk, moose, coyote, fox, and 112 bird species, as well as the anadromous fish (Trueblood 1973). Heading the River of No Return Wilderness Council, not so incidentally, was Ted Trueblood, native Idahoan and Associate Editor of *Field and Stream*.

To be sure, sportsmen are not always enthusiastic about a particular classified wilderness. They exhibit considerable concern about the ultimate levels of hunting and fishing to be allowed in National Forest wilderness. And there is concern in the heavily populated East that classification of Wilderness there may restrict wildlife management for maximum game production. These pressures demonstrate the need for a basic philosophy fitting important wildlife uses into a wilderness framework—a philosophy emphasizing wildlife uses carried out in such a way that they are consistent with wilderness values.

Wildlife-Related Problems in Wilderness Management

The necessity to manage human use and influences to preserve wilderness naturalness and solitude has been emphasized in earlier chapters. This need extends to wilderness wildlife, as the Wildlife Management Institute (1975) recently stressed:

Man and his activities can so interrupt Wilderness wildlife's natural cycles and systems that only through deliberate intervention can mankind assure the survival of key species of wildlife. America can retain and expand its rich Wilderness wildlife heritage only if it applies scientifically sound facts to

223

the management of all species and if its citizens harmonize their activities with the systems of Wilderness.

Some of the most difficult wilderness management issues involve wildlife because there is no classified or proposed wilderness that is not a part of a larger Federal agency jurisdiction with a wildlife-management mission that predates the Wilderness Acts. The situation is further complicated by the legal tradition dating back to the Magna Carta—that most fish and wildlife fall under State authority. There are differences of opinion over how far the State's legal authority extends to Federal lands, but a 1976 Supreme Court decision upheld the right of Congress to legislate control of wild horses and burros on Federal lands—Kleppe vs. State of New Mexico 1976. Wilderness may become another testing ground for determining legal authority over wildlife if controversy grows about the allowable extent of fish stocking and if pressure for expanded wilderness hunting continues. Some think Federal jurisdiction over wildlife would prevail in such a test (Robinson 1975).

Wilderness is affected by a variety of constraints that apparently conflict with the goals of naturalness and solitude set forth in the Wilderness Acts. For example, hunting and fishing are established activities in most National Forest wildernesses and in some National Wildlife Refuge Areas. Legislation succeeding the Wilderness Act requires preservation of certain threatened or endangered species in some wildernesses, implying the use of manmade devices and alterations, if necessary. Furthermore, ecological trends stimulated by previous management, such as the unnatural influence made on vegetation by the exclusion of fire, may be reflected dramatically in current wilderness wildlife populations. Geographic realities dictate that migrating wildlife populations such as deer or elk may spend only part of their yearly cycle in wilderness.

Such factors affecting wildlife in wilderness make it one of the most difficult elements of wilderness management—yet one of the most important. In this section we discuss some key wildlife-related problems in wilderness management.

Multiple Agencies and Missions

A recognition of the varying legal missions of the four wilderness management agencies is basic to an understanding of wilderness wildlife management possibilities and constraints. As outlined in previous chapters, the National Wilderness Preservation System includes classified wilderness under the jurisdiction of the Forest Service, the Fish and Wildlife Service, the National Park Service, and, as a result of 1976 legislation,

will soon contain Bureau of Land Management areas. Each wilderness administrative agency owes its existence and its missions to particular national needs expressed through various Congressional acts, many of which predate and take precedence over the Wilderness Acts. Each agency responds to different sets of pressure groups. Each has a different set of philosophical traditions, a particular management legacy, and different kinds of professional personnel. These are important influences that directly and subtly shape management policy for wilderness within each agency. Perhaps most important, wilderness and wilderness-wildlife management are subordinate to other pressing concerns in all agencies. Money is scarce for wilderness management and in even shorter supply for wilderness wildlife management.

The Forest Service, while pledged to multiple use, has important timber production responsibilities that are a central mission of the agency. Under its resource utilization legacy, the Forest Service has been accused of being "less than totally enthusiastic" about creating wilderness out of its Western roadless areas and about establishing wilderness in the East (Risser 1973). But, as noted in chapters 4, 5, and 6, the Forest Service established the first wilderness areas by administrative fiat beginning in the 1920's, and there is much more classified wilderness in the National Forests than in any other jurisdiction. However, while it continues to support wilderness preservation, the Forest Service has been "more cautious about it than most preservationists have desired" (Robinson 1975).

Wilderness management on the National Forests is also complicated by geographic and administrative dispersal. For example, a designated Forest Service Wilderness may encompass multiple planning units; ranger districts and regions in two or more National Forests. That same Wilderness may also abutt proposed wilderness, a National Park, and State and private lands. Such cases really do exist. Millions of largely inaccessible acres are involved. If it all sounds complicated, it is. The boundaries may signify different restrictions governing such variables as allowable party size, types of fires permitted, and whether dogs, firearms, or fires are even allowed. Wilderness wildlife management also reflects this imprecision created by the extensive geographic space and widespread administrative organization.

The National Park Service, dating back to the Congressional Act of 1916 which created it, has focused on preservation of native animal life as one of the specific purposes of the parks. This intention is expressed in a frequently quoted passage of the Act:

. . . which purpose is to conserve the scenery and the natural historic objects and the *wildlife* (italics ours) therein and to provide for the enjoyment of the same in such manner and by such means as will leave them unimpaired for the enjoyment of future generations.

In implementing this Act, the newly formed Park Service developed a philosophy of wildlife protection, which in that era was indeed the most obvious and immediate need in wildlife conservation. Thus, the parks became refuges, the animal populations were protected from hunting, and their habitats were protected from fire (which in some areas turned out to be detrimental to some species). For a time predators were controlled to protect the "good" animals from the "bad" ones (Leopold, A.S. et al. 1969). The net preservationist policy frequently produced gross overpopulation problems with respect to browsing species.

National Park Service policy has evolved to an emphasis on the protection of natural *processes,* with purposeful management of plant and animal communities as an essential step in preserving wildlife resources, but without bias in favor of particular species or climax vegetation. However, its legacy of providing human enjoyments—parks are for people—is a continuing influence on its wilderness management. Recently one Park Service official, Roger Contor[5], said that statement needs extending to "Parks are for people *who enjoy seeing wildlife.*" Since too many people means habitat desecration, that goal will require an easing of people pressures in many places.

The Fish and Wildlife Service manages several different types of areas: Wildlife refuges, wildlife ranges, game ranges, wildlife management areas, and waterfowl protection areas—each with particular management constraints and options. Until recently the game ranges were administered in collaboration with the Bureau of Land Management.

Nearly everyone has a slightly different view of what the National Wildlife Refuge System is, or should be. This was illustrated in the Leopold Committee report:

Most duck hunters view the (waterfowl) refuges as an essential cog in the perpetuation of their sport. Some see the associated public shooting grounds as the actual site of their sport. A few resent the concentration of birds in the refuges and propose general hunting to drive the birds out. Bird watchers and

protectionists look upon the refuges as places to enjoy the spectacle of masses of water birds, without disturbance by hunters or by private landowners; they resent any hunting at all. State fish and game departments are pleased to have the Federal budget support wildlife areas in the states but want maximum public hunting and fishing on these areas. The General Accounting Office in Washington seems to view the refuges as units of a duck factory that should produce a fixed quota of ducks per acre or a bird-days per duck stamp dollar. The Bureau of Outdoor Recreation sees the refuge system as 29 million acres of public playgrounds. The Fish and Wildlife Service recognizes the primary importance of protecting and perpetuating migratory waterfowl, as subjects of hunting and as objects of great public interest (Leopold, A. S. et al. 1969).

National Wildlife Refuges:

. . . more often than not have been developed from areas misused in the past by drainage, lumbering, burning, and overgrazing, and needing restoration to become first-class wildlife habitat. Such refurbishing is accomplished mainly with dams, dikes, and fences, and through farming programs to produce special and supplemental wildlife foods. Management may also employ irrigation systems, regulate livestock grazing to provide habitat for more successful wildlife use, soil conservation practices, forestry programs, or rough fish-control—to name a few of the practices carried out (U.S. Department of the Interior 1974).

While some Fish and Wildlife management "oldtimers" continue to resist the restrictions wilderness classification would place on their management, many other wildlife managers have come to view wilderness as complementary to a comprehensive wildlife management program.

The Bureau of Land Management administers the Public Domain which includes more land than the National Parks, Wildlife Refuges, and National Forests combined. The Federal Land Policy and Management Act of 1976 grants wilderness management authority to BLM and call for an inventory, within 15 years, of roadless areas 5,000 acres or larger and roadless islands and recommendations as to which units are suitable or unsuitable for wilderness classification. Congress will undoubtedly classify significant amounts of BLM land

---

[5] Speech by Roger Contor, Superintendent of Rocky Mountain National Park, to a National Wildlife Federation Winter Summit Group, Estes Park, Colo. Summarized in Conservation News: CN4-15-75, p. 8–11.

potentially suitable as wilderness (see chapters 5 and 6). In the interim the Agency is committed to managing such lands to preserve their wilderness character until Congress acts. BLM had already established a primitive areas system managed for wilderness purposes and has developed a planning process to guide their management (see chapter 8). These areas may ultimately become the first BLM-managed wildernesses after their review under provisions of the new Act.

The BLM is thus, by virtue of Congressional intent and the resources it administers, assured of a major wilderness management role. Reconciling wilderness-wildlife problems will be a major part of this challenge for an agency faced with its traditional emphasis on commercial livestock grazing and a popular view of public domain as a source of extractive resources such as minerals and timber. In particular, BLM wilderness managers may face difficult conflicts arising from competition for forage by domestic livestock and wilderness wildlife.

All this is not meant as criticism of the wilderness managing agencies. It is merely to help explain the different influences inherited by each Agency that will be reflected in their wilderness management emphasis and directions for wildlife. At this juncture, that there are divergent wilderness-wildlife management policies and practices may be all to the good. A practice possible to initiate only under existing Forest Service traditions may prove adaptable in National Park Wilderness, while the BLM may quietly borrow a technique from an adjacent Wildlife Refuge. Conversely, a form of wilderness management tolerated by one agency on one area may seem invidious to another and will not automatically be copied throughout the NWPS. The National Wilderness Preservation System, like any ecosystem, can profit from this diversity. Wilderness-wildlife management must make the best of the diversity inherent in multiple agency responsibilities, while at the same time continuing to search for optimum homogeneity in wilderness-wildlife management standards. Hopefully, the general orientation expressed in the following quotation can be established:

> When we designate a piece of land as wilderness we are saying in effect that this area is hands-off to human beings but business as usual for you critters who make your homes here (Hammond 1974).

Funding Constraints

Wilderness management is not adequately funded to meet its goals of preserving naturalness and solitude in the face of increasing demands for use. As a result, there has been a fiscal attitude in all wilderness agencies that wilderness management is low priority, being concerned with relatively low-density, inaccessible areas of minimal use; and that in times of scarce Federal money such management can be postponed.

Money for wilderness-wildlife management is particularly scarce. For example, by its own admission the Forest Service has less than 1 percent of its current budget directly available for wildlife management *anywhere* (McGuire 1975). The lack of money literally controls wilderness management for wildlife because fiscal realities dictate possibilities. The current hope is that funding will improve for Forest Service management activity as provisions of the Forest and Rangeland Renewable Resources Planning Act of 1974 and the National Forest Management Act of 1976 are implemented.

Contradictory Legislation

The aims of the Wilderness Act are threatened by old and new statutes passed by Congress. Laws favoring mining, endangered species, water management, national defense, economic development, timber production, energy exploitation, transportation, and general human welfare can conflict directly and indirectly with wilderness management in general and wilderness wildlife in particular.

For example, mining, legally allowed in National Forest, BLM, and some National Park and Wildlife Refuge wilderness, could have a substantial impact on wilderness wildlife. Unavoidable sedimentation in streams would affect fish, and the legally allowed means of access could harm wildlife. Such impacts can be minimized only by the most careful administering of legal mineral extraction within a wilderness management framework supported by strict environmental standards.

Sheep and cattle, allowed by the Wilderness Act to graze in some National Forest and potential BLM wilderness, consume forage otherwise available for wildlife, and this commodity use is also accompanied by pressures for predator control in the affected areas. Water impoundments exist in some wildernesses and can be established by Presidential order in others—an obvious local impact on the naturalness of fish and wildlife distributions. But wilderness designation can automatically help some wildlife species. For example, the red-cockaded woodpecker nests only in trees infected by redheart fungus disease—trees that would be removed in any forest stand improvement operation (Trefethen 1975).

The National Wildlife Refuge Act and the Wilderness Act suggest contradictory wildlife management emphasis. Under the Wilderness Acts, managerial freedom to manipulate vegetative cover to perpetuate, improve, or alter an area's value to species or associations of species is hobbled legally and even more restricted politically. On the other hand, the Endangered Species Act of 1973 (PL93-205) directs agencies to make sure no actions are taken that would "jeopardize the continued existence of such endangered species and threatened species which is determined by the Secretary . . . to be critical," no matter where they are, including in wilderness. Conforming to this law may require management techniques (e.g., vegetative manipulation, otherwise disallowed) for a certain endangered species that would otherwise not be in keeping with pristine wilderness. The Historic Preservation Act and related executive orders also lead the agencies to engage in some activities that may be viewed by some as contrary to Wilderness System intent—such as preserving or refurbishing historic structures that would otherwise be removed or allowed to deteriorate. If excessive recreation use is drawn to such attractions, this can increase wildlife harrassment in the surrounding locality.

Time and Space Factors

In the case of certain rare or endangered wildlife species particularly, time is not on the side of the wilderness manager. The forces of a technological society are moving with such velocity that the manager cannot opt to let the normal recovery processes of nature work their slow pace. Saving an endangered species may require actions otherwise incompatible with allowing natural processes full sway. For example, it is hardly a case of letting nature take its course when you rob a wildlands whooping crane nest and bequeath the eggs to a sandhill crane in order to establish a new whooping crane population with a different migrational pattern, but the experiment is being conducted to try to help save the whooper from extinction. One of the most difficult questions surrounding a species unable to compete and thus facing imminent extinction is whether this is a result of natural processes which, in wilderness, ought to continue.

The wilderness manager also has space problems. Our larger wilderness wildlife species require a lot of home range, to which wilderness boundaries may not be related. Certainly some of the "vest-pocket" wilderness areas are too small to contain the home ranges of some species. Can adjacent habitat be managed in such a case so as to develop a natural fence that will contain and protect the animal? If so, what then is the carrying capacity of the core territory? How much total area would have to be managed to provide viable range for a species—for example, grizzly or bison? What management practices would be required?

Suppose the objective is to save a remnant population of grizzlies in a proposed wilderness. According to Biologist Albert W. Erickson (1975), suppression of natural fires would have to stop, prescribed fires would have to be set, or both. Otherwise natural succession will overtake the pioneer and shrub stages the grizzlies usually prefer. Some roads in the periphery of the wilderness would need to be closed to restrict human intrusion. But here wilderness preservation and the husbandry of an endangered species can go hand in hand—if the area in question is big enough to sustain a reproducing population of grizzlies, and if fire can be introduced as a wilderness management measure.

Interdependencies

Few wildernesses are large enough to be self-regulatory ecological units; rather, most are ecological islands subject to direct or indirect modification by activities and conditions in the surrounding area (Leopold, A.S. et al. 1969). As pointed out in chapter 7, no wilderness exists in a vacuum. It is always surrounded by and/or abuts something that can markedly affect wilderness management for wildlife within the area.

One example is the elk situation in several western areas. The elk's summer range can be well within a wilderness, but in the late fall the herd typically drifts down to winter range in valleys that are outside the wilderness boundaries. Here the elk may be hunted under State regulations and/or fed artificially to the end that, whatever the net result, natural processes are short circuited.

A National Elk Refuge was created in Jackson Hole in 1913 to perpetuate an elk herd whose winter range was largely expropriated for cattle ranching. To hold elk on the Refuge, a program of hay feeding was begun which became a fixed ritual. The elk streamed down from the proposed wilderness in south Yellowstone and the Tetons and from adjacent National Forest wilderness to gather on the feeding grounds where they spent all winter without making any effort to find natural forage. The daily arrival of the hay sled signaled the only activity; namely, a jostling among the animals to be first in line as the bales were dropped. Tourists rode among them on sleighs. These elk lost their independence and fear of man—their wildness.

Fortunately, in this instance corrective action has been launched. A cooperative program is well underway among the Fish and Wildlife Service, the Park Service,

Figure 11-2.—Some animals, such as elk and deer, migrate seasonally to high wilderness meadows for summer range but may winter in nonwilderness lowlands. These elk graze on summer range in the upper Madison River drainage on the Gallatin National Forest near Yellowstone National Park, Mont.

the Forest Service, and the State of Wyoming to rehabilitate the Jackson Hole herd by breaking the hay habit. Limited hunting on the Refuge is eliminating the earliest arrivals and pushing the main herd back into the hills where good winter forage is available. The aim is to wean the herd totally from artificial foods, precluding the need for a feeding program using hay or food pellets.

Perhaps the most pervasive external influences are simply the kaleidoscopic activities of humans on the periphery of wildernesses, none of them particularly massive by themselves, yet all of them together often making a significant impact on wilderness ecosystems. Sometimes these influences are in the form of established rights and uses that predate an area's classification and are thus continued under provisions of the Wilderness Act, or else they have already resulted in impacts.

For example, although the Cabeza Prieta Game Range in Arizona is relatively free of human disturbance, a variety of impacts compromise its wilderness character, but must be retained in the current proposal for classification of a wilderness within its boundaries. Water developments, necessary for the conservation of desert bighorn sheep and Sonoran pronghorn antelope, include wells with windmills and rock tank catchments. Military operations associated with the Williams Bombing and Gunnery Range include air-to-air gunnery and missile

firing over the Game Range. The Border Patrol and the Agricultural Research Service both require road access on occasion. And previously there was a program of coyote poisoning, ostensibly to protect the native bighorn (USDI FWS n.d.). The area wouldn't seem very wild to the conquistadors who named it, but it's some of the wildest left in the Southwest. And all such compromises with external influences are necessary to honor overriding legal commitments while retaining the possibility of wilderness classification, for this area at least.

Natural processes like windstorms, wildfire, outbreaks of disease, floods, insects, droughts, avalanches, and the activities of predators are among nature's tools for creating and maintaining the mosaic of wilderness. Wilderness wildlife species are particularly responsive to the changes that follow inexorably in the wake of nearby fire, plant disease, and predator controls. The absence of fire eliminates those species that require early stages of plant succession. For example, fire prevention and control in Glacier National Park since 1910 has resulted in a decrease in elk and deer numbers as forest replaces pioneer shrub. Whitetails have declined in numbers from an estimated 2,205 in 1946 to 220 in 1957 (McClelland 1975).

Wilderness may host insects and diseases intolerable to surrounding lands, and the control of pests and disease

228

in adjacent areas can disturb the naturalness of nearby wilderness. For example, DDT spraying to inhibit spruce budworm in areas adjacent to what is now the proposed Yellowstone Wilderness produced widespread mortality among mountain whitefish, trout, and longnose suckers in the Yellowstone River (Cape 1969). The fish kills were merely the data that were measurable and worthy of notice, but they may have reflected damage to the ecosystem ultimately far more serious and widespread.

Predator control not only suppresses predator species but can lead to an eruption of their prey. Predator control on public and private lands outside wilderness can push the target animals into the preserved area as a protected haven. An obvious unnatural chain of events will follow.

People-Wildlife Conflicts

As mentioned earlier, recreational use of wilderness has increased recently faster than most other kinds of outdoor recreation. Furthermore, wilderness visitation is unevenly distributed and usually concentrated along trails at particularly popular locations (see chapter 13). Overuse in spots is an increasing problem in wilderness, even in some areas where total use is not an issue. At heavily used locations, conflicts occur between users pursuing different activities, many of which involve wildlife.

For example, solitude and tranquility, the essence of wilderness for one visitor, may be degraded by the rifle shot of another for whom wilderness quality is linked to a set of deer or elk horns. For the vicarious user who never gets there, the thought of people doing anything at all in wilderness may be objectionable and the prospect of overuse and unnatural impacts may be intolerable. Fishermen at a high lake may resent the intrusion of hikers swimming or skipping stones along the shore. Human impacts on naturalness in wildlife can be highly visible. Where wilderness camps are habitually used by people, such species as chipmunks, jays, mice, and bears may likewise become habitual scroungers of food and garbage. On the other hand the presence of people can reduce opportunities to see wildlife. Chester (1976) reports that in the Gallatin Range of Yellowstone National Park there is an inverse relationship between intensity of human use and the frequency of wildlife observation.

Whatever the form of wilderness use, it has the potential not only to mar the wilderness experience but actually to degrade wildlife habitat and affect wildlife habits. In turn, wilderness wildlife can threaten human safety as indicated by the people-grizzly conflict in U.S. and Canadian National Parks (Herrero 1970, Craigheads

1971, Craighead et al. 1974, Gilbert 1976). In Alaskan wilderness, the presence of the brown bear will deter many potential users. How to—and even whether to—make wilderness safe for both native wildlife species and human visitors is not the least of the wilderness manager's wildlife problems.

Cole (1974) reports at least partial success in management involving grizzlies and humans in Yellowstone National Park. By eliminating unnatural foods such as garbage, regulating hiking and camping, and eliminating individual rogue bears, hazards to backcountry visitors have been reduced without deterring either grizzly reproduction or all human satisfactions. It should be noted that not everyone is pleased with the results. The potentially undesirable impact of such a strategy on the grizzly population has been called into question (Craigheads and Varney 1974; Craigheads 1971). Moreover, one disappointed visitor exclaimed last year " . . . We drive 2,000 miles to this Park and we haven't seen a single bear." But, bear feeding—even though it might lure them out of the backcountry for the pleasurable viewing of people—if carried out anywhere near wilderness can totally defeat a goal of keeping wilderness wildlife wild.

Human pressure on wildlife can be subtle. In the case of the mountain sheep, for example, Geist (1975) reports that because knowledge of home range is passed on from generation to generation through the dominant rams and, if a sheep population is forced out of its range and, especially, if the big rams are lost, the knowledge of the home range will be lost and the sheep population will be adversely affected. Even if people merely startle a wild animal repeatedly, such disturbance increases the cost of living to the animal by causing it to expend additional energy, which it then must replace by consuming more. In a rigorous northern environment, where neither the animals nor the range can afford the extra toll, the effects may be very harmful indeed (Geist 1971a, 1971b). For example, in the Sangre de Cristo Range in Colorado, human pressures have forced mountain bighorns into lambing ranges at higher elevations, where extended bad weather can lead to an 80 percent incidence of pneumonia in lambs and a steady decline in the population of the herd (Woodward, Gutierrez, and Rutherford 1974). Likewise, human disturbance is suspected as a limiting factor for bighorns in the Sierra Nevadas (Dunaway 1976).

Hunting

Hunting and fishing are more than a quest for game and provide sportsmen with a variety of satisfactions (Hendee 1974). For hunting and fishing in the wilderness, many of these satisfactions may be strongly tied to an overall wilderness experience. Evoking memories of his days as a wilderness wanderer, it was perhaps inevitable that Andy Russell (1971) would link rod, gun, and wildlands:

> It was wild, free country laced together by crystal streams between the low, folded ridges buttressing the feet of the mountains—all basking under summer skies and glittering coldly in the bitter winds of winter; it was a frontier—a land of boots and saddles, guns and fishing rods, the smell of pines and grass, and the clean, warm feel of the sun in everything.

In terms of hunting today, the National Wilderness Preservation System offers diversity. No hunting is allowed at all in any National Park Wilderness or in some National Wildlife Refuge wilderness. (Of course in many cases the same migratory wildlife that use such wilderness part of the year are hunted when they move outside the protected area.) Hunting is allowed, however, in National Forest and BLM wilderness and in some National Wildlife Refuge wilderness—a controversial practice to some people who fear its impact on naturalness, but certainly not to the States who were guaranteed the continuation of hunting on such lands under terms of the Wilderness Act, and not to the many sportsmen and their organizations who supported the Act because of this very provision.

One might argue whether sport hunting by humans is consistent with the wilderness concept in general, or even with the "naturalness" required by the Wilderness Act. However, for wilderness managers where hunting is allowed, such conjecture may be moot. On a positive note, wilderness hunting is a traditional activity and may offer one of the most ecologically pure experiences. Here man, away from roads or comfort-and-convenience facilities, can experience himself as man the predator under the most natural conditions. A large contingent of hunters and game managers feel that the finest quality hunting experiences are to be found in the opportunity to track and stalk game in wilderness without artificial diversions such as roads, clearcuts, or cultivated crops, and to blend with the wildest setting possible on a quiet vigil during the hunt. For them, hunting is a wilderness-dependent activity. In fact, the popularity of some early fall, highcountry deer seasons, such as in Washington State, results in undue pressures in some wilderness locations for brief periods. For example, Buck Creek Pass in the Glacier Peak Wilderness is no place to find solitude the first weekend in September when the early high hunt begins. Nor are locations in several western wildernesses

near temporary yet lavish camps set up by outfitters to cater to hunters with preferences for something more than true wilderness living conditions.

At its best, however, in wilderness where it is legal, hunting can offer a popular and healthy outdoor activity under quality conditions, *if* it is carried out under regulations that protect wilderness from overuse and insure wilderness-dependent experiences. In the final analysis wilderness hunting controls game populations and can help keep game species from destroying habitat for themselves and other species in the absence of natural controls—healthy habitat being the key to healthy wildlife. Unquestionably, hunting pressure can cause significant population declines—the caribou in North America, for example (Bergerud 1974). On the other hand, in the Cache National Forest elk herd in northern Utah, a heavy increase in hunting in 1968–71 did not result in a population decline evidenced in 1958–66 at lower hunting pressure. Obviously, factors other than hunting are at work to produce population fluctuations in this herd (Kimball and Wolfe 1974).

An attitude of many people, which seems to grow with urbanization, is an outspoken antipathy to hunting—anywhere (Applegate 1973; Hendee and Potter 1976). This attitude regards nearly any killing of wild creatures as destructive and inhumane (although there has been little objection to fishing on the same basis). On the other hand, the Allen Committee Report emphasized that biological facts have to be considered:

> In productive populations of 'resident' wildlife there are compensatory relationships between man-caused and natural mortality—one is not added to the other. Thus, a game crop can be taken under properly adjusted regulations, year after year, without diminishing the population. Among migrant species, less is known of mortality relationships, and the job of regulation is more complex. While errors may occur, means of avoiding them steadily improve. Agencies administering hunting and fishing are committed to protecting the resource. All will agree that the taking of wildlife should employ the least wasteful and most humane methods available. Traditionally, hunting as a total experience involves environmental satisfactions: room to roam, quiet, solitude. Hunting at its best can cultivate an increasing outdoor sophistication in the individual. He improves his knowledge and enjoyment of nature in all its aspects. He refines his sporting standards, including recognition that quality is poorly

measured by the size of the bag (Allen et al. 1973).

Any buildup of shooters poses a particular threat to large and conspicuous birds. Wanton gunnery needs more serious attention by lawmakers, enforcement staffs, and the judiciary. And hunting has a crucial biogenetic aspect. Attempts to preserve or restore large units of primitive ecosystems frequently must presuppose that important endemic components will be missing and that numerous exotics, both plant and animal, will be present. The vertebrates most commonly absent and difficult, if not impossible, to provide for are the large carnivores—cougar, grizzly, and wolf (Allen 1966). We say, of course, that human hunters can substitute for these natural predators. But do they? The wolf, for example, tends to cull calves and superannuated females. Hunters try to select prime males. What this means is not clear, but it is an important long-range question to those concerned with true naturalness in wilderness. The genetic integrity of game species may be in jeopardy where they exist under primary control by the gun and without biologically adequate attention from natural enemies. Yet, without some form of cropping, ungulates particularly, can eat themselves out of house and home.

Is man, acting as a predator himself, applying a strong selective force to hunted species that may be bringing genetic changes in the survivors? (Leopold 1966.) If so, to what end? Does the bighorn hunter harvest only the slow-witted or does he take the sentinel ram who is the custodian of the herd's traditions? We could be playing Russian roulette and not know it. Certainly, heavy hunting unquestionably affects animal patterns and makes it less easy to study natural behavior. James Peek reports good evidence that hunting has influenced elk movement patterns in wilderness situations.[6] Geist has observed that prolonged and extensive ungulate hunting will indeed alter the biology of the species affected (Geist 1971). A 4-year study in the Big Creek region of Idaho showed that cougars harvested much higher percentages of the elk and deer in poor condition than did human hunters. The old and the young, not the prime specimens, were selected in the natural predation (Weddle 1970).

We can make two major mistakes with respect to this whole issue. First, we could assume that all species react similarly to hunting in all places, and we would probably be wrong. While hunting pressure may in fact be deleterious to the survival of bighorn sheep, for example, it may well be producing strains of mallards and Canada geese better able to adjust to unnatural environments.

Second, we could assume that wildlife management lessons learned in man-modified environments are directly applicable to wilderness, and we would again probably be wrong. Wilderness is unique as a relatively unaltered environment, and the potential irreversibility of our management mistakes, no matter how well intentioned, is scarey. Except for a geographic fluke, for instance, wildlife managers would have wiped out the wood bison (Cowan 1966).

Fishing

Fishing in wilderness streams, particularly in high wilderness lakes, is likewise a source of concern and potential controversy. Wilderness fisheries are an important issue for managers because most recreational use of roadless areas centers on lakes and streams, particularly high lakes (Brown and Shomaker 1974). At lakes in some heavily used areas, such as the Alpine Lakes Wilderness in Washington, the physical impact of human use at high lakes has become obvious and managers have proposed manipulating the high lake fisheries to decrease human use and impact. However, studies of use at seven lakes in that region (Hendee et al. 1974) indicate that only about 40 percent of the visitors to the lakes actually fished, only 40 percent of the parties contained fishermen, anglers fished an average of less then 2 hours per day, and 40 percent of them caught no fish. An equally important finding: non-fishermen spent just as much time at the lakeshore as anglers. Other studies (Kennedy and Brown 1974; Hoagland 1973; Carpenter and Bowhis 1976) and baseline data presented in chapter 13 confirm that, on the average, only about half the visitors to wilderness high lakes actually fish. Obviously, any policy designed to relocate western wilderness visitors by manipulating the fishery—that is, attracting or repelling visitors by regulating the availability or opportunity to catch fish—can affect only part of the use. At some locations, of course, redistributing even part of the use may go a long way toward solving an over-use problem. In a unique wilderness such as the Boundary Waters Canoe Area where fishing is a central attraction, fishing regulations could substantially help to lessen the impact stemming from the large motorboats and much paraphernalia that are traditional in the portions of the BWCA open to motorized boating (Lucas 1965).[7]

---

[6] Peek, James. March 1976. Personal correspondence. [Dr. Peek is associate professor of wildlife management at the University of Idaho.]

[7] Merriam, Lawrence C. March 22, 1976. Personal correspondence. [Dr. Merriam is Professor of Forestry at the University of Minnesota.]

Clearly, fishing on wilderness waters is an important activity for many visitors. But fish management in wilderness is controversial, particularly when it involves nonindigenous species such as eastern brook trout, which have been widely introduced to western high lakes where fisheries are maintained through periodic aerial stocking.

Artificial stocking of wilderness high lakes distorts the naturalness of the affected aquatic ecosystem, and the use of aircraft for stocking can invade the solitude of affected users. But aerial stocking is strongly supported by many sportsman groups and by the American Fisheries Society (1975) which declared its position in a recent resolution:

> Whereas, the U.S. Forest Service has interpreted the Wilderness Act, 1964, to mean that aerial fish stocking of wilderness area lakes, which were not stocked prior to 1964, is an activity prohibited by the Act; . . . now, therefore, be it resolved, that the American Fisheries Society urges the U.S. Forest Service to modify its existing interpretation of the Act and to permit the use of aircraft as a means for fish stocking of lakes in national Wilderness areas.

The National Park Service is under similar pressure (Wallis 1976). At its 1976 annual meeting in Louisville, Ky., the National Wildlife Federation deplored the curtailing of artificial stocking of indigenous species and called on the National Park Service to cooperate fully with State fisheries agencies "to restore fishing opportunities for the benefit of the public."[8]

Research Needs

What we don't know about wilderness wildlife would, as the saying goes, fill a book. In all too many cases the wilderness wildlife manager must fly by the seat of his pants. Fish and wildlife research in general is underfunded, particularly those deep-digging basic studies that must undergird all applied research. Nongame species are distinctly underrepresented in the literature of fish and wildlife ecology. Comprehensive basic research is needed to examine all the plant-animal relationships in total natural ecosystems. Likewise, studies that will test alternative management practices in keeping with Wilderness Act constraints.

And since wilderness wildlife management is in large part people management, we need more behavioral research to support the effort. Users and use trends, nonconsumptive values, access opportunities, wildlife economics, political-legal issues, information-education,

fishing trends—these human dimensions of fish and wildlife programs suffer from a lack of rigorous study and basic data (Hendee and Schoenfeld 1973).

A Case Study in Wilderness Wildlife Management Approaches

In the real world, wilderness managers are forced to deal with some of the problems and issues that have been discussed. Some of their efforts are noteworthy. Following is a discussion of wilderness wildlife management directions for some wilderness-related species in western National Parks, by Roger Contor, at the time Superintendent of Rocky Mountain National Park and formerly Deputy Regional Director of the Midwest Region of the Park Service in Omaha. Before that, he was Superintendent of North Cascades National Park. Mr. Contor's statement expresses a management perspective on selected wilderness-wildlife problems consistent with his training and experience as a front-line National Park administrator, but not necessarily expressing National Park Service policy. Implicit in Mr. Contor's comments is a view that the problems of wildlife in wilderness are interdependent with the larger setting in which the wilderness occurs.

> The age-old bear problem in the West is, of course, not the wild bear but the bear that has lost his fear of humans through repeated encounters with them, or through being introduced to human food left deliberately or unintentionally by humans. The problem bear does not get that way overnight. It sometimes takes 2 or 3 years for a bear to change from an alert, timid animal which is almost never seen by a human to one aggressive enough to rip open camping gear or physically approach a human for a handout. In many instances an alert manager can prevent this progressive education of bears by taking action to (1) eliminate disposal of garbage where bears can find it; (2) encourage campers to hang their camping gear suspended to trees by ropes so that bears cannot reach it while they are away; (3) physically reverse the familiarization trend by the use of chemical repellants or electric fences around areas of attraction; (4) tranquilize or trap the animals and relocate them in distant areas as soon as they lose their fear of humans; and (5) occasionally destroy an animal whose behavior is irreversible and

[8] Resolution adopted by the affiliated representatives of the National Wildlife Federation at their 40th Annual meeting March 1976, Louisville, Ky.

who has not only become a dangerous nuisance but may be influencing other bears to become hazards.

As a barometer of naturalness, the bear is unexcelled. It is almost abnormal to see a bear in the wild. Any time bears have become familiar enough to permit themselves to be seen frequently, the naturalness of the area has deteriorated. It is a thrill to most people merely to see a bear track in the moist soil of the trail, or to see other evidence of his presence. The rare experience of surprising a truly wild bear is a thrill which the wilderness traveler can anticipate but may seldom realize.

The rate of physical encounters with grizzly bears in some of our northern National Parks is growing much faster than human use of the backcountry. The more such bear-human encounters take place, the more rapidly the bear loses its fear of man. The potential for that bear to actually attack a human is greatly increased. The dilemma to managers of parks having grizzly populations is one which challenges the basic preservation and use concept of National Park management.

All indications point to strong public support for the preservation of grizzlies in the United States. *In grizzly territory then, it is the public rather than the bears which must yield if we want to keep the grizzly.* The most logical way to eliminate the increasing frequencies of bear-human encounters is to greatly restrict human use in known grizzly habitat. Fortunately, grizzly bears tend to occupy their home ranges under fairly consistent patterns, and it is not too difficult to determine the areas from which human use must be restricted. Relatively large parties, guided by persons familiar with the bears' habits and locations, can permit people to observe the bears under safe conditions without actually producing encounters. Terrain and vegetative cover will confound this goal in areas such as Glacier National Park. However, in the open rolling area of Yellowstone National Park it will be much easier.

Another problem: Managers of National Parks having significant elk populations are universally faced with the problem of maintaining natural ecosystems with a major element of that ecosystem missing—an effective predatory influence.

As mentioned previously, grizzly bears are not truly effective predators on an elk population even though they do take a number of old, dying animals and a few of the newborn calves. Only in the Madison River drainage of Yellowstone does the grizzly approach the role of an effective predator, and in this case he may be a predator on what is basically an unnatural population. Elk probably did not confine themselves to the deep snow country of the west side of Yellowstone prior to being forced into this area by the activities of modern man.

But the elk is one of the superlatives of native American wildlife and provides strong satisfaction to those who are able to observe it under wilderness conditions. To optimize the use of wilderness by both elk and humans, careful controls must be enforced to provide living space for elk populations. They need undisturbed areas to breed, rest, feed, bear their young. A designated-site type of overnight wilderness use has proven effective in Rocky Mountain National Park to minimize the stress of increasing human use in wilderness. Elk populations apparently can tolerate human activity within their general summer range areas if the human activities remain consistent. Elk are not disturbed by distant views of humans camped around a certain lake or meadow consistently each night of the summer. It is when the humans deviate from their normal travel pattern and wander into the elk living space that the elk are disrupted.

It is incumbent that managers of National Park wilderness units continue to explore possible ways of reintroducing wolves into elk habitat to reestablish a proper predator-prey relationship. The barriers to such reintroductions are manifold, but it is hoped they will not always prevail. In the meantime, managers of National Park wilderness are faced with three alternatives for proper elk management: (1) Control population growth by maintaining National Park boundaries that include only summer elk range and by public hunting. (2) Utilize "natural regulation" permitting vegetation conditions on elk winter range inside National Parks to control productivity and allow the population to exist "in balance" with carrying capacity of the environment. This approach is now being tested in a number of areas. There must be a complete ecosystem or it may have undesirable effects upon other species which are diminished in numbers and vigor with the productivity of the elk herd. (3) Periodically conduct live-trapping programs on the fall-winter range area to reduce the excess populations; however, areas where elk surplus are welcome as transplants are becoming fewer in number and ultimately this may not be a viable alternative.

In addition to channelling human use in wilderness areas so that elk populations are disturbed as little as possible, other management measures are occasionally needed to prevent undesirable disturbance of elk. In high visitor-use, "wilderness threshhold" sections of National Parks, it may become increasingly necessary to protect certain elk viewing areas from off-road travel by humans during the breeding and calving periods. The tendency of some photographers to pursue elk relentlessly has caused many herds to abandon meadow areas near roads and parking areas. Only by providing protection from such stress can managers encourage the return of the elk to suitable habitats and locations where they can be seen and enjoyed by the visiting public.

Fortunately, the public has shown a great willingness to honor such restrictions when adequate explanation for the purpose of the action is given. It appears that the public is more willing to yield their right to wildlife benefits than most managers realize.

Along with mountain goats, bighorn sheep possess the distinction of being the most predictable of large wildlife. Once a person learns their resting, bedding, feeding, and traveling areas, it becomes very easy to find these animals on a day-to-day basis even though their population may be low in a given area. This is both a blessing to persons wishing to locate the animals for purposes of observation and photography, and a torment to the animals which may thus have little privacy in their lives.

Nationwide, bighorn populations have been greatly reduced. Any additional stress placed upon them by unwarranted human disturbance is unfortunate. Whether bighorns can evolve resistance to the many diseases and parasites which were brought into North America by Old World domestic sheep remains a critical question. Whether because of their rarity or other qualities, bighorn appear to rank second only to grizzly bears in the preference scale of serious wildlife observers. Fortunately, it is quite possible for park managers to provide opportunities to watch bighorn from an undisturbing distance. In many cases, the sheep can be observed from the road or from an adjacent mountain ridge, or from carefully guided parties. It is the uncontrolled photographer working at close quarters who causes the great stress in the bighorn populations and causes them to abandon essential habitat areas.

Bighorn overpopulation does not appear to be a problem now nor is it expected to be for many decades in the future. Most populations are lucky to hold their own. Any surplus in a thrifty bighorn population should be utilized as a source for reintroduction of individuals into former bighorn habitat. High density populations appear to be particularly susceptible to disease. Bighorns are also highly subject to space and food competition from elk and other herbivorous wildlife—and in some cases from domestic animals which graze the same range. In recent years, land managers have become increasingly aware of this critical need and significant steps have been taken to improve conditions for wild sheep, particularly in or adjacent to the Inyo National Forest in California.

Several State wildlife departments have made strides in increasing distribution of bighorns through live trapping and reintroduction programs. These programs, plus medicinal treatment to combat the effect of lungworm and other parasites and diseases, have recently demonstrated that it is possible for man to help a bighorn population survive. National Park managers should be alert for any possibilities of cooperative efforts with State agencies in this endeavor.

In contrast to bighorn sheep, the mountain goat is a relatively healthy, thriving, problem-free animal which provides great observation potential for park visitors. Because it generally does not require separate summer and winter ranges it is being introduced by various State wildlife departments to mountains previously not occupied by goats. This poses an immediate confrontation with any National Park in the vicinity, it being Park Service policy to resist the invasion of exotic species into a National Park area. National Park wilderness managers may find themselves faced with the task of live-trapping mountain goats for removal. Mountain goats may also provide additional stress on native bighorn populations through competition for space and food—especially where bighorn winter at high elevations. National Parks facing the possible invasion of mountain goats at the moment are Yellowstone and Rocky Mountain. Some National Forests share the same problem.

Wilderness Management Objectives for Fish and Wildlife

So far in this chapter we have (1) Defined wilderness wildlife; (2) identified and advocated the importance of wildlife values and relationships to the National Wilderness Preservation System; (3) discussed some related management problems; and (4) illustrated these topics with a manager's views on wilderness-wildlife management for some major species common to National Park wilderness in the Rocky Mountains.

In this concluding section our purpose is to (5) recommend objectives for wildlife in the National Wilderness Preservation System, and (6) suggest guidelines for the wilderness-wildlife management we see as necessary to meet those objectives. A basic theme of this book is that wilderness management must be goal-oriented and that clear management objectives for all aspects of wilderness—including fish and wildlife—must be spelled out in area plans to guide all management actions (see chapter 8).

Although details of wilderness management for wildlife will vary according to location and agency, we think the following broad objectives are applicable to the entire wilderness system regardless of agency jurisdiction. These objectives are statements of conditions sought with respect to wildlife in wilderness; they serve

as criteria for choosing and evaluating management policies and actions. They are targets reflecting the synthesis of legal requirements of the Wilderness Act and a wilderness-wildlife management philosophy.

PROPOSED WILDERNESS MANAGEMENT
OBJECTIVES FOR FISH AND WILDLIFE

To seek natural distribution, numbers, and interactions of indigenous species of wildlife.

To allow natural processes, as far as possible, to control wilderness ecosystems and their wildlife.

To keep wildlife wild, their behavior altered as little as possible by human influence.

To permit viewing, hunting, and fishing where such activities are (1) biologically sound, (2) legal, and (3) carried out in the spirit of a wilderness experience.

To favor the preservation of rare, threatened, and endangered species dependent on wilderness conditions whenever appropriate.

To seek the least possible degradation of the qualities that make for wilderness—naturalness, solitude, and absence of permanent visible evidence of human activity—within the constraints of all overriding legislation applicable to wildlife in a particular wilderness.

Wilderness Wildlife Management Guidelines

To achieve these proposed objectives, we recommend a number of management directions, guidelines, and policies. In some cases the proposed direction applies to wildlife the wilderness management principles set forth in chapter 7. In other cases, it extends to wilderness many of the principles recommended in the Leopold Committee Report on wildlife management to the Secretary of Interior (Leopold, et al. 1969), and the Allen Committee Report on North American Wildlife Policy (Allen et al. 1973).

The following guidelines suggest management direction, but they shouldn't displace the overriding theme that a wilderness philosophy or ethic, based on an appreciation of all affected values, is an acid test for all proposed wilderness-wildlife management actions. A basic wilderness management framework is that only *necessary actions* to achieve established wilderness objectives are justified and they must employ the *minimum methods* and techniques required (Church 1977).

1. *Respect overriding legislation.* A fundamental requirement of wilderness management for wildlife is to recognize the different legal requirements that may

apply in classified wilderness under the jurisdiction of different agencies. The Wilderness Act states in Section 4(a)

> The purposes of this Act are hereby declared to be within and supplemental to the purposes for which national forests and units of the national park and national wildlife refuge systems are established and administered . . .

Section 4(b):

> Except as otherwise provided in this Act, each agency administering any area designated as wilderness shall be responsible for preserving the wilderness character of the area *and shall so administer such area for such other purposes for which it may have been established as also to preserve its wilderness character.* (emphasis ours)

The only direct reference to wildlife in the Act states that

> Nothing in this Act shall be construed as affecting the jurisdiction or responsibilities of the several states with respect to wildlife and fish in the national forests.

The most obvious example of overriding legal requirements are those that permit hunting in National Forest, BLM, and some National Wildlife Refuge wildernesses. However, because of overriding legislation prohibiting hunting in the National Parks, it is *not* allowed as a general rule in National Park wildernesses. In certain situations, hunting has been temporarily allowed in particular National Parks to control excessive populations which were threatening their own habitat and that of other animals.

Within some units of the National Wildlife Refuge System, both classified and proposed as Wilderness, superseding legal rights also override specific wilderness purposes. Because these refuges were specifically established to preserve habitat for particular wildlife species, management activities usually disallowed in wilderness may be necessary to protect some species and habitat. In the Cabeza Prieta Wildlife Refuge in southern Arizona, specific and prior rights granted for other purposes (such as the Border Patrol and Williams Gunnery Range) must be honored for wilderness classification to be considered. Similarly, fish stocking in National Forest wilderness lakes has been carried out by State wildlife agencies pursuing their legal right to manage the fishery resource.

Overriding legal requirements impinge on wildlife more than on any other aspect of wilderness. These legal requirements must be respected and this will require some compromises in naturalness. Wilderness manage-

ment for wildlife must be tailored to the unavoidable constraints placed by laws on the administrative Agency concerned, while embracing the broad principles of the Wilderness Act. It is extremely important that a statesmanlike communication prevail among the wilderness managing agencies, State fish and wildlife agencies, and wildlife conservation groups, so that everybody concerned can at least acknowledge where they disagree on wilderness-wildlife management issues, interpretations of the law, and advisable policy. This is a major, current challenge, particularly critical as it relates to different purposes, philosophies, and perspectives of State Fish and Game departments as compared to those of the Federal Wilderness management Agencies.

2. Allow natural processes to shape wilderness habitat. A fundamental concept is that classified wilderness is a place where nature rolls the dice, and resulting naturalness, whatever its characteristics, is wilderness. Artificial habitat manipulations that are desirable for fish and wildlife management on nonwilderness lands and waters are not consistent with either the Wilderness Act or the wilderness ethic that should guide its implementation. When there are legal exceptions to the natural process criterion, the most *natural practices* and tools should be used in a manner exerting the *minimum impact* on wilderness naturalness and solitude.

Wilderness means *natural*. Where there is vegetation, it should reflect natural conditions. The distribution, abundance, and diversity of plant cover should be substantially unaltered by man and his influence. Lakes and streams should reflect undisturbed watersheds and channels. Animal life should approach natural numbers and species. Where harvest is permitted, it should be well within biological limits. Wilderness managers are guardians, not gardeners, and their task is to *assure the conditions that permit natural processes to operate freely.* Where it is clear that these processes for one reason or another have been compromised, the manager may have to mimic or simulate natural processes, but only as briefly and naturally as possible. For example, to eliminate exotic species or introduce fire where it has been unnaturally suppressed. The often-expressed concept that wilderness should be a "vignette of primitive America" should not suggest a static picture of a pre-European settlement landscape, maintained in suspended animation by whatever techniques are needed. Wilderness, rather, should be the place where a vignette of natural but dynamic forces characteristic of early America operate as freely as possible. Ecological change will be inevitable and constant, its velocity dependent on the ecosystem involved. Necessarily, there will be times in its succession when a wilderness will not be a particularly good habitat for some wildlife species nor particularly appealing to visitors.

One National Park manager described a naturalness strategy to us as follows:[9]

> The National Park Service is now in the business of 'preserving' natural *processes* (in Parks as well as in their wilderness). We should intervene only to the extent necessary to counteract the unavoidable effects of past mistakes, the impacts of currently accepted human use, beyond those that primitive man might have exerted, and the impacts of influences originating outside the parks. Most of our management must be of people, and of their effects on park ecosystems.

The committee on North American Wildlife Policy (Allen et al. 1973) pointed out that by encouraging natural processes,

> It will often be possible even to restore a 'damaged' wilderness to a high standard. Native animals that have disappeared may be reintroduced. The effects of minor grazing or forest cutting will be erased, over time, by plant succession. Fire and other natural disturbances can initiate new cycles of plant and animal life, as they did before the coming of modern man. The capacity of life communities to regenerate enlarges the possibilities for 'natural' wilderness.

Consider the example of the Boundary Waters Canoe Area. In 1948 about 14 percent of this area was privately owned, and about 45 resorts plus some 100 individual cabins were located in what was to be designated in 1964 as wilderness (Lucas 1972). Only a few private properties now remain and the canoeist paddling Basswood Lake today cannot now discern the shores where the Peterson Lodge entertained 50 guests at a time in 1955. But the loons know things have changed; they have returned to Hoist Bay. So, to some extent at least, you *can* turn back the clock!

However, it will not always be so easy to restore wildlife species to wilderness. Habitat regeneration is very slow in alpine or desert regions and buildup of depleted populations can take many years. Studies indicate, for example, that the social structure of cougars is such that pioneering into new habitat is slow if minimum populations are not present nearby (Seidensticker et al. 1973). Likewise, for hereditary reasons, the North American mountain sheep appear incapable of

dispersing into new or restored habitat (Geist 1971). Although he hasn't actually tried it, Geist believes mountain sheep could be encouraged to use salt licks that are progressively moved into new territory, thereby establishing migratory routes which would be followed by succeeding generations (Geist 1971).

The natural processes criterion certainly precludes artificial control of predatory animals, insects, or plant diseases—unless they threaten resources outside the wilderness. Where and when insect or disease blights strike, they should simply run their course as a contribution to a constantly changing natural ecosystem. Where predators are present, they are permitted to follow their natural instincts. Where the predators are present in insufficient numbers, however, prey populations may erupt to where they threaten unnaturally the continued existence of a natural environment. In such a case, predatory species must be imported, their prey cropped, or both. We must recognize, however, that not only are predators difficult to reestablish, but loss of the predator influence is only one disruption of game ecosystems; disruption of natural migratory patterns and population distributions may be more disturbing to the system (Craighead et al. 1973).

It isn't always easy to decide what is natural. Consider a hypothetical wilderness in Maine, noted for its moose. It is likely that logging long ago helped to create the lingering high-quality natural moose habitat by providing those stages in plant succession preferred by large ungulates. It is ironic that this natural habitat (and the habitat-dependent moose) would be eliminated with the cessation of logging in order to satisfy one of the conditions of naturalness prescribed by the Wilderness Act. The moose could probably be saved by introducing prescribed (unnatural) fires, in lieu of logging, to create seral plant communities (Peek et al. 1976).

Although our knowledge of natural processes is inadequate, we do know there is a vital connection between diversity and numbers of wildlife and habitat mix in wilderness. And we recognize that fire has been the great renewer of forest areas, the creator of variety of cover type on a large scale. On a smaller scale, diversity of habitat has been instigated by insect, disease, windthrow, and stagnation (Cowan 1966). Where fire has been suppressed from its natural role, diversity and numbers of wildlife are retarded. To achieve the goal of natural distributions and numbers of native wildlife in wilderness, fire must be allowed play a more prevalent and thus a more natural role in wilderness ecosystems. In some cases, prescribed fire must be artifically introduced to make up for past fire prevention and control.

[9] Evison, Boyd. 1976. Personal correspondence. [Mr. Evison is Superintendent, Great Smoky Mountains National Park.]

Figure 11-3.—In some National Wildlife Refuge Wilderness, legislation establishing the Refuge or Game Range and superceding Wilderness designation within it, may call for management measures to insure the survival of particular species. *Upper left*: a charcos rock tank catchment in the proposed Cebeza Prieta Game Range Wilderness, Ariz., helps insure the survival of Desert Bighorn; *lower left*, a "guzzler"; and *lower right*, a water flue in the Desert National Wildlife Range, Nev. provides vital water for wildlife.

And, again, we must not be too quick to define natural. An Adirondack forest, by virtue of natural plant succession may have recovered from logging a hundred years ago, and in some ways be more natural today than a Rocky Mountain forest never logged but held for the past 75 years in suspended plant succession by efficient fire prevention and control programs. Because wilderness fire may be the most effective and appropriate habitat management tool, fire management and wilderness-wildlife management must go hand in hand.

As a practical matter, of course, because of the impact of technology, natural chance may have insufficient time and opportunity to influence the character of wilderness, particularly in the East where areas typically are small and scattered. Fire and insect control actions can be expected on surrounding lands to protect economic values there, and few wilderness administrators may voluntarily shoulder the resulting public relations

problem of risking a wilderness burn or insect blight that might move out to commercial forest.

3. *Use minimum impact tools where natural processes must be supplemented or simulated.* Because it is surrounded by nonwilderness regions, wilderness is subjected to less natural processes than if the whole continent were still wilderness. For example, the wilderness that would naturally be consumed by a holocaust may be insulated by a fire-suppression program in a surrounding National Forest. The wilderness ecosystem that would ordinarily enjoy balanced predator-prey relations is distorted by game-protection policies in a surrounding National Park or by predator-control practices on an adjoining Bureau of Land Management area. To minimize these influences, humans must sometimes interfere to simulate or supplement retarded influences even though some naturalness will be lost.

Wilderness managers may at times have to mimic natural processes such as by prescribed burning, substituting human hunters for natural predators, or even, in very special cases, employing hand tools to disturb vegetation as a substitute for such natural features as the bison-built prairie wallows that were "the propagation sites of a host of native flowers and forbs that fed antelope and prairie chicken" (Leopold, A. S. et al. 1969). Otherwise, the wilderness manager may merely preside over unnatural monotypes.

Whatever management tool or practice is deemed essential, it must represent the *minimum* departure from the natural process for which it substitutes. Department of Interior policy is very clear in this regard, setting forth "the minimum tool rule."

> The (Wilderness) manager should use the minimum device necessary to successfully, safely, and economically accomplish the objective. Economic factors should be considered the least important of the three criteria. The chosen tool or equipment should be the one that least degrades wilderness values temporarily or permanently (Reed 1972).

That Forest Service policy calls for only minimum, necessary actions has also been recently clarified (Weaver and Cutler 1977).

What constitutes the minimum tool will, of course, vary with the situation and the terrain. For example, in a program to rescue rare bighorn sheep by providing a dependable water supply, the choice may be between a windmill and a rock catchment. Nor does management need to be extensive to be effective. Critical areas which may determine bird or animal numbers are often a small fraction of total range (Leopold, A.S. et al. 1969).

Restoring once-indigenous species by transplanting is a controversial wilderness management option since it can affect the whole wilderness vegetation-ungulate-carnivore complex. Allen (1966) recommends that "available ranges should not be left unstocked if there are breeders to spare" and he cites successful transplants of trumpeter swans, pronghorns, sage grouse, turkey, and bighorn sheep. On the other hand, some wood bison in Canada have been rendered genetically impure by the introduction of plains bison (Allen 1966). One wildlife biologist reviewer of this chapter suggested that bighorn sheep captured in British Columbia or other locations should not be reintroduced into vacant ranges in the Sierra Nevada until we know more about the various subspecies. Otherwise forage, disease, and predation

problems may make the program counterproductive.[10] Furthermore, (Cowen 1966) points out that in reintroductions too little attention undoubtedly has been paid to the possibility of transporting disease organisms to the host (Cowan 1966). If indeed some subspecies or strains of animals are delicately attuned to life in specific local environments, one may question the utility of trapping and shifting these populations in an effort to restock underpopulated ranges (Leopold 1966). In short, wilderness is 'no place to experiment without the most judicious caution.

The opposite problem, that of exotics invading wilderness, is a knotty one, particularly in the case of such vigorous species as starling, tamarisk, Eastern brook trout in Western lakes and streams, and Japanese honeysuckle. The problem is critical when the invading species displaced an indigenous but endangered one. For example, the greenback trout in Rocky Mountain National Park was forced out in part by the introduction of the aggressive Eastern brook trout.[11]

For some plant and animal species, there is probably no satisfactory way of getting rid of them once they are established. The elimination procedures would be worse than their presence in terms of the wilderness outlook. From another perspective, at some point they may be considered virtually indigenous.

4. *Favor Wilderness-Dependent Endangered Species.* It is in attempting to comply with the Endangered Species Act that the wilderness manager may come closest to subverting natural processes. For example, to restore a breeding population of eagles to a wilderness may require installing artificial rest platforms. (But if the platforms are constructed of rough-hewn lumber and not of aluminum, the eagles will rapidly take care of camouflaging them.) Given the small amount of habitat left for certain wilderness-dependent species, is it wise to let natural processes further jeopardize a threatened or endangered species? And if not, what intrusions on the wilderness are acceptable in trying to preserve them? In resolving such conflicts, wilderness managers should begin by respecting applicable overriding legislation, which may require efforts to save such species, but do only what is necessary and follow the minimum tool rule, as called for earlier. But this is hardly adequate help.

For example, in the original Gila Wilderness, the rare native Gila trout has survived only because dams outside the wilderness or natural stream barriers inside have prevented competing species or interbreeding trout

---

[10] Dunaway, David J. 1976. Personal correspondence. [Mr. Dunaway is wildlife biologist in the Forest Service Regional Office, San Francisco.]

[11] Contor, Roger (see footnote 5).

from contaminating the Gila's habitat.[12] Question: In a species-contaminated stream in the Gila, do you construct stream barriers and poison existing introduced fish populations in order to restock Gila trout and thus husband an endangered species? And if you do opt for this much manipulation as being necessary, as a minimum tool do you blast a cliff into the streambed to form a natural-appearing barrier that can fool visitors, or do you make the barrier out of rock masonry that is clearly identifiable as unnatural? Clearly, there are esthetic overtones to such decisions. Sensitivity and case-by-case judgment are needed.

Where necessary, "special protection can be given to diminishing species by designating areas where entry is excluded; coastal sea mammals and birds are in obvious need of more inviolate areas that include their feeding and breeding grounds" (Allen et al. 1973). On the California Bighorn Sheep Zoological Area in the Inyo National Forest, Calif., there is no entrance or passage without permission, no discharge of firearms, and no grazing of any kind—all in the interests of preventing stress on an endangered species during such critical periods in its life cycle as breeding, lambing, and winter foraging.

5. *Manage for indigenous species kept wild.* Certainly wilderness-wildlife management should be limited to native plants and animals. In classified wilderness, for example, Gambel quail in a desert wash should be observed in the shade of mesquite, not tamarisk. A visitor to proposed wilderness in the crater of Haleakala National Park ought to see mamane trees and silver swords, not feral goats (domestic but gone wild). Carrying the point further, artificiality in any form must be minimized: Wildlife should be native and wild. Forage relationships in wild animals should be natural. No artificial feeding practices are fitting in designated wilderness, and their tolerance in adjacent areas must take into account the possible impact of subsidized species on wilderness naturalness, e.g., winter-fed elk that will migrate in the summer to wilderness.

Sometimes, of course, although he wishes it were otherwise, the manager of wilderness-type terrain is stuck with trying to manage an introduced species. For example, a big wildlife problem for the Superintendent of Great Smoky Mountains National Park is the immigrant wild pig. On National Forests in the same region a significant wildlife management problem is the human poacher and his dogs, who together threaten the

black bear population. In such cases there is no substitute for overt enforcement.

6. *Encourage angling styles that are part of and compatible with wilderness experiences.* Fishing is a traditional recreation activity in most wildernesses, and its status, under the direction of State fish and wildlife agencies, is reaffirmed by the Wilderness Act. Fishing, like hunting, can achieve its finest quality in wilderness, can be a scarce wilderness-dependent experience, and can be a means by which many recreationists realize wilderness values. Wilderness is a place where one can indulge in the primitive myth that one can live off the land. Catching a few fish and eating them in camp with family or friends contribute to the overall quality of many a wilderness experience, and is a goal of many users. Our view is that fishing, if carried out in a manner consistent with wilderness values, is a very acceptable wilderness activity.

Managers should encourage the use of techniques and equipment that do not degrade the environment—for example, the use of artificial lures that simulate naturally occurring foods. (The use of natural bait itself causes too much worm-digging, rock turning over, and log and stump destruction.) Fishing regulations for wilderness should encourage a focus on the overall wilderness experience as opposed to fishing just to catch as many fish as possible. At certain locations, regulations might include catch-and-release requirements, the use of barbless hooks, or perhaps a requirement that all fish taken must be cooked and eaten at the site. Naturalness of the experience, not the bulging creel, should be emphasized.

Artificial stocking of certain high lakes in many western states was initiated years ago to transport to suitable waters the species barred from entering by natural barriers. Some of these lakes are now classified wilderness and their stocking and the methods used continue as established uses under the Wilderness Act. Yet today, the practice of artificial stocking, and the methods used, are among the most controversial wilderness management issues. There is no question that artificial stocking compromises the naturalness of wilderness, particularly the specific aquatic ecosystems that are affected.

At a minimum, we believe management of each individual wilderness should strive to retain most of its waters the way nature willed them, whether as naturally barren waters or with naturally reproducing fisheries, without artificial stocking. Artificially-stocked fisheries would seem tolerable in classified wilderness only where the practice is clearly established and political realities dictate its continuance. Any artificial stocking of

---

[12] Koen, John, 1976. Personal correspondence. [Mr. Koen is director of recreation, Southwest region, U.S. Department of Agriculture Forest Service, Albuquerque.]

wilderness lakes must be based on comprehensive planning that takes account of overall wilderness use and the capability of individual lakes to sustain human impact. Where stocking is allowed, naturalness goals dictate that only indigenous species and established, low-impact methods should be used. We feel that aerial stocking of high lakes could be restricted to locations where it has become clearly established and where it is carried out in a manner to minimize its impact on wilderness qualities and the experiences of visitors. Alternate methods for stocking fish should be explored during the negotiation of a politically feasible solution to the fish stocking issue by wilderness managers, users, and State fish and game managers.

Fishery-management objectives can often be met in wilderness without the intensive management practices and stocking that are applicable elsewhere. Quality fishing can indeed be provided by natural means in many locations: Witness the situation in Yellowstone National Park, where naturally productive fisheries are maintained through the use of carefully controlled daily and possession catch limits as well as through restrictions on bait, lures, and size limits.

The presence of fish in wilderness waters must be related first to its natural role in the ecosystem.

> When we manage a fishery for maximum sustained yield to fishermen, we may be depriving certain wild animals the level of food supply that is natural. A Wilderness lake may be an unusually productive lake for fish, but it may have to be that way to support the osprey and eagle pairs that nest along its shores, or the bears that feed on fish runs in feeder streams. If we don't leave nature as much alone as possible in Wilderness, it won't be done anywhere else.[13]

It is imperative that wilderness managers and interested publics fully participate with State fisheries managers in developing wilderness fisheries management programs. The planning and management of wilderness fisheries should include the development of a full range of alternative fishing opportunities outside of the wilderness to relieve pressures and allow a focus in wilderness on forms of fishing that are dependent on the wilderness setting. The most defensible rationale for the manipulation of fish populations in some high lakes may be the usefulness of the practice as a diversionary management tool. Managers might continue to stock a previously stocked lake to divert fishermen from other more natural lakes or drainages less able to withstand human impact. But such decoy tactics might best be emphasized in recreation areas adjacent to classified wilderness. The long-range policy question is whether any artificial stocking in designated wilderness is too harsh a compromise with naturalness.

We are recommending a restrictive posture on any further expansion of artificial fish stocking in wilderness. This topic is controversial; so is our recommendation. An opposing view was expressed to us by Richard Stroud, Executive Vice President of the Sport Fishing Institute:[14]

> ... as the mountain lacking the grizzly becomes just a pile of rocks, so, too, a high elevation lake without fish life becomes just a big puddle. Perhaps in no other aquatic ecosystem—owing to extreme water clarity and sharpened human perception—is the visual impact of fish life as important as in high mountain lakes. The naturalness of the aquatic ecosystem is only an illusion, lacking representativeness of all trophic levels. Introduction of fish life corrects an error of nature—overcomes an unnaturalness, if you will ... I strongly disagree with the "let nature roll the dice" philosophy. Strictly followed, it would preclude introduction of any fish into any barren lakes ... I do not believe that discriminate stocking of selected fishless waters compromises Wilderness values. On the contrary, I contend the results enhance these values ... I cannot support a leave-it-alone orientation in Wilderness fisheries management. It implies a negative, do-nothing management philosophy that is based on questionable and arbitrary notions of naturalness that are altogether too simplistic ... I urge, rather, the current position of our Board of Directors of the Sport Fishing Institute. "To permit state fish conservation agencies to carry out desirable fish stocking of remote waters by aerial means which, when completed, leaves the visible environment unaffected and which is necessary if quality fishing experiences are to be readily available for optimum use and enjoyment by the public in Wilderness Areas."

This view, backed by a strong political constituency of sportsmen, suggests that artificial fish stocking in wilderness will be carried on to some degree for many

---

[13] Allen, Durward. 1976. Personal correspondence. [Dr. Allen is professor of Wildlife Ecology at Purdue University.]

[14] Stroud, Richard. 1976. Personal correspondence.

years. This makes it all the more important that fish stocking programs be a part of—and not apart from—overall wilderness management plans so an optimum balance can be struck between that practice and all the affected wilderness values.

7. *Favor hunting methods and conventions that foster wilderness-dependent experiences.* It is essential that wilderness hunting be scientifically managed to insure that the natural ecosystem is not impaired. It should be just intensive and selective enough (with regard to age and sex) to protect the natural behavior and dynamics of game population. We agree with Fox and Fox (1976) that harvest should mimic as closely as possible the pattern of kill by natural predators; that there should be no hunting of predators near the top of the food chain, such as wolves and grizzlies, and that hunting should not be permitted where either a lack of knowledge or lack of regulatory staff makes it uncertain that hunting can maintain a healthy ecosystem and its associated wildlife.

Evidence supports the need for careful game management in wilderness to preserve naturalness. Protecting against unwanted influences of hunting and other human disturbance is especially critical for sensitive or endangered species. To protect the genetic spark of the bighorn sheep, perhaps hunting regulations should encourage the taking of females and yearling males,

Figure 11–4.—Wilderness wildlife guidelines proposed in this book emphasize hunting and fishing as important wilderness recreation activities where it is (a) biologically sound, (b) legal, and (c) carried out in the spirit of a wilderness experience.

rather than prime male breeders with trophy horns (Morgan 1973).

Plinking can be especially damaging in wilderness where there may be few witnesses to dissuade an armed visitor from yielding to the temptation of a live target, such as whistling marmots in a timberline boulder field. Where such actions occur, and where other visitors have been disturbed by nonhunting gunfire, managers may want to consider limiting guns in wilderness except during hunting season. Plinking is definitely not a wilderness-dependent activity. It causes noise pollution and anxiety to wilderness animals and users alike, and can inflame antihunting sentiment by nonhunter visitors who categorize any gun toter as a hunter.

However, one of our reviewers provided an articulate counterargument to restricting guns:

Prohibition of guns is going to be controversial. Firearms can be useful for signaling, protecting against the occasional rattlesnake that threatens a child, or warding off a grizzly. Many visitors choose to carry a firearm simply because it enhances the wilderness experience. Education and information on appropriate use is probably a more useful approach than prohibition.[15]

Where it is allowed in wilderness, hunting must be of such a quality that it does not degrade the wilderness resource or the experience of other users. It should permit satisfactions that—although linked to hunting—depend on wilderness for their realization (Hendee 1974). Wilderness-quality hunting may mean different things to different people, but let's say it is the opportunity to pursue the recreation under biologically sound and ethical rules, in a manner pleasing to oneself and one's fellow hunters, acceptable to most nonhunters, and in keeping with wilderness criteria of naturalness, solitude, and contrast with civilization. It is not realistic to expect that all wilderness hunters would voluntarily restrict themselves to muzzle loaders or bow and arrows. But conforming to a wilderness ethic implies restrictions on extravagant base camps or walkie-talkies that crackle messages from canyon to canyon. Wilderness is the one place the hunter can confront game on its terms, and this opportunity should be encouraged for those who can appreciate the unique values of such an experience.

8. *Promote wilderness-wildlife research using appropriate methods.* The need for management, the feasibility of management methods, and evaluation of results must be based upon continuing scientific research.

---

[15] Peek, James. March 1976. Personal correspondence. [Dr. Peek is associate professor of Wildlife, University of Idaho.]

There is a need for applied research in all phases of wilderness-wildlife and fisheries management. This challenge calls for a concerted endeavor by scientists in the Federal Agencies, the States, and universities. "Active management aimed at preservation of natural communities of plants and animals demands skills and knowledge not now in existence. A greatly expanded research program, oriented to management needs, must be developed" (Leopold, A.S. et al. 1969). Early in this chapter we called for inventory of wildlife species and their habitat as a first step to guide wilderness management for wildlife. While inventory is related to research we are calling here for more rigorous analysis, evaluation, and study to determine probable consequences in the welfare and behavior of wilderness wildlife in response to alternately changing conditions—natural or due to man's inadvertent or deliberate influence.

Another important topic for research is wildlife-related human behavior. As the North American Policy Committee states (Allen et al. 1973):

> Our most neglected and crucial research needs are those concerning human social behavior. The biologist alone, the social scientist alone, the economist alone cannot deal with these questions. Their combined effort is required, and it must do great things.

Thus, the need for wildlife-related wilderness research is based on both ecological and human behavior issues—the latter as it relates to environmental and social impacts and wildlife-related wilderness experiences.

In using wilderness as a wildlife research laboratory, however, the scientist is under the same constraints as everybody else not to degrade its naturalness or solitude. While some instrumentation in support of basic ecological research may be necessary to record accurately the scientific parameters of wilderness, physical structures are not in keeping with wilderness criteria, nor are such techniques as painting big markings on live trapped animals for later observation from an obtrusive helicopter. Even investigations of wilderness users must be discrete and sensitive to the values that are affected by the research process—notwithstanding the long range contribution of such studies.

We must recognize, however, that radiotelemetry and aircraft, used with discretion, are invaluable means, sometimes the only means, of obtaining data on the natural distributions and behavior patterns of large wilderness species. These resources merit and deserve the understanding that can only be gained through judicious programs of marking and observation. One reviewer of this chapter wrote to us: "If we allow radio

communications by wilderness managers, and modern cameras, canoes, and camping gear on the part of visitors, why should the wildlife researchers have to revert to outmoded techniques, so long as he leaves no lasting imprint on either the landscape or the wildife resource."[16]

We have only begun to investigate the relationships and the natural mechanisms that work within our natural ecosystems. Many wildlife research opportunities are essentially wilderness-dependent; they require vast, natural areas that may ultimately exist only in wilderness. It would be foolhardy to deny competent scientists the opportunity to learn from those processes that have developed through millions of years and which have proved their durability by survival.

Conclusions

We recommend the foregoing guidelines as necessary to achieve the proposed wilderness-wildlife management objectives. We emphasize, however, that these guidelines are intended to supplement, and not substitute for, wilderness-management principles suggested in chapter 7 and elsewhere in the book.

It seems unrealistic to seek one monolithic wilderness-wildlife management pattern; wilderness management needs to be tailored to the unavoidable constraints on the administrative Agency concerned and focused on needs of individual areas, while yet embracing the broad principles in the Wilderness Act. For this reason, sensitive and preceptive wilderness-wildlife management is essential on the part of all assigned agencies. We are encouraged by the recent development of "Policies and Guidelines for Fish and Wildlife Management in Wilderness and Primitive Areas," by the Land Resources Committee of the International Association of Fish and Wildlife Administrators (1976).[17] These guidelines represent the type of down-to-earth suggestions that are needed by Forest Service and BLM land managers as well as by State fish and wildlife personnel. In broad terms the IAFWA direction is compatible with the strategies outlined in this chapter. The IAFWA policies and guidelines espouse a minimum-tool approach to management, emphasize the need for area-specific plans to adapt the broad guidelines to local situations, and suggest a focus on indigenous species and on the need to

---

[16] Peek, James. March 1976. Personal correspondence. [Dr. Peek is associate professor of Wildlife at the University of Idaho.]

[17] International Association of Fish and Wildlife Administrators. 1976. Policies and Guidelines for Fish and Wildlife Management in Wilderness and Primitive Areas. Washington, D.C. 23 p. mimeo.

fit all practices to the wilderness environment. While not as comprehensive nor as restrictive as could be desired, the IAFWA statement is a significant step forward. In our opinion, its single most important lack is the expression of a clear wilderness philosophy or ethic to guide its application. Federal wilderness area supervisors may have to assume a "policeman posture" over wilderness quality when negotiating wildlife management practices with State fish and game departments. Some key *potential* conflicts in it appear to us to be in its provisions for clearing log jams in spawning streams, stocking barren lakes, maintaining existing fish and game management facilities, provision for commercial trapping, and controlling problem animals. Hopefully a wilderness philosophy can be integrated into the IAFWA guidelines as a constraint on their interpretation and application. Too liberal an interpretation could compromise wilderness values. A guiding wilderness ethic is needed as policies are applied to meet the needs of individual areas.

This chapter has sought to set the stage for such a process. It has also sought to remind readers of the interdependency of wilderness and wildlife.

Wildlife is only one component of the wilderness-wildlife resource and cannot be considered separately. Wildlife uses, such as sport fishing or hunting, must be governed not just by the surplus capacity of fish and game but by the impact of such uses on the naturalness of relationships among all components of the wilderness resource. More specifically, while a particular lake may have the capacity to support a certain level of fishing pressure, the acceptable level of that use must also be measured against the aggregate impact of fishermen and other users on the vegetation and soil around the lake or along the stream.

The case for a comprehensive—as opposed to functional—approach does not downgrade wilderness management for wildlife; indeed we believe that wildlife should receive much stronger consideration in wilderness planning and management. We are merely emphasizing that only by managing wildlife in wilderness, not in and of itself, but as an ingredient of the natural ecosystem whose integrity hinges on and contributes to the wildlife resource, can the wildlife manager contribute soundly to wilderness preservation.

Finally, we wish to emphasize the importance of wildlife in the wilderness web. The real ecological justification for an occasional retreat to wilderness is the opportunity it provides to acquire a perception of the oneness of our world. Wilderness affords the opportunity to view the natural processes by which the land and the living things upon it have achieved their characteristic forms and by which they maintain their existence; to become aware of the incredible intricacies of plant and animal communities; to sense intrinsic beauty and contrasts with creeping degradation in many nonwilderness settings. These things add up to the great lesson of man-environment interdependency: That insects, birds, fish, mammals, water, soil, trees, plants, and people are all part of the same scheme—an intricately woven fabric. Snip one thread and the entire cloth begins to unravel; stitch up one tear and you begin to repair the whole. Exposure to wilderness, however casual or however intense, directly or vicariously, can be a doorway to the ecological understanding of our utter interdependence with our environment and with life everywhere, to the development of a culture that will secure the future of an environment fit for life and fit for living, and to an appreciation of all those amenities that are inexorably linked to the inner prosperity of the human spirit.

Literature Cited

Allen, Durward.
  1966. The preservation of endangered habitats and vertebrates of North America. *In* Future environments of North America, p. 22–37. F. Fraser Darling and John Milton, eds. The Natural History Press, Garden City, N.Y.

Allen, Durward.
  1973. Report of the committee on North American wildlife policy. *In* Proceedings of the 38th American wildlife and natural resource conference, Washington, D.C., March 18–21, 1973, p. 152–181. Wildlife Management Institute, Washington, D.C.

Allen, Durward.
  1974. Of fire, moose, and wolves. Audubon 76(6):38–49.

Applegate, James.
  1973. Some factors associated with deer hunting by New Jersey residents. *In* Human dimensions in wildlife programs, p. 111–117. John Hendee and Clay Schoenfeld, eds. Wildlife Management Institute, Washington, D.C.

Bergerud, Arthur T.
  1974. Decline of caribou in North America following settlement. J. Wildl. Manage. 38(4):757–770.

Bishop, Richard C.
  1972. Conceptual economic issues in conserving the California condor. *In* Western agricultural economic association proceedings, Logan, Utah, July 23–25, 1972, p. 119–122. Utah State University Press, Logan, Utah.

Brown, Perry J., and John H. Schomaker.
  1974. Final report on criteria for potential campsites: Suppl. N. 32 to Project 12-11-204-3. 50 p. Utah State University Institute for Study of Outdoor Recreation and Tourism, Ogden, Utah.

Buchheister, Carl W.
1963. Wilderness and wildlife. *In* Tomorrow's wilderness, p. 76–83. Francois Leydet, ed. Sierra Club, San Francisco.

Cape, Oiver B.
1969. Effects of DDT spraying on the Yellowstone River system. *In* Readings in conservation ecology, p. 325–343. George W. Cox, ed. Appleton-Century-Crofts, New York.

Carpenter, M. Ralph and Donald R. Bowhis.
1976. Attitudes towards fishing and fisheries management of users in Desolation Wilderness. Calif. Fish and Game 62(3):168–178.

Carr, Archie.
1973. The everglades. Time-Life Books, New York. 184 p.

Chester, James.
1976. Human-Wildlife relationships in the Gallatin Range, Yellowstone National Park. Draft paper in the author's files.

Church, Frank.
1977. Wilderness in a balanced land use framework. Wilderness Resource Distinguished Lecture, University of Idaho Wilderness Research Center, March 21, 1977. 18 p. Reprinted as "Whither Wilderness" in American Forests, July 1977, p. 11–12, 38–41.

Ciriacy-Wantrup, S.V., and William E. Phillips.
1970. Conservation of the California tule elk. Biol. Conserv. 3(1):23–32.

Cole, Glen F.
1974. Management involving grizzly bears and humans in Yellowstone National Park. Bioscience 24(1):1–11.

Cowan, Ian McTaggert.
1966. Management, response, and variety. *In* Future environments of North America, p. 55–59. F. Fraser Darling and John Milton, eds. The Natural History Press, Garden City, N.Y.

Craighead, Frank, Jr., John Craighead, and Joel Varney.
1974. A population analysis of the Yellowstone grizzly bears. Bull. 40. 20 p. University of Montana School of Forestry, Missoula, Mont.

Craighead, John J., and Frank C. Craighead.
1971. Grizzly bear-man relationships in Yellowstone National Park. Bioscience 21(16):845–857.

Craighead, John J., Frank C. Craighead, Jr., Robert L. Ruff, and Bart O'Gara.
1973. Home range and activity patterns of nonmigratory elk of the Madison drainage herd as determined by radiotelemetry: Wildl. Monogr. No. 33. 50 p. The Wildlife Society, Washington, D.C.

Crisler, Lois.
1958. Arctic wild. 301 p. Harper and Row, New York.

Dasmann, Raymond F.
1966. Wildlife biology. 231 p. Wiley, New York.

Dunaway, David J.
1976. Human disturbance as a limiting factor of Sierra Nevada bighorn sheep. 15 p. mimeo. (Paper presented at First North American Wild Sheep Conference, April 14–15, 1971, Colorado State University, Fort Collins, Colo.)

Erickson, Albert W.
1975. Management of the grizzly bear in the Thompson Falls area and adjacent environs. 30 p. mimeo. Wildlife Management Associates, Bellevue, Wash.

Farney, Dennis.
1974. The big thicket. Defenders of Wildlife News 49(3):175–179.

Fox, Irving K. and Rosemary J. Fox.
1976. Wilderness preservation in the north. 20 p. mimeo. Macmillan Planetarium, Vancouver, B.C.

Frome, Michael.
1974. A place for wild animals, wild plants. Defenders of Wildlife News 49(3):194–200.

Freddy, Dave.
1973. The Selkirk caribou. 18 p. mimeo. Wilderness Research Center, University of Idaho, Moscow.

Geist, Valerius.
1971a. Is big game harassment harmful? Oilweek 22(17):12–13.

Geist, Valerius.
1971b. Mountain sheep. 383 p. University of Chicago Press, Chicago.

Geist, Valerius.
1975. Mountain sheep and man in the northern wilds. 248 p. Cornell University Press, Ithaca, N.Y.

Ghiselin, Jon.
1973-74. Wilderness and the survival of species. Living Wilderness 37(124):22–27.

Gilbert, Bil.
1976. The great grizzly controversy. Audubon 78(1):62–69.

Hamer, J.D.W.
1974. Distribution abundance and management implications of the grizzly bear and mountain caribou in the Mountain Creek Watershed of Glacier National Park, B.C. 164 p. M.S. thesis, University of Calgary, Alberta.

Hammond, John L.
1974. The role of wilderness areas in wildlife management. Pac. Wilderness J. 1(6):10–11.

Hendee, John C.
1974. A multiple satisfactions approach to game management. Wildl. Soc. Bull. 2(3):104–112.

Hendee, John C., and Clay Schoenfeld, eds.
1973. Human dimensions in wildlife programs. 193 p. Wildlife Management Institute, Washington, D.C.

Hendee, John C., Roger N. Clark, and Thomas E. Dailey.
1974. Fishing and other recreation behavior at roadless high lakes: some management implications. 33 p. mimeo. (Paper presented at American Fisheries Society Annual Meeting, Honolulu, Hawaii, Sept. 8, 1974.) [In publication process as USDA Forest Service Research Paper, PNW Forest and Range Experiment Station, Portland, Oreg.]

Hendee, John C., and Dale Potter.
1976. Hunters and hunting: management implications of research. *In* Proceedings, recreation research applications workshop (Asheville, N.C., Sept. 15–18, 1975). U.S. Dep. Agric., Misc. Publ. 28802, p. 137–161. Southeast. For. Exp. Stn., Asheville, N.C.

Herrero, Stephen.
1971. Human injury inflicted by grizzly bear. Science 170(3958):593–598.

Hochbaum, H. Albert.
1970. Wilderness wildlife in Canada. *In* Wilderness: the edge of knowledge. p. 23–33. Maxine E. McCloskey, ed. Sierra Club, San Francisco.

Hoagland, John F.
1973. A description of anglers and angling in two use areas of the Uinta Mountains. 99 p. M.S. thesis. Utah State University, Logan, Utah.

Kennedy, James, and Perry J. Brown.
1974. Attitudes and behavior of fishermen in Utah's Uinta Primitive Area. 13 p. mimeo. (Paper presented to annual meeting of American Fisheries Society, Honolulu, Hawaii, Sept. 8, 1974.)

Kimball, John F., Jr., and Michael L. Wolfe.
  1974. Population analysis of a northern elk herd. J. Wildl. Manage. 38(2):161–174.

Koehler, Gary M., William R. Moore, and Alan R. Taylor.
  1975. Preserving the pine marten. Western Wildlands 2(3):31–36.

Leopold, A. Starker.
  1966. Adaptability of animals to habitat change. In Future environments of North America, p. 66–75. F. Fraser Darling and John Milton, eds. The Natural History Press, Garden City, N.Y.

Leopold, A. Starker, Stanley A. Cair, and Clarence M. Cottam.
  1969. Report of the special advisory committee on wildlife management for the Secretary of the Interior. 14 p. Wildlife Management Institute, Washington, D.C.

Leopold, Aldo.
  1949. A Sand County Almanac. 226 p. Oxford, N.Y.

Lime, David W., and Charles T. Cushwa.
  1969. Wildlife esthetics and auto campers in the Superior National Forest. USDA For. Serv. Research Paper NC–32, 8 p. illus. North Central For. and Range Exp. Stn., St. Paul, Minn.

Lucas, Robert C.
  1965. The importance of fishing as an attraction and activity in the Quetico-Superior area. USDA For. Serv. Res. Note LS–61, 3 p. Lake States Exper. Stn., St. Paul, Minn.

Lucas, Robert C.
  1972. Wilderness perception and use. In Politics, policy, and natural resources, p. 309–323. Dennis L. Thompson, ed., McMillan, New York.

McClelland, B. Riley.
  1975. Wildlife influences on aesthetic values in Glacier National Park. Western Wildlands 2(3):23–30.

McGuire, John R.
  1975. The Forest Service program for the nation's renewable resources. 658 p. U.S. Dep. Agric., For. Serv., Washington, D.C.

McHenry, Robert and Charles Van Doren.
  1972. A documentary history of conservation in America. 442 p. Praeger Publishers, New York.

Mercure, Delbert V., Jr., and William M. Ross.
  1970. The Wilderness Act: a product of Congressional compromise. In Congress and the environment, p. 47–64. Richard Cooley and Geoffry Wandesforde-Smith, eds. University of Washington Press, Seattle, Wash.

Meslow, E. Charles, and Howard M. Wight.
  1975. Avifauna and succession in Douglas-fir forests of the Pacific Northwest. In Proceedings of the symposium on management of forest and range habitats for nongame birds, p. 190–196. Dixie R. Smith, ed. U.S. Dep. Agric., For. Serv. Tech. Bull. WO-1. Washington, D.C.

Milton, John P.
  1972. The web of wilderness. Living Wilderness 35(16):14–19 (Special Alaska issue.)

Morgan, James K.
  1973. Slamming the ram into oblivion. Audubon 75(2):16–19.

Nash, Roderick.
  1970. Wild-deor-ness. In Wilderness: the edge of knowledge, p. 36. Maxine McCloskey, ed. Sierra Club, San Francisco.

Odum, Eugene P.
  1969. Relationships between structure and function in the ecosystem. In Readings in conservation ecology, p. 6–20. George W. Cox, ed. Appleton-Century-Crotts, New York.

Olson, Sigurd.
  1963. Listening point. 242 p. Knopf, N.Y.

Peek, James M., David L. Ulrich, and Richard J. Mackie.
  1976. Moose habitat selection and relationships to forest management in north-eastern Minnesota. Wildl. Monogr. No. 48. 65 p. Wildlife Society, Washington, D.C.

Pimlott, Douglas.
  1974. The Arctic offshore gamble. Living Wilderness 33(127):16–24.

Poole, Daniel A.
  1976. Wilderness values and wildlife management. 20 p. mimeo. Wildlife Management Institute, Washington, D.C.

Reed, Nathaniel P.
  1972. Memorandum. June 24, 1972. 4 p. U.S. Dep. of Int., Park Serv., Washington. D.C.

Reiger, John F.
  1975. American sportsmen and the origins of conservation. 39 p. Winchester Press, New York.

Risser, James.
  1973. The Forest Service and its critics. Living Wilderness 37(122):6–15.

Robinson, Glen O.
  1975. The Forest Service. 337 p. Johns Hopkins, Baltimore.

Russell, Andy.
  1971. Trails of a wilderness wanderer. 297 p. Knopf, N.Y.

Schoenfeld, Clay.
  1971. Everybody's ecology. 316 p. Barnes, N.Y.

Schoenfeld, Clay.
  1976. Environmental education and wildlife policy. 22 p. mimeo. (Paper prepared for council on environmental quality national symposium on a national wildlife policy. Washington, D.C. October 1, 1976.)

Seidenstricker, John C., IV, Maurice G. Hornocker, Wilbur V. Wiles, and John P. Messick.
  1973. Mountain lion social organization in the Idaho Primitive Area. Wildl. Monogr. No. 35. 60 p. Wildlife Society, Washington, D.C.

Smith, David.
  1973. Appendix L: Maintaining timber supply in a sound environment. In Report of the President's advisory panel on timber and the environment. p. 396–426. U.S. Government Printing Office, Washington, D.C.

Spurr, Stephen H.
  1963. The value of wilderness to science. In Tomorrow's wilderness, p. 59–75. Francoise Leydet, ed. Sierra Club, San Francisco.

Talbot, Lee M.
  1970. An international view of wilderness. In Wilderness: the edge of knowledge, p. 16–22. Maxine E. McCloskey, ed. Sierra Club, San Francisco.

Trefethen, James B.
  1975. An American crusade for wildlife. 409 p. Boone and Crockett Club, New York.

Troyer, Will.
  1973. Alaska's brown bear. Living Wilderness 73(126):32–37.

Trueblood, Ted.
  1974. Struggle on the Salmon. Living Wilderness 38(126):15–24.

U.S. Department of the Interior, Fish and Wildlife Service.
  1974. The national wildlife refuge system. 8 p. Washington, D.C.

U.S. Department of the Interior, Fish and Wildlife Service.
  [n.d.] Cabeza Prieta wilderness proposal, Cabeza Prieta game range. 14 p. Washington, D.C.

Wallis, Orthello L.
  1976. Management of high country lakes in the national parks of

California. 17 p. mimeo. (Paper presented to High Mountain Lakes Symposium by California/Nevada Chapter American Fisheries Society and California Trout, Fresno, Jan. 29, 1976.)

Weaver, James, and M. Rupert Cutler.
1977. Wilderness policy: a colloquy between Congressman Weaver and Assistant Secretary Cutler. J. For. 75(7):392-394.

Weddle, Ferris.
1970. Secrets of the mighty cougar. Nat. Wildl. 8(6):58–62.

Wildlife Management Institute.
1975. Placing American wildlife management in perspective. 64 p. Wildlife Management Institute, Washington, D.C.

Woodward, Thomas N., R.J. Gutierrez, and William H. Rutherford.
1974. Bighorn ram production, survival, and mortality in south-central Colorado. J. Wildl. Manage. 38(4):771-774.

Wright, Herbert E., Jr.
1974. The Boundary Waters. Living Wilderness 38(125):9–16.

Fire has been an historic force shaping the character of the wilderness. The restoration of fire to its historic natural role is one of the major challenges in wilderness management today. Here a fire burns in the Payette National Forest in Idaho.

248

12 Fire In Wilderness Ecosystems

Introduction

In the primeval wilderness—where the earth and its community of life are untrammeled by man—periodic

This chapter was written by Miron L. Heinselman, adjunct professor, Department of Ecology and Behavioral Biology, University of Minnesota, St. Paul, Minnesota, and retired Principal Plant Ecologist, U.S. Department of Agriculture, Forest Service, North Central Forest Experiment Station, St. Paul, Minnesota.

forest, grassland, and tundra fires are part of the natural environment—as natural and vital as rain, snow, or wind. In Minnesota, for example—fire has clearly been associated with such typical postfire pioneer trees as jack pine, aspen, and black spruce for more than 40,000 years. The evidence is found in charred wood and cones in glacial deposits and from charcoal stratigraphy of laminated bottom sediments of Lake of the Clouds in the Boundary Waters Canoe Area (Rosendahl 1948; Heinselman and Roe 1963; Swain 1973). The oldest evidence may predate man in North America. Nevertheless, our western, urban-based society has perceived fire only as a destroyer and has attempted to protect the wilderness from it.

An enlightened biocentric approach to wilderness management must allow for the natural role of fire to the maximum possible extent—consistent with the safety of people and adjacent nonwilderness resources. This chapter explores our current knowledge of fire's role and the alternatives in working with this important variable in wilderness programs.

Lightning and Man as Fire Sources in the Primeval Wilderness

Unlike Europe, the Mid-East, and much of Asia, most of North America had very sparse human population and little agriculture or industry until 150 to 300 years ago. Paleo-Indians apparently existed over much of the continent from late-glacial times, and in the more recent past Indians, traders, trappers, hunters, prospectors, and stockmen had camps within some present wildernesses. But these people did not fell trees or cultivate crops to any appreciable extent. They all used fire, however, and many forest and prairie fires were set, accidentally or deliberately. Historical research (Day 1953; Little 1974; Weaver 1974) suggests that Indians in the Northeast and along the Pacific Coast burned the forests on a considerable scale. The reckless use of fire by settlers, prospectors, and early loggers is well known.

But lightning is also a cause of fire in most of the same regions where forest fires are easily set by man. The relevant questions then are: In primeval times, did man add significantly to the area burned and alter the natural cycle and timing of fires? Or, did he serve mainly as an alternate source of ignition? We can never fully answer these questions, but recent data on lightning-fire occurrence and other evidence suggest that lightning is the primary fire starter in many regions. For example, despite today's much higher human population, lightning ignitions still account for most of the total area burned in Alaska, northern Canada, the Selway-Bitterroot and Pasayten Wildernesses, and many other areas (Habeck and Mutch 1973; Rowe and Scotter 1973; Viereck 1973; Fahnestock 1975; Johnson and Rowe 1975).

Evolutionary adaptation to reproduction after fires and the survival of individuals during fires is in itself evidence that many plants long have existed in a fire environment. Examples include the persistent, closed (serotinous) cones of jack pine, lodgepole pine, and pond

pine, which open in the heat of crown fires; the persistent, semiclosed cones of black spruce; the thick, fire-resistant bark of giant sequoia, redwood, Douglas-fir, ponderosa pine, red pine, many other pines, western larch, oaks, and other trees; the root suckering of aspens; the sprouting from the root crown of birches, oaks, redwood, and many other trees and shrubs; and the light, windborne seeds of aspens, pines, spruces, and birches. Mutch (1970) has hypothesized that fire-dependent plant communities burn more readily than nonfire-dependent communities because natural selection has favored the development of flammable foliage. This theory recognizes that plants that have survived fires over evolutionary time periods may have selected flammable properties that contribute to their perpetuation in a fire environment. Such plants and communities actually *depend on* periodic fire for survival. Many animals also are not only adapted to surviving fires, but also *depend on* the early stages of plant successions following fires for some of their habitat needs. In this sense, the animal components of many ecosystems are also fire dependent.

The Natural Role of Fire in Ecosystems

An ecosystem can be called *fire dependent* if periodic perturbations by fire are essential to the functioning of the system. A full recognition of fire's role is only now pervading ecological theory, but it seems clear that many of the forest, grassland, and savanna ecosystems of the primeval American wilderness were *fire dependent*.[1] In such ecosystems, fire initiated and terminated vegetational successions; controlled the age structure and species composition of the vegetation; produced the mosaic of vegetation types of the landscape; affected insect and plant pathogen populations; influenced nutrient cycles and energy flows; regulated the biotic productivity, diversity, and stability of the system; and determined the habitats available to wildlife.

The scale of fire effects and the specific ways fire influences the natural system depend on the kind of *fire regime* characteristic of given ecosystems. The following fire regimes apply mainly to forests, but a modified scheme might be used to describe the regimes of prairie, savanna, shrubfield, or tundra ecosystems. The important elements of a fire regime are: (1) Fire *type* and *intensity* (crown or surface fire), (2) *size* (area) of typical significant fires, *and* (3) *frequency* or *return intervals* typical for specific land areas and for major fires in a

---

[1] See, for example, Clements 1910; Maissurow 1935; Spurr 1954; Ahlgren and Ahlgren 1960; Cooper 1961; Hartesveldt 1964; Loucks 1970; Kozlowski and Ahlgren 1974.

region. In subsequent discussions, six kinds of *fire regimes* will be distinguished:

0 = No (or very little) natural fire.

1 = Infrequent, light surface fires (more than 25-year return intervals).

2 = Frequent, light surface fires (1- to 25-year return intervals).

3 = Infrequent, severe, surface fires (more than 25-year return intervals).

4 = Short return interval, crown fires (25- to 100-year return intervals).

5 = Long return interval, crown fires (100- to 300-year return intervals).

6 = Very long return interval, crown fires (over 300-year return intervals).

Historically, combinations of these regimes were typical of many regions. Regimes also varied according to vegetation types and physiographic sites within biogeographic regions. For example, the jack-pine type of ecosystems in the Boundary Waters Canoe Area was subject to regime 4 or 5 on most sites, as opposed to a 2 or 3 and 5 regime for red pine. With this background, let us examine the natural role of fire in more detail.

Fire as an Agent that Terminates and Renews Succession

In much of the original North American wilderness, it was fire more than any other factor that periodically eliminated or set back old forests and reset the successional clock. The nature of these periodic disturbances depended on the fire regime typical of the vegetation and physiography within each climatic region. For example, the giant sequoia forests of the Sierras usually experienced light or moderate surface fires at short intervals (4 to 15 years) that kept down invading shrubs, true firs, and incense cedar. They scarred but seldom killed the giant sequoias. Perhaps once in a thousand years, fuel and weather permitted local crown fires that wiped out groups of giant sequoias and created the large openings necessary for their reproduction (Biswell 1961; Hartesveldt 1964; Kilgore 1973). This history contrasts sharply with that of jack pine in the boreal forest and of lodgepole pine in the Rockies. There, on many sites, the regime was a crown fire or severe surface fire covering large areas at return intervals of 50 to 200 years. Such fires killed most or all of the trees, prepared the soil for reseeding, eliminated competitors, and opened the closed cones of the pines to reseed the area.[2] Fire was the common element in these otherwise unlike examples. In both cases, it was the

agent that periodically renewed successions. In the giant sequoia forest there was short-interval renewal of understory successions, while the overstory was renewed on a millenial time scale. In the cases of jack pine and lodgepole pine, fire wiped the entire slate clean and reset the successional clock every 50 to 200 years.

Fire as a Controller of Plant Community Composition

Fire influences the species composition of plant communities in the following ways: (1) It triggers the release of seeds (jack pine, lodgepole pine, pond pine, and others). (2) It stimulates flowering and fruiting of many plants. (3) It alters seedbeds (when litter and humus are replaced with bare soil, ash, or thin humus, this favors the germination and survival of most pines, Douglas-fir, giant sequoia, larch, some species of spruce, aspen, birch, and many other trees, shrubs, and herbs.). (4) It stimulates vegetative reproduction of many woody and herbaceous species when the overstory is killed. (5) It reduces competition for moisture, nutrients, heat, and light. (6) It selectively eliminates parts of a plant community (surface fire or partial overstory kill). (7) Fire frequency (return interval) influences community composition and controls overstory age for vegetation types reproduced by crown fires (e.g., jack pine, lodgepole pine, black spruce). Taken together, these mechanisms give fire important control—sometimes the dominant influence—over plant communities.

Fire as a Controller of the Scale of the Vegetation Mosaic

Viewed from a high-flying aircraft or mountaintop, the vegetation of naturally forested areas often appears as a patchwork or *mosaic*. This pattern also appears on vertical airphotos and on spacecraft imagery. What one sees are contrasting forest-age classes, successional stages, and vegetation types created by recurring forest fires over the centuries. Their *scale* depends on past fire size and on the kind of fire regime in specific areas. Scale is also heavily influenced by the physiographic base on which fire does its work. Steep and broken terrain often shows more complex patterns than level, gently rolling, or uniformly graded terrain, because fire and other important environmental factors are more varied in behavior and effects on complex slopes. In regions where fires are typically large crown or severe surface fires, such as the boreal forest, individual patches of the mosaic may cover many thousands of acres in dynamic patterns. Yet the mosaic as a whole changes little over time; the patches—like the pieces in a kaleidoscope—are periodically rearranged by fire and succession (Wright and Heinselman 1973; Wright, H.E. 1974).

---

[2] See, for example, Clements 1910; Heinselman 1973; Rowe and Scotter 1973; Loope and Gruell 1973.

Figure 12-1.—Periodic fires help renew ecological succession, control insects and pathogens, and create new food for browsing wildlife—all natural processes are influenced by fire. This series of photos of an area on the Flathead National Forest, Mont., taken in 1929, 1945, 1950, and 1973, show how succession reclaims even areas badly burned.

The average time required for a natural fire regime to burn over given ecological land units or an entire large nature reserve can be called the *natural fire rotation* (Heinselman 1973). This time period is somewhat analogous to the forester's term *"rotation."* For the Boundary Waters Canoe Area, the natural fire rotation averages about 100 years. But, like all averages, natural fire rotations are complex—each vegetation type and physiographic site tends to have its own characteristic return interval. This means that some areas will be skipped by fire for very long periods, while others may burn over several times. The fire rotation concept is useful as a tool for comparing the role of fire in different ecosystems, but it requires better fire history data than are now available for most wildernesses.

Fire as a Regulator of Fuel Accumulations

In most northern conifer forest ecosystems, the production of plant biomass exceeds decomposition for hundreds of years following the initiation of new succession. Production increases with temperature, precipitation, and fertility, but so does decomposition. Decomposition *rates* decrease and *net accumulation* increases northward or with increasing elevation, other factors being equal (Bray and Gorham 1964; Heinselman 1974). Cool, dry, summer climates also inhibit decomposition of standing dead timber. The net result is that plant materials accumulate throughout the forest: In the trunks, branches, and leaves of living trees and shrubs; in dead standing trees and shrubs, fallen logs, and uprooted root systems; and as accumulated twigs, needles, leaves, mosses, rotting wood, and other organic debris making up the litter and humus layers of the forest floor. All of these materials are potential fuel. (The trunks of large, living trees seldom burn, unless bare, dry wood is exposed in rotted-out areas, old fire scars, or similar defects.)

When fire occurs, all materials combustible under the prevailing conditions are reduced to ash, and the fuel cycle is completed. However, if many living trees are killed but unburned, which happens in crown fires in dense timber, new fuel is created by the fire itself in the form of snag forests. At first the arrangement of snags is unfavorable for carrying fire. But as the snags gradually fall, they may create a new peak in fuel buildup if their density is sufficient and decomposition is slow. In the North Cascades this fire-created secondary fuel peak may come 30 to 60 years after a crown fire (Fahnestock 1975), but in the Lake Superior region, most snags fall within 20 years and snag fuels are unimportant after 30 years. In some ecosystems, succession may introduce a less flammable understory of shade-tolerant broadleaf trees beneath pines, but in many other regions, succession introduces flammable conifers such as fir, cedar, or spruce which then serve as ladder fuels to increase the crown-fire potential. In general, the trend is toward increasing fuel buildup with elapsed time following fire.[3]

Fire as a Controller of Forest Insects, Parasites, and Pathogens

There are many fascinating interactions between fire and native forest insects and pathogens. For example, fire, or the lack of it, regulates the total vegetative mosaic and the age structure of individual forest stands. These in turn influence insect populations. When extensive stands of balsam fir or lodgepole pine reach maturity, outbreaks of the spruce budworm or mountain pine beetle can kill trees and create fuel concentrations that make large-scale fires possible. Such fires then terminate the outbreak by eliminating the host trees until new stands attain susceptible ages. Fires temporarily eliminate such plant parasites as mistletoe on black spruce, lodgepole pine, and other species (Irving and French 1971; Alexander and Hawkesworth 1975). They can also sanitize forests against other pathogens for a time.

Fire as a Controller of Nutrient Cycles and Energy Flow

In fire-dependent ecosystems, fire is a major factor in nutrient cycling and energy flow. Rates and pathways are influenced by fire frequency and intensity. In the absence of fire or in long intervals between fires, nutrient cycles and energy flow can be partially or severely blocked by incomplete decomposition of biomass. Accumulating biomass builds up fuel loads, which make lightning ignitions and high-intensity burns increasingly probable over time (Wright and Heinselman 1973). When fires occur, some or most of the nutrients in the forest biomass are unlocked and released as ash.[4] Some nitrogen is volatilized. But often there is no major loss of nutrients from the watershed because revegetation quickly utilizes the released nutrients (Wright, R.F. 1974; Bradbury et al. 1975; McColl and Grigal 1975).

Productivity, Diversity, and Stability of the Ecosystem in Relation to Fire

Vegetation production is heavily linked to complete nutrient cycling, and fire recycles nutrients that might otherwise not move. It also influences soil temperatures and local climates. Periodic, light surface fires or severe fires at long intervals prevent the accumulation of nutrients, dry matter, and energy in organic soil layers, reduce peat formation, and prevent permafrost encroachment (Heinselman 1974). Recurrent burns might be necessary to maintain longterm system reproductivity in many ecosystems.[5]

Fire prevents systemwide succession to species-impoverished climax stands by maintaining a mix of successional stages in the vegetation mosaic. The spatial scale of the mosaic is determined by fire size, type of fire regime, and natural fire rotation. Return intervals, intensity, and fire size together determine the pattern of stand ages and successional stages. These are the major factors determining ecosystem diversity on a gross scale, both for plant and animal communities. Fire also might be crucial in setting parkland/forest and grassland/forest boundaries in the western mountains and forest/tundra boundaries in the far north (Wright and Heinselman 1973).

The dynamic, fire-created mix of successional stages, communities, and stand ages in the vegetation mosaic might be essential to the stability of the system as a whole.[6] Unnatural fire exclusion could cause fuel accumulations leading to large, intense fires followed by unnatural effects on regeneration. An aged, near-climax ecosystem might also be particularly susceptible to insect and disease outbreaks and to blowdowns. Its animal

---

[3] See, for example, Dodge 1972; Heinselman 1973; Rowe and Scotter 1973; Biswell 1974; Weaver 1974; Kilgore and Sando 1975.

[4] See, for example, Grigal and McColl 1975; Vitousek and Reiners 1975; Foster and Morrison 1976.

[5] See, for example, Loucks 1970; Wright and Heinselman 1973; Vitousek and Reiners 1975.

[6] See, for example, Loucks 1970; Wright and Heinselman 1973; Wright, H.E. 1974; Vitousek and Reiners 1975.

populations would certainly be less diverse and probably less stable.

Early students of fire and its ecological role often emphasized succession and the climax hypothesis. They defined a climax community as one that has attained a dynamic, steady-state equilibrium between the environment and biota and is therefore self-perpetuating. Climax is attained only when species of earlier successional stages have been replaced by shade-enduring climax species in a full cycle of self-reproduction. Proponents of this theory suggested that climax forests are somehow more diverse, productive, and stable than pioneer forests that follow fires.

The evidence neglected by these early workers is that the time required for such a convincing case of climax is longer than the average time between fires for most stands in many western and northern conifer forest ecosystems. For the giant sequoia forest, it would be more than 3,000 years. For most Douglas-fir, ponderosa pine, and sugar pine forests it would be 500 to 1,000 years; and even for jack pine and lodgepole pine it would be 200 to 300 years. Because fire almost always returned to these forests before climax status was attained, we cannot be sure what vegetation might develop on typical fire-free sites for these species.

Recent writers point out that, in many temperate and boreal forest ecosystems, periodic fire perturbations were part of the natural environment and essential to the maintenance of species diversity, productivity, and longterm system stability.[7]

Where does this leave climax theory? In the light of present knowledge, the climax concept is not particularly useful.

Yet, in another sense the fire-dependent vegetation itself might be considered climax, because with periodic perturbations by fire it has maintained a quasi-stability for thousands of years, as demonstrated by studies of the pollen rain in such ecosystems (Swain 1973; Wright, H.E. 1974). But what *patch size* should be considered in deciding whether the forest mosaic as a whole is stable? If one looks at the vegetation of a vast region such as the Yellowstone plateau, there has been stability over thousands of years in the presence of fire. But if we are talking about patches on the scale of individual stands of lodgepole pine or Douglas-fir, which sometimes cover whole watersheds, then the steady-state climax is almost never attained before fire intervenes. The lesson is that we need to understand natural systems as they actually exist, not hypothetical, undisturbed systems that do not occur in the real world.

Wildlife Habitat and Fire

In fire-dependent ecosystems, fire controls the scale of the vegetation mosaic through fire size, intensity, and frequency; it influences the relative abundance of plant communities and successional stages. These determine habitat patterns for all herbivores, thereby regulating their numbers to the extent that populations are habitat limited. For example, fire increases foods for herbivores dependent on forage or browse plants that proliferate in early postfire succession.[8] It also increases yields of many berry-producing shrubs, thereby enlarging the food supply of bears and many birds. Fire eliminates some forage plants characteristic of old forests for 50 to 100 years—notably tree lichens and ground lichens in the north. Lichens are used by barren-ground and woodland caribou on winter ranges (Scotter 1964, 1971), but caribou also use sedges and other plants on burns and can probably shift winter ranges in response to changes in the vegetation mosaic (Bergerud 1974; Johnson and Rowe 1975). Fire regulates many insect populations, some of which are important food sources for birds such as warblers and woodpeckers. In some cases, whether fire increases or decreases food availability will depend on the relationship of prey and predator. Carnivores are dependent on herbivores and therefore they also depend on the fire-created vegetative mosaic. For example, more frequent fires in the Boundary Waters Canoe Area might favor moose and deer and thereby lead to increases in wolf populations. On the other hand, a lower fire level in that area might favor red squirrels and pine marten (Heinselman 1973).

Fire Occurrence and Behavior — A Few Principles

Before considering the place of fire in wilderness programs, it is important that we understand fire's essential ingredients.

1. *Fuel.* Fuel must be adequate, sufficiently dried, and properly arranged. Even heavy fuel loads might not produce a moving, self-perpetuating fire if they are discontinuous or poorly arranged, or if their energy availability is marginal for the prevailing weather. Fuel chemistry is an important factor in energy yields. Crown fires usually require adequate ground fuels beneath the

---

[7] See, for example, Loucks 1970; Heinselman 1973; Wright and Heinselman 1973; Wright, H.E. 1974; Vitousek and Reiners 1975.

[8] See, for example, Heinselman 1970; Loope and Gruell 1973; Rowe and Scotter 1973; Viereck 1973; Bendell 1974.

stand and some ladder fuels to carry fire up into the crowns.[9]

2. *Weather.* Suitable burning weather is characterized by one or more factors that promote drying of available fuels: (1) Low relative humidity (often below 30 percent), (2) a precipitation-free period of sufficient duration to reduce the moisture content of fine- and medium-size fuels to the critical level, and (3) sufficiently high current and antecedent temperatures. In level terrain, some wind is generally required to make wildfires spread rapidly. In mountainous terrain, fires create their own drafts—uphill.

The National Weather Service routinely forecasts fire weather in all major forest regions. Such evaluations are based on many variables. (For an example of the extensive literature which has been developed around this complex science, see Schroeder and Buck 1970.)

3. *An ignition source.* Fuel loads can be heavy and weather conditions hazardous, but if ignition sources are lacking, there will be no fire. The major natural source is lightning. If thunderstorms are not accompanied by heavy rain, fires can result from strikes in snags, organic layers, or trees with dry rot or flammable crowns. The probability of lightning ignitions can often be forecast, and the continental pattern of lightning fires has been mapped (Schroeder and Buck 1970). On many wilderness travel routes, man is also an ignition source.

Prescribed (controlled) fires can be set anywhere fuels are suitable if the weather is right. Once ignited, weather and fuels regulate the fire's progress. For maintaining control of the fire, there must be suitable fuel discontinuities in key areas.

For given burning conditions, fires spread through continuous fuels at predictable rates which have been quantified (Rothermel 1972; Frandsen 1973). However, much of the progress of fires can be due to long-distance spotting ahead of the main flame front. On steep terrain, advance fires will spread downhill because of rolling logs, heated boulders, and other debris. Paper birch is a major cause of spotting because of its thin, flammable bark.

Seasonal and Climatic Factors

The *seasons* are important in fire behavior because of their influence on vegetative development and the curing of grasses, sedges, and leaves. In the north, spring and fall are generally favorable for rapid surface-fire spread because green ground fuels are at minimum, and cured fuels are abundant. If these seasons are normally rainy, as in much of the Pacific Northwest, this is not so.

But in the Lake States and the boreal forest, midsummer fire behavior is often sluggish because green ground vegetation acts as a heat sink. In conifer forests with little ground vegetation, this is unimportant, however, and under prolonged drought even the current year's green vegetation can become cured—a normal occurence in summer-drought climates.

The annual climatic regime also has much to do with the expected occurrence of wildfires and therefore the recommended timing of safe, prescribed burning. Most North American wildernesses have snowcover from early fall through late spring or early summer. Except for this common element, seasonal patterns, which vary significantly from one to another, fall into one of three major types. (See USDA 1941; Schroeder and Buck 1970).

Wet winters and dry summers characterize the maritime climates of the Pacific coast and the Cascade and Sierra Nevada ranges from Washington to California. Winters are not very cold; summers are clear, warm, and dry. Much of the total annual precipitation in the mountains is snow, which accumulates to great depths. Occasional summer thunderstorms do occur, expecially over the mountains, and they usually carry very little rainfall. Mid-to-late summer is the wildfire season in the mountains.

Dry winters and wet summers are typical of the Northeast, the Great Lakes, the Midwest, most of the Canadian boreal forest region, and the eastern ranges of the Rocky Mountains from Alberta to New Mexico. These climates are continental with cold winters and significant snow accumulation but relatively light total snowfall. Summers are characterized by frequent frontal rainstorms. Thunderstorms are common from spring through fall, particularly in midsummer. Most storms are accompanied by enough rain to extinguish lightning ignitions, but some dry storms occur in most years. Lightning occurrence decreases northward, but some lightning-caused tundra fires occur even beyond the arctic tree line in Alaska and Canada. Prolonged summer droughts occur at intervals of 5 to 30 years.

The Intermountain West—from interior British Columbia south through eastern Washington and Oregon, all of Idaho, and extreme western Montana to Utah, Nevada, and Arizona—has characteristics of both the Pacific maritime and continental climates. Winter snowfall and snowpacks are moderate to heavy, and occasional periods of frontal summer rainfall occur. Extended summer dry periods are frequent, however, and dry thunderstorms are common. Lightning occurrence decreases northward.

---

[9]See, for example, Fahnestock 1970; Van Wagner 1968; Brown 1971, 1974; Rothermel 1972; Sando and Wick 1972; Kilgore and Sando 1975.

255

The Southeastern States, the deep South, and the Gulf Coast have complex climates, with considerable maritime precipitation derived from the Gulf of Mexico and the Atlantic. Annual precipitation is heavy and well distributed over the year, but temperatures are high, and short droughts create burning conditions. Sustained snowcover is rare except in the higher Appalachian Mountains. Winter fires are possible in most areas because vegetation is cured and snowcover is usually lacking. Thunderstorms are very frequent, but most lightning ignitions are extinguished by rainfall, and the vegetation of many areas is not very flammable except for the southern pine regions of the Coastal Plain and Piedmont.

Major Drought Episodes

In some regions of the ecologically significant fire, conflagrations in primeval times evidently occurred during infrequent major droughts. Fire weather is not average weather, at least in the North. Large-scale or severe surface and crown fires that regenerated large areas might have occurred largely during regional or subcontinental drought anomalies. It is clear from tree-ring studies of fire-scarred pines, Douglas-fir, giant sequoia, and redwood that surface fires burned many areas in many different wilderness regions at closely spaced intervals.[10] Certainly all of these fires did not occur in major drought years. But we need to know more about the likelihood that some regions experienced weather suitable for large-scale crown fires chiefly at long intervals during major droughts.

Interactions with the Fuels Mosaic

Given ignitions and fire weather, fires are still constrained by the fuels mosaic. Natural fuels are related to vegetation types because the various trees, shrubs, and ground-layer species vary widely in crown form, flammability or fuel chemistry, and litter characteristics. For example, most long-needle pines produce a loosely arranged needle straw. Stand age is related to both fuel availability and flammability. Old stands usually contain dead material, both down and in standing snags. Also, in old stands, succession to shade-tolerant species can generate understories of fir, cedar, hemlock, or spruce— species with dense, long crowns that serve as ladder fuels. Old forests are also likely to have sustained insect, mistletoe, or fungal attacks and blowdowns—all of which generate fuels.

---

[10] See Fritz 1931; Spurr 1954; Frissell 1973; Heinselman 1973; Houston 1973; Kilgore 1973; Loope and Gruell 1973.

256

Natural Fire Barriers

Many landscape features limit fire spread: Nonflammable vegetation types, lakes, rivers, streams, seepages, swamps, barren rock areas, snowfields, timberlines of high mountains, and fresh burns where fuels have been exhausted. The effectiveness of barriers is related to their condition and size, to adjacent fuels, and to prevailing weather conditions. Under extreme burning conditions, with high winds or fire-generated convection columns or whirls, natural barriers can fail because of long-distance spotting (Countryman 1964; Haines and Updike 1971).

Topographic and Landform Factors

Fire movements are strongly related to slopes, soil, and geology of local landforms. Fires tend to move upslope. Their movements are also influenced by aspect (compass bearing), steepness of slopes, soils and landform variables—all of which affect soil moisture, fertility, vegetation types, and local wind patterns. In general, the steeper south- and southwest-facing slopes and infertile or dry landforms are particularly fire prone. Heavier forest stands of moist and fertile sites also burn, but only after longer drying periods and return intervals.

Fire Size and Intensity as Ecological Variables

Most lightning-caused fires are small and soon go out. However, some develop into surface fires that burn over hundreds or even thousands of acres—scarring trees, significantly changing the understory vegetation, killing occasional trees or groups of trees, recycling nutrients, and reducing surface fuels. An occasional blaze develops into a major crown fire, killing whole forests over large areas. But, even in such crown fires there are usually skipped areas—somehow favored by the vagaries of wind, topography, and fuel—commonly on north slopes; around lakes or streams; in draws, canyons, or swamps. These by-passed areas are important as sources of plant propagules for recolonization of the burn. We might think it is the small, relatively undamaging fires that are best for the wilderness. But in some ecosystems, infrequent but large crown fires covering thousands of acres are responsible for an area's distinctive character and typical vegetation mosaic. Wilderness managers must provide—safely—for some burns of this character, or such ecosystems cannot be maintained in their truly natural state.

Fire-Dependent Ecosystems in the American Wilderness

A review of the natural, fire-dependent ecosystems of important wilderness regions will help focus on the urgency of positive fire management programs and on the necessity of recognizing differences in fire history and fire effects.

The Sierra-Nevada Region of California

This high-mountain country contains some of the world's best known nature reserves and the most magnificent conifer forests on earth. Included are the Sequoia-Kings Canyon, Yosemite, and Mt. Lassen National Parks; the John Muir, Sierra, Minarets, Hoover, Mokelume, Desolation, Caribou, and Thousand Lakes Wilderness Areas; and the Emigrant Basin and High Sierra Primitive Areas. Much of the country is alpine, but wherever forests occur fire has been a vital environmental factor. In the south, the westside forests between 3,000 and 8,000 feet include groves of giant sequoia and vast forests of sugar, ponderosa, and Jeffrey pines; Douglas-fir; incense cedar; and white and California red firs. At higher elevations throughout the area there are stands of lodgepole, western white, and whitebark pines; and mountain hemlock. The climate is winter-wet/summer-dry, and much of the precipitation is snow, which accumulates to 7 to 15 feet and may remain on the ground into June in high-elevation forests. Dry lightning storms occur infrequently, but ignitions are common because of the dry summers. Schroeder and Buck (1970) show 21 to 40 lightning-caused fires per million acres per year. At intervals of several years, episodes of dry thunderstorms combined with unusual dryness cause widespread fires. This climatic pattern has resulted in a history of light surface fires at intervals of 4 to 15 years in giant sequoia and ponderosa-sugar pine stands, with crown fires or surface fires severe enough to kill stands or portions of stands at very long intervals (perhaps 300 to 1,000 years or more) (Show and Kotok 1924; Biswell 1959, 1961; Wagener 1961; Hartesveldt 1964; Kilgore 1973). Many giant sequoias bear impressive multiple fire scars, some of them thousands of years old. Most individual fires were small because the terrain is broken and the vegetation varied. Lightning-caused fires are also common in the high country, but seldom crown or become large because of the open character of the forest and fuel discontinuities caused by exposed bedrock, boulder fields, wet meadows, lakes, and snowfields (Kilgore and Briggs 1972). The giant sequoia and mid-elevation pine forests were unquestionably kept open and structured by frequent periodic surface fires in primeval times. Fire protection over the last 70 years has caused unnatural fuel accumulations and invasions of true firs and incense cedar beneath the pines and sequoias. These conditions are setting the stage for unnatural conflagrations that could kill even the fire-resistant pines and sequoias (Biswell 1959, 1961; Hartesveldt 1964; Kilgore 1970, 1972, 1973; Dodge 1972; Weaver 1974).

The California-Oregon Coast Range Region

Another string of wilderness areas has been set aside in the coastal mountains from southern Oregon to southern California. Included are the Kalmiopsis, Marble Mountain, Yolla Bolly Middle Eel, Ventana, San Rafael, San Gabriel, Cucamonga, San Gorgonio, San Jacinto, and Agua Tibia Wilderness Areas; and the Salmon-Trinity Alps Primitive Area. Some areas have a chaparral or oak-madrone, coulter and digger pine vegetation at lower elevations. Higher elevations, where present, support ponderosa, Jeffrey, and lodgepole pine forests, and sometimes white fir, incense cedar, and other species. The climate is winter-wet/summer-dry, and snow accumulates at the higher elevations. Summers are long, dry, and hot in the south, but lightning ignitions do occur. Schroeder and Buck (1970) indicate about 5 to 20 lightning fires per million acres per year. The vegetation of the chaparral-oak-madrone-digger pine zones is extremely flammable, and in nature was probably subject to periodic, high-intensity fires that killed most of the vegetation. Attempted fire exclusion has created very difficult fire control problems in the chaparral and related vegetation zones (Vogl 1967; Dodge 1972; Biswell 1974; Weaver 1974). The natural fire regime in the ponderosa-Jeffrey pine zones was probably similar to that in the Sierras.

The Coast Redwoods Region

Several small de facto wilderness areas occur within the new Redwoods National Park and in some of the larger California State Redwoods Parks. This region is within the coastal fog belt of northern California—a winter-wet/summer-dry climate, mitigated by fog drip. Elevations are slight, and snow, when it does fall, soon melts. Lightning-caused ignitions occur, although summer thunderstorms are not common. The redwoods were clearly subject to intermittent fires—many of the largest veterans bear deep fire scars hundreds of years old. The natural fire regime was probably one of long-interval, severe surface fires. Redwood sprouts from the root crown, and many groups of trees are sprouts from fire-killed individuals (Fritz 1931; Stone 1965; Stone and Vasey 1968; Stone, Grah, and Zinke 1969).

The Cascades Range of Oregon and Washington

The Cascades are dominated by a series of spectacular geologically recent volcanic peaks, many now included in wilderness areas or National Parks. Designated areas include the North Cascades, Mt. Rainier, and Crater Lake National Parks; and the Glacier Peak, Pasayten, Goat Rocks, Mt. Adams, Mt. Hood, Mt. Jefferson, Mt. Washington, Three Sisters, Diamond Peak, Mountain Lakes, and Alpine Lakes Wilderness Areas. Well-watered, lower elevations on the west side, where included, support magnificent stands of Douglas-fir, western hemlock, western redcedar, grand fir, and in the south also ponderosa pine, sugar pine, and incense cedar. On the drier east side, ponderosa pine and lodgepole pine dominate at lower elevations, and cedar and hemlock are rare or missing. Higher elevations support a complex of vegetation types ranging from stands of lodgepole or western white pine, to forests of noble fir or silver fir, and nearer timberline, Engelmann spruce, subalpine fir, alpine larch, Alaska yellow-cedar, white-bark pine, and mountain hemlock. These forests are complex and varied in their physiographic and altitudinal distributions—and probably also complex in their pattern of past fire occurrence (Franklin and Dyrness 1969, 1973). The climate is winter-wet/summer-dry, and much of the precipitation occurs as snow, which accumulates 10 to 20 feet in depth and persists into July in high-elevation forests. Summer weather is mostly clear and dry, but thunderstorms do occur, and lightning ignitions are frequent. Schroeder and Buck (1970) indicate an occurrence rate of 11 to 40 lightning fires per million acres per year. Late summer is the normal wildfire season. At intervals of several years, major episodes of lightning ignitions may coincide with severe summer drought, causing widespread outbreaks such as the Wenatchee fires of 1970.

On well-watered west slopes the natural fire regime seems to have been mostly one of large-scale but very long-interval crown fires or severe ground fires. Return intervals were perhaps 150 to 500 years or more for various sites. Extensive, even-aged stands of Douglas-fir attest to past fires, and many fire boundaries are still evident. The lower elevation, eastside ponderosa pine forests probably had a regime of frequent, light surface fires. Detailed fire-history work is still needed in this region, especially for westside ecosystems. East of the Cascade Crest, Fahnestock[11] has documented a lightning-caused-fire occurrence rate of 13 fires per million acres per year in the Pasayten Wilderness from 1910 to 1969. Ligntning caused 88 percent of recorded fires, and 78 percent of the area burned. Two fires, each exceeding 20,000 acres, accounted for 59 percent of the lightning-caused burn area. This history suggests a long-return-interval crown fire or severe-surface-fire regime for the Pasayten. Fire control has not yet significantly affected fuels or disrupted the age structure of the forest. Postfire snags stand intact for 20 to 30 years, and fallen snag fuels peak 30 to 60 years after fire.

The Intermountain Region and the Southwest

Between the Cascades-Sierra ranges and the main Rocky Mountain system there is a discontinuous series of more isolated ranges having a vegetation and fire history somewhat different from either province. This region extends from eastern Washington, Idaho, and extreme western Montana south to Arizona and New Mexico. Designated reserves with significant forests include the Cabinet Mountains, Selway-Bitterroot, Eagle Cap, Strawberry Mountain, Sawtooth, Mt. Baldy, Gila, and Chiricahua Wildernesses; the Salmon River Breaks, Idaho, Blue Range, Gila, and Black Range Primitive Areas; and the north rim of Grand Canyon National Park. Ponderosa pine and Douglas-fir occur at lower elevations throughout the region, as does Engelmann spruce at higher elevations. In the north, the better watered, low-elevation west slopes support western larch, western white pine, western hemlock, western redcedar, and grand fir, and the higher elevations support lodgepole, whitebark, and limber pines; alpine larch; subalpine fir; and mountain hemlock (Dauben-mire 1952; Daubenmire and Daubenmire 1968; Franklin and Dyrness 1969; Habeck and Mutch 1973). Quaking aspen occurs sparingly throughout, and in Arizona and New Mexico there are also some blue spruce, white (concolor) fir, and Chihauhua pine. Grassland, meadow, and shrub communities are often interspersed with forest.

The climate retains some Pacific maritime influence, tending toward heavy snow winters and dry summers in the north, with a greater percentage of the precipitation occurring as late summer rains in Arizona and New Mexico. Summer thunderstorms are frequent over the entire region, and lightning ignitions are extremely common because of the frequency of prolonged droughts. Schroeder and Buck (1970) indicate a lightning-fire occurrence rate of 20 to 60 fires per million acres per year for most of the region, but the rate exceeds 60 per million acres in the Arizona-New Mexico mountains. A study of lightning-fire occurrence in the White Cap drainage of the Selway-Bitterroot Wilderness indicated an occurrence rate of about 70 fires per million acres per year for that local situation (Habeck and Mutch 1973). In Idaho and eastern Oregon, the fire season is June through September; but in New Mexico and Arizona, May and June are the major fire months

---

[11] Fahnestock, George F. 1975. Fires, fuels, and flora as factors in wilderness management. Unpublished paper, 31 p., Seattle, Wash.

because of a tendency toward greater rainfall with July and August thunderstorms.

Throughout this region the natural history of ponderosa pine and Douglas-fir stands has been one of small and repeated, light to moderate surface fires at average return intervals of about 6 to 15 years. These fires were severe enough to kill back most of the Douglas-fir regeneration, thin out overdense ponderosa pine saplings, and occasionally kill out individuals, clumps, or small groves of aged ponderosa pine or Douglas-fir. Such a history maintained the parklike ponderosa pine stands originally characteristic of lower elevations throughout the region (Cooper 1961; Weaver 1961, 1974; Habeck and Mutch 1973).

At higher elevations, on some north slopes, and farther north on slopes with more maritime climates, the fire regime has often been one of long-interval (150 to 300 years), severe surface fires or crown fires that killed out whole stands on individual slopes or drainages and regenerated such areas to relatively even aged stands of western white pine, western larch, and lodgepole pine (Wellner 1970; Aldrich and Mutch 1972). In some areas these stands also contain mixtures of western redcedar, western hemlock, and grand fir. It is not clear how much of the northern intermountain region had the first kind of fire regime as opposed to the last, but both were present. Fire suppression in the last 60 years has probably altered fuels and vegetation most in areas that were subject to periodic light surface fires. The heavy-fuel, long-interval, crown-fire-regime areas and higher elevation forests have probably not been affected so much because many areas would not have burned in this period in any case.

The Rocky Mountain Region

The Rocky Mountain system, as discussed here, includes all of the eastern Front Ranges and the secondary western ranges west to, but excluding, the Intermountain and Southwest Region. It extends from Jasper National Park in the Canadian Rockies south to Colorado. Designated reserves include Jasper, Banff, Yoho, Kootenay, and Waterton National Parks in Canada; Glacier, Yellowstone, Grand Teton, and Rocky Mountain National Parks in the United States; the Bob Marshall, Mission Mountains, Scapegoat, Gates of the Mountains, Anaconda-Pintlar, North Absaroka, South Absaroka, Teton, Washakie, Bridger, Mt. Zirkel, Rawah, Eagle Nest, Maroon Bells-Snowmass, West Elk, La Garita, and Weminuche Wildernesses; and the Spanish Peaks, Absaroka, Beartooth, Cloud Peak, Glacier, Popo Agie, High Uintas, Flat Tops, Uncompahgre, and Wilson Mountains Primitive Areas.

The natural vegetation includes forests of lodgepole pine, Engelmann spruce, subalpine fir, and quaking aspen at middle to upper elevations, and in the Canadian Rockies also a scattering of white spruce, black spruce, paper birch, and balsam poplar, plus isolated groves of Douglas-fir along the warmer slopes of the lowest river valleys. In the north, whitebark pine and alpine larch occur near timberline, but southward limber pine replaces these species. In Montana and British Columbia, west-facing slopes with a maritime influence may support local areas of western hemlock, western redcedar, western white pine, western larch, Douglas-fir, and ponderosa pine. In Utah and Colorado, white (concolor) fir occurs on moist, upper elevation sites, and blue spruce is found along streams and benches. At lower elevations the lodgepole pine forests merge with scattered stands of Douglas-fir, and from Montana southward they merge also with ponderosa pine in some localities. Valleys, flats, and benches are often occupied by nearly treeless, grassy parks, meadows, or sagebrush grasslands. Near and above timberline, there are extensive meadows, nearly treeless old burns, and alpine tundra communities (Daubenmire 1943; Oosting and Reed 1952; Horton 1956; Rowe 1959; Marr 1961; Habeck 1968; Day, R. J. 1972; Stringer and La Roi 1970; Loope and Gruell 1973).

The climate is more continental than in the preceding regions, with long, very cold winters at the higher elevations, and warm summers with considerable rainfall, much of it coming in thunderstorms. Snow accumulations are substantial because of sustained freezing weather, but depths and water content are much less than in the Sierras or Cascades, and most forests are free of snow by May or early June. Brief or extended summer droughts are frequent, especially northward. Lightning ignitions are common, but most fires are extinguished by rains that accompany the thunderstorms. Lightning-fire occurrence ranges from about 2 to 15 fires per million acres per year (Schroeder and Buck 1970). Lightning occurrence decreases northward, but summer droughts tend to increase northward, giving the highest fire occurrences in Montana and Colorado. Some fires occur in most years, but it is the infrequent, severe summer droughts that lead to major fire episodes.

Extensive, relatively even aged forests of lodgepole pine and quaking aspen attest to past fires. Burn boundaries are often distinct because of abrupt changes in stand ages and species (Clements 1910; Patten 1969; Taylor 1969; Day, R. J. 1972; Habeck 1970; Loope 1971; Loope and Gruell 1973). Some lodgepole forests are 150 to 350 years old, however, indicating that return intervals can be very long in this region (fire control has only been effective for 30 to 60 years). Cone serotiny in lodgepole varies—most stands in the Yellowstone-Grand Teton region have open cones, while in the Canadian Rockies, Colorado, and elsewhere most cones are closed (Clements 1910; Loope and Gruell 1973). Some Yellowstone Park stands have developed multiple-age structures through creeping surface fires, or in some cases through stand breakup due to long periods without fire. In the Grand Teton region, the Canadian Rockies, and elsewhere subalpine fir is now invading lodgepole pine stands, perhaps on an unnatural scale due to fire exclusion (Day, R.J. 1972; Loope and Gruell 1973). Fir contributes to fuels and provides ladder fuels that facilitate crown fires, but if such fires occur these areas will revert to nearly pure lodgepole pine.

Outbreaks of the native mountain pine bark beetle (*Dendroctonus ponderosae*) in old lodgepole pine stands have occurred sporadically over the centuries. Since 1960 large areas have been attacked in the Grand Teton-Yellowstone region, killing 10 to 45 percent of the trees in many stands. Fire exclusion may be accelerating such attacks because an excess of older stands is slowly being created. This insect has influenced lodgepole ecosystems for millenia, and is simply another factor in the natural fuels cycle (Loope and Gruell 1973).

Engelmann spruce and subalpine fir stands often occur in valleys, coves, and around lakes and streams where they escape most fires, but many stands are also clearly of fire origin (Day, R.J. 1972; Loope and Gruell 1973). Most quaking aspen stands were fire maintained through root suckering, but fire exclusion has prevented their renewal for 60 years, and many stands that might have burned are now decadent (Gruell and Loope 1974).

Fire has also been a factor in maintaining meadow and grassland communities in the parks of river valleys and flats. Ancient, fire-scarred Douglas-firs occurring in groves or as scattered individuals along the margins of these local grasslands tell of their fire history from Jasper Park in the north to the Yellowstone-Grand Teton Region in the south (Stringer and La Roi 1970); Houston 1973; Loope and Gruell 1973; Tande 1975). Fires apparently burned these grassland, meadow, and sagebrush areas, and crept into the Douglas-fir groves around their margins, at intervals of about 6 to 60 years over at least the past 400 years. The average return interval in Yellowstone Park for several sites ranged from 17 to 41 years (Houston 1973). Both lightning and Indian ignitions were probably involved, but lightning alone is clearly a major ignition factor. Fire exclusion is now allowing the invasion of lodgepole pine in many of these open areas and thereby eliminating much valuable wildlife habitat.

In summary, the two dominant fire regimes in most of the primeval Rocky Mountain wilderness were (1) long-return-interval (perhaps 100 to 300 years) crown fires or severe surface fires in most of the continuous forests of lodgepole pine, spruce-fir, and associated species; and (2) shorter return interval (perhaps 5 to 60 years), light to moderate surface fires in lower elevation Douglas-fir, aspen, and ponderosa pine stands, in grassy parklands, and in adjacent, open, lodgepole pine groves.

The Lake Superior Region

The ancient Laurentian highlands surrounding Lake Superior contain several reserves that include the last major remnants of the old "Northwoods." Included are Isle Royale and Voyageur's National Parks; Quetico Provincial Park, Ontario; the adjacent Boundary Waters Canoe Area (BWCA) in Minnesota; and Porcupine Mountains State Park in Michigan. This is spectacular lake country, and together these areas contain several thousand small- to medium-sized lakes, largely in glacially dammed bedrock basins. All areas have had some logging, but more than a million acres of virgin country still remain, largely in the BWCA-Quetico area and on Isle Royale.

The forests are transitional between the original white pine-northern hardwood forests of the Northeast and boreal forests of northern Ontario. All areas still contain some eastern white pine and red pine, although many older stands were cut between 1890 and 1940. Boreal elements predominate in the BWCA and Quetico, where extensive stands of jack pine, black spruce, and white spruce-balsam fir alternate with quaking aspen and paper birch. The Porcupine Mountains and Isle Royale also contain forests of sugar maple, yellow birch, red maple, basswood, red oak, and American elm, intermingled with white pine, white spruce, balsam fir, and northern white-cedar, and in the Porcupines also with eastern hemlock. Sugar maple and hemlock are absent from the BWCA, Quetico, and Voyageur's; and red maple, yellow birch, and basswood are much less common there. There are many peat bogs supporting stunted black spruce and tamarack. Northern white-cedar is prominent around many lakeshores and drainages, and black ash, elm, and balsam poplar occur along streams (Cooper 1913; Graham 1941; Rowe 1959; Horton and Bedell 1960; Ohmann and Ream 1971; Krefting, Hansen and Meyer 1970; Heinselman 1973; Grigal and Ohmann 1975).

The climate is continental, with long, cold winters and short, warm summers. Annual precipitation averages about 28 inches, 64 percent falling as rain during the May through September growing season. Annual snowfall

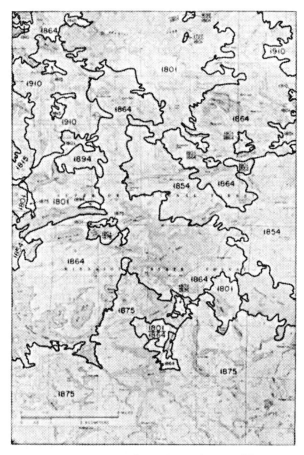

Figure 12-2.—Fire—a natural component of many wilderness ecosystems—is one of the most significant factors affecting the composition of plant and animal life. This map shows the fire history in a portion of the Boundary Waters Canoe Area, Minn., marking the birth of existing forest stands. Fires dating into the late 1600's have been mapped.

averages only about 70 inches, but the ground is snowcovered from mid-November to April because of sustained low temperatures. Thunderstorms are common from May through September. Lightning ignitions are frequent, but most are extinguished by rains accompanying the storms. Dry storms do occur, however, and lightning-fire occurrence is about 1 to 5 fires per million acres per year (Schroeder and Buck 1970). The fire season is from May through October, with peaks in May and late September when the vegetation is cured. Fast-moving crown fires are most frequent in spring and fall (Haines and Sando 1969; Sando and Haines 1972). Summer fires may occur in coniferous stands, especially in July and August during extended drought.

The primeval vegetation was strongly fire dependent (Maissurow 1935; Spurr 1954; Ahlgren 1959a, 1959b, 1974; Frissell 1973; Heinselman 1973; Swain 1973).

Despite 60 years of fire control, most virgin stands still contain overstory elements dating from the last fire, the major exception perhaps being some of the northern hardwood forests of Isle Royale and the Porcupine Mountains. Virgin jack pine, black spruce, and aspen-birch forests usually date very closely from the last fire, and most jack pine stands here have closed cones. Some stands of red and white pine and spruce-fir contain groves or scattered trees of two or more age classes, each dating from separate fires. The time of origin of red and white pine stands commonly ranges up to 10 or 15 years after dated fires, indicating extended periods of regeneration. Red pine stands frequently show multiple fire scars, proof that moderate surface fires were common in that type. In the BWCA and Quetico the areas burned most intensely are large uplands distant from natural firebreaks such as lakes and streams. Jack pine, black spruce, and aspen-birch types dominate such sites. The mineral soil areas burned least intensely are swamp edges, ravines, lakeshores, islands, lower slopes, and the east, northeast, or southeast sides of large lakes. White pine, red pine, white spruce, cedar, and fir are relatively more abundant there. However, on Isle Royale and in the Porcupine Mountains the northern hardwoods occupy certain high ridges and jack pine is rare. This difference is related to the local climatic influence of Lake Superior, where the northern hardwoods forest reaches its northern limit. Wildlife habitat patterns and use are also strongly fire controlled (Mech 1966; Hansen, Krefting, and Kurmis 1973; Heinselman 1973).

The natural fire regime of most coniferous forests was one of long-interval crown fires or severe surface fires. Return intervals for most jack pine, black spruce, spruce-fir, and associated aspen-birch areas were probably 50 to 150 years. However, many red and white pine sites had a regime of light to moderate surface fires at return intervals of 20 to 40 years, combined with long or very long interval crown fires or severe surface fires. These killed much of the stand at intervals of 150 to 300 years and resulted in new regeneration. Most of the area burned and most stand origins in the BWCA in the last 300 years can be accounted for in about a dozen fire years (Heinselman 1973). This history suggests that most of the ecologically significant fires occurred during infrequent periods of severe drought. There were many other fires, but they account for only small areas. The natural fire rotation for the BWCA as a whole is about 100 years. This is still the only region where studies of charcoal stratigraphy in annually laminated lake sediments have been combined with pollen analysis to document the pre-Columbian fire regime (Swain 1973;

261

Wright, H.E. 1974). This work shows that periodic forest fires have occurred in the region for at least 9,300 years.

The Boreal Forest Region

This vast region stretches from Quebec and Labrador across northern Canada to interior Alaska (Rowe 1959; Helmers 1974). Only a few forested nature reserves having wilderness qualities have yet been designated, but great areas are still de facto wilderness, and more reserves may be established. Present reserves where the forests are protected from exploitation include Riding Mountain, Prince Albert, Wood Buffalo, and South Nahanni River National Parks in Canada; and Mt. McKinley National Park in Alaska.

The forests are relatively simple for so vast a region. Jack pine, from Quebec to Alberta and lodgepole pine, from Alberta into the Yukon, are the only pines. White and black spruce cross the continent. Balsam fir occurs from Quebec to western Alberta, but is replaced by subalpine fir from there into the Yukon. Northern white-cedar occurs only from Quebec to Manitoba, but tamarack crosses the continent. Quaking aspen, balsam poplar and paper birch are virtually the only broadleaf trees, and all cross the continent. The pines and fir generally disappear in the forest-tundra transition region and are absent from interior Alaska. The limit of trees is generally attained only by the two spruce, tamarack, and here and there by stunted aspen, birch, or balsam poplar. Large and small lakes and boggy peatlands abound. Thick humus accumulations occur on many upland sites. Moss or lichen ground cover that ignites readily when dry occurs in most spruce and in many pine stands (Rowe 1959; Ritchie 1962; Rowe and Scotter 1973; Viereck 1973).

The climate is characterized by long, very cold winters and a winter-dry/summer-wet precipitation pattern. Annual precipitation decreases northwestward from 35 to 45 inches in northern Quebec to only 10 to 15 inches in the Yukon and interior Alaska. Snow accumulations are generally light, especially in the northwest, but snow covers the ground from mid-October to May. Summers are normally cool, with occasional light rains, but extended droughts with long periods of warm, clear weather do occur, especially in the northwest. The long days of these northern latitudes permit severe drying, and there may be little cooling or humidity increase during the short nights of June and July. Thunderstorms are much less frequent than in southern climates, but lightning ignitions nevertheless occur because ground fuels and arboreal lichens ignite readily during droughts.

The lightning-fire occurrence rate is reported to be less than one fire per million acres per year (Schroeder and Buck 1970), but subregional variations probably exist.

Lightning is a major cause of fire in the more remote regions, and individual fires often burn vast areas. In the 7 years 1961 through 1967, 44 percent of all fires in the northern Canadian territories were lightning caused, and they accounted for 78 percent of the total area burned (Rowe and Scotter 1973). In the Mackenzie valley, lightning is the major cause of all fires (Rowe et al. 1974). In a 40,000-square-mile study area northeast of Ft. Smith, Northwest Territory, on the wintering ground of the Beverley caribou herd, lightning caused 85 percent of all fires from 1966 to 1972, and accounted for 99.9 percent of the area burned (Johnson and Rowe 1975). In the Alaskan interior, fires still burn an average of 1 million acres yearly, and for the period 1940 to 1969, lightning ignitions accounted for 78 percent of the area burned (Hardy and Franks 1963; Barney 1971; Viereck 1973).

The typical, natural fire regime is one of long-interval crown fires or severe surface fires, killing most of the stands in given areas. Black spruce, jack pine, lodgepole pine, and aspen-birch forests all regenerate promptly in response to such a regime; and vast, even-aged forests of these species are common wherever they occur. Some jack pine and lodgepole pine areas also experience moderate surface fires that do not kill all of the stand, as near Fort Simpson, Northwest Territory (Rowe et al. 1974). The return intervals for many vegetation types are probably in the 80 to 150 year range (MacLean and Bedell 1955; Horton 1956; Rowe 1970; Rowe and Scotter 1973; Viereck 1973; Rowe et al. 1974). On the winter range of the Beverley caribou herd, fires burned an average of 0.9 percent of the area annually from 1966 to 1972 (Johnson and Rowe 1975). Most of the area burned in given subregions probably burns during major droughts which recur at intervals of 10 to 40 years (MacLean and Bedell 1955; Rowe and others 1974).

There has been debate about how much the arrival of Europeans has changed the fire regime and whether any changes have affected the vegetation and the winter range of caribou (Lutz 1956; Scotter 1964; Rowe and Scotter 1973; Viereck 1973; Bergerud 1974; Johnson and Rowe 1975). Areas near settlements clearly did see an early increase in fires, and recently a decrease due to fire control. But the evidence now indicates that most of the more remote country is still an essentially pristine environment, with little change in fire regimes and few other human impacts that could have altered the vegetation (Viereck 1973; Johnson and Rowe 1975).

The Eastern Deciduous Forest, Appalachian, and Gulf Coast Regions

Many small- to medium-sized wilderness units have been designated or are under study in the Appalachian Mountains from Maine, New Hampshire, and New York south to South Carolina, and in scattered other localities throughout the Southeast and Midwest. Already protected are Baxter State Park in Maine, Adirondack State Park in New York, the Great Smoky Mountains National Park, and the following wildernesses under Forest Service jurisdiction: Presidential Range-Dry River, Great Gulf (New Hampshire); Bristol Cliffs, Lye Brook (Vermont); Dolly Sods, Otter Creek (West Virginia); Rainbow Lake (Wisconsin); Linville Gorge (North Carolina); Joyce Kilmer-Slickrock (North Carolina, Tennessee); James River Face (Virginia); Caney Creek, Upper Buffalo (Arkansas); Beaver Creek (Kentucky); Ellicott Rock (Georgia, North Carolina, South Carolina); Gee Creek (Tennessee); Cohutta (Georgia, Tennessee); Sipsey (Alabama); and Bradwell Bay (Florida). There are also several forested wildlife refuges with wilderness status. The vegetation of this large region is too diverse and complex to treat here, but in general it is largely a mixture of broadleaf hardwoods, including sugar and red maples, yellow birch, beech, many oaks and hickories, tulip poplar, ash, elm, cherry, several other hardwoods, several pines (especially eastern white pine and shortleaf), eastern hemlock, and in the high mountains and the northeast also balsam fir, Fraser fir, red spruce, and northern white-cedar. In addition, parts of the coastal plain support large areas of the southern pines (longleaf, loblolly, slash).

The climate varies considerably from north to south and also locally because of the influence of the Appalachians and the ocean. However, from the fire-occurrence standpoint, five generalizations apply: (1) Precipitation is abundant (35 to 75 inches annually) and well-distributed through the seasons; (2) temperatures are relatively high and severe, short term droughts do occur; (3) winter snowcover is variable and of short duration except in the higher and northern mountains; (4) thunderstorms are frequent, but most are accompanied by enough rain to extinguish lightning ignitions; (5) decomposition of forest fuels and humus is rapid because of the mild and humid climate. These climatic patterns probably produced a natural fire regime that involved infrequent dormant-season surface fires in the deciduous hardwood forests, and perhaps somewhat more frequent, but still very long-return-interval fires in most conifer-hardwood and conifer forests. The southern coastal plain pine region is clearly an exception, however,

because frequent light surface fires were abundant there (Komarek 1974). Lightning fires still do occur in pine and pine-hardwood forests in Great Smoky Mountains National Park and adjacent areas, but most fires are surface fires that do not greatly change the forest composition (Barden and Woods 1973). The pine component of such forests may have been maintained in the past by crown fires or very severe surface fires that occurred only at long intervals in exceptional droughts. The lightning fire season in the southern Appalachians is April through August, with 40 percent of all fires occurring in May (Barden 1974).

Deliberate burning by Indians and early settlers was widespread. Essentially all areas outside reserves have also had their forest cover modified by commercial logging, fuelwood cutting, or land clearing at some time during the past 400 years. Thus the influence of man has been more intense here than in other areas of North America. Both the American chestnut and the American elm have largely been eliminated by introduced fungi. Fire-history studies based on tree-ring and fire-scar evidence are difficult to conduct because most of the evidence has been lost through cutting or rapid tree growth. For most of these areas, the ecosystem management problem is thus largely one of restoration, and natural fire may not be very important. Where fire was important, detailed local studies will be essential to elucidate its role.

The Everglades, Wetlands, Prairies, and Deserts

Wilderness units have already been established or proposed for a wide spectrum of chiefly nonforest wetland, prairie, or desert grass and shrub ecosystems. Many of these units are within the National Wildlife Refuge System or the National Park System, but there are also several Forest Service units with desert shrub ecosystems in the Southwest. Fire was a vital factor in many of these ecosystems (see Robertson 1962; Humphrey 1974; Komarek 1974; Vogl 1974). A review of the many varied local situations is beyond the scope of this chapter. Managers must carefully study the natural role of fire in each area, and where evidence indicates important effects, a fire management program is indicated.

Factors that Control Natural Fire Regimes

An understanding of certain basic factors will help fire managers develop policy and can guide interim policies where the natural regimes is poorly known.

263

1. *Lightning*. Occurrence is most frequent in the South, especially over the southwestern mountains and in the southeastern states, and decreases northward more or less systematically, but some thunderstorms do occur to the northern timberline and even in arctic tundra regions. The probability of lightning-caused ignition is related to seasonal climatic patterns and thunderstorm characteristics. Other factors being equal, areas with heavier total precipitation and summer rainfall climates will experience fewer ignitions for a given amount of thunderstorm activity than areas with lighter total precipitation and/or winter-wet/summer-dry climates.

2. *Fuel production.* The amount of fuel produced influences both the probability and severity of fires. In general, total biotic production is higher in the South and at lower elevations and decreases northward and with increasing elevation. Total annual precipitation often obscures this trend, however. When temperature and precipitation are integrated, the highest areas of fuel production can be identified, and such areas are now well known.

3. *Fuel accumulation.* Independent of production, fuel tends to increase northward, with increasing elevation and decreasing moisture. It is relatively greater in summer-dry as opposed to summer-wet climates because decomposition increases both with temperature and available moisture (up to the point of oxygen deficiency, at which the moisture trend is reversed).

4. *Elevation.* The life zones of high mountain ranges integrates the temperature gradient caused by elevation, slope, and aspect, and are a guide to the effective temperature regime. A few thousand feet of elevation can be equivalent to several hundred miles of latitude in the resultant effect on fire regimes.

5. *Other Factors.* Precipitation patterns and temperatures, when integrated with lightning occurrence, fuel production, and fuel accumulation results in a systematic and understandable distribution of natural, lightning-caused fire regimes. These regimes can be summarized as follows.

The Continental Pattern of Lightning-Fire Regimes

In the California mountains, at the lower elevations of the Intermountain Region, in the Southwest, and in the Southern Pine Region of the Gulf States, the *natural* lightning-fire regime is one of frequent light to moderate surface fires, with a return interval of usually not longer than 5 to 25 years. Such fires tend to be relatively small in area (if there have not been unnatural fuel accumulations due to fire exclusion). These characteristics are the result of high lightning occurrence during favorable weather,

and a production/accumulation balance that provides rapid replacement of light, flammable fuels, but prevents heavy accumulations, especially in the presence of periodic fires. Crown fires and severe ground fires that kill stands might be mostly the result of man-caused fuel accumulations, but even in these regions, before man's influence became significant, fuels and weather probably did combine to produce violent fire behavior in local areas at very long intervals.

In the Cascades, the higher elevations of the Rockies, the higher elevations and higher precipitation areas of the Intermountain Region, the northern Lake Superior Region, and the Boreal Forest, the *natural* lightning fire regime is chiefly one of long-return-interval crown fires or severe surface fires, with return intervals on most sites in excess of 75 years and in many areas in excess of 200 to 300 years. Such fires tend to be large in area, although fire size varies widely with the local physiographic setting. These regime characteristics are due to combinations of reduced lightning occurrence (as in the boreal forest), low annual production but high net-accumulation of fuels, or climates that are normally too moist for effective ignitions (west slopes of Cascades, Lake Superior Region, many places in the Rockies). At the lower elevations, in the drier portions of these regions, where droughts are common; and in the most flammable vegetation types, light to moderate surface fires with return intervals of 5 to 40 years occurred in some areas, but these are not typical patterns for most of these regions.

In the Eastern Deciduous Forest, lightning-caused fires probably occurred only at rather long intervals, during the dormant season, usually only in the most flammable types (such as oak or oak-pine) and then were not very severe in most cases. This is so because total precipitation is high; summer rains are usually abundant; and the warm, humid summers promote rapid decay of forest fuels. In addition, the litter of most broadleaf deciduous trees is less resistant to decay and less flammable than that of most conifers. There are exceptions, but for this reason also, many broadleaf deciduous forests probably had less lightning-caused fire than would conifer forests in the same physical setting.

Fire Policy Alternatives and their Consequences

There are five theoretically available policy alternatives with respect to fire: (1) Fire exclusion, (2) no fire-control program, (3) management of lightning-caused fires, (4) prescribed fire, (5) mechanical manipulation of vegetation and fuels. Combinations are obviously possible, but it is useful to describe each separately. Failure to pursue a conscious policy will still result in the unintended or haphazard implementation of one or more of these same options.

Fire Exclusion

A fire-exclusion policy requires the immediate suppression of all fires, regardless of cause, location, or expected damage. It might fail in application, but if the policy requires prompt suppression, without exceptions, then the objective is to exclude fire from the ecosystem. Until very recently, this has been the standard policy in most wildernesses and National Parks, and it remains the policy in many. At the very least it is often defensible as a holding action until the expertise and equipment to implement a more desirable option are available, or until a rational judgment concerning the best alternative can be made. However, if it is known that an ecosystem was strongly fire dependent, then managers must recognize that fire exclusion is really a powerful form of vegetation manipulation. It requires personnel, machines, and large inputs of scarce management funds. In most areas, fire exclusion is really a large-scale ecological experiment because, if the natural system was fire dependent, we have no way of foretelling the ultimate consequences. If the policy succeeds, there will probably be major changes in both vegetation and wildlife populations and perhaps also major breakdowns in the productivity, diversity, and stability of the ecosystem.

Another problem resulting from a policy of fire exclusion is a buildup of forest fuels. We do not really know the extent of the fuel accumulation problem, because in most ecosystems it is not clear how long fuels would continue to increase without fire. But in the kinds of ecosystems we are discussing here, fire was one of nature's ways of reducing fuels and recycling biomass and nutrients. With both lightning and man as sources of ignition, one wonders if fire exclusion is really a viable option in such ecosystems. Perhaps, in following a policy of exclusion, we are only setting the stage for a major conflagration which could not only be dangerous to human life and property, but disruptive to the very ecosystems we are purportedly protecting. Fire exclusion often requires the use of bulldozers or other heavy line-building equipment, aircraft, smoke jumpers, and retardants. When major fires threaten lives or property outside the wilderness, managers are tempted to use all available techniques, regardless of the consequences to wilderness resources. Fire exclusion, if practiced too long, can therefore force managers to inflict major damage on the landscape in the name of saving the wilderness from fire. Recent experience with the erosion of tractor-built

fire lines in Alaska is a good example of the kind of lasting environmental damage that can occur from fire suppression (Viereck 1973). Unless there is good reason to believe that fire is not a significant factor in the ecosystem, fire exclusion should be rejected except as an interim measure.

No Fire-Control Program

A no fire-control program is the opposite of fire exclusion. It is even less acceptable, unless fire is essentially impossible in the ecosystem. The reason is that such a program endangers human life and property—including lives and property beyond wilderness boundaries. Responsible management must provide for the safety of persons and property—certainly outside the wilderness, to say nothing of visitors and Agency personnel within the area. Some fire protection people might believe that fire ecologists advocate complete cessation of fire control, but actually no informed and responsible person would be so callous. This option must be rejected outright.

Management of Lightning-Caused Fires

A policy of managing lightning-caused fires rests on the belief that they are natural and desirable in wilderness ecosystems. Such a policy attempts to restore such fires to their natural status *safely* by protecting lives and property, and by minimizing unacceptable effects on wilderness resources due to unnatural fuel accumulations. The approach is simply one of avoiding direct manipulation as much as possible by allowing nature to select the time, place, vegetation, and fuels for fires through lightning ignitions. The management involves selective fire control based on both safety and ecological considerations.[12] This is a new and viable approach to the fire problem for many areas and we will be discussing it further.

Prescribed Fire

The goal of a prescribed-fire policy is the restoration of the natural fire regime through the substitution of deliberate ignitions for lightning-caused fires. It is based on the assumption that the ecological effects of fire will be the same, whether man or lightning caused. This assumption is not totally valid, however. While it might be possible, through skillful firing, to create significant burns that closely resemble lightning-caused fires, it might also be possible to burn in seasons when lightning never occurs, or at closer than natural intervals. These circumstances should not alone preclude the use of

---

[12] See Kilgore 1972; Habeck and Mutch 1973; Agee 1974; Daniels 1974.

Figure 12-3.—Efficient fire control using pack strings, helicopters. smoke jumpers, and aerial fire-retardant bombing has contributed to less than natural levels of fire in some wildernesses.

prescribed fire. The basic reason for this option is the belief, often valid, that fires can more often be managed safely if the time and place of ignition are selected in advance, thus allowing time to ready personnel and equipment, work with weather forecasts, make fuel assessments, and prepare lines (Kilgore 1970; Heinselman 1971a, 1973; Agee 1974). This option is also explored below in greater detail.

Mechanical Manipulation of Vegetation and Fuels

Another policy rejects fire, both lightning caused and prescribed, as an unacceptable or unsafe agent of change, and substitutes mechanical manipulations—e.g., harvest of the forest, soil disturbance, planting—for the periodic, natural perturbations caused by fire. Safety is usually given as the reason for favoring this option (Kaufert

1964). Vegetation removal need not be commercially motivated, and no product or biomass must necessarily be moved from the site. (In fact, it would be *illegal* to sell the timber in either a wilderness or National Park under present U.S. statutes.)

There are several ecological problems with this approach, however. First, if the vegetation is felled mechanically, it is not clear how the forest biomass can be recycled promptly. If fire is used *after* cutting, the safety problem still remains. A more basic concern is that the ecological effects of mechanical manipulation are subject to a manager's decisions, his skills, and his knowledge. Theoretically, it is possible to *simulate* many of the effects of fire by mechanical means, but the result is artificial—a simulation. And, in wilderness, naturalness is a prime objective.

266

The extent of ecosystem control involved in mechanical manipulation can best be seen through an example. Consider an attempt to reproduce an old lodgepole pine-Engelmann spruce-subalpine fir forest. The manager would have to decide how large an area to cut, which trees to fell and which to leave, how to prepare the soil, whether to seed or plant, which species and what seed sources to use, how *much* seed, and *when* to sow. Furthermore, it is not clear how the ecological or esthetic effects of standing snags would be simulated, nor how stumps could be avoided.

An important criticism of such widespread control is that the scientific values associated with natural vegetation would be lost when virgin forests are heavily manipulated. As a method of restoring vegetation already altered by commercial logging, the method might have some merit. The question of *degree* of mechanical manipulation is also involved. What about a minimal amount of cutting in advance of prescribed burning to reduce fuels, to prepare firelines, to fell snags or birch trees to avoid long-distance spotting? These are questions that must be weighed carefully and spelled out in management plans. Once a little manipulation is begun, it is easy to conclude that more would be better. At some point the whole concept of natural ecosystems is sacrificed, and a managed forest is substituted. If carried very far, this alternative becomes *silviculture*, not wilderness preservation. Silviculture has its place—but not in wilderness management.

Restoring Fire to Wilderness Ecosystems
Objectives

A basic theme of this book is that clearly established objectives underlie management actions. Fire restoration is clearly a situation where understanding the objective must precede planning or implementation. The basic objective for most fire-restoration situations can be simply stated as: *To restore fire to its natural role in the ecosystem to the maximum extent consistent with safety of persons, property, and other resources.* Note that the goal is *not* to produce any specific mix of vegetation types, to create desirable wildlife habitat, to reduce fuels, to improve esthetics, or to attain related specific benefits. Some of these benefits might accrue from a successful program, but the objective is to *restore the naturalness of the environment and let natural processes take over.* This will help to produce an ecosystem "where the earth and its community of life are untrammelled by man." Such an objective is in keeping with a biocentric focus for wilderness management, which places strong emphasis

on preservation of the natural physical and biotic wilderness resources (Hendee and Stankey 1973).

The Need for Historical Data

The objective requires a careful effort to determine *what the natural role of fire actually was.* In general, this means that the manager should have the clearest possible definition of the presettlement fire regime. His information should include the following:
1. Causes of past fires.
2. Seasonal, geographic, and long-term patterns of lightning ignitions.
3. Character of past fires—i.e., their type, intensity, ecological effects, and return intervals.
4. Characteristic return intervals for specific vegetation types and physiographic situations.
5. Typical *sizes* of burns.
6. Fire exclusion programs—extent of their application and degree of success.
7. Natural fuels mosaic—before and during fire protection.

If specific historical information cannot be obtained, managers must reconstruct the probable situation through inferences from literature and from studying the natural vegetation, climate, and geographic setting.

Safety

Fires are dangerous. The intelligent manager will never allow his enthusiasm for restoring the ecosystem to override safety considerations. In recent years most fire fatalities have been sustained by firefighters. Great care must be exercised to build personnel safety into all fire management plans, but there is also potential danger in any fire to wilderness visitors, nearby residents, travelers, and in some cases even to nearby towns and villages. Visitors can be directed away from fire areas or evacuated if necessary. Closure of fire areas is possible. But the responsibility for keeping fires away from homes, villages, roads, powerlines, structures, and commercial forests outside the wilderness is absolute. Wilderness fire programs that jeopardize the lives or property of people not involved in the use or management of an area will not be tolerated by our society—and rightfully so.

Enclaves of development within major nature reserves, such as those in Yellowstone or Jasper National Parks, present special problems that must be realistically faced. For example, in some areas it might be possible to use managed lightning-caused fires in the backcountry, but only prescribed fire somewhat nearer the enclaves, and chiefly mechanical manipulation in their immediate vicinity. In many cases the only other safe approach would be to phase out such enclaves.

Definition of "Fire Management" and "Managed Fires"

Wilderness fire management is the deliberate reintroduction of fire to achieve stated wilderness objectives in a naturally fire-dependent ecosystem through the execution of technically sound plans under specific prescriptions.

Management fires can be either naturally caused (lightning or volcanic ignition) or prescribed burns, depending on the fire plan for specific areas. But all fires that do not meet preplanned criteria—and this includes all man-caused fires other than deliberately ignited management burns—are wildfires and should be suppressed. Not only is it unacceptable to allow carelessness to dictate wilderness fire effects, but such fires also tend to have unnatural location patterns.

Managed Lightning-Caused Fire Versus Prescribed Fire

The basic objective of wilderness fire programs is to return fire to its natural role as an environmental factor. Natural ignitions, natural fire patterns, and fire behavior are preferred over human ignitions and heavily directed fire behavior. Fire programs are really needed only if there is concern (1) about safety or (2) about unnatural ecosystem effects due to prior fire exclusion. Unfortunately, one or both concerns are often justified. The guiding principle in choosing between a managed lightning-fire program, prescribed burning, or some combination should be this: If not precluded by safety or ecological concerns, managed lightning fires are preferred. However, safety concerns might dictate that only prescribed fires will be used near the wilderness perimeter, near enclaves of development, in very small wildernesses, in high visitor-use areas, and in ecosystems where it is known that natural fires tend to be high-intensity crown fires or severe and fast-moving surface fires. If it appears that unnatural fuel accumulations might cause fire to kill overstory trees and it is unlikely that natural fires will be large or fast moving enough to reduce the fuels, prescribed fires can be used to do the job.

Combinations of lightning fire and prescribed fire for certain problem situations often make the most sense. It is also possible to enhance the area or movement of a lightning fire by skillful firing of key perimeters. Such work might be justified when a fire is obviously doing a safe job or reducing unnatural and potentially dangerous fuels. The key here is the word *unnatural*. If the fuels are believed to be unaffected by past human action, then the

fire should be allowed to proceed naturally until it reaches its own final perimeter. Enhancement of natural fires might also be justified in some cases simply to get it over with sooner, to cut costs, or to reduce the duration of smoke production. In another sense, though, the distinction between prescribed fires and natural fires can become blurred. For even where managers rely on lightning ignitions, they must have the option of suppressing certain perimeters, or even the entire fire, if they anticipate unacceptable safety problems or resource damage.

Another aspect of prescribed burning that must be faced is the possibility of artifically modifying fuel in advance of burning to achieve desired results. The only tenable position is that modification should be used only if burning unnatural fuel accumulations (caused by fire exclusion) would otherwise cause unacceptable ecological effects or safety problems. Usually such fuels can be reduced in stages with several light burns. Snag felling, cutting of paper birch trees (to avoid spotting) and other advance treatments of fuels are questionable actions in wilderness and should be prohibited unless essential to assure the success of prescribed fires.

The natural ignition pattern is a vital key to restoring the natural vegetation mosaic. This is why lightning

Figure 12–4.—Lightning is nature's primary source of ignition in wilderness ecosystems.

268

ignitions are preferred. If we let nature choose the time, the place, and fuels, then a natural ecosystem should result. If prescribed burning is used exclusively, the ignition patterns are crucial. One possibility is to identify defensible burning blocks bordered by natural fire barriers, and then to randomly select the blocks to be fired each year. Another approach is to wait for lightning ignitions in such blocks, extinguish the resulting fires and then reignite them under favorable circumstances.

The Wilderness Fire Management Plan

Wilderness fire plans should include some—or all—of the following elements which have been synthesized from plans, proposals, guidelines, and other Forest Service and National Park Service writings.[13]

Objectives or Introduction

The objectives for the total wilderness fire program should be clearly spelled out and related to other objectives of the wilderness unit and the managing Agency.

Descriptions and Maps of Landscape Units

Planning must be tied to on-the-ground conditions relevant to fire behavior, control problems, and ecological effects. For this purpose it is often useful to identify significant landscape units on large-scale maps and/or aerial photographs. Standard ecological land units (ELU's), habitat types, vegetation types, or physiographic units are concepts that can usually be used. Mapping units should have reasonable homogeneity with respect to their gross vegetation, expected range of fuels, and major physiographic variables (e.g., topography, climate, geology, soils).

Fire History and Natural Fire Regime

Historical data, fire-scar chronologies, stand-origin data, and pertinent publications, maps, and photographs should be summarized. The detail is less important than the manager's concept of *the kind of natural fire regime to be restored*. Return intervals for fires in key vegetation types and landscape units should be given if known, and the character of ecologically significant fires described (typical fire size, behavior, intensity). Differences in fire regimes and effects between landscape units should be described.

[13] See Aldrich and Mutch 1972, 1973; Kilgore and Briggs 1972; Habeck and Mutch 1973; Agee 1974; Daniels 1974; Gunzel 1974; Moore 1974; Mutch 1974; Van Wagtendonk 1974; Kilgore 1975; Reese et al. 1975.

Fuels

A workable classification of the important fuel types in the area should be given or established if not already available. Descriptions of fuel types, based on field work if possible, should be included. Fuel loading and rate-of-spread estimates should be given. Maps of at least the more hazardous fuel areas might be included.

Weather Regime

A concise summary of important weather variables and of historic fire weather for the specific area is needed, along with descriptions of safe-but-workable burning weather and "red flag" unacceptable conditions.

Potential Impacts Outside the Wilderness

A discussion of potential problem areas in control, and of other impacts on resources (e.g., smoke abatement) or values outside the wilderness is needed.

The Action Plan

Following the same planning heirarchy explained in chapter 8, the fire management plan must be aimed at achieving clearly-stated objectives for fire within the wilderness and set forth the policies and actions that must be carried out to attain those objectives.

Guiding principles and decisions that influence prescriptions and action plans should be explicit. These might include (a) *goals* (e.g., restoration of the natural fire regime); (b) *scope of prescriptions* (e.g., will they be limited to protecting life and property, or will they extend to protecting resources adjoining the wilderness boundary); and (c) *decisions that establish priorities and guide actions* (e.g., will fires be limited to lightning-caused ignitions, or will prescribed or visitor-caused burns be acceptable? Under what conditions?).

Prescriptions that define action should be tied to landscape units (and, in some cases, to specific fuel or vegetation types); specify seasons or dates and the Buildup-Index (BUI) or other measures of antecedent conditions under which burning will be permitted; and define acceptable limits for fuel moisture, relative humidity, windspeed, and temperatures. If prescribed burning is involved, both lower and upper limits must be specified and based on restoration of the natural ecosystem and avoidance of unacceptable risks. Only upper limits that will avoid serious control problems need be set for managed lightning-caused fires. If too conservative, they can be changed later. For the management of lightning-caused fires the plan must define three general sets of conditions: (1) Conditions under which a fire will only be put under competent technical observation, (2) conditions under which a fire will be suppressed, and (3) conditions under which portions of a fire might be observed, while other portions will be selectively suppressed. There must be clear language to the effect that *all fires will be suppressed if they jeopardize* human life, valuable cultural resources, or species of endangered wildlife, or if they threaten to exceed prescriptions or to escape from predetermined zones or from the wilderness unit unless there are cooperative agreements with another agency that provide for such cases. Prescriptions should be summarized in chart form for dispatching purposes.

A section should include a narrative flow chart or table and a map that integrates prescriptions into *pre-attack or ignition and control plans*. The chart should be *immediately available* to the fire dispatcher, all aerial observers and lookouts, and key supervisory personnel. The narrative should cover preattack items for each landscape unit. Maps should identify key features and locations of specific actions such as potential control-line locations, burnout areas, campsites, access routes, helispots, airfields, and air-tanker sources. This part of the fire plan should include travel times, a communications plan, and equipment availability and locations. Also needed are clear statements of policy—on line-construction equipment and standards, use of retardants, and fuel modification in advance of burning. For prescribed burning, both long-range and annual plans are needed, the latter prepared during the off-season and based on progress toward long-range objectives and the previous year's experience.

The safety plan should specify protective measures for fire crews, supervisory personnel, visitors, threatened homes, villages, facilities, and other property under given contingencies, including wildfires not related to management fires.

Line Responsibility

Line officers with responsibility for executing the plan should be identified. It should be clear which decisions are made by whom, and who their alternates are. Obviously a key decision is the initial decision to suppress or not suppress a given lightning-caused ignition. As fires proceed, there will be additional important decisions on whether, when, where, or how to take suppression measures. If time permits, using a committee of designated specialists can be a good approach to making such decisions.

Cooperation

This section should spell out cooperative arrangements with staff people who might not be directly involved in implementing the plan, with researchers, and with other agencies. The aim should be to maximize the information and experience gained from each fire. This is also the place to take note of special programs or plans based on boundaries with other agencies or other nations.

Information Program

Steps to inform and secure the cooperation of the public and the agency's own staff should be detailed here. It is vital that the public understand that, rather than abandoning the area to the vagaries of wildfire, the agency has an effective fire control program (Stankey 1976). Possibilities for using management fires in educational programs concerning wilderness resources and natural ecosystem processes can also be described.

Literature

The plan should include key references on the climate, geology, vegetation, ecosystem types, wildlife, and fire history for the region, plus fire control guides, equipment manuals, and other necessary information. Such literature should be on hand at headquarters.

Approvals

The plan should be reviewed and signed by the appropriate officials.

The Effect of Area Size on Fire Programs

Other factors being equal, large and well-blocked-in wildernesses present far fewer problems in fire management than small, narrow, irregular, or poorly blocked-in areas. But some fires tend to become very large and intense, as in the North Cascades, the boreal forest, or the BWCA, so that area size alone can not always assure containment. In such areas, very large crown fires and severe surface fires that could cover tens of thousands of acres are unacceptable. Here, fire size might often have to be held below natural upper limits, because even a large, designated wilderness is really only a fragment of the primeval ecosystem. Prescribed fires might be necessary near the boundaries of large units, and throughout the area for small units.

Avoiding Adverse Impacts of Suppression Activities

Necessary suppression work and prescribed burning must be carried out with great sensitivity to wilderness values. The guiding principle should be that the least damaging equipment and methods will be employed,

Figure 12–5.—Lookouts were once the main surveillance method to detect wilderness fires. Today, however, many lookouts are being phased out in favor of aerial surveillance carried out only when fire danger is high. *Left*: Wiley Park lookout, Selway-Bitterroot Wilderness, Mont. *Right*: Firescan, an infrared detection device supplements visual observation.

consistent with safety. This means handlines instead of bulldozers, and minimal use of saws and axes. This means avoiding fire control techniques that, in the past, did more damage to the ecosystem than the fires they were intended to suppress. Frequently a little advance planning will identify natural fire barriers where fires can be suppressed with little or no permanent evidence.

Examples of Wilderness Fire Management Programs and Supporting Research

Wilderness fire management and research programs have been underway in numerous National Parks, wildernesses, and related reserves for several years. A few examples will help identify the state of the art, as well as provide contacts and literature sources. The beginnings can be traced in part to the so-called Leopold Committee's 1963 report on "Wildlife Management in the National Parks" (Leopold et al. 1963). While not aimed directly at fire problems, it identified the ecosystem changes resulting from the elimination of natural fire as a key element influencing National Park wildlife habitat. In 1965 a National Park Service directive called for implementing the Leopold Report, particularly for areas in the natural category in several of the large parks (Baker 1965) and expressly encouraged the use of fire, including prescribed fire, as an appropriate natural

agent in ecosystem restoration programs. Fire management programs were not long in appearing.

Sequoia-Kings and Yosemite National Parks, California

The first designation of a Natural Fire Management Zone in forested western wilderness and the first breakthrough in prescribed burning in the West came in Sequoia and Kings Canyon National Parks in 1968. Beginning then, lightning-caused fires were allowed to burn under surveillance unless safety problems or resource damage was anticipated, in a special management zone above 8,000 feet in the Middle Fork Kings River drainage. This zone was gradually expanded and now encompasses about 590,000 acres, or roughly 70 percent of these Parks. The forests are generally open and subalpine, and much of the terrain is extremely rocky or above timberline. Some 97 fires occurred within this zone up to 1975, burning 7,800 acres. Partial suppression was needed for only a few fires, and no serious problems have developed (Kilgore and Briggs 1972; Agee 1974; Van Wagtendonk 1975).

In 1969, starting in the Redwood Mountain Area, prescribed burning to reduce unnatural fuels and invading shade-tolerant understory trees began in the lower elevation mixed-conifer forests, including some giant sequoia groves (Kilgore and Biswell 1971; Kilgore 1972, 1975). Initially some cutting and piling of small

271

trees and litter was used to avoid control problems and unnatural overstory damage. Similar work was done later on a 20-acre unit of the Mariposa Grove of giant sequoias in nearby Yosemite National Park. Later, more extensive understory precribed burning in mixed conifers was carried out without significant modification of fuels in both the Yosemite and Sequoia-Kings Canyon areas. This type of burning is now part of a large-scale operational program.[14]

In 1972 a Natural Fire-Zone was also established in Yosemite. By 1975 it included 480,000 acres. The fire control staff believes that essentially any fire within this zone can safely be allowed to burn because of prevailing fuel, vegetation, and physiographic factors *if* specified weather and fuel prescriptions are met.

An additional 132,000 acres were in a "Conditional Fire Zone," an area of restricted burning because of the fuel accumulations generated by previous fire exclusion. As these fuels are reduced, it is hoped that parts of the Conditional Zone can become areas in the Natural Fire Zone. In the remainder of the Park, which includes most of the park's developments, a full-scale fire suppression program is in effect, but prescribed burning is being used to reduce fuels in critical areas (Van Wagtendonk 1975).

Certainly some of the success of the Sequoia-Kings Canyon and Yosemite fire management programs can be credited to the extensive research available when these programs began and to the continued cooperation of research and management.[15]

Selway-Bitterroot Wilderness, Idaho and Montana

This Forest Service wilderness is the largest unit of the National Wilderness Preservation System (1,238,000 acres), and the first unit having operational experience with a sizable Wilderness Fire Management program. The program began in 1970 in the 100-square-mile White Cap Study area on the Bitterroot National Forest. Five ecological land units were involved in the initial area: shrubfield, ponderosa pine savanna, ponderosa pine/Douglas-fir (south slope), north slope communities, and subalpine. Prescriptions were prepared for each ecological land unit based on field investigations of fuels, plant communities, landforms, and fire spread and intensity potentials. A detailed management plan called for selective suppression of fires, depending on weather conditions and fire locations. The study plan was approved in 1972. It was immediately put to a difficult

test—the most severe fire weather in decades produced six lightning fires in 1973. One, the Fritz Creek Fire, burned 1,200 acres under prescription within the unit, but caused a 1,600-acre fire outside the unit. Full-scale suppression was taken on this escape, but the Fritz Creek Fire was allowed to burn inside the wilderness. The unit boundary, where crossed, was a small stream, the north side being inside the unit, and the south (a north slope) outside. No important resource damage occurred, and no developed areas were involved, but this example illustrates the difficulty of holding fires along an exterior wilderness boundary where continuous fuels extend outside the wilderness. Nevertheless, considering the severe fire weather, the White Cap program was a success. In 1975 the study was expanded to include the adjacent 135,000-acre Bear Creek drainage to the north on the Nez Perce National Forest. This raised the total area under fire management to about 200,000 acres. Again, cooperation between managers and research people helped provide a solid technical base for this effort.[16]

Grand Teton and Yellowstone National Parks, Wyoming

These two Parks have related ecosystems and problems, and close but not common boundaries. Their total area is almost 2-½ million acres, much of it de facto wilderness. A strong fire research base has shown that both areas have fire-dependent ecosystems.[17] Yellowstone now has two Natural Fire Management Zones encompassing 340,000 acres in total: The Mirror Plateau Unit in the northeast, and the Two Ocean Plateau Unit in the southeast. Both have been operational since 1973, but so far few fires have occurred. Grand Teton has a more complex zoning scheme, with a 125,000-acre Natural Fire Management Zone in the main Teton Range and a 22,000-acre Conditional Fire Zone in a sagebrush grassland in the southeast of the Park where lightning fires may be allowed to burn on decision of a fire committee. All lightning and man-caused fires are suppressed in the developed remainder of the Park (134,000 acres), but prescribed fires are permitted where appropriate.

Several lightning fires have occurred since the plan's inception, the largest being the 2,700-acre Waterfall Canyon fire in 1974. This fire, located in the Natural Fire Zone on the west shore of Jackson Lake, was allowed to burn from its ignition by lightning on July 14 through

[14] See Agee 1974; Kilgore 1975; Van Wagtendonk 1975.

[15] See Biswell 1961; Hartesveldt 1964; Hartesveldt and Harvey 1967; Weaver and Biswell 1969; Kilgore 1970, 1971a, 1971b, 1972, 1973; Kilgore and Biswell 1971; Kilgore and Briggs 1972; Cotton and Biswell 1973; Agee 1974; Kilgore and Sando 1975; Van Wagtendonk 1975.

[16] See Mutch 1970, 1974; Habeck 1972, 1973; Aldrich and Mutch 1972, 1973; Habeck and Mutch 1973; Daniels 1974; Moore 1974.

[17] See Patten 1969; Taylor 1969; Houston 1971, 1973; Loope 1971; Loope and Gruell 1973.

the busy tourist season until finally extinguished by fall rains and snows in December. It burned slowly in an area of old Engelmann spruce and other forest types, and no significant suppressive action was taken. On some days smoke was heavy in Jackson Hole and partially obscured views of the spectacular Teton Range across Jackson Lake. Local opposition to the fire developed, and the problem was aired on national television. The National Park Service stoutly defended the fire as natural, and as part of its innovative new ecosystem restoration program. Considerable public support for the fire was received, but this fire illustrates the difficulty in gaining public support for natural fires, particularly where they are visible in residential, commercial, or esthetically important areas. Public reluctance to accept natural burns is a legacy from 50 years of fire prevention campaigns that condemned all fires (Stankey 1976).

Teton Wilderness, Wyoming

A fire management plan has been prepared for this 560,000-acre National Forest Wilderness, which adjoins both Yellowstone and Grand Teton National Parks (Reese et al. 1975). A long, common boundary with Yellowstone Park's Two Ocean Natural Fire Area will not have to be defended by either agency when the plan is implemented. Lightning-caused fires will be allowed to burn under surveillance if they meet certain prescriptions, with the option of limited or total suppression at any time. The initial decision to declare a fire a natural fire and allow it to burn will be made by the District Ranger.

Trends and Future Needs

The necessity of restoring fire to fire-dependent ecosystems in wildernesses, National Parks, and related nature reserves is now widely recognized. The trend toward active fire management programs is strong, and more areas are initiating programs each year. Wilderness fire management is complex and demanding work, requiring high professional competence and intimate knowledge of the specific ecosystem and land unit to be managed. More people trained in ecology and forestry, with understanding of fire behavior and an interest in preservation management, will therefore be needed in the near future.

The need for natural fire programs in wilderness is generally understood by informed supporters of parks and wilderness but not among people who have been indoctrinated since childhood with the negative aspects of fire. To such people *all* fire is bad, all smoke is pollution, and most fires kill wildlife. The existence and

extent of this problem have been shown by Stankey (1976). To overcome this legacy from past fire prevention campaigns, slogans, and posters that told an incomplete story, new and innovative educational work with the media and schools is needed. Careful distinctions must be made between *wildfires*, which still must be suppressed in all cases, and *management fires*; and between urban air pollution and the necessary combustion of forest fuels in wilderness fire programs (Hall 1972). To make these distinctions, the public must have accurate knowledge. Stankey's (1976) findings suggest that wilderness users will respond positively when the factual knowledge of fire's natural role increases.

We need more fire management experience with severe surface fires and crown fires of substantial size, the kind that were characteristic of many of our more northern and high-elevation conifer forests. We need to know, for example, what the characteristic *sizes* of such fires were and whether fires of modest size were as effective as large fires in rejuvenating the local ecosystem. Experts in fuels, fire behavior, fire control, and fire ecology need to learn more about the probability of quiescent periods during intense fires when further enlargement of the burn could easily be restricted by suppression along key perimeters. We need to revise our definition of threshold conditions for crowning and rapid fire spread in well-chosen examples of key ecosystems. Such experience can often be gained in the remote portions of our largest wilderness units without fear of boundary transgressions.

Perhaps we can also learn more about the management of crown fires and high-intensity surface fires through designed burning trials in wildernesses where natural fire barriers provide adequate protection. The pioneering work of Van Wagner (1968, 1971) shows the potential of such studies. Prescribed fires can also be the safest approach, both from the human safety and ecological damage standpoint, for reducing unnatural fuel accumulations built up because of fire exclusion beneath stands of ponderosa pine, giant sequoia, redwood, sugar pine, red pine, and similar species. Once reductions have been accomplished, it should be possible to rely again on natural ignitions.

Wilderness Fire Programs and Ecological Knowledge

Wilderness fire management is important not only because it can maintain the natural landscapes and biota of wilderness as a cultural and recreational resource, but also because it can maintain large-scale functioning ecosystems that will contribute to basic scientific knowledge. We do not yet fully understand the role of periodic major perturbations, such as fire, in ecosystems. We need to know more about how such events regulate nutrient cycles, energy flow, and biotic productivity, and about the need for periodic disturbance in maintaining the diversity and stability of whole systems. And we need to understand the questions of frequency, scale, and spatial distribution of perturbations as they relate to changes in animal habitats and to the dispersal and reproduction of plants. For these purposes, programs that allow natural lightning-caused ignitions and restrict the spread of fires as little as possible will be best. Prescribed fire is preferable to eliminating fire from the system; but to preserve scientific values, natural fire is best.

We also need to know much more about the evolution in plants of special adaptations to fire. And we need to know more about the possibility that long-term fire exclusion could eliminate some plants and animals from the biota, or cause unexpected and undesired expansions of certain species (e.g., the expansions of balsam fir and the spruce budworm in northeastern North America).

The costs of inadequate ecological knowledge in the lack of clear fire management objectives could be a loss of public acceptance of fire as a management tool. As an example, a fire in 1976 on the Fish and Wildlife Service's Seney National Wildlife Refuge Wilderness in Michigan burned nearly 72,000 acres, including 16,000 acres of State land and 1,500 acres of private land. The lack of information on fuel conditions and weather, coupled with a fire management plan that did not cover the Refuge's wilderness lands, resulted in severe criticism of the agency's decision to allow the fire to burn (Popovich 1977). If wilderness managers fail to adequately prepare their wilderness fire management plans, severe consequences of public and political criticism might seriously cripple future uses of fire for management purposes.

Our understanding of natural ecosystems as *systems* is still in its infancy. Future scientists will require complete, functioning, large-scale natural ecosystems as laboratories to get at the questions just raised, and at many more not yet asked but perhaps more important. The answers are certain to be vital to man's future, and fire is certain to emerge as a crucial element. Many of the most widespread natural ecosystems of the earth—including most conifer forests, savannas, and grasslands—were fire dependent. And many of our most important domestic plants and animals and useful forest trees evolved in such ecosystems. It is chiefly in our larger wildernesses and National Parks where some of these ecosystem questions can be met (see Wright, H. E. 1974) because man is rapidly converting the rest of our planet to cultivated or grazed fields, exploited forests, mine dumps, highways, and urban areas. The value of natural wilderness will surely increase in the next few decades. And we might soon discover that it holds many unexpected secrets.

Literature Cited

Agee, J. K.
    1974. Fire management in the National Parks. Western Wildlands 1(3):27–33.
Ahlgren, C. E.
    1959a. Some effects of fire on forest reproduction in northeastern Minnesota. J. For. 57(3):194–200.
Ahlgren, C. E.
    1959b. Vegetational development following burning in the northern coniferous forest of Minnesota. Proc. Soc. Am. For., San Francisco, Calif., p. 21–22.
Ahlgren, C. E.
    1960. Some effects of fire on reproduction and growth of vegetation in northeastern Minnesota. Ecology 41:431–445.
Ahlgren, C. E.
    1970. Some effects of prescribed burning on jack pine reproduction in northeastern Minnesota. Univ. Minn. Agric. Exp. Stn., Misc. Rep. 94, For. Series 5, 14 p.
Ahlgren, C. E.
    1974. Effects of fires on temperate forests: North Central United States. *In* Fire and ecosystem. Chapter 6, p. 195–223. T. T. Kozlowski, and C. E. Ahlgren, eds. Academic Press, New York.

Ahlgren, I. F., and C. E. Ahlgren.
    1960. Ecological effects of forest fires. Bot. Rev. 26(4):483–533.
Aldrich, D. F., and R. W. Mutch.
    1972. Ecological interpretations of the White Cap drainage: a basis for wilderness fire management. Draft Fire Management Plan, Bitterroot National Forest, U.S. Dep. Agric., For. Serv., 84 p.
Aldrich, D.F., and R.W. Mutch.
    1973. Wilderness fire management planning guidelines and inventory procedures. U.S. Dep. Agric., For. Serv., North. Reg., 35 p., Appendices.
Alexander, M. E., and F. G. Hawkesworth.
    1975. Wildland fires and dwarf mistletoes: a literature review of ecology and prescribed burning. USDA For. Serv., Gen. Tech. Rep. RM—14, 12 p. Rocky Mt. For. and Range Exp. Stn., Fort Collins, Colo.
Baker, H. W.
    1965. Guidelines for resources management in the areas in the natural category of the National Park System. USDI, Natl. Park. Serv., memorandum on the implementation of the Leopold Report, 9 p. (processed), October 14, 1965.

Barden, L. S.
1974. Lightning fires in southern Appalachian forests. Ph.D. thesis, University of Tennessee, 65 p. (typescript).

Barden, L. S., and F. W. Woods.
1973. Characteristics of lightning fires in southern Appalachian forests. In Annu. Tall Timbers Fire Ecol. Conf. Proc. No. 13, p. 345-361.

Barney, R. J.
1969. Interior Alaska wildfires, 1956-1965. U.S. Dep. Agric., For. Serv., Pac. Northwest For. and Range Exp. Stn., 47 p.

Barney, R. J.
1971. Wildfires in Alaska—some historical and projected effects and aspects. In Fire in the northern environment: symposium proceedings. Fairbanks, Alaska, 1971, p. 51-59.

Beaufait, W. R.
1960. Some effects of high temperatures on the cones and seeds of jack pine. For. Sci. 6:194-199.

Bendell, J. F.
1974. Effects of fire on birds and mammals. In Fire and ecosystems. Chapter 4, p. 73-138. T. T. Kozlowski, and C. E. Ahlgren, eds. Academic Press, New York.

Bergerud, A. T.
1974. Decline of caribou in North America following settlement. J. Wildl. Manage. 38(4):757-770.

Biswell, H. H.
1959. Man and fire in ponderosa pine in the Sierra Nevada of California. Sierra Club Bull. 44(7):44-53.

Biswell, H.H.
1961. The big trees and fire. Natl. Parks 35(163):11-14.

Biswell, H. H.
1974. Effects of fire on chaparral. In Fire and ecosystems. Chapter 10, p. 321-364. T. T. Kozlowski, and C. E. Ahlgren, eds. Academic Press, New York.

Biswell, H. H., H. R. Kallander, Roy Komarek, R. J. Vogl, and H. Weaver.
1973. Ponderosa fire management: a task force evaluation of controlled burning in ponderosa pine forests of central Arizona. Tall Timbers Res. Stn., Misc. Publ. No. 2, 49 p.

Bradbury, J. P., S. Tarapchak, J. C. B. Waddington, and R. F. Wright.
1975. The impact of a forest fire on a wilderness lake in northeastern Minnesota. Verh. International Verein. Limnol. 19:875-883. (Proc. Int. Union Limnol.)

Bray, J. R., and E. Gorham.
1964. Litter production in forests of the world. In Advances in ecolo. res., 2:101-157. Academic Press, New York.

Brown, J. K.
1971. A planar intersect method for sampling fuel volume and surface area. For. Sci. 17(1):96-102.

Brown, J. K.
1974. Handbook for inventorying downed woody material. USDA For. Serv., Gen. Tech. Rep. INT-16. Intermt. For. and Range Exp. Stn., Ogden, Utah.

Buckman, R. E.
1964. Silvicultural use of prescribed burning in the Lake States. Proc. Soc. Am. For., Denver, Colo., p. 38-40.

Clements, F. E.
1910. The life history of lodgepole burn forests. U.S. Dep. Agric., For. Serv., Bull. 79, 56 p.

Cooper, C. F.
1960. Changes in vegetation, structure and growth of southwestern pine forests since white settlement. Ecol. Monogr. 30:129-164.

Cooper, C. F.
1961. The ecology of fire. Sci. Am. 204(4):150-160.

Cooper, W. S.
1913. The climax forest of Isle Royale, Lake Superior, and its development. Bot. Gaz. 55(1):1-44, 115-140, 189-235.

Cotton, L., and H. Biswell.
1973. Forestscape and fire restoration at Whitaker's Forest. Natl. Parks and Conserv. 47(2):10-15.

Countryman, C.M.
1964. Mass fires and fire behavior. USDA For. Serv., Res. Pap. PSW-19, 53 p. Pac. Southwest For. and Range Exp. Stn., Berkeley, Calif.

Daniels, O. L.
1974. Test of a new land management concept: Fritz Creek 1973. Western Wildlands 1(3):23-26.

Daubenmire, R. F.
1943. Vegetation zonation in the Rocky Mountains. Bot. Rev. 9(6):325-393.

Daubenmire, R. F.
1952. Forest vegetation of northern Idaho and adjacent Washington and its bearing on concepts of vegetation classification. Ecol. Monogr. 22(4):301-330.

Daubenmire, R. F., and J. B. Daubenmire.
1968. Forest vegetation of eastern Washington and northern Idaho. Wash. State Agric. Exp. Stn. Tech. Bull. 60, 104 p.

Day, G. M.
1953. The Indian as an ecological factor in the northeastern forest. Ecology 34(2):329-346.

Day, R. J.
1972. Stand structure, succession, and use of southern Alberta's Rocky Mountain forest. Ecology 53(3):472-478.

Dodge, M.
1972. Forest fuel accumulation—a growing problem. Science 177(4044):139-142.

Fahnestock, G.R.
1970. Two keys for appraising forest fire fuels. USDA For. Serv., Res. Pap. PNW-99, 26 p. Pac. Northwest For. and Range Exp. Stn., Portland, Oreg.

Foster, N. W., and I. K. Morrison.
1976. Distribution and cycling of nutrients in a natural *Pinus banksiana* ecosystem. Ecology 57(1):110-120.

Fowells, H. A.
1965. Silvics of forest trees of the United States. U.S. Dep. Agric., Agric. Handb. No. 271, 762 p.

Frandsen, W. H.
1973. Effective heating of fuel ahead of spreading fire. USDA For. Serv., Res. Pap. INT-140, 16 p. Intermt. For. and Range Exp. Stn., Ogden, Utah.

Franklin, J. F., and C. T. Dyrness.
1969. Vegetation of Oregon and Washington. USDA For. Serv., Res. Pap. PNW-80, 216 p. Pac. Northwest For. and Range Exp. Stn., Portland, Oreg.

Franklin, J.F., and C.T. Dyrness.
1973. Natural vegetation of Oregon and Washington. USDA For. Serv., Gen. Tech. Rep. PNW-8, 417 p. Pac. Northwest For. and Range Exp. Stn., Portland, Oreg.

Frissell, S. S.
1973. The importance of fire as a natural ecological factor in Itesca State Park, Minnesota. Quaternary Res. 3(3):397-407.

Fritz, E.
1931. The role of fire in the redwood region. J. For. 29(6):939-950.

Graham, S. A.
1941. Climax forests of the Upper Peninsula of Michigan. Ecology 22(4):355–362.

Grigal, D. F., and J. G. McColl.
1975. Litterfall after wildfire in virgin forests of northeastern Minnesota. Can. J. For. Res. 5(4):655–661.

Grigal, D. F., and L. F. Ohmann.
1975. Classification description, and dynamics of upland plant communities within a Minnesota wilderness area. Ecol. Monogr. 45(4):389–407.

Gruel, G. E., and L. L. Loope.
1974. Relationships among aspen, fir, and ungulate browsing in Jackson Hole, Wyoming. U.S. Dep. Agric., For. Serv., Intermt. Reg. Misc. Pap., 33 p.

Gunzel, L. L.
1974. National policy change-natural prescribed fire. Fire Manage. 35(3):6–8.

Habeck, J. R.
1968. Forest succession in the Glacier Park cedar-hemlock forests. Ecology 49(5):872–880.

Habeck, J. R.
1970. Fire ecology investigations in Glacier National Park. Dep. Botany, University of Montana, 80 p. (processed).

Habeck, J. R.
1972. Fire ecology investigations in the Selway-Bitterroot Wilderness. University of Montana, U.S. Dep. Agric., For. Serv. Publ. R1-72-001, 119 p.

Habeck, J. R.
1973. A phytosociological analysis of forests, fuels and fire in the Moose Creek Drainage, Selway-Bitterroot Wilderness. University of Montana, U.S. Dep. Agric., For. Serv. Contract No. 26-2952, Rep., 113 p.

Habeck, J. R., and R. W. Mutch.
1973. Fire-dependent forests in the northern Rocky Mountains. Quat. Res. 3(3):408–424.

Haines, D. A., and R. W. Sando.
1969. Climatic conditions preceding historically great fires in the North Central Region. USDA For. Serv., Res. Pap. NC-34, 19 p. North Central For. Exp. Stn., St. Paul, Minn.

Haines, D. A., and G. H. Updike.
1971. Fire whirlwind formation over flat terrain. USDA For. Serv., Res. Pap. NC-71, 12 p. North Central For. Exp. Stn., St. Paul, Minn.

Hall, J. A.
1972. Forest fuels, prescribed fire, and air quality. U.S. Dep. Agric., For. Serv., Pac. Northwest For. and Range Exp. Stn., Portland, Oreg. 44 p.

Hansen, H. L., L. W. Krefting, and V. Kurmis.
1973. The forest of Isle Royale in relation to fire history and wildlife. Univ. Minn. Agric. Exp. Stn. Tech. Bull. 294, Forestry Series 13, 43 p.

Hardy, C. E., and J. W. Franks.
1963. Forest fires in Alaska. USDA For. Serv., Res. Pap. INT-5, 163 p. Intermt. For. and Range Exp. Stn., Ogden, Utah.

Hartesveldt, R. J.
1964. Fire ecology of the giant sequoias: controlled fires may be one solution to survival of the species. Nat. Hist. 73(10):12–19.

Hartesveldt, R. J., and H. T. Harvey.
1967. The fire ecology of sequoia regeneration. In Tall Timbers Fire Ecol. Conf. Proc. 7:65–77.

Heinselman, M. L.
1969. Diary of the canoe country's landscape. Naturalist 20(1):2–13. (J., Nat. Hist. Soc. Minn.)

Heinselman, M. L.
1970. Preserving nature in forested wilderness areas and national parks. Natl. Parks and Conserv. 44(276):8–14.

Heinselman, M. L.
1971a. Restoring fire to the ecosystems of the Boundary Waters Canoe Area, Minnesota, In 10th Annu. Tall Timbers Fire Ecol. Conf. Proc. Fredericton, N. B., 1970, p. 9–23.

Heinselman, M. L.
1971b. The natural role of fire in northern conifer forests. p. 61–72. In Fire in the northern environment. C. W. Slaughter, R. J. Barney, and G. M. Hansen, eds. Symp. Proc., Fairbanks, Alaska. U.S. Dep. Agric., For. Serv., Pac. Northwest For. and Range Exp. Stn., 275 p.

Heinselman, M. L.
1973. Fire in the virgin forests of the Boundary Waters Canoe Area, Minnesota. Quat. Res. 3(3):329–382.

Heinselman, M. L.
1974. Restoring fire to the canoe country. Naturalist 24(4):21–31.

Heinselman, M. L.
1975. Boreal peatlands in relation to environment. p. 93–103. In Coupling of land and water systems. A. D. Hasler, ed. Springer-Verlag: New York, 309 p.

Heinselman, M. L., and E. I. Roe.
1963. A record of some pleistocene trees and shrubs from Itasca County, Minnesota. For. Sci. 9(3):336–337.

Helmers, A. E.
1974. Interior Alaska (includes reprinting the map "Major Ecosystems of Alaska"). Naturalist 25(1):16–23.

Hendee, J. C., and G. H. Stankey.
1973. Bioentricity in wilderness management. Bioscience 23(9):535–538.

Horton, K. W.
1956. The ecology of lodgepole pine in Alberta and its role in forest succession. Can. Dep. North. Affairs and Natl. Resour., For. Branch Tech. Note 45, 29 p.

Horton, K. W., and G. H. D. Bedell.
1960. White and red pine ecology, silviculture, and management. Can. Dep. North. Affairs and Natl. Resour., For. Branch Bull. 124, 185 p.

Houston, D. B.
1971. Ecosystems of National Parks. Science 172:648–651.

Houston, D. B.
1973. Wildfires in northern Yellowstone National Park. Ecology 54(5):1111–1117.

Humphrey, R. R.
1974. Fire in the deserts and desert grassland of North America. In Fire and ecosystems. Chapter 11, p. 365–400. T. T. Kozlowski, and C. E. Ahlgren, eds. Academic Press, New York.

Irving, F. D., and D. W. French.
1971. Control by fire of dwarf mistletoe in black spruce. J. For. 69(1):28–30.

Johnson, E. A., and J. S. Rowe.
1975. Fire in the subarctic wintering ground of the Beverley caribou herd. Am. Midl. Nat. 94(1):1–14.

Kaufert, F. H.
1964. Controversy in canoeland. Am For. 70(10):24–27, 78–82.

Kilgore, B. M.
1970. Restoring fire to the Sequoias. Nati. Parks and Conserv. 44(277):16–22.

Kilgore, B. M.
1971a. The role of fire in managing red fir forests. Trans. North Am. Wildl. and Nat. Resour. Conf. 36:405–416.

Kilgore, B. M.
1971b. Response of breeding bird populations to habitat changes in a giant sequoia forest. Am. Midl. Nat. 85(1):135–152.

Kilgore, B. M.
1972. Impact of prescribed burning on a sequoia-mixed conifer forest. In Annu. Tall Timbers Fire Ecol. Conf. Proc. p. 345–375.

Kilgore, B. M.
1973. The ecological role of fire in Sierran conifer forests—its application to National Park Management. Quaternary Res. 3(3):496–513.

Kilgore, B. M.
1975. Restoring fire to National Park wilderness. Am. For. 81(3):16–19.

Kilgore, B. M., and H. H. Biswell.
1971. Seedling germination following fire in a giant sequoia forest. Calif. Agric. 25(2):8–10.

Kilgore, B. M., and G. S. Briggs.
1972. Restoring fire to high elevation forests in California. J. For. 70(5):266–271.

Kilgore, B. M., and R. W. Sando.
1975. Crown-fire potential in a sequoia forest after prescribed burning. For. Sci. 21(1):83–87.

Komarek, E. V.
1974. Effects of fire on temperate forests and related ecosystems: Southeastern United States. In Fire and ecosystems. Chapter 8, p. 251–277. T. T. Kozlowski, and C. E. Ahlgren, eds. Academic Press, New York.

Kozlowski, T. T., and C. E. Ahlgren, eds.
1974. Fire and Ecosystems. 542 p. Academic Press, New York.

Krefting, L. W., H. L. Hansen, and M. P. Meyer.
1970. Vegetation type map of Isle Royale National Park. U.S. Dep. Inter., Bur. of Sport Fish. and Wildl.

Leopold, A. S., S. A. Cain, I. N. Gabrielson, C. M. Cottam, and T. L. Kimball.
1963. Wildlife management in the National Parks. Living Wilderness 83:11–19.

Little, C.
1974. Effects of fire on temperate forests: Northeastern United States. In Fire and ecosystems. Chapter 7, p. 225–250. T. T. Kozlowski, and C. E. Ahlgren, eds. Academic Press, New York.

Loope, L. L.
1971. Dynamics of forest communities in the Grand Teton National Park. Naturalist 22(1):39–48.

Loope, L. L., and G. E. Gruell.
1973. The ecological role of fire in the Jackson Hole Area, northwestern Wyoming. Quat. Res. 3(3):425–443.

Loucks, O. L.
1970. Evolution of diversity, efficiency, and community stability. Am. Zool. 10(1):17–25.

Lutz, H. J.
1956. Ecological effects of forest fires in the interior of Alaska. U.S. Dep. Agric., Tech. Bull. 1133, 121 p.

MacLean, D. W., and G. H. D. Bedell.
1955. Northern clay belt growth and yield survey. Can. Dep. North. Affairs and Natl. Resour., For. Branch Tech. Note No. 20.

Maissurow, D. K.
1935. Fire as a necessary factor in the perpetuation of white pine. J. For. 33(4):373–378.

Marr, J. W.
1961. Ecosystems of the east slope of the Front Range in Colorado. University of Colorado Studies, Series in Biology No. 8, 134 p.

McColl, J. G., and D. F. Grigal.
1975. Forest fire: effects on phosphorus movement to lakes. Science 188(4193):1109–1111.

Mech, L. D.
1966. The wolves of Isle Royale. Fauna of the Natl. Parks of the U.S., Fauna Series, 210 p., U.S. Government Printing Office.

Moore, W. R.
1974. From fire control to fire management. Western Wildlands 1(3):11–15.

Mutch, R. W.
1970. Wildland fires and ecosystems—a hypothesis. Ecology 51(5):1046–1051.

Mutch, R. W.
1974. I thought forest fires were black! Western Wildlands 1(3):16–21.

Ohmann, L. F., and R. R. Ream.
1971. Wilderness ecology: virgin plant communities of the Boundary Waters Canoe Area. USDA For. Serv., Res. Pap. NC-63, 55 p. North Cent. For. Exp. Stn., St. Paul, Minn.

Oosting, H. J., and J. F. Reed.
1952. Virgin spruce-fir forest in the Medicine Bow Mountains, Wyoming. Ecol. Monogr. 22(2):69–91.

Patten, D. T.
1969. Forest succession in Yellowstone National Park. Natl. Parks 43(264):21–22.

Popovitch, Luke.
1977. Up in flames—Taking heat on the Seney. J. For. 75(3):147–150.

Reese, J. B., F. R. Mohr, R. E. Dean, and T. Klabunde.
1975. Teton wilderness fire management plan. Draft, February 1975, U.S. For. Serv., Teton Natl. For., 57 p. and appendices.

Ritchie, J. C.
1962. A geobotanical survey of northern Manitoba. Arctic Inst. North Am., Tech. Pap. No. 9, 47 p., maps.

Robertson, W. B.
1962. Fire and vegetation in the Everglades. In Annu. Tall Timbers Fire Ecol. Conf. Proc. 2:67–80.

Rosendahl, C. O.
1948. A contribution to the knowledge of the pleistocene flora of Minnesota. Ecology 29(2):284–315.

Rothermel, R. C.
1972. A mathematical model for predicting fire spread in wildland fuels. USDA For. Serv., Res. Pap. INT-115, 40 p. Intermt. For. and Range Exp. Stn., Ogden, Utah.

Rowe, J. S.
1959. Forest regions of Canada. Can Dep. North. Affairs and Natl. Resour., For. Branch Bull. 123, 71 p.

Rowe, J. S.
1970. Spruce and fire in northwest Canada and Alaska. In Tenth Tall Timbers Fire Ecol. Conf. Proc. 10:245–254.

Rowe, J. S., J. L. Bergsteinsson, G. A. Padbury, and R. Hermesh.
1974. Fire studies in the Mackenzie Valley. Can. Dep. Indian and North. Affairs, INA Publ. No. QS-1567-000-EE-A1, 123 p.

Rowe, J. S., and G. W. Scotter.
1973. Fire in the boreal forest. Quaternary Res. 3(3):444–464.

Sando, R. W., and D. A. Haines.
1972. Fire weather and behavior of the Little Sioux fire. USDA For. Serv., Res. Pap. NC-76, 6 p. North Cent. For. Exp. Stn., St. Paul, Minn.

Sando, R. W., and C. H. Wick.
  1972. A method of evaluating crown fuels in forest stands. USDA For. Serv., Res. Pap. NC–84, 10 p. North Cent. For. Exp. Stn., St. Paul, Minn.

Schroeder, M. J., and C. C. Buck.
  1970. Fire weather—a guide for application of meteorological information to forest fire control operations. U.S. Dep. Agric., Agric. Handb. 360, 229 p.

Scotter, G. W.
  1964. Effects of forest fires on the winter range of barren ground caribou in northern Saskatchewan. Can. Wildl. Serv., Wildl. Manage. Bull., Series 1, No. 18, 111 p.

Scotter, G. W.
  1971. Wildfires in relation to the habitat of barren-ground caribou in the taiga of northern Canada. In 10th Annu. Tall Timbers Fire Ecol. Conf. Proc. Fredericton, N. B., 1970, p. 85–105.

Show, S. B., and E. I. Kotok.
  1924. The role of fire in the California pine forests. U.S. Dep. Agric. Bull. 1294, 80 p.

Spurr, S. H.
  1954. The forests of Itasca in the nineteenth century as related to fire. Ecology 35(1):21–25.

Stankey, G. H.
  1976. Wilderness fire policy: an investigation of knowledge and beliefs. USDA For. Serv., Res. Pap. INT–180, 17 p. Intermt. For. and Range Exp. Stn., Ogden, Utah. (In press.)

Stone, E. C.
  1965. Preserving vegetation in parks and wilderness. Science 150(3701):1261–1267.

Stone, E. C., and R. B. Vasey.
  1968. Preservation of coast redwood on alluvial flats. Science 159(3811):157–161.

Stringer, P. W., and G. H. LaRoi.
  1970. The Douglas-fir forests of Banff and Jasper National Parks, Canada. Can. J. Bot. 48(10):1703–1726.

Swain, A. M.
  1973. A history of fire and vegetation in northeastern Minnesota as recorded in lake sediment. Quaternary Res. 3(3):383–396.

Tande, G. F.
  1975. A fire history of the Athabasca River Valley around Jasper Townsite, Jasper National Park, Alberta. Unpublished prelim. report, 9 p., plus fire history manuscr. maps.

Taylor, D. L.
  1969. Biotic succession of lodgepole pine forests of fire origin in Yellowstone National Park. Ph.D. thesis, University of Wyoming, 320 p.

U.S. Department of Agriculture.
  1941. Climate and man. U.S. Dep. Agric. Yearb. 1941, 1248 p.

Van Wagner, C. E.
  1968. Fire behavior in a red pine plantation: field and laboratory evidence. Can. Dep. For. and Rural Dev. Publ. 1229.

Van Wagner, C. E.
  1971. Fire and red pine. In 10th Annu. Tall Timbers Fire Ecol. Conf. Proc. Fredericton, N. B., 1970, p. 211–219.

Van Wagtendonk, Jan
  1974. Refined burning prescriptions for Yosemite National Park. U.S. Dep. Inter., Natl. Park Serv., Occas. Pap. No. 2, 21 p.

Van Wagtendonk, Jan
  1975. Wilderness fire management in Yosemite National Park. Unpubl. manuscr., prepared for proc. 14th Biennial Wilderness Conf., New York City, 1975, 19 p. (typescript).

Viereck, L. A.
  1973. Wildfire in the taiga of Alaska. Quaternary Res. 3(3):465–495.

Vitousek, P. M., and W. A. Reiners.
  1975. Ecosystem succession and nutrient retention: a hypothesis. Bioscience 25(6):376–381.

Vogl, R. J.
  1967. Fire adaptations of some southern California plants. In 7th Annu. Tall Timbers Fire Ecol. Conf. Proc. p. 79–109.

Vogl, R. J.
  1974. Effects of fire on grasslands. In Fire and ecosystems. Chapter 5, p. 139–194. T. T. Kozlowski, and C. E. Ahlgren, eds. Academic Press, New York.

Wagener, W. W.
  1961. Past fire incidence in Sierra Nevada forests. J. For. 59(10):739–748.

Weaver, H.
  1943. Fire as an ecological and silvicultural factor in the ponderosa pine region of the Pacific slope. J. For. 41:7–14.

Weaver, H.
  1961. Ecological changes in the ponderosa pine forest of Cedar Valley in southern Washington. Ecology 42(2):416–420.

Weaver, H.
  1974. Effects of fire on temperate forests: Western United States. In Fire and ecosystems. Chapter 9, p. 279–319. T. T. Kozlowski, and C. E. Ahlgren, eds. Academic Press, New York.

Weaver, H., and H. Biswell.
  1969. How fire helps the big trees. Natl. Parks 43(262):16–19.

Wellner, C. A.
  1970. Fire history in the northern Rocky Mountains. In The role of fire in the Intermountain West: symposium proceedings. Intermt. Fire Res. Counc. and Univ. Mont., p. 42–64.

Wright, H. E.
  1974. Landscape development, forest fires, and wilderness management. Science 186(4163):487–495.

Wright, H. E., and M. L. Heinselman.
  1973. The ecological role of fire in natural conifer forests of western and northern North America: Introduction. Quaternary Res. 3(3):317–328.

Wright, R. F.
  1974. Forest fire: impact on the hydrology, chemistry, and sediment of small lakes in northeastern Minnesota. Interim Rep. No. 10, Univ. Minn., Limnological Res. Cent., 129 p. (based on Ph.D. thesis of author, University of Minnesota, 1974).

Estimates of wilderness use by recreationists are based on permits, trail registrations, or guesses. The most accurate wilderness use data comes from mandatory visitor permit systems. Here a wilderness ranger checks a permit displayed on a backpack in Rocky Mountain National Park.

13 Wilderness Use And Users: Trends And Projections

Wilderness has been preserved because society believes it has values that justify putting it off limits to development. Most of these values are based on some kind of use. This is clear in the Wilderness Act, which states that wilderness is to be preserved for "use and enjoyment as wilderness" by "the American people of present and future generations."

The Importance of Understanding Wilderness Use

An understanding of wilderness use is an essential foundation for any consideration of wilderness management. Not only do most wilderness values stem from wilderness use, but so do most threats to wilderness, and, as a result, most management problems as well. In chapters 14 and 15, where use management is discussed, we will develop the idea that most wilderness management is use management. Wilderness-use management is inherently complex and difficult; without in-depth knowledge of the character of use, its management is impossible. This is particularly true if management seeks to minimize regimentation and rely instead on light-handed, subtle approaches.

There are many kinds of wilderness use that reflect a variety of values. This chapter first will identify the uses

of wilderness and related resources and discuss the amount of each use. Because information is scanty for all uses except recreation, and because recreation is a very important use, we will devote a special section of this chapter to a review of the amount, character, and distribution of wilderness recreational use and the characteristics of users. Trends in use and projections and speculation about future use will complete the chapter.

Wilderness Use: An Overview

Wilderness Dependency

Different kinds of wilderness use vary in their dependency on wilderness conditions. Commodity uses, such as grazing or mining, take place in some wildernesses but do not depend on or require wilderness conditions. This is true of certain recreational uses, also. Some recreation—for example, campers playing volleyball in a wilderness meadow—just takes place in a wilderness, without depending on the wilderness qualities of the environment. Other activities—for example, observing the results of natural ecological processes on the landscape, experiencing solitude and isolation, and facing the challenges of traveling and living in an undeveloped area—clearly do require wilderness settings. Other activities, such as observing wildlife, are

281

intermediate and for some people can be enhanced by the wilderness setting, even if not dependent on it.

This concept of wilderness dependency is basic to managing wilderness use. In chapter 7 we set forth as one of several principles of management that wilderness-dependent activities should be favored over those that can be carried on outside wilderness. We will attempt to evaluate the degree of wilderness dependency of different uses as they are discussed; but, with present knowledge, this must be a largely subjective, impressionistic—and, therefore, debatable—evaluation.

Public Recreational Use

The most obvious wilderness use is recreational. It is so prominent that it is often the only use people think of. Wilderness use and recreational visitation are usually treated as synonyms. On-site recreational use certainly involves the largest numbers of direct wilderness users, has great impacts and poses severe management challenges.

Recreational use is itself a broad category including many diverse activities. People take all sorts of hikes—short, day hikes, long backpacking trips, and everything in between. Some ride horses. Others walk, leading pack animals. They float rivers in boats, canoes, and rafts. In a few places with special regulations, some visitors use boats with outboard motors, jet boats, and airplanes for access. People come in all sorts of groups—family, friends, or groups sponsored by varied organizations—and a few travel alone.

The wilderness dependency of different recreational uses varies from high to low. Roadless recreation areas (rather than unmodified, wilderness ecosystems) would provide acceptable and often preferable settings for a large part of this use. Recreational use of wilderness, which totaled over 10 million visitor-days in 1975, will be discussed later.

Commercial Recreational Use

In addition to public visitor use, there is also commercial recreational use of wilderness. Outfitters and guides accompany some visitors, adding to as well as facilitating the use of wilderness; this use usually involves travel by horse or boat. Other types of outfitting businesses involve only equipment rental—the visitors go on their own without guides. This is common in canoeing areas where rentals vary from just a canoe on up to all camping equipment. In parts of the California Sierras burros are rented. In contrast, few businesses anywhere rent horses for do-it-yourself wilderness travel, or backpacking equipment, or ski-touring gear. The types of commercial recreation occurring in wilderness

certainly depend on roadless land, and probably on large blocks of it. Specialized transportation (horses, rafts, etc.) is the essential key service the outfitters offer and roads would essentially eliminate the need for specialized transportation. However, it seems to us that unmodified ecosystems are not necessary for most uses involving commercial outfitters. Much of this use would also benefit from a somewhat greater development of facilities (corrals, improved campsites, etc.) than might be appropriate in classified wilderness.

There are no overall figures on the extent of commercial recreation in wilderness. Outfitter use varies from none in some wildernesses (most eastern areas and some smaller western areas) to a majority of the use in others (particularly on dangerous, whitewater rivers such as the Colorado, Middle Fork of the Salmon, and Selway where special equipment and knowledge are essential). In general, outfitters and guides play a more important role in larger wildernesses where horse travel is common. However, even in two of the largest wildernesses, the Bob Marshall in Montana and the Selway-Bitterroot in Montana and Idaho, studies show only a minority of the visitors employ outfitters—about one-third in the Bob Marshall and one-sixth in the Selway-Bitterroot (Lucas 1978). Still, outfitting is a sizable industry. In 1975 there were 51 outfitters licensed to take parties into the Bob Marshall Wilderness, for example, and 45 in the Selway-Bitterroot.

Indirect Recreational Use

Besides direct, on-site recreational use of wilderness, there are several important types of indirect use. Millions of people who never set foot in wilderness nevertheless derive satisfaction from experiencing wilderness indirectly through the experiences of other people. This *vicarious* use can come about through reading, looking at photos and films, listening to lectures and accounts by others of their experiences, or while staying at resorts or recreation areas which are near wilderness. Usually vicarious use is not thought of as a *use* of wilderness, and yet in a sense it is, and probably a major use. Without wilderness, the base for these vicarious experiences would be gone. Accounts of historical encounters with wilderness provide a substitute, but only a very limited one; they lack the immediacy of the assurance that one could actually visit the area.

Many people value keeping open the option to visit wilderness. Whether or not they ever actually visit a wilderness, it is worth something to them to know they could. For many others, the simple fact that wilderness exists has value even without the visitation option. As Krutilla (1967) pointed out, some people who derive satisfaction from the knowledge that wilderness still exists "would be appalled by the prospect of being exposed to it." *Existence* and *option* values have been defined and measured in preliminary efforts (Fisher and Krutilla 1972; Tombaugh 1971; Cicchetti and Freeman 1971).

Many people also want to leave wilderness for their heirs or for posterity in general. This amounts to keeping future options open beyond one's own lifetime and has been labeled *bequest value* (Krutilla 1967). All of these uses seem to be dependent on wilderness to a high degree.

Clawson (1963) pointed out that a recreation experience has not only an on-site phase, but also four off-site phases: Anticipation, travel to, travel from, and recollection. It seems likely that compared to most other types of recreation, wilderness visits have particularly long and well-developed anticipation and recollection phases. Planning frequently starts well in advance, and experiences are often relived afterwards.

Some wildernesses are closed to all direct, on-site recreational use. Specifically, this is true of some Fish and Wildlife Service wilderness, especially some small islands. In addition to the indirect, vicarious use these areas provide, they also provide breeding grounds that produce many birds and, in some cases, other wildlife that are observed and enjoyed outside the wilderness.

Any estimate of the amount of indirect use clearly would be very difficult to make and none is available. Sales of wilderness-related books are substantial, and films with nature-wilderness themes draw crowds. Several popular TV programs are based on nature and wilderness. We would speculate that the number of vicarious and other indirect users is probably greater than the number of actual visitors.

Scientific Use

One of the major values of wilderness is its potential for scientific use. Wilderness serves as a laboratory, particularly for ecology and other biological sciences, because of the relatively natural, unmodified conditions there and the opportunity to study natural processes operating in large areas. As the rest of the world becomes more developed and modified by man, the contrast between wilderness and nonwilderness increases and the value of such areas for research is enhanced. For example, the High Uintas Primitive Area in Utah was called "a perfect outdoor laboratory" for a study of radioactive fallout "because they [the Uintas] remain almost undisturbed year after year" (Pendleton 1968). This scientific use depends substantially on wilderness. There are also research natural areas which serve some of the same research purposes, as well as other purposes of their own (Dyrness et al. 1975; Schmidt and Dufour 1975), but, because of their smaller size, they are often exposed to outside influences, and large-scale, long term ecological processes are usually better represented in wilderness (see chapter 6 for further discussion on these topics). Research on some mammals with large home ranges such as grizzly bears, wolves, and mountain lions is especially dependent on wilderness.

Certain types of environments—particularly high mountains—are well represented in classified wilderness, with the result that subjects for certain research often are located in wilderness. Glaciers are a notable example of this situation.

Wilderness can also provide a good setting for some kinds of social and psychological research. The isolation of small groups of people and their close interdependence in the face of the challenges of wilderness travel provide unusual and valuable research opportunities. Sociologist William Burch (1974) believes "questions concerning the structure and function of small groups and their relation to larger wholes seem naturally adapted to wildland situations."

No one keeps a record of scientific use of wilderness, and there is some difference of opinion as to its extent. But, for example, in the Glacier Peak Wilderness in Washington there have been at least six formal studies in the past decade and several additional informal studies. A bibliography of nearly 350 studies on the Sierra Nevada range in California in progress between 1970 and 1973 was recently prepared, and many of these studies were either on classified wilderness, National Park backcountry, or other undeveloped. lands (Stanley 1974). Some sort of central register of wilderness research projects is needed both to document this use and trends in it, and also to improve the quality of research by increasing scientists' awareness of similar or related studies and facilitating communication between investigators.

A related scientific value and potential use is based on the gene pool within wilderness. In wilderness, the natural genetic diversity of native plants and animals is preserved (Ghiselin 1974; Seagrave 1976). Outside wilderness this diversity is often reduced as species become extinct and as common species are selectively bred for greater uniformity, increased yield, and other specific characteristics. It must be pointed out, however, that the wilderness system is very short on representation of many types of environments and ecosystems—such as grasslands and low elevation forests—and this severely reduces the gene pool value. As a result, much of this particular use must depend on nonwilderness lands.

Educational Use

Wilderness is also used for educational purposes in two major ways. First, closely related to scientific use, is the use of wilderness for field trips; for subjects and study areas for theses, dissertations, and other reports; and for instructional examples. If the educational use relates to large-scale, long term ecological processes it is dependent on wilderness to a high extent, but, for many other topics, other lands probably are more readily available.

The second educational use is more akin to recreation use; it is the use of the wilderness as a setting for teaching woodsmanship and survival skills. Many universities teach wilderness-travel skill courses, usually with field trips. Some youth-serving organizations, such as the Boy Scouts, have taught outdoor living skills with their application in wilderness as the pinnacle of achievement. There is considerable doubt that most of this use is really dependent on wilderness. What does seem to be needed is a fairly large, unroaded area.

Like scientific use, educational use is also not measured for the wilderness system, but seven educational organizations in the Pacific Northwest accounted for 13,000 visitor-days in eight wildernesses in Oregon and Washington in 1971.[1] In several of the wildernesses, the educational organizations' use accounted for about 5 percent of the total use.

Therapeutic Use

Wilderness also provides a setting for therapeutic programs designed primarily to alleviate behavior or psychological problems rather than physical ailments. Delinquent and mentally disturbed people have been taken on wilderness canoe trips, river float trips, and backpacking. The participants seemed to benefit from the isolation from outside pressures, the challenges and the need for group support in meeting them, and perhaps from qualities of the wilderness (Bernstein 1972; Thorstenson and Heaps 1973; Lowry 1974).

Personal Development

Other programs are something of a blend of therapy and education, aimed at personal development and self-discovery. Working with people in a wilderness setting, these programs are designed to build self-reliance, personal understanding, awareness of other persons, persistence, and similar traits. Outward Bound Schools are one well-known example of this type of program, but there are many others (Kaplan 1974; Hanson 1973). It is

difficult to say whether such programs really depend on wilderness or just roadless, challenging country. The numbers of such users are probably a fairly small part of the total use of wilderness, but some areas receive substantial use. Visits are often long, and survival exercises in living off the land can have a heavy impact on ecosystems.

Commodity Use

Several on-site, commodity uses take place in, but do not depend on the particular qualities of wilderness.

Mining

The 1964 Wilderness Act permits mining as one of these commodity uses, but agency regulations are designed to minimize adverse impacts on the wilderness. Almost all mining claims are in National Forest wilderness. Most National Parks are closed to all mining, but six Parks were established with special provisions permitting mining: Crater Lake National Park, Oreg.; Glacier Bay National Monument, Alaska; Mount McKinley National Park, Alaska; Organ Pipe Cactus National Monument, Ariz.; Death Valley National Monument, Calif. and Nev.; and Coronado National Memorial, Ariz. All but Coronado National Memorial are being studied for possible wilderness classification, but none contain classified wilderness now. Mining is going on in Death Valley and Mt. McKinley, and there has been mineral exploration, but no mining in Glacier Bay and Organ Pipe. In 1976, Congress passed a law (P.L. 94–429) closing these six National Parks to new mining claims and placed all existing claims under strict, new regulations. The 1964 Wilderness Act permits the continued staking of claims in National Forest wilderness only, until the end of 1983. However, since claims can be staked only on public domain lands, they are effectively limited to western wildernesses which are part of the public domain, and excluded from eastern wildernesses which are not. In the East, almost all the land in wildernesses was private land before it was acquired by the Federal Government. In many cases, the mineral rights were not acquired, however, and therefore mining is a possible use, subject to restrictions to protect the wilderness. But, if mining appeared to threaten the wilderness, the private mineral rights in eastern wildernesses could be taken by condemnation (P.L. 93–622) if funds were available to compensate owners.

Actual, on-site commodity uses of National Forest wilderness appear rather limited, despite the controversy which surrounds them. Mining claims are numerous— just how numerous is hard to determine because, until recently, there was no requirement to notify the Forest

---

[1]These figures are taken from an unpublished study by Ronald Dick, J. Oltremari, D. Sheppard, and A. Wilcox, "Wilderness as a classroom—a preliminary report," 1972, on file at the Pacific Northwest Forest and Range Experiment Station, Seattle.

Service when claims were filed on National Forest land. Claims were recorded in the county courthouse, along with many others on other lands. In 1960, the Forest Service estimated there were over 7,000 claims in wilderness and primitive areas larger than 100,000 acres (Outdoor Recreation Resources Review Commission 1962). However, in 1974, there was no mineral extraction from any National Forest wilderness or primitive area. Permits for prospecting in wilderness areas are required now, but only 10 were in effect in 1974. This low level of activity is consistent with mineral surveys of wilderness and primitive areas (mentioned in chapter 5) which have failed to turn up any major mineral deposits. Restrictions on mining activity to protect the wilderness make mining more difficult and costly and probably have discouraged development.

The Bureau of Land Management (BLM) policy for primitive areas prohibited mining, except for existing rights. Some primitive areas were withdrawn from

mineral entry, which closed them to filing mineral claims, before the BLM organic act (P. L. 94–579) passed (Foster 1976). That act brought BLM-administered land under the terms of the 1964 Wilderness Act which permits filing claims through 1983 on land not already withdrawn. No data on mining or mineral claims in potential BLM wilderness are available, but mining is a common use of BLM lands which might affect many areas to be studied for possible wilderness classification.

Logging

Except for limited timber cutting necessary for mine timbers, logging is allowed in just one wilderness, the Boundary Waters Canoe Area (BWCA) in Minnesota— an area which is an exception within the NWPS in a number of ways. Special restrictions protect shoreline forests in the BWCA, and much of the area is closed to cutting. About 200,000 acres which have never been logged and about 200,000 acres previously logged, out of

Figure 13–1.—Wilderness is valued for many reasons. The most prominent use is recreational, but the Wilderness Act provides for certain commercial uses, such as outfitter camps (*upper left*), scientific use (*upper right*) and water development, such as this earthen dam, now breached, in the Mt. Zirkel Wilderness, Colo. (*lower left*); and, livestock grazing, such as this sheep band in the Bridger Wilderness, Wyo. (*lower right*).

1,000,000 in the entire BWCA, are available for timber harvesting under current policies. Logging in the BWCA is controversial and lawsuits brought by environmental organizations resulted in injunctions against logging which apply (in early 1977) to all areas outside existing timber sales areas until a new timber management plan and environmental impact statement are prepared.

Since World War II, logging in the Boundary Waters Canoe Area has produced an annual average of about 40,000 cords of pulpwood, which is about 4 percent of the total pulpwood production for Minnesota.[2]

Water Storage

Water storage is another use permitted by the 1964 Wilderness Act, but again, only within National Forest units of the wilderness system. New water storage projects require Presidential approval, but a number of small reservoirs built before enactment of the 1964 Act exist and continue to be used.

The high mountains that make up so much of the wilderness system store vast amounts of water in the form of snow. A large proportion of the streamflow in the West originates in wilderness. Two uses related to snow in wilderness are controversial. First, in a few places weather modification efforts have been attempted to increase snowfalls and the resulting summer streamflows downstream, and weather modification has been proposed for other wildernesses. Many people are concerned because changing the weather inevitably changes the ecosystem—and wilderness exists primarily to allow natural processes to operate without modern man's influence.

Second, whether natural or modified, snowpacks are measured periodically to forecast streamflow for irrigation and power generation and to estimate flood danger. Some means of measuring snow depend on using helicopters, snowmobiles, or snow pillows (automatic snow-weight-recording devices connected to radio transmitting stations). All these methods raise questions of conflict with the wilderness concept. Different wilderness-managing agencies have responded somewhat differently to this conflict. In the National Forest wildernesses, except where helicopter use was well established before the Wilderness Act, snow measurements are made without mechanized equipment. Electronic devices which measure and transmit snow data are not permitted. The Department of the Interior policy for National Park wilderness is to permit existing water-resource monitoring devices to be

retained in wilderness. New devices will be placed in wilderness only if the Secretary of the Interior decides that essential information cannot be obtained from locations outside the wilderness and that the proposed device is the minimum necessary to successfully and safely accomplish the objective.

Most water impoundments for storage of irrigation water that are in wilderness were built well before the Wilderness Act. Typically, the dams are low and constructed of local rock and timber, and shoreline vegetation has had many years to adjust to the higher water level. Thus, many of the reservoirs are not conspicuously unnatural. No current inventory of these dams is available,[3] but 73 were tallied in 1960, based on incomplete data for National Parks and Forest Service wilderness, wild, and primitive areas (Outdoor Recreation Resources Review Commission 1962). Reservoirs are concentrated in a few wildernesses (about 20); most wildernesses do not have any such developments. Over one-half the reservoirs are in the Montana portion of the Selway-Bitterroot Wilderness which has low dams on about 40 of the lakes, some built in the 1880's and 1890's before the area was even a National Forest, let alone a wilderness. But other wildernesses in Montana and Idaho do not have dams. A few dams in the Boundary Waters Canoe Area, built to facilitate log drives, are still in place and maintain lake levels. Many more are abandoned and rotting away. Some of the wildernesses in the California Sierras have small dams to control streamflows; otherwise, streams go dry in late summer with a resulting loss of fish. There are also a few high, concrete dams used for generating electricity in the Sierras. They were built before the Wilderness Act from the 1930's up to 1963, when the Rubicon River was dammed in the Desolation Wilderness.

Grazing

Grazing by domestic livestock—sheep, cattle, and a few horse herds—is also allowed by the Wilderness Act. It is less common than it once was. Changes in the livestock business have reduced the economic attractiveness of this sort of extensive grazing. Higher costs for herders and transportation to distant, wilderness ranges; emphasis on intensive production of forage on better lands; and more use of feedlots have all reduced demand for wilderness grazing. The fact that fees for grazing public land have been raised and are scheduled to increase further probably contributes to a continuing decline in wilderness grazing demand. In 1974, 206,000 Animal Unit Months (AUM's) of grazing took place in

[2] From the Boundary Waters Canoe Area Management Plan and Environmental Statement, Superior National Forest, Duluth, Minn., 1974.

[3] Personal communication from W. J. Holman, Forest Service, Washington, D.C., June 1976.

National Forest wilderness. (One AUM equals one cow or five sheep for 1 month.) This is about one-tenth of 1 percent of all grazing of forest-rangeland areas.[4] Figures on grazing in Bureau of Land Management primitive areas and potential wilderness are unavailable, but grazing of these lands probably is substantial; over 80 percent of BLM land in the Western States (excluding Alaska) is subject to grazing (Foster 1976).

Wilderness Recreational Use: A Closer Look

Much more is known about recreational use than the other wilderness uses. It is also an important use and thus warrants a detailed discussion. The discussion of recreational use will cover three main points: (1) Amount, (2) character, and (3) distribution of use.

Recreational use has been reported for many types of areas, including wilderness, for many years. However, use data are of very uneven quality, and some review of the methods used to measure wilderness use and their shortcomings is necessary background.

Use Measurement Methods

Wilderness-recreational use is one of the most difficult types of recreational use to measure. The typical wilderness has many access points. Some larger ones have 70 or 80 entries, and even some of the smaller areas have 15 or 20 accesses, usually distant from Ranger Stations and difficult to check. Compared to developed sites, use is light and variable (wilderness recreation is, by definition, low density). This makes it prohibitively expensive to observe all entry points—some would have no use at all to observe on some days. Use is dispersed over such a wide area that it is nearly impossible to make any sort of direct head count, as can be done in developed auto-access campgrounds. Therefore, a variety of indirect ways of measuring wilderness use has been devised: Sample observations, electronic counters, automatic cameras, estimates based on data from trail registers or mandatory permits, or guessing.[5]

Observing a sample of trailheads on sample days has been tried (Lucas, Schreuder, and James 1971; Lucas and Oltman 1971), but the highly variable use makes reliable

sampling difficult and costly. The 74,000 acre Mission Mountains Primitive Area has 19 access points. If the main use season is considered to be about 100 days, then there are 1,900 date/place combinations from which to sample. One person working full time could sample about 4 percent of these, and then only for about 6 or 7 hours per day. Stratified sampling that would concentrate on more used times and places could increase the efficiency of sampling somewhat, but this would require some reasonably accurate information on use patterns to plan the stratification of the sample.

In addition to entry-point sampling, traffic has been sampled at roadblocks on access roads (Lucas 1964). In many areas one road serves many entry points and results in much more use being sampled for the same effort.

Automatic electronic trail traffic counters have been tried with varying success (Lucas, Schreuder, and James 1971). An improved model which projects an infrared beam onto a reflector and registers a count whenever there is a sufficiently long interruption was tested (Tietz 1973). The problems with such counters were illustrated in the test. Ten of the 19 counters, installed by field personnel according to manual instructions, proved to be set up incorrectly and did not count accurately. Another counter stopped working. The remaining counters turned out to be quite accurate. However, at best, the counters can indicate the number of large, moving objects passing since the last time the counter was read. They cannot indicate whether the objects were hikers, packhorses, elk, or cows; when they passed; or how they clustered into parties or groups. There are counters that print out counts and times but they are expensive. Length of stay or information about activities cannot be obtained from the counters. Neither can direction (entry or exit) or route of travel. Automatic counters are being used in a number of wildernesses and provide information on trends in use.

Automatic movie cameras, set to expose one frame at preset intervals, say every 30 seconds, have been used by the National Park Service (Marnell 1977) to estimate use of several wild rivers. Other use-recording systems employ a movie camera triggered by a passing object which interrupts an infrared beam to film a few frames. Some of these cameras photograph a calendar clock in a corner of each frame to record the date and time of each observation. Group size and type of boats can be determined. For protection of privacy, no identification of individuals is ever made, and only public areas through which visitors pass are filmed, not campsites or swimming areas.

---

[4] This percentage is based on the estimate of 213 million AUM's on forest ranges (in all ownerships, not just National Forests) in 1970 in the Assessment (draft) for the Forest and Rangeland Renewable Resources Planning Act of 1974 released by the U.S. Department of Agriculture, Forest Service, August 1975.

[5] Over a dozen studies of use estimation for wilderness and dispersed recreation are reviewed by George A. James, 1971, Inventorying recreation use. In Recreation: symposium proceedings, p. 78–95. U.S. Dep. Agric., For. Serv., Northeast. For. Exp. Stn., Upper Darby, Pa.

Many estimates of wilderness use are based on voluntary self-registration at trail registers. Trail registers provide much more complete information than traffic counters. Party size, method of travel, date of entry, length of stay, some data on destination (or itinerary) and activities, and visitor residence are usually obtained. The problem, of course, is that some visitors do not register (Lucas 1975; Lucas, Schreuder, and James 1971; Wenger and Gregersen 1964). Some kinds of visitors— especially horsemen, hunters, people making very short visits, and lone individuals—are less likely to register than others. Thus, the resulting registration data not only underestimate use, but also provide biased estimates of its composition.

Efforts have been made to develop systems for basing estimates on the trail register data (Lucas, Schreuder, and James 1971). In effect, adjustment factors are applied to raw data from the trail register cards to compensate for nonregistration. It is necessary to observe a sample of registration behavior to develop the adjustment factors.

It appears (Lucas 1975) that registration rates may be highly variable among wildernesses and over time. This makes it essential to carefully check registration rates before using them as a basis for use estimates. Field checking registration is difficult and expensive, however, and is rarely done. Electronic traffic counters or, probably better, automatic cameras might be useful and less costly sources of information on true total use to compare to registration data. Currently, use estimates based on trail registers have a large, but usually unknown, margin of error.

The most accurate wilderness use data come from mandatory visitor-permit systems (Hendee and Lucas 1973). Most National Park wildernesses, about 40 in 1976, and over one-half of all National Forest wildernesses (Lime and Buchman 1974) require visitors to obtain permits, a practice also common in Canadian wilderness-type areas. In almost all cases, permits must be obtained from the managing agency. In a very few wildernesses, permits are issued by cooperators, such as resort employees. In a few National Forest wildernesses in Oregon, permits are required but are self-issued by visitors at trailheads. The visitor deposits one copy of the permit and carries another while in the wilderness. Permits provide all of the information obtained from trail registers, in addition to greater detail on planned routes of travel.

Some visitors fail to get permits (Lime and Lorence 1974), just as some visitors do not register at trail registers. Compliance varies, although it is substantially higher than for trail registers. It is high in most National Parks and in the Boundary Waters Canoe Area where

the system has been in effect almost 10 years and visitor awareness is high, but it might be lower in areas with newer permit systems. In North Cascades National Park in Washington, permits were required for overnight backcountry visitors beginning in 1973. The first year about 65 percent of all parties obtained permits, but this rose to 86 percent in 1974.[6] All but 2 percent of the visitors accepted the concept of a permit system. Most noncompliers said they were unaware of the requirement. Availability of permits at times and places convenient for visitors undoubtedly increases compliance.

As with trail registers, some types of visitors are less likely to comply than others. Data from the Boundary Waters Canoe Area show that people on short visits, staying in resorts or campgrounds, or using motorboats were low in compliance (Lime and Lorence 1974). In the North Cascades, compliance was low for young adults, visitors in one- or two-person parties, rural and small-town residents, groups made up of friends (rather than families), and fishermen. Permit data could be adjusted (this is done with Boundary Waters Canoe Area permit data), but usually the emphasis has instead focused on raising compliance.

In most areas, commercial outfitters are required to report numbers of guests served, often as a basis for the fees they pay for their special use permits.

A final way of estimating wilderness use is to make an educated guess, based on last year's report and an assumed rate of annual increase. Estimates might be modified in the light of any available observations—how many cars were parked at a particular access compared to what is remembered from previous years (but probably at different times of the season and on different days of the week), changes in the number of guests reported by outfitters, wilderness rangers' impressions, unusual weather, and so on. Some wildernesses show wide fluctuations in use from year to year. Often this comes from the use of guessing, which is sensitive to changes in the person doing the guessing or in which observations are used from year to year.

Individual wildernesses generally rely on one kind of estimate: Permits, trail registrations, or guesses. Accuracy varies from good to very poor. Unfortunately, the method used and the expected accuracy level are not reported. If adjustments are made for noncompliance on permits or trail registers, they are often essentially guesswork, based on unsystematic spot checks, although

[6] Hays, John. 1974. Mandatory backcountry permits—an investigation into noncompliance in North Cascades National Park—Summer 1974. Unpublished report on file at North Cascades National Park Superintendent's Office, Sedro Wooley, Wash. 98284.

in a few areas more reliable checking is used for noncompliance adjustments.

Estimates of the use of the overall wilderness system, however, are a mixture of all three types of estimates, and the resulting level of accuracy is uncertain, but probably only fair to poor. Whether errors compensate more than they accumulate is unknown.

Comparisons of visitor use over time are particularly unreliable. Older estimates were mainly guesses, and as more accurate methods were adopted, large changes in reported use often occurred. Therefore, historical records of use trends (see fig. 13-10) must be treated cautiously.

Certainly, use data need not be perfect to be useful, and any improvement adds to the management value of the information. Managers in many areas have worked hard with considerable success in recent years to upgrade wilderness use data. The issue of use data will reappear in chapter 14 on visitor management. There we recommend a permit system as the best source of use data and suggest a well run, carefully monitored trail register system as the next best choice. There we will also discuss systems for summarizing data from permits or trail registers.

Units of Measurement

There are several units of measurement for recreation use.[7] The main units of measure may be described as follows.

Visitor-Day.—A visitor-day is the presence of one person for 12 hours, or any equivalent combination (e.g., two people for 6 hours each or three people for 4 hours each) that equals 12 visitor-hours. (Visitor-hours are also occasionally used.) The visitor-day is a standard federal unit of measure, adopted in the 1965 use season, and widely used. However, the National Park Service often uses several other units instead: Visits; overnight stays; and, sometimes for the entire National Park System, visitor-hours. None of these are reported by the Forest Service, although visitor-hours can be easily calculated by multiplying visitor-days by 12.

A few studies employ *group-days* (or *party-days*) as a unit of measure. These are identical to visitor-days but expressed in terms of groups or parties (synonyms) instead of individuals.

Before 1965 *man-days* was the unit comparable to visitor-days. This was essentially one person for a day of the week (or equivalent combination), but different agencies had different guidelines for handling fractions of days. For example, at one time the Forest Service

defined 15 minutes to 3 hours as one-fourth of a man-day, 3 to 5 hours as one-half, 5 to 7 hours as three-fourths, and over 7 hours as a whole man-day. This makes it impossible to convert visitor-days to man-days. A man-day could equal anything from two 12-hour visitor-days to a little over one-half a visitor-day, almost a four-to-one variation. For aggregated data, probably about 1.5 visitor-days per man-day would serve as a rough conversion factor.

Recreation-Day.—A recreation-day is the presence at a recreation area of one person for any part of a calendar day, from part of an hour on up to all day. This is a relatively new measure.

Visit.—A visit is the entry of a person into a reporting unit, such as a wilderness. If the same person returns later, it is another visit. Visits used to be widely reported. The National Park Service still uses the visit unit extensively, but the Forest Service no longer publishes data on visits. Sometimes *group* (or *party*) *visits* are used. This is simply the number of entries of groups. *Occasion* is sometimes used as a synonym for visit.

If length of stay is expressed in 12-hour units, then visits multiplied by length of stay equals visitor-days.

Visitor.—A visitor is a person who makes one or more visits, usually during a year. The person is counted as a visit each time, but as a visitor only once. This is not a commonly used unit. Also uncommon is the *group* or *party visitor.*

Overnight stay.—An overnight stay is the passing of one night by a visitor within a Park or other reporting unit. An overnight stay occurs each night the visitor remains in the Park. It is essentially a night-time headcount. It could also be described as a *visitor-night.* This unit is used only by the National Park Service. For an individual party, overnight stays could be converted approximately into visitor-days by multiplying by two and adding one, on the assumption that each night is matched by the preceding day, plus the last day:

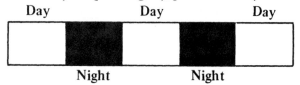

Equals 2 overnight stays or 5 visitor-days

In a few research studies, *group-* or *party-nights* are used.

Value of different units.—This array of units is probably confusing. Which of the units is best? As is so often the case, the answer is "that depends." Specifically, it depends on the purpose for which the data are to be used. Often, several different units are relevant to a particular purpose.

[7] Most of the units of recreation-use measurement are explained in "A glossary of terms used by the Bureau of Outdoor Recreation," U.S. Department of the Interior, Bureau of Outdoor Recreation, 1975. 32 p.

For impact on camping areas and camper congestion, the overnight stay or the group-night provides the most relevant information. For an overall measure of solitude, the visitor-day is most appropriate. For a measure of the proportion of society using wilderness, the number of visitors is most useful. Visits are a partial substitute for visitors, much easier to obtain, and give a general idea of total use and certain types of managerial workloads such as permit issuance. However, the great variation in the kinds of use labeled visits makes this a difficult unit of measure to interpret. A brief visit of an hour or so counts the same as a 2-week stay. Visits can be used with visitor-days, if both are reported, to gain an idea of *length of stay*.

Different wilderness-management agencies do not use comparable terms to report use now. We would suggest that at least visits and visitor-days be regularly reported annually for all wildernesses. Actually, visitor-hours would be preferable to visitor-days for clarity. The term "day" is subject to differing interpretations—a calendar day (either 24 hours or any part of a day), an 8-hour working day, and day-time (presumably this is what the 12-hour standard relates to). In contrast, a visitor-hour is unambiguous, and can easily be converted to any sort of day desired.

We also recommend the overnight stay as a useful supplemental unit, although calling it a visitor-night would clarify its meaning.

Current Levels of Use

How much is wilderness used? The Forest Service is the only agency managing wilderness to report recreational use separately for wilderness areas. However, the National Park Service in 1975 reported over 2.3 million overnight stays for backcountry camping, defined as camping in minimally developed areas not reached by roads. This would equal about 5 million visitor-days. For some parks this figure gives a good idea of wilderness camping use, but not day use, which is usually very substantial. But, the heaviest backcountry camping is in areas with large reservoirs, such as Lake Mead and Glen Canyon, where motorboat camping—rather than wilderness types of recreation—is common. Reported backcountry overnight stays at all areas which have parts included in wilderness proposals totaled 1.8 million in 1975 (table 13–1). Probably about 1 million of these overnight stays occurred on lands that are, or soon might be, classified as wilderness. This would equal about 2 to 2-½ million visitor-days of camper use of National Park wilderness and less than a million visits. Planned revisions in Park Service procedures for reporting use will eliminate these problems and enable

much more accurate descriptions of use of National Park wilderness.

Table 13–1.—*National Park backcountry overnight stays for Parks with wilderness or potential wilderness, 1975, by States*

National Park (NP), National Monument (NM), or other category	1975 overnight stays in backcountry
Alaska	
Glacier Bay NM	1,133
Katmai NM	741
Mt. McKinley NP	17,410
Arizona	
Chiricahua NM	0
Grand Canyon NP	158,380
Petrified Forest NM	160
Organ Pipe Cactus NM	1,223
Saguaro NM	3,904
California	
Death Valley NM	4,112
Kings Canyon NP	93,142
Lassen Volcanic NP	14,911
Lava Beds NM	51
Pinnacles NM	0
Sequoia NP	110,420
Yosemite NP	187,768
Joshua Tree NM	858
Point Reyes National Seashore	38,396
Colorado	
Black Canyon of the Gunnison NP	2,143
Colorado NM	159
Great Sand Dunes NM	411
Mesa Verde NP	0
Rocky Mountain NP	56,700
Florida	
Everglades NP	11,968
Hawaii	
Haleakala NP	6,278
Hawaii Volcanoes NP	2,839
Idaho	
Craters of the Moon NM	122
Maryland	
Assateague National Seashore	8,058
Michigan	
Isle Royale NP	12,039
Montana	
Glacier NP	24,785
North Dakota	
Theodore Roosevelt National Memorial Park	414
New Mexico	
Carlsbad Caverns NP	641
Bandalier NM	5,622

Table 13–1.—*National Park backcountry overnight stays for Parks with wilderness or potential wilderness, 1975, by States (Continued)*

National Park (NP), National Monument (NM), or other category	1975 overnight stays in backcountry
Oregon	
Crater Lake NP	1,022
South Dakota	
Badlands NM	338
Texas	
Guadalupe Mountains NP	2,166
Big Bend NP	21,835
Utah	
Arches NP	1,614
Bryce Canyon NP	585
Capitol Reef NP	3,139
Cedar Breaks NM	0
Zion NP	9,217
Canyonlands NP	27,039
Virginia	
Shenandoah NP	112,306
Washington	
North Cascades NP	25,041
Olympic NP	119,695
Mount Rainier NP	22,702
Wyoming	
Grand Teton NP	32,787
Yellowstone NP	44,387
Kentucky-Virginia-Tennessee	
Cumberland Gap National Historical Park	3,187
North Carolina-Tennessee	
Great Smoky Mountains NP	105,220
Colorado-Utah	
Dinosaur NM	21,750
Florida-Mississippi	
Gulf Islands National Seashore	0
Arizona-Nevada	
Lake Mead National Recreation Area	512,035
Total	1,830,853

NOTE: See table 6–4 for proposed wilderness acreages.

The 105 National Forest wilderness and primitive areas reported about 7.5 million visitor-days of recreational use in 1975. Table 13-2 gives the estimated use for each area. Use varies widely among the different areas. Use distributions will be covered in a later section.

Visits have not been reported since 1969, but length-of-stay information indicates a little over 3 million visits in 1975. The number of visitors would be less, because many people make a number of wilderness visits each year. Visitors to the Desolation Wilderness in California averaged about three trips a year to wilderness areas (not just the Desolation), and Northern Rockies wilderness visitors averaged about three and a half trips (Lucas 1978) Visitors studied at three Washington and Oregon areas averaged over six wilderness visits per year (Hendee and others 1968). So, the 3 million or so 1975 National Forest wilderness visits were probably made by around 1 million individuals.

No use figures for Fish and Wildlife Service wildernesses are available. Some are closed to use, and use is light in most areas.

It is difficult to compare use of National Park wilderness and backcountry with National Forest wilderness for several reasons: Use of different units, different types of reporting areas, and lack of information on day use of National Park backcountry. Unpublished use figures for Yellowstone National Park showed about 100,000 backcountry day-use visits in 1975, and 65,000 overnight stays. This means that visitor-days of day use were roughly half or less of the total visitor-days accounted for by overnight visitors (assuming about 150,000 12-hour visitor-days for 65,000 overnight stays, and around 70,000 12-hour visitor-days for 100,000 day-users). If Yellowstone is typical, then all National Parks were used at a level of 3 to 4 million visitor-days in their wilderness or backcountry portions during 1975. If day use equaled overnight use, the estimate would be 4 to 5 million total visitor-days. Improved use figures for National Park wilderness might drastically revise these figures, and better figures for all wilderness managing agencies might change the comparisons markedly.

Wild river recreation statistics are scarce. The numbers of Colorado River runners through the Grand Canyon were mentioned in chapter 2. In 1974, over 14,000 people went through the canyon. Several wild rivers in National Forests also have reported use figures. In 1974, visitor-days totaled 42,000 on the Eleven Point River in Missouri; 45,000 on the Middle Fork of the Salmon in Idaho; 142,000 on the Rogue River in Oregon; and 164,000 on the Chatooga in North Carolina, South Carolina, and Georgia.

Character of Use

Length of Stay

Most wilderness visits are short. Many small- or medium-sized wildernesses are predominantly day-use

Table 13-2.—*Use intensities in National Forest wilderness and primitive areas, 1975, by States*

Wilderness	1975 Visitor–days	Gross Acres	Visitor–days/Acre
Alabama			
Sipsey	7,600	12,000	0.63
Arizona			
Chiricahua W.	4,600	18,000	0.25
Galiuro W.	300	55,000	0.01
Mazatzal W.	12,400	205,346	0.06
Mt. Baldy W.	4,600	7,000	0.65
Pine Mountain W.	4,700	19,500	0.24
Sierra Ancha W.	7,300	20,850	0.35
Superstition W.	41,700	124,140	0.34
Sycamore Canyon W.	11,600	48,500	0.24
Blue Range P.A.*[1]	5,100	175,112	0.03
State Totals	92,300	673,448	0.13
Arkansas			
Caney Creek	3,800	14,433	0.26
Upper Buffalo	1,200	10,590	0.11
State Totals	5,000	25,023	0.20
California			
Agua Tibia	47,900	16,971	2.82
Caribou W.	61,700	19,080	3.23
Cucamonga W.	19,600	9,022	2.17
Desolation W.	256,100	63,500	4.03
Domeland W.	12,100	62,561	0.19
Emigrant Basin W.	134,800	106,910	1.26
Hoover W.	191,100	42,800	4.46
John Muir W.	1,378,000	504,263	2.73
Marble Mountains W.	208,500	214,543	0.97
Minarets W.	234,400	109,559	2.14
Mokelumne W.	45,800	50,400	0.91
San Gabriel W.	42,700	36,000	1.19
San Gorgonio W.	171,900	34,718	4.95
San Jacinto W.	77,500	21,955	3.53
San Rafael W.	45,200	143,000	0.32
South Warner W.	34,200	69,547	0.49
Thousand Lakes W.	7,700	16,335	0.47
Yolla Bolly–Middle Eel W.	21,700	111,091	0.20
Ventana W.	127,900	98,000	1.31
High Sierra P.A.	4,900	10,247	0.48
Salmon Trinity Alps P.A.	227,600	285,756	0.80
State Totals	3,351,300	2,026,258	1.65
Colorado			
La Garita W.	23,600	49,000	0.48
Maroon Bells-Snowmass W.	64,100	66,280	0.97
Mount Zirkel W.	32,400	72,180	0.45
Rawah W.	29,000	26,797	1.08
Weminuche W.	181,400	405,031	0.45
West Elk W.	23,900	62,000	0.39
Flat Tops P.A.	36,800	102,124	0.36
Gore Range–Eagle Nest P.A.	36,100	62,125	0.58
Uncompaghre P.A.	50,100	69,253	0.72
Wilson Mountain P.A.	14,800	30,875	0.48
State Totals	492,200	945,665	0.52
Florida			
Bradwell Bay W.	1,200	22,000	0.05

292

Wilderness	1975 Visitor–days	Gross Acres	Visitor–days/Acre
Georgia			
Cohutta W.*	23,600	32,307	0.73
Ellicott Rock W.*	2,500	181	13.81
State Totals	26,100	32,488	0.80
Idaho			
Sawtooth W.	46,700	216,383	0.22
Selway–Bitterroot W.*	70,200	989,179	0.07
Idaho P.A.	267,200	1,232,744	0.22
Salmon River Breaks P.A.	13,200	217,185	0.06
State Totals	397,300	2,655,491	0.15
Kentucky			
Beaver Creek W.	7,900	5,500	1.44
Minnesota			
Boundary Waters Canoe Area	1,090,100	1,034,852	1.05
Montana			
Anaconda–Pintlar W.	31,600	159,086	0.20
Bob Marshall W.	124,700	950,000	0.13
Cabinet Mountains W.	21,400	94,272	0.23
Gates of the Mountain W.	2,300	28,562	0.08
Mission Mountains W.	38,400	75,588	0.51
Scapegoat W.	15,300	240,000	0.06
Selway–Bitterroot W.*	63,300	254,480	0.25
Absaroka P.A.	15,600	64,000	0.24
Beartooth P.A.	69,800	230,000	0.30
Spanish Peaks P.A.	13,500	50,696	0.27
State Totals	395,900	2,146,684	0.18
Nevada			
Jarbidge W.	7,300	64,827	0.11
New Hampshire			
Great Gulf W.	24,100	5,400	4.46
Presidential Range-Dry River W.	21,000	20,380	1.03
State Totals	45,100	25,780	1.75
New Mexico			
Gila W.	84,900	438,626	0.19
Pecos W.	129,400	165,000	0.78
San Pedro Parks W.	22,700	41,132	0.55
Wheeler Peak W.	8,200	6,051	1.36
White Mountain W.	21,300	28,230	0.75
Black Range P.A.	17,200	169,984	0.10
Blue Range P.A.*	1,800	36,598	0.05
Gila P.A.	14,700	132,788	0.11
State Totals	300,200	1,018,409	0.29
North Carolina			
Ellicott Rock W.*	8,700	342	25.43
Joyce Kilmer-Slick Rock W.*	25,200	15,000	1.68
Linville Gorge W.	38,500	7,655	5.03
Shining Rock W.	29,400	13,400	2.19
State Totals	101,800	36,397	2.80

Wilderness	1975 Visitor–days	Gross Acres	Visitor–days/Acre
Oregon			
Diamond Peak W.	9,500	35,440	0.27
Eagle Cap W.	72,700	292,700	0.25
Gearhart Mountain W.	700	18,709	0.04
Kalmiopsis W.	8,300	78,850	0.11
Mountain Lakes W.	11,400	23,071	0.49
Mount Hood W.	26,800	14,160	1.89
Mount Jefferson W.	74,400	100,000	0.74
Mount Washington W.	17,200	46,655	0.37
Strawberry Mountain W.	25,600	33,653	0.76
Three Sisters W.	63,600	196,708	0.32
State Totals	310,200	839,946	0.37
South Carolina			
Ellicott Rock W.*	14,100	2,809	5.02
Tennessee			
Cohutta W.*	4,800	1,795	2.67
Gee Creek W.	2,600	2,570	1.01
Joyce Kilmer–Slick Rock*	2,200	3,832	0.57
State Totals	9,600	8,197	1.17
Utah			
High Uintas P.A.	131,900	237,177	0.56
Vermont			
Bristol Cliffs W.	2,500	6,500	0.38
Lye Brook W.	21,100	14,300	1.48
State Totals	23,600	20,800	1.13
Virginia			
James River Face W.	4,600	8,800	0.52
Washington			
Glacier Peak W.	97,900	468,505	0.21
Goat Rocks W.	55,100	82,680	0.67
Mount Adams W.	52,100	42,411	1.23
Pasayten W.	53,500	500,000	0.11
State Totals	258,600	1,093,596	0.24
West Virginia			
Dolly Sods W.	26,000	10,215	2.55
Otter Creek W.	18,200	20,000	0.91
State Totals	44.200	30,215	1.46
Wisconsin			
Rainbow Lake W.	2,200	6,600	0.33
Wyoming			
Bridger W.	187,200	383,300	0.49
North Absaroka W.	17,000	359,700	0.05
Teton W.	46,600	563,500	0.08
Washakie W.	34,000	714,300	0.05
Cloud Peak P.A.	45,900	136,905	0.34
Glacier P.A.	28,700	176,303	0.16
Popo Agie P.A.	33,700	71,320	0.47
State Totals	393,100	2,405,328	0.16
GRAND TOTALS	7,513,400	15,378,290	0.49

[1] Areas marked with (*) are located in more than one State. Figures for the entire area are given below.

Table 13-2.—*Use intensities in National Forest wilderness and primitive areas, 1975, by States (Continued)*

Wilderness	1975 Visitor–days	Gross Acres	Visitor–days/Acre
AREAS LOCATED IN MORE THAN ONE STATE (figures for entire wilderness)			
Blue Range P.A. (Arizona–New Mexico)	6,900	211,700	0.03
Cohutta W. (Georgia–Tennessee)	28,400	34,102	0.83
Ellicott Rock W. (Georgia–South Carolina–North Carolina)	25,300	3,332	7,59
Selway–Bitterroot W. (Idaho–Montana)	133,500	1,243,659	0.11
Joyce Kilmer–Slick Rock W. (North Carolina–Tennessee)	27,400	14,033	1.95

areas. Average length of stay, in calendar days, and percent of visits that were day use are available for some areas (table 13-3).

Among the areas for which this information is available, only the Bob Marshall Wilderness in Montana has little day use. Its size (about 1 million acres) and the location of the wilderness boundary (many miles beyond the trailhead in most places) screen out day users. Trips of a week or more account for less than one-tenth of all visits even in the very large wildernesses such as the Boundary Waters Canoe Area in Minnesota, the Bob Marshall Wilderness, and the Selway-Bitterroot Wilderness in Idaho and Montana. Visits in Washington and Oregon averaged 2 to 3.5 days. This is typical for small-to medium-sized wildernesses. A study of the southern Appalachian trail also showed 53 percent of visitors on 1-day trips (Murray 1974), and lengths of stay there averaged about 2.5 days. This area is not a classified wilderness, but it is similar and may suggest use characteristics for the new wildernesses in the Eastern United States.

Probably, lengths of stay have been about the same for a number of years. Increased travel costs could lead to fewer and longer trips in the future.

Party Size

Parties of wilderness visitors are generally small; from one-half to three-fourths of the parties at all areas for which we have data are in the two- to four-person size range (table 13–3). Lone individuals usually are infrequent visitors, although National Park backcountry campers are two to three times as likely to be alone as are people making visits to National Forest wildernesses. At most areas, parties of over 10 people account for about 5 percent of all groups.

There are a few unusual cases among these examples: The Boundary Waters Canoe Area has a 10-person-per-party limit and the San Gorgonio is used heavily by parties of 10 to 15 young people from nearby summer camps. But, the overall pattern is quite consistent.

Party size might be declining a little; more places have restricted party size; and the larger, organized groups have generally become smaller as both managers and organization leaders have become concerned about the impact of large groups on the environment and on other visitors. The proportion of small, independent groups has increased rapidly in relation to large, organized groups.

Figure 13–2.—Data on the amount, character, and distribution of recreational use are important information for managers. Lakes and streams are often favorite camping spots. Grassy Lake in the John Muir Wilderness, Calif.

Table 13–3.—*Characteristics of use of National Park backcountry and National Forest Wilderness and Primitive Areas*

Area (State)	Year	Length of stay — Average[1]	Length of stay — Percent day-use	Party size (Percent of total) — 1	2–4	5–10	Over 10	Method of travel (Percent of total) — Hike	Horseback	Hike with stock	Other	Activities (Percent of total) — Fish	Hunt	Photography	Swim	Nature Study	Mountain Climbing	Types of group (Percent of total) — Family	Family with Friends	Friends	Club Organization	Alone
Boundary Waters Canoe Area (Minn.)	1974	4.2	41	3	70	27	0	3	NA	NA	97	—	—	—	—	—	—	—	61	27	11	1
Bob Marshall W. (Mont.)	1970	5.9	14	6	51	27	7	31	59	6	4	61	34	58	11	28	0	43	15	30	2	8
Scapegoat W. (Mont.)	1970	2.9	41	6	61	20	14	69	18	12	1	62	11	53	20	27	2	36	21	29	8	7
Cabinet Mtns. W. (Mont.)	1970	1.6	67	5	72	18	4	90	7	2	1	61	6	45	15	25	2	40	15	33	5	5
Spanish Peaks P.A. (Mont.)	1970	1.8	63	8	57	27	6	72	20	7	1	41	16	53	9	29	4	38	13	35	4	10
Mission Mtns. P.A. (Mont.)	1970	1.7	62	5	57	32	5	97	2	1	0	74	2	56	18	31	2	46	17	29	2	5
Selway-Bitterroot W. (Idaho-Mont.)	1971	3.0	48	5	66	22	6	70	20	6	4	42	16	58	17	35	2	40	14	37	3	6
Desolation W. (Calif.)	1974	3.2	40	9	69	18	5	99	1	0	0	48	1	54	46	52	4	33	16	34	7	10
John Muir W. (Calif.)	1972	—	—	9	72	12	7	—	—	—	—	—	—	—	—	—	—	—	—	—	—	—
San Gorgonio W. (Calif.)	1972	—	—	7	53	15	25	—	—	—	—	—	—	—	—	—	—	—	—	—	—	—
Yosemite N.P. (Calif.)	1972	—	—	14	71	12	3	—	—	—	—	—	—	—	—	—	—	—	—	—	—	—
Sequoia-Kings Canyon N.P. (Calif.)	1972	—	—	13	75	7	5	—	—	—	—	—	—	—	—	—	—	—	—	—	—	—
Grand Teton N.P. (Wyo.)	1974	—	62	—	—	—	—	—	—	—	—	—	—	—	—	—	—	—	—	—	—	—
North Cascades N.P. (Wash.)	1974	[2]3.5	·	13	63	18	6	—	—	—	—	—	—	—	—	—	—	—	—	—	—	—
Olympic N.P (Wash.)	1974	[2]2.8	—	14	72	9	5	—	—	—	—	—	—	—	—	—	—	—	—	—	—	—
Mount Rainier N.P. (Wash.)	1974	[2]1.9	—	13	71	14	2	—	—	—	—	—	—	—	—	—	—	—	—	—	—	—
Glacier Peak W. (Wash.)	1965	—	—	—	—	—	—	82	18	0	0	—	—	—	—	—	—	—	—	—	—	—
Three Sisters W. (Oreg.)	1965	—	—	—	—	—	—	85	15	0	0	—	—	—	—	—	—	—	—	—	—	—
S. Appalachian Trail (Va., Tenn., N.C., Ga.)	1970–1971	2.5	53	—	—	—	—	—	—	—	—	—	—	—	—	—	—	—	—	—	—	—

[1] Length of stay is expressed in ordinary calendar days.
[2] Based *only* on overnight campers; no day-use included.

SOURCES: Lucas 1978; Hendee, Catton, Marlow, and Brockman 1968; Murray 1974; unpublished summaries of permit data from agency files.

Method of Travel

The most common method of travel in almost all areas is hiking (table 13-3). There are a few exceptions. Most visits to the Boundary Waters Canoe Area (BWCA) are made in paddled canoes (in 1974, 56 percent of all visits). Some BWCA visitors use outboard-motor-powered canoes (10 percent), while others use motorboats (27 percent); a few hike (2 percent), and snowshoe or ski (1 percent). Snowmobile use was permitted in the BWCA for a time—in 1974, 4 percent of all visits were made by snowmobile—but their use was terminated by the Chief of the Forest Service in 1976. The horsepower of outboard motors is generally restricted in the BWCA, and all use of motors is limited to specific zones. The BWCA is one of very few areas where mechanized travel is permitted by the Wilderness Act. Established airplane access can be permitted to continue under the Act, and it is allowed in several areas, especially the Selway-Bitterroot Wilderness and Idaho Primitive Area, but not the BWCA, which has a unique policy banning low-elevation flights as a result of Executive Order 10092 signed by President Truman in 1949.

About two-thirds of the Bob Marshall Wilderness visitors ride horses, which may also be the case in the Idaho Primitive Area and Teton Wilderness which are large areas with reputations as horse country, but data are lacking. Hikers predominate, however, in the Nation's largest wilderness, the Selway-Bitterroot in Idaho and Montana.

Data are not yet available, but the wildernesses in the Eastern United States are probably almost entirely hiker-use areas, except for a few that lend themselves to canoeing, kayaking, or rafting. Horses are rare or absent altogether in most of these wildernesses.

Hiking and nonmotorized boating (canoeing, kayaking, rafting) in wildernesses have grown more rapidly than other travel methods in recent years. This trend is strong, apparently in all areas.

Activities

Most wilderness visits are multi-purpose; typically visitors participate in a variety of activities. Surveys of visitors to seven wilderness-type areas indicated that, on the average, respondents participated in three activities (table 13-3). In areas with fishing opportunities, one-half or more of the visitors wet a line. However, (as pointed out in chapter 11) for many the fishing is somewhat incidental, rather than central. They spend a limited amount of time fishing, and pursue it as only one of a number of activities. For example, an observational study at seven lakes in the Alpine Lakes Wilderness in

Washington[8] reported about 40 percent of the visitors fished, and, also, that about 40 percent of the parties had members who fished. However, on the average, anglers fished less than 2 hours per day and about one-half caught no fish. About 80 percent of the fishermen indicated they visited the lakes for reasons other than or in addition to fishing. More than half gave reasons other than catching fish or getting food as a reason for fishing. Similar conclusions emerged from a study of fishing in the Desolation Wilderness in California (Carpenter and Bowhis 1976). This less-than-central role for fishing was also reported by BWCA visitors who paddle canoes, but mechanized visitors (motor canoeists and motorboaters) concentrated heavily on fishing and assigned it great importance as a reason for their visits and as an influence on their satisfaction (Lucas 1965).

Photography and nature study are also major activities in most places, and swimming is also common in many areas. These are all low-impact, nonconsumptive uses that fit well into wilderness management objectives. Hunting varies from minor to fairly common in the National Forest wildernesses (it is generally prohibited in the National Parks). Mountain climbing is an infrequent use in most areas, including all those in table 13-3, but common in a few areas.

Season of Use

Summer is the big use season. Some areas have nationwide reputations as big-game hunting areas, but in the only two such areas studied (the Bob Marshall and the Selway-Bitterroot) summer visitors still substantially outnumbered fall hunters. A few areas in the South, Southwest, and at low elevations in California have winter or spring peaks in use. In the North and at higher elevations in the mountains, winter use is light, but much more common than a decade or two earlier and growing.

Many areas experience weekend peaks in use. Weekend peaking is especially sharp in the smaller, more accessible wilderness areas, and produces serious congestion and overuse in many places. An example of moderate weekend peaking at the Desolation Wilderness in California is shown in figure 13-3. Other smaller, more accessible areas, such as the San Gorgonio and San Jacinto near Los Angeles, show much more severe weekend peaks. Data are not now available, but based on similarities of size and location, we would expect that many of the small, eastern wildernesses would also show sharp weekend peaks.

_____

[8] From an unpublished paper by John C. Hendee, Roger N. Clark, and Thomas E. Dailey, "Fishing and other recreational behavior at roadless high lakes: some management implications," presented to the 1974 American Fisheries Society Meeting, Honolulu, 1974. 33 p.

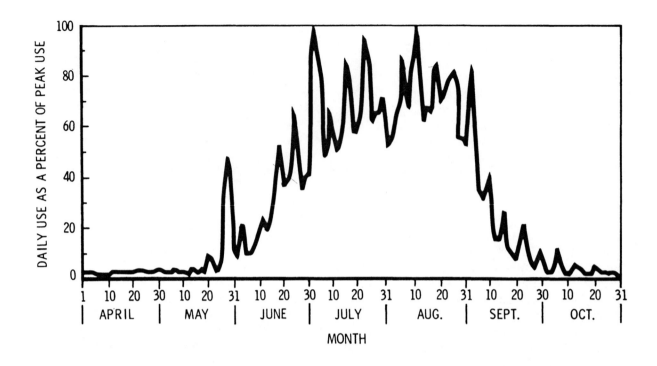

Figure 13–3.—Daily distribution of use in the Desolation Wilderness, Calif. (From summarized wilderness permit information, five California Region Wildernesses, 1971, unpublished report by Gary H. Elsner, Pacific Southwest Forest and Range Experiment Station, Berkeley, Calif.)

Social Groups and Organization Sponsorship

In almost all areas, a large majority of the visitors are part of family groups (which sometimes include friends), and about one-third to one-half of the groups in the areas studied include children under 16. Most other visitors come with small groups of friends. Organization-sponsored groups are not common, ranging from almost none in some areas to about one-tenth elsewhere. Organizations include conservation and outdoor recreation clubs such as the Wilderness Society, Sierra Club, and American Forestry Association; youth groups such as Boy and Girl Scouts, young people's camps of all sorts, church and school groups. In 1976, the Wilderness Society "Way to the Wilderness" program sponsored 70 trips and the American Forestry Association "Trail Riders of the Wilderness" organized 41 trips. Most of these trips were by horseback. In the same year the Sierra Club sponsored about 300 hiking, hiking-with-packstock, horseback, and boat trips (almost two-thirds of which involved wilderness or similar areas); and local chapters of the club sponsored many more outings.

Examples of the types of groups visiting some wildernesses for which we have data are given in table 13–3. Family means related or married people, not necessarily an entire family. A father and son would be classified as family.

Similar results were reported for 1965 visitors to three wildernesses in Washington and Oregon (Hendee and others 1968). There, 48 percent of the group leaders said they usually visited wilderness with family groups, 38 percent with friends, 8 percent with organizations, and 7 percent alone.

Figure 13–4.—Most wilderness visitors are in small parties of family or close friends but some use is by organized groups. A patrol of Boy Scouts hike into the Desolation Wilderness, Calif.

298

Family groups are a growing segment of the wilderness visitor population. This suggests two of the important values of wilderness—temporary escape from pressures of the modern world and strengthening of primary group bonds that can result from wilderness living.

Visitor Residence

Many wilderness areas draw visitors from all over the Nation. The John Muir Wilderness in California, for example, had visitors from 43 States in 1972. Sequoia and Kings Canyon National Parks had backcountry visitors from 39 States in 1972. However, for every area for which data are available, the overwhelming majority of visitors are from the region near the wilderness. Over 97 percent of the 76,000 visits to the John Muir Wilderness in 1972, 96 percent of the 17,000 Sequoia-Kings Canyon backcountry visits, and 92 percent of the Yosemite visits were made by Californians. Residents of Washington accounted for 74 to 78 percent of all visits to North Cascades, Olympic, and Mount Rainier National Parks in Washington in 1974. From 58 to 85 percent of the visits to seven Forest Service wildernesses and similar areas in Montana were made by Montanans. About two-thirds of the BWCA visits are made by residents of Minnesota. One conclusion suggested by visitor-residence data is that energy shortages and higher travel costs are unlikely to reduce wilderness use significantly. Residence data also indicated that, although wilderness *is* a national resource, from a recreational use viewpoint, wilderness is needed fairly close to population centers.

Distribution of Use

The geographical distribution of wilderness use is very uneven—there are many people in a few places and only a few are in many others. This unevenness is evident among wildernesses as well as within individual wildernesses whether we look at numbers of visits by trailheads; flows of visitors over the trails, waterways, or cross country; or visitor use of camping areas.

There is general agreement that such extremely uneven use is undesirable. There is no agreement, however, as to what constitutes optimum distribution. We will discuss the problem of comparing use between areas below; but, briefly, areas vary greatly in their ability to absorb use, and equal use of every area would be disastrous.

The problem of determining optimum distribution within a wilderness is much more complicated. It is clear that an even distribution—the same amount of use on every acre, or of every mile of the trail system and of every campsite—is neither possible nor desirable. It is impossible—barring total regimentation—for several reasons. People take trips of varying lengths; and, thus, the interior is not as heavily visited as the periphery. Also, we know most use is on trails or water routes which typically branch and diverge with the result that main trunks inevitably carry more people than branches.

Evenly dispersed use is undesirable for two reasons. First, different parts of a wilderness vary in their ability to absorb use. Some places are fragile; others more durable. Second, "outstanding opportunities for solitude" (the Wilderness Act's words) would be lost. The solitude experience would be homogenized. It might be a fairly high level of solitude if total use were similar to present use, but it would be essentially the same everywhere for everyone. However, people vary in their definitions of solitude and in the value they place on it. With completely even use, persons who really prize solitude would be frustrated. At the same time, persons not strongly motivated to seek solitude would encounter fewer visitors than they would willingly accept—in a sense, solitude would be wasted on them.

We have no neat formula for an optimum distribution of use within a wilderness. No one has. We know that in most areas present use is too unevenly distributed, and that redistribution to reduce the extremes is desirable. Badly overused trouble spots are a common problem. We don't know how far we should try to go in the direction of more evenly distributed use, but we know use could be *too* even. Some range of use intensities and associated variation in levels of solitude must be maintained. This issue of optimum use distributions will come up in many sections of this book—in discussions of principles of management (chapter 7), carrying capacity (chapter 9), and use management (chapters 14 and 15).

Area-to-Area Distribution of Use

Reported visitor use of individual wildernesses shows substantial variation among different areas (tables 13–1 and 13–2). Five National Parks each reported between 100,000 and 200,000 overnight backcountry stays—Yosemite, Grand Canyon, Olympic, Shenandoah, and Great Smoky Mountains. Lake Mead reported 500,000 overnight backcountry stays; but unlike the first five, most of them would not be defined as wilderness use. At the other extreme, some areas (table 13–1) reported no overnight use. All of the heavily used National Park areas are close to large population centers.

The most heavily used National Forest units are the John Muir Wilderness in California and the Boundary Waters Canoe Area (BWCA) in northern Minnesota, both of which reported more than 1 million visitor-days of use in 1975—about 32 percent of the total Forest Service visitor-day usage of wilderness reported for that year. On the other end of the scale, use in the Galiuro Wilderness in Arizona was only about 300 visitor-days.

The reasons for such different drawing power are poorly understood. The most heavily used National Forest wildernesses are almost all located relatively close to large population concentrations, as was also true for the National Park areas. California, Minnesota, Southern Appalachian, and New England wildernesses receive the most intense recreational-use pressure (table 13–1). In California in 1975, 12 of 21 wildernesses had over 1 visitor-day per acre (twice the national average). Three had over 4 visitor-days per acre. The BWCA in Minnesota also exceeded 1 visitor-day per acre. In the Southern Appalachians, Ellicott Rock Wilderness, located in Georgia, North Carolina and South Carolina, had over 7 visitor-days per acre. Another North Carolina area (Linville Gorge) had 5 per acre. The one wilderness in Kentucky, and one each in Tennessee and West Virginia, had over 1 visitor-day per acre. In New England, the Great Gulf Wilderness in New Hampshire had 5 visitor-days per acre, and the other New Hampshire wildernesses exceeded 1, as did another wilderness in Vermont. Only four areas in the United States outside California, Minnesota, the Southern Appalachians, and New England had over 1 visitor-day per acre: 1 each in Oregon, Colorado, Washington, and New Mexico.

Location near many people makes heavy use *possible*, but a reputation as an attractive area is also *necessary* if heavy use is to actually occur. This reputation must be based to some extent on actual attractions and recreational opportunities, but these are not the only factors determining an area's appeal. Personalities and historical accidents probably play an important role. Publicity in national magazines and guidebooks has contributed to the popularity of some wildernesses (and some particular trails in specific wildernesses). Some people have speculated that just classifying an area as wilderness attracts extra use. The identity that a name gives an area, and the word wilderness, might also stimulate use. If this is true—and the very limited evidence to date is insufficient to decide[9]—use could escalate in the new eastern wildernesses as classification

leads to their discovery. Some managers of eastern wildernesses believe this trend is underway.

By themselves, visitor totals give us little information regarding pressure on the resource. For one thing areas vary in size. For example, the use in the BWCA is distributed over 1 million acres; the Galiuro covers only 52,000 acres. Although total use in the Pecos Wilderness in New Mexico and the Bob Marshall Wilderness is about the same, the Bob Marshall is about 6 times as large as the Pecos. To aid in comparing areas and indicating pressure, acreage and use figures for all National Forest areas have been expressed in use per unit area (table 13–2).

As table 13–2 suggests, between different areas there are large differences in the degree of visitor congestion as well as in pressure on the soil, vegetation, water, and wildlife. Some of this variation may be acceptable and desirable, but the extremes may be questioned.

Although table 13–2 contributes to an understanding of inter-area differences in use pressure, it still gives a far from complete picture of congestion and of opportunities for solitude which are required by the Wilderness Act. In addition to size, at least two additional factors should be considered in describing levels of wilderness congestion. The first variable is length of season. In the northern Rocky Mountains or Cascades, the main use season might be less than 2 months (because of trails blocked by snow or streams too high to ford). In the milder regions of the country, the season is much longer. For instance, the Salmon River in Idaho, only about 2,000 feet above sea level, is used almost year round. Therefore, adding a length of season variable to the measure of annual use per unit of area has the effect of producing even higher use levels during the main season than table 13–2 might suggest. For instance, the 1 million visitor-days of use in 1975 in the BWCA were not distributed evenly over an entire year—about 90 percent of the visitor-days came between mid-May and the first of September.

Second, the proportion of usable or effective acreage is not the same in all wildernesses. Although all wilderness acreage is available in the sense that it provides at least a backdrop for the recreationist and space for isolation, only a portion is used directly by the visitor. The amount of land available for distribution of use is affected by steepness of slope; type of vegetation; and area of lakes, streams, and wet, boggy soils. On the San Jacinto Wilderness in southern California, for example, it was estimated that of the 690 acres in one travel zone (management area), approximately 400 acres were unavailable for use because of excessive steepness, type of

---

[9] Prior to enactment of the 1975 Eastern Wilderness Act, the Scapegoat Wilderness in Montana was the only area designated as a wilderness without any previous special classification. Reported visitor-day totals for the Scapegoat were: 1973—16,400 (1973 was the area's first year as a wilderness); 1974—19,700, and 1975—15,300. Figures prior to 1973 were not kept for the area because it was not a separate unit. Even allowing for the low accuracy of these use estimates, there clearly has not been any explosion of use after wilderness classification.

Table 13–4.—*Trail and entry-point density in selected National Forest Wildernesses and National Parks*

| Wilderness (State) | Acres | Entry points [1] | | Trail miles | |
		Number	Number per 1,000 acres	Number	Number per 1,000 acres
Great Gulf (New Hampshire)	5,400	13	2.41	25	4.63
Rainbow Lake (Wisconsin)	6,600	10	1.52	21	3.11
Hercules Glades (Missouri)	12,315	22	1.79	34	2.72
Linville Gorge (North Carolina)	7,655	12	1.57	19	2.48
Shining Rock (North Carolina)	13,400	4	0.30	30	2.21
Lye Brook (Vermont)	14,300	9	0.63	31	2.17
Pecos (New Mexico)	165,000	38	0.23	267	1.62
Desolation (California)	63,479	22	0.35	99	1.56
Anaconda-Pintlar (Montana)	159,086	30	0.19	207	1.30
Dolly Sods (West Virginia)	10,215	8	0.78	12	1.17
Yosemite Nat. Park (California)	[2] 646,700	67	0.10	650	1.01
Glacier Nat. Park (Montana)	[2] 927,500	81	0.09	801	0.86
Shenandoah Nat. Park (Virginia)	79,019	104	1.32	68	0.86
Idaho (Idaho)	1,232,744	43	0.03	1,057	0.86
Bob Marshall (Montana)	950,000	47	0.05	818	0.86
High Uintas (Utah)	237,177	21	0.09	199	0.84
Bridger (Wyoming)	383,300	41	0.11	315	0.82
Selway-Bitterroot (Idaho-Montana)	1,243,659	87	0.07	916	0.74
Sawtooth (Idaho)	216,383	26	0.12	152	0.70
Mission Mts. (Montana)	73,945	23	0.31	48	0.65
Teton (Wyoming)	563,500	24	0.04	318	0.56
Beartooth (Montana)	230,000	20	0.09	62	0.27

[1] Entry points are defined as trails crossing the wilderness boundary.
[2] Acreage figures for Glacier and Yosemite National Parks refer to areas proposed for classification as wilderness.

vegetation, and the presence of excessively wet meadows. Other areas are even more rugged and the proportion of the area usable might be much smaller. For example, we would estimate that considerably less than 10 percent of the area in the Mission Mountains Primitive Area in Montana is potentially usable. Managers of the John Muir Wilderness in California estimated only 2 percent of the area was actually used directly.

Usable acreage also is influenced by the degree of development of access and travel routes. Most wilderness travel is restricted to the existing trail systems or areas directly adjacent to trails. (Trail and cross-country travel will be discussed further in the next section.) Some areas are well supplied with an intricate trail network while other areas have only sketchy, sparse trail systems. Miles of trail and numbers of entry points (which relate more closely to capacity than does gross area) on a per-1,000-acre basis, vary considerably among the sample of areas included in table 13–4. The Great Gulf Wilderness has about 80 times as many entry points on an area basis as does the Idaho Primitive Area, and the Desolation Wilderness has 12 times as many as the Idaho area. And, the Great Gulf Wilderness has 17 times as dense a trail network as the Beartooth Primitive Area.

Intra-Wilderness Use Distribution

Use *within* any particular wilderness is likely to vary as much as use between wilderness areas. For instance, in the BWCA in 1974, about 70 percent of the user groups entered through only 7 of the area's 70 entry points. In fact, two entry points accounted for one-third of all groups entering the area. In the Mission Mountains in Montana over 90 percent of the groups entered at only 2 of the area's 19 trailheads (Lucas, Schreuder, and James 1971).

Figure 13–5, which shows the use pattern in the Spanish Peaks Primitive Area in Montana for the 1970 season, is representative of the spatial distribution of use in most wildernesses. Most trail use is heavily concentrated along some rather short segments of the trail system—for instance, on the trail leading into Lava Lake near the eastern edge of the area, which is only a little over 2 miles long. Nearly two-thirds of the area's use is day use which accounts for the concentration on short in-and-out routes such as the Lava Lake trail. But most of the trail system has only a trickle of use, an average of less than one party every 2 days of the use season. Campsite use is also uneven. It seems to be

301

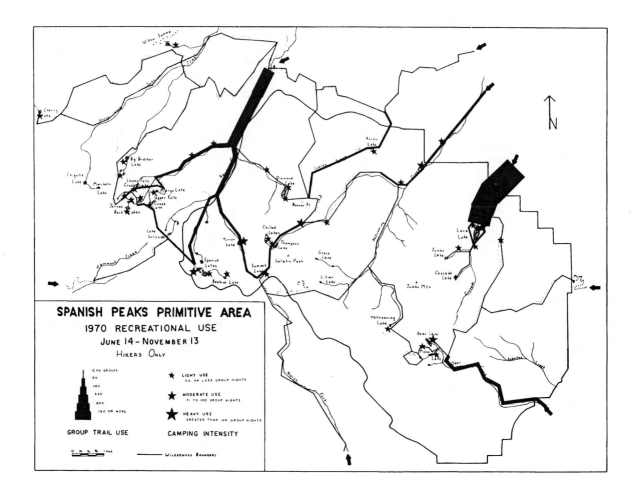

SPANISH PEAKS PRIMITIVE AREA

1970 RECREATIONAL USE

JUNE 14 – NOVEMBER 13

HIKERS ONLY

★ LIGHT USE
50 OR LESS GROUP NIGHTS

★ MODERATE USE
51 TO 100 GROUP NIGHTS

★ HEAVY USE
GREATER THAN 100 GROUP NIGHTS

GROUP TRAIL USE   CAMPING INTENSITY

—— WILDERNESS BOUNDARY

Figure 13–5.—Distribution of recreational use, Spanish Peaks Primitive Area, Mont. 1970.

heaviest at some of the larger lakes that are reasonably accessible.

The heavy concentration of use along only a few trail miles is shown in figure 13–6. Trail segments are ranked from the most to the least used. Total travel, in cumulative visitor-miles, is graphed against cumulative trail miles. For the entire trail system, the 10 percent of trail miles with the heaviest use accounted for about half of all visitor-miles. One can determine the percent of total use concentrated on any proportion of the trail network—30 percent of the trail miles get a little over 70 percent of all use, and 92 percent of the trail system accounts for all use. The index number expresses how much the curve rises above the 45° diagonal which represents an even use distribution. The higher the index number, the more concentrated the use. The index's value can vary from 0 (the 45° diagonal) to 100, the number which would describe a situation in which one

short segment had *all* the use. In the Spanish Peaks, the use is relatively concentrated (index number 53), but two larger areas that have been studied—the Bob Marshall and Selway-Bitterroot—showed even more concentrated use (index numbers 85 and 67, respectively). Horse use tends to be more concentrated than hiking use. Horse parties go farther, but they tend to stay on main trails. As a result, areas with heavy horse use have more concentrated total-use patterns. The Bob Marshall, the only area studied where a majority of visitors travel by horse, also shows the most concentrated use. The Desolation Wilderness in California (index number 60), an area about the same size as the Spanish Peaks but with about 20 times as much use, showed a somewhat more concentrated use distribution than the Spanish Peaks. One might expect that users, in an attempt to avoid crowds, would disperse more evenly. However, this does not happen. The dense trail network in the

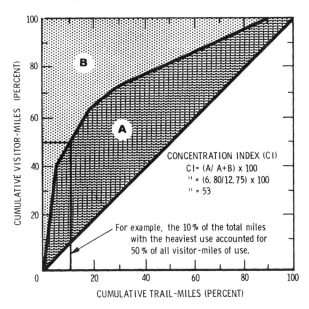

Figure 13-6.—Trail use concentration, Spanish Peaks Primitive Area, Mont., 1970.

it is estimated that fewer than 20 percent of the visitors to most areas do any cross-country traveling. And, an even smaller percentage of the total distance covered in the wilderness is off-trail travel. The specific amount of

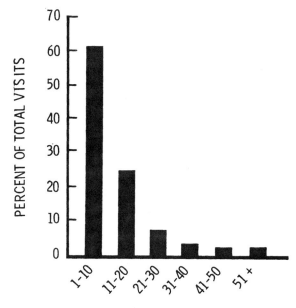

DISTANCE TRAVELLED, ROUND TRIP

(Based on a 1970-71 survey of 2,264 visitors to eight wilderness and backcountry areas in Montana and Idaho.)

Figure 13-7.—Distance traveled per trip, eight Montana and Idaho Wildernesses.

Desolation might also lead one to expect use to disperse more evenly, but this does not happen either. Uneven use seems universal and apparently is not self-correcting.

The pattern of short trips, both spatially and temporally, is characteristic for most wildernesses. This conclusion is illustrated in figure 13-7, which summarizes visitor trail travel for eight Montana and Idaho wildernesses and backcountry areas. Only about 14 percent of the visitors traveled over 20 miles round trip in the wilderness—a statistic which refutes the notion that wilderness trips are typically long safaris. Only about 2 percent of the visitors traveled over 50 miles.

An effective way of describing wilderness congestion resulting from use concentration is to measure the number of other parties a group could be expected to meet per hour or day in a given portion of the wilderness. In the Boundary Waters Canoe Area, data from trip diaries during the summer use season in 1971 (Lime 1975) revealed wide variation in frequency of encounters at different lakes. Groups reported the number of other parties they saw on individual lakes each day and the number of hours spent on the lake. Visitors to some lakes encountered more than 40 times as many groups as did visitors to other lakes. Often, only one or two portages separated very heavily and lightly congested lakes. This distribution of encounter levels is illustrated, for a small portion of the area, in figure 13-8.

Use patterns in most wildernesses are strongly trail related. From studies of Forest Service wilderness areas,

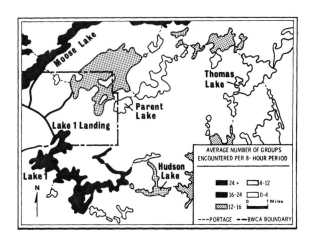

Figure 13-8.—Mean number of groups encountered per 8-hour period in a segment of the Boundary Waters Canoe Area, Minn., 1971.

303

cross-country travel depends on the motives, interests, and experience of the visitors, as well as on the terrain and vegetation in the area. Visitors are almost locked into trails in steep, heavily forested country, especially in areas characterized by abundant downed trees. This describes most areas in the Northern Rockies and much of the Cascades and the East. Alpine, plateaulike areas, and open desert country, on the other hand, open up cross-country opportunities.

Campsite use is also usually very uneven. In the Boundary Waters Canoe Area, Merriam and others (1973) reported 23 campsites varied from 28 to 1,138 total visitor-days of use over 5 years. Six sites totaled under 200 visitor-days each, and 11 were over 600. Western wilderness shows similarly uneven campsite use. Many *potential* campsites—a majority, in fact, in most areas—show no evidence of ever having been used at all (Brown and Schomaker 1974). In the Desolation Wilderness, the most popular 16 percent of the camps accounted for one-half of all use. The least used one-half accounted for only 18 percent of all use. The same type of analysis shown in fig. 13–6 for trail use can be applied to campsite use concentration. It appears that campsite use, although uneven, is less concentrated than trail use.

A study (Brown and Schomaker 1974) showed that the most frequently used campsites in the Spanish Peaks Primitive Area (Montana) and the Bridger Wilderness (Wyoming) shared the same characteristics: (1) Proximity to both water and fishing opportunities, (2) scenic and water views (but usually of a lake, not a stream), (3) location within 700 feet of a trail, (4) availability of at least 500 square feet of level land (4 percent or less slope), and (5) availability of firewood within 300 feet.

About one-half of the campsites were within 50 feet of the shoreline of a lake or stream, almost two-thirds were within 100 feet, and 85 percent were within 200 feet. Camping so close to water causes problems, which will be discussed in other chapters, but it is also obvious that sites close to water are highly attractive, and getting people to change their selection of campsites may not be easy.

User Characteristics

The Stereotype

A common stereotype of wilderness visitors pictures them as young, athletic, wealthy, leisured, and big-city "dudes." This stereotype is common in discussions as diverse as Congressional testimony on wilderness classification proposals and barroom arguments in small towns near wilderness.

The stereotype is largely a myth (Stankey 1971), resting on casual observation of small, biased samples, and, most pernicious of all, selective perception. We all tend to see and remember what we expect or want to see. Thus, stereotypes are self-perpetuating. The only cure is a dose of hard facts, which we will attempt to provide by presenting what is known, from scientific surveys, about the characteristics of wilderness visitors.

Age

Wilderness visitors tend to be young, younger than the general population; and, yet, all age groups are at least fairly well represented (table 13–5). Data from areas studied show large proportions of children and young adults most places (from 30 to 57 percent are 25 or younger), and almost as many older adults (30 to 50 percent are 26 to 45 years of age), also, especially in some of the areas with above-average proportions of visitors traveling by horse. Age distribution for the general American population is also included in table 13–5 for comparison.

All of these age figures refer to individual visitors. A number of studies have been based on party leaders or persons registering for the entire party. A study comparing party leaders and other party members (Jubenville 1971) concluded that, although attitudes were similar, socioeconomic characteristics differed significantly. For example, party heads tend to be older (Hendee et al. 1968).

The data are inadequate to determine if the age structure of wilderness visitors is changing over time.

Figure 13–9.—Water, lakes, and streams are the focal point for much activity on wilderness trips.

Table 13-5.—*Characteristics of wilderness visitors*

Area (State)	Year	Age (Percent of total)						Income (Percent of total) - - - dollars - - -					Occupation[2]				Education (yrs)[3] (Percent of total)			
		1-15	16-25	26-35	36-45	46-55	56 and over	Under 5,000	5,000-9,999	10,000-14,999	15,000-24,999	25,000 and over	Prof.-Tech.	Stu-dent	House-wife	Skilled Labor	0-8	9-12	13-16	17 and over
Boundary Waters Canoe Area (Minn.)	1960	—	—	—	—	—	—	—	—	—	—	—	—	—	—	—	0	21	54	25
Bob Marshall W. (Mont.)	1970	13	17	21	25	13	10	6	30	23	29	14	30	16	9	9	4	36	29	31
Scapegoat W. (Mont.)	1970	4	29	25	24	11	8	11	42	29	14	7	22	25	8	5	4	43	33	18
Cabinet Mtns. W. (Mont.)	1970	8	40	22	12	12	6	12	45	28	12	4	19	30	9	9	3	48	32	15
Spanish Peaks P.A. (Mont.)	1970	26	29	17	17	8	3	17	29	26	17	11	30	33	7	8	2	31	35	29
Mission Mtns. P.A. (Mont.)	1970	9	24	25	20	14	9	15	32	26	16	11	40	20	9	12	4	29	28	35
Selway-Bitterroot W. (Idaho-Mont.)	1971	4	27	24	19	14	11	12	37	25	17	10	26	22	9	9	3	38	33	26
Desolation W. (Calif.)	1972	29	28	18	12	10	2	11	16	23	28	21	39	26	9	7	0	18	40	42
S. Appalachian Trail (Va., Tenn, N.C., Ga.)	1970-1971	—	—	—	—	—	—	10	24	23	44		38	38	7	3	20		44	36
Four Calif. W.	1975	—	—	—	—	—	—	27	15	18	26	14	—	—	—	—	—	—	—	—
U.S. Families & Individuals	1970	—	—	—	—	—	—	34	29	21	12	4	—	—	—	—	—	—	—	—
U.S. Families	1970	—	—	—	—	—	—	19	32	27	22		—	—	—	—	—	—	—	—
U.S. Individuals[1]	1970	31	17	12	11	11	18	—	—	—	—	—	—	—	—	—	25	54	21	

[1] Estimated from U.S. Census data in which age and education figures are defined slightly differently. Others are usually 10 percent or less.

[2] Only the four most common types of occupations are shown.

[3] Based on years of schooling completed to date for visitors 16 years old or over, except for the Boundary Waters Canoe Area which is based upon data from people who had completed their educations, and only for paddle canoeists, the most common type of user, and the most comparable to visitors to other wildernesses.

SOURCES: Lucas 1964; Lucas 1978, Murray 1974; Vaux 1975.

Changes in birth rates, the degree to which individual wilderness visitors continue to visit wilderness as they age, and the age groups from which most new visitors are recruited will interact in complex ways over the years to produce an answer to this question.

Physical Ability

The only study of physical condition as related to wilderness use (Wiesner and Sharkey 1973) concluded that college men who visited wilderness were neither stronger nor more fit than those who did not, but that they had, in comparison with other college men, more favorable attitudes about exercise and parents who were more physically active. As a barrier to participation, lack of *interest* was more critical than lack of *ability*.

Sex

Wilderness has sometimes been viewed as a male sanctuary. Perhaps at one time it was, but now about one-fourth of the visitors are female. The larger, horse-oriented wildernesses average less female visitation; the smaller, hiking areas a little more.

Residence

Most wilderness visitors are from urban areas, as are most Americans. However, because visitors do not typically travel long distances to visit wilderness, the size of the urban areas they come from depends largely on the sizes of cities in that region. Thus, about 60 percent of the visitors to Montana wilderness come from small- to medium-sized towns (5,000 to 100,000 people), and a little over 20 percent are rural. In southern California, by contrast, with much larger cities within the region, over 90 percent come from cities with over a million people. An earlier study (Outdoor Recreation Resources Review Commission 1962) reported 90 to 96 percent urban visitors to the Mt. Marcy area (a State wilderness-type area in New York), the Boundary Waters Canoe Area in Minnesota, and the High Sierra in California.

Although current residence is overwhelmingly urban, several studies (Hendee et al 1968; Burch and Wenger 1967; Lucas 1978; Outdoor Recreation Resources Review Commission 1962) show considerably more rural background for wilderness visitors during childhood. How much of this is a reflection of the general rural-to-urban movement of population and how much a suggestion that a rural background tends to create interest in wilderness cannot now be determined.

Income

Wilderness visitors are above average in income (so are almost all types of outdoor recreationists), but only moderately so in most places. Income data from recent studies are given along with U.S. averages in table 13-5.

Income comparison, unfortunately, cannot be simple, as is indicated by the inclusion of two sets of national income averages in table 13-5. The first, calculated by Vaux (1975), includes both families and unrelated, single persons who constitute an economic unit, while the second is for families. Wilderness visitors look quite affluent compared to Vaux's data for individuals and families combined, but quite similar to families. In fact, most wilderness visitors are part of a family economic unit and the questions in most surveys have asked about family income. Therefore, it seems most appropriate to compare the income distribution of wilderness visitors to families, rather than to Vaux's families and individuals, which includes large numbers of widows, bachelors, and other single people in the comparison.

Earlier studies of wilderness visitors' income (Stankey 1971) show the same moderate overrepresentation of higher incomes in a wide variety of areas. The idea that high incomes are *necessary* to visit wilderness does not fit the facts, however. Typical expenditures for wilderness visits are low, usually under $10 per person per day (Stankey 1971; Lucas 1978).

Occupation

Persons in professional-technical occupations and students form the majority of visitors to most wildernesses (table 13-5). Generally, from 20 to 60 percent of the visitors of working age (beginning between 16 and 18, depending on the study) are in professional or technical work. The professions most often encountered are in the fields of education, research, social service, and religion, rather than law, medicine, and engineering. Usually almost one-fourth of adults and young adults are students, although a few areas have reported low figures for students—down to 4 percent in the Middle Fork of the Flathead in Montana, an unclassified, roadless wilderness study area where many visitors enter at a central airstrip.

Housewives and skilled laborers usually are the next most common professions, each comprising about one-tenth of the total. Other occupational categories are not well represented. Blue-collar workers, other than skilled craftsmen, account for only about 5 percent of all visitors, and farmers are usually well under 5 percent.

The occupational breakdown of wilderness visitors is strikingly different from that of the general population. Most wilderness visitors are in occupations that emphasize working with people, ideas, or abstractions rather than working with things. The contrast between their working environment and the wilderness is strong, and this could be one important appeal of wilderness. It has been termed the escape or compensatory hypothesis. Familiarity and the social setting or personal community also might play a role in shaping preferences for wilderness recreation (Burch 1969).

Education

The most distinguishing characteristic of wilderness visitors is high educational levels (table 13–5). All studies agree on this (Hendee et al. 1968). Two-thirds of the BWCA paddling canoeists who were no longer in school were college graduates, and one-fourth had done graduate work (Lucas 1964). Educational levels were even higher in the Mt. Marcy (New York) and High Sierra areas (Outdoor Recreation Resources Review Commission 1962), but this sample was based on party leaders. In the seven Montana areas, over one-third of the persons 16 or older had graduated from college (many were still in school, which lowered the average). About one-fourth had done graduate work or were still in graduate schools.

Does advanced education somehow help develop an interest in the natural world and primitive recreation? Or are certain types of people drawn to both university education and wilderness by some sort of innate curiosity? One can only speculate.

Conservation Organization Membership

Between 20 and 30 percent of the visitors to areas studied belong to a conservation group or outdoor recreation activity club (Hendee and others 1968; Lucas 1978). This compares to less than 10 percent of car campers (Hendee, Gale, and Harry 1969). About 40 percent of the club members (about one-tenth of all visitors) belong to a wilderness-oriented organization such as the Sierra Club, Wilderness Society, and National Parks and Conservation Association.

The Stereotype Reconsidered

The facts about wilderness users' characteristics are well established. In fact, the profile of the wilderness visitor is clearer than that of most other recreationists. The characteristics are quite similar from area to area, even in different parts of the country. The stereotype has little basis in fact and should be discarded once and for all.

Use Trends

Because of weaknesses of wilderness-use figures, caution must be used in analyzing use trends over time. The older records are probably less accurate than the more recent figures, but indicate broad trends.

As far back as figures go, the overall trend is strongly upward. Although only National Forest wilderness-use statistics are generally available, records kept by staff members in certain National Parks provide some information on Park backcountry use trends. These will be presented later. Since 1946, National Forest wilderness use has increased enormously (fig. 13–10). From 1946 to 1964, man-days increased over seven times, and visits almost as much. During this period, United States population grew 35 percent. From 1965 to 1975, visitor-days (the new unit of measure) increased 66 percent while visits probably nearly doubled (data gaps prevent precise calculations). Population grew only about 10 percent in this period. Visits in 1975 were at least 15 times as numerous as in the late 1940's.

California's heavily used National Forest wildernesses, all on a permit system, showed an average 16 percent annual increase in the 1970 to 1975 period. Crowding and congestion, and even use-rationing in several areas, have not yet produced a leveling off of California wilderness use.

The last 25 or 30 years have been a period of great growth for outdoor recreation. However, wilderness use has grown even faster, exceeding the general rate of increase. This is shown when, to avoid the problem of shifting units of measure, National Forest wilderness use is expressed as a percentage of total recreation use and also of developed campground use within the National Forests.

National Forest recreation use of wilderness as a percent of total recreation use of the National Forests, and use of National Forest campgrounds:

Year	Total Use	Campground Use	
		(Man-days Base)	
1946	1.2	5.1	
1951	1.8	—	(N.A.)
1956	2.0	—	(N.A.)
1961	1.9	7.2	
1964	2.1	9.0	
		(Visitor-days Base)	
1965	2.8	13.3	
1970	3.4	16.9	
1974	3.5	18.9	
1975	3.7	19.9	

The interesting thing is that wilderness is *still* increasing its share of National Forest recreation. The 16 new eastern wildernesses show up in the use figures for the first time in 1975, but they totaled only about 200,000 visitor-days and have only a minor effect on trend statistics.

The National Park figures for backcountry camping have been kept only since 1972; but they show a 31 percent growth from 1972 to 1973, an 11 percent

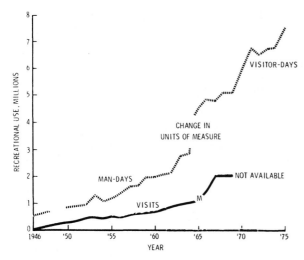

Figure 13–10.—Use of National Forest wilderness and primitive areas, 1946 to 1975.

growth from 1973 to 1974, and an 8 percent increase from 1974 to 1975. For comparison, *total* overnight stays for the National Parks increased 6 percent, 0 percent, and 9 percent for the same three periods. From 1967 to 1972, backcountry camping in Yosemite National Park went from about 78,000 to 221,000 overnight visits—184 percent more.[10] From 1967 to 1974, overnight stays in the backcountry of Shenandoah National Park quadrupled and reached 120,000.[11] In the last 10 years, backcountry use of Rocky Mountain National Park increased 730 percent—while total use of the Park grew a substantial but much smaller 73 percent.[12]

Sales of wilderness-related outdoor equipment are high and have increased rapidly in the 1970's, which also reinforces the validity of the upward trend in use estimates. For example, sales of one major backpacking equipment supplier (Recreational Equipment, Inc., Seattle and Berkeley) increased 25 to 38 percent during each of the first 3 months in 1975 compared to the same periods in 1974.[13] This firm has grown from one employee and annual gross sales of $85,000 in 1955 to 600 employees and sales of $22,000,000 in 1975.[14] Sales for another large outdoor equipment company, Eddie Bauer, Inc., went from $22 million in 1974 to $27 million in 1975, a 22 percent increase.[13] Even after allowance for

[10] Department of the Interior, National Park Service, Press release, "National Park Service extends backcountry protection plan." June 24, 1973.

[11] From presentation by Superintendent Robert R. Jacobsen at 20th Meeting of the Appalachian Trail Conference, June 22, 1975.

[12] From *National Parks and Conservation Magazine*, February 1976, p. 21

[13] From *Marples Business Roundup*, No. 655, March 26, 1975 (a business newsletter covering the Pacific Northwest).

[14] Smith, A. R. 1976. Mountain climber pushing for Alpine Lakes Bill. *In* the *Everett* (Washington) *Herald*, February 9, 1976.

inflation, this growth is substantial—an indication of growing public interest in backpacking and related recreation.

Use Projections

If the view of past trends is blurred, the view of the future is even murkier. Only two wilderness use projections have been made, and neither is recent. The Wildland Research Center (ORRRC 1962) projected wilderness man-days of use in 2000 to be 9.6 times the 1959 level. The Forest Service also made unpublished planning projections for essentially the same period and predicted about the same increase. This 40-year increase sounds very large, but it represents an annual increase of just under 6 percent. From 1960 to 1975 the average annual increase has been 7.1 percent. From 1946 to 1959, the average annual increase was almost 15 percent.

Wilderness use was projected based on projections of population, income levels, and related factors in conjunction with information on relationships of these characteristics to wilderness use. This technique is probably better than merely extrapolating from the past,

Figure 13–11.—Winter use of wilderness is increasing and offers a chance for extremely low impact use. Ski touring in the Selway-Bitterroot Wilderness, Mont.

but it has two serious flaws. One, the relationship of participation to population characteristics is not well understood. There is available now a good deal of descriptive information which has just been reviewed. But, causal connections are uncertain, as we indicated for education, for example. Second, projections of the population and its characteristics themselves are not very reliable. Projections of wilderness use, like many other types of outdoor recreation, also must take into account the fact that capacity is limited. Projection must have some upper limits; 500,000,000 visitor-days in 1 year is clearly impossible, for example.

These problems have apparently discouraged anyone else from making projections of wilderness use.[15] We will not peer into the crystal ball for any magic numbers, either. However, it appears to us that the potential for

---

[15] One limited exception is the study by Cicchetti, Seneca, and Davidson (1969) that projects 24 types of recreational activities, using data from the Bureau of the Census national recreation surveys (in 1960–61 and 1965). One of their activities is "remote camping," projected to decline either 17 or 39 percent by 2000, depending on differing assumed decreases in areas providing opportunities for remote camping and resulting crowding. In contrast, hiking is projected to about triple in the same period.

future growth is still substantial. Many of the qualities of typical visitors reflect overall changes in America's population—we are becoming more urban, better educated, more affluent, and more of us are white-collar workers. All of these changes point to continued growth in wilderness use. However, we are also becoming older, and this could temper growth somewhat (Marcin and Lime 1975). Growth could be dampened, also, if rationing becomes more widespread. However, if the wilderness system grows with the addition of new areas, this will add to reported use.

Wilderness use has not spurted recently as part of an environmental fad. In fact, the most rapid recorded growth was in the late 40's and 50's. But, if growth slows down or stops entirely, this does not necessarily imply a decline in the value of wilderness. The numbers game can be a dangerous trap. Stable use would not reduce the need for professional wilderness management. It would only make the challenge a little less overwhelming.

Among the co-authors, the author primarily responsible for preparation of this chapter was Robert C. Lucas.

Literature Cited

Bernstein, Arthur.
   1972. Wilderness as a therapeutic behavior setting. Ther. Recreation J. 6(4):160–161, 185.
Brown, Perry J., and John H. Schomaker.
   1974. Final report on criteria for potential wilderness campsites. Conducted through Institute for Study of Outdoor Recreation and Tourism, Utah State University, Logan, Utah. Supplement No. 32 to 12–11–204–3. 50 p.
Burch, William R., Jr.
   1969. The social circles of leisure: competing explanations. J. Leisure Res. 1(2):125–147.
Burch, William R., Jr.
   1974. In democracy is the preservation of wilderness. Appalachia 40(2):90–101.
Burch, William R., Jr., and Wiley D. Wenger, Jr.
   1967. The social characteristics of participants in three styles of family camping. USDA For. Serv. Res. Pap. PNW–48, 29 p. Pac. Northwest For. and Range Exp. Stn., Portland, Oreg.
Carpenter, M. Ralph, and Donald R. Bowhis.
   1976. Attitudes toward fishing and fisheries management of users in Desolation Wilderness, California. Calif. Fish and Game 62(3):168–178.
Cicchetti, Charles J., and A. Myrick Freeman III.
   1971. Option demand and consumer surplus: further comment. Quart. J. Econ. 85(8):528–539.
Cicchetti, Charles J., Joseph J. Seneca, and Paul Davidson.
   1969. The demand and supply of outdoor recreation. 301 p. Bureau of Economic Research, Rutgers, the State University, New Brunswick, N.J.
Clawson, Marion.
   1963. Land and water for recreation: opportunities, problems, and policies. 144 p. Rand McNally & Co., Chicago.

Dyrness, C. T., Jerry F. Franklin, Chris Maser, Stanton A. Cook, James D. Hall, and Glenda Faxon.
   1975. Research natural area needs in the Pacific Northwest: a contribution to land-use planning. USDA For. Serv. Gen. Tech. Rep. PNW–38, 231 p. Pac. Northwest For. and Range Exp. Stn., Portland, Oreg.
Fisher, Anthony, and John V. Krutilla.
   1972. Determination of optimal capacity of resource-based recreation facilities. Nat. Resour. J. 12(3):417–444.
Foster, John D.
   1976. Bureau of land management primitive areas—are they counterfeit wilderness? Nat. Resour. J. 16(3):621–663.
Ghiselin, John.
   1973-74. Wilderness and the survival of species. Living Wilderness 37(124):22–27.
Hanson, Robert A.
   1973. Outdoor challenge and mental health. Naturalist 24(1):26–30.
Hendee, John C., William R. Catton, Jr., Larry D. Marlow, and C. Frank Brockman.
   1968. Wilderness users in the Pacific Northwest—their characteristics, values, and management preferences. USDA For. Serv. Res. Pap. PNW–61, 92 p. Pac. Northwest For. and Range Exp. Stn., Portland, Oreg.
Hendee, John C., Richard P. Gale, and Joseph Harry.
   1969. Conservation, politics, and democracy. J. Soil and Water Conserv. 24(6):212–215.
Hendee, John C., and Robert C. Lucas.
   1973. Mandatory wilderness permits: a necessary management tool. J. For. 71(4):206–209.

Jubenville, Alan.
    1971. A test of differences between wilderness recreation party leaders and party members. J. Leisure Res. 3(2):116–119.
Kaplan, Rachel.
    1974. Some psychological benefits of an outdoor challenge program. Environ. and Behav. 6(1):101–116.
Krutilla, John V.
    1967. Conservation reconsidered. Am. Econ. Rev. 57(4):777–786.
Lime, David W.
    1975. Sources of congestion and visitor dissatisfaction in the Boundary Waters Canoe Area, p. 68–82. In Third Boundary Waters Canoe Area Instit. Proc., Duluth, Minn., May 9, 1975. 102 p.
Lime, David W., and Roland G. Buchman.
    1974. Putting wilderness permit information to work. J. For. 72(10):622–626.
Lime, David W., and Grace A. Lorence.
    1974. Improving estimates of wilderness use from mandatory travel permits. USDA For. Serv. Res. Pap. NC–101, 7 p., illus. North Central For. Exp. Stn., St. Paul, Minn.
Lowry, Thomas Power, ed.
    1974. Camping therapy: its uses in psychiatry and rehabilitation. 138 p. Charles C. Thomas, Springfield, Ill.
Lucas, Robert C.
    1964. Recreational use of the Quetico-Superior Area. USDA For. Serv. Res. Pap. LS–8., 49 p., illus. Lake States For. Exp. Stn., St. Paul, Minn.
Lucas, Robert C.
    1965. The importance of fishing as an attraction and activity in the Quetico-Superior Area. USDA For. Serv. Res. Note LS–61, 3 p. Lake States For. Exp. Stn., St. Paul, Minn.
Lucas, Robert C.
    1975. Low compliance rates at unmanned trail registers. USDA For. Serv. Res. Note INT–200, 6 p. Intermt. For. and Range Exp. Stn., Ogden, Utah.
Lucas, Robert C.
    1978. The characteristics of visitors to wilderness and related areas in the Northern Rockies and California Sierras. USDA For. Serv. Res. Pap. Intermt. For. and Range Exp. Stn., Ogden Utah. (In press.)
Lucas, Robert C., and Jerry L. Oltman.
    1971. Survey sampling wilderness visitors. J. Leisure Res. 3(1):28–43.
Lucas, Robert C., Hans T. Schreuder, and George A. James.
    1971. Wilderness use estimation: a pilot test of sampling procedures on the Mission Mountains Primitive Area. USDA For. Serv. Res. Pap. INT–109, 44 p. Intermt. For. and Range Exp. Stn., Ogden, Utah.
Marcin, Thomas C., and David W. Lime.
    1976. Our aging population structure: what will it mean for future outdoor recreation use? p. 42-53. In Proceedings of the national symposium on the economics of outdoor recreation, 163 p. New Orleans, Nov. 11-13, 1974.

Marnell, Leo F.
    1977. Methods for counting river recreation users. p. 77-82. In Proceedings, river recreation management and research symposium, 455 p. Jan. 24–27, 1977. USDA For. Serv., North Central For. Exp. Stn., St. Paul, Minn.
Merriam, L. C., Jr., and others.
    1973. Newly developed campsites in the Boundary Waters Canoe Area: a study of 5-years' use. Stn. Bull. 511. For. Series 14. 27 p. Agric. Exp. Stn., University of Minnesota, St. Paul.
Murray, Judith Buckley.
    1974. Appalachian trail users in the southern National Forests: their characteristics, attitudes, and management preferences. USDA For. Serv. Res. Pap. SE–116, 19 p. Southeast. For. Exp. Stn., Asheville, N.C.
Outdoor Recreation Resources Review Commission.
    1962. Wilderness and recreation—a report on resources, values, and problems. (ORRRC Study Report 3) 352 p., illus. U.S. Government Printing Office, Washington, D.C.
Pendleton, Robert C.
    1968. Wilderness is not recreation alone—scientific studies prove the value of wilderness. Naturalist 19(4):28–31.
Seagrave, Sterling.
    1976. Scientists learn from wild plants. Bioscience 26(2):153–154, 156.
Schmidt, Wyman C., and W. P. "Buster" Dufour.
    1975. Building a natural area system for Montana. Western Wildlands 2(1):20–29.
Stankey, George H.
    1971. Myths in wilderness decision making. J. Soil and Water Conserv. 25(5):183–188.
Stanley, John.
    1974. Research projects in the Sierra Nevada, 1970–1973. 32 p. Sierra Club, San Francisco.
Tietz, John G.
    1973. Project record: trail traffic counter accuracy test, ED&T 1977 Trail Traffic Counter. 37 p. USDA For. Serv. Equip. Develop. Center, Missoula, Mont.
Thorstenson, Clark T., and Richard A. Heaps.
    1973. Outdoor survival and its implications for rehabilitation. Ther. Recreation J. 7(1):31–33.
Tombaugh, Larry W.
    1971. External benefits of natural environments, p. 73–77. In Recreation: symposium proceedings, 211 p. USDA For. Serv. Northeast. For. Exp. Stn., Upper Darby, Pa.
Vaux, H. J., Jr.
    1975. The distribution of income among wilderness uses. J. Leisure Res. 7(1):29–37.
Wenger, Wiley D., Jr., and Hans M. Gregerson.
    1964. The effect of nonresponse on representativeness of wilderness-trail register information. USDA For. Serv. Res. Pap. PNW–17, 20 p. Pac. Northwest For. and Range Exp. Stn., Portland, Oreg.
Wiesner, Robert R., and Brian J. Sharkey.
    1973. Some characteristics of wilderness backpackers. Percept. and Motor Skills 36(3):876–878.

Wilderness management is essentially the management of human use and influence. Management of visitors and their impacts is especially important for preserving the naturalness and solitude that distinguish wilderness from other settings. Here a wilderness ranger suggests this party go to a lightly used location instead of a more popular area.

Visitor management is a critically important part of wilderness management. In fact, most wilderness management *is* visitor management. The major exception is the management of widespread ecological processes to minimize or compensate for modern man's direct and indirect interference as discussed in previous chapters on wilderness ecosystems, wildlife, and fire. Even considering these exceptions, the generalization holds true that most wilderness management is the management of visitor use.

Objectives and Constraints

In many recreation areas, the management of visitors and their impacts might involve engineering or structural solutions. For example, sites could be hardened and protected by paving or planting nonnative, durable grasses; and visitor activity could be channeled by barriers and abundant regulatory signs.

However, this engineering approach has limited applicability in classified wilderness. The framework for visitor management is derived from wording in the Wilderness Act: wilderness is "undeveloped Federal land retaining its primeval character and influence, without permanent improvements or human habitation . . . managed so as to preserve its natural conditions and which generally appears to have been affected primarily by the forces of nature, with the imprint of man's work substantially unnoticeable" and "has outstanding opportunities for solitude or a primitive and unconfined type of recreation." The Act goes on to prohibit commercial enterprise, permanent or temporary roads, structures or installations, motorboats, motorized equipment, aircraft, or mechanical transport (of any other kind, presumably). The 1975 Act directed at eastern wilderness calls for mangement in accordance with the 1964 Wilderness Act.

The Act also contains some specific and limited exceptions to these constraints including: Existing private rights; emergencies involving the health and safety of people within a wilderness; fire, insect, and disease control (under regulation by the Secretary); mineral exploration until 1984 and mining; water control structures (only when approved by the President); access to private inholdings, valid mining claims, and occupancies; commercial operations by outfitters and guides; continuation of established motorboat and aircraft use; and livestock grazing.

Most important for our discussion here, the Act also grants exceptions to development restrictions for *administrative activities* ". . . necessary to meet minimum requirements for the administration of the area for the purpose of this Act." Thus, any management exception to the Act's restrictions must pass a series of stringent tests: It must be *necessary* to meet just the *minimum requirements* to manage the area for the *purpose of the Wilderness Act.* The purpose, as discussed in chapter 4, is to ". . . assure that an increasing population, . . . expanding settlement, and growing mechanization does not occupy and modify all areas within the United States . . . to secure . . . an enduring resource of wilderness . . ." and to "preserve its wilderness character . . ." while devoting areas to recreational, scenic, scientific, educational, conservation, and historical use of types consistent with wilderness.

Management actions cannot be justified just because they are convenient, economical, or because they are effective ways of achieving nonwilderness goals, such as increasing streamflows, or stopping natural erosion or increasing the use capacity of a wilderness recreation site.

The constraints in administrative activities mean actions such as paving trails or fencing fragile meadows are at least highly questionable if not illegal, in the opinion of many people. This is the position from which we discuss wilderness management in this chapter and throughout the book. We recognize, as pointed out in chapter 1, that there are others who feel this approach is too pure and rigid.[1]

Beyond the legal constraint, the spirit and ideal of wilderness cries out against the frequent use of improvements, facilities, and structures in its management. A developmental approach seems self-defeating; to try and save wilderness by changing it until it no longer is wilderness makes no sense.

Thus, we think wilderness managers must rely primarily on the management of visitor use to control unwanted impacts, through such measures as changing use levels and patterns and modifying visitor behavior. This is essential both for enhancing the quality of

<hr>

[1]For example, see editorial, "Approach wilderness addition with caution," *The Oregon Statesman* (Salem, Oreg.), August 6, 1975.

visitors' wilderness experiences and to protect the wilderness resource.

In this chapter, we discuss various aspects of visitor use and their associated impacts, their potential for influence by management, and the direct and indirect management tools and techniques that might be applied. We assess the effectiveness of each technique based on both research and management experience. In this attempt, we have been aided by correspondence and conversations with many managers, including a large number who reviewed drafts of this book. Where appropriate, we recommend management directions we believe are necessary to maintain wilderness values.

Aspects of Visitor Use Subject to Management

Of all the many aspects of wilderness visitors' use, which ones can management influence? To what extent can different uses and their impacts be modified, and how?

It is useful to think of a *typology* or classification of undesirable visitor actions and their associated impacts, and the managerial responses that are needed and justified (table 14–1):

1. *Illegal actions with adverse impacts.* Examples are the illegal use of chain saws or motorbikes in wilderness, with the resulting disruption of other visitors' experiences and soil and vegetation damage. The managerial response would be law enforcement coupled with clear communication of legal restrictions.

2. *Careless or thoughtless violations of regulations with adverse impacts.* Here people usually know better, but don't care or don't think about the impact of their actions. Littering is an example, as are shortcutting trail switchbacks, camping in closed areas, and building wood fires where they are not permitted. The manager can try

Table 14–1.—*Five types of visitor actions, examples, and general management response*

Type of visitor action	Example	Management response
1. Illegal actions	Motorcycle violation	Law enforcement
2. Careless actions	Littering, Nuisance activity (e.g., shouting)	Persuasion, education about impacts, rule enforcement
3. Unskilled actions	Ditching tent	Primarily education about low-impact use practices, some rule enforcement
4. Uninformed actions	Concentrated use	Education-information
5. Unavoidable impacts	Human waste, physical impact of even careful use	Reduction of use levels to limit unavoidable impacts; relocation of use to more durable site

314

to motivate visitors to cease such behavior by persuasion; by making it easier to do the right thing or harder to do the wrong thing; by management actions such as providing litterbags or encouraging litter pickup through the use of incentives or direct appeals by rangers, or physically blocking shortcuts; and by enforcing rules and regulations (which are less authoritative than laws) against these acts.

3. *Unskilled actions with adverse impacts.* Digging a drainage ditch around a tent is an example of an impact resulting from a lack of wilderness skills or knowledge. Many once-recommended woodsman practices—such as building bough beds and pole shelters and burying garbage—are now inappropriate in wilderness because of their accumulated impact stemming from heavy use. Some are unnecessary with modern camping equipment. Some practices acceptable in areas outside wilderness are out of place within it. The manager's main response is to educate visitors about desirable practices, and, when necessary, to establish and enforce rules against such actions while always trying to educate visitors about why such rules are necessary.

4. *Uninformed behavior which intensifies use impacts.* This kind of behavior is illustrated by large numbers of visitors who enter a wilderness at a few well-known access points during peak use periods when they might have dispersed themselves over a number of access points if they had been more informed about alternative places. Concentrated camping at conspicuous places is another example. No matter how skilled and careful they are, problems are created. The manager's response is to provide prior information about alternatives available.

5. *Unavoidable minimum impacts.* Every party that visits a wilderness causes some minimum, unavoidable impacts by their mere presence. The party is *there;* other parties will see them and their solitude will be reduced. Visitors must step on plants, defecate, and urinate. Vegetation under a tent is compressed and damaged to some extent. Even with all the skill and knowledge possible, there remains a minimum, unavoidable level of impact. Use can be shifted to areas best able to support it. Trails, for example, can be relocated to more durable sites (discussed in chapter 15). When, after relocating use, the accumulation of unavoidable impacts is excessive, the manager can only reduce or eliminate use; all other options have been used up.

We will refer to these five types of impacts in the following discussion of the specific aspects of visitor use that managers can influence, with some mention of general types of managerial responses. Then information needs for visitor management will be considered.

Following this will be a detailed discussion of wilderness use management tools and *how* managers can influence various aspects of use.

Amount of Use

Clearly, managers can restrict numbers of visitors if they believe their unavoidable impacts (type 5) exceed the physical or social carrying capacity. Use can be restricted indirectly, for example, by closing roads or not maintaining trails; or directly, for instance, by rationing the number of use permits issued. However, as we noted in chapter 9, the direct rationing of use should be a last resort after every other appropriate approach has been exhausted.

Distribution of Use

As we noted in chapter 13, wilderness use distributions are typically uneven. Some of this unevenness results from uninformed actions (type 4) of users who possess limited knowledge of alternative opportunities. However, sometimes concentrated use reflects available trails (which can be relocated in the long run), differences in attractiveness of locations, or proximity to population centers. Here, the impacts fall into our type 5 category—unavoidable minimum impacts. In either case, managers might try to alter the distribution of use through the provision of information to users. This information might include the following:

1. Alternative nonwilderness opportunities: Several studies suggest that many wilderness visitors probably would be better satisfied in areas with more facilities and managed more intensively for dispersed recreation than is wilderness (Hendee et al. 1968; Stankey 1973; Lucas 1973). These users are seeking primitive, roadless recreation experiences but don't require or necessarily want the completely undeveloped conditions provided in classified wilderness. Managers, by providing information about roadless, but nonwilderness, locations can often steer users to desired experiences, thus relieving pressures on legally classified wilderness as well as better meeting visitors' desires.

At the same time, information about wilderness needs to stress its character and deemphasize recreation opportunities that are not wilderness dependent. For example, wilderness brochures have sometimes featured photographs of proudly smiling fishermen displaying dozens of fish caught, hunters kneeling by trophy elk, deer, or sheep, or very large groups of visitors—the wrong kind of image of wilderness, we believe. Isolation, solitude, and challenge could be portrayed with photographs of small parties in natural, typical surroundings (not necessarily in uniquely beautiful, scenic spots).

2. Other less used wildernesses: As indicated in chapter 13, use intensity varies greatly from wilderness to wilderness. Sometimes a lightly used wilderness capable of absorbing more use is located near a heavily used area. Most visitors have only sketchy, word-of-mouth information about use levels from one wilderness to another. Managers might provide such information to enable those visitors particularly concerned with solitude and relatively undisturbed conditions to more readily find them, while at the same time reducing impacts by diverting use from heavily used areas. This approach might not shift enough use, however, and might need to be supplemented by more direct controls.

3. Less used entry points, trails, and campsites within the wilderness: Chapter 13 pointed out how uneven and concentrated use typically is within any wilderness. A few miles of trail and a few campsites usually account for a large proportion of all use. Information about less used locations could help disperse users to them. More direct controls could be imposed through wilderness permits or by onsite dispersal by wilderness rangers, although these measures should be viewed as last resort actions.

Timing of Use

Most wildernesses have short use seasons and many have sharp weekend and holiday peaks in use (chapter 13). Managers can try to shift use from peaks to low period, first by providing information about peak period and off-season use levels and use on weekdays compared to weekends, and finally by regulation, if necessary.

Party Size

Large parties are not common in most wildernesses (chapter 13), but the few that exist have a serious adverse effect on other visitors' experiences (Stankey 1973). Managers can limit party size, and have in many places, but this technique needs to be supplemented with education and persuasion. Frequently, large parties are sponsored by organizations that are easier to contact than independent users and that may be anxious to cooperate with wilderness managers. The average size of parties sponsored by such groups as the American Forestry Association, the Wilderness Society, and the Sierra Club has declined in recent years in response to concerns about the adverse impacts of large parties.

Length of Stay

Length of stay can be regulated; but, in general, it doesn't contribute much to overuse. Few parties stay very long (chapter 13) and much of the use associated with longer stays either is in more remote, less used, and less

impacted areas; or at least it can be in such areas. Furthermore, the grand wilderness adventure to the most remote possible location seems particularly consistent with the purposes of the Wilderness Act and with the philosophy of wilderness. On the other hand, when an occasional party stays for a long time at one popular campsite (a few parties almost homestead), it is unfair to other visitors and hard on the site. For this reason, a reasonable limit on length of stay at any one campsite seems desirable. Time spent at a particular location—not total time in the wilderness—is the factor with the greatest relationship to undesirable use patterns.

Behavior

Changing behavior of wilderness visitors is a key to visitor management that can reduce or eliminate much of the need to regulate and control visitor use. Some managers with wilderness experience in different parts of the country believe there are substantial regional differences in visitor behavior that suggest that undesirable behavior is not inevitable; people can learn and change and visitor behavior is susceptible to manager-directed change.

Figure 14-1.—Trails are an important influence on use distributions and visitor experiences. The ease of access and travel that trails offer tend to increase use. Fragile areas, often left without trails, hold down use and provide cross-country travelers with greater isolation. A trail crew at work in the John Muir Wilderness, Calif.

316

Three aspects of visitor behavior are relevant here; behavior related to: (1) Resource impacts, (2) impacts on the experiences of others, and (3) cooperation with management.

Resource Impacts

Resource impacts can be dramatically increased or reduced depending on visitor behavior. Illegal and careless behaviors (types 1 and 2) may be more serious than inappropriate behavior by well-meaning, but unskilled, visitors (type 3). Unskilled behavior (type 3) is most common, however.

Several kinds of behavior determine resource impacts. First, self-contained camping (the opposite of living off the land) is low impact. Proper equipment is the key. Tents with aluminum or fiberglass poles eliminate the need to cut trees for tent poles. Tents do away with the need for pole and bough lean-to's. Air mattresses or foam pads replace bough beds. Waterproof tent floors make drainage ditches obsolete. Camp stoves mean no firewood gathering, no smoke, and no ashes. Fewer horses reduce impacts on trails, hitching areas, and forage.

Camping and traveling skills can be upgraded to reduce impacts. Visitors can learn to recognize and respect fragile soils and vegetation, avoid harassing wildlife, use water without polluting it, properly dispose of garbage (pack it in, pack it out), use campfires sparingly and only where wood is abundant, choose suitable places for fires, and be safe with fire.

Horse use requires special skill and knowledge because of the horse's potential for damaging soils and vegetation. Most horses weigh over 1,000 pounds; their weight is supported on small hooves with iron shoes. A horse can eat 20, 30, or more pounds of grass and other forage each day in a wilderness. Several booklets (Back Country Horsemen 1972; Miller 1973) and some agency brochures discuss how to minimize impacts while using horses. Probably the main mistake many visitors make is to leave horses tied too long in a small, often vulnerable area. Tying horses to trees for long times, especially overnight, has killed trees, produced manure concentrations, and detracted seriously from the beauty of campsites. Longtime picketing of horses in one area produces overgrazed circles. The animal can hardly be held responsible for his natural behavior of pawing, stamping, eating, and defecating. The problem lies with the behavior of the visitors responsible for the horse, mule, or burro. In addition, use of new, light equipment reduces the number of animals needed to transport camper gear, thereby further reducing the level of impact.

Impacts on Other Visitors

Visitor behavior, including choice of activities and the way they are pursued, party size, and the selection of campsites, also affects other visitors' experiences. The key to acceptable wilderness behavior is respect for other visitors' desires for isolation and solitude. Appropriate behavior requires knowledge of a largely unwritten set of rules or norms for wilderness use. For example, visitors who are sensitive to these norms will usually try to camp out of sight of others and hold down noise (for information on how far different types of noise will travel in different settings and how to minimize transmission of campsite noise by strategic location of campsites, see Daily and Redman 1975). Extensive social overtures beyond the courtesies of greeting and limited getting acquainted are usually not considered appropriate in wilderness camp areas, and most visitors respect one another's privacy. Littering and erection of campsite improvements, such as shelves, stools, racks, shelters, and rock fireplaces that are left behind are all examples of behavior that can detract from the quality of the wilderness experience of others. A skillful camper leaves the campsite so unmodified it is difficult to tell it has been used.

Cooperation

Finally, cooperation with management is a visitor obligation. This includes such things as registering at trail registers or obtaining a wilderness permit where it is required, and responding to other requests of management whether it is to pack out litter or fill out a questionnaire seeking information useful to management. It also includes complying with rules, regulations, and laws pertaining to the use of the area.

Wilderness visitors generally seem very cooperative. Wilderness users and managers are usually united in their concern for the resource. This is reflected by the unusually high response of wilderness visitors to questionnaires seeking their views and their almost complete compliance with requests to pick up and carry out some extra litter (Clark and Muth 1976).

Information Needed for Visitor Management

Professional management of visitors requires reliable base data just as much as timber management, water management, or any other type of resource management. Much past management of wilderness visitors has been based on the manager's personal experiences, feelings, and intuition rather than on systematically collected information. Professional judgment must always be a major part of wilderness management; but, it should be based on reliable information about use, resource conditions, likely user responses to management actions, and probable responses of the ecosystem to management decisions.

Guesswork is just not good enough for the challenge of wilderness management now and in the future. Research and managers' experience both indicate that the best guesses about use levels and patterns and users' attitudes are often very inaccurate; for example, in many areas, during the first year that wilderness permits were used, sharp changes in use figures were produced, both up and down. Field surveys have generally shown that use is less evenly distributed than managers estimated, length of stay is shorter than thought, and there is less horse and more hiker use than believed. Similarly, managers have commonly held assumptions about visitors' attitudes on solitude, on facilities, and on use controls that have often turned out to be wide of the mark (Hendee and Harris 1970). Even campsite impacts—a seemingly objective, readily observed condition—proved to be less severe than managers thought (see the discussion of campsite inventories in chapter 15). Unsystematic observation and subjective recall are not reliable.

Information for resource management costs money to collect, and the benefits of better information must be compared to these costs (Herfindahl 1969). Poor wilderness management decisions based on inadequate information can be very costly, and can even result in irreversible damage. Information collection for information's sake can be a trap, and complete, precise information is not a realistic goal. But a major upgrading of base data about wilderness use and resources is the essential first step to improved management. This information is needed to develop management plans and actions, to monitor the reactions of visitors and the ecosystem, and to revise plans. Without this base data, the manager is flying by the seat of the pants; there is no way to determine whether management is achieving its objectives. Effective learning from experience is prevented.[2]

Two categories of data are relevant to visitor management: Resource data and visitor data.

Resource Data

Information about resource conditions is essential. For example, how good or bad are physical-biological

conditions at each camping area? How much effect has grazing had on meadows? Is water quality too low in some places? Are trails eroding? This information is essential to identify places where use needs to be reduced or changed in type, and to select locations where some of it might be diverted as well as where new facilities might be considered or where maintenance and repair are needed.

A variety of basic resource inventory techniques from the fields of range management, wildlife management, forestry, and ecology are available but only a few examples of these will be discussed here. Depending on money available and the need for the information to meet objectives for the wilderness, a variety of information could be collected—data about the condition of trails and travel routes, campsites, forage areas, water near use areas, natural attractions, and so forth. This would help identify critical spots that should be checked regularly. At some interval, maybe 5 or 10 years, a complete reinventory would probably be desirable. Without some systematic observation of resource conditions it will not be possible to say with any confidence if conditions are improving or deteriorating.

Because information is costly, it should be collected systematically, should be related to specific objectives, and should be in a form that is easily used and that permits comparisons between places and over time. The Code-A-Site system, discussed in chapter 15, is an example of systematic, readily retrieved information collection. Photographic techniques provide other examples. Some managers have established permanent photo points throughout the wilderness under their administration. A photo point near the center of a campsite, for example, can be relocated later if the distances from three trees or rocks are carefully measured and the reference trees carefully identified on a sketch map. The next time, arcs are swung at the recorded distances from the trees and their intersection marks the point closely. A stake can be driven just below the surface to help pinpoint the location. A series of photographs of areas such as campsites, meadows, and other key locations, enables managers to quickly determine changes that are occurring. If done properly, it is possible to measure such things as groundcover loss, soil erosion, tree vigor, changes in species composition, and other vegetation damage (Walker 1968). Panoramas—full, 360° views—can be obtained by carefully levelling the camera and rotating it a specific amount before each photo is taken. An example of a campsite photographic panorama is on page 319.

Vertical photos, taken from about eye-level, can record detailed conditions on sample areas. A 1-meter-square

[2]Collection of resource and visitor use information was a topic in the Anaconda-Pintlar Wilderness Plan (see chapter 8) for which separate objectives and distinct policies and actions were identified.

Figure 14–2.—Periodic rephotographing of wilderness camps and trails can provide an excellent record for measuring impact over time. This 360-degree panorama photo of a campsite in the Selway-Bitterroot Wilderness permits measures of existing impact as well as the spread of impact over time to be made.

plot is covered nicely with a 28 mm lens on a 35 mm camera. Longer lenses might be used on a larger format camera. Percentage of the sample areas covered by vegetation, by bare soil, and by dead plant material can be measured and plant species identified. If carefully done, the same sample plots can be relocated and photographed again to measure trends.

A special technique has been developed to photograph stereographically sample locations on trails that permits accurate measurement of degree of erosion (Rinehart, Hardy, and Rosenau 1978). Two photographs of a trail sample transect are taken from a distance of 15 feet. The two photos are oriented identically, but one is taken 9 inches to the right of the other. An example of a pair of stereographic photographs of a trail is shown on page 320. When viewed through a stereoscope, the trail is seen in three dimensions (3-D). (Some people can see "in stereo" without a stereoscope by relaxing their eyes and looking through the photographs as though focusing on a distant object.)

Changes from year to year are readily observed in the detailed, 3-D photographs. The sample transect is marked by tent stakes driven flush with the ground, and a string stretched between them marks the transect. Closely spaced vertical measurements from the string to the trail surface enable one to calculate the cross-sectional area below the string to determine the degree of entrenchment of the trail. The same cross-sectional area also can be measured directly from the photographs (Rinehart, Hardy, and Rosenau 1978).

Such photos, systematically collected over time, constitute an important bank of information and, in some cases, can help determine the natural conditions

that prevailed prior to man's influence (for a good example, see Gibbens and Heady 1964, and also figure 10–5, page 202 in this book.)

Visitor Data

A variety of visitor data can be used in management. First, there is basic information on use levels, patterns of use, and characteristics of use. This information is usually collected by area managers. Second, there is information on the characteristics and behavior of visitors; on their knowledge of appropriate ways of doing things; their desires and preferences; the satisfactions they get from use; their attitudes about conditions in the area and about other uses; and their feelings and probable reactions to management actions, policies, or regulations. Such information is generally gathered by research scientists rather than managers. All of these data change over time and need to be measured periodically. Basic use data are collected annually; other visitor information needs to be updated at longer intervals.

The ways of gathering basic use data were discussed in chapter 13. Four approaches are possible. Direct observation of a sample of times and places is one approach, but costly and with low precision. Automatic counters have had mixed success, but, even when they perform well, they provide limited information. Trail registers provide incomplete data that can be adjusted for nonregistrants if registration behavior is checked, but this again is costly. Mandatory permits provide the most reliable and complete data on use (Hendee and Lucas 1973).

Permit Systems

The costs of operating a permit system are substantial (primarily in salaries of people to administer it), but in

319

BIG CREEK TRAIL SEGMENT #8
8/12/75

Figure 14-3.—Stereo-pair photos permit the view to see impacts in 3-dimensions; estimates of the volume of annual soil loss from this trail can be made directly from such photos. Place a stereo-viewer over this photo to see the detail that can be measured.

addition to obtaining sound use data there are other benefits (Hendee and Lucas 1973). The main additional benefit to both managers and visitors comes from the contact between the two. This contact has the potential for communicating information about where and when to go that could improve visitors' experiences and reduce excessive impacts on the wilderness, and the potential for improving visitors' knowledge of regulations, desirable behavior and practices, and hazards. The benefits of communication are lost, however, if the agency representatives, where permits are issued on a face-to-face or telephone basis, are not well informed and skilled in public contacts or if written material used with mail or self-issued permits is not well done, up to date, and readable. A permit system that records who went where, and for how long, can also add a dimension of safety to wilderness travel. The permit is necessary, of course, when direct regulation of use must be resorted to, but this is not the only or even the main reason for a permit system; it is unfortunate that many people view permits and use rationing as inevitably linked. It is likely that a well-run permit system could reduce and delay the need to regulate use.

The costs of administering a permit system and the costs in the form of visitor inconvenience need to be weighed against the many benefits. At least for heavily used areas, the benefits seem large relative to costs. But there are less obvious benefits from permits issued in more lightly used areas. Even these areas have overused spots that a permit system might help to identify and aid in redirecting people to less used places. In addition to helping redistribute use within a wilderness, permit data also can aid in redistributing use between wildernesses. Encouraging some visitors to switch from popular to less visited wildernesses would be aided by reliable data on the use of all areas, not just the heavily used ones. If use of certain popular areas is controlled, some of the users turned away at one area will go to another nearby wilderness. The permit system provides a good check on this movement between areas and can help identify new trouble spots quickly.

For some areas where use levels and environmental impacts are not high enough to require rationing, the self-issued, mandatory permit may be an attractive compromise. Seven National Forest wildernesses in Oregon use this system. The standard Forest Service wilderness permit is available from a box near trailheads. Visitors fill out a permit, take one copy, and deposit one. This appears to be by far the best way to gather accurate use information because compliance is very good. Field checks by wilderness rangers show 91- to 95-percent compliance, compared to 50 to 60 percent in the same areas with agency-issued permits. This is also much better than trail registers.

The self-issued permit is more convenient for visitors, as it eliminates any need to drive out of the way to an issuing office or to change travel schedules to get a permit during office hours. It also is considered by most managers to reduce administrative costs considerably. Personal contact is lost, but a well-designed map can give regulations and suggested practices, perhaps better than busy clerks with little wilderness background.

With self-issued permits, it is difficult to try to divert visitors away from overused areas. With agency-issued permits, this is possible; but, unfortunately, it often is not done anyway because of a lack of well-informed, skilled people to issue permits. Contacts with wilderness rangers in the field are more effective in communicating suggestions on wilderness behavior and reminders of regulations.

If managers seek to redistribute use to achieve management goals for solitude and use impacts, all persons registering might be sent information on use-problem areas during the off-season. Many of them will make trips, or know people who will. (This approach was used in 1975 with some Boundary Waters Canoe Area visitors, as is described in more detail later.) The near-complete compliance with self-issued permit requirements would provide an excellent mailing list for such information.

Use Summaries

The permits or trail register cards provide raw data on each party. Included are the size of the group, where the party leader lives, main method of travel, number of stock (horses, mules, or burros), date of entry, and either exit date or length of stay (fig. 14-4). Permits also usually provide information on entry and exit locations, travel itinerary, and camping locations by travel zones. Trail register cards can also request some information on itinerary and, at least, entry point.

Ways to organize this raw data for management purposes are almost endless, and selectivity is essential. There are a number of different basic units of measure of recreational use. These were defined and discussed in chapter 13. No single measure is best; different units are useful for different purposes. Number of group visits, individual visits, visitor-days, and group-nights are particularly useful for many important visitor management decisions.

Tabulations can be made in different ways, depending on the management purpose being served (Lime and Buchman 1974; Elsner 1972; Frayer and Butts 1974). Data can be tabulated on the basis of location variables (such as entry points or travel zones), by visitor characteristics (such as residence of leader, length of stay, group size, or method of visitor travel), or by time variables (such as day of week, weeks of the season, or months). These variables can also be combined into more complex tables—for example, entry points used by visitors from a nearby large urban area during the peak month.

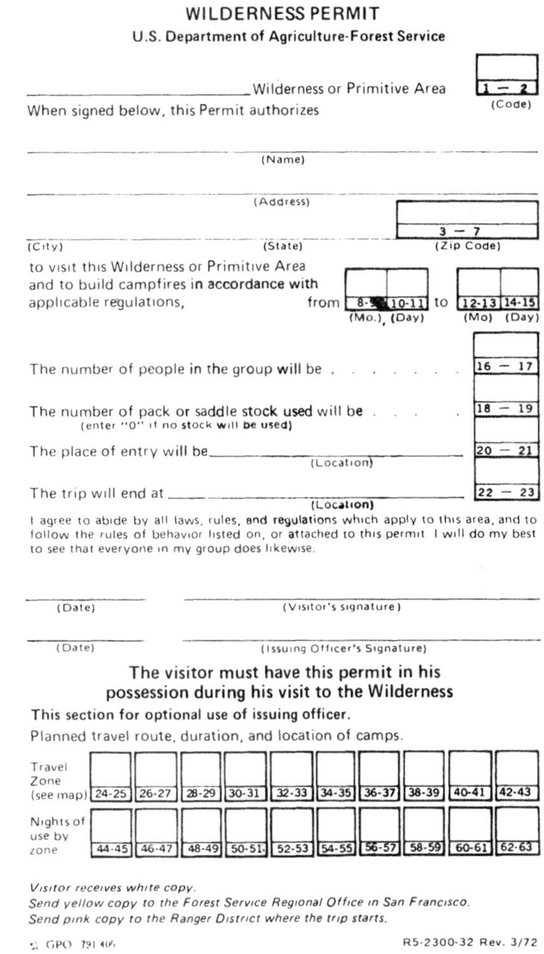
WILDERNESS PERMIT
U.S. Department of Agriculture-Forest Service

_____ Wilderness or Primitive Area [1 — 2] (Code)
When signed below, this Permit authorizes

(Name)

(Address)

(City) (State) [3 — 7] (Zip Code)

to visit this Wilderness or Primitive Area and to build campfires in accordance with applicable regulations, from [8-9] [10-11] (Mo.), (Day) to [12-13] [14-15] (Mo) (Day)

The number of people in the group will be . . . . [16 — 17]

The number of pack or saddle stock used will be . . . . [18 — 19]
(enter "0" if no stock will be used)

The place of entry will be _____ (Location) [20 — 21]

The trip will end at _____ (Location) [22 — 23]

I agree to abide by all laws, rules, and regulations which apply to this area, and to follow the rules of behavior listed on, or attached to this permit I will do my best to see that everyone in my group does likewise.

(Date) (Visitor's signature)

(Date) (Issuing Officer's Signature)

The visitor must have this permit in his possession during his visit to the Wilderness

This section for optional use of issuing officer.

Planned travel route, duration, and location of camps.

Travel Zone (see map)	24-25	26-27	28-29	30-31	32-33	34-35	36-37	38-39	40-41	42-43
Nights of use by zone	44-45	46-47	48-49	50-51	52-53	54-55	56-57	58-59	60-61	62-63

Visitor receives white copy.
Send yellow copy to the Forest Service Regional Office in San Francisco.
Send pink copy to the Ranger District where the trip starts.

GPO 791 406 R5-2300-32 Rev. 3/72

Figure 14-4.—The standard wilderness permit used in all National Forest wilderness and National Park backcountry in California in 1975. Essentially the same form, with only minor variations, is used elsewhere by the Forest Service and similar forms are used in National Parks outside California.

Both the Park Service and Forest Service have done extensive analyses of wilderness permit data. The Park Service generally collects, analyzes, and stores data in individual parks while the Forest Service uses centralized computer capabilities for regional and nationwide analysis. However, both agencies are interested in essentially the same kinds of information, and efforts are underway to standardize permits and share information derived from permit and registration data. Basic data believed to be needed by management are distributed annually in nine summary tables for each Forest Service wilderness using permits from the central computer center.[3] The following user information is included:

1. *Mode of travel:*
   Use for each of the three units of use management: (1) Group visits, (2) individual visits, (3) visitor-days by primary mode of travel.

2. *Residence of group leader:*
   Use (for the three use-units listed above) both by State of residence and by 3-digit zip code sectional center for State or States within which the wilderness is located.

3. *Persons present on each day for the whole wilderness:*
   In both table and graph form.

4. *Groups present on each day for the whole wilderness:*
   In both table and graph form.

5. *Group size:*
   Numbers of groups by group-size classes (group-size variation).

6. *Length of stay variation:*
   For both groups and visits ranked by length of stay.

7. *Entry point:*
   For both groups and visits ranked by entry point.

8. *Travel zone:*
   Groups present on each day by zone for the entire wilderness, with zone totals for:
   a. Day-use groups (not staying overnight)
   b. Camping groups
   c. Total groups
   d. Visitor-days.

9. *Wilderness use (visits and visitor-days) by county, State, forest, ranger district:*
   (This last table is primarily for other annual recreation reports).

Almost 20 additional tables are also available on request. These give more detailed information on use by travel zones, entry points, and visitor origin. Other special tables can be produced on a custom basis when needed for particular management planning purposes.

The general, standard tables should enable a manager to assess the overall situation and identify trends. The optional tables would usually be requested only for special problems and planning needs. It is important that managers "use a rifle rather than a shotgun," and ask only for data needed to answer specific, relevant questions. A manager can flounder in too much information and fail to use it effectively. We must stress again the need for reasonably accurate basic use data. Tables based on inaccurate data, resulting from careless field collection, are misleading no matter how neat and precise the sheets of computer printout appear.

Special Visitor Information

Permits seem the best source of basic use data, but they cannot provide other needed information about visitors' attitudes, knowledge, behavior, satisfactions, and so on. Also, permits necessarily are based on user plans and expectations before the trip, rather than actual outcomes. For example, itineraries can shift and trip lengths can change, and they often do. Special studies can get around this weakness. Here, again, there are a variety of possible approaches, and deciding which is best depends on the questions being asked and the setting. The types of methods best suited to different situations are identified well by Clark (1977). Three main research methods are surveys, observation, and diaries.

Surveys generally involve questionnaires that collect self-reported information in contrast to direct observation of actual behavior. Visitors are asked via a mailed questionnaire, or a face-to-face or telephone interview, to describe themselves, their behavior and activities, their values, attitudes, ideas, and so on. Some things—for example, satisfactions—seem impossible to measure any other way. There can be problems, of course. Questions can be misunderstood, interviewers can influence responses, memories can falter, assumed social pressure can color answers, samples can be poorly selected and unrepresentative, and so on. (Permit systems possess an additional advantage for surveys by providing a relatively unbiased list of visitors from which samples can be drawn for surveys.) The survey technique is valuable, but its proper use requires special skill and training.[4]

---

[3]The computer programs are part of the Forest Service RIM (Recreation Information Management) System, at the Forest Service, Fort Collins, Colo., Computer Center (FCCC). The original programs, developed by Elsner (1972), have been expanded and modified.

[4]The design and conduct of social surveys are described in Potter et al. (1972). Surveys conducted or sponsored by federal agencies must be approved by the Office of Management and Budget under the terms of the Federal Reports Act (44 U.S.C. 3501–3512). Approval is granted only for studies passing rigorous review of the need for the information and scientific validity of the research plan and questionnaires or interview schedules.

Observation can be a systematic, scientific tool, as well as a casual, everyday activity (Burch 1964; Campbell 1970). Detailed checklists of things to observe can be prepared and used to structure the process. For things readily observed, the technique is more objective and accurate than verbal recall. For example, if one were interested in how much time visitors actually spent fishing while camped at lakes (Hendee, Clark, and Dailey 1974), or whether they register at trail registers (Lucas 1975), observation would be the most effective technique.

Although permits and trail register data are self reports, they also provide something like indirect observation of certain behavior, such as choice of entry point.

Diaries or visitor logs or self-reporting forms are a third useful technique. Visitors are given some sort of log book or recordkeeping form before they enter the wilderness and are asked to record certain things, such as their travel times, numbers of encounters, or each day's high point (Lime 1970). For detailed activity or experience information, where memory recall could be a problem, this technique is a useful approach. Some of its applications can overlap potential use of observation and surveys. For example, some visitors might be asked to record the time they fished, as opposed to engaging in other activities at lakes. Using this self-reporting technique, a larger sample can be obtained and the data are gathered without an observer's possible intrusion on visitors' solitude. However, some reporting inaccuracies can creep in, some visitors do not fill out the diary, and those who comply have to put up with some paperwork. If where or how people fished was also important, then observation would usually be the better choice.

In some cases, a combination of study techniques is possible and advantageous. For example, if the activity or issue being studied can be observed, at least partly, and people also are asked about what they do as well as why, then the two approaches can strengthen each other and insure against drawing unwarranted conclusions.

Special studies need to be conducted with sensitivity to the experience of the wilderness visitor. Conspicuous observation or interviews inside the wilderness seem inappropriate to us. They are also poor scientific procedures. Observation or interviews can modify the behavior they seek to describe, thus diminishing validity, and sampling people inside an area cannot yield a sample with definable statistical properties—the probability of any visitor being sampled is unequal and unknown. Interviews at entry or exit points or later at home seem both more considerate and sounder scientifically. Interviews some time after the trip may even contribute

to the enjoyment of the *recollection phase* of the trip. This might be part of the reason for high rates of return of mail questionnaires by wilderness visitors.

This review has concentrated on methods for obtaining information about visitors. Wilderness research needs are discussed in chapter 16.

Visitor Management Tools and Techniques

Wilderness visitor management can employ a wide range of tools and techniques. Gilbert et al. (1972) pointed out the important distinction between direct and indirect visitor management. Table 14–2 presents this distinction with examples. *Direct management* emphasizes regulation of behavior. Individual choice is restricted, and managers exert a high degree of control over visitors. *Indirect management* emphasizes influencing or modifying behavior. The individual retains freedom to choose. The manager controls visitors less completely, thus allowing more variation in use and behavior.

Indirect management should be, as we argued in chapter 7, the first choice, with direct management used only when indirect means cannot achieve management objectives. Most wilderness users prefer indirect management (Stankey 1973), and the concept of wilderness as an undeveloped, free, open, and unconfined place accentuates the desirability of a management philosophy that is as indirect, unobtrusive, and subtle as possible.

Our preference for indirect management is in accordance with the principle of minimum regimentation which was presented in chapter 7. It seems to us that if heavy-handed management of people appears needed to achieve a management objective, the objective itself needs to be reexamined. It may not be important enough to justify the loss of visitor freedom, because visitor freedom is also a wilderness management goal. In any case, either regulation for regulation's sake, or regulation for administrative convenience, is unacceptable.

Nevertheless, direct controls are necessary at specific problem areas at some times, but they should be applied in ways that permit as much visitor freedom as possible. We stress that respecting visitor freedom is an essential element in wilderness visitor management, and that all planned management actions must be tested in terms of their effect on freedom. Controls should be applied with maximum restraint, and only when and where they are clearly justified.

Indirect Visitor Management Techniques
Physical Alterations

The concept of a wilderness as an undeveloped area, with a very limited role for facilities, needs to be kept in

Table 14–2.—*Direct and indirect techniques for managing the character and intensity of wilderness use*

Type of Management	Method	Specific Techniques
INDIRECT (Emphasis on influencing or modifying behavior. Individual retains freedom to choose. Control less complete, more variation in use possible)	Physical Alterations	Improve, maintain, or neglect access roads. Improve, maintain, or neglect campsites. Make trails more or less difficult. Build trails or leave areas trailless. Improve fish or wildlife populations or take no action (stock, or allow depletion or elimination).
	Information Dispersal	Advertise specific attributes of the Wilderness. Identify range of recreation opportunities in surrounding area. Educate users to basic concepts of ecology and care of ecosystems. Advertise underused areas and general patterns of use.
	Eligibility Requirements	Charge constant entrance fee. Charge differential fees by trail zones, season, etc. Require proof of camping and ecological knowledge and/or skills.
DIRECT (Emphasis on regulation of behavior. Individual choice restricted. High degree of control.)	Increased Enforcement	Impose fines Increase surveillance of area
	Zoning	Separate incompatible uses (hiker-only zones in areas with horse use). Prohibit uses at times of high damage potential (no horse use in high meadows until soil moisture declines, say, July 1). Limit camping in some campsites to one night, or some other limit.
	Rationing Use Intensity	Rotate use (open or close access points, trails, campsites). Require reservations. Assign campsites and/or travel routes to each camper group. Limit usage via access point. Limit size of groups, number of horses. Limit camping to designated campsites only. Limit length of stay in area (max./min.).
	Restrictions on Activities	Restrict building campfires. Restrict horse use, hunting, or fishing.

Modified from "Toward a Model of Travel Behavior in the Boundary Waters Canoe Area," C. Gorman Gilbert, George L. Peterson, and David W. Lime. 1972. *Environment and Behavior* 4(2):131–157.

mind, but many kinds of physical alterations do not conflict with these constraints. For example (table 14–2), some alterations can be made outside the wilderness. Access roads can be modified, and this would probably alter use patterns substantially. The last few miles of a road to an overused trail could be closed and the trail lengthened to connect with a new trailhead. Studies show substantial visitor support for such actions (Stankey 1973). An improved road, extended further, leading to a large parking area could increase use if that were desired. A ramp for unloading horses from stock trucks facilitates and encourages horse use. If a road runs directly to a boat ramp on a lake that is an entry point to a wilderness, use will be very different in both amount and type than if the road ends a quarter of a mile away and a portage trail leads to the water.

Trails offer another acceptable, unobtrusive way to influence use patterns. Some areas can be deliberately left without trails to hold down use. Trails can be built or rebuilt to be easy or hard, trail length from point A to B can usually be varied considerably, bridges can be built to facilitate use, or trails can ford streams to reduce or divert use. Some trails are too rough and rocky for horses, but hikers can scramble over them, unobtrusively separating these types of use.

Trail design can markedly influence the quality of the experience for the people who hike or ride horses over them. A well-planned trail can lead travelers to changing vistas or monotonously bore straight through dense forest. Trails can seek out varied vegetation, rock outcrops, glimpses of water, and perhaps increase chances of seeing wildlife. Trail layout can either increase or decrease visitors' awareness of other visitors. A trail can pass right by popular campsites or, in many cases, swing around, through trees or behind a ridge. A winding, up-and-down trail cuts down on observation of other travelers just as long, straight, flat stretches increase sightings. Carefully thought-out trail loops or alternate routes can reduce encounters between users.

Campsites in wilderness may not be so adaptable to visitor management because most of them are essentially undeveloped. Still, there may be some cases where a manager might want to consider minimal initial clearing or development (a few wildernesses have fireplaces because of fire danger, many have fire rings, and some have outhouses and hitching rails for horses) to encourage people to camp there. Removal of facilities can reduce use or change the kind of use at a site.

Physical alterations affecting fish and wildlife can influence use, but serious questions about conflicts with the basic wilderness goal of unmodified ecosystems must be considered (see chapter 11). Whether or not to stock fish is probably the main question for the manager. Many, if not most, high mountain lakes were naturally without fish, but many have been stocked in the past. In some, fish reproduce but, in many others, they do not and periodic restocking is done. Other lakes that are capable of supporting fish have remained barren. Fishing is an

Figure 14-5.—To minimize resource damage, trails should be located away from lakeshores and in the edge of the timber around meadows. Unplanned trails, merely established by use, are often located where excessive resource damage will occur, as in this meadow in the John Muir Wilderness, Calif.

important attraction for many wilderness visitors, and management actions that enhance fishing opportunities can increase use. Because a lake without fish usually will get less use, surrounding meadows and camp areas will remain less impacted, and those visitors concerned more with solitude than fishing would prize such places. But, apart from any effects on visitors, the goal of preserving natural wilderness ecosystems would seem to rule out introducing species absent there in nature, even though they may exist elsewhere in the same wilderness (see chapter 11). If the area were a nonwilderness, dispersed recreation area, then manipulating fish and wildlife attractions would be a powerful and appropriate technique.

All these physical alterations can affect use without any new rules or regulations. To most visitors, it would not even be obvious that the area's managers were seeking to modify use.

Information Dispersal

Providing visitors with information that can influence where they go, what they do, and how they do it is a particularly promising indirect management method. Wilderness visitors are typically well educated (chapter 13), and they should be able to make good use of additional information in making decisions about their actions in wilderness. Information on alternative areas to visit, or alternative parts within a particular wilderness, could have a considerable effect on use. For all practical purposes, a place someone is unaware of does not exist; it is not part of that person's decision-space. The many articles in outdoor magazines on where to go and numerous guidebooks attest to the public's interest in such information. This interest could be used to encourage use shifts. Conversely, articles that describe a supposed hot spot for fishing can accentuate overuse as well as attract users whose primary interest is focused on a daily limit of fish rather than on wilderness.

In addition, information on use patterns might influence visitors who value solitude to change their travel behavior to avoid congestion. We know of a few attempts to use this approach, although they are so recent that their effectiveness is still unknown. A brochure and map inform visitors to part of the Selway-Bitterroot Wilderness in Montana about how much use each of 10 trailheads receive, which campsites are in poor condition, and how to find the trailheads. In a similar effort, visitors to the Boundary Waters Canoe Area in Minnesota (using the previous year's permits for a mailing list) were mailed information on use pressures at different places and times which encouraged the choice of less used areas. Supplying visitors with a map showing

325

heavily used areas within the Rawah Wilderness in Colorado did not lead to any significant changes in use distributions, but the map was given to people at the trailhead, too late perhaps to shift travel plans, and therefore it is still unclear what effect such information might have (Schomaker 1975).

Information on attractions might also be used to try to modify use distributions. These kinds of information need to be used with restraint and sensitivity, of course. A wilderness visitor should not be deprived of the sense of discovery, of uncertainty, and exploration by a flood of detailed information about every aspect of the wilderness. Furthermore, such information could stimulate use and create problems that would not otherwise occur. Some people feel guidebooks can be destructive (Landrum 1976). Shifting use is a two-edged sword: It can help or hurt. Information is a very attractive tool, but it must be used carefully. Guidebooks or information that focus on a few areas—such as "100 Best Hikes"—may produce unwanted effects (overuse of the areas described) compared to providing comprehensive information on all places in a large region.

Information on the ecosystem and how to care for it could help reduce visitor impacts. Most wilderness visitors are intelligent and well meaning, but most of them live in a very different environment from wilderness and might not realize how their actions affect the ecosystem. Simple "do's" and "don'ts" are probably much less effective than a brief explanation of the problem and suggested visitor behavior. "Don't tie horses to trees!" probably has less effect than a short explanation of what happens when horses are left tied for long in one place and some pointers on alternative, less destructive ways of keeping horses around. With some understanding of the problem, the visitor is more likely to do the right thing, or if circumstances prevent doing the recommended thing—as they sometimes do—the person has some basis for intelligently choosing the next best thing.

Wilderness skills can be enhanced through information designed to reduce impacts on physical-biological resources and other visitors, or to add to the quality of the visitors' experience. Dealing prudently with wilderness hazards (e.g., crossing large streams, avoiding avalanche dangers or grizzly bears) might be included.

Eligibility Requirements

A person needs to demonstrate some knowledge and skill to drive an automobile—a license is required. In most states, young hunters must pass a course in hunter safety to obtain a license. Similar requirements could be applied, in varying ways, to wilderness visitors. A test or successful completion of a course in wilderness skills might be required. The course might be a few hours long and conducted in a classroom, or last days or even weeks in the outdoors. The idea is far from new—J.V.K. Wagar suggested the need for certifying outdoorsman skills in 1940, but little has been tried. Some professional guides must pass tests, but the general public does not (except for mountain climbers in a few places). Perhaps such a license requirement might be imposed only for heavily used areas, maybe only those where use is actually rationed. In such places, permits might be issued only to visitors with licenses, and others could gain experience by visiting other, less used areas, not necessarily classified as wilderness. Obviously, the details could be complicated, but the general idea is worth considering. Certainly, if skills, knowledge, and sensitivity to wilderness values could be raised, more people could enjoy wilderness without destroying it; direct controls would be less needed; and actual rationing could be at least postponed.

Fees are another technique for modifying use. Constant fees—that is, the same charge at all times and places—would tend to reduce use. The degree of the reduction would be some function of the level of the fee. A flat entry fee would probably reduce short stays more than long ones, while a per-day fee would probably not have this effect. Ideally, a fee would encourage people who placed a low value on wilderness (those whose recreational interests lay mainly elsewhere) to seek an alternative for which no fee or a lower fee was charged. However, persons who valued wilderness but whose incomes were low would also be discouraged. This is true, of course, for anything bought and sold, but the validity of this income effect for public goods and services is questioned by many people. The income effect could be offset to some extent by free or lower priced entry permits for certain types of low-income visitors, such as inner-city Boy Scout troops. Credit might be earned through work on trails, litter cleanup, or other service projects.

Variable fees would have a much more sensitive effect on use. Fees could vary between places, high at heavily used wildernesses and at overused entry points, and low at seldom-visited areas. (This is similar to high-priced theater tickets for front-row, center seats and loges, and inexpensive tickets for balcony seats.) Fees could be raised at peak periods and lowered or dropped entirely during the off-season. (Most resorts and motels have lower off-season rates.) Perhaps persons who had qualified for a "wilderness license" could pay a reduced fee on the assumption they would have less impact on the wilderness. Conceivably, a person's first visit in a year could be cheaper than later, additional trips to encourage spreading benefits more evenly.

Obviously, there are many opportunities to influence and manage wilderness visitation using fixed or variable fees. However, most wilderness visitors object to fees, and it seems unlikely that Congress will grant the wilderness-administering agencies the authority to use fees as a wilderness management tool. Perhaps later, when all of the potential wilderness has been identified and either classified or allocated to other uses, the concept of wilderness user fees will seem more feasible.

Another type of eligibility requirement relates to physical alterations. This is the level of physical challenge presented by a wilderness. If the challenge is great—few trails, steep and rough trails, no bridges, no horse-handling facilities (corrals, hitch racks, and drift fences), no campsite improvements, and no directional signs—the demands on physical ability and skill are high. A visitor must meet these requirements to be able to move through the wilderness (Hardin 1969; Leopold 1943).

Direct Management Techniques

Direct management techniques involve regulation and restriction of individual choice. Management can exercise a high degree of control, but generally with high administrative costs. To some extent, direct management requires less knowledge of visitors, their behavior, and likely responses to management actions than does indirect management. Some knowledge of use patterns is needed; but, again, if use patterns are to be directly controlled to fit management objectives, less real understanding of them is required.

This means that direct management is usually somewhat easier than indirect management, and perhaps demands less professional skill. Direct management does, however, possess more potential for confrontations, conflict, and controversy than indirect techniques. In any case, as we have explained before, we feel that direct techniques should be applied only after indirect methods have done as much as they can to solve management problems. Unfortunately, it seems to us that managers often leap directly from laissez-faire, uncontrolled activity to tight regulation rather than adopting new controls only to the extent necessary, and using indirect methods as effectively as possible before employing direct management techniques.

Zoning by Types of Use

Zoning is one common direct management technique (chapter 3 referred to the use of zoning in wilderness in other countries). In its simplest form, zoning is the elimination or restriction of certain types of use in some spatial zone. For example, parts of a wilderness may be closed to horses or to camping. In a few wildernesses with grizzly bears, some trails or drainages may be temporarily closed after bear sightings or incidents.

Zoning may also be temporal as well as spatial. For example, high, moist meadows might be closed to horses until July 1. Length-of-stay limits can also be established on a zone basis. In the Boundary Waters Canoe Area, for example, some heavily used peripheral zones have a 1-night camping limit. See chapter 8 for additional discussion of zoning in wilderness management planning.

Rationing Use Intensity

Several direct techniques can be used to control use intensity. A limit can be set on the number of parties or individuals entering per day or other time period at all or certain entry points. Thereafter, travel itinerary is up to each party; they can make it up as they go. The time unit could be an hour (or several hours), which would spread use out more. This would be especially effective for river runners, for whom speed of travel is more uniform than for trail travelers. It could even be a week for a large area with typically long stays, when it is recognized that a good many parties take about 1-week trips in such areas and would like to begin and end around weekends.

Limits could also be placed on the number of persons staying overnight; numbers entering would depend on the planned lengths of stay of parties already in the area. If use were at capacity, numbers leaving would determine numbers admitted. Two examples of daily entry control, three of overnight use limits, and one mixture of the two may help clarify the techniques.

1. The Forest Service permits only seven parties per day to float the Middle Fork of the Salmon River in Idaho. Advance reservations are available and account for almost all use. A certain proportion of the permits are allocated to commercial guides; the others are reserved for private parties.

2. Entrance to Linville Gorge Wilderness in North Carolina, a small, very popular area, is limited to 100 individuals per day for day use and 30 persons per day for overnight use. Party size cannot exceed 10 people. Reservations can be made up to 30 days in advance, through the Ranger Station, by mail, telephone, or in person.

3. In the San Jacinto Wilderness in California, only overnight campers are limited. In the Meadows Unit, 100 campers per night are allowed, while in the larger Plateau Unit 300 are allowed. Day use is unrestricted. One-fourth of the capacity is held for in-person requests

on the day of departure and three-fourths for advance reservations.

4. Rocky Mountain National Park also limits overnight camping (Fazio and Gilbert 1974). Permits are issued for 150 designated campsites and 63 for cross-country travel away from designated sites. The visitors must determine where they will camp each night when obtaining their permit and are expected to adhere to this itinerary. Advance reservations can be made (prior to 1975, a permit could be obtained only up to 24 hours in advance). About 400 persons were turned away in one peak week in 1973; still most people, including those turned away, said they thought use rationing was necessary (Fazio and Gilbert 1974).

5. The main access to Mt. Whitney in California, the highest peak in the coterminous 48 States, is by a trail through the John Muir Wilderness. Only 75 overnight camper parties are admitted each day. Advance reservations are made; however, the large number of no-shows (about 40 percent) allows a substantial number of users to gain entry on a first-come, first-served basis. Day use is unrestricted.

6. Both numbers of overnight parties and day users are limited in the San Gorgonio Wilderness in California. In the popular South Fork Basin, 23 overnight parties are permitted per night, and only 26 day-use parties may enter (Hay 1974). Reservations are available. In addition to these quotas, experienced campers are permitted to use pioneer sites away from trails and established campsites when capacity has been reached (Stankey and Baden 1977).

Limited entry permits can be administered in a variety of ways. Some or even all could be available for advance reservations by mail, telephone, or in person. Often, some proportion of the available permits are held back for last-minute arrivals on a first-come, first-served basis (sometimes called queuing from the similarity to waiting in line to be served). Usually these permits can be obtained 1 day ahead of entry. There seems to be equity in a mixture of reservation and drop-in permits. People who plan carefully far ahead, perhaps because of their need to schedule vacations and travel far from their home to the wilderness, need some advance assurance they will be able to visit the wilderness. Other people cannot or at least prefer not to plan so much, and operate in a spontaneous, spur-of-the-moment fashion. If they live close to the wilderness, they may react to last-minute weather changes. A mixed system gives each type of person a chance at a permit.

Limited permits could also be issued through a lottery, as is done for some big-game hunting permits. Handling such a lottery for entries on various dates would seem much more cumbersome than assigning hunting permits for clearly defined hunting seasons. When would applications close? When would applicants learn of success or failure? Most visitors surveyed reject the lottery concept.

All of these and other approaches to rationing use—reservations; lottery; first-come first-served; fees; and skill/knowledge have different mixtures of advantages and disadvantages, which are reviewed in detail by Stankey and Baden (1977). They summarize the likely effects of each technique in a table reproduced here (table 14–3).

Each system benefits certain types of visitors at the expense of others (columns 2 and 3). Some are in wide use and others are untried (column 4). Visitor acceptance varies from low to high, with some question marks (column 5). Difficulty of administration varies, but only queuing (first-come, first-served) seems likely to ever be easy (column 6).

Efficiency (column 7) includes two concepts. First, how closely can use be matched to capacity? Second, how well does the system allocate permits to the people who place a higher value on the opportunity? The range is wide, from low to high.

The different systems control use (column 8) and affect visitor behavior (column 9) in different ways.

Stankey and Baden (1977) provide five guidelines for managing wilderness rationing:

1. Start with an accurate base of knowledge about use, users, and impacts.

2. Use direct rationing only after less restrictive measures have failed to solve the problems.

3. Combine rationing techniques to minimize and equalize costs to managers and users.

4. Ration, preferably, so the people to whom the experience is most valuable are more likely to get it.

5. Monitor all rationing programs so their effectiveness can be objectively evaluated.

With free reservations, there are usually no-shows. Generally, if a reservation has not been picked up and used by a certain time, such as noon, it is released for use by drop-in visitors. The Mt. Whitney trail has had about 40 percent no-shows; some other areas, such as the Middle Fork of the Salmon River, have very few. Some people might apply for a permit "just in case we decide we want to go," and this could be part of the problem.

If permits are issued at several locations, a communication system is needed in order to know when the limit has been reached.

Generally, public acceptance of controlled entry seems to have been good, as shown both in studies (Hay 1974;

Rationing system	User Evaluation Criteria			
	Clientele group benefited by system	Clientele group adversely affected by system	Experience to date with use of system in wilderness	Acceptability of system to wilderness users [1]
Request (Reservation)	Those able and/or willing to plan ahead; i.e., persons with structured life styles.	Those unable or unwilling to plan ahead; e.g., persons with occupations that do not permit long-range planning, such as many professionals.	Main type of rationing system used in both National Forest and National Park wilderness.	Generally high. Good acceptance in areas where used. Seen as best way to ration by users in areas not currently rationed.
Lottery (Chance)	No one identifiable group benefited. Those who examine probabilities of success at different areas have better chance.	No one identifiable group discriminated against. Can discriminate against the unsuccessful applicant to whom wilderness is very important.	None. However, is a common method for allocating big-game hunting permits.	Low.
Queuing (First-come, first-served)	Those with low opportunity cost for their time (e.g., unemployed). Also favors users who live nearby.	Those persons with high opportunity cost of time. Also those persons who live some distance from areas. The cost of time is not recovered by anyone.	Used in conjunction with reservation system in San Jacinto Wilderness. Also used in some National Park Wildernesses.	Low to moderate.
Pricing (fee)	Those able or willing to pay entry costs.	Those unwilling or unable to pay entry costs.	None.	Low to moderate.
Merit (Skill and knowledge)	Those able or willing to invest time and effort to meet requirements.	Those unable or unwilling to invest time and effort to meet requirements.	None. Merit is used to allocate use for some related activities such as technical mountain climbing and river running.	Not clearly known. Could vary considerably depending on level of training required to attain necessary proficiency and knowledge level.

Rationing system	Administrative Evaluation Criteria			
	Difficulty for administrators	Efficiency–extent to which system can minimize problems of suboptimization	Principal way in which use impact is controlled	How system affects user behavior [2]
Request (Reservation)	Moderately difficult. Requires extra staffing, expanded hours. Record-keeping can be substantial.	Low to moderate. Under-utilization can occur because of no shows, thus denying entry to others. Allocation of permits to applicants has little relationship to value of the experience as judged by the applicant.	Reducing visitor numbers. Controlling distribution of use in space and time by varying number of permits available at different trailheads or at different times.	Affects both spatial and temporal behavior.
Lottery (Chance)	Difficult to moderately difficult. Allocating permits over an entire use season could be very cumbersome.	Low. Because permits are assigned randomly, persons who place little value on wilderness stand equal chance of gaining entry with those who place high value on the opportunity.	Reducing visitor numbers. Controlling distribution of use in space and time by number of permits available at different places or times.	Affects both spatial and temporal behavior.
Queuing (First-come, first-served)	Difficulty low to moderate. Could require development of facilities to support visitors waiting in line.	Moderate. Because system rations primarily through a cost of time, it requires some measure of worth by participants.	Reducing visitor numbers. Controlling distribution of use in space and time by number of persons permitted to enter at different places or times.	Affects both spatial and temporal behavior. User must consider cost of time of waiting in line.

[1] Based upon actual field experience as well as upon evidence reported in visitor studies (Stankey 1973).

[2] This criterion is designed to measure how the different rationing systems would directly impact the behavior of wilderness users (e.g., where they go, when they go, how they behave, etc.).

Rationing system	Difficulty for administrators	Administrative Evaluation Criteria		
		Efficiency–extent to which system can minimize problems of suboptimization	Principal way in which use impact is controlled	How system affects user behavior [2]
Pricing (Fee)	Moderate difficulty. Possibly some legal questions about imposing a fee for wilderness entry.	Moderate to high. Imposing a fee requires user to judge value of experience against costs. Uncertain as to how well use could be fine tuned with price.	Reducing visitor numbers. Controlling distribution of use in space and time by using differential prices.	Affects both temporal and spatial behavior. User must consider cost in dollars.
Merit (Skill and knowledge)	Difficult to moderately difficult. Initial investments to establish licensing program could be substantial.	Moderate to high. Requires users to make expenditures of time and effort (maybe dollars) to gain entry.	Some reduction in numbers as well as shifts in time and space. Major reduction in per capita impact.	Affects style of camping behavior.

[1] Based upon actual field experience as well as upon evidence reported in visitor studies (Stanley 1973).

[2] This criterion is designed to measure how the different rationing systems would directly impact the behavior of wilderness users (e.g., where they go, when they go, how they behave, etc.).

Fazio and Gilbert 1974; Taylor 1972), and managers' experiences.

Some systems control travel routes or itineraries; for example, in Rocky Mountain National Park. Similar control of overnight visitors is common in other National Park wildernesses. Usually, capacities are established for camp areas. Visitors applying for a permit must indicate the camp areas they want to use each night. This is checked against capacities and scheduled use by other parties. If space exists at each place each night, the permit is issued for this itinerary, and the party is expected to stick to it. If space is not available at one or more camps, an alternate route must be worked out. If this is possible, the permit is issued and the party is obligated to adhere to the revised route.

This system, which is analogous to a reservation system for a motel chain or airline, has the potential for matching use to capacity very closely. It has some serious problems, however, particularly the loss of visitor freedom. For instance, at a trail junction, there is no option to change plans because one way looks more fascinating than the originally planned direction. An unexpectedly beautiful camp might beckon for a second night, but if the schedule says "move," the party is supposed to go.

Furthermore, many parties find it difficult or impossible to stay on schedule. Plans are often too ambitious, and travelers find they run out of energy before they reach their scheduled destination. Weather, blisters, illness, a camera forgotten hanging in a tree—all sorts of things can slow a party.

Whether a party is in the "wrong" campsite by choice or accident, it could be an uncomfortable experience. Apprehensions could nag visitors. If a ranger comes along, will he check their permit? Will he reprimand them, make them move, issue a violation notice, or what? If the camp quota is not full anyway, will the ranger take this into account? If the ranger ignores the violation, is this fair to the party that reluctantly passed a lovely, empty campsite late in the day and pushed on with aching feet until sunset to reach the campsite listed on their permit? We believe the system causes a serious loss of the sense of wilderness freedom and exploration for a fairly small gain. It appears to transplant the "rat race" of most people's working world to the wilderness. In addition, it seems to place the wilderness ranger in a particularly uncomfortable enforcement role.

Perhaps some compromise mixture might be considered for control of itineraries. Popular, heavily used zones or groups of campsites might need to have controlled use, night by night, but parties going elsewhere, or promising not to use specified main campsites could be turned loose. For example, Forest Service managers require special permits (in addition to general wilderness permits) for parties planning to camp at particular popular locations in the Pecos Wilderness and San Pedro Parks Wilderness, both in New Mexico.

There is a danger with very site-specific use management. Overuse problems may be only moved from one place to another if managers approach management in an excessively fragmented way. Visitor use patterns are interconnected, like an ecosystem, and changing use at a few places can displace visitors to other, perhaps undesired, places. Use management planning and control needs to consider larger areas that function as visitor use units, such as drainage basins in some areas, to avoid creating unintentional new problem areas.

Shenandoah National Park in Virginia considered a reservation system for designated camping areas in the Park backcountry—the controlled-itinerary system—but rejected this approach, because the managers saw it as being unduly restrictive of visitors, cumbersome in implementation, and unnecessary until all other alternatives have been tested.[5] They also felt, "that our backcountry problems are not with people, per se, but are with a few destructive camping practices, some unthinking and some traditional, by backcountry users."

Instead, Shenandoah National Park adopted an imaginative plan which seems to us to incorporate much of the general approach advocated in this book. Permits are required for overnight use; maximum, permitted party size is nine people. Visitors may camp where they want to, as long as they meet several conditions:

1. Camp out of view and at least 250 yards from any paved road or the Park boundary;

2. Camp out of sight and at least ½ mile from any automobile campground, lodge, visitor center, or any other developments or facility (except a trail, unpaved road, or trail shelter);

3. Camp off and out of sight of any trail or unpaved road, and out of sight of any signs posting special no-camping areas;

4. Camp out of sight of other camping parties, outside and out of sight of any trail shelter except when "essential" during "severely unseasonable weather";

5. Camp at least 25 feet away from any stream;

6. No wood or charcoal fires may be built, and campstoves are encouraged;

7. Camp at the same site no more than two nights.

The plan was developed with extensive public involvement and seems to be well accepted as well as successful in the eyes of Park officials.[6] The managers feel this approach is particularly appropriate in the eastern deciduous forest where visibility is usually limited, but we feel much of the system might have merit in many western areas as well.

The Shenandoah backcountry managers developed this system to cope with extremely heavy, rapidly growing use that was severely damaging a limited number of designated camping sites, many with shelters, and producing a "country fair" atmosphere rather than a wilderness experience. They hoped it would provide visitors freedom, assure opportunities for solitude, open up (without deterioration) much of the Park, and permit more use than would a site-reservation, controlled-itinerary system.

The campsite-spacing rules seem particularly valuable because the visual isolation they produce is an important value to most wilderness visitors (chapter 9), but, in the absence of specific reminders, guidelines, or sanctions, campers often select campsites in such a way that visual isolation is impaired.

One interesting idea that has not been field tested calls for rationing use with the chance of obtaining a permit proportional to the use intensity in any wilderness or zones within a wilderness—"risk zoning," as it has been called (Greist 1975). In other words, for those areas where use intensities were relatively high, the chance of getting an entry permit also would be high. Where use intensity was low (and where managers wanted to keep it low), the chance of getting a permit would be lower, too. The advantage of this system is that it requires users to consider the costs associated with gaining entry and would, at least theoretically, accurately reflect the value placed on solitude by the user. Visitors who valued solitude little would usually be able to enter a wilderness rather than frequently being denied entry to maintain high solitude levels that would be "wasted" on them. At the same time, there would be places with high levels of solitude for those who prized it and who would rather take an occasional trip in such areas than frequent trips to more crowded areas.

If use controls are needed, we believe they should usually be applied at entry points, rather than to itineraries. With knowledge of normal use patterns and route choices, entry quotas could be set to keep overnight use within about the same campsite capacities of the route-control system. For example, if Arrow Lake has a three-parties-per-night limit, and use-pattern analysis shows (1) virtually all Arrow Lake campers enter from the Deer Creek trailhead and (2) about 10 percent of the Deer Creek parties choose to camp at Arrow Lake, about 30 parties per day could be permitted to enter at Deer Creek in order to keep use at Arrow Lake around 3 per night. To keep use below 3 parties a greater proportion of the time, fewer parties—maybe only 20 per day—would be allowed to enter.

---

[5]From a Shenandoah National Park information sheet, SNP-204a (no date, but probably early 1974 or late 1973). SNP-204 gives the backcountry camping regulations. Also based on correspondence and conversations with Robert Jacobsen, Superintendent, Shenandoah National Park, Luray, Va. The backcountry was classified as wilderness in 1976, shortly after this use management plan was put into effect.

[6]1975. Notes used by Superintendent Robert R. Jacobsen of Shenandoah National Park. In Government use regulations along the Appalachian Trail workshop: panel presentation. 20th meeting of the Appalachian Trail Conference, Boone, N.C., June 22, 1975.

Figure 14–6.—Campsites are an important focal point for recreation use of wilderness. Studies indicate a large proportion of recreationists' time is spent in and around campsites, a fact that contributes to impacts and emphasizes the need for careful site location. Many campsites have become established close to lakes such as this one at Upper Triple Lake in the Selway-Bitterroot Wilderness, Mont.

There would be some variation; on some nights four or five parties might camp where only three were desired. But this happens with controlled itineraries also, perhaps less often, but with the added cost of guilt and worry for the campers. In Glacier National Park, where an itinerary system is in use, managers say most parties were found to be off schedule after about the fifth day of travel. Therefore, after 5 days, they have to come out and obtain a new permit for long trips. Other areas report higher conformity.

The wilderness travel simulation model discussed later in this chapter is particularly useful in relating entry patterns to camp-use levels, especially when use from different entry points overlaps. The simulator indicates the likelihood that any use level of a particular campsite will be exceeded.

Other direct restrictions, mentioned before, could be applied to party size, to numbers of horses, and so on, to control use intensity. We have heard of party-size limits ranging from 8 up to 50. Knowledge is not sufficient now to support a precise limit, but we know from research that large groups detract more than small parties from the enjoyment of other users (Stankey 1973). The physical-biological impacts of larger groups is less clear, but it has been the focus of exploratory studies by the Sierra Club (Hartesveldt et al. 1971). Some variation in maximum party size based on the character of an area and its use makes sense. For example, large parties may be appropriate if large rafts are needed to run some rough, white-water rivers. But, there seems to be some consensus that party-size limits in the 6- to 12-person range are reasonable most places.

Some managers have controlled use intensity with a rotation system, a sort of shifting zoning plan. Some deteriorated campsites are closed for a time and then reopened. This technique also could be used (but has not been, to our knowledge) for certain trails or watersheds. The object, of course, is to allow natural processes to restore vegetation and other ecosystem components. This will be discussed in detail in the next chapter, which deals with site management.

Restrictions on Activities

Many specific activities can be prohibited to reduce or eliminate various adverse impacts. For example, wood fires can be prohibited, particularly where fuel is scarce, to save picturesque, old dead trees and down logs.

Sometimes restrictions are adopted without enough consideration of alternative possibilities for improving visitor behavior—for example, rather than banning fires, could visitors be educated and motivated to build fewer and smaller fires, select firewood more carefully, locate fires properly, and clean up ashes better? The choice for the manager really need not be limited to the status quo or prohibition of an activity.

Some managers discourage travel off trails (while others encourage it!). Off-trail travel disperses use and impacts and contributes to solitude, but some types of terrain are easily damaged and travel across them can create new paths that persist.

In the Boundary Waters Canoe Area, visitors are not permitted to take bottles or cans with them (reusable containers are permitted). This regulation is reported to have greatly reduced littering.

Hunting and fishing regulations offer considerable scope for affecting activities, varying use intensities, and altering impact on the wildlife and fish component of the ecosystem. The attractiveness of certain areas can be increased or reduced by varying the restrictiveness of seasons, bag limits, or both. Complete closure is also possible.

Several other management tools are neither direct nor indirect techniques. Rather, they are means of carrying out either type of management. One of the most important is the wilderness ranger.

Wilderness Rangers

Many management actions just discussed need to be carried out by wilderness rangers. The wilderness ranger (by whatever name) is a specialist who patrols the wilderness during its use season. He or she (and many wilderness rangers are females) often works during the summer only, or the summer and fall. A few are year-round employees who work on wilderness data preparation and management planning during the off-season.

Wilderness rangers can be used as versatile field managers, or, alternatively, only as backcountry garbage collectors. They can gather field data on resource conditions, use, and visitor actions; influence visitor behavior by suggestions, advice, and information; enforce regulations; perform emergency trail repairs (but not the trail crew's job of major maintenance); plan

and direct or do cleanup (the garbage-collector role); and give emergency assistance (Kovalicky 1971). As field managers, wilderness rangers can help solve site-specific problems (such as overuse of a popular camp area) by providing visitors with information and advice. In this way, wilderness rangers can reduce both the need for area-wide regulations and more direct controls.

The National Parks have had wilderness rangers for some time, but they were rare until the 1960's in National Forest wilderness. Now, almost all wildernesses and backcountry areas have wilderness rangers, although sometimes the large area patrolled by one person permits only superficial coverage. But in some areas, great importance is placed on rangers as a major management tool. For example, the very heavily used Desolation Wilderness in California now has nine wilderness rangers working in an area of only about 65,000 acres. From all available evidence, wilderness rangers have proven to be very useful. Visitor surveys also indicate they are well accepted by the public (Hendee et al. 1968; Stankey 1973; Lucas 1978).

One of the major problems concerning wilderness and backcountry rangers is training. There is much to learn to get ready for the short summer season such as agency philosophy, enforcement procedures, information to provide visitors, the lay of the land, safety, wilderness living, and so forth. Managers must be selective in hiring wilderness rangers. Selectivity is possible. Many talented young people compete for wilderness ranger jobs—some openings attracted as many as 80 applicants each for the 1975 summer. Above all, candidates should be selected for their interest and ability to work with people as well as their kowledge and concern for wilderness. Wilderness rangers are, in effect, people managers (see the section on litter control that follows), and they are the agency's prime contact with the public.

Litter Control

The "pack-it-in, pack-it-out" program is accepted as a necessary way of life in wilderness. Litter cleanup and efforts to further reduce littering are needed in wilderness. Research indicates that litter detracts seriously from wilderness experiences (Stankey 1973; Lee 1975), and is a user complaint identified in several studies. Many believe that a clean site is more likely to be kept clean by users. Although supporting evidence is scanty, it is an assumption worth using. The amount of garbage removed in concerted efforts can be truly impressive. In the Pasayten Wilderness in Washington, 160 mule loads (100 to 200 pounds each) and 10 helicopter loads were removed in the summer of 1975.

Fortunately, litter cleanup is one problem for which research has provided some useful guidelines. Several studies contributed to the design of the "incentive system for litter control." Field tests in developed campgrounds indicated litter levels were reduced tenfold and at one-fifteenth the cost of standard procedures (Clark et al. 1972a, 1972b). Using the incentive system, rangers contact families with children and solicit the help of kids to clean the campground in return for fire prevention and environmental education type rewards—badges, comic and coloring books, and so on. Rangers can make a few contacts and leave to carry out other duties while a young but enthusiastic crew cleans the campground; mom and pop can relax for a while and upon returning, the ranger knows he will have a keen and receptive group for whatever wisdom he might impart with the rewards.

An adaptation of the incentive system has been developed for wilderness and backcountry (Clark and Muth 1976). It is actually an "appeal system" because it has not proven feasible for wilderness rangers to carry a supply of incentive rewards, kids are not as numerous, and many wilderness users objected to the notion of rewards—a mere "appeal" for their help is all that is necessary. This is partly because the "pack-it-out" norm has become accepted. The major problem in the "appeal system" comes from wilderness rangers who (1) are either too reticent to appeal to users for help in cleaning up additional areas, or (2) actually think of themselves as wilderness garbage collectors who should be doing the cleanup. But, with wilderness rangers who think of themselves as people managers, who make contact with many visitors in their areas and are not afraid to appeal for help in litter cleanup or packing out sacked-up refuse, a clean wilderness is feasible. It can be achieved by applying the available "state of the art"; is anything less really management?

Use Simulation Models

Redistributing and reducing wilderness use appear to be necessary in many areas to achieve management objectives. Managers, therefore, are using a variety of techniques to try to lower use levels and shift use patterns, such as entry-point quotas, controlled itineraries, and information and persuasion to divert some use from critical sites.

However, all the managerial actions, except the establishment of rigid itineraries (which have other problems previously discussed), suffer from a major flaw. The manager's objective is to reduce use at overused locations and to avoid excessive levels of various types of encounters between visitors (on trails and at campsites).

However, there has been no way to relate changes in total use or redistribution of use to the number of encounters per party or to the amount of use of particular places within a wilderness. The complexity of travel routes, which characteristically overlap and intertwine, and the variability in travel decisions are so great that neither intuition nor analytic solutions (from use of a formula) are useful predictors of the level of use of critical locations or encounters.

The rigid itineraries provide a more determinate result, at least for use of camp areas and encounters between camping parties, but not for encounters between parties while traveling on the trails. For many reasons, discussed above, not all parties adhere to their itinerary, so results are not as determinate as they seem.

If use patterns and encounters resulting from any given total use level and entry-point distribution cannot be predicted, experimentation through trial and error is an apparent alternative. However, trial and error is not an effective approach. It is very time consuming; managers would have to try a policy for a year or more to see how it worked. Results for any one year could be heavily influenced by uncontrolled outside factors such as weather. Feedback about results is limited and may be distorted by a few, untypical experiences (usually bad experiences) which may be blown out of proportion. Detailed information on use patterns and encounters would be available only if special, costly studies monitored the area. It would not always be possible to create the use pattern the managers desired to test. For example, if managers wanted to know the effect of a doubling in use, there probably would be no practical way to cause this much use in the short run. At least three sorts of high costs could also result from a trial-and-error approach to use management. First, serious, long-lasting or even irreversible damage to resources might result from tests of heavy use. Second, many visitor benefits could be sacrificed, either through testing excessive use levels that seriously reduced the quality of visitors' experiences or through testing low levels of use that resulted in many people being denied entrance. Finally, frequent, major changes in use policies could lead to controversy and severe public relations problems.

Systems that are too complex for analytic solutions and not suited to real-world experimentation are often approached by simulation modeling. Simulation models are simplified replicas of a particular, complex real-world system, usually described so that it can be represented by a computer program. Simulation models are analogous to tabletop games that imitate various sports, such as football and baseball. They are used widely in engineering and business. For example, a simulation model might be used to help decide, for an ocean port, how different combinations of additional cranes and tugboats alter the efficiency of loading and unloading ships.

Therefore, a wilderness travel simulation model was developed by Resources for the Future, Inc., in cooperation with the Forest Service to provide a better way to formulate and evaluate use management policies (Lucas and Shechter 1977; Smith and Krutilla 1976; Shechter and Lucas 1978). The simulation model provides a practical way for managers to test use patterns quickly. Variability in visitor behavior is incorporated in the model, but, in just a few minutes, use can be simulated for a number of seasons to average out variations. The model records and displays in appropriate tables all the desired information on use and encounters. Because the experimentation takes place in the computer instead of the real world, the high social costs are avoided. Even the most extreme patterns can be tested without damage to precious resources.

The wilderness use simulation model includes a replica of an area's travel system (entry points, trails or water or cross-country routes, and campsites), and provides for different types of parties (size and travel method). The computer program for the model generates visiting parties who arrive at the area at various simulated dates and clock times, enter at particular access points, select routes of travel and move along them. The simulated parties may overtake and pass slower parties moving in the same direction (overtaking encounters), pass parties moving in the opposite direction (meeting encounters), or pass by parties camped in areas visible from trails or other travel routes, such as rivers (visual encounters). Parties that stay overnight select campsites which they may share with other camping parties (camp encounters are recorded when they occur). On an ensuing day, camping parties leave the campsite and continue on their chosen routes, and eventually leave the area.

To make the model operational, data are needed on the area and its use. The travel network must be known, and something about how different types of visitors behave within it—their patterns of arrival, various routes followed and relative popularity of each, travel speeds, and so on. This information is supplied to the model in probabilistic terms; for example, there might be once chance in ten that a party entering at Deer Creek would select a route to Arrow Lake with a 1-night stay there.

The simulator provides detailed output information for each individual simulation of a particular use situation or "scenario." Since part of the input data is of a probabilistic nature, the model has the capability of producing summaries of a series of replications or "runs" of any such scenario, providing average values of various measures, such as the amount, character, distribution, and timing of use. For example, the number of parties of each type using each trail segment is provided. Additional information is available on the number of encounters by type of encounter, by type of party (classified by mode of travel and by length of stay), and by individual trail segments and campsites.

The model is coded in the IBM-originated language GPSS, version V. (GPSS stands for General Purpose Simulation System.) The model to date has been successfully operated on IBM's 360 and 370 series of computers as well as Control Data Corporation's 6600 computer. A Users Manual (Shechter 1975) is available.

Managers choose the use patterns they are considering trying to achieve through management. In order to try to bring use impacts and solitude levels into line with management objectives for the area, they might be considering actions designed to alter numbers of parties entering at various trailheads or to reduce weekend peaks, or they might be considering adding some new trails or campsites. Managers can test use patterns on the simulator and learn how closely the results agree with their objectives. If the agreement is not close enough, the simulator's results will aid them in revising the use pattern to come closer. We must stress the importance of management objectives. The simulator will determine use distribution and encounter frequency for a particular use pattern, but whether this is acceptable or unacceptable must be a managerial decision based on management objectives. How the use pattern will be shifted is also a managerial responsibility. Use might be rationed, a new trail might be built or another closed, or information supplied to visitors to change their location choices. The simulator is not concerned with *how* the use pattern is altered, but only with the *consequences* of the alteration.

The simulator is an aid to the manager in decisionmaking; it does not make the decisions. It is a way to play "what if?", to try out a potential management program before implementing it and to evaluate the results to help decide whether to proceed or modify the planned program. Both the programs to be tested and the evaluation of results depend on the manager's professional skill, not the computer. The simulation model should help put use modification programs on a sounder, more justifiable basis.

Applications of the simulator to test areas (the Spanish Peaks Primitive Area in Montana, the Desolation Wilderness in California, and the Green and

Yampa Rivers in Dinosaur National Monument in Colorado and Utah) indicate that when the existing use situation was simulated, the resulting use patterns and encounter experiences generally agreed with data from visitor surveys, indicating validity of the model. Where there were discrepancies, they stemmed primarily from oversimplification of certain data describing typical use (for example, including too few different travel routes to adequately reflect the variability of visitor movements), rather than inherent flaws in the simulation model itself. These shortcomings can be corrected in future applications of the model.

In the Desolation Wilderness (Shechter and Lucas 1978) and Dinosaur National Monument,[7] a variety of simulation scenarios were tested. Use was increased and decreased by varying amounts, and uneven distributions were made more even by shifting use from popular entries to less used access points and from heavily used weekends to weekdays.

Some clear relationships, not all expected, emerged. Changing the timing of visitor entries had little effect on use pressures or encounter levels. Changes in total use (all other things remaining the same) produced proportionate results. For example, if total use doubles, use of any specific location doubles, on the average. In hindsight, this now seems obvious. Encounters, expressed in per-party-per-day terms, also double in this example, which was not expected.

This predictable, proportional relationship provides a convenient base for comparing results of more complex scenarios in which use is redistributed with an across-the-board change with the same total use. Almost all use redistribution scenarios produced lower average encounters per party per day than the same total use without redistribution. Some use redistributions were more than 50 percent more effective in reducing average encounter levels than equivalent across-the-board decreases in total use. For example, one entry point redistribution plan required only a 9 percent reduction in total use, but reduced average trail encounters 16 percent and encounters in camp by 13 percent.

Average encounters do not tell the whole story, however. The frequency of extreme encounter levels (very high levels, especially, but sometimes also very low and zero levels) changed substantially for different scenarios. In the example given, the proportion of party-days with high levels of solitude rose more than they would with an across-the-board cut in use, but this was

not true of all scenarios. A manager probably would be more concerned about reducing or eliminating experiences of unsatisfactory quality than altering averages. In addition, changes at key trouble spots were even more pronounced. This also would probably be more relevant to a manager's evaluation of the results of a scenario than overall averages.

A somewhat simpler simulation model has been developed for the Boundary Waters Canoe Area that presents only information on numbers of parties camping per night in each travel zone, based on numbers entering at various access points (Gilbert, Peterson, and Lime 1972; Peterson, de Bettencourt, and Wang 1977). This has been used to help set entry point daily limits that will not overtax available camping locations.

The use of computer-based simulation modeling in outdoor recreation management planning may arouse fears of depersonalization. On the contrary, it may help make it possible to maintain the traditional values of visitor independence, flexibility, and spontaneity as well as to protect resources and experience quality in the face of growing demands on limited resources.

Visitor Management in the Future

As use problems increase or intensify in wilderness, managers will be constantly pressed to develop innovative techniques and tools to meet the challenge. Increased refinement of many of the techniques and tools is needed to increase their effectiveness.

As we look to the future, we also see increased efforts to offset visitor impacts by improving the quality of visitor behavior. Much attention is now focused on the need for a "wilderness ethic": an accepted code that governs the wilderness traveler's behavior so that some of the current management headaches, such as litter, will cease to exist. Efforts to develop an ethic have been made by conservation organizations (The Wilderness Society n.d.; Sierra Club 1967), by private individuals (Wilson n.d.; Petzoldt 1974), and by agencies (for example, Nezperce National Forest 1975). Many of these efforts stress not only the proper ways of handling oneself in the wilderness (e.g., how to set up a tent, build and put out fires), but also appropriate behavior styles, such as respecting the privacy of others, refraining from shouting, and even choosing colors for clothing and tents that blend into the natural scene. To the extent that such desirable behavior becomes commonplace, the job of the wilderness manager becomes less demanding and the need for direct management controls less urgent. Education of wilderness visitors is a potentially powerful

[7]McCool, Stephen F., and David W. Lime. 1976. The wilderness area travel simulator: applications to river recreation management. Paper presented to Interagency Whitewater Management Conference, Salt Lake City, Utah, February 11, 1976. A revised version of this paper is included in Shechter and Lucas (1978).

336

as well as preferable tool in wilderness use management, and it should play a larger role in the future.

Summary

This chapter has tried to make several main points. First, use and *minimal* facilities to accommodate it (trails and campsites, in particular) *are* consistent with wilderness objectives. But, use must be managed. The largest part of wilderness management *is* use management. The only actions that seem justified for use management are those necessary to achieve wilderness management objectives established for an area—including the protection of natural conditions and providing an opportunity for quality wilderness experiences.

There are a range of visitor actions and associated impacts to be dealt with, and we pose a typology recognizing five of them—actions that are illegal, careless, unskilled, uninformed, and unavoidable impacts. Several aspects of wilderness use can be influenced including the amount, distribution, and timing of use; party size; length of stay and user behavior as it affects the resource and other visitors; and cooperation with management. We point to the need for basic data on wilderness use and the resource to help guide decisions about what management actions are needed. *Indirect* use management, as subtle and light handed as possible rather than *direct* regulation, can preserve the visitors' freedom and should be the manager's first choice.

Trails and campsites are critical tools in influencing use distributions and visitors' experiences (management of trails and campsites and visitor impacts on them is covered in chapter 15). A variety of other techniques, practices, and standards are available as tools for achieving visitor management objectives.

The issues discussed in this chapter all depend on what part of the recreation opportunity spectrum wilderness must serve. If few alternative categories of roadless but nonwilderness lands are available to meet roadless recreation needs, then wilderness visitor management must be more diverse and some areas must be more developed and more heavily used. If programs for intermediate, semiwilderness, backcountry recreation are developed by land management agencies, as we strongly feel they should be, then management direction for classified wilderness should stress unmodified conditions, limited development, and opportunities for solitude—to be consistent with the narrower range of the environmental modification and recreation spectrum that wilderness would then represent.

Among the co-authors, the author primarily responsible for preparation of this chapter was Robert C. Lucas.

Literature Cited

Back Country Horsemen.
  1972. Back country horsemen's guidebook. 60 p. Hungry Horse News. Columbia Falls. Mont.
Burch, William R., Jr.
  1964. A new look at an old friend—observation as a technique for recreation research. U.S. Dep. Agric., For. Serv., 19 p. Pac. Northwest For. and Range Exp. Stn., Portland, Oreg.
Campbell, Frederick L.
  1970. Participant observation in outdoor recreation. J. Leisure Res. 2(4):226–236.
Clark, Roger N., Robert L. Burgess, and John C. Hendee.
  1972a. The development of anti-litter behavior in a forest campground. J. Appl. Behav. Anal. 5(1):1–5.
Clark, Roger N., John C. Hendee, and Robert L. Burgess.
  1972b. The experimental control of littering. J. Environ. Educ. 4(2):22–28.
Clark, Roger N., and Robert M. Muth.
  1976. The appeal system for litter control in wilderness and backcountry. U.S. Dep. Agric., For. Serv., Res. Note. Pac. Northwest For. and Range Exp. Stn., Portland, Oreg. (In press.)
Clark, Roger N.
  1977. Alternative strategies for studying river recreationists. p. 91-100. *In* Proceedings, river recreation management and research symposium, Jan. 24–27, 1977. 455 p. U.S. Dep. Agric., For. Serv., North Central For. Exp. Stn., St. Paul, Minn.

Dailey, Tom, and Dave Redman.
  1975. Guidelines for roadless area campsite spacing to minimize impact of human-related noises. USDA For. Serv., Gen Tech. Rep. PNW–35, 20 p. Pac. Northwest For. and Range Exp. Stn., Portland, Oreg.
Elsner, Gary H.
  1972. Wilderness management . . . a computerized system for summarizing permit information. USDA For. Serv., Gen. Tech. Rep. PSW–2, 8 p. Pac. Southwest For. and Range Exp. Stn., Berkeley, Calif.
Fazio, James R., and Douglas L. Gilbert.
  1974. Mandatory wilderness permits: some indications of success. J. For. 72(12):753–756.
Frayer, W.E., and D.B. Butts.
  1974. BUS: a processing system for records of back country camper use. J. Leisure Res. 6(4):305–311.
Gibbens, Robert P., and Harold F. Heady.
  1964. The influence of modern man on the vegetation of Yosemite Valley. Manual 36, 44 p. Calif. Agric. Exp. Stn., University of California, Berkeley.
Gilbert, Gorman C., George L. Peterson, and David W. Lime.
  1972. Towards a model of travel behavior in the Boundary Waters Canoe Area. Environ. Behav. 4(2):131–157.

Greist, David.
    1975. Risk zoning: a recreation area management system and method of measuring carrying capacity. J. For. 73(11):711–714.

Hardin, Garrett.
    1969. The economics of wilderness. Nat. Hist. 78(6):20–27.

Hartesveldt, R.J., H.T. Harvey, and John Stanley.
    1971. Wilderness impact studies. Sierra Club Bull. 56(4):10–11.

Hay, Edwards.
    1974. Wilderness experiment: it's working. Am. For. 80(12):26–29.

Hendee, John C., William R. Catton, Jr., Larry D. Marlow, and C. Frank Brockman.
    1968. Wilderness users in the Pacific Northwest—their characteristics, values, and management preferences. USDA For. Serv., Res. Pap. PNW–61, 92 p. Pac. Northwest For. and Range Exp. Stn., Portland, Oreg.

Hendee, John C., and Robert W. Harris.
    1970. Foresters' perception of wilderness-user attitudes and preferences. J. For. 68(12):759–762.

Hendee, John C., and Robert C. Lucas.
    1973. Mandatory wilderness permits: a necessary management tool. J. For. 71(4):206–209.

Hendee, John C., Roger N. Clark, and Thomas Dailey.
    1974. Fishing and other recreation behavior at high lakes: some management implications. 25 p. mimeo. Paper presented to American Fisheries Society, Honolulu, Hawaii, Sept. 8.

Herfindahl, Orris C.
    1969. Natural resource information for economic development. 212 p. Johns Hopkins University Press, Baltimore.

Kovalicky, Thomas J.
    1971. The wilderness ranger concept. Naturalist 22(3):14–15.

Landrum, Paul.
    1976. Are guidebooks destructive? Free Country Times (Univ. Oregon Outdoor Program), Spring, p. 5.

Lee, Robert G.
    1975. The management of human components in the Yosemite National Park ecosystem. 134 p. The Yosemite Institute, Yosemite, Calif.

Leopold, Aldo.
    1943. Flambeau: the story of a wild river. Am. For. 49(1):12–14, 47.

Lime, David W.
    1970. Research for determining use capacities of the Boundary Waters Canoe Area. Naturalist 21(4):8–13.

Lime, David W.
    1971. Factors influencing campground use in the Superior National Forest of Minnesota. USDA For. Serv., Res. Pap. NC–60, 18 p. North Central For. Exp. Stn., St. Paul, Minn.

Lime, David W., and Roland G. Buchman.
    1974. Putting wilderness permit information to work. J. For. 72(10):622–626.

Lucas, Robert C.
    1973. Wilderness: a management framework. J. Soil and Water Conserv. 28(4):150–154.

Lucas, Robert C.
    1975. Low compliance rates at unmanned trail registers. USDA For. Serv., Res. Note INT–200, 6 p. Intermt. For. and Range Exp. Stn., Ogden, Utah.

Lucas, Robert C.
    1978. The characteristics of visitors to wilderness and related areas in the Northern Rockies and California Sierras. U.S. Dep. Agric., For. Serv., Res. Pap., Intermt. For. and Range Exp. Stn., Ogden, Utah. (In press.)

Lucas, Robert C., and Robert Rinehart.
    1976. The neglected hiker. Backpacker 4(1):35–39.

Lucas, Robert C., and Mordechai Shechter.
    1977. A recreational visitor travel simulation model as an aid to management planning. p. 31–35. In State-of-the-art methods for research, planning, and determining the benefits of outdoor recreation, compiled by Gary H. Elsner, 62 p. U.S. Dep. Agric., For. Serv., Gen. Tech. Rpt. PSW–20. Pac. Southwest For. and Range Exp. Stn., Berkeley, Calif. Also Simulation & Games 8(3):375–384.

Miller, Bob.
    1973. Suggestions for using horses in the mountain country. 13 p. Animal and Range Sciences Dept., Montana State University, Bozeman.

Nezperce National Forest.
    1975. Environmental outfitting: methods and equipment for the outfitter sensitive to protecting the back country. 17 p. U.S. Dep. Agric., For. Serv., Grangeville, Idaho.

Peterson, George L., James S. de Bettencourt, and Pai Kang Wang.
    1977. A Markov-based linear programming model of travel in the Boundary Waters Canoe Area. p. 342–350. In Proceedings, symposium on river recreation management and research, Jan. 24–27, 1977. 455 p. U.S. Dep. Agric., For. Serv., North Central For. Exp. Stn., St. Paul, Minn.

Petzoldt, Paul.
    1974. The wilderness handbook. 286 p. W.W. Norton and Company, New York.

Potter, Dale R., Kathryn M. Sharpe, John C. Hendee, and Roger N. Clark.
    1972. Questionnaires for research: an annotated bibliography on design, construction and use. USDA For. Serv., Res. Pap. PNW–140, 80 p. Pac. Northwest For. and Range Exp. Stn., Portland, Oreg.

Rinehart, Robert P., Colin Hardy, and Henry Rosenau.
    1978. Stereo photographs made in field with pivoting camera mount are used to measure wilderness trail conditions. J. For. (In press.)

Shechter, Mordechai.
    1975. Simulation model of wilderness-area use. Resources for the Future, Inc., Washington, D.C. 172 p. (Available from National Technical Information Service, Springfield, Va. Manual order No. PB 251 635, Program tapes order no. PB 251 634.)

Shechter, Mordechai, and Robert C. Lucas.
    [1978]. Wilderness travel simulation as an aid to wilderness management. Johns Hopkins University Press for Resources for the Future, Inc., Baltimore. (In press.)

Schomaker, John Henry.
    1975. Effect of selected information on dispersal of wilderness recreationists. Ph.D. diss., Colorado State University, Fort Collins. 95 p.

Sierra Club.
    1967. The Sierra Club handbook. David Brower, ed. 317 p. Ballantine Pub. Co., New York.

Smith, V. Kerry, and John V. Krutilla.
    1976. Structure and properties of a wilderness travel simulator. 173 p. Johns Hopkins University Press for Resources for the Future Inc., Baltimore.

Stankey, George H.
    1973. Visitor perception of wilderness recreation carrying capacity.

USDA For. Serv., Res. Pap. INT–142, 61 p. Intermt. For. and Range Exp. Stn., Ogden, Utah.

Stankey, George H., and John Baden.
1977. Rationing wilderness use. USDA For. Serv., Gen. Tech. Rpt. INT–198, 20 p. Intermt. For. and Range Exp. Stn., Ogden, Utah.

Taylor, Ronald B.
1972. No vacancy in the wilderness. Sierra Club Bull. 57(1):5–8.

Wagar, J.V.K.
1940. Certified outdoorsmen. Am. For. 46(11):490–492, 524–525.

Walker, Richard.
1968. Photography as an aid to wilderness resource inventory and analysis. Professional paper submitted for M.S. degree, Colorado State University, Fort Collins. 114 p.

Wilderness Society.
[n.d.] Off on the right foot: a guide to proper wilderness use. 6 p. Wilderness Society, Washington, D.C.

Wilson, Floyd.
[n.d.] A code of conduct for those who visit wilderness. 4 p. Floyd Wilson Wilderness Education Foundation, Denver, Colo.

One important wilderness management task is the inventory of all established campsites and evaluation of their impacts. Some sites might need to be relocated if they show excessive environmental damage or are located in particularly sensitive locations. Information provided by this wilderness ranger on a Code-A-Site inventory card for a camp in the Selway-Bitterroot Wilderness, Mont., will be used in management planning.

Trails and campsites are acceptable in wilderness and clearly compatible with the Wilderness Act. They are indispensable to recreational use of wilderness and important tools for use management. It is also clear that trails and campsites, and the visitor use they serve, must be limited to avoid threatening the naturalness and solitude of an area—the qualities that distinguish wilderness. As was discussed in the previous chapter, visitor use may need to be directly or indirectly modified to protect opportunities for solitude and to keep use impacts to acceptable levels. In this chapter we consider the locations directly impacted by visitors—campsites and trails—and management methods for keeping physical, biological, and social impacts at acceptable levels.

Objectives

Here, as for visitor use, management objectives must reflect a balance. A reasonable network of simple, narrow trails (with some areas left trailless) is acceptable and desirable in a wilderness, as are lightly impacted, minimally altered campsites. Some impact is inevitable, with recreational use. But, trails deeply eroded, churned into bogs, greatly widened, or converted into multiple, parallel trails are not acceptable. Neither are dustbowl campsites with dead or dying trees as a result of visitor impacts. The question is how to manage trails and campsites to minimize use impacts while making possible high-quality wilderness experiences.

The alternative to striving to minimize use impacts is to adopt the sacrifice-area concept. In this the manager tries to concentrate use on a few spots and accept the sacrifice of these places to damage from heavy use in order to save many other places from visitor pressures.

We disagree with the sacrifice-area approach to wilderness-site management. Sacrificing parts of a wilderness to severe impacts seems to us to ignore the Wilderness Act's definition of wilderness as a place where natural conditions are preserved, a place that has been affected primarily by the forces of nature, and a place where the imprint of man's work is substantially unnoticeable. The sacrifice-area policy clashes with the philosophy and spirit of wilderness as we understand it. It also seems insensitive to the quality of the visitor's experiences.

On the other hand, research indicates that even light, limited use usually produces substantial impacts, while further use produces proportionately less impact (Merriam et al. 1973). If wilderness is visited, as it usually will be, unmodified natural conditions cannot be maintained. Therefore, at least a hint of the sacrifice concept must be accepted. The sacrifice concept is an end point on a continuum, while the dispersed, minimal-impact approach is near the other end of the continuum. The two approaches differ in degree, but are not two entirely separate approaches. The critical questions seem to be whether to accept severe site impacts on relatively few sacrifice areas or to disperse minimal impacts over a widespread area. We lean heavily toward the latter approach.

It is essential that physical-biological management of use sites be integrated with visitor management. Actions to restore or relocate sites rarely will be effective unless the use patterns and visitor behavior that caused the original problem are also altered. On the other hand, altering use patterns and behavior can produce only very slow recovery without some physical-biological management. For example, a severely eroded trail generally will not revert to a more natural condition even if use is drastically altered; a badly deteriorated campsite might recover very slowly unless some direct resource management action to speed restoration is applied.

The following discussion addresses campsites first, and then trails.

Campsites

Wilderness campsites play a very important role in management. Chapter 9 pointed out that campsite isolation is particularly valued by many visitors. The number of campsites that offer seclusion, out of sight and

sound of other campsites, might be a major determinant of wilderness social carrying capacity. Resource damage is also a serious problem with campsites. Visitors congregate at campsites, sometimes in large groups for long times, and extensive areas can be drastically altered. A recent study indicates that campers at wilderness lakes spent about 60 percent of their time right in camp which suggests the importance of campsite location and the potential for resource damage (Hendee, Clark, and Dailey 1974).

Campsite Inventories

One of the most critical types of information for management of any wilderness is a campsite inventory. This inventory provides basic information for making decisions about carrying capacity, for efforts to redirect use, for providing visitors with information, for planning wilderness rangers' work, for applying the wilderness travel simulation model, and for almost any other planning activity. A campsite inventory ideally should include sites already in use and potential sites that visitors might use if they were aware of them. Dispersing visitors

Figure 15-1.—The need for recreation facilities in wilderness is a controversial topic. Facilities are generally limited to those absolutely essential to protect the resource, with facilities for comfort and convenience facilities normally prohibited. *Upper left*: "Wallowa" type toilet; *upper right*: bridge of native materials; *lower left*: rustic sign used in National Park wilderness; *lower right*: primitive table placed to attract use away from sensitive locations.

342

to these potential campsites, as discussed earlier, could substantially raise the carrying capacity of many areas, therefore it is important to know the number of such potential sites even though all of them would not—and should not—be pressed into use.

A campsite inventory system will be discussed shortly, but first we need to consider the question of defining a wilderness campsite. Two sorts of characteristics seem essential (Brown and Schomaker 1974). First, a site must be usable. Generally it must have a source of water and be neither too steep, too wet, or too small. In other words, it must possess certain physical characteristics to *function* as a campsite. Second, the site must be *desirable* as a campsite. In addition to being *able* to camp there, people must also *want* to camp there.

A study of wilderness campsite preference (Brown and Schomaker 1974) looked at existing sites in the Spanish Peaks Primitive Area of Montana to identify functional and desirable campsite characteristics. These sites all had developed from repeated selection by campers without any managerial interference with free choice. Sites in use reflected visitors' standards for usable and desirable camping places. The investigators measured over 15 factors at each site, and concluded that the minimum for an acceptable functional site was: 400 square feet of level ground (4 percent slope or less), location on dry ground within 500 feet of water and 750 feet of firewood. Horse-use sites required 800 square feet of level areas. Almost all horse-use campsites had forage areas averaging 3 to 4 acres, usually within 300 feet of camp. If horse users were required to feed their horses exclusively with prepared, packed-in feed, forage would cease to be a requirement.

Brown and Schomaker (1974) also identified potential but unused campsites that possessed at least the minimum functional characteristics. A comparison of potential sites which those campers chose to use suggests which factors are important campsite attractions. Desirability seemed to depend mainly on a view of a nearby lake (lakes are fairly common in the area). Ninety percent of all sites in use had views of a lake (or a lake *and* a stream), and 4 percent had a view of a stream alone. Only 6 percent lacked a view of water. Although there were many potential sites near streams, few were in use. The proportion of potential campsites which were in use near lakes was much higher.

Campsite preference has also been studied in the Boundary Waters Canoe Area (BWCA) (Frissell and Duncan 1965). It was found that 63 percent of existing sites (all the result of visitor selection and use) were on islands and 91 percent were in stands of pine. When

asked, "What would you consider to be an ideal campsite?" 45 percent answered "located on an island," 39 percent mentioned "flat tent spots available," 30 percent listed firewood availability, 27 percent cited a good landing area, and 24 percent wanted a campsite "protected from wind."

More research is needed on the factors that determine campsite selection in different settings—for example, visitor preferences in areas with few or no lakes, with desert vegetation, or along rivers—and the relation of campsite choice to impacts on the environment, on other visitors, and on the satisfactions of people using the sites (Lime 1971). Tests are needed to measure the results of programs to encourage campers to disperse and use additional sites, many of which will not be near lakes. The Spanish Peaks study suggests that it will be difficult to get many parties to voluntarily shift away from lakes. This is particularly unfortunate because a recent study (Dailey and Redman 1975) indicates that noise impacts between camping parties are greatest at lakes, where noise carries far, whereas they are minimized by the background noise near streams.

Recently, a campsite inventory system, Code-A-Site, was developed to collect basic information about campsites along forest roads, in backcountry, and in wilderness (Hendee et al. 1976). Code-A-Site uses edgepunch cards (see fig. 15–2) and a codebook for recording basic information about each campsite: location; capacity; available resources such as firewood, water, forage, and scenery; measures and estimates of the degree of environmental impacts; site facilities such as toilet, table, fireplace, or makeshift, visitor-constructed improvements; proximity to other sites; available activities and attractions; needed work at the site or other management recommendations; judgments about the amount of use the site receives; a site map; and space for recording other information a particular manager might desire.

Field tests indicate it takes from 5 to 20 minutes to code each campsite depending on the data desired and the training of data collectors. Ideally, Code-A-Site data are collected by wilderness rangers as they go about their normal duties.

Code-A-Site was applied to several wildernesses during its design and development; field testing indicated some conditions unexpected by managers. First, it was found that managers generally underestimated the number of sites that had been established. For example, at one of the heavy use locations identified in the Glacier Peak Wilderness Management Plan, the Code-A-Site inventory turned up twice as many sites as managers estimated were there.

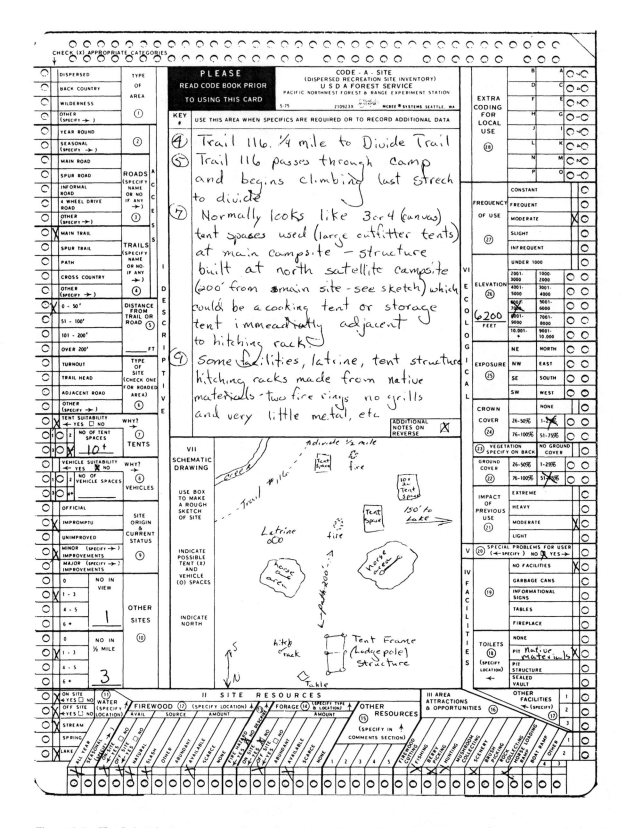

Figure 15–2.—The Code-A-Site inventory system is a management tool for recording, storing, analysing, and using recreation site data. Here is a Code-A-Site edgepunch card for recording basic information about campsites following codebook instructions.

Second, site concentration was greater than was realized. For example, in the eastern portion of the Three Sisters Wilderness in Oregon, 70 campsites were found near a cluster of three heavily used lakes (Green Lakes). In a portion of the nearby Mt. Jefferson Wilderness, there were 15 campsites around Square Lake—located 1 mile inside the wilderness. In both areas, site concentration was intense near popular lakes yet much of the surrounding wilderness had few sites in use.

Third, it became clear that because of dissimilar management information needs in different wildernesses, standardized data collection could not be prescribed. Flexibility in the inventory system is necessary. In one wilderness, managers might want to know only site locations and their sizes in order to determine the people-at-one-time (PAOT) capacity of the wilderness. Elsewhere, managers might want to identify sites with severe impacts or those that need management attention for other reasons—important information for planning the work of wilderness rangers. Code-A-Site has also been used to make rough estimates of the amount of overnight use in a particular area by combining it with field judgments about the amount of use each site received over a summer. Elsewhere, it has been used by managers and scientists as a system for recording detailed and replicable measures of site impacts, measures that could be repeated in a few years to see the extent to which management efforts to reduce impacts were succeeding or failing.[1]

Finally, the site impacts were not as severe as managers had thought. For example, in the Three Sisters Wilderness only 11 percent of all campsites inventoried were judged to have severe impacts, and in the Mt. Jefferson Wilderness only 5 percent. Use of many sites apparently was not as great in these areas as managers had believed.

These examples illustrate the basic nature of campsite inventory data and the variety of uses to which it can be put. Visitor management decisions must rest on data about the availability of established and potential campsites, their location, attractions, and condition.

Designation

In some wildernesses, all or a portion of the campsites are officially designated. They may have a sign that identifies them as officially sanctioned campsites. Sometimes they are marked on maps. They may have certain facilities, often a manufactured fireplace with a metal grate, perhaps a simple pit toilet, and, much less frequently, some type of table. Other impromptu campsites are undesignated. They have simply developed over the years as people have chosen them as desirable places to camp. Some sites are obviously used often and are distinguished by some loss of natural vegetation, some bare ground at the center of the site, and one or more fire rings of loosely placed rocks. Others might not reveal signs of use to anyone but an expert observer. Usually there are no facilities provided at undesignated sites, although some have homemade facilities. Officially designated sites are common in National Park wilderness and in some National Forest wilderness. The BWCA has over 1,000 designated campsites. Currently, BWCA users are encouraged to use only these sites, and future plans call for requiring their use.

Other wildernesses have both designated and undesignated sites. In some California wildernesses, for example, wood fires are permitted only at designated sites, and camp stoves must be used elsewhere.

Whether single- or multiple-party campsite areas should be provided is another related question. Most wilderness campsites accommodate only one party, in at least relative isolation from other campsites. However, some camp areas have multiple, clustered sites, and resemble minimally developed road-accessible campgrounds. Visitor surveys suggest this cluster arrangement is usually strongly disliked by most visitors (Stankey 1973).

Location

Where wilderness campsites should be located relative to trails and shores of lakes and streams is a question on which opinions differ widely. Many managers believe camping close to the shores of lakes and streams is undesirable and have prohibited camping near shorelines for distances of from 25 to 200 feet. The reasons for such restrictions rest on the belief that resource damage is more likely near shorelines because vegetation there is fragile; that, without limitations, congestion and resulting adverse impacts will accumulate because most users are attracted to the water; and that environmental damage is more noticeable and objectionable because of the importance most visitors attach to the shore zone. Camping close to water can also increase risks of water pollution from wash water and human wastes.

Shoreline camping can also detract from visitor experiences. Camps close to the shoreline of heavily used lakes convert public space, open to all, into private space, monopolized by the camping party (Hendee, Clark, and Dailey 1974). Camps on lakeshores are also conspicuous across open water and capable of detracting from

---

[1] Monitoring site impacts is discussed in more detail in chapter 14 under "Information Needs for Visitor Management: Resource Data."

solitude more than camps tucked away in the trees. Noises carry easily to other parties around the lake because of the lack of sound-diminishing barriers and because a lake surface minimizes the attenuation of sound (Dailey and Redman 1975).

However, despite all the reasons for limiting shoreline camping, there is overwhelming evidence that the most popular campsites are close to water. Also, in some areas, lack of alternative potential campsites directs users to waterfronts. In rugged terrain, level land is often concentrated in narrow strips close to lakes and streams. In the Spanish Peaks Primitive Area camper preference and, in some places, terrain limitations resulted in high concentrations of campsites near shorelines. Brown and Schomaker (1974) found that 85 percent of the existing campsites were located within 200 feet of lakes or streams, and nearly half were within 50 feet. Obviously, even a 50-foot setback requirement would prohibit use of almost half of these established sites, and a 200-foot requirement would wipe out all but a few sites. Managers considering camping setback requirements need a campsite inventory to evaluate the effect of "distance from shoreline" camping restrictions on the number of campsites eliminated.

Some areas also prohibit camping within a specified distance of trails, as well as shoreline restrictions. In steep mountains, where trails often are squeezed between steep slopes and lakes or streams, the waterfront and trail no-camping zones can overlap and thus eliminate almost all camping places, perhaps unintentionally.

In light of the above evidence, managers should think carefully about imposing restrictions on campsite location. Enforcing such restrictions is a difficult assignment for wilderness rangers, especially with so many existing campsites conspicuously present to tempt campers. But some things can be done to combat site impacts at lakes.

If use levels at lakes were kept low enough that most parties could camp out of sight and sound of other groups (as most visitors strongly prefer), the need for a waterfront setback might largely vanish. On most small lakes in open country, for example, only one party at a time could camp if the solitude objective (camping out of sight and sound of other groups) were to be met. In this case, the conflict of public vs. private space would also be minimized.

Indirect management techniques could also help. Visitors could be educated and encouraged to stay back from lakeshores where possible, to properly dispose of wastes, and generally to use low-impact camping techniques.

When new campsites are being planned, whether this involves designation and development or only identification on maps to assist visitors in their route planning, location relative to water and to trails should be given careful attention. Durable sites, secluded from trails and other campsites, set back from shorelines but still with a view and a feeling of reasonable proximity to the water would seem to be the ideal for which to strive.

Poorly located campsites—those causing unacceptable physical or social impacts—could be closed to use on a site-by-site basis, rather than zoning all lands close to water off limits to camping. This should be accompanied by identification or designation of more acceptable alternative campsites, numerous enough to accommodate the expected use of the critical area.

The most restrictive technique is the assignment of individual campsites by permit. Some National Parks use a variation on this system, assigning campsites requested by visitors if possible. Campsite assignment might be necessary to meet management objectives in some locations, but, as discussed in chapter 14, we feel such restrictive methods should be the manager's last resort.

Facility Development

How many and which campsite facilities should be provided is another controversial topic. As discussed in chapter 14, the Wilderness Act limits facility development to certain specific purposes. There still are different interpretations of what level of facility development is justified in wilderness and under what conditions.

What functions could various facilities at wilderness campsites serve? Resource protection is one possibility. Use control or modification of behavior is another. Visitor safety is a rather unlikely function of campsite facilities, except possibly to minimize risk of disease transmission from human wastes. (Safety is a more important consideration in trail location, design, and maintenance.) Visitor comfort and convenience might be one motive for facility development. However, the wilderness concept of meeting nature on its own terms seems to rule out comfort and convenience as valid justifications for facilities in wilderness. Visitor safety from natural hazards also is not unequivocally an objective in considering wilderness facilities. The National Park Service, in its "Management Policies" states this well:

> The visitor must accept wilderness largely on its own terms. Modern conveniences are not provided for the comfort of the visitor; and the risks of wilderness travel, of possible dangers from accidents, wildlife, and natural

phenomena must be accepted as part of the wilderness experience.

(National Park Service *Management Policies* VI–4, 1975).

Finally, what do visitors want and expect in the way of wilderness facilities? Are they eager for them or not? With these various considerations in mind, let's look at different facilities that might be found at wilderness campsites.

Fireplaces

Fireplaces are provided in some wildernesses. Designs vary, but typical construction uses a steel grate, rocks, and mortar. Particularly in areas of high fire hazard (e.g., southern California) many managers believe such fireplaces reduce the risks of campfires spreading and igniting forest or brush fires. Some people question whether fireplaces reduce the risk of spreading fires. We know that every year wilderness rangers put out some campfires that have been left burning. Whether fireplaces encourage visitors to leave campfires burning or effectively contain fires and stop their spread is unknown. Even small, unimpressive fires can spread in duff to burn roots, and destroy trees, shrubs, and campsite beauty.

It might be thought that fireplaces are a convenience for visitors. However, surveys indicate wilderness visitors who oppose constructed fireplaces outnumber visitors who favor them more than two to one, which suggests that fireplaces are an unwanted improvement for most visitors (Hendee et al. 1968; Lucas 1978). The same studies indicate loose-rock fire rings are much more acceptable to visitors. However, in some wildernesses, managers have decided that these fire rings are an undesirable mark of man and detract from the quality of the wilderness. They also feel they attract parties repeatedly to the same sites and increase resource damage. These managers have wilderness rangers break up and scatter the fire rings, and they encourage visitors to use only a few rocks to support a portable cooking grate, scattering the rocks when they leave camp. If ashes can also be concealed by being buried or scattered widely, the spot used for the fire can be very inconspicuous. A possible compromise might be to break up some of the fire rings at sites where they are numerous, leaving one or two well-located rings for continued use.

A procedure recommended in some places consists of digging up a chunk of sod; using the hole for a fireplace; and, before leaving, replacing the sod to conceal all signs of use. Along some wilderness rivers, users are urged to carry fire pans (round, convex metal pans) to contain the fire and prevent the spread of ashes along the sandy

beaches or into the water. The ashes are either spread along upper bank areas after the pan cools or, sometimes, carried out. Material that sinks can be dropped in the river. However, if these systems are not used carefully, the aggregate impact of fire use by campers might be greater than if a few semipermanent fire rings are left to localize camping impacts, particularly in areas of heavy use.

Obviously, management judgment is needed and solutions will vary depending on local conditions, but it must be remembered that objectives of the Wilderness Act include naturalness and "outstanding opportunities for solitude" and generally prohibit "permanent improvements."

Where managers have banned open fires, they have avoided the problem of fireplace facilities. Backpacker stoves serve cooking purposes well, and many visitors now use them voluntarily. However, campfires have a long tradition and provide a social setting similar to the crackling blaze in a living room fireplace, in addition to providing the warmth that is needed or desired sometimes. Many visitors are reluctant to abandon building social fires. However, giving up such fires does substantially lower user impacts. When fires are foregone, one manager pointed out, "stars are brighter, sunsets and sunrises take on more meaning, and a camper can take pride in 'leaving no trace.'"

Behavior based on a wilderness ethic and outdoor skills is the key in this situation as in so many others. A small, well-placed fire built with only a few rocks, or none at all, and only if firewood is not scarce, allowed to burn out before drowning with water to minimize ashes and partly burned wood, causes only a fraction of the impact of a large, thoughtlessly handled fire.

Tables

Tables seem to us to be entirely a comfort and convenience facility devoid of any resource protection capability. Some managers believe tables could attract users to locations selected by managers and divert use from more fragile or overused sites. However, wilderness user surveys indicate that only a few people find tables desirable. Split-log tables are more acceptable than plank construction (Hendee et al. 1968; Lucas 1978). National Park Service policy prohibits tables.

Tent Pads

Tent pads of wood, earth, or gravel are common in developed road-access campgrounds, and are found in some nonwilderness hiking areas such as in the White Mountains of New Hampshire. As far as we know, they are not used in wilderness. Although their development might be defended on the grounds of resource protection, we think it is more appropriate to provide campers with information on methods of setting up tents to protect wilderness values. In our opinion, tent pads seem to be self-defeating in terms of preserving natural conditions and the camping experience based on unaltered conditions. Visitor acceptance has not been studied in wilderness, but we would expect it to be low.

Shelters

"Adirondack" shelters—three-sided cabins open in front—still exist in some wildernesses and a few National Park backcountry areas under study for possible wilderness classification. Generally, shelters are considered inappropriate in wilderness, and have been removed in many National Park and Forest Service areas after their classification as wilderness. However, over half the visitors surveyed in three Washington and Oregon areas favored the existing shelters (Hendee et al. 1968).

Some shelters might have historical values. An example is the former Image Lake Shelter in the Glacier Peak Wilderness in Washington. Erected by a local conservation organization as a tribute to mountaineering troops of World War II, it was removed because it attracted heavy use and thereby caused serious vegetation impacts. Other wildernesses include structures such as old trappers' or homesteaders' cabins, some with historical significance. Many existing wilderness structures need to be reviewed for possible inclusion under the National Register of Historical Sites as provided by Federal law.

A few shelters and structures might be necessary to administer some wildernesses—in remote locations, a food or equipment cache cabin might be needed for use by wilderness rangers in a large wilderness, for example. In addition, exceptions might be justified in Alaska, where severe weather, bear danger, and precedent are cited as reasons for maintaining public cabins. However, other persons still regard Alaskan cabins as comfort and convenience facilities. In general, public shelters and structures attract visitors (and often bears and other animals) and intensify problems associated with concentrated use. Unless there is a reservation system, many more campers might arrive than a shelter can accommodate, and the resulting impacts spread to adjacent areas. Overflow campers often come without tents, counting on using the shelter, and might be tempted to build bough shelters in bad weather. And not every old cabin in a wilderness is automatically a valuable historical site merely because of age. Shelters and structures for public use are incompatible, permanent

Figure 15-3.—Shelters are focal point for use and impact. Here visitors congregate at Avery Shelter in 3-sided Adirondack lean-to, at Bigelow Col on Maine's Mt. Bieglow.

improvements in wilderness. We recommend phasing out existing buildings and not developing new ones.

Horse Facilities

Horse-holding facilities such as corrals and drift fences have been traditional in some western wildernesses, but are being phased out in many areas as unnecessary, permanent improvements. Stock facilities vary, but all are intended to avoid the frustrating and sometimes fruitless search for strayed horses. This experience has ruined many a wilderness breakfast and has even inspired colorful new additions to our language. Pole corrals probably are the most secure way to keep stock near camp. A pole hitching rail or hitching posts serve the same purpose. Drift fences, which cut across normal horse travel routes, usually valley bottoms, with a gate on the trails, keep horses from returning towards home, as they often will try to do. None of these facilities directly protect resources; in fact, they all detract from the natural, unmodified character of the wilderness. The area within a corral or around hitching rails or posts is usually a sacrifice area—it is devoid of vegetation, soils are compacted, and dust or mud is thick.

However, these facilities can be less damaging than some alternative ways of holding stock, particularly tying

Figure 15–4.—Makeshift facilities constructed by users often detract from the wilderness setting and should be discouraged. *Left*: John Muir Wilderness; *right:* Pole shelter left by hunters in a wilderness study area.

them to trees, which is very destructive to ground vegetation and can kill the tree. Picketing (tying a horse on a long rope fastened to a stake in a meadow), if not done carefully, can produce round, overgrazed, and trampled areas.

In many places, other ways of holding horses are encouraged to avoid serious impacts. Hobbles— something like leather handcuffs—enable horses to hop around and graze but are intended to keep them from traveling far. Some hobbled horses learn to hop faster than a man can run, however. Bells on horses, especially on the leaders, can help in locating hobbled or loose stock (but the noise of clanging bells can bother other visitors nearby). Some well-trained, experienced mountain horses will stay close even when turned loose. Another method, borrowed from the old horse cavalry, is the picket line—a taut rope is strung between two trees padded with gunny sacks to prevent the rope from damaging the bark and horses are tied to this picket line. There will be some impact, but it will be removed from tree roots; and, if different places are used each time, a sacrifice area of concentrated impact will not develop. Another option is the use of temporary corrals, either of poles temporarily tied in place only as long as needed, or of ropes (as used on the prairies by early cowboys).

Deciding what horse-use facilities to provide or permit is not easy. Varied opinions are strongly held and rooted in old, cherished habits and folkways. For example, horsemen in certain regions pack with Decker packsaddles; they feel that others who use cross-buck saddles and diamond hitches are weak in the head—and vice versa. The need for corrals is also strongly debated. Certain ways of holding horses are characteristic of different geographical areas, perhaps for historical reasons rather than because of actual differences in need.

Visitors generally disapprove of corrals and other horse-handling facilities; but, of course, most visitors are hikers. However, even in areas where horse use predominates, opinions about horse facilities are very divided (Hendee et al. 1968; Lucas 1978).

Horse camping and trail riding are traditional uses of most western wildernesses. But conflicts do exist between horsemen and hikers. Many managers are convinced that horse use is excessively damaging to the wilderness resource and have imposed regulations on stock use. Horsemen, on the other hand, view many of these regulations as unnecessary and discriminatory. Properly handled, they argued, stock need not be destructive of wilderness (Miller 1973).

In view of these conflicts, we offer three observations. First, while we recognize that all use creates impacts (chapter 9), limited research suggests that stock use is proportionately more damaging to resources than hiking. Two recent studies (Dale and Weaver 1974; Weaver and Dale 1977), found that trails used by both hikers and horsemen were generally more deeply eroded than those used by hikers alone, and that hiker impacts on trails were significantly less than horse impacts on both level and sloping sites. Horses were particularly damaging to soil and vegetation when coming downhill, as they tended to brace their forelegs and catch themselves with each step, exerting heavy pressures on the trail surface. In addition, grazing by recreational stock unnaturally alters vegetation conditions, such as wildflower displays, which can reduce scenic quality, affect native animals that use the same areas, and perhaps change the behavior of a natural fire. Horse manure is conspicuous and unattractive, and can introduce seeds that develop into nonnative plants.

Second, although horse use does create management problems, we feel it would be wrong to administratively prohibit horse use of wilderness. Some wildernesses are better suited to accommodating horse use than others. For example, the Teton Wilderness in Wyoming (a National Forest Wilderness east of Grand Teton National Park) is an area with large, open meadows with substantial forage, where most trails are not steep, and distances are long. The area seems well suited to horse use. Other areas, such as the Mission Mountains in Montana, are small with steep trails and very little forage; such an area is probably not well suited to horse use. The key, it seems to us, is to manage horse use according to the capabilities of individual areas. This means that in portions of some wildernesses, or perhaps in entire areas, horses would not be permitted, but in others they would continue to be part of the scene. Careful planning can provide diverse recreational experiences. Closing certain areas to horses will provide the kind of setting desired by those with strenuous objections to stock. Keeping other areas open will allow horsemen continued opportunities to enjoy their style of use.

There are other options to consider for the use of stock. For many people, the enjoyment of their wilderness trip centers on their horse: caring for it, saddling it, and riding it during the day. For others, however, the horse or other stock animal is only a means of transportation for the individual, his gear, or both. "Drop" or "spot" packing, which consists of using stock only for transportation to a campsite and then taking the animals out of the wilderness until the party is ready to leave, offers a wilderness-use opportunity for people unable to hike or those who do not want the burden of caring for stock. It also reduces the aggregate level of stock impact on the resource. It is true that an extra round trip usually is necessary (unless scheduling permits another party to be taken out on the return trip), but the reduction in impacts around campsites and on forage can be great, particularly during long stays.

Wilderness managers might want to try to separate stock users and hikers. As pointed out in chapter 9, most hikers prefer not to meet horse travelers. A recent study in Yosemite National Park identified the presence of horse manure as a particular annoyance of hikers (Lee 1975). If horsemen and hikers are to be separated, it is important to search for existing "natural" separations or zones. For instance, in the Spanish Peaks Primitive Area of Montana, most hiker use is concentrated in the northern and eastern portions of the area while most of the horse use is in the southern and western portions. Any system of zoning to separate users should take advantage of natural divisions where they exist. Good use data would be needed to identify horse- and hiker-use areas. In other places, where certain campsites tend to be used by horse parties, certain sites might be designated for horse use and others for hikers. (This system has been tried in Rocky Mountain National Park.)

Finally, in those areas where stock use is permitted, specialized facilities can be used to minimize conflicts between hikers and horsemen. For instance, in the Sawtooth Wilderness in Idaho, a special trailhead is maintained for horse users. It has corrals, hitching racks, and stock loading ramps and is located several hundred yards away from the trailhead normally used by hikers. If separate horse camps were established in the backcountry, some separate horse facilities also might be used.

Toilets

Toilets are one more controversial facility. Some view outhouse toilets as a necessary feature at campsites, arguing that health and esthetic problems will occur if they are not provided. The counter argument is that if a toilet is needed to prevent sanitation or esthetic problems, the site is already being used beyond its capacity *as wilderness,* and that other waste disposal practices would be effective if use levels were lower.

Outhouse pit toilets of varied designs are found at some popular campsites in a number of wildernesses. Some are the traditional shed, complete with roof (sometimes of fiberglass). Others are only a box a few feet high. Toilets of this type are used in the BWCA and the Pacific Northwest—where they are called Wallowa Toilets. In the Sawtooth Wilderness, log walls about 5 feet high form a triangle open at one corner around a pit toilet. Toilets are numerous in some wildernesses. Many other areas have no toilets of any kind. Where toilets do not exist, a typical recommendation is that each visitor dig a small, shallow, individual hole for defecation, cover it, and let natural biological decomposer organisms go to work—the so-called cat method (fig. 15–5). Research data are lacking as to what method of human waste

WILDERNESS SANITATION

You are about to take a step beyond civilization, a step into the rugged, untamed wilderness.

While in the wilderness, you will be without the modern conveniences to which you are accustomed. You will be "roughing it"—without lights, without refrigeration, and without plumbing. Here in this untamed country, *you will be without even the most basic sanitation facilities*. There are no garbage collections and no toilets. You will have to manage without these conveniences.

Disposing of waste and refuse is a most important part of your wilderness experience. Improper disposal of refuse will spoil and pollute these areas. If you handle sanitation properly, you will leave the land clean and attractive for yourself and others to enjoy.

How do you do this? There are right and wrong ways to dispose of wastes in the wilderness. The proven methods of such waste disposal are described on the reverse side of this card. We ask your cooperation in following them.

UNITED STATES DEPARTMENT OF AGRICULTURE
FOREST SERVICE

HUMAN WASTE

Fortunately, nature has provided in the top 6 or 8 inches of soil a system of "biological disposers" that works to decompose organic material. Keeping this in mind, you should:
- Carry with you a small digging tool. A light garden trowel is good.
- Select a suitable screened spot at least 50 feet from any open water.
- Dig a hole 8 to 10 inches in diameter, and no deeper than 6 to 8 inches—to stay within the "biological disposer" soil layer. Keep the sod intact if possible.
- After use, fill the hole with loose soil and then tramp in the sod.
- Nature will do the rest in a few days.

CAMP WASTE

- Carry out cans, bottles, aluminum foil, and anything else that will not burn. Cans are easier to carry if they are scorched and flattened. Burying is not satisfactory because the cans usually will be exposed by animal or frost action.
- Burn in your campfire all paper and other burnable material.

FS-66

GPO 876-267

Figure 15-5.—Forest Service information sheet on "Wilderness Sanitation".

disposal is best. It is uncertain which method poses less hazard to health—pit toilets or shallow burial (Sanks and Temple 1975). Pit toilets, by concentrating human waste, might actually increase the risk of polluting adjacent waters. Biological decomposition is usually much less effective with deep, concentrated fecal material than with shallow burial of waste matter. Environmental conditions are obviously critical, but no one really knows the precise relationships. What works well at one location might not work elsewhere, depending on elevation, soil type, soil temperature, moisture, and other variable conditions. A study in Grand Teton National Park concluded that man's presence in the alpine zone has not grossly affected the aquatic microflora or indicator bacteria and that most streams in the higher country were safe for drinking—but one careless individual could cause a problem (MacFeters 1975).

Pit toilets are hard to maintain and keep clean, even in areas reached by roads; in remote wilderness settings they can become very unappealing. Vault style toilets—toilets with a removable container—have been used in some areas, with the containers removed by horse or helicopter. Removal can be a problem, however; often when the tank is full, the toilet is simply moved to a new location and a new tank is installed. In the Sawtooth Wilderness, instead of moving toilets when the pit fills, the material is dug out and reburied nearby.

With campsites scattered to achieve wilderness solitude, it is difficult to locate the toilet in a central location where people will use it. People who camp far

351

from the toilet won't use it; alternatively, the toilet can serve as a magnet and undesirably concentrate camping near it. Often, in an attempt to put the toilet out of sight, managers hide it so well that campers don't find it. Alternatively, toilets are sometimes marked so well that the signs are a blight on the naturalness of the wilderness setting.

Wilderness visitors are also divided on preference for outhouses. Older surveys show considerable support. Hendee et al. (1968) found almost half the visitors to three areas in Washington and Oregon favored toilets, but the more wilderness-oriented visitors opposed them. In the northern Rockies, around 40 percent of the visitors favored outhouses, almost as many opposed them, and the remainder were neutral (Lucas 1978). On the other hand, two-thirds of all visitors (including day users) to the Desolation Wilderness in California opposed outhouses as did three-fourths of the overnight campers there, despite heavy use (Lucas 1978). Given this ambivalence and variation, the use of outhouses to modify use patterns seems quite unpredictable; they might attract some visitors—the less wilderness-oriented—and repel others.

Toilets, like other facilities, should be a tool for achieving wilderness management objectives and not visitor comfort and convenience. If provided they must be sensitively located by managers, for surely the presence of outhouses—especially when accompanied by a direction sign saying toilet—is a reminder of civilization and not consistent with the spirit of wilderness. Outhouses seem essential only to meet management objectives for specific, individual locations in the wilderness. Unfortunately, present knowledge does not clearly identify the characteristics of such locations although heavy use, if permitted, is clearly one important factor. Efforts should be continued to encourage appropriate individual waste disposal, which can help eliminate the need for toilet facilities.

Garbage Pits

Garbage pits are an anachronism that almost everyone rejects under today's use conditions. They are purely a visitor convenience (and an improvement only over outright littering), that imposes a substantial adverse impact on the wilderness. Now, the nearly universal recommendation is to burn all refuse that will burn and pack the rest back for proper disposal outside the wilderness.

If fires are banned, this system encounters problems. Then everything must be packed out. This might be preferable anyway, if visitors will make the extra effort. Careful meal planning could largely avoid the problem of wet garbage, such as leftover oatmeal. It is debatable whether burning, burial, or scattering for animals is the best way to dispose of wet refuse that is difficult to pack out.

Figure 15-6.—Litter can quickly accumulate in wilderness. Organized group cleanups; the pack-it-in, pack-it-out program; and requesting the cooperation of users to pick up litter and haul out sacked garbage are examples of programs to control this problem. The photos show a during-and-after photo of a Sierra Club cleanup effort in the Selway-Bitterroot Wilderness, Mont.

Water Pumps

Hand operated water pumps are mentioned as permissible facilities, "if necessary," in the National Park Service's *Management Policies*. However, the conditions under which such facilities would be necessary are not described. Pumps apparently are rare in wilderness. This might suggest that most managers view such major permanent improvements as inconsistent with accepting wilderness largely on its own terms, a view we share. (In at least one area, the Forest Service removed a pump that existed before wilderness classification.) It is true, of course, that in some areas, especially arid wilderness, water development (improved springs, a pipe from a catch basin, wildlife "guzzlers," or pumps) could increase the carrying capacity for both people and wildlife. The same could be said for many types of development, but such modifications must always be carefully weighed against the wilderness quality of naturalness. A delicately adjusted natural ecosystem might become unbalanced. For example, an artificial water source in an arid wilderness could result in an increase—an unnatural increase—in deer, with resulting impacts on browse species, which in turn could reduce the capacity of the area to support other animals better able to survive with limited water. Predator populations might increase, and the ripples of a small alteration of the natural environment spread ever outward. In many ways, such environmental changes are analogous to weather modification in wilderness.

Site Restoration

Restoration of acceptably natural conditions on campsites is a problem of major concern to wilderness managers. How much interference or manipulation by man is justified in the attempt to restore natural conditions? If the unnatural condition has resulted from the impact of modern man's actions, is further human intervention acceptable to restore a more nearly natural condition? Even though most people probably accept this kind of intervention, some means are more readily accepted than others.

Almost all actions to restore damaged campsites involve temporary closure to provide rest and recovery time for the area. This is easier said than done in wilderness. It is usually impractical to have a ranger present every day to enforce the closure. The temptation to use a site marked as closed is great, and justifications or rationalizations are easy—"a storm was building up and no other site was within reach," or "it was getting dark and . . .," and so on.

The most effective approach to closure consists of helping visitors understand the reasons for closures and letting them know about alternatives. It is important to get this information to the visitors before they enter the area so they can adjust plans. Violations are sure to be more common if visitors learn of a closure only after they reach the campsite, probably weary and unsure of the distance to the next site.

In New Hampshire, parts of a badly damaged site in Tuckerman Ravine, just outside the Great Gulf Wilderness, were fenced. This was a research study, rather than a management action (Fay 1975). The fence was only a single rope attached to metal fence posts. Apparently, this symbolic fence was honored. Strings 12 to 15 inches high strung between stakes also successfully diverted users from revegetation sites at Image Lake in the Glacier Park Wilderness and at Cascade Pass in North Cascades National Park[2]. Similar methods might be tried elsewhere, perhaps by stringing rope from existing trees around the site, along with posting signs that the area is closed.

There are a range of possible restoration actions that can accompany closure:

1. *Rest—no other action.* A site can be closed to all use (or certain kinds of high-impact use, such as horse parties) for a time while nature, unaided, restores natural conditions. Unfortunately, damage can result from use for only a short time (Frissell and Duncan 1965), but restoration may be extremely slow (Merriam et al. 1973; Willard and Marr 1971; Fay 1975). Because of this, using rest alone to restore sites could mean that more sites would be resting than in use, and, certainly, that popular sites would be closed and recovering far more of the time than they would be open for use.

2. *Rest—seedbed preparation—natural regeneration.* After closure the soil can be hand cultivated to prepare a receptive bed for native seeds and runners from plants in the surrounding area. Some native plants spread mainly by sprouting from roots, and they will not be helped by this method if roots have been destroyed by use. Soil at heavily impacted sites around Image Lake in the Glacier Peak Wilderness in Washington was spaded. The manager feels it has been quite effective in furthering the establishment of grass, shrub, and tree seedlings.[3]

3. *Rest—seeding—planting.* The next step would be to seed the impacted area, transplant plants, or do both. The objectives of wilderness would seem to dictate that

[2]Miller, Joseph W., and Margaret M. Miller. 1973. Revegetation experiments in impacted subalpine plant communities at Cascade Pass, North Cascades National Park. 19 p. [Unpublished report prepared for the National Park Service. On file at Superintendent's office, North Cascades National Park, Sedro Wooley, Wash.]

[3]Smith, Bernard A. 1976. Personal correspondence. USDA For. Serv., Darrington Ranger District, Mt. Baker-Snoqualmie National Forest, Darrington, Wash. [On file at Forestry Sciences Laboratory Intermountain Forest and Range Experiment Station, Missoula, Mont.]

these seeds and plants be from locally occurring, native species. Over a period of several years, Miller and Miller[4] have carried out seeding-transplanting studies at Cascade Pass in North Cascades National Park. Most transplants have survived in areas where visitors were excluded, but only 4 of 62 transplants and almost no seedlings survived on a campsite used by just one party for a few days. Miller and Miller[2] also concluded that seeding is possible only on favorable locations, and even there it is extremely slow in reestablishing a vegetation cover. Additional research is needed to develop knowledge and techniques about how to carry out such horticultural practices under wilderness conditions.

Some managers have used readily available nonnative seeds of durable lawn grasses. Grass seeding with turf species probably is fairly effective in many places. However, a study of revegetation of a mine near the border of the Beartooth Primitive Area, Mont., reported higher plant densities on test plots seeded with native plants than introduced species (Brown and Johnston 1976). In contrast, in the Adirondack Mountains in New York (not part of the National Wilderness Preservation System), seeding with red fescue and Kentucky bluegrass (along with fertilizer) was quite successful in establishing a vegetative cover (Ketchledge and Leonard 1971). After several years, native plants began to invade the sites again (Ketchledge and Leonard 1972). To us, this is an unacceptable practice in wilderness because of the impact on naturalness. If the artificial seeding of nonindigenous plants is deemed necessary (after all other techniques fail), we think this indicates that the physical carrying capacity of the site under natural, wilderness conditions has been exceeded and is reason for closing the area to recreational use.

Transplanting native plants would probably speed up recovery considerably, but it would be an expensive practice (Brown and Johnston 1976). Furthermore, if transplants are collected in the wilderness, the impact is really only being shifted, not eliminated, although the impact could be dispersed widely and made much less conspicuous than the concentrated damage at the visitor-use site. A great deal of transplanting has been done since 1971 at Image Lake in the Glacier Peak Wilderness. The managers conclude that it has been "reasonably successful" in reestablishing vegetation but that there are now "a great many plug holes around" where plants have been dug.[3] Miller and Miller[2] also express concern about the heavy, long-lasting impact of digging

transplants near the site being revegetated. Native plants could be propagated outside wilderness in plant nurseries, but as the Millers point out, this procedure runs the danger of introducing nonnative weed species with transplants.

Mulching with locally collected material has been used some places to condition soil and aid in survival of seedlings and transplants.

4. *Fertilizing.* Fertilizing alone might be used to increase the vigor of remaining plants and hasten their recovery, with or without rest. Fertilizer might be applied just once, to try to compensate for past impacts and get closer to some natural balance, or it might be used repeatedly to increase the vegetation's ability to withstand use. Philosophically and ecologically, it is easier to justify a one-shot application because continued use of fertilizer could upset natural processes (by increasing eutrophication of nearby waters, for example). Some feel that nitrogen fertilizer alone would largely avoid this particular risk and still aid in vegetative recovery, but knowledge is lacking. One study (Beardsley and Wagar 1971) of a developed, road-access campground just outside the Sawtooth Wilderness, concluded that fertilizer alone was ineffective. Without fencing, it was also ineffective in the White Mountains of New Hampshire, but in fenced plots limited increases in plant cover were produced in 2 years (Fay 1975).

5. *Irrigation.* Watering a closed campsite might speed recovery, but doing this under wilderness conditions would be difficult. If a gasoline engine pump were needed, it would constitute another nonconforming use. Other methods for moving water, such as ditches, would be a defacement of the wilderness. However, the study by Beardsley and Wagar (1971) did suggest that under the conditions in the Sawtooth area, water was the most effective single agent contributing to plant recovery.

6. *A combination of techniques.* A site could be allowed to rest along with seedbed preparation, planting, seeding, fertilizing, and watering, or any combination of these. The Sawtooth study (Beardsley and Wagar 1971) found the greatest vegetative response was to a combination of seeding, watering, and fertilization, and recommended seeding and fertilizing if watering was not possible.

7. *Eradication of nonnative plant species.* In addition to closure, more natural conditions might be sought by trying to eliminate nonnative species often found at campsites, such as common dandelions which, following their introduction from Europe, have spread widely. This could be very difficult, and reintroduction might occur, especially if horses use the area. Hay carries weed seeds

---

[4]Miller, Joseph W., and Margaret Miller. 1975. Revegetation experiments on Cascade Pass, North Cascades National Park. 8 p. [Unpublished report prepared for the National Park Service. On file at Superintendent's office, North Cascades National Park, Sedro Wooley, Wash.]

(pelletized feed does not); horse manure also introduces seeds that are still viable.

Site restoration is one challenge to wilderness managers that might tempt them to compromise the naturalness of wilderness. We think the introduction of nonindigenous species is never justified. We also ask managers to consider if carrying capacity has been exceeded before more than a one-shot fertilization application is used to accelerate site restoration. Other, more extensive actions—seedbed preparation, seeding, planting, irrigating—need to be considered cautiously. Their effectiveness and impacts are poorly understood at this time, and the advantages and disadvantages are difficult to compare.

Trails

Trails are the main travel arteries in wilderness—studies show only about 15 to 20 percent of visitors travel off trails at all in most areas, and then usually only for short distances (Lucas 1978). But for these cross-country hikers the solitude afforded by such opportunities is extremely important. River use usually does not depend on trails, but in lake canoeing areas, portage trails are short but vital connecting links between lakes and navigable stretches of rivers. Trails also are used for wilderness administration.

The dependence of most travel on trails means that trails can be a powerful tool for directing use patterns and for influencing the kind of experiences visitors receive. Unfortunately, very few wilderness trails were built with either recreation or wilderness protection in mind (Lucas and Rinehart 1976). Almost all trails were built in the 1920's and 1930's as an administrative transportation system, especially in National Forest, but also in National Parks. Fire control was their main use; they were built for horse and mule traffic to lookouts and fires. A few were built to facilitate prospecting, mining, or grazing of National Forest lands.

Redesign and relocation could substantially increase the recreational value of many of these trails and help reduce resource impacts. Some types of land are more vulnerable to damage from trail construction and use than others. For example, it seems important to route trails around wet meadows and away from lakeshores. Many factors—slope, parent material, soil, type of geologic land-forming process, vegetation, exposure, elevation, and climate—can influence trail durability. This was true in the Selway-Bitterroot Wilderness in Idaho where trails in some land types began eroding at very gentle grades, while even steep trails eroded little in other types of locations (Helgath 1975). General

guidelines for other areas are not now available, but further study in a variety of environments seems warranted to develop them.

Where trail construction would have detrimental impacts on the wilderness resource (because it produced serious erosion, for example, or brought too many visitors into critical wildlife habitat) and where an alternate location is not possible, trails should not be built. Such areas can be used for light cross-country travel.

Trail Standards

Trail-design standards specify tread width, grade or slope, alinement, tread surface material, drainage, width of trailside vegetation cleared, extent of clearance of down trees or other obstructions, signs, and types and locations of bridges. Visitor surveys have indicated little support for high-standard trails, but strong support for low-standard trails. Our discussions with wilderness managers indicate that this is the direction many are taking. We think this is a good sign because, in many cases, wilderness trails have been built to excessively high standards.

The Forest Service Manual (FSM 2323.11c and 7730.31) now calls for a maximum trail width of 24 inches and trail locations that follow the natural contours of the land as much as possible and result in minimum disturbance of soil and vegetation. Trails should appear to be a part of the country rather than an intrusion on it. Bridges "will be provided only: a. When no other route or crossing is reasonably available. b. Where the crossing during the primary season of public use: (1) cannot be safely negotiated afoot (2) cannot be safely forded by horses; b. where less formal devices are frequently destroyed or damaged by flood waters; c. where essential for administrative purposes."

National Park Service management guidelines state simply that "narrow, unpaved foot and horse trails are permissible." More detailed guidelines are being prepared. A wilderness trail policy is needed in all agencies, but the policy should allow for flexibility. The objective should be to provide a range of travel opportunities in wilderness including full-standard trails that meet minimum requirements for both horse and hiker use, some trails suitable for hikers only, and minimally marked man ways or way trails, and unmarked cross-country routes. However, excessively developed trails have no place in wilderness (Shaine 1972).

A special question of appropriate trail standards arises where a National Scenic Trail, such as the Appalachian Trail and the Pacific Crest Trail established by Congress (P.L. 90–543), crosses a wilderness. Outside wilderness,

National Scenic Trails usually are built to a higher standard and intended for heavier use than are wilderness trails. In some places, the problem can be avoided by locating the National Scenic Trail so it bypasses the wilderness. The National Trails System Act states that "development and management of each segment of the National Trails System shall be designed to harmonize with and complement any established multiple-use plans for that specific area . . . " That provision seems to us to assign priority to wilderness management objectives, but the question will need to be resolved in the future.

The need for trail surfacing with crushed rock or corduroy (log surfacing of trails), and elaborate drainage devices, can often be reduced or avoided by trail relocation. In some terrain, soil moisture and drainage conditions that cannot be avoided pose a choice between quagmires or surfacing or even bridging if that particular area is to be served by a trail. Although trail bridges and surfacing are permanent improvements and probably show a "substantially noticeable imprint of man's work," wide, deep mudholes caused by man's travel over an inadequately surfaced trail can be even more noticeable. The same is true to a more limited extent for bridges. Fords or, for small streams, stepping stones can sometimes be found and a trail directed to them.

Trails are necessary to allow reasonable recreation use of wilderness, but their development should be guided by the minimum standards needed to meet use objectives and minimize threats to the naturalness and solitude of wilderness.

Bridges

Bridges pose a difficult management problem. In wilderness, structures are to be minimized, but recreational use and enjoyment is one purpose of wilderness. Challenge is part of a wilderness experience—challenge is mentioned specifically in the 1975 Eastern Wilderness Act and implied in the 1964 Act—but how much challenge? Large rivers cannot be forded by hikers and sometimes cannot be crossed safely by horses. Should hikers have to swim, perhaps using an air mattress to help float a pack? There are places, in Alaska, for example, where that is just what travelers must do. Probably most people would favor bridges in these cases. Agency policies do, and almost all surveyed visitors do. However, in some cases, a possible alternate route could make a bridge not essential. Wilderness use patterns can be modified substantially by provision of bridges over large streams or by their absence. Use can be reduced and delayed until later in the summer in mountains where snowmelt runoff is heavy in early summer. Depending on the situation and the management objectives, use of bridges may or may not be desirable.

Where streams are small, and the worst that can happen to a hiker is wet feet, most managers and most visitors do not favor bridges, although many have been built in such locations.

Bridges range from elaborate suspension structures that a string of packhorses can easily cross to a log felled across a creek that hikers can inch across while the horses ford the stream. A log flattened on top, perhaps with a handrail for balance on one side, is a popular, simple hiker bridge. Our view is that bridges, like trails, should be built to the minimum standard that will meet wilderness use objectives. We think wet feet are not an unreasonable expectation for wilderness recreationists, but we share the view of many managers and visitors that a bridge should be provided if safety, rather than wet feet, is the real issue.

Figure 15-7.—Wilderness management may require the use of primitive work and travel skills. Also, there are important cultural values in the preservation of these skills. *Left*: moving through a western wilderness with a loaded packstring; *right*: working with crosscut saw and adz.

356

Signs

Several kinds of signs are possible in wilderness: (1) directional, (2) informational, (3) interpretive, and (4) regulatory. They are used to different degrees by the various Agencies, and there is also some variation within Agencies. Signs are a conspicuous mark of man and thus potentially in conflict with wilderness values. Visitor surveys in Washington and Oregon (Hendee et al. 1968) indicate general support for fairly simple, wooden directional signs, but limited support for informational or interpretive signs. About half the visitors to wildernesses in the northern Rockies (Lucas 1978) favored interpretive signs.

1. *Directional signs* give trail destinations, and sometimes mileages, usually at trailheads and junctions. Some directional signs might be necessary for recreational use, but accurate wilderness maps would reduce or eliminate this need. "Maps before signs" is a manager's operating rule we favor. The trend seems to be provision of a minimal number of directional signs at important or confusing trail junctions with the name of the major destinations to which the trails lead but often without distances indicated. Among wilderness managers there seem to be a growing consensus that to preserve wilderness challenge and a sense of adventure and exploration, detailed directional signs and mileage markers should be eliminated. We endorse this thinking. As with all other wilderness management tools, signs must be related to specific management objectives for the area. The fewest signs necessary to meet these objectives is all that seems justified in wilderness.

2. *Informational signs* give functional information to users—for example, the location of camps, toilets, and water, or warning of unsafe water. Very few, if any, of these signs are needed, and we encourage managers to carefully evaluate their necessity.

3. *Interpretive signs* explain natural features and historical sites. To us, they seem inappropriate in wilderness because other informational tools, such as maps, brochures, or guidebooks can accomplish the same things. Interpretive signs are not essential to manage for wilderness purposes, and they are a conspicuous mark of man.

Many wildernesses have had books prepared about their natural and historic qualities as well as publications giving information on trails, campsites, and attractions. One study indicated that 100 percent of the visitors to the Glacier Peak Wilderness in Washington were interested in an interpretive wilderness guidebook and 40 percent said they would pay as much as $2 for such a book (Butterworth 1970). In the Rawah Wilderness in Colorado, 30 percent of the visitors had a guidebook that had been published only the previous winter (Schomaker 1975).

4. *Regulatory signs* are essential in some cases to inform visitors of closed campsites, restrictions on certain types of use, fire restrictions, wilderness permit requirements, and so forth. Signs marking the wilderness boundary serve to inform people where legal restrictions apply. However, regulatory signs should be used only where and when necessary to meet visitor management objectives—they are a too conspicuous reminder of civilization. In most cases, regulatory signs can be at or near trailheads. In particular, we deplore fire prevention signs nailed to the trees in some areas we have visited. To us, they seem superfluous, conspicuous reminders of civilization with its flood of advertising. They seem out of place in wilderness and are probably ineffective anyway. Again, maps and informational brochures could greatly reduce the need for signs.

Trail Maintenance

Maintenance is a major job with trails. They require much more time and attention than campsites. In most areas, the biggest trail maintenance job is cutting out and removing trees that fall across the trail. On some main trails, maintenance can be an almost continual operation where very few logs ever block trails for long. Other trails might be cleared only once every few years. In some wildernesses, policy has shifted toward less intensive trail maintenance in order to offer challenges and restrict the amount and kind of use.

Hikers can usually cope with log-blocked trails without great difficulty by crawling under, climbing over, or walking around the obstruction. Horses usually have more trouble; riders must often stop, get out a crosscut saw or axe, and cut the log out or, if possible, detour around the obstacle. Some consider this all part of the adventure, others view it as an intolerable inconvenience. Surveys suggest most visitors will accept at least a few trees across trails. However, detours around some down logs can cause serious erosion and damage vegetation, especially if horses scramble up and down steep banks. This adverse effect must be considered in management decisions.

Trail crews also prune back encroaching branches; clear large rocks out of the trail; repair erosion damage; and install or maintain bridges, ditches, drains, culverts, and water bars.

Drainage is critical in controlling trail damage. A poorly layed out trail can become a manmade drainage ditch when snow melts or after heavy rains. Water bars are a common device used in dealing with drainage

Figure 15–8.—Trail construction and location is extremely important if the kind of erosion and impact shown here are to be avoided.

problems. Water bars are logs, boards, timbers, or rocks installed across a trail, usually on an angle and sloping out, that are intended to divert running water off the trail. In effect, they are miniature diversion dams. But, unless carefully installed to encourage rapid flow of water, they often are buried in the sediment deposited behind them and cease to function. Unless securely anchored, they also can be dislodged, particularly by horses. If not spaced closely enough or located properly, so much water can build up by the time the flow reaches the water bar that it cannot be handled and overflows the bar.

Often a trail dips and rises enough to divert running water before it can build up to destructive levels. This is sometimes called a rolling grade, and should be sought in locating new trails.

In some areas, fiberglass liners buried beneath the trail tread have been advocated as a way of permitting the natural flow of water through boggy areas without leading to erosion, water pollution, or vegetative damage (Dalley 1975). This engineering approach seems to us to be less appropriate than improved trail design and relocation.

The use of mechanized equipment—in particular, chain saw instead of handsaw—for constructing and maintaining trails is a hot issue. Most miles of existing trails were built more than a generation ago and

maintained with handtools for decades; but by the time the Wilderness Act became law in 1964, the chain saw had largely replaced handsaws. The Wilderness Act prohibited mechanical equipment except "to meet minimum requirements for the administration of the area for the purpose of this Act."

Different Agencies and managers have drawn the line on chain saw use differently. In general, routine use of chain saws for maintenance has ended. Only when the job is unusually difficult or virtually impossible because of the size or number of trees are chain saws allowed, and then usually only with special approval from higher levels in the Agency.

Some sketchy data suggest that the cost advantage is not always in the chain saw's favor, and perhaps some trail maintenance can be done as cheaply with handtools. The same controversy also involves some other power equipment such as very small bulldozers, gasoline-engine-powered rock drills for blasting, and portable rock crushers for surfacing trails which have been developed recently (USDA FS 1975).

Early day handtools and horsedrawn equipment are still commonly used, but the gradual loss of oldtimers who had experience in operating and maintaining tools such as crosscut saws has limited their use (Oltman 1972). Some of these tools are simply no longer produced, disappearing along with button shoes. However, recent tests using handtools by specially trained, two-man maintenance crews have proven quite successful (Oltman 1975).

The General Accounting Office (1970) investigated the administrative use of motorized equipment in wilderness and reported to Congress that cost cutting in wilderness management using labor-saving technology would be possible. They also recommended Congress provide further guidance concerning the use of motorized equipment for administrative purposes in wilderness. The silence of Congress in response to this report seems to indicate rejection of cost efficiency as a major criterion in wilderness management. The use of mechanized equipment in new trail construction is more easily justified than it is for trail maintenance (except in special circumstances such as removal of very large trees, or of numerous trees, such as can result from avalanches or windstorms). When used for trail construction, however, such modern power machinery is not only an intrusion, but also can produce higher standard trails than are needed. Our view is that the less such technology is used, the better.

The old, traditional western trail crews rode horses and transported equipment on packhorses. In some places in recent years, backpacker crews have replaced horse crews. Backpackers have less adverse impact on wilderness resources than crews with pack strings and can camp in many more places, often closer to the place where the work needs to be done. Using lightweight backpacking equipment, crews stay out and work trails for stretches of 5 days or longer (Oltman 1975). Trail work does need to be done in wilderness, and crews are required. Again, our view is that the method selected should be the one with the least impact that will meet management objectives.

Site Management Balancing Act

Wilderness site management calls for some of a tightrope walker's sense of balance. Our view is that only the minimum facilities needed to meet management objectives are justified in wilderness, and we do not believe that most wilderness visitors want more than this. Minimum facilities can enable people to enjoy wilderness as wilderness, but we must stress the "as wilderness" qualification. Sensitivity to wilderness values, careful planning, and restraint: All are necessary if wilderness is to be protected by site management rather than changed to something other than wilderness. As was pointed out at the end of chapter 14, if some areas are not managed for roadless recreation—backcountry, semiwilderness, intermediate, whatever they may be called—then at least some wilderness must be more developed and more heavily used, and the distinctive wilderness values of naturalness and solitude could be diminished.

Among the co-authors, the author primarily responsible for preparation of this chapter was Robert C. Lucas.

Literature Cited

Beardsley, Wendell G., and J. Alan Wagar.
1971. Vegetation management of a forested recreation site. J. For. 69(10):728-731.
Brown, Ray W., and Robert S. Johnston.
1976. Revegetation of an alpine mine disturbance: Beartooth Plateau, Montana. USDA For. Serv. Res. Note INT-206, 8 p. Intermt. For. and Range Exp. Stn., Ogden, Utah.
Brown, Perry J., and John H. Schomaker.
1974. Final report on criteria for potential wilderness campsites. Conducted through the Institute for Study of Outdoor Recreation and Tourism, Utah State University, Supplement No. 32 to 12-11-204-3, unpublished, 50 p.
Butterworth, Stephan.
1970. Development of model guidebooks for Glacier Park Wilderness. Master's thesis, College of Forest Resources, University of Washington, Seattle, 70 p.
Dailey, Tom, and Dave Redman.
1975. Guidelines for roadless area campsite spacing to minimize impact of human-related noises. USDA For. Serv., Gen. Tech. Rep. PNW-35, 20 p. Pac. Northwest For. and Range Exp. Stn., Portland, Oreg.
Dale, D., and T. Weaver.
1974. Trampling effects on vegetation of the trail corridors of northern Rocky Mountain forests. J. Appl. Ecol. 11(2):767-772.
Dalley, Durray.
1975. Bridging the wet spots. U.S. Dep. Agric., For. Serv. Eng. Field Notes 7(10):6-9.
Fay, Stephan.
1975. Ground-cover vegetation management at backcountry recreation sites. USDA For. Serv., Res. Note NE-201, 5 p. Northeast. For. Exp. Stn., Upper Darby, Pa.
Frissell, Sidney S., Jr., and Donald P. Duncan.
1965. Campsite preference and deterioration. J. For. 63(4):256-260.
General Accounting Office.
1970. Problems related to restricting the use of motorized equipment in wilderness and similar areas. Department of Agriculture, Department of Interior. B-125053. 44 p. Washington, D.C. Report to the Congress by the Comptroller General of the United States.
Helgath, Sheila F.
1975. Trail deterioration in the Selway-Bitterroot Wilderness. USDA For. Serv., Res. Note INT-193, 15 p. Intermt. For. and Range Exp. Stn., Ogden, Utah.
Hendee, John C., William R. Catton, Jr., Larry D. Marlow, and C. Frank Brockman.
1968. Wilderness users in the Pacific Northwest—their characteristics, values, and management preferences. USDA For. Serv., Res. Pap. PNW-61, 92 p. Pac. Northwest For. and Range Exp. Stn., Portland, Oreg.
Hendee, John C., Roger N. Clark, and Thomas Dailey.
1974. Fishing and other recreation behavior at high lakes: some management implications. 25 p., mimeo. Presentation to American Fisheries Society, Honolulu, Hawaii, Sept. 8.
Hendee, John C., Roger N. Clark, Mack Hogans, Dan Wood, and Russ Koch.
1976. Code-A-Site: a system for inventory of dispersed recreational sites in roaded areas, backcountry, and wilderness. USDA For. Serv. Res. Pap. PNW-209, 33 p. Pac. Northwest For. and Range Exp. Stn., Portland, Oreg.
Ketchledge, E.H., and R.E. Leonard.
1971. Progress report: high peak erosion studies. Adirondack Peeks 8(2):8-10.
Ketchledge, E.H., and R.E. Leonard.
1972. Progress report: high peak erosion studies. Adirondack Peeks 9(1):12-13.
Lee, Robert G.
1975. The management of human components in the Yosemite National Park ecosystem. 134 p. The Yosemite Institute, Yosemite, Calif.
Lime, David W.
1971. Factors influencing campground use in the Superior

National Forest of Minnesota. USDA For. Serv., Res. Pap. NC–60, 18 p. North Central For. Exp. Stn., St. Paul, Minn.

Lucas, Robert C.
1978. The characteristics of visitors to wilderness and related areas in the Northern Rockies and California Sierras. USDA For. Serv., Res. Pap. Intermt. For. and Range Exp. Stn. (In press.)

Lucas, Robert C., and Robert Rinehart.
1976. The neglected hiker. Backpacker 4(1):35–39.

MacFeters, Gordon A.
1975. Final report to the Park Service, Grand Teton National Park, on microbial studies of a high alpine water supply used for recreation. Research Contract No. CX 12004 B025, 26 p., mimeo. Montana State University, Bozeman.

Merriam, L.C., Jr., C.K. Smith, D.E. Miller, Ching taio Huang, J.C. Tappeiner II, Kent Goeckermann, J.A. Bloemendal, and T.M. Costello.
1973. Newly developed campsites in the Boundary Waters Canoe Area: a study of five years' use. 27 p. Stn. Bull. 511, For. Series 14. Agric. Exp. Stn., University of Minnesota, St. Paul.

Miller, Bob.
1973. Suggestions for using horses in the mountain country. 13 p. Animal and Range Sciences Dept., Montana State University, Bozeman.

Oltman, Jerry L.
1972. Practices and problems in trail maintenance and construction. 81 p. U.S. Dep. Agric., For. Serv., Equip. Dev. Center, Missoula, Mont.

Oltman, Jerry L.
1975. An evaluation: two-man backpacking crews for trail maintenance. 48 p. U.S. Dep. Agric., For. Serv., Equip. Dev. Center, Missoula, Mont.

Sanks, R., and K.L. Temple.
1975. Final report on liquid and solid waste disposal in U.S. forest lands. Report to Intermt. For. and Range Exp. Stn. FS–INT Grant No. 7, 72 p. Montana State University, Bozeman.

Schomaker, John H.
1975. Effect of selected information on dispersal of wilderness recreationists. Ph.D. thesis, College of Forestry and Natural Resources, Colorado State University, Ft. Collins, 95 p.

Shaine, Ben.
1972. Trails in wilderness. The Wild Cascades, June–July, p. 12–24.

Stankey, George H.
1973. Visitor perception of wilderness recreation carrying capacity. USDA For. Serv., Res. Pap. INT–142, 61 p. Intermt. For. and Range Exp. Stn., Ogden, Utah.

U.S. Department of Agriculture, Forest Service.
1975. Surfacing forest trails with crushed rock. Equip. Dev. and Test Rep. No. 7700–5, 13 p. U.S. Dep. Agric., For. Serv. Equip. Dev. Cen., Missoula, Mont.

Walker, Richard.
1968. Photography as an aid to wilderness resource inventory and analysis. Professional paper submitted for M.S. degree, Colorado State University, Fort Collins. 114 p.

Weaver, T., and D. Dale.
1977. Trampling effects of hikers, motorcycles, or horses in meadows and forests. 12 p. J. App. Ecol. (In press.)

Willard, Beatrice E., and John W. Marr.
1971. Recovery of alpine tundra under protection after damage by human activities in the Rocky Mountains of Colorado. Biol. Conserv. 3(3):181–190.

Perhaps one of the most important issues confronting wilderness managers is to insure that in their efforts to protect the wilderness resource, the freedom and spontaneity that characterizes the wilderness experience is not lost in a myriad of regulations and rules. Respect for visitors and restraint in the issuance of controls should govern management actions.

16 The Future: Issues And Challenges In Wilderness Management

In this final chapter, we review some of the major topics, controversies, problems, and challenges we believe are particularly important to wilderness management, now and in the future. These topics include: (1) Controlling impacts of recreational use, (2) improving wilderness administration, (3) increasing relevant research, (4) providing alternatives to wilderness, (5) integrating wilderness in the East into the NWPS, (6) restoring fire to natural levels, and (7) securing adequate appropriations.

Controlling Impacts of Recreational Use

Controlling the impacts of wilderness use—social-psychological and physical-biological—is necessary to preserve the elements of solitude and naturalness required under the Wilderness Act. The terms of the Act are subject to differing interpretations—although consistency of judgments is improving as Departmental Regulations, agency policy, and philosophy are tempered with field experience. But the Act does not provide precise criteria for defining or measuring naturalness and solitude, the distinguishing wilderness characteristics managers are called upon to preserve—at standards they must themselves determine. Nonetheless, the challenge to preserve these distinguishing wilderness qualities is fundamental. There is no question that meeting these legally required goals for classified areas of the National Wilderness Preservation System

will require some restriction on recreation use—at least at certain times in particular locations within individual wilderness areas. This reality is recognized and accepted by most managers and users; restrictions on visitor numbers and behavior are already in force in a few wildernesses.

Techniques of visitor and site management have been discussed in chapters 14 and 15 following previous material describing philosophical considerations (chapter 1), legal constraints and mandates (chapter 4), proposed principles (chapter 7), and a planning framework for implementing management actions (chapter 8). Our purpose here is to emphasize three points that we feel are essential to successful efforts to control user impacts: (1) Restraint in regulating use; (2) respect for visitor freedom; and (3) equity in any use regulations imposed.

Restraint in Regulating Wilderness Use

Because the regulation of visitor use is one of the most politically volatile wilderness management tasks, restraint is needed to make sure only necessary restrictions are imposed. We believe that all wilderness management—including visitor use—should be governed by the criteria of necessity and minimum regimentation. All actions should be *necessary* to meet area objectives, and clearly set forth in area management plans that are developed with public review and participation to test their acceptability. The actions should entail the least possible regimentation that will accomplish the desired end.

As a general rule, use impacts should first be handled where and when they occur before wilderness-wide restrictions are imposed. And, when widespread use restrictions are needed to meet area objectives, only the minimum essential regulation should be applied. Use rationing—the direct restriction of entry—should be a last resort. Yet, even when other strategies are conscientiously applied, visitor restrictions are nonetheless present and direct regulation will sometimes be necessary. Public acceptance and support for all visitor controls may depend on management's prior restraint and its record of adhering to criteria of necessity and minimum regimentation in imposing use restrictions.

Respect for Visitor Freedom

The spectre of government control implicit in the regulation of wilderness visitation has threatening overtones in our society. Most people, including wilderness users as well as many managers, don't like the notion of government restrictions, particularly when they restrict visitation to a category of public land that has been set aside in part to represent the antithesis of urban environments and their omnipresent controls on human activity. Freedom-related values are basic to the wilderness system—symbolically for the millions of vicarious users and as an integral part of the wilderness experience for visitors. Respect for these values underscores the necessity of applying only the minimum, necessary regimentation whenever use restrictions are needed to control visitor impacts.

Equity in the Imposition of Regulations

A recent blue ribbon commission identified the need for an equitable system of rationing use of wilderness as one of the major forest policy issues facing the country (President's Advisory Panel on Timber and the Environment 1973). Even if applied only when necessary and with minimum regimentation, there must be the greatest possible equity in restrictions on use. Visitor management techniques vary in their impact on different categories of users, e.g., day users, overnight campers staying one or two nights, organized groups, large parties, and small groups. Impacts of restrictions must be carefully considered in order to assess their effects on various kinds of users and minimize any systematic discrimination. Many techniques can be applied to manage use, but their effects on different user groups vary (see chapter 14; Behan 1976; and Stankey and Baden 1977). On a broad scale, equity in the impacts of restricting use may be achieved by applying a wide variety of use-management techniques to distribute impacts among various user groups.

Wilderness visitors have already been labeled as a privileged group by virtue of their typically high socio-economic standing (although as we point out in chapter 13, this stereotype is not completely true). The idea of a "police state wilderness system locked up for an elitist minority," however mythical, could become a focal point for anti-wilderness sentiment and help defeat essential management programs. To minimize this possibility, wilderness managers need to be guided by sensitivity and restraint in their efforts to regulate use. Regulations should be employed only when they are clearly necessary, they produce minimal interference with visitor freedom, and they are equitable in spreading impacts among various groups of users.

Improving Wilderness Administration

Wilderness is a favored personal, as well as professional, interest of many resource managers in the Forest Service, National Park Service, Fish and Wildlife Service, and Bureau of Land Management. All these Agencies are making progress in developing management programs for the classified and proposed wilderness under their jurisdiction. However, there is much to be done.

Wilderness management philosophies, current management capability, and interest vary not only among the four managing Agencies but within them as well. This is to be expected in any new endeavor. Wilderness management is a very young speciality as Nash illustrated in chapter 2. It was not until 1964 that legislation clearly defined wilderness and mandated a framework for its management. The next several years were devoted to interpreting the Act and developing regulations and guidelines. In addition, most of the Agencies' wilderness-related energies were at first devoted to the classification process—carrying out reviews mandated by the Act and developing proposals and recommendations to Congress for classification of individual wildernesses. This continues to be a major activity by all the Agencies although they are increasingly focusing on management of classified and proposed areas to see that their wilderness characteristics are retained.

In this decade wilderness management has emerged as a serious resource speciality. This new era is marked by several trends: The establishment of wilderness management classes at several universities around the country; an increasing number of scholarly journal

Figure 16-1.—The future quality of wilderness, both in terms of naturalness and as a setting for a special kind of recreational experience, depends on management decisions made today. *Left*, Bridger Wilderness; *right*, Boundary Waters Canoe Area.

articles on the topic; acceleration of relevant research; more seasonal wilderness patrolmen hired under increasingly specific job descriptions, qualification requirements, and performance standards; establishment of some professional wilderness management positions within the agencies; increased concern for wilderness in overall land-use planning processes; and preparation of wilderness management plans for individual areas. There is another trend that is perhaps even more noteworthy: The increasing number of National, regional, and local meetings and conferences bringing together resource professionals to discuss wilderness management problems and needs. As mentioned in the preface, it was such a meeting in 1973 that led us to prepare this text. It is significant that many of these conferences include participants from more than one Federal Agency. It is our impression that such meetings are becoming more professional—topics and discussion reflect management concerns that transcend individual agency policies and focus instead on a search for optimum ways to preserve the wilderness resource regardless of agency jurisdiction.

The future quality of the National Wilderness Preservation System depends on continued professional growth in wilderness as a resource management speciality. This professional challenge is matched by the administrative challenge of managing a far-flung system of areas with wide-ranging social and physical conditions while coordinating agency actions to provide a National Wilderness Preservation System that is truly national Improved wilderness administration will be a major factor in safeguarding the investments of human effort and natural resources represented by classified wilderness. Unfortunately, it is impossible to develop a formula or point to any one thing that might insure meeting this challenge. What is involved is an entire system of management.

In figure 16-2 we identify 11 elements of a comprehensive wilderness administration system. These elements are concerned with actions of the management agencies, relevant educational and research institutions, and the affected public. All exist now to varying degrees and mentioning them here does not mean to disparage current efforts. What is needed is their strengthening and integration. Wilderness administration can be no stronger than its weakest essential element, and across-the-board efforts are needed to improve all of them. In particular, skillful administration is needed to knit all the elements together into a true wilderness management system in each agency and to secure coordination and cooperation among the agencies and the public toward the common goal of preserving an NWPS that is truly national. Following is a brief review of the elements, their importance, and their interrelationships.

1. *Agency philosophy and National guidelines* for interpreting the Wilderness Act, that give clear management direction and constraints, are needed to guide development of management field programs. The

365

Figure 16-2.—Elements of a comprehensive administration system for the National Wilderness Preservation System.

first decade following passage of the Wilderness Act was a time of policy development for the agencies; the resulting management direction is now coming into sharper and more consistent focus in agency manuals, field applications, and manager statements of policy and philosophy. The current situation reflects an important evaluation of early efforts, of trial and error. Careful scrutiny of emerging management philosophy permits both specialists and laymen to appraise the consequences of NWPS classification, the kind of management actions thereby indicated, and thus the consequences for the affected resources and people (see chapter 1 for discussion of the importance of philosophy to management).

2. *Coordination among agencies* managing wilderness is improving but must be strengthened to help knit the far-flung network of individual areas into a truly National System. Certainly there will be interagency differences in emphasis that reflect variation in viewpoints, overriding legislation, and local differences in physical and social conditions. For example, hunting is prohibited in National Park wilderness but is allowed in most wilderness managed by other agencies. Such diversity can be healthy. The need is for interagency communication and coordination to minimize problems of conflicting wilderness management approaches,

particularly where contiguous or nearby wilderness are under different jurisdictions or where the management of adjacent nonwilderness lands creates wilderness impacts. Coordination and cooperation is emerging in the form of joint wilderness use permits for adjoining areas under different jurisdiction, interagency conferences, planning, and joint wilderness training programs to name a few examples.

3. *Integration of wilderness into agency land-use planning* is essential to coordinated management within the broader framework of the National Forest, National Park, Wildlife Refuge, and BLM systems within which all wilderness exists. Progress is encouraging. All the agencies have developed and are improving wilderness management planning procedures that are linked to their overall land-use planning processes (see chapter 8). But land-use planning is also a relatively new and evolving process. Wilderness management planning is challenged to keep abreast of the evolution in land-use planning philosophies and methodologies so the most effective techniques can be applied to wilderness, and the resulting plans properly coordinated with other land uses.

Preallocation studies of areas proposed for wilderness classification have important ramifications for overall land-use planning. While classification issues are

366

different from management issues in that they are inherently political (see chapter 1), we think potential management problems that may result from classification decisions should be surfaced for consideration in land use studies. One way of doing this would be to include wilderness management feasibility and potential problems as one of the criteria for evaluating proposed land-use alternatives in any wilderness study. Wilderness preservation will not be furthered by the classification of areas that cannot be feasibly managed to meet wilderness standards or by those that will command a disproportionate share of management manpower and money at the expense of the rest of the NWPS.

4. *Management plans for individual wildernesses* are needed to establish clear objectives to guide management actions. Chapter 8 is devoted to wilderness-management planning—its importance and some suggestions on how to do it. Here we wish only to emphasize that wilderness-management plans are the vehicles through which national direction is translated into objectives to be achieved—through management policies and actions—in individual wildernesses. We believe the key to better plans is more clearly stated objectives that describe conditions to be maintained or restored through management. Such objectives are difficult to write and should be derived with public participation if they are to become accepted targets of management. However, once clearly stated, these objectives are the most important criteria for deciding what management actions will be necessary, for subsequently judging the degree of management's success, and for determining needed changes in policies and actions. Wilderness management can be no more effective than the direction charted in its underlying planning process.

5. *Career ladders* are needed that reward wilderness-management expertise and also provide management officials headed for broader responsibility the opportunity to learn about wilderness. But the issue of providing job opportunities in wilderness management and the assignment of personnel to jobs with increasing responsibility is complex.

The challenge is to create legitimate wilderness-management job opportunities at a variety of levels. In general, a sequential ladder of positions might proceed from seasonal ranger to year-round management coordinator, wilderness management planner, area manager, and so forth to regional and national office staff responsibilities for wilderness. However, if *only* these sequential jobs are featured in a professional's career ladder it could lead to a degree of specialization in wilderness that could slight the broader aspects of

management, such as those involving the interdependency of wilderness with other land uses. We think it is necessary that a ladder of increasingly responsible wilderness management jobs be established within the agencies so expertise can be rewarded, but we think other resource management experience is also necessary to properly develop individuals for wilderness-management leadership. Wilderness management does not operate in a vacuum, independent of other resource concerns, and the selection and training of managers must reflect this interdependence. Effective wilderness management will require the integration of ideas, experiences, and perspectives from many interrelated resource and administrative specialities. Furthermore, in recognition of the fact that wilderness management in all the agencies takes place within a broader resource and administrative framework, it is desirable that some wilderness management jobs be available as stepping stones to and from other resource management careers—especially for talented managers who will ultimately rise to broad leadership positions.

6. *Highly qualified seasonal rangers* are needed since they are the first line of contact between agency management, the wilderness resource, and its users. Wilderness ranger (or patrolman, if you like) jobs are highly prized by college students, teachers, and resource management graduates unable to find professional, career employment in their chosen field. Some wilderness ranger positions can have 50 to 100 applicants under the merit employment systems governing Federal summer jobs. In some locations, agency managers have established volunteer positions calling for wilderness patrolman duties without salary to expand the number of persons available to administer a wilderness. The number of applicants typically vying for wilderness ranger-patrolman positions allows managers to set high standards for qualification and performance (see chapter 14). Managers should make the most of this opportunity, bearing in mind that wilderness management to date is essentially people management; therefore, social skills as well as personal interest and resource knowledge should rate high on the list of desirable qualifications.

7. *Evaluation of wilderness management* efforts is necessary to provide accountability for achieving objectives and the feedback necessary for improvement or change. Each of the agencies operates under a system of internal and external management evaluation through their planning processes. To provide necessary feedback—both positive and negative—wilderness management, in general, and in individual areas, should be a focus for periodic inspection and evaluation—

review that utilizes data whenever available from resource and use inventories and monitoring systems.

The rapid turnover of personnel makes it especially important that lessons from experience are not lost. Constructive lessons can be learned from close examination of successes and failures; inspection and evaluation are essential to any management system. We favor an increased emphasis on the evaluation of wilderness management to identify successes and failures and, more importantly, the reasons for them. Ideally, such inspections and evaluation should be both internal and external. Other agencies and the affected public can provide valuable input and stimulate an educational flow of information about wilderness problems, achievements, and the management policies and actions associated with them.

8. *Systematic collection of resource and use information* is basic to intelligent wilderness management decisionmaking. Without a reliable data base feasible management objectives cannot be devised nor can management be accurately evaluated to see if objectives are being obtained or if new direction is needed. Resource and use information is thus an essential element to implementing wilderness management and as feedback to the system. Planning for the use of data needed to provide these inventory and monitoring functions are illustrated in chapter 8, and the kinds of data required and available collection techniques are covered in subsequent chapters. The information that can be useful includes: The amount and kinds of wilderness recreation use; campsite locations and impacts; vegetation cover types and associated successional processes evidenced by fire, insect, and disease; wildlife populations and their distributions; trail mileage and condition; existing facilities; nonrecreational uses such as grazing, prospecting, mining, and ongoing scientific studies; water resource quality, development, and use; and cultural and historically important sites.

Ideally, such information is provided for in wilderness management plans, collected by field managers and seasonal rangers following the plan's direction, and used by administrators and the interested public in evaluating management and the need for redirection. The resource and use information is also invaluable to scientists doing research to explain natural phenomena or to identify and solve wilderness-management problems.

9. *Training of wilderness management personnel* through university courses, inservice sessions, and interagency and citizen group conferences is essential. Universities can play a vital role here by offering professional courses and programs related to wilderness management. Universities also host conferences and provide a valuable pool of educational and research specialists for teaching at training sessions. Interagency training conferences are particularly valuable because at these forums a wide range of alternative viewpoints can surface, and professional discussions of wilderness management issues that transcend agency differences can take place. Some good wilderness conferences have been sponsored by citizen groups, but to date most of these have focused on classification of additional areas. As the attention of environmentalists increasingly encompasses managment issues, their conferences can become an additional valuable source of education for wilderness managers; and an opportunity for two-way communication between managers and affected citizens.

10. *Research* to develop basic knowledge and suggest solutions to wilderness management problems is an essential element of improved management. Some of the most advanced applications of wilderness management techniques have been derived from research. Additional study, in close communication and cooperation with management, is the most efficient way to develop the knowledge and techniques necessary to meet wilderness management objectives. In the next section we provide some suggestions about what kind of research we think is required. Here we suggest only that research is a major key to developing the new knowledge necessary to advancing the state of the art in wilderness management. A coordinated program of wilderness-related research involving agencies, universities, and research-endowment foundations must be an integrated part of the overall management system.

11. *Public education and involvement* to foster understanding and support of wilderness are essential to improved administration. Wilderness management is ultimately constrained by the limits of public understanding, acceptance, and support. All the involved agencies must expend the effort to educate the public about the purposes of wilderness and their management programs, or meaningful support and involvement by the public will be impossible. Public involvement has become a way of life for resource managers in Federal agencies. The Wilderness Act requires public participation in the classification of individual wilderness areas, and much of the agency's experience in public involvement has focused on this process. The extension of public involvement to wilderness management is logical and feasible through the management-planning process (see chapter 8). Wilderness management can be assured of success only if it proceeds with the understanding, support, and constructive input of an informed and involved constituency.

This discussion of the 11 elements of a system for improved wilderness administration has been necessarily brief, touching only on major items. The list of elements could surely be expanded as could some of the details necessary for their application. Our call is for the synergistic combination of all these elements to foster continued growth in the quality of management for the National Wilderness Preservation System. This will require the integration of efforts by all concerned parties—the agencies, universities, research institutions, and the public.

Increasing Relevant Research

A coordinated program of relevant research involving the agencies, universities, and research foundations must be an integrated part of the overall wilderness-management system. The need is for both *applied* research to find solutions to immediate wilderness management problems and *basic* research to upgrade our scientific understanding of the resource and its use. Among the many uses of such data is its utility for appraising the need for, and the potential consequences of, alternative management actions. But the challenge extends far beyond research in support of management; scientific uses are a specifically mentioned purpose of the Wilderness Act and research should be encouraged to see that those values are realized (see chapter 13).

In the following we suggest a framework for organizing wilderness research into two major categories: Behavioral and resource.

Wilderness Behavior Research

A major theme of this book is that current wilderness management is primarily people management, and more specifically the management of recreational use. This reality has been reflected for nearly two decades in calls for research that have assigned highest priority to studies of wilderness recreation behavior (Dana 1957; Fisher 1960; Morse 1966; Lucas 1974).[1]

Applied behavioral research, including studies that have adapted and applied principles from more basic research to wilderness, has already been important to development of current management techniques.

A good example relates to the measurement of wilderness recreation use. Studies in the early 1960's indicated that voluntary self-registration stations at wilderness trailheads could be used to routinely estimate an area's use if total registrations were adjusted to

account for nonresponse which the research indicated was predictable for certain kinds of users (Wenger and Gregerson 1964; Wenger 1964). In that era, these gross estimates of wilderness use provided by self-registration systems were badly needed and the kind of inaccuracies of the method that have been identified by more recent studies were not then critical. (Lucas 1975; Lucas, Schreuder, and James 1971). For several years self-registration was viewed as a promising management tool and was used as a basis for estimating visitation to many wildernesses. Then several surveys of wilderness visitors indicated that many users would be receptive to mandatory visitor permits (Hendee and Lucas 1973). Applied studies and trial applications further tested and refined the wilderness permit idea, its feasibility for visitor management, and the utility of the visitation data it provided (Elsner 1972; Frayer and Butts 1974; Lime and Buchanan 1974; Fazio and Gilbert 1974; Lime and Lorence 1974). Subsequently, in part responding to information provided by these studies, mandatory permits have become a major wilderness visitor management tool (see chapters 13 and 14).

The foregoing example illustrates how research can be valuable in developing management options, and also the need for cumulative research—related series of studies that build on one another to yield progressively more refined ideas and applicable information. The validity and applicability of research-based information also depends on a wide scientific data base including studies in several locations and verification by several scientists using different methods. For example, the tendency of wilderness visitors to be, on the average, more highly educated and of higher socioeconomic status than the general population is documented by numerous studies, but most of them have been carried out in western wildernesses. The applicability of that generalization to the more recently established, and smaller areas of the Wilderness System in the East must be established by additional study in those locations.

The following framework identifies three major categories (separate but interrelated) of needed wilderness-visitor studies: (1) Social-economic—who they are, (2) values and behavior—why they visit wilderness; what satisfactions, values, and benefits they seek and receive; and the kinds of behavior and activities they engage in, and (3) management studies—tests of management techniques to determine which are most successful in solving problems of wilderness visitation under different conditions.

(1) *Social-economic studies.* These include variables such as sex, age, education, occupation, income, residence, the social structure of visitor parties, expenditures, and

[1]See also Lucas, Robert C. 1972. Forest Service wilderness research—the problem, research to date, and needed research. U.S. Dep. Agric., For. Serv., Intermt. For. and Range Exp. Stn., Missoula, Mont. 22 p. Mimeo. January 1972.

travel distance. Survey methodologies such as mail questionnaires and personal and telephone interviews are needed to gather this information. Two problems plague such studies: Sampling and nonresponse. Sampling involves the identification of a complete universe of visitors for a given wilderness so a representative population can be studied. Previous surveys of wilderness users have focused on summer use, to the neglect of fall and winter use, and have concentrated on heads of parties, thus limiting knowledge about all visitors (Jubenville 1971). Nonresponse from the sample surveyed concerns the failure of sampled individuals to supply requested information. Response rates of surveys can vary from 40 to 90 percent although most wilderness studies report high levels of response. Obviously, if data from half the visitors are missing, a study's findings can be misleading.

Demographic characteristics and other socioeconomic information is relevant to management. It indicates the kinds of people who benefit from direct use of wilderness; it gives clues about how to communicate with these visitors by indicating where they live and the range of values they are likely to hold; it yields information useful for guiding other studies; it can help in estimating future demand from comparisons of typical visitor characteristics with future populations; and it provides information useful for wilderness allocation studies by indicating who might directly benefit from wilderness classification.

(2) *Visitor values and behavior studies.* Why do visitors go to wilderness; how long do they stay; what satisfactions, values, and benefits do they hope to get (and which of these values actually materialize); what activities are pursued; what is the meaning of these activities in relation to the overall wilderness experience; what problems are bothersome or interfere with their experience; what are their attitudes and preferences for alternative wilderness management policies? This information about wilderness visitors is basic to successful management. It supplements information about observed and recorded behavior patterns and can give valuable clues about how visitors might react to various management alternatives that *managers think* might enhance values and control problems. And previous study indicates that managers' perceptions of wilderness-visitor values and behavior can be biased (Hendee and Harris 1970).

A growing body of research-based literature relates to user motives, values, and preferences. It should be strengthened by more specific study aimed at determining how user values and behavior are related to and affected by wilderness conditions. One objective of the National Wilderness Preservation System is to provide desired values to visitors. But, more information is needed about how these values are enhanced or diminished under particular wilderness conditions that are capable of being influenced by management. There is also a need to strengthen the behavioral focus of this kind of research by zeroing in more heavily on what people actually do—not just what they say they would do or how they feel—in response to wilderness situations and conditions.

(3) *Visitor-management studies.* Visitor-management studies are of high priority. Managers need to know how wilderness values and benefits can be optimized and how use distribution and impacts of use can be managed within tolerable limits without offsetting losses in values due to visitor regimentation. In summary, the basic question as posed by one high management official is: How can wilderness-recreation use be balanced with preserving the wilderness resource itself (Peterson 1976)?

Research is needed to help assess the consequences and public acceptability of various management techniques that are applied in different locations and under different conditions to solve wilderness problems. For example, there are several possible approaches to solving overuse problems—indirect use rationing, direct rationing, restrictions and regulations at certain sites or for entire areas, and so forth (see chapters 14 and 15). Knowledge about the effects of the various techniques on the amount and distribution of use and visitor reactions can help managers to determine what methods to use as well as to evaluate the effectiveness of these techniques. Relevant research developments include the wilderness-use simulation model described in chapter 14; a wilderness management planning framework (see chapter 8); the previously mentioned studies evaluating the acceptability and utility of wilderness permits, the incentive system for litter control (see chapter 14), and studies indicating the management preferences of users (Hendee et al. 1968; Stankey 1973).

All these behavioral research topics call for applied study—the use of scientific methods to solve people problems. However, as pointed out in chapter 13, wilderness is also valuable as a scientific laboratory for basic behavioral as well as ecological research. Wilderness is a place where behavioral research can provide insight into social unity and diversity by looking at the organization and function of intra- and intergroup processes and relationships in the relatively unstructured social environment of wilderness (Burch 1974). Ultimately, the human benefits underlying wilderness designation may be clarified by wilderness behavior research. Of course, behavioral research must operate under the same constraints as resource research with studies dependent on wilderness conditions favored.

Wilderness Resource Research

Studies are needed in several natural science disciplines to further knowledge of ecological processes in the natural laboratory of wilderness. The resource research opportunities in the National Wilderness Preservation System are substantial. From the standpoint of freedom from man's direct influence, wilderness already contains a large share of natural areas, and it may ultimately contain the most natural of the world's remaining unimpacted areas. As the rest of the world becomes progressively more modified by human influence, the contrast between wilderness and other lands will enlarge as will the values of wilderness as a natural laboratory. Where else will there be opportunities to study large-scale ecosystem processes in areas with a minimum of man-caused disturbances? Here, of course, there is an interdependence between wilderness management and research because the scientific values of naturalness depend on the direction and effectiveness of management in preserving the wilderness environment.

There is a need for studies of the variety of physical and biological components of the wilderness ecosystem—such as soil, water, vegetation, wildlife and the ecological relationships among them. As a framework for such research, we advocate studies to (1) monitor wilderness naturalness, (2) expand basic ecological knowledge, and (3) solve wilderness resource problems. The following discussion of the framework is very general and readers interested in more detail should consult chapters 10, 11, and 12 on wilderness ecosystems, wildlife, fire, and the reference materials cited in those chapters.

(1) *Monitor wilderness naturalness.* It is impossible to manage wilderness to preserve naturalness until we know what natural conditions are and their direction and rates of change as dictated by ecological processes. Studies to establish baselines of natural conditions in wilderness are needed to compare and assess human influences outside of wilderness, and also to help determine the extent to which wilderness naturalness is being maintained. For example, studies of historical patterns of plant succession and fire history indicate that exclusion of natural wildfire through efficient fire prevention and suppression has led to unnatural conditions in some fire-dependent wilderness ecosystems (see chapter 12, Ohmann and Ream 1971; Ohmann et al. 1973). Based in part on knowledge from such research, management programs to restore fire to its natural role have been initiated in several areas.

(2) *Expand basic ecological knowledge.* Research to expand basic scientific knowledge about ecological processes can lead to useful application in both wilderness and other settings. For example, long-term studies of the ecological relationships between fire, moose, and wolves at Isle Royale National Park have strikingly illustrated the vital, natural interdependencies between moose habitat and its formative influences such as fire and the predatory-prey relationship keeping moose and habitat in balance (Allen 1974). Likewise, studies of natural fire rotations are essential to developing sound wilderness fire management policies to maintain natural conditions (see chapter 12).

There is a particular need for basic ecological research on the dynamics of landscapes—where they are coming from and specifics of where they are headed. Such information is essential to understand the changing face of wilderness ecosystems and to making intelligent choices about management actions that affect them. For example, studies in the Oregon and Washington Cascades, including sites at Mt. Rainier National Park and the Mt. Jefferson and Goat Rocks Wilderness, suggest that coniferous trees invading meadows and diminishing certain esthetic values were probably the result of temporary climatic variation and other natural factors (Franklin et al. 1971). These findings not only cast doubt on the assumed need for management action to control the invasion that had been suspected of being an unnatural phenomenon, but also indicated that removing the invading trees could be accomplished without the likelihood of immediate reinvasion (see chapter 10 for further details).

Studies of wilderness vegetative communities in the BWCA identified about half a million acres as truly pristine and provided valuable information for charting future vegetation management policies in the area. Less directly applicable to wilderness management, but important for predicting water yields from wilderness, is research on climatic variation and related effects in large undisturbed wilderness watersheds. Studies of glaciers, most of which are located in classified or proposed wilderness, are expanding basic knowledge of these barometers of climatic change that have been such an important formative influence on the American landscape. Because glaciers typically are found in wilderness, glaciological study may be wilderness dependent.

(3) *Solve wilderness resource problems.* A growing number of wilderness resource management problems require new information from research for their solution. Information from resource research has already

been important to management decisions in several areas.

Study of bighorn sheep in the Rocky Mountains suggested that human influences forcing animals to higher ranges increased the "cost of living" to these animals in the harsher climate, and adversely affect survival of lambs leading to a decline in populations (Geist 1971; Woodward et al. 1974). While solving this problem will require management of human-use patterns, the prerequisite for such action is scientific knowledge about the bighorn.

Vegetation impacts from recreational use at Image Lake in the Glacier Peak Wilderness and at Cascade Pass in North Cascades National Park have been studied to determine success of potential restoration methods.[2] The results of these studies, which indicate how slow and difficult the restoration of high elevation vegetation impacts can be, have led to some recuperation on damaged sites. Perhaps a more important result of these studies is a more cautious approach and a renewed determination by managers to prevent new impacts from occurring elsewhere.

Fish stocking in wilderness is controversial but seems likely to continue in many places where it has already become established (see chapter 11). To optimize the benefits of stocking sought by anglers while minimizing the impacts on wilderness naturalness, it would be desirable to base stocking decisions on research identifying the kind of lakes and levels of stocking that would yield the greatest benefits in wilderness as well as elsewhere. Studies of high lakes in Washington indicate substantial variation in productivity due to lake characteristics and stocking levels (Johnston 1972-73), and variation in the importance of fishing to wilderness users (Hendee, Clark, and Dailey 1977). This kind of data could help guide the controversial practice of fish stocking in wilderness.

A final example of a problem needing research concerns human waste disposal in wilderness. Early guidelines called for burying human waste 6 inches in the ground to minimize the health hazard from pollution of water and unesthetic impacts around heavily used areas. However, an alternative line of reasoning is that human waste should be left on the surface where bacterial action is greater and decomposition faster. Decomposition rates probably vary widely between areas. Research is needed to guide management policy about human waste disposal in wilderness, a problem with both ecological and social (esthetic and health) dimensions.

The foregoing discussion is intended to be merely suggestive and general, not an analysis on which to build a research program. A comprehensive problem analysis encompassing the NWPS should be developed, however, incorporating the input of agency and university scientists from pertinent social, physical, and biological sciences and managers from all the affected agencies. Studies need to be replicated in a number of areas representing the variety of conditions present in the NWPS. Diversity of areas is a major feature of the NWPS, and this diversity has been greatly increased by the addition of wilderness in the Eastern United States. While basic principles emerging from studies in one region or wilderness may apply across the System, others might be applicable only in certain areas or under particular conditions.

Alternatives to Wilderness to Ease Use Pressures

In chapters 1 and 7, we argued that wilderness, one point along a continuum of environmental opportunities, is interrelated with the other parts of this land-use spectrum. Some of these other land uses can accommodate primitive, roadless recreation, but unless such areas are available as alternatives to wilderness, all roadless activity will ultimately be forced into classified wilderness. Studies of wilderness use have consistently revealed the presence of visitors whose expectations and preferences are for roadless recreation, but not necessarily for wilderness. Some visitors seek experiences requiring comfort and convenience facilities that are largely prohibited by terms of the Wilderness Act and the underlying philosophy and purposes that led to its passage (Hendee et al. 1968; Stankey 1973; Merriam and Knopp 1976). Some uses do not require outstanding solitude, and some visitors are mainly interested in activities that could be better provided elsewhere. The preferences of these visitors are legitimate and should be accommodated at some point on the recreation spectrum—but they cannot all be met in wilderness without creating overuse impacts and eroding wilderness standards of naturalness and solitude. In addition, areas are needed that have been set aside specifically to serve roadless, nonwilderness users such as motorbikers, fly-in fishermen, or visitors wanting easy-to-follow trails and comfort and convenience facilities such as shelters and cabins.

---

[2]Miller, Joseph, and Margaret Miller. 1976. Revegetation experiments at Cascade Pass, North Cascades National Park. Presented at Resource Management and Research Workshop, sponsored by Forest Service and National Park Service, Seattle, Wash., April 28-29, 1976.

Seeing that such alternatives are made available to ease demands on formal wilderness is important to the future quality of the NWPS. The problem can be resolved only if all Federal agencies, separately and collectively, identify the full spectrum of preferences for recreation and other land uses they manage, and cooperatively adopt implementing strategies. In addition to the NWPS, land classifications, such as Wild and Scenic Rivers, can accommodate some primitive forms of recreation and help ease pressures if their management results in the attraction of wilderness-type uses. However, a backcountry (or other roadless recreation area concept) also needs to be implemented as a supplement to wilderness for the purpose of meeting roadless, nonwilderness demands. In such areas, the principal management goal would be to provide for primitive recreational experiences rather than for the maintenance of natural ecological processes. How such areas are created—legislatively or through administrative designation by agencies through their land-use planning processes—is not as important as seeing that such opportunities are made available. Administrative designation does have a greater measure of security now since provisions of the National Environmental Policy Act require preparation of an EIS and opportunities for public involvement before such designations can be implemented or changed.

It may well be that the backcountry idea is not politically viable as a legislative proposal—arousing the suspicions of environmentalists and commodity users alike. This apparent status of the concept makes it all the more important that the multiple-use agencies such as the Forest Service and Bureau of Land Management continue their efforts to provide some roadless, nonwilderness opportunities through their land-use planning processes.

Integrating Wilderness in the East into the NWPS

Legislation, commonly referred to as the Eastern Wilderness Act (P.L. 93-622), enacted January 3, 1975, provides criteria for admitting areas in the Eastern United States to the NWPS that might have sustained prior human impact. This legislation, which was to further the purposes of the Wilderness Act of 1964, created 16 instant wildernesses in the Eastern United States, totaling 206,988 acres, and designated an additional 17 areas totaling 125,000 acres for study as to their wilderness suitability (see chapter 4). For several years prior to passage of this Act, opponents to admitting areas in the East to the NWPS pointed to their apparent defects: They were small, many had sustained previous impacts from pioneer settlement and timber cutting, and some were receiving intensive recreation use. Many felt that these areas did not meet standards set forth in the Wilderness Act of 1964, and so they should be set aside in a separate, Eastern Wild Areas classification—an action intended to protect the NWPS from depreciation. Whatever the merits of their arguments, the so-called Eastern Wilderness Act of 1975 is now an accomplished fact. Further debate no longer serves any useful purpose. In fact, many resent any reference to Eastern Wilderness, thinking that the term infers differences between wilderness in the East and West when it is supposed to be one NWPS. The challenge is to fully integrate these eastern areas, despite their somewhat different conditions, into a wilderness system that is truly national.

The contrasts between wildernesses in the East and West are striking (Cermak 1975). One East-West difference is the physical distance separating users from wilderness areas. Unlike their western counterparts, people in the East typically live much closer to wilderness. There are only a few population centers in the West comparably close to wilderness areas (Los Angeles, Seattle, Portland, Denver) but, because more and larger wildernesses are near these cities, generally they are not subjected to pressures typical of the East.

On the other hand, the dense vegetation in most eastern wildernesses insulates people from sight and sound of one another, thus increasing social carrying capacity and enhancing an area's ability to tolerate and recover from physical impacts. The annual leaf fall from the deciduous vegetation that covers most wilderness in the East replenishes the forest floor, covering impacts and perhaps increasing the environmental as well as the aesthetic tolerance to use.

The most striking contrast between eastern and western wilderness is size. In July 1975, the 66 classified western wildernesses averaged about 160,000 acres each (see chapter 6). The 16 instant wildernesses in the East averaged only about 12,000 acres—and many of the proposed wildernesses in the East are much smaller, several less than 5,000 acres. These areas are small enough to raise legitimate questions about how small an area can be and still be managed to provide wilderness conditions and experiences. However, even though the small size of most wildernesses in the East (established and proposed) does create management problems, experiences in these areas should furnish valuable information about the feasibility of providing additional wilderness-type experiences on small tracts of industrial or State lands in the East.

In this and other ways, the problems introduced by the so-called Eastern Wilderness Act of 1975 requires new management approaches and adjustments in thinking, but we are convinced that they are not insurmountable difficulties. Our view is that the National Wilderness Preservation System has been enhanced by the addition of the 16 instant wildernesses and the possibility of more to come. They demonstrate the political viability, flexibility, and transferability of the wilderness concept. Rather than being bound by ironclad and absolute criteria, it is applicable to regional needs and opportunities. The inclusion of smaller, heavily used and previously impacted eastern areas to the NWPS emphasizes the importance of applying a nondegradation concept in wilderness management (see chapter 7). This principle recognizes the variation in primeval qualities of individual wildernesses, but emphasizes the need to prevent further degradation of naturalness and solitude existing in each area rather than letting all NWPS areas deteriorate to some lowest common denominator.

Because of the management problems that will be encountered in wildernesses in the East, there may be a temptation to "rewrite the book" on the basis of these differences, but we feel it should be staunchly resisted. The challenge is to incorporate these eastern areas into the NWPS, welcoming the diversity they offer, but applying the same basic principles of wilderness management, modified only to the extent required by local circumstances.

Restoring Fire to Natural Levels in Wilderness

One of the most controversial and important issues in resource management involves the role of fire on wildlands. After decades of vigorous prevention campaigns to reduce man-caused fires, and development of efficient fire control organizations and modern technology to fight wildfires of all causes, management is now asked to consider that some fires are *not* bad. A concept of "the friendly flame" has emerged to recognize the important, natural role fire plays in wildland ecosystems (see chapter 12). Fire is a natural agent important in terminating and renewing succession; controlling plant community composition, the scale of the vegetation mosaic, insects, parasites, and pathogens; and regulating fuel accumulation, nutrient cycles, and energy flow. Fire is important in maintaining the natural diversity necessary for wildlife and the visual diversity

appreciated by visitors. The need in many situations to restore fire to natural levels, by allowing some fires to burn or even to prescribe burn, is now officially recognized—the need for integrated fire management (Kilgore 1976). The notion of fire management has replaced the older, more restricted focus on fire control.

The need for management to restore fire to its natural role in wilderness ecosystems is recognized, but the challenge is formidable. Successful fire management programs are now operating in several wildernesses that have fire-dependent ecosystems. Wilderness fire management is technically and administratively complex and demanding. It requires the highest professional competence, adequate training, and intimate knowledge of the specific ecosystem and land unit to be managed. Wilderness fire management has inherent risks as well as the rewards of progressing toward wilderness naturalness goals. Even a long overdue wilderness wildfire that is allowed to burn will be accompanied by the need for a public education program to reassure a concerned and fire-conscious public, and a wilderness fire that gets away to nonwilderness land can have serious consequences for the agency and responsible officials (Popovich 1977). But, there is no chance of achieving the required naturalness of wilderness ecosystems if fire is not restored to natural levels. The development of wilderness management programs for all units of the National Wilderness Preservation System needs particular emphasis in the immediate years ahead.

Congressional Appropriations for Wilderness Management

Adequate management of the National Wilderness Preservation System will not be possible unless Congress appropriates the necessary funds. To date, Congress and the agencies have assigned wilderness management a lower priority than many other programs involving more intensive land uses. Since it involves relatively inaccessible and little used land areas, particularly in times of scarce Federal money, such management can be postponed. The study of areas proposed for wilderness classification has so far been regarded as more important (Church 1977). Yet, as we stated early in this book (see chapter 1), in a few decades the classification of areas into the NWPS will be complete; the ultimate quality of the NWPS depends on its management.

The conservative attitude toward financing wilderness management has not yet been critically damaging. In fact, large-scale funding of early management schemes emphasizing trail construction, user facilities, camps, stock facilities, and even serious proposals for hostels and shelters might have damaged the resources and jeopardized wilderness values. These early plans did not envision increased recreation use, the evolution of relatively purer standards, and the development of sophisticated management methods and techniques.

Given the experience of the last decade, it seems likely that wilderness management is now in a position to use money and manpower to better advantage than ever before. It seems important to reaffirm the necessity of wilderness management, the principle that wilderness cannot be preserved merely by its classification (draw a line around it and leave it alone), but depends instead on a comprehensive, adequately funded, management program to insure that the goals of the Wilderness Acts are approached and their objectives realized. We outlined earlier the several elements we consider important in a comprehensive wilderness administration system and strongly urge particular attention to such elements by Congress in considering the necessary funding for such a program. In particular, it is important that funding for management recognize the need for research, planning, and public involvement as essential elements to quality management. Moreover, as new areas are considered for addition to the Wilderness System, careful thought should be given to their money requirements for cost-effective management to meet established wilderness objectives. Often, wilderness management is less expensive than management of alternative uses—but there will always be necessary expenses and they should be a visible consequence in all land-use studies that consider wilderness as one alternative.

Conclusion

In this chapter, we've highlighted some major issues and challenges we think are important to wilderness management. In singling out these items, we have risked slighting other important topics. It is hoped that these are adequately covered elsewhere in the book.

Not singled out in this chapter, but thoroughly discussed in chapter 1, is the question of overall wilderness management direction. The issue is how pure should wilderness management be? That is, what is the proper emphasis between a pure or biocentric management orientation emphasizing the natural integrity of wilderness ecosystems, as opposed to an anthropocentric or human use and enjoyment orientation?

Throughout this book we have stressed a biocentric, as opposed to an anthropocentric wilderness management philosophy, but we are not advocating an extreme orientation. We are calling for a biocentric emphasis, but with common sense application and responsiveness to local conditions. We stress that *wilderness management should not mold nature to suit people. Rather, it should manage human use and influences so that natural processes are not altered. Managers should do only what is necessary to meet wilderness objectives, and use only the minimum tools, force, and regulation required to achieve those objectives.*

The debate over how pure wilderness management should be will continue but hopefully between narrower extremes than the polarized discussions in the past. It is increasingly recognized that wilderness areas are distinguished by levels of relative naturalness and solitude not present in other areas, and that the challenge of wilderness management is to maintain those thresholds. Clearly, this cannot be done if wilderness areas are allowed to become mere recreation areas without roads. There are many other wilderness values at stake including natural, cultural, historical, scientific, and gene pool values, besides the increasingly scarce opportunity for human experiences in wilderness areas.

Wilderness management policies are becoming increasingly crystallized as Agency experience, public review, and legislative and judicial guidelines combine to provide feedback as to what is appropriate. We believe much of the polarity over purity in management may have its roots in what people believe or perceive the policies to be, rather than what they actually are. Management policies of the Forest Service were recently outlined in a discussion between Assistant Secretary of Agriculture Rupert Cutler and Congressman James Weaver of Oregon. Many commonly assumed prohibitions (e.g., no toilets in wilderness) were, in fact, not substantiated by actual policy. Management, Assistant Secretary Cutler noted, is guided by the principles embraced in the following questions:

1. Is it necessary to protect the resource and manage the use?

2. Is it the minimum action or facility required to accomplish the objective?

3. Does it protect the wilderness values?

4. Does it pass a test of reason and common sense?

A wilderness management policy shaped by the answers to such questions will, in our opinion, protect the wilderness resource in the long term and provide equitable and reasonable opportunities for public use.

In closing, we want to emphasize our optimism about the future of wilderness management and the quality of the institution that depends on it—the National

Wilderness Preservation System. Wilderness didn't just happen. Maybe it did once, but that was before man developed the will and capacity to change the face of the landscape. Today, in the United States, wilderness is a product of past good fortune, foresight, hard work—and planning.

Figure 16-3.—In the long run, education will be extremely important to increased professionalism in wilderness management. Many universities now offer courses in wilderness management and offer students an opportunity to apply their knowledge to real world problems.

We've been fortunate because we had the Leopolds, Zahnisers, Marshalls, Carharts, and many others to inspire, warn, and cajole us; the example of other countries to give substance to their warnings; and time to act while the possibility of a wilderness system was still attainable.

We can no longer count on good fortune—nor do we need to—but we must increasingly rely on the other elements. We still need the foresight to look beyond material needs and desires; the restraint to say no to clamors for short term uses and short-sighted policies that could irreparably damage the wilderness resource; the willingness to work hard, to collect and pore over data, and consider with colleagues and interested citizens the merits of alternative actions. And, we need planning—planning carried out by qualified and committed people.

Wilderness management is emerging as an increasingly important specialty in resource management that is attracting the attention of an enthusiastic and highly committed cadre of university students and professionals in the managing agencies. The future quality of wilderness management depends on their continued efforts.

Among the co-authors, the author primarily responsible for preparation of this chapter was John C. Hendee.

Literature Cited

Allen, Durward.
    1974. Of fire, moose and wolves. Audubon 76(6):38–49.
Behan, R.W.
    1976. Rationing wilderness: an example from Grand Canyon. Western Wildlands 3(2):23–26.
Burch, William R., Jr.
    1974. In democracy is the preservation of wilderness. Appalachia 40(2):90–101.
Cermak, Robert W.
    1975. Wilderness in the east: problems for research. In Proceedings southern States recreation research applications workshop, USDA Forest Service General Technical Report SE-9, p. 52-57. Asheville, N.C. 302 p.
Church, Frank.
    1977. Followup with Senator Church. Western Wildlands 4(3) Fall.
Dana, Samual.
    1957. Problem analysis; research in forest recreation. U.S. Dep. Agric., For. Serv. 36 p. Washington, D.C.
Elsner, Gary.
    1972. Wilderness management . . . a computerized system for summarizing permit information. USDA For. Serv. Gen. Tech. Report PSW-2. 8 p. Pac. Southwest For. and Range Exp. Stn., Berkeley, Calif.

Fazio, James R., and Douglas L. Gilbert.
    1974. Mandatory wilderness permits: some indications of success. J. For. 72(12):753–756.
Fisher, Joseph L.
    1960. A framework for wilderness research. Nat. Parks 34(158):11–13.
Franklin, Jerry F., William H. Moir, George W. Douglas, and Curt Wiberg.
    1971. Invasion of subalpine meadows by trees in the Cascade Range, Washington and Oregon. Arctic and Alpine Res. 3(3):215–224.
Frayer, W.E., and D.B. Butts.
    1974. BUS: a processing system for records of backcountry camper use. J. Leisure Res. 6(4):305–311.
Geist, Valerius.
    1971. Mountain Sheep. 383 p. University of Chicago Press.
Hendee, John C., William R. Catton, Jr., Larry D. Marlow, and C. Frank Brockman.
    1968. Wilderness users in the Pacific Northwest—their characteristics, values, and management preferences. USDA For. Serv. Res. Pap. PNW-61, 92 p. Pac. Northwest For. and Range Exp. Stn., Portland, Oreg.
Hendee, John C., and Robert W. Harris.
    1970. Managers' perceptions of wilderness user attitudes and preferences. J. For. 68(12):759–762.